T0261325

Intelligent Internet
Knowledge Networks

Processing of Concepts and Wisdom

Intelligent Internet Knowledge Networks

Processing of Concepts and Wisdom

SYED V. AHAMED

Professor of Computer Science
City University of New York

A JOHN WILEY & SONS, INC., PUBLICATION

Published by John Wiley & Sons, Inc., Hoboken, New Jersey.
Published simultaneously in Canada.

For general information on our other products and services or for technical support, please contact our
Customer Care Department within the United States at (800) 762-2974, outside the United States at
(317) 572-3993 or fax (317) 572-4002.

Wiley also publishes its books in a variety of electronic formats. Some content that appears in print may
not be available in electronic format. For information about Wiley products, visit our web site at
www.wiley.com.

Library of Congress Cataloging-in-Publication Data is available.

Ahamed, Syed V.
  Intelligent Internet Knowledge Networks: Processing of Concepts
  and Wisdom

ISBN-13: 978-0-471-78856-0
ISBN-10: 0-471-78856-2

Printed in the United States of America.

10 9 8 7 6 5 4 3 2 1

Contents

Foreword   xv

Preface   xvii

Introduction   xxi

PART I   HUMAN THOUGHT AND MACHINE PROCESS

Chapter 1   Processing of Knowledge   3
1.1   Introduction   4
1.2   The Basis of New Machines   8
1.3   Classical Computing Environments   11
1.4   Newer Computing Environments   12
        1.4.1   Telecommunications Applications   13
        1.4.2   Medical Applications   14
        1.4.3   Other Computer-Intensive Systems   15
1.5   Object-Oriented Systems   16
1.6   Special Purpose Computer Systems   16
1.7   Conclusions   17
References   18

Chapter 2   Network Perspective   19
2.1   Evolving Network Architectures   21
2.2   Networks for Communication   21
        2.2.1   Copper in Networks   22
        2.2.2   Microwaves in Networks   24
        2.2.3   Fiber Optics in Networks   26
2.3   Transmission in Optical Network   26
2.4   The SONET Standard   31
2.5   SONET Architectures   35
2.6   ATM Concepts   38
2.7   Expectations from Modern Network   42

2.7.1 Specific Applications 43
2.7.2 Special-Purpose LANs and Generic Backbones 44
2.8 Architectural Commonality 45
2.8.1 The All-Internet Solution 46
2.8.2 The All-Private Network 46
2.8.3 Integrated Network Architectures and Internet 46
2.9 Intelligent Networks 47
Control and Sequencing of Functions 48
Communication of Data and Control Signals 50
Computation, Address Lookup and Dynamic Routing 50
Logical Channel Switching 50
2.9.1 Intelligent Networks Defined 51
2.9.2 Specific Building Blocks of Intelligent Networks 52
2.9.2.1 Service Switching Point (SSP) 53
2.9.2.2 Service Control Point (SCP) 53
2.9.2.3 Signal Transfer Point (STP) 56
2.9.2.4 Service Management System (SMS) 56
2.9.2.5 Intelligent Peripheral (IP) 57
2.9.2.6 CCIS Network. 57
2.9.2.7 Functionality of IN Components 59
2.9.3 Seamless Networks 60
2.10 Database Management 60
2.10.1 Data Management in Intelligent Networks 61
2.10.2 Data Management for DSL Development 62
2.10.2.1 Permanent Databases 64
2.10.2.2 Program Databases 65
2.10.2.3 Postprocessing Program Databases 65
2.10.2.4 Pictorial Databases 65
2.10.2.5 Intermediate Databases 66
2.10.3 Data Management for Lightwave Systems 67
2.10.3.1 Vendor Databases for Lightwave Systems 67
2.10.3.2 Program Databases for Lightwave Systems 68
References 68

Chapter 3   Embedded Intelligence 71
3.1 Search for Knowledge 72
3.1.1 Intelligent Internet Defined 73
3.1.2 Intelligent Internet from Intelligent Network Platform 74
3.2 Peripherals and Interfaces 75
3.3 Generic Medical Networks 75
3.3.1 Hospital-based Medical Networks 77
3.3.2 Architectural Considerations 81
3.3.3 Architectures for Telemedicine 85
3.3.4 MSP-Based Medical Network 85
3.3.4.1 Integration of Medical Networks 85

3.3.4.2   Status Quo of the Medical Network Environments   86
3.3.4.3   Intelligent Medical Network or MSP-based
          Intelligent Internet   86
3.3.4.4   Proposed MSP Network Configuration   89
3.3.4.5   MSP-Based Network or the Internet   90
3.3.4.6   Knowledge-Based Programmable MSP Architectures   91
3.4 Generic Educational Network   93
3.4.1   Network-Based Intelligent Educational Networks   94
3.4.2   Network Architecture for Distance Learning   94
3.4.3   Design Considerations of Network-based Educational Systems   96
3.4.4   Features Common to Educational Environments   97
3.4.5   Role of Networks in Educational Environments   98
3.4.6   Role of Knowledge Bases in Educational Environments   98
3.5   Architecture for Electronic Government   99
3.5.1   Control, Coordination, and Flow of Information   99
3.5.2   Configuration of an EG Platform for a Small Nation   102
3.6   Billing Systems   106
3.6.1   Interoperability of Databases and Data Formats   107
3.6.2   Service Options   107
3.6.3   Other Market Demands and Their Influence on Telco Databases   107
3.7   Knowledge Bases   110
References   111

PART II   STABILITY OF ENVIRONMENTS

Chapter 4   Sensing and Monitoring Networks   115
4.1   Basic Concepts for Sensing   117
4.2   Users, Intelligence, and Databases   118
4.2.1   Network Segment Dealing with User Dialogue   118
4.2.2   Network Segment Dealing with Knowledge and Intelligence   118
4.2.3   Network Segment Dealing with Databases and Data Management   120
4.3   Details of Flow of Information   120
4.4   Deployment of Switch Architecture   122
4.5   Adjunct Processes in the Switches   123
4.6   Conclusions   123
References   125

Chapter 5   Intelligent Knowledge Sharing   127
5.1   Internet Knowledge Sharing   128
5.2   KBs for Technology Transfer   128
5.3   Current Knowledge Networks   129
5.3.1   IN and KSP-Based Intelligent Internet   130
5.3.2   Proposed Technology Transfer Network   131
5.3.3   Merits of KSP-Based Network   132
5.3.4   Programmable KSP-Based Network Architectures   134

5.4   KBs in Hospital Networks   137
       5.4.1   Global Medical Network Environment   137
       5.4.2   MSP-Based Intelligent Internet   138
       5.4.3   Configurations of the Machine   139
               5.4.3.1   Level I—Routine Medical Functions   142
               5.4.3.2   Level II—Machine Assisted Human Functions   143
               5.4.3.3   Level III—Expert Medical Functions   143
5.5   Knowledge-Based Processes   144
       5.5.1   Intelligent Networks for Telemetry and Data Processing   144
       5.5.2   A Confluence of Four Disciplines   144
       5.5.3   Implementation   145
       5.5.4   The Architecture Dealing with Sensors, Intelligence
               and Databases   146
       5.5.5   Program and Data Management in the KPS   149
5.6   Conclusions   150
References   151

Chapter 6   Intelligent Control Systems   153
6.1   Applications   154
6.2   Sensed Parameters as "Objects"   155
6.3   Deployment of Intelligent Control   155
       6.3.1   Sensing Network Response Complex Via the Sensors   159
       6.3.2   Configuration of the Transaction Management Machine (TMM)   162
       6.3.3   Functions of the Database Management Machine (DBM)   162
       6.3.4   Functions of DBM and KMM, Specific to Inventory Control   164
6.4   Control of a National Economy   164
       6.4.1   Sensing Network Response Complex Via the Sensors   165
       6.4.2   Configuration of the Transaction Management Machine (TMM)   165
       6.4.3   Interaction with Knowledge Management Machine (KMM)   165
       6.4.4   Functions of DBM to Monitor National Economy   167
       6.4.5   Functions of KMM to Monitor National Economy   167
6.5   Sensing Network to Replace Middle Management of a Corporation   168
       6.5.1   Flowchart of Events for Routine Activity   168
6.6   Conclusions   171
References   172

Chapter 7   Audio-Visual Sensing in Humans   173
7.1   The Human Ear as the Processor   175
7.2   The Rules of Audio Language   175
       7.2.1   Ground Rules   176
       7.2.2   Audio Language for the Language Learners   176
       7.2.3   A Programmable Audio and Visual Menu for Every User   176
7.3   Computer and Audio-Visual Languages   177
7.4   Conclusions   178
References   178

PART III HUMAN THOUGHT AND MACHINE PROCESS

Chapters 8   Framework for Processing Knowledge   181
8.1   Knowledge Processing Environments   183
      8.1.1   Conventional Processing from Computing Systems   184
      8.1.2   Call Processing from Telecommunication Systems   187
              8.1.2.1   Earlier Configurations of Channel Banks   189
      8.1.3   Knowledge Service Processing from Intelligent Networks   195
              8.1.3.2   Knowledge Transfer Points (KTP) for Knowledge
                        Environments   197
              8.1.3.3   Knowledge Control Points (KCP) for Knowledge
                        Environments   197
              8.1.3.4   Knowledge Services Control Points (KSCPs) for
                        Knowledge Environments   199
8.2   Platform of KPS from Computer Systems and ESS   202
      8.2.1   Communication Module (CM) of KPS   202
      8.2.2   Switching Module (SM) of the KPS   204
      8.2.3   Administrative Module (AM) of the KPS   206
      8.2.4   Knowledge Module (KM) of the KPS   207
8.3   Role of the Knowledge Processor Unit (KPU)   207
      8.3.1   Processor Environments   208
      8.3.2   Multiprocessor-Based Environments   211
8.4   Alternate Architectures   213
8.5   A Multifunctional Intelligent Network   214
      8.5.1   Integrated Design Approach   214
      8.5.2   Proposed Architecture   215
8.6   Certainty in Knowledge Processing   215
      8.6.1   Knowledge Processing System Based on Uncertainty   217
      8.6.2   Basic Building Blocks   217
              8.6.2.1   Database Unit (DBU)   218
              8.6.2.2   Knowledge Processor Unit (KPU)   218
              8.6.2.3   Numerical Processor Unit (NPU)   219
      8.6.3   Block Diagram of the KPS   220
      8.6.4   KPU Execute Cycle   220
              8.6.4.1   "Fetch" of KPU Instruction   223
              8.6.4.2   The "Decode" of KPU Instruction   225
              8.6.4.3   "Object Operand Fetch" of KPU Instruction   225
              8.6.4.4   The "Execute" of KPU Instruction   226
              8.6.5.5   "Store" the Result of KPU Instruction   227
      8.6.6   DBU and Its Functionality   228
      8.6.7   The "Fuzzy" NPU   228
      8.6.8   Fuzzy Hamming Distance and Its Iterative Control   229
      8.6.9   Design and Implementation of the System   230
      8.6.10 Program Execution Mode of the KPU   231
              8.6.10.1 Execution Sequence for External "Object" Programs   233

8.6.10.2 Execution Sequence for Internally Generated
Programs   234
8.6.11 Learning Mode of the KPU   235
8.6.12 Program Execution Sequence in the Learning Mode   239
8.7   Conclusions   240
References   241

Chapter 9   A New Breed Of Machines   243
9.1   Introduction   243
9.2   Human Needs and Computer Solutions   245
9.3   Development of Machine Instructions   246
      9.3.1   Human Needs and Computer Languages   247
      9.3.2   Simple Needs, Simple Solutions   248
      9.3.3   Complex Needs, Complex Solutions   249
9.4   Architectures   261
9.5   Conclusions   264
References   264

Chapter 10   Concepts and Constructs for a Wisdom Machine (WM) 267
10.1   Introduction   268
10.2   Role of Decision Support Systems (DSS)   271
       10.2.1 The I/O Subsystem   272
       10.2.2 Operational Parameters   273
       10.2.3 Scientific, Social and Mathematical Models   273
10.3   Role of Sensing Networks   273
       10.3.1 Sensor/Response System   274
       10.3.2 Current Parameter Database   275
       10.3.3 Knowledge, Information, and Models Databases   275
10.4   Role of Accumulated Knowledge   276
10.5   Confidence in the Results   277
10.6   The Realm of Reality   278
10.7   Typical Computer Functions in the WM   278
       10.7.1 Dialog Processor (Subsystem 1)   278
       10.7.2 Database (DB) Administrator (Subsystem 2)   279
       10.7.3 Knowledge Base (KB) Administrator (Subsystem 3)   279
10.8   Human Intervention   280
       10.8.1 Symbols and Equations (Subsystem 4)   281
       10.8.2 Axiomatic Tools (Subsystem 5)   281
       10.8.3 Hypothesis Testing (Subsystem 6)   282
10.9   All Human Functions   283
10.10 Architecture   284
10.11 Frontier of Intelligence into Wisdom   291
10.12 Order, Awareness, and Search   293
10.13 Conclusions   294
References   296

Chapter 11   Knowledge Environments   299
11.1   Introduction   299
11.2   Knowledge Systems   302
        11.2.1 C&C Checker   302
        11.2.2 Functions of the C&C Checker   303
        11.2.3 Role of Switching Systems   303
11.3   Knowledge Communication Systems (KCSS)   305
        11.3.1 Communication Module of KCS   305
        11.3.2 Switching Module of KCS   306
        11.3.3 Administrative Module of the KCS   307
        11.3.4 Intelligent Network Aspects in KCS   307
        11.3.5 Knowledge Control Points in KCS   314
11.4   Knowledge Processing Systems (KPSs)   314
        11.4.1 Programmable Steps for KPU   315
        11.4.2 Computer Processor Environments   317
        11.4.3 Knowledge Processing   319
        11.4.4 Low-Level Single KCPU Knowledge Machine   320
        11.4.5 Multiple KCPU Knowledge Machine   320
        11.4.6 Object-Based Knowledge Machine   323
11.5   IN and IK-Based KPS (I^2-KPS)   326
11.6   IN and IN-Based, Intelligent KPS (I^3-KPS)   328
11.7   Wafer Level Knowledge Machines   330
        11.7.1 Object Processes and Knowledge Processes   331
        11.7.2 KOP Specific Processor Arrays   331
        11.7.3 Object Processors   338
        11.7.4 Advanced Knowledge Processing Unit   339
        11.7.5 Wafer Level Knowledge Machine   339
11.8   Conclusions   340
References   341

Chapter 12   Wealth of Knowledge   345
12.1   Introduction   346
12.2   Truisms in Information Domain   353
12.3   Philosophic Validation   354
12.4   Scientific Principles   355
12.5   Economics of Information   358
12.6   Integration and Social Change   359
        12.6.1 Level of ($I«»K$)   360
        12.6.2 Propensity of Organizations   360
12.7   Theory of Knowledge   361
        12.7.1 Algebraic Constructs of Knowledge Theory   362
        12.7.2 Systemic Limitations of Knowledge Systems   364
12.8   Processing of Information   365
12.9   Economics of Knowledge   366
        12.9.1 Diminishing Value of Knowledge   367

12.9.2 Economic Life of Inventions   369
12.9.3 Impact of High-Speed Networks on Human Behavior   370
12.10 Conclusions   372
References   373

PART IV   PERSISTENT MINDS AND TIRELESS MACHINES

Chapter 13   Human Needs and Machines   377
13.1   From AI to BI   378
        13.1.1 An Imitation of Human Behavior?   379
        13.1.2 Sigmund Freud's Contributions   381
        13.1.3 Carl Jung's Contributions   382
        13.1.4 Eric Berne's Contributions   383
        13.1.5 Abraham Maslow's Contributions   383
13.2   Inadequacy of Earlier Models   384
        13.2.1 Two Additional Levels   385
13.3   The Need to Search (Sixth Level)   386
13.4   The Need to Unify (Seventh Level)   388
13.5   A Model of Human Behavior   390
        13.5.1 Satisfaction of Needs   390
        13.5.2 Repetition and Boredom at (6)   393
        13.5.3 The New Cycle (1–6) for $(i + 1)$st Need   395
        13.5.4 Integrated Patterns for (1–7) Needs   396
        13.5.5 The Semi-infinite Search Space at Each Level   397
13.6   Movement within Pattern (1–9) for Any One Need   400
13.7   Oscillations of Behavior   403
13.8   Effects of Phasors on Pattern (1–9) of Behavior   404
13.10   Conclusion   410
References   412

Chapter 14   The Practice of Wisdom   415
14.1   The Human Aspects   416
14.2   The Sources of Wisdom   417
14.3   Viruses in Human Networks   418
14.4   Peripheral Accomplices in Human Networks   418
14.5   Conviction and Wisdom   419
14.6   Modules of Positive Wisdom   420
        14.6.1 Positive Predisposition of the Human Team   421
                14.6.1.1 Type A: Individuals Favoring Unrestrained Wisdom   421
                14.6.1.1 Type B: Individuals Favoring Restrained Wisdom   424
        14.6.2 Realizations of the Axioms of Positive Wisdom   426
        14.6.3 Flavors of Positive Wisdom   426
        14.6.4 Symphony of Positive Wisdom   428
14.7   Modules of Negative Wisdom   429
        14.7.1 Negative Predisposition of the Abuser Team   431

14.7.1.1 Type C: War Mongers Favoring Maximal Injury
and Destruction   431
14.7.1.2 Type D: Thugs Favoring Local and Controlled
Injury   433
14.7.2 (Derivations of) Statements of Negative Wisdom   435
14.7.3 Flavors of Negative Wisdom   436
14.7.4 Chaos and Fractals of Negative Wisdom   436
14.7.5 Positive and Negative Modes of Wisdom   436
14.8   IKW&V Base Management   438
14.8.1 Wisdom Base Management (WBM)   438
14.9   The Economics of IK&W   439
14.9.1 The (Shortened) IKWV Chain   440
14.10 Conclusions   441
References   442

Chapter 15   Looking Ahead: Social and Ethical Implications   445
15.1   The Knowledge Trail   447
15.1.1 Flexible Representation of Objects   448
15.1.2 Object Processing Along the Knowledge Trail   449
15.2   Role of Humans   454
15.2.1 Economic Basis of Human Search   456
15.2.2 Conflictive Directions of Human Role   456
15.3   Human Discretion: Prophets or Plunderers   457
15.3.1 Human, Still the Unknown   458
15.3.2 Machine, Still the Mindless   458
15.4   A New BDI-K-CWE Trail   459
15.4.1 A Simplified Graph Representation   460
15.4.2 Movement from Node (i) to Node ($i + 1$)   461
15.4.3 Charting of the Knowledge Trail   463
15.5   From Bits to Etiquette   469
15.6   Migration of Societies under External Influence   471
15.6.1 Coefficient of Corruption   473
15.6.2 Discrete Event Analysis and PERT   474
15.7   Conclusions   482
References   482

List of Acronyms for the Entire Book   483

Indices   493
Classification of Eight Indices   493

I—Index of Established Concepts   495
II—Index of New Concepts   497
III—Index of Human Aspects   499
IV—Index for Knowledge   501

V—Index of Social Setting 503
VI—Index of Technology 505
VII—Index of Wisdom 507
VIII—Index of Information (Words) 509

About the Author 523

Foreword

I appreciate the opportunity to provide a personal introduction to *Intelligent Internet Knowledge Networks*. This is an ambitious book by an author with a penchant for tackling difficult material, and with the intellectual grit needed to create a full-blown manuscript out of a mesh of concepts each of which is challenging in its own right, let alone in an overall unified design.

The hierarchy of information, knowledge and wisdom is broadly understood at a conceptual level. Also well accepted is the notion that the converging sciences and technologies of media processing, computing and networking, while far from being at the pinnacles of their individual courses, are converging well to enable the ideals that one associates with Information: immediacy, relevance, and personalization. What are much less obvious are the underpinnings of a framework that bridges the chasm between information and knowledge, and the daunting gap that follows: from knowledge to wisdom. To the extent one can even begin to define those underpinnings and foundations in technical terms, this book does both: it takes a shot at an almost intractable challenge, and pulls it off in many ways.

While the treatment in the book necessarily, if not explicitly, recognizes and builds upon several disciplines, it is the subject of computer science that comes closest to providing a common thread and language through its intense chapters. Constructs such as machine architectures, information filters and sensor networks constitute points of departure in its many chapters and sections. The reader that is armed with these backgrounds is taken, albeit in random and asynchronous ways, through thought processes and intellectual leaps into definitions, parsings, meta-constructs and conclusions that seek to validate the bold title of the book. Philosophical statements abound, and attempts to tie them with scientific methodology find various degrees of success. Concrete scenarios are invoked as appropriate, drawing from domains such as medicine, education and sensing, so that the author's abstractions are grounded in crucial reality.

Readers of this book will find the author's approaches to the integration of natural intelligence, machine intelligence and network intelligence to be novel and valuable. They will also be exposed to a rich technical framework for knowledge networks that is constructive, if not definitive. Perhaps more important, they will observe intellectual dimensions and connections that offer serious value, alike to the student and the practitioner. It is my hope that readers of this potentially ground-breaking work will use it as a valuable stepping stone for follow-up investigations and writings: advances that will take us ever closer to the holy grail of knowledge networks enroute (as the author points out) to the loftier goal of communication networks that would increasingly process concepts and wisdom.

PROFESSOR NIKIL JAYANT
John Pipin Chair in Wireless Systems
Executive Director, Georgia Centers for Advanced Telecommunication
  Technologies
Director, Georgia Tech Broadband Institute
Georgia Research Alliance Eminent Scholar
May 2006

Preface

This book encompasses four directions of human achievement: intelligence, Internet, knowledge and networks. These dimensions appear unrelated at first, but soon get interwoven: they blend into each other in a synergistic and harmonious way without bounds. The four-dimensional space and our way of thinking get unified freely, encompassing intelligence. Internet, knowledge and networks.

First, consider intelligence. At the pinnacle resides natural intelligence ready to tackle any problem that the mind can conceive. At the intermediate level, the role of artificial intelligence (AI) becomes dominant in carrying out slightly higher level tasks, blending machine intelligence with previously programmed human intelligence. At the lowest rung resides the encoded machine intelligence that is cast in silicon and Pentium and that carries out mundane tasks synchronized to the cycles of a cesium clock.

Second, consider Internet. At the (current) pinnacle resides the Internet, ready to interface with any WWW in its validated TCP/IP format. Intelligence and Internet get fused into the next generation internets lurking near the end of the decade. At the intermediate level, all digital networks are well synchronized and properly interfaced to accept information in an orderly and hierarchical format and to take on the optical paths or the ether space. At the lowest rung of networks reside analog networks, cast in copper, space, and any conceivable media in an asynchronized and imprecise fashion just to get the information across.

Third, consider knowledge. At the pinnacle reside values, ethics, and social benevolence. Here, the process of unification starts to have significance. Intelligence, Internet, knowledge and networking commingle to produce a composite fabric of human bondage and long-lasting human values. At the lowest rung of knowledge are the binary bits, somewhat like the raw cells in a body. Bits soon blend to become bytes and data blocks, data becomes information, information turns into knowledge, knowledge gives rise to concepts, concepts lead to wisdom, and wisdom offers values and ethics.

Finally, consider networks. Computer applications exist to serve human beings;

but machines have their limitations. If the traditional seven-layer OSI model is downsized to three layers and then topped with four additional layers (global concern, human ethics, national environment, and economic/financial basis), then the new seven layer network model would encompass the networks as they exist now and would include human values in their makeup. The convergence of the four dimensions (intelligence. Internet, knowledge and networks) starts to be evident at the top. Currently, the application layer (AL), the OSI model falls short of satisfying any human needs. At the lowest rung is the physical layer (PL) with six additional Layers to make the OSI model.

A distant and philosophic outlook on this book offers a slightly different perspective. The four parts of the book communicate: (1) the current technology, (2) the enhanced awareness of the environment, (3) the search for knowledge and wisdom, and (4) the struggle to be informed and to be judicious about the choices for humankind. Human beings retain mastery over machines and machines are highly stylized but mindless slaves. Humans choose the trail for future and machines simply follow. The four parts are portrayed as follows:

The *first* part of the book deals with current computer and network technologies that bring reality and urgency to knowledge and information. These technologies, deeply embedded in modern society, process, communicate and, disseminate information effectively.

The *second* part of the book presents the capacity of human beings to scan and sense the environment deeply and thoroughly. This part emphasizes the combined roles of sensor and processing technologies. These two technologies offer human beings the capacity to look beyond the obvious and derive information to micromanage the environment and be able to strategize and win. Such an immense power to precisely manipulate the environment was unavailable to prior generations. A new sense of responsibility becomes eminent.

The *third* part of the book provides architectures of machines that process information and derive knowledge. Whereas information is stored in databases and knowledge is retained in minds making human beings knowledgeable and wiser. Coupled with intellect and creativity, concepts form a bridge between the domain of knowledge and the state of wisdom. This part implies that if the current state of technology is projected into the future, then knowledge, concept, and wisdom processing is realistic as data and information processing was about three decades back. This part introduces an eight link genesis of human thought: binary bit, structured data, assembled information, derived knowledge, creative concepts, distilled wisdom, and contemplated inspiration. Together, they constitute a chain of struggle of a modern human being.

Finally, the *fourth* part of the book intertwines human struggle with human needs. The quest to make life more fulfilling and rewarding is as ancient as the evolution. This concluding part of the book points to the role of instilled values and contemplated inspirations ignite the human struggle in a positive light. It also warns of the danger of human beings who exploit and deplete the wealth of wisdom already distilled from eons of evolution. Modern society faces the same temptations that migrants faced when the "pilgrims" entered Americas. Machines play only a secondary role in the final links of a long chain from binary bits to positive inspirations.

This book covers two frontiers of human thought. At one extreme, Chapters 1–7 present the scientific notions that make computers and networks optimal, self-correcting, and efficient. At the other extreme, Chapters 13–15 present the philosophic struggle that turns human ingenuity into precise, elegant, and socially beneficial ways to conceive, realize, and implement the computers and networks that serve humankind. The two extremes do not overlap to become a closed contour. Instead, Chapters 8–12 present the spiral and helical pathways that encompass incremental movements in and out of a much larger intellectual space.

The core elements of modern information and knowledge processing environments are computers and sophisticated switching systems. Such environments may consist of a large mainframe stand alone-computers, clusters of interconnected computers, a network of computers, or even the Internet with key elements for the processing of data, information, knowledge, and wisdom. Within this rather diversified framework, leading up to knowledge processing and the extraction of wisdom, we explain the historic landmarks in the hardware, software, and firmware embedded in these individual or clusters of machines. They perform generic and modular functions that make the basic building blocks of the global functions used in modern Internet based information processing systems.

At the current stage of scientific achievement, computing and switching technologies are two of the major contributors to communication systems. These technologies have already made intelligent communication services and Internet common household options. Some of the other relevant technologies complement communication and switching technologies immensely. For example, innovations in the VLSI industry have greatly benefited both technologies and vice versa. This type of symbiotic relationship is evident in the communications and optical industries. Reliable communication systems need the highest quality of optical fiber and optical devices. A demand in the optical industry, based on a human need (to communicate), is thus created. It is also evident in the medical field and pharmaceutical industry. However, supply and demand do not interact in a positive way. In fact, some inventions arise just to put an end to a need: for example, the end of smallpox epidemic eventually terminated the production of the vaccine. Some industries become subservient to the whims and fancies of society. In this book, an innovative process is taken one step further by suggesting computer architectures that will serve an array of human needs in two ways: (1) by distilling the axioms of wisdom (see Parts II and III) from events in society in order to achieve progress in a peaceful and harmonious way and (2) by extrapolating the needs (see Part IV) of general populations from snapshots of present status.

In this book, we momentarily retreat from the legacy of inventing tools and gadgets for the twenty-first century, which solve immediate social problems. Instead, we examine the possibility of machines emulating the human behavior by evolving basic and core knowledge from routine events (in networks and the Internet) and deriving axioms of wisdom from the core knowledge with the help of human beings. The concepts presented in this book are at the horizons of computer science and offer a possible forward leap in the way we process knowledge and derive wisdom from knowledge. Such wisdom guides human thinking to generate new (and beneficial) knowledge, making the inter-dependence of machines and humans symbiotic and sustained.

SYED V. AHAMED
Holmdel, New Jersey

Introduction

It is rare that an expert in a technical discipline is also a deep thinker and, indeed, a philosopher, who is both deeply concerned with the uses and consequences of his discipline and, at the same time, is a visionary who has the insight and wisdom to be able to formulate what his discipline might, and ultimately should, do for the benefit of mankind. Professor Syed Ahamed is such an individual. His mastery and understanding of the workings and intricacies of modem communication and information networks is extraordinary. It is the result of decades of both working in, and consulting for the communications industry. At the same time he is a teacher of the subject and a researcher with computer science and electrical engineering graduate students. In contrast to the proverbial technocrat. Professor Ahamed, the communications engineer, is also a poet and philosopher, who does not compartmentalize the normally diverging two cultures of technology and philosophy, but actually synthesizes them into a new discipline that carries the name of his new book. In so doing he, in his own words "places himself at the horizons of computer science, while at the same time offering a possible leap forward in the way we process knowledge and derive wisdom from knowledge."

This book represents an unusual combination of sound technical knowledge coupled with a genuine regard for, and fascination with, the human condition. It should be of interest to anyone who is concerned with the directions in which modem communications and information networks have the potential to lead us.

PROFESSOR EMERITUS GEORGE S. MOSCHYTZ
Signal and Information Processing, Swiss Federal
Institute of Technology (ETH) in Zurich, Switzerland
Head, School of Engineering, Bar-Ilan University, Israel
June 17, 2006

Intelligent Internet
Knowledge Networks

Processing of Concepts and Wisdom

PART *I*

Network Environments

The status of current technology is surveyed briefly to provide a technical basis for realizing new machines and networks proposed in Parts II, III, and IV of this book. Current technology is fairly mature in three basic areas: (1) computer and processing, (2) Internet Protocol (IP) addressing and router configurations, and (3) high-speed global network communications. The synergy and convergence of the three technologies permit new configurations and networks to become realities. Numerous cases of such systems (such as intelligent sensing, medical alert, hospital networks, and electronic governments), are currently being deployed. These recent trends in the technology sector of society are the stepping stones in the development of new machines and networks in the next decade. Within this rather diversified framework of new machines, knowledge processing and extraction of wisdom will become feasible.

In Part I, we explain the historic landmarks in hardware, software, and firmware embedded in these machines. In perspective, one can realize that knowledge processing is as feasible now as data processing appeared in the late 1940s, or as feasible as very-large-scale integration (VLSI) appeared in the early 1950s. The ultimate success of many enduring methodologies depends on the collective will of the industrial community. Major trends are initiated by potential financial gains, provided the technology exists. For example, global information networks prevail because of fiber optics technology, and modern diagnostic cancer and surgical

Intelligent Internet Knowledge Networks. By Syed V. Ahamed
Copyright © 2007 John Wiley & Sons, Inc.

procedures exist because of magnetic resonance imaging (MRI) techniques. Social demand plays a role in increasing the potential rewards. In the same vein, if knowledge processing can solve some of the greater and global intellectual needs of human beings, then it is conceivable that machines will be built simply to address our curiosity at first and then to draw the foundations of wisdom for later generations.

Chapter *1*

Processing of Knowledge

In a snapshot, an intricate web of industries contributes the products that serve humanity. In a portrayal of the Information Age, a hierarchy of computers, networks, and the Internet offers strategic information that drives the worldwide economies. The transfer of information and knowledge within the web of networks is fast, accurate, and dynamic. The economic and social interdependence within the web of industries is also dynamic and volatile, more so now than a century ago. The dynamics of demand for products that serve society are evermore rapidly changing. This acceleration of technologies, growth of industries, and the accompanying social implications exert a profound pressure on the basic motivation, control, and monitoring of the networks that cater to the web of industries.

From a historical perspective, inventors and designers have come up with devices and gadgets to perform the routine and repetitive tasks once done by human beings. These innovations accomplish the tasks faster and more accurately. On the one hand, the concept of modern machines borrows from the way in which human beings think; on the other hand, the implementation and the realization of the innovation are borrowed from the scientific methodology and technology of society. In this book, the objective is to make the machines (artificially) "think" through the entire process of predicting needs and "inventing" the means to satisfy those human needs. The search for truth, elegance, and social value becomes a part

Intelligent Internet Knowledge Networks. By Syed V. Ahamed
Copyright © 2007 John Wiley & Sons, Inc.

of the due process of inventing. With human being guiding and supervising their performance, these machines should be able to generate a set of values that are likely to bring about a more harmonious society. Both the positive and negative attributes of human beings are explored to build machines that are secure and incorruptible.

This chapter reviews the classic computing environments as a prelude to novel computing environments. The chapter also reviews classic architectures and development of software that have made computers conducive to processing of data, information, and knowledge. In addition, the artificial intelligence (AI) techniques, and growth of worldwide data, information, and knowledge bases are also documented. Three major applications are illustrated in this chapter. Sections dealing with telecommunications, telemedicine, and other computer-intensive environments are presented to integrate the current network technology and the future needs of society. Both current architectures and novel configurations are presented to offer readers an insight into the trends of development in these applications and how they may be fine-tuned to suit specific countries and social environments.

1.1 INTRODUCTION

The core and focal elements of modern information and knowledge processing environments are computer and highly sophisticated switching systems. Such environments may consist of a large mainframe, stand-alone computers, a cluster of interconnected computers, a network of computers, or even the Internet with key elements for the processing of data, information, knowledge, and wisdom. Within this rather diversified framework that leads up to knowledge processing and extraction of wisdom, we explain the historic landmarks in the hardware, software, and firmware embedded in these machines. They perform generic and modular functions that make the basic building blocks of the global functions performed by modern information processing systems. At the highest level, these machine functions rival the functions considered primarily as human functions in the past. In a gradual and sustained way, these machines are coming closer and closer to thinking and responding to any situation or need much like a human being would think and respond.

This approach makes the machines imitate and even enhance the ways in which humans would have responded and reacted. These enhanced and optimal ways of responding and reacting are the unarticulated goal of inventions since antiquity. For example, the abacus came about to help the traders, the threshing machines came about to help the farmers, the diagnostic systems came about to help the doctors, and so on. Even decision support systems and their applications help corporate decision makers. To a large extent, inventors and designers have come up with devices and gadgets that are not only able to the work of human beings but able of do it faster and better. The concept of modern machines has been borrowed from the ways in which human beings think; yet on the other hand, while the implementation and realization of inventions are borrowed from science and technology within society.

At the current stage of scientific achievement, computing, communication, and transmission technologies are some of the major contributors to social progress. These technologies have already made intelligent communication services and Internet common household options. Other relevant developments also assist these three technologies immensely. For example, innovations in the VLSI, laser, and maser industries have greatly benefited these technologies and vice versa.

This type of symbiotic relationship is evident in the communications and optical industries. Reliable communication systems need the highest quality optical fiber and optical devices. A demand in the optical industry, based on a human need (to communicate), is thus created. It is also evident in the medical field and pharmaceutical industry. However, the contributor and recipient industries do not always provide a positive feedback for one another. In fact, some inventions arise just to put an end to a need. The end of smallpox epidemic eventually terminated production of the vaccine.

In this book, we take a step forward in the realization of new systems by suggesting viable computer architectures. These configurations will serve the array of pervasive human needs in two ways: (1) by distilling the axioms of wisdom (see Part II) from events in society in order to achieve progress in a peaceful and harmonious way and (2) by extrapolating human needs (see Part III) from a snapshot of the present status of society.

In most cases, an established web of industries contributes the products that serve humanity. The economic and social interdependence within the web of industries is dynamic and unstable, more so now than a century ago. The dynamics of demand for products that serve the society can fluctuate rapidly. This acceleration of technologies, industrial growth, and the accompanying social implications exert a profound pressure on the basic mode of human behavior and thought.

There is a need for union of four dimensions: intelligence, internets, knowledge, and networks. A snapshot of this four (A, B, C and D) dimensional space is shown in Figure 1.1.

The seven-layer OSI model is sometimes shrunk into three layers by combining the top three layers into one dealing with computer applications and also by combining the lower three layers into the data layer, trapping the network layer in the middle. If a global perspective is to be maintained, then the additional four layers imply global concern, ethics, national context, and economic aspects of all computer communications. This philosophy is based on the assumption that every transaction is for a global purpose, no matter how insignificant it may appear to be.

At the pinnacles of these four dimensions lie natural intelligence, next-generation internets, human ethics (bondage), and global concern. This idealized region of human existence is far from reality, but it offers a target zone. To this extent, the struggle of modern humans in an information age is similar the struggle of primitive humans in the Stone Age. The search for ideal and efficient ways to live a pain-free life continues.

	7 Layers and 4 Dim			
1	Natural Intelligence	Next Generation Internet	Ethical Values	Global/Philosophic Concern
2	Creativity (Str. & Unstr.)	Intelligent Internet	Wisdom	Ethical/Social Issues
3	Network Intelligence; INCM	Current Internet	Concepts	National, Societal Matters
4	Artificial Intelligence	Packet/Frame/Cell Network	Knowledge	Economic/Financial/
5	Application Programs	Digital Carrier Systems	Information	App. Pres., Sess. Layers
6	Chip Sets and Firmware	Analog Carrier Systems	Data Structures	Transport Layer
7	Encoded Intelligence hw, sw	Telegraph Systems	Binary Bits	Network, D-L, Phy. Layer
	A - Intelligence	**B - Internet(s)**	**C - Knowledge**	**D - Network Layers**

(a) Four dimensions (A, B, C, and D) of evolution that have shaped our current society. At the top of the hierarchy resides the fusion where science, machines, and networks support a stable, ethical, and beneficial society

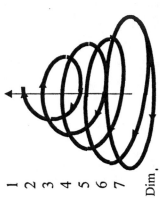

Dim.

1
2
3
4
5
6
7

(c) Jagged and unpredictable path of movement within a cube formed by the four panels A, B, C, and D in part (a)

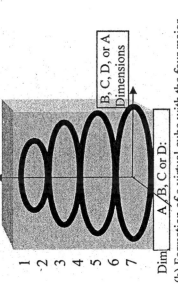

Dim: A, B, C or D:

B, C, D, or A Dimensions

1
-2
3
4
5
6
7

(b) Formation of a virtual cube with the four major dimensions of forces within the society

Figure 1.1 Representation of the four dimensional (A, B, C, and D) space that encompasses the new machines for processing information and knowledge in the new Internet era.

Past achievements of science and technology have taken the status of humankind to different hierarchical levels in these four dimensions. These levels are portrayed in Figure 1.1a by the heights of the bars at the right side of each of the four boxes.

In *dimension A* for intelligence (Figure 1.1a), natural intelligence, human creativity,[1] and network intelligence (based on the intelligent network conceptual model or INCM) occupy the first, second and third layers. The human intellect reigns supreme.

In *dimension B* for the Internet (Figure 1.1a), the hierarchy is based on the functionalities of the inter-networks. In the hierarchical chain, next-generation internets (NGIs), intelligent Internet (II), and the current Internet occupy the first, second, and third layers.

In *dimension C* for knowledge (Figure 1.1a), a framework based on the hierarchy from binary bits to ethical values is shown. This framework is expanded further in Chapter 15. In processing of bits, data, and information, modern computer systems play a dominant role. The processing of knowledge is main theme of the present book. The processing of knowledge to extract generic concepts, the generalization of concepts to distill axioms of wisdom, and the unification of concepts to derive ethical values occupy the fourth, fifth, sixth, and seventh layers in dimension C. Modern computer systems fall short of providing the neural nets in these four layers.

In *dimension D* for networks (Figure 1.1a), the application layer for computer communications and transmission control protocol/internet protocol (TCP/IP) layers for internet communication are well established. The top four layers dealing with the economic basis, the national implications, the ethical and moral consequences, and finally the global (philosophic) implication constitute the fourth, fifth, sixth, and seventh layers. Once again, modern computer systems fall short.

It is not imperative that all activities and transactions be correlated at the higher levels. For example, during the design of the physical layer (PL) in communication networks (dimension D), it is not necessary to trace this (lowest) open system interconnect (OSI) layer to the (highest) application layer. What is essential are the functions and interfacing of the intermediate layers (AL). In the same vein, the design of circuits that process bits (dimension C) need not be traced to the unification of concepts leading to ethical values. What is essential are the logical and scientific steps in the processing of the intermediate layer. The same reasoning applies for dimensions B and A.

When the four panels— A, B, C, and D (in Figure 1.1a)— are merged together to form a cube (shown in Figure 1.1b), the hierarchies in the four dimensions lie side by side. There is some layer-to-layer correlation that has existed in the past (Internet, OSI and TCP/IP model; concepts, economic considerations, and financial oppurtunities, etc.). The synergy has brought about the current Internet technologies. The interdependency of the roles (seventh layer) of natural intelligence, next-generation internets, unification of concepts, and global concern

---

[1] Human creativity is considered to be different from natural intelligence by some psychologists. The type of adaptation that is germane to intelligence assumes many flavors and modes in creative contributions.

is likely to dominate the future. It is also evident that synergy and confluence are necessary. We attempt to provide such a scenario by tapping into the different disciplines and building knowledge machines, knowledge processing systems, and intelligent internet environments as shown in Figure 1.2.

1.2 THE BASIS OF NEW MACHINES

Human evolution is millions of years old. The evolution of science and technologies is a few centuries old. For this reason, we momentarily retreat from the twenty-first century legacy of inventing tools and gadgets. These modern inventions solve immediate scientific social problems. Instead, we envision the possibility of machines emulating human responses. The basic core knowledge is embedded in the routine events within networks and the Internet. Such a body of core knowledge leads to axioms of wisdom with the help of human beings. The concepts presented are now at the horizons of computer science and they offer a path to processing of knowledge and deriving wisdom from knowledge. Such wisdom guides human thinking to generate new (and beneficial) knowledge, making the interdependence symbiotic and sustained, toward the betterment of humankind. In an unwritten code of ethics, this is the basic premise on which civilization evolved. In a counterproductive sense, the lack of adherence to such a code of ethics is the trigger for the downfall of civilizations. We explore these negative forces that are prevalent in the society in Chapters 14 and 15.

Currently, the financial rewards of inventing are limited to a few astute individuals and organizations. New knowledge does not always bring status and financial rewards. Remarkable stories of the trials and tribulations of Nikola Tesla [1], Gregor Mendel [2], and George Boole [3] still linger on even though we all benefit from their extraordinary contributions to science. In an un-chartered and ill-defined feedback loop between those inventing solutions that serve transient social needs and those making entrepreneurial gains, many scientists are short-changed.

Illusive social conditions add to the complexity (like noise) in the feedback process. What is proposed in this book is a twofold approach: (1) forcing machines to learn the future social needs and (2) forcing machines to solve long-term problems in the same way philosophers have done bringing sustained social justice and lasting elegance to society. Such long-term and fundamental problems arise from basic human needs and the solutions are found the ways in which human civilizations have learned to solve such problems.

These new systems of machines can address the social needs of a nation or a community. They propose an array of solutions (derived from all the global knowledge bases and scientific methodologies) to these needs in a way that is acceptable to the entire society or community. In a sense, early bias, stemming from personal gain or greed of any one group of human beings is viewed in conjunction with the effects on the entire society, and the intent and biases are eliminated like bugs and viruses in a computer system. This two-step dynamic strategy is feasible by a nonprofit, nonpolitical agency such as educational foundations, judicial systems or even a well-written operating system.

The knowledge and wisdom that are derived by the new machines facilitate solution of basic problems optimally and effectively. This permits society to progress towards a more advanced civilization. Growth is thus accelerated. The social gains for the core constituents of society are even more dramatic. In history, the golden rule of King Ashoka (after the brutal war of Kalinga) documents his reign in which a great majority of the subjects enjoyed unsurpassed peace and harmony, even though it was short lived. The Aryan societies, Ancient American Indians, and the older Eskimo societies document that such societies can function stably over long periods until societal forces and the negative tendencies of leaders destroy the very society that gave them their inception.

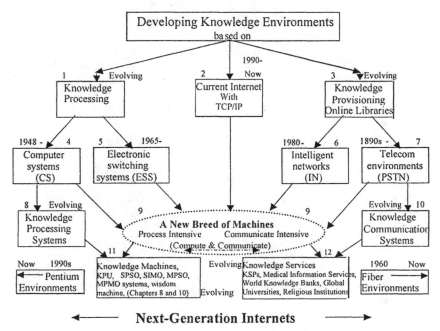

Figure 1.2 The evolution of a new generation of machines and next generation Internets (NGI). Intelligent internets qualify as computer networks that blend knowledge processing for the personal and social needs of human beings with global Internet-based communication systems that utilize national digital highways, WANs, LANs, and information byways of any country. See part II of this book for details of other knowledge systems.

The main advantage of letting the machine perform *initial* knowledge processing functions is the elimination of bias from the decision-making process. All the events are weighed and considered in deriving initial constructs of wisdom. Knowledge and wisdom are guarded as genuine corollaries, derivatives, and extensions of the Laws of Nature.

An environment in which this initial processing of knowledge is performed solely by humans exists in news and TV reporting. Many times, the news items get tainted with the reporter's word and social bias. Any truth, validity, and lesson from the reality (which indeed lead to lasting knowledge and ensuing wisdom) are sometimes discarded in all-human environments. From a global and scientific perspective, truth is sometimes made obscure and it becomes hard to find validity and consistency in what is documented. Social benefit and the elegance of news events (if any) are hardly explained in scientific terms. In the news media network environment, human bias sometimes distorts the truth. Misrepresented news items bring out bias rather than the truth. Machines that systematically verify factual foundations offer some protection against tainted reports.

Conversely, all-machine processing of knowledge can become senseless, irrelevant, and even hypothetical. Perhaps blending the functions of machine clusters (embedded in networks and the Internet) and a team of carefully chosen humans (like Supreme Court justices) could lead society to be just, virtuously inclined, and poised. Generally, outcome is progress of a nation or civilization. Networks, machines and embedded social structures can become the catalysts toward this positive change.

The American judicial system is based on such a model. When a gross injustice is committed at the hands of local judges or law enforcement agencies, the Supreme Courts hears the case and issues new guidelines for the interpretation of the constitutional laws. In this book, we propose to enhance and broaden the judicial model to the informational world (see Chapter 10). Routine information that is transacted in the networks and Internet becomes irrelevant. Only data carrying significant information gets automatically tagged for more inquiry for its universal implications and/or underlying significance. The frequency and certainty of the information derived from many such data streams lead to confidence and knowledge about such transactions. Furthermore, the data streams lead to truth (with a given confidence level), the social value, and the implicit elegance in their occurrence.

Finally, the confluence of lasting truth, positive social values and the elegance of simplicity points to wisdom originating from the data streams in networks and the Internet. This wisdom, when judiciously entered into a dictionary of wisdom, becomes an axiom to be used as a guide in the new sets of events created by the individuals in society. Thus, the positive feedback prevails and the process is enhanced.

1.3 CLASSICAL COMPUTING ENVIRONMENTS

In the early days of computing, machines were built primarily for processing numbers. The instruction sets for these early machines were heavily geared to operations for binary (integer) and simple floating-point numbers. Soon the arithmetic units (AUs) of the central processor units (CPUs) were augmented with logic units (LUs) and combined to optimize the designs of the arithmetic logic units (ALUs) to be fast and efficient. The logic units offer programmers new sets of operations and micro decision capability at the machine and assembly languages levels. These decisions may be based on the quantitative and qualitative nature of initial or intermediate parameters. This parameter-based branching and adaptability of the executions of instructions is the most elementary basis for complex decisions that modern computer systems make.

Introduction of semi-conductor technology facilitated the building of viable smaller computers during the 1950s. The increased capability of the small-scale and medium scale integration (SSI and MSI) chips offered much greater flexibility to hardware designers and also a larger instruction set to binary-level programmers. The applications of computers were gradually enhanced and more accuracy was offered. The character and nature of the parameters as operands were enhanced ranging from integers, floating pointing, and single precision numbers. Later, with the advent of large scale and very-large-scale integration, (LSI and VLSI) double precision, complex numbers, arrays, and matrices could also be processed quite easily by growingly sophisticated hardware in the central processor unit (CPU) and array processors. The types of operations also were enhanced manifold, ranging from the simple add/subtract to the complex matrix manipulations, thus providing users with newer applications of computer systems.

From an architectural perspective, the introduction of the Institute of Advanced Study (IAS), stored-program control (SPC) based machine [4] has left a lasting imprint since the 1950s. A series of attempts to optimize the layout of the hardware resulted in the same memory units of the basic computer to hold the program and the data interchangeably. This arrangement initiated the concept of relocatable programs that further enhanced the use of the same computers for executing different programs and different segments of the same program. Due to this synergy and confluence of inventions in the field of computing, there has been a sustained growth of the computers in many applications and fields.

From a purely hardware perspective, the advent of microprogramming has made computing more universal. The same machine platform can service different applications such as scientific and/or business. The microprogrammable CPU gets primed with microprograms in the control memory (CM) in the form of different chip sets. In turn, the CPU of a main machine now serves either the scientific and research community or the business and accounting community.

The enhancements were equally impressive in the early software. The assemblers, loaders, and linkers offered more latitude and enhanced programmability. The nature of the hardware framework was reflected in the three final stages (assembly, loading, and linking) of the generation of binary executable code. For example, the IBM 360/370 series of machines had a specific basic assembly language (BAL) quite different from that for the DEC machines. The loaders and linkers were also specific to the machine. Thus the user/programmer could relinquish the need to know that framework or the architecture of the machine that would execute the programs. In essence, these high-end users needed to become familiar with the application problems and the rules of higher-level languages (HLLs).

Compilers of these HLLs were getting increasingly sophisticated. For example, the extent of improvement from the compilers for FORTRAN II to FORTRAN IV was dramatic. The lexical analysis (LA) for parsing, syntactic analysis (SA_1) for syntactic usage of variables, and semantic analysis (SA_2) for determining the context and semantics of usage of variables and their operations were becoming highly dependable and efficient. On the one hand, they were specifically designed and application directed, providing more flexibility and command to be executed on (almost) any machine. On the other hand, the intermediate code generated by the compilers after LA, SA_1 and SA_2 could be coupled to machine specific assemblers, loaders, and linkers of other machines. This segmentation of the compiler and machine level functions still offers a great amount of portability and functionality to the programs.

However, the introduction of optimizing compliers (e.g., the FORTRAN V compilers) for scientific and engineering problems provided new insight for a global optimization for the outer software layers. This particular approach using iterative optimization procedures to arrange and address the location and relocation of the program variables reduces the execution time of the programs, even though the one-time initial compilation time is increased. Thus the repeatedly used HLL programs run faster and use less computer resources. This approach makes computer less expensive to use and gets us closer to the solution of the generic problems in the scientific, engineering, and business community.

1.4 NEWER COMPUTING ENVIRONMENTS

During the 1960s and 1970s, the computer software for scientific and business applications had become sophisticated enough to handle the routine needs of scientific and commercial users. Commercial software had become abundant during the 1980s. However, there was a demand from the skilled programmers for software that allowed one to exert more direct control on the machine functions than the control that was allowed by the designers of higher-level languages. In a sense, the facility that HLL designers provided for typical users was soon becoming a stumbling block for sophisticated users. These users knew the actual limits of hardware and its functions in the CPU and wanted to exploit these functions in the execution of more sophisticated programs. Typical applications came from switching systems designers in the communication industry, packet switch manufacturers, and vendors of specialized computer systems.

Two of the seminal contributions to satisfy the needs of sophisticated users were the UNIX operating system and the C language from Bell Laboratories. In 1965, when electronic switching systems (ESSs) were introduced, the need to control the ESS due to the growth and long-distance nature of telephone calls became apparent and a whole new language was essential to meet the needs of the communications industry. Essentially, a new operating systems (OS) environment (UNIX) and the C language made computers more powerful, to serve sophisticated and demanding users. The concepts introduced in the UNIX OS and their deployment in the C language have been enhanced further in the C++ language for midlevel users. For the more sophisticated users LISP [5], PROLOG [5], and more recently introduced Java [7] languages offer greater flexibility in programming complex tasks on machines.

In essence, the new operating systems and languages provide users with the flexibility to interact with the CPU functions (arithmetic, logical, branching, and switching), which was denied by the HLL software designers. The UNIX OS [8] simplified the numerous layers of older operating systems (OSs) and the C [9] languages made HLLs software more universal and powerful. The ease of programming in the HLL was slightly compromised to achieve more powerful and optimal instruction sets to solve a more complex and generic breed of problems.

A new era of freedom ensued for programmers to address problems that were less prone to computerized solutions. The more versatile control on the functionality of the hardware in the computer and then the enhancement of the CPU hardware have been strong catalysts in allowing computer systems to solve larger arrays of commercial and business problems than what the earlier computer systems could handle. The increased capability of the software and the reduced cost of the VLSI chips have contributed to the rapid and pervasive growth of the mid-era computer systems. Machines have also experienced longer word lengths from the 20 bit architectures of the IAS machine [1] to the 64-bit and then the 128-bit machines. Whereas the IAS architectures were designed for the entire 20-bit words as 8-bit instruction code and 12-bit address field, the newer machines offer much more flexibility. The innermost layers of software have considerable latitude in controlling the CPU functions. Special beneficiaries of this flexibility were the graphics processors that were in their infancy during the 1980s.

1.4.1 Telecommunications Applications

The older communication switching systems control and function as massively parallel processed facilities to handle the "call progress" of each call independently. Typically, they serve well over 100,000 callers simultaneously. These systems need a new breed of operating systems (e.g., the UNIX operating system) and a new powerful language (e.g., the C language) to command the individual processes. The basic building block in the mainframe 4ESS is the 1A and then the more powerful 1B processor [10, pp. 101–104]. The busy hour call attempts (BHCAs) of 1B were over one million in 1994. The main host computer-switch 4ESS could handle 107,502 trunk lines with 500,000 calls per hour as far back as 1974 with the 1A processor. These electronic switching systems were getting increasingly larger, with some urban systems handling larger and larger traffic volume in the traditional circuit-switched mode. The culmination of these switches was the 5ESS switch in the United States with the equivalent Canadian, European, and Japanese switches. [11]. More recently, these switches and their technological stride have been dwarfed by the high-capacity optical switches that handle optical interconnect capability at multi-gigabits per second. It is evident that the traditional general-purpose computing environments cannot handle the needs specific to the telecommunications industry or any other specialized industry. Specific hardware architectures and specialized software configuration are both essential.

Business and financial environments also have specific needs. Over a period of time, numerous software configurations have come and gone. One of the languages for the business applications developed during the 1970s was ALGOL. In a broad sense, business users have not been as demanding and sophisticated as the telecommunications users. Consequently, the effects have been noticeably different. In most cases, the basic hardware for processing of data for business applications has not changed drastically except for the size and interconnectivity of the peripheral devices.

The newer hardware from most computer manufacturers will function interchangeably. The compilers and the machine-specific segments of the compiler will generally suffice for the newer business and financial applications. Specific hardware that has evolved is that for database management, security, and encryption. Businesses have become vast and global, and size and management of business records have also increased. For security needs, specialized software modules generally suffice. In the domain of networks, financial networks [12] assume an elaborate switching strategy over private and secure lines. Major innovative strides in specialized core hardware for commercial applications have not been made even though the scanners and (credit) card readers have become discriminating and abundant over the last few decades.

1.4.2 Medical Applications

Medical systems have crucial and explicit needs. The research and development of these special purpose computers is evident. Typical systems are used in the field of magnetic resonance imaging (MRI). The computer system plays an integral part for delivery of the high-energy excitation (fixed and oscillating) electromagnetic fields and the two measurements of time (spin–lattice and spin–spin) relaxation for the tissues to return to their normal condition. But much more than that, the excitation and the measured data are logged into an elaborate database and a graphic management and interpolation capability that generates very detailed pictures of the tissue under the MRI process. The contour, opaqueness, and the extent spread of a malignancy are accurately traced by specialized software modules to discriminate between healthy and malignant tissues. The computer system thus becomes an integral part of the MRI system. The HW and SW modules are as intricate and sophisticated as the massive electromagnetic field generation systems that deliver the high-energy radiation into the tissue. Even though the complexity exists, the extent of coding involved is drastically less than the C language code that drives the electronic switching systems in the communications industry. Nor is there an elegant way to alter the ESS code to serve as the MRI code because of the different HW structures and SW organization of the two systems. It is imperative to note that the machine modules are customized to the type of application. For this reason, we propose radically different architectures for the inference of knowledge and search for wisdom in the machines discussed in Parts II and III of this book.

1.4.3 Other Computer-Intensive Systems

Computer graphics and electronic game systems have both experienced an explosive growth. From the 1960s when the CPU also functioned as a graphics processor unit (GPU), to the actual embodiment of a separate GPU chip, and then to its reintegration with CPU (486, early 1990s), advances in technology have made most graphics functions fast and efficient. The chip design is suited to the graphic functions, while, the software design is suited to the applications. This evolution has permitted the movie and animation industry that is evident today.

Numerous varieties of chip set designs have appeared over the last two decades. Computer game designers deploy novel applications of the graphics chips and software. The spiraling growth still continues for chips and for embedded software, as computer games grow more sophisticated. Currently, the computer games industry deploys some of the fastest and most powerful chips for animation, coordinate transformations, lighting and visual effects.

The aeronautics and airplane industry has deployed numerous special-purpose chip sets for landing and take-off during inclement weather. When special criteria prevail, the system designers prefer customized chips to perform under harsh environmental and operating conditions. Even though the architecture of chips and code is sophisticated, system designers prefer customized VLSI configurations to general-purpose computers.

Over the last decade, the automobile industry has made vehicles intelligent and safer by integrating appropriate sensing and monitoring systems (see Chapters 4–6) into vehicles. Intelligent hardware agents optimize the automobile systems to be adaptive to weather and road conditions. Automatic safety mechanisms protect the passengers under the most severe impact conditions. In many instances, these numerically controlled systems attain the complexity of small computers but they are not classified as computer or robotic systems. Such gadgets become components of the automobile. The overall functionality becomes optimal and user friendly because of the embedded logic and optimal response of VLSI chips for most modern vehicles (cars, trains, buses, etc.) and the built in graphical user interface for the chip sets.

1.5 OBJECT-ORIENTED SYSTEMS

Numerous versions and enhancements to the UNIX operating system and the C language are available to make computers far more responsive and versatile. In a sense, the outer layers of software are adjusted to impart and maintain the properties of objects (as visualized from the AI programming language perspective) and are manipulated by a set of instructions suited for object manipulation and object processing. Some hardware architectures are better suited for UNIX operating system and C language requirements than others. Computer systems can be redressed in outer layers of software to make one machine emulate another machine. If the entire hardware instruction set is not available on the new machine, then a series of machine code instructions are assigned to perform the same function as the old machine performed. In this mode of emulation, some the UNIX machines can function under a Windows® operating system and vice versa. However, it is important to note that special-purpose computers such as those used for defense and space applications remain aloof in their functionality.

1.6 SPECIAL PURPOSE COMPUTER SYSTEMS

On the one hand, general-purpose computing systems are versatile and inexpensive. On the other hand, dedicated computer systems accomplish special functions efficiently and optimally. Special groups of computers that are specific to the communications industry have a firm foothold in switching systems. The medical field has specialized computers for magnetic resonance imaging (MRI), cancer treatment, X-ray, and radiation centers. The aerospace industry, electronic games industry, and graphics and printing industries each have a history of established demand and usage. It is possible to classify each subset of applications and come up with optimally designed hardware to serve as a unique computer system. Such individualized computer systems are too expensive to be practical and for this reason hardware manufacturers have been providing relatively inexpensive chip sets for different applications.

The concept of providing a computer on a chip has been rampant since the late 1980s. The realization of such a system was documented since 1990s and the full fledge manufacture of the "one month chip," in the early 1990s has offered greater hope for very special-purpose computer systems. When the solution to any problem can penetrate the software and firmware layers to the gate and logic level, the integrated circuit (IC) chip (one billion gates) or a chip set can be fabricated with reasonably high yields and good operational (and numerical) accuracy. The IC industry is mature and successful enough to tackle a new breed of computers to function beyond the routine needs of the scientific, medical, business, and gaming industries. The pursuit of higher speeds, larger wafer size, smaller gate size, and higher yields can only make the computing scene faster, more sophisticated, more accurate, and less expensive.

1.7 CONCLUSIONS

Three forces have intensified the growth of small and large computer systems. Because of demand, innovation and technology have developed new and sophisticated computer systems for the marketplace. The computer industry, medical applications industry, VLSI industry, graphics industry, and electronic games industry have been the chief beneficiaries. Projected social needs (and thus the resulting profits) for the new devices and products lead venture financiers and industry and government leaders to initiate and fund major research and development. Venture financing has brought about sophisticated computer systems to the automobile industry (e.g., Rolls Royce, Ford Motor Company). Industrial leaders have pushed for special purpose systems in semiconductor industry (e.g., Intel, Motorola) and government funding (NSF and ARPA) has initiated the seminal concepts in the packet switching industry. Whereas the motives of financiers and industry are to exploit the economic opportunities, the government involvement is generally aimed at providing longer-term benefits for the society. National and political goals are driving these research projects.

Current technology is being used to make radical changes to the existing systems. Inventors and financial teams validate the technical and financial success of the new computer and systems projects. The aerospace industry is a good example of the union of technology and federal sponsorship during the 1960s.

Follow-up technologies and/or products also stand to benefit from the new and radical concepts. The VLSI gating principle has benefited the most applications, ranging from tiniest mobile telephone to monumental space observatories; the internal combustion concept has benefited the transportation industry, while fiber optic transmission has benefited global communication systems.

Advanced computing systems can accelerate social progress by learning from humans how to better society at large. Whereas social progress is based on refinement of knowledge and wisdom, computing systems (in a preliminary sense) are directed toward the numerical and logical processing of data. Thus, it becomes imperative that a dependable link be established between the processing of data and the deductions of axioms of wisdom. For this reason, we propose (Chapter 12) that the boundaries between data and information, information and knowledge, and knowledge and wisdom need to be explored and (if possible) mathematically formalized. The tools and techniques borrowed from AI, especially pattern recognition (PR) and expert systems (ESs) can determine if the patterns of information flow in computer and communication networks offer clues to the underlying knowledge, and if those networks can be iteratively used again to find axioms of wisdom from that newly derived knowledge. In this context, graphs linking different events and objects in society become useful in predictive searches (just like a human being would pursue) for new knowledge and then the ensuing wisdom (if any).

REFERENCES

[1] M. J. Seifer, *The Life and Times of Tesla*, Citadel Press, Sacramento, CA, 1998.
[2] R. M. Hening, *The Monk in the Garden: The Lost and Found: Genius of Gregor Mendel, the Father of Genetics*, Mariner Books, Boston, 2001.

[3] I. G. Birkhauser, George Boole: *Selected Manuscripts on Logic and Its Philosophy,* 1977. See also A. C. Gillie, *Binary Arithmetic and Boolean Algebra,* McGraw Hill, New York, 1965.

[4] A. W. Burks, H. H. Goldstine, and J. von Neumann, U. S. *Army Report Ordnance Department,* 1946. See also G. Estrin, The Electronic Computer at the Institute of Advanced Studies, *Mathematical Tables and Other Aids to Computation, Vol. 7,* IAS, Princeton, NJ, 1953, pp. 108–114.

[5] P. Seibel, *Practical Common Lisp,* Apress, Berkeley, CA, 2005.

[6] S. J. Russell and P. Norvig, *Artificial Intelligence,* Prentice Hall, Upper Saddle River, NJ, 1995.

[7] E. Castro, *HTML for the World Wide Web with XHTML and CSS: Visual QuickStart Guide,* Peachpit Press, Berkeley, CA, 2002.

[8] J. Peek, et al. *Learning the UNIX Operating System,* 5th ed., O'Reilly Media, Sebastopol, CA, 2002.

[9] B. Stroustrup, *The C++ Programming Language,* 3rd ed., Addison Wesley, Boston, 2000.

[10] S. V. Ahamed and V. B. Lawrence, *Design and Engineering of Intelligent Communication Systems,* Kluwer Academic Publishers, Boston, 1998.

[11] S. V. Ahamed and V. B. Lawrence, *Intelligent Broadband Multimedia Networks,* Kluwer Academic Publishers, Boston, 1997.

[12] N. Goldburt, *Design Considerations for Financial Institution Intelligent Networks,* Ph.D. Dissertation at the Graduate Center of the City University of New York, 2004.

Chapter *2*

Network Perspective

Modern networks are highly diversified to suit the specialized demands of the applications they serve. These networks can be customized much like the chip sets that are fabricated to suit a specific purpose. The networking techniques are almost as diversified as the computing techniques. In fact, programmable computing systems are the precursors to modern switching systems that constitute the major building blocks of networks.

Applications of computing systems are far more diversified than the applications of networks. Whereas computing systems and networks evolved somewhat independently, switching within the computer is essential. Likewise, the programmable switching modules are essential for network functions. A healthy symbiotic interdependence prevails. Networks are implied in almost all modern computing systems and computing systems or subsystems are implied in almost all modern networks.

Before computer systems (especially the stored program or the SPC generic and programmable systems), the telephone and telephone networks were manually or relay switched. Rudimentary as they had been, they were still deployed in medium sized networks; they were still deployed as late as the 1960s. Rows of telephone operators would use switchboards systematically to make duplex connections to complete calls. Soon after, step-by-step rotary switches were deployed based on pulses of current to mechanically connect different circuits within the older networks.

Intelligent Internet Knowledge Networks. By Syed V. Ahamed
Copyright © 2007 John Wiley & Sons, Inc.

Fortunately, human multipliers and dividers were never systematically used in computing applications, although (it is said) very early logarithmic tables were calculated by rows of human beings very good in arithmetic. Today, there is no human element in low-level computing or in networks. Most modern switching systems are computerized to make networks as robust and dependable as computer systems.

In perspective, creativity is still in the realm of human activity. However, machines have gradually taken over human activities that are routine and programmable. Even though intelligence can be forced upon machines (by the AI programs), concepts and wisdom are in the domain of human beings until machines can be "taught" to deal with truth, elegance in concepts and universality of wisdom.

In this chapter, more sophisticated technologies that have made intelligent networks, broadband networks, and the Internet feasible are introduced in Section 2.1. Communication features of three generic medium types (copper, microwave, and fiber) are presented in Sections 2.2 and 2.3. Optical standards are presented in 2.4. The technologies embedded in existing networks (intelligent networks, broadband networks, and the Internet) that offer a platform for emerging networks (medical, educational, and electronic government) are presented in the remaining sections. It is well within the creative framework of new inventors to use enhanced or even parallel technologies to offer enhanced or even different applications.

The role of peripherals is emphasized in building smart, responsive, and intelligent networks. Typical applications that are embedded in telecommunication networks are presented to show that such network and application intelligence can be built into other specialized environments such as intelligent medical networks, intelligent distance learning, and campus networks, and intelligent defense and surveillance networks.

Since the introduction of the 800-network or IN/1, the role of databases in networks has become a topic of prime importance. The database (SCP/1) was first introduced in 1980 for network control. In current applications, network databases play an ever more demanding and intensified role. A typical application of a database management system is presented for simulation and design studies of distribution networks. Such networks are used to take the digital data over the "last mile" to eventual users.

In the applications presented in this book, all earlier database techniques and strategies have been extended into the object base and knowledge base systems. Such data, object, and knowledge base techniques and systems become especially important in manipulating information, knowledge, wisdom, and values in current and future networks. Accordingly, the section (Section 2.10) deals with database management systems and their organization. These become the basis for building object and knowledge base systems as discussed in Chapters (4–15).

2.1 EVOLVING NETWORK ARCHITECTURES

In a macroscopic sense, network architectures experienced the explosive growth during the 1990s similar to what the VLSI architectures experienced during the late 1970s and 1980s. The number of chip architectures far outnumbers the network architectures even though a conceptual parallelism prevails. In a broad sense, the silicon to Pentium migration (in LSI) is comparable to the copper to fiber migration (in networks). The local bus structures in wafer scale integration are comparable to lightwave circuits within global knowledge networks. The exponential growth in the semiconductor industry has sent delayed shock waves throughout the network industry. Some of these delayed waves have already arrived as intelligent networks, SONET, ATM, and wireless networks. Networks have expanded into also medical, educational, and electronic government fields. Such analogies and their implications continue to unfold in the corporate and in the personal domains.

In this chapter, we discuss the major implications of the changes in technology of the last three or four decades (e.g., smart networks and intelligent robots) and extrapolate the possible future systems (such as knowledge networks and concept banks) now lurking on the horizon. When will society feel that it is ready to accept the potential contributions from such systems? From a technological consideration, such systems are already feasible. Being aware of the human pitfalls, we have reason to suspect that these inventions can be abused to the detriment of humankind. (See Chapter 15).

2.2 NETWORKS FOR COMMUNICATION

Almost all recent communication networks incorporate the architectures and advantages of fiber optic systems. The advantages are far-reaching. Universal network access is greatly enhanced by deploying cordless telephones (CT2), and third generation (CT3), 2G, 2G+, and 3G wireless technologies are discussed further in Section 2.2.2. Recommendations and standards proposed by the International Telecommunication Union (ITU) Open System Interconnect (OSI) committees are strictly followed to make these networks global.

In general, four of the most significant driving forces in the communication (and computer networking) arena are (1) all-digital wireless technologies; (2) SONET digital hierarchy; (3) ATM architectures that engulf most existing circuit, packet, and message switched networks including the high-speed American (DS1, DS3, etc.), European (E1, E2, E3, etc.), and private LANs; and (4) the extended ITU-OSI signaling hierarchy to span the numerous networks.

Appropriate peripheral devices and interfaces channel the information from network to network from across the street to across the world. In this section, the overall perspective of the newer networks is presented. In the packet transfer mode, traditional packet switching (e.g., X.25) exists over low quality voice grade networks. Fast packet switching exists as a frame relay with variable packet size, in networks with a speed of less than 2 Mb/s, and also with fixed packet size broadband networks. Switched multi-megabit digital service (SMDS) uses the distributed queue dual bus (DQDB) protocol. It is deployed over connectionless networks between 2 and 45 Mb/s whereas the ATM cells are transported at rates higher than 45 Mb/s. Due to the fixed size of the packets or cells and the "connectionless" path in DQDB and the ATM networks, such services are classified as *cell relay services*.

The simple and cost effective Ethernet lines have rates of 10, 100, 1000 Mb/s with the possibility of 10 Gb/s. These rates make Ethernet options viable in the metropolitan area network (MAN) environment. The gigabit Ethernet, primarily used to interconnect data networks, operates in a connectionless mode and nominally (due to possible packet loss) offers 1.25 Gb/s. The newer 10-gigabit Ethernet standards promote the convergence of earlier network technologies. To accommodate the growing demand for high bandwidth, deployment of the edge network between private virtual networks (PVNs), storage area networks (SANs), and the core SONET/SDH is foreseen as an economic and a viable alternative.

The legacy SONET/SDH does not handle bursty packet data traffic efficiently, especially in the metropolitan area networks. With an intense growth in data traffic because of high-speed LANs, DSL, and SANs (at 1.06 and 2.12 Gb/s), network service providers are shifting their attention to next generation SONET/SDH. The next-generation SONET/SDH extends deployment of the existing or core SONET/SDH network by slightly modifying the Layer-1 (physical layer) networking by including newer technologies, such as virtual concatenation (VC), generic framing procedures (GFPs) and link capacity adjustment scheme (LCAS).

The modern high-speed cell relay (ATM), the frame relay (carrying OC-n rates) and traditional digital carrier systems [1], the American and European digital systems, the ISDN systems, the circuit-switched digital capability, the DSL and the ADSL can all merge into a the low-cost, highly elegant and efficient optical carrier system. The digitized data in the voice grade networks can also be carried but the streaming of data becomes cumbersome due to the low speed of the traditional packet data rates and the very high speed of the optical carrier systems.

2.2.1 Copper in Networks

High-speed transmission on copper facilities had been an economic alternative to homes and locations where the copper already exists for transmission. With the 2B1Q code, BRISDN high-speed data is feasible, if not already available, to individual homes. Both the 2B1Q and the cluster codes have fallen into disfavor with chip manufacturers (since mid-1990s) for the network terminations at the customer and central office ends. With DMT and 2-D trellis coding methodologies, data transmission up to the T1 rate of 1.544 Mb/s (in the HDSL mode of operation) is feasible to most individual customers.

Where the loop environment is harsh, the subrate (i.e., rates less than 1.544 Mb/s) transmission over an individual subscriber line (768 or 384 kb/s) becomes an option to offer digital services to the customers. The same methodologies can take data rate to 6.34 Mb/s in the ADSL mode, and data from variable rates of 384 kb/s to 6.34 Mb/s in the symmetric digital subscriber line (SDSL) mode. Fiber capacity, even at the lowest SONET rate of 51.64 Mb/s, can reach individual homes in a star or bus topology from a centralized data distribution point. It is approximately 30 times faster than the T1 rate of 1.544 Mb/s.

Currently, there are numerous variations for the digital subscriber line. The IDSL (for ISDN-DSL) with a rate of 144 kb/s (first studied and analyzed in 1978 [2]) has been deployed for two bearer channels at 64 kb/s each and a delta channel at 16 kb/s for signaling and low-speed data. The codes deployed [2] are the AMI, the 2B1Q, and the 4B2T to reduce the transmission rates (80 kb/s for 2B1Q code) over the copper medium. HDSL is meant for T1 (1.544 Mb/s) and E1 (2.048 Mb/s) rates over carrier serving area (CSA) loops in dual-duplex (two wire pairs) mode and needs 0–400 kb/s with 2B1Q code. Typically one bridge tap is permitted and a binder group separation is not required. The SDSL or the SHDSL is a single wire pair version of the HDSL but needs 0–350 kHz for upstream and 0–450 kHz for downstream data using the 16 phase and amplitude modulation (PAM) constellation coding for reducing the bandwidth over the copper channel.

The ADSL has four (ADSL/ADSL Lite, ADSL2/ADSL2+) subcategories. The DSL standards permit echo cancellation (ECH) mode and frequency-division multiplex (FDM) mode. The upstream range is 16 kb/s to 1 Mb/s and the downstream range is 1.5–9 Mb/s on most of the standard loops. Discrete multi-tone (DMT) modulation techniques are used. The ADSL standards are quite elaborate and cumbersome: Standards T1.413 originated in North America and was then standardized by ITU as G.992.1 for full rate ADSL (also known as G.DMT and G.992.2 standard called the G.LITE).

VDSL supports all voice data and video simultaneously with the required quality of service (QoS). Video conferencing, HDTV, graphics, and imaging are also supported. The upstream rate is 2.34–3.78 Mb/s and the downstream rate is 7.56–51.84 Mb/s in the asymmetric mode and 7.56–25.92 Mb/s in the symmetric mode. Two codes (MCM with DMT coding and SCM with CAP or QAM coding) are possible. Fiber to node architecture with an optical network unit (ONU) situated in the existing metallic access network is usually deployed for the VDSL architectures.

From the hybrid fiber coaxial (HFC) environment, fiber serves as the backbone of the video/multimedia network that takes data to video hubs at rates of multi-gigabits per second, transmitting digital images and sound as clearly and crisply as toll quality PCM encoded speech. Both the "fiber to the house" (FTTH) and "fiber to the curb" (FTTC) options offer unsurpassed advantages to both network owners (larger flexible service provisioning with IP intelligence with higher revenue projections) and customers (higher bandwidth and more bits per dollar) but at a slightly enhanced initial cost.

Presently, value-added services over copper facilities (xDSL) have three broad categories. First, video services offer broadcast and video on-demand options to customers. The capacity for high bandwidth downstream to customers is a service requirement for video. The bandwidth requirement for broadcast is predictable but it is less predictable for video on-demand. The required quality of service also calls for tight delay tolerance for delay and packet loss. Fast channel switching, security, and user chosen service provisioning also become important. Second, voice over IP (VoIP) and video conferencing need strict QoS controls as far as jitter and packet loss are concerned. Security issues also need to be addressed. Third, for the IP private virtual network services, data security, continuity of service, and high bandwidth provisioning (if needed) are also issues that the network service providers need to address.

If the DSL services are offered via a circuit-switched central office facility, then the numerous customer premises equipment is multiplexed onto a STM-1 service at the central office. The DSLAM uplink multiplexer typically converts the DSL data and signal onto the Layer 2 ATM format. The ATM aggregation occurs and then the ATM networks provide interconnection to ISP and the other core Internet type service providers. For future networks, the FTTC DSLAM provides communication over optical fiber to the curb. With the FTTC option, both ADSL2+ and VDSL services may be provided over a bandwidth of approximately 25 Mb/s because of the extremely short copper length between the curb to the customer premises. Multicast service and IP intelligence can also be included in the customer premises equipment or CPE.

2.2.2 Microwaves in Networks

The introduction of cell phones has brought microwave communications to prominence. However, the use of microwaves for signal transmission was the basis of Marconi's (1897) and Tesla's (1901) original patents. Microwave technology has made monumental strides during the last century [3]. In this section, some of the highlights as they pertain to the immediate access and availability of information are summarized.

Wireless communication offer unique features to customers and the technology focused on five groups of users— portable in-house users, mobile walk-around users, fixed-location users, commuting (train and plane) users, and traveling global users. The earlier mobile radio systems offered two-way radio communication, unichannel dispatch capability, and individualized paging systems. Multiple access and limited addressing capability are possible. Packet-mode communication is generally deployed and works dependably with acknowledge mode that forces a retransmission if the packets are not received or get error prone.

For two-way telephone users, deployment of the wireless "last-link" capability was introduced in 1978 to connect remote payphone users to the central office. The second-generation cordless telephones (CT2) connected users to the central offices. The third-generation CT3 systems with small private branch exchange (PBX) followed shortly afterwards.

Other wireless telecommunications facilities, such as POTS, other circuit-switched, packet-switched and message-switched services are available and small wireless PBXs could be integrated with major switching systems such as electronic switches and cell and frame relay systems. Almost any service can be offered now from a network perspective.

The geographical partitioning into neighboring hexagonal base cells with handover protocol facilitated immense mobility for users. The location of the wireless PBXs at the vertices of the (approximate) hexagonal cells for telephone (or services) coverage further made the handover smooth and dependable. The subdivision of larger hexagons into smaller cellular hexagons permits higher traffic density in densely populated areas.

The global system for mobile communication (GSM) that is deployed in Pan-European second-generation digital radio systems brought greater dependability and coverage to wireless telephony. Other types of wireless communications such as private mobile radio (PMR) and European radio message systems (ERMES), also became popular on the European scene. The present technology is based on the research and development projects for advanced communication in Europe (RACE, RACE-I, and RACE-2) that will resolve open-ended technical issues by using systematic and technologically well founded solutions.

The universal mobile telephone services (UMTSs) initiated in America provide access to ISDN, bearer services, low rate video, image, document retrieval, and video services. The UMTS-2000 is primarily a packet-based system. The architectures of the generic universal mobile telephone services (GUMTSs) network are documented in [3].

The third-generation (3G) wireless networks provide communications for everyone, everywhere (accessible via microwave and telephone networks), at any time. The customers include cellular users, private network users, paging users, cordless users at home and offices, satellite users with global coverage, and globe trekkers, because of convergence technologies within fixed and mobile networks. The goals are to have common provisioning for landline and mobile users, universal subscriber identification, ATM-based switching architecture, and more or less common call processing modular procedures. The migration to 3G is facilitated by a 2+G phase deploying group and broadcast calls. The general packet radio service (GPRS) allows packet-switched communications. The intelligent network services for mobile users (called CAMEL) will allow users to utilize operator-specific services during roaming onto other networks.

A significant number of simulation tools and techniques are available for the design of wireless communication systems. Techniques for dealing with flat and multiple peak terrains can offer constant signal strength as the roamers traverse the domain. Short term fading effects, envelope and phase variation in the signal can be tracked. Five modulation techniques (coherent binary AM or PSK, FM with discrimination, coherent FSK, non-coherent FSK and differential PSK) are available for digital transmission. For secrecy and security, spread spectrum systems (SST) can be deployed. The effects of interference and the impact of the nine wireless (Trunk-ed Radio, SST, CDMA, cellular radio, mobile satellite, infrared, meteor burst, VSAT, and RF) feasible technologies are presented in [3].

2.2.3 Fiber Optics in Networks

Optical transmission was proposed during the early 1960s after the invention of the laser in 1960. The multi layered glass structure was suggested during the mid 1960s and Corning Glass produced a rough specimen of fiber with about 20-dB/km loss in 1970. Optical systems have been functioning with ever increasing capacity and sophistication. The high quality single mode fibers offer about 0.16 dB/km loss at 1.55 µM wavelength and about 0.25 dB/km loss at 1.30 µm wavelength. The chromatic dispersion [1] at approximately 15 picoseconds/km-nanometer in the low loss window of 1.5 µm (with zero dispersion at 1.3 µm) is also equally attractive. Both of these attributes make fiber optic systems essential components of most modern networks.

Two major driving forces behind most broadband digital networks are the availability of high-grade fiber for transmission and the profusion of inexpensive ATM switches. The transmission issue was successfully resolved during the 1970s and early 1980s. Presently, the data rates and ranges are well beyond the projected needs of even the most digit-intensive society. Where fiber is easily available, new national and global trunk data communication are mostly based on fiber optics. Fiber is deployed in most of the older trunk and shared transmission facilities throughout the United States, Canada, Europe, Japan, and Australia [3].

2.3 TRANSMISSION IN OPTICAL NETWORK

Through the 1990s, high-speed optical switching was being incorporated within the optical fiber systems to offer true optical networks. Fibers can carry data at multi-gigabits/second rates quite dependably. Local public domain networks (such as the telephone networks) are likely to continue to deploy semiconductor switching under stored program control and to deploy fiber for high-capacity, long-haul transmission. When fiber optic backbone networks are tied into wireless networks, the hurdle for all-optical communication is the wireless link. When fiber optic backbone networks are tied into the Internet, the only hurdle for the broadband link is the subscriber line capacity. However, FTTH and FTTC seem to be two distinct paths around the subscriber loop constraints.

Super high-speed switching for optical computing is still not practical, and optical computers are yet to be proven economically feasible before networks can assimilate their switching capacity. Currently, compound semiconductor materials [1] can not offer clean sharp edges for gating photons in optical signals. This scenario is similar to the delayed impact of semiconductor digital computers of the mid-1950s on switching systems of the mid-1960s. Having its inception in 1948, the computer industry was already well into its prime before the first electronic switching system (1ESS) was introduced in 1965.

Fiber optic communication is deployed in most national and international communications networks. On the national scene, fiber has been introduced routinely for interoffice high data capacity channels in the United States, Canada,

Europe, and Japan. Optical rates OC-12 (at 622.080 Mb/s) and OC-48 (at 2488.32 Mb/s) have been achieved by commercial systems. Most information services, deploying data links at these rates handle voice, video, and data communication needs of large and small customers. The data rates with the DWDM techniques are much higher. These services use fiber to the house (FTTH) and fiber to the curb (FTTC) architectures. BRISDN (144 kb/s) and PRISDN (T1/E1 rates) bearer capabilities, progressing into the broadband ISDN (155–600 Mb/s) services, and then to the ATM-based bandwidth on-demand capability become readily feasible with all-fiber backbone and distribution architectures. The operating cost for such services is in the maintenance of the transceivers rather than the maintenance of the fiber transmission media.

On the international scene, the first undersea transatlantic telephone cable (TAT-8) was commissioned in late 1988. The capacity is limited to 40,000 voice calls, which is double the capacity of all other copper transatlantic cables and satellites. The next fiber cable system (TAT-9) commissioned in the early 1990s handles twice this capacity at 80,000 voice calls.

More recently, any country aspiring to participate in the digital revolution has a stake in the worldwide broadband backbone. Interconnections are almost as varied as the telephone channel connects in a small region. Fiber has diminished the size of the globe for data traffic to less than 1 second (including buffer and server times) at broadband Internet speeds. The router and bridge delays are usually longer than the transmission delays. The globe now has a flexibility to interconnect town to town and knowledge bank to knowledge bank. In our information rich society, the data and information banks can communicate almost instantly. Knowledge (after knowledge processing (Chapter 8) is in place), concepts and wisdom (after concept and wisdom machine (Chapters 10 and 11) are in place) can also get communicated at Internet speeds.

There are dozens[1] (and even hundreds, locally) of fiber optic undersea cables around the world. Network service providers around the globe are as common as Internet services providers in a community. For this reason, we provide a global overview of two typical global fiber optic networks currently serving different cultures and societies.

The TAT-8 high capacity fiber optic transmission system transmits 296 Mb/s data over 3646 miles. This system is equipped with 109 repeaters spaced approximately 70 km (230,000 ft.) apart using coherent laser sources at 1.3 μm wavelength. Six single-mode fibers constitute the cable. The combined capacity of TAT-8 and TAT-9 has served the transatlantic telecommunication needs since mid-1990s. Transpacific fiber optic cable systems link Japan, Guam, Hawaii, and the Pacific Rim states.

---

[1] Trans Atlantic Cables: CANTAT-3 at 2.5 Gb/s; TAT-12,TAT 13 at 5Gb/s; Atlantis-2 (12,000 km) at 10 Gb/s; Gemini at 30 Gb/s; Columbus III (11,000 km); Atlantic Crossing AC-1, (14,000 km); and Trans Pacific Cables: TPC-5 at 5 Gb/s (25000 km), Japan-USA; TPC-6, at 100 Gb/s with Soliton Technology; APCN (12,000 km) at 5 Gb/s; US/China Fiber Cable (27,000 km), at 80 Gb/s; (SEA-ME-WE-3 38000 km, in 1999, at 2.5 Gb/s initially but expanded later. FLAG or Fiber Link Around the Globe, (27000 km), UK, Spain, Sicily, Alexandria, Jeddah, Dubai, Bombay, Thailand, Hong Kong, Korea, Japan .

In order to provide high-capacity cable linking Europe to the Asia-Pacific region, the SEA-ME-WE 2 (South East Asia Middle East Western Europe 2) was initiated in 1993. Singapore Telecom and France Telecom started the submarine cable project after preliminary studies during the late 1980s. Because of the success of the SEA-ME-WE 2 project, a successor project, SEA-ME-WE 3 was initiated [4]. The later system includes 39 landing points in 33 countries and 4 continents from Western Europe (including Germany, England, and France) to the Far East (including China, Japan, and Singapore) and to Australia. SEA-ME-WE 3 (Figure 2.1) is the longest system in the world with a total length of 15,058 miles or about 39,000 km. The use of wavelength division multiplexing (WDM) greatly increases the capacity of the networks allowing high-quality transmission over distances as great as from Germany to Australia. The system capacity as at August 2003 has been upgraded twice already and consists of two fiber pairs each carrying 8 wavelengths. Some wavelengths operate at 10G while others operate at 2.5G. The maximum bandwidth in sections of the SEA-ME-WE 3 network is 20 Gb/s (as of the end of 2005). Total capacity including 10G is 505G (= 3232 STM1).

A recent 17,400-mile (27,850-km), global long-haul network is the SAT-3/WASC/SAFE submarine cable system providing connectivity to and from (1) Portugal, (2) Spain, (3) Senegal, (4) Cote d'Ivoire, (5) Ghana, (6) Benin, (7) Nigeria, (8) Cameroon, (9) Gabon, (10) Angola, (11) South Africa (Access Point) 1, (12) South Africa (Access Point) 2, (13) Reunion, (14) Mauritius, (15) India, (16) Singapore and (17) Malaysia. Countries (4 through 13) are on the west coast of Africa and benefit greatly from the established global economies of the West and from the growing economies of countries like India and Malaysia. The acronyms stand for third South Atlantic Telephone cable (SAT-3), West African Submarine Cable (WASC) and South Africa–Far East (SAFE). It has been operational since April 2002 and is expected to provide digital capacity of 120 Gb/s. In order to provide high-speed connections around the globe, the first phase was called SEA-ME-WE-3 (from the Western countries to Singapore) and ready for service since 1999, the second phase encompasses the WAT-3-WASC (countries 4–12) and the SAFE (countries 14–17) submarine cables which have been in service since 2002. In the final phase of deployment, EASSy (East African countries) ties in both SEA-ME-WE-3 and the SAT-3/WASC/SAFE long-haul fiber optic cable networks from six locations.

Towards the end of 2005, SEA-ME-WE-4, the underwater cable connecting Southeast Asia, the Middle East and Western Europe came into service with a capacity that is 32 times its originally designed (in 1998) capacity. It has a full capacity of 1.28 terabits per second (10 Gb/s for each of the 64 WDM channels on each of the two fiber pairs). The span is about 20,000 km. A map of the fiber backbone covering the fiber optic net embedded in SEA-ME-WE 3 and 4 networks is shown in Figure 2.1.

These fiber optic transmission systems facilitate the communication of high-speed data. Knowledge processing or the intelligent network functions are not an integral part of these fiber optic systems. However, in conjunction with intelligent nodes and intelligent database systems (strategically located within the network), the fiber optic transmission systems offer high-performance digital access for computers, knowledge bases, multimedia, video, educational, medical imaging, facsimile, and even plain old telephone services throughout the world. Currently, the global fiber networks are underutilized. The lack of demand from the commercial sector and hence the lack of economic incentive are strong deterrents to additional growth of very-high capacity optical networks.

The recent trend in optical networks is to provide broadband and Internet service at competitive rates and make these networks scaleable for the expanding needs of the corporate community. For ease of installation and maintenance, the choice is toward passive optical networks (PONs). This approach makes PON networks as affordable as the traditional copper-based technologies. Over the decades even the very early copper-based technologies adopted (T1) repeaters, line extenders, and subscriber loop carrier systems. These technologies are discussed in some detail in [2]. Because of the innovations in fiber optic line termination devices, copper-based technologies and the associated devices are likely to be short lived.

Numerous digital subscriber line (DSL) and the asymmetric digital subscriber line (ADSL) technologies have staged a comeback and remain vital until the PON technology becomes so inexpensive that the fiber to home (FTTH) or the fiber to the curb (FTTC) technologies will replace the obsolete copper telephone lines.

There are inherent advantages associated with the PON technologies for reaching customers. Currently, PONs offer broadband and global access using both time-division multiplexing (TDM) and IP services at prices comparable to the copper (twisted wire pair and coaxial) based services. Even though the installation is a capital investment, revenue opportunities for voice, video, interactive video, TV, and games are enormous.

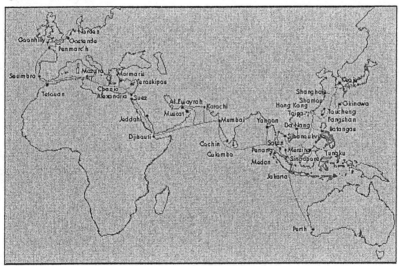

Figure 2.1 One of the recent fiber optic (SEA-ME-WE 3 and 4) networks added to the community of high-speed backbones of the world.

Robust optical network terminations (ONTs) allow the PON to reach consumer premises with numerous options. At the low end, the network configuration options are typically two/four POTS lines, Ethernet service, RF and switched digital video services. Full options of the telephony service (with all the CLASS options [3] and customization and all the X11 services) become feasible. Typical virtual private networking (VPN) options become available because of the large fiber bandwidth and limited programmability at the termination which offers multiple ISP support and multiple data services profiling for users. Multiple-customer service can also be provided with an enhanced network termination for community centers, hospitals, and businesses.

Central office (CO) terminations need typical data switches for CATV electronics and all the telephony interconnect options for the typical telephone services. These CO optical terminations are built to be compatible with the Class 5 switched from different vendors all around the world and offer TDM and DS1 interfaces. Simple DS0 cross-connects with carrier application make service provisioning and customization available to individual customers.

The optical networks offer a range of choices for video services and applications. The IPTV using the digital IP video format and IP network provides premium and CATV quality. Extended services, such as pay per view, VCR options, and video over TV also become options. Standard TV (SDTV) and HDTV at 20 Mb/S (or more for additional channels) are programmable options. Both Internet and CATV signals provide video content for customers. Digitized CATV and Internet video content typically flow through a high capacity router. Other switched services flow through multiple T1 lines at the Class 5 central offices. The high bandwidth and cellular (53-octet ATM cells, see [2]) nature of the ATM traffic that carries a wide variety of services solves the congestion problem in most of the lower bandwidth video networks. Medical and educational networks stand to benefit from global and local passive fiber optic networks.

The impact of these newer networks is still to be felt within the global community of information and knowledge users. The digital environment is becoming dominant in society. This trend is likely to make newer computer systems and internets more capable of serving the personal and social needs of human beings. History has demonstrated the synergy between computers systems, VLSI technology, and network growth during the 1980s. It is foreseeable that knowledge processing systems, nanotechnology devices, and intelligent Internets may provide a new breed of machines that solve deep-seated human and social problems rather than scientific and business problems.

2.4 THE SONET STANDARD

SONET stands for the Synchronous Optical NETwork, OC stands for optical carrier and OC-n stands for Optical Carrier at rate n times the basic rate of 51.840 Mb/s. SONET has made deep inroads in almost all networks because of the standard PCM time slot of 125 microseconds (μs) that is deployed at all the optical rates. It is also associated with the well-accepted standards for the transport of predefined frames through the network. SONET concepts are well documented in the literature [3]. An overview of the subject is presented in this book only to inform and assert that the network technology that is proposed for the wisdom machines (Chapter 8) and the personal behavioral networks (Chapter 12) can be implemented relatively inexpensively by SONET on fiber and ATM on SONET. The ease of multiplexing and the elegance of the hierarchy have both contributed to its global acceptance as the optical standard. The older nonsynchronous hierarchical systems such as DS1 (1.544 Mb/s), CEPT-1 (2.048 Mb/s), DS1C (3.152 Mb/s), and DS2 (6.312 Mb/s) are combined via VT (virtual tributary) streaming into a STS-1 SPE (synchronous payload envelope) signal and even DS3 (44.736 Mb/s) with path overhead into one STS-1 signal. The overall transport capability of almost all international communication carriers is thus preserved in the SONET optical networks.

SONET standards, originally proposed by BCR[2] specify the standardized formats and interfaces for optical signals. Historically, the work started as far back as 1985 to provide standard optical interfaces between major carriers (such as NYNEX, MCI, or Sprint). SONET standards address four goals. They attempt to provide a broad family of interfaces at optical rates (i.e., OC-1 through OC-192). They provide easy and simple multiplexing/demultiplexing of the signals (such as headers and payloads) within the network components. They address the issues of the growing trend toward communication networks becoming synchronous. Finally, they provides ample overhead channels and functions (via the header blocks) to perform and support the maintenance of the network facility.

Total synchronism of all networks is unachievable and for this reason the standard committees have accepted plesiochronous [3] interfacing signals, thus permitting the use of less than perfect timing recovery circuits in the network.

These standards, first approved by ANSI's T1X1 committee for standard fiber optic transmission, were reviewed and accepted by CEPT, ITU, and the European Telecoms in the 1987–1988 time span [5] after considerable debate (the 9-row/13-row debate) about the number of rows in each of the frames. The 9-row x 90 column frame was favored by some of the European Telecoms and the 13-row x 60 column frame was favored by the United States.

In February 1988, the Synchronous Transport Signal - Level 1, shown in Figure 2.2 was finally accepted with 9 rows x 90 columns and at a bit rate of 51.84 Mb/s. At this rate, the time duration of the frame is exactly 125 µs and this duration is necessary to get 810 bytes (or octets with 8 bits per byte or octet) at a rate of 51.840 Mb/s. Thus, one entire frame gets into the network in 125 µs (at OC-1 rate), and this is the same as the sample time of the PCM encoded speech of 1 byte (8 bits) at

---

[2] (Bell Communications Research, a research and development unit of Bell Operating Companies, later taken over by Telcordia Inc.)

[3] The plesiochronous nature permits a small variation in the significant timing instants of the nominally synchronous signals; that is the recovered signals may have small, but controlled, variations in their instantaneous rates or their instantaneous frequencies.

8 kHz, thus maintaining the 125 μs clock duration for both the traditional voice circuits and the new SONET network (Table 3.1).

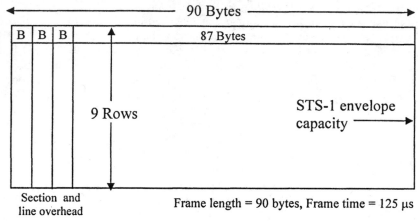

Figure 2.2 The composition of a STS-1 frame. STS - synchronous transport system.

TABLE 3-1 Rate Hierarchies for the SONET Synchronous Data Transport

SONET Transport	Optical Carrier	Data Rate	Signal (STS)
STS-1	OC-1[a]	51.840 Mb/s[b‡]	x 1
STS-3	OC-3 [a]	155.520 Mb/s[b]	x 3
STS-9	OC-9 [a]	466.560 Mb/s	x 9
STS-12	OC-12 [a]	622.080 Mb/s[b]	x 12
STS-18	OC-18 [a]	633.120 Mb/s	x 18
STS-24	OC-24 [a]	1.244160 Gb/s	x 24
STS-36	OC-36 [a]	1.866240 Gb/s	x 36
STS-48	OC-48 [a]	2.488320 Gb/s[b]	x 48
STS-96	OC-96	4.976640 Gb/s	x 96
STS-192	OC-192	9.953280 Gb/s[b]	x 192

[a] Only the OC-1, OC-3, OC-9, OC-12, OC-18, OC-24, OC-36, and OC-48 are allowed by the American National Standards Institute (ANSI).
[b] Currently accepted OC rates. The ITU has the STM-i designation, with i (= $n/3$) for the STS-n designation. The numerical value of i ranges from 1 to 64 corresponding to SONET rates from STS-3 to STS-192 with i limited to 1, 4, 16 or 64 (or with n = 3, 12, 48, or 192) for the currently accepted rates. The payload capacity for each STS rate is exactly 87/90 times the data-rate tabulated.

The approvals by ITU and *complete* standards go as far back as 1992. The SONET standard is incorporated for asynchronous transfer mode (ATM) in broadband ISDN applications for voice and data via the virtual tributaries into a STS-1 SPE (with path overhead) signal. The standards for fiber optic digital hierarchy range from the OC-1 rate of 51.84 Mb/s through the OC-3 (widely accepted) rate of 155.52 Mb/s to the OC-96 rate at 4.97664 Gb/s. More recently, the specialized fibers fabricated with self-focusing properties have opened the OC-192 rate for possible applications.

The multiplicative relation [6] between the hierarchical rates greatly facilitates the framing format for SONET synchronous data transport. The STS-n signal is scrambled and converted to the OC-n signal and this line rate is exactly N times the OC-1 rate. Multiplexing of the STS signals needs intricate byte encoding in the header blocks, and this becomes a crucial concern in the "SONET ready or compatible" switches that link [7, 8] various types of networks (such as DS1, DS3, all-digital synchronous networks, and all-optical networks) via the digital cross-connect systems (DCS). The standard 125 µs time slot is chosen for all the hierarchical OC rates. This leads to simplistic calculations for the number of bytes for the OC-1 ($n = 1$) through OC-192 ($n = 192$) rates as follows.

Number of bytes (or octets) in one 125 µs time slot for the *OC-n* rate is

$$\text{Number of bytes} = 51.84n \times 1.\text{E}{+}6 \times 125 \times 1.\text{E}{-}06 / 8$$

$$= 6480\ n \text{ bits} / 8 \text{ or } 810n \text{ bytes}$$

$$= 9 \times \ (3{+}87)\ n \text{ bytes}$$

$$= 9 \text{ rows} \times (3n \text{ bytes OH} + 87n \text{ bytes PL}) /\text{frame}$$

Here OH signifies overhead for the SONET header block and PL indicates payload for carrying the customer data. The breakdown between the overhead and the payload is segmented with $27 \times n$ bytes for overhead and $783 \times n$ bytes for payload.

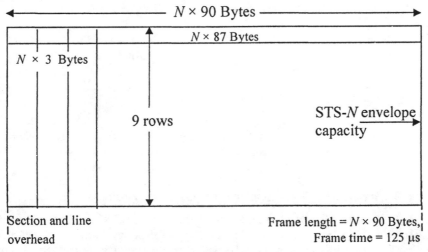

Figure 2.3 SONET OC-n frame. STS - synchronous transport system.

The rows are transmitted one by one and the byte integrity is retained through the ATM network. It is thus implicit that when the network is operating in its normal synchronous mode, the 8 sequential bits are also the bits of the same byte. The byte (or octet) classification for other rates follows the same pattern.

The arrangement of the SONET frame can simply be derived from the considerations listed above. For example, the SONET frame for the commonly used OC-n rate is shown in Figure 2.3.

The starter frame STS-1s of an nth level STS-n frame needs special attention. Byte interleaving and frame alignment are both necessary to form the STS-n frame. Byte integrity at the OC-3 level (to meet the ITU standards) is thus implemented; and it also permits STS-n to carry broadband payload at 150 and 600 Mb/s. Multiplexing of various SONET frame and digital cross-connects is handled by the SONET central offices. A typical configuration of this type of central office is shown in Figure 2.4.

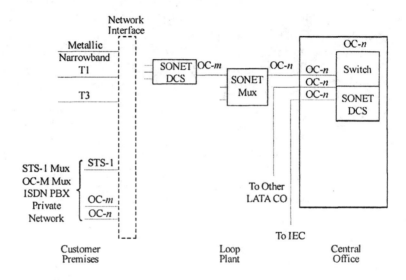

Figure 2.4 Configuration of a SONET based central office. DCS - digital cross-connect switch; DLC - digital loop carrier; IEC - inter-exchange carrier; ISDN - integrated services digital network; LCO - local central office; OC-m - optical carrier m; OC-n - optical carrier n; PBX - private branch exchange; STS - synchronous transport system.

Here, the various services such as T1, T3, HDSL, VHDSL, and other STS-n based services are reduced to the common basis of their synchronism (or 125 μs) appropriate switch, and then the information is reconstituted in the appropriate signaling format and sent to the customers. The coexistence of broadband ISDN and ATM was proposed as early as 1990 via the ATM cell mapping into the

SONET payloads for easy, elegant transport via the optical information highways of the future.

This will be necessary until all the systems assume one standard format, preferably the ATM format (see Section 2.6); and then the ATM switch, in conjunction with the bridges and routers, will perform all the switching. Meanwhile, a number of the digital cross-connect systems, such as AT&T's DDM-2000, FT-2000 SONET multiplexers, and many versions of digital access cross connect systems (DACSs) and SONET DCS are available to perform high-speed optical-rate switching. Newer services, such as broadcast TV facilities, interfacing HDTV quality CAD/CAM terminals, virtual reality devices, medical image transfer, super computer applications, will be the prime beneficiaries of these DCS and DACS switches.

2.5 SONET ARCHITECTURES

The deployment of SONET occurs in numerous architectures and applications. Typical configurations are shown in Figure 2.5. Within the broadband network, the point-to-point linear deployment for access and interoffice capabilities (Figure 2.5a), integrated access (Figure 2.5b), tree configurations with limited DS1, DS3 switching (Figure 2.5c), and hub site architectures with extended switching (Figure 2.5d) are used.

Rings using add-drop Multiplexers (ADMs, See [2.5]) can also be constituted for broadband data traffic (Figure 2.5a), and hubs with digital cross connect switch (DCS) provide a localized broadband switching capability (Figure 2.5b). The DCSs are generally built with wideband (DS1 and VT) and broadband (DS3 and STS-1) interfaces. SONET interfacing with both the WDCS and BDCS is already available. The virtual terminals have two modes of operation— floating and locked. The floating mode is suitable for bulk transport of channelized or unchannelized DSn and for distributed VT grooming. The locked VT mode is better suited for integral numbers of STS-1s transport and for distributed DS0 grooming between DS0 path terminating equipment.

SONET deployment in phases can enhance the capacity and switching of modern information highways quite efficiently and inexpensively, since the ADMs and DCSs are relatively inexpensive compared to the traditional ESS type of switches. SONET may also be deployed for DS1 and DS3 transport in the trunk environment. SONET is also a contender in integrated digital loop carrier (IDLC) environments [9]. Depicted in Figure 2.6, IDLC applications can provide access to DS1, baseband, and broadband (OC-3) services from any broadband network and local digital switch (LDS), thus facilitating broadband and baseband networks to coexist via ADMs and remote data terminals (RDTs in Figure 2.6).

This advantage in the IDLC environment removes the need for DS1 (1.544 Mb/s) realignment, thus offering these carrier systems better utilization of the switching facilities. Distributed VT cross-connections, bulk transport/switching of channelized and unchannelized, synchronous or asynchronous DS1s (mapped asynchronously), unchannelized bit-synchronous DS1 transport, DS0 circuit-switched traffic, and IDLC byte synchronous mapping are feasible in the floating VT modes of the RDTs (see Figure 2.6).

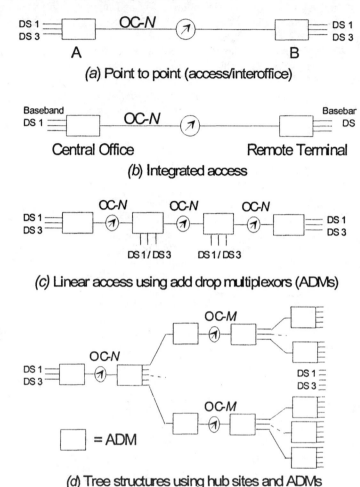

(a) Point to point (access/interoffice)

(b) Integrated access

(c) Linear access using add drop multiplexors (ADMs)

(d) Tree structures using hub sites and ADMs

Figure 2.5 Four stages of deployment of SONET in the existing broadband networks. ADM- add drop multiplexers. The use of hubs and ADMs is most common in recent implementations of SONET and the ATM environments to change network topology.

Low power complementary metal oxide semiconductor (CMOS) technology devices at OC-3 and higher rates are making these architectures easy to implement for generic and programmable data distribution systems to reach homes, businesses, and special services customers. SONET offers direct mapping of the SONET frame to the byte synchronous DS0 (64 kb/s) 125-µs time slot (in the floating VT1.5 mode of operation) for encoded voice/speech applications.

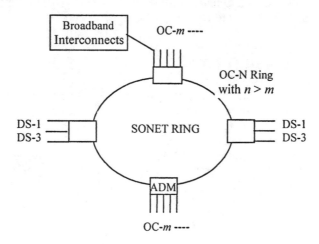

(a) Deployment of SONET rings with add drop
multiplexers (ADMs)

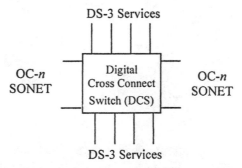

(b) Digital cross-connects for full-fledged switching
capability at the hub sites

Figure 2.6 The integration of the SONET transport System (STS) based
optical networks with the current digital networks. DS - digital signal; OC -
optical carrier.

Three general architectures for the SONET transport systems providing point to point DS1, DS1 & DS3 to STS-1 & STS-3, and combinations of *OC-n*, using add-drop multiplexers, and digital cross connects are shown in Figure 2.7. New networks can thus be fabricated with wide transport and switching capabilities.

These architectures indicate the strategies for incorporation of the evolving SONET and ATM components into the existing framework of telecommunication networks. Over a period of time, the older network rates, such as DS1 through DS3 will be replaced by the more accepted OC-*n* rates.

2.6 ATM CONCEPTS

The optical rates currently available (up to 4–40 Gb/s) for the transport of data are far too high to be directly integrated into the existing telecommunication networks. The SONET frame, lasting for 125 μs, can carry a large amount of information as the payload (2349 bytes) even at the OC-3 rate. While this size may appear perfectly reasonable in the LAN/MAN/WAN data environment, it can be perceived as being too large for other (like switched virtual carrier SVC, or permanent virtual carrier, PVC) types of service in business and industry.

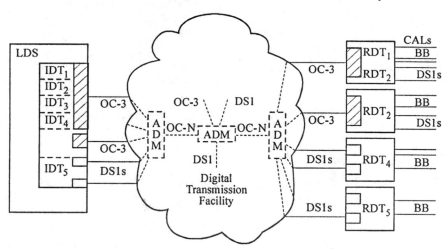

Figure 2.7 Typical Configurations for SONET and integrated digital loop carrier (IDLC) Facilities. ADM - add drop multiplexers; BB - baseband; CAL - customer access line; DS1 - digital signal, level-1; IDT - integrated digital terminal; LDS - local digital switch; OC - optical carrier; RDT - remote digital terminal.

In the trunk environment, numerous low-rate data channels are multiplexed onto the fiber trunk with its own particular protocol, framing, and bit designations for rates ranging from T0 to T3 or E0 to E3. However, recent applications are not always circuit-switched but becoming more and more packet and message switched. Hence, the idea of having the SONET carry smaller size packets or "cells" becomes more appealing. In a sense, asynchronous transfer mode (ATM) is an extension of the signal transport concept on which SONET itself relies. Cells provide user level interfacing packets and SONET frames become the photonic network transport packets. ATM standards outline the efficient (and perhaps elegant) techniques to bridge the gap between multiplicity of users and the vast variety of lightwave devices that make up the network. However, until such networks are a reality, ATM can be used to supplement DS2 and DS3 networks.

The asynchronous transfer mode (ATM) of data transfer is a worldwide standard. It stems from the availability of a high-speed backbone in the national or global environment. It has started an era of cell relay technologies and falls under a wide umbrella of packet switching. The technological fit of ATM can be seen as a progression of X.25 technologies to frame technologies and then into the cell technologies, as depicted in Figure 2.8. It also depends on the SONET standard for the transport of data. ATM is a standard for most networks to directly communicate with each other, provided the SONET and ATM protocol and header block information are consistently followed.

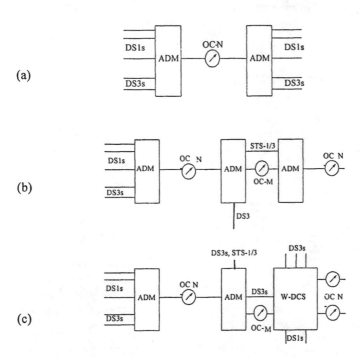

Figure 2.8 Three additional scenarios (see Figure 2.5) for the deployment of wideband networks. (a) point-to-point using ADMs, (b) network extensions using ADMs and (c) combination of ADMs and wideband digital cross-connect Switches (WDCS). DSn - digital signal n; OC - optical carrier.

ATM is based on packet-switched technology. The ATM packets or cells are relayed and routed throughout the network and thus get communicated between the source and the appropriate destination. Since the protocols and functions are unique to ATM, the technology for these ATM-based networks is called *cell relay* technology as opposed to the *frame relay* technology used to carry data in the circuit-switched digital capability (CSDC)at 56 kb/s, fractional T1 rates via T1 carrier, and even DS1 and DS3 networks.

ATM functionality has been embedded within a fixed size link-layer (i.e., the OSI layer 6, data link-layer) entity. This link-layer entity is the "cell" and the size of this fixed-length entity is 53 octets (bytes). There are 5 octets for the header block and 48 octets for the payload (or the data to be transported.) Similar to the header of most packet networks, the ATM cell header carries information unique to the nature of data, its functionality, disassemble and reassemble of cells, and the payloads. The typical ATM cell format for the user–network interface and network–network interface is shown in Figure 2.9. The information contained in the header is encoded to conform to the functions within the ATM sublayers.

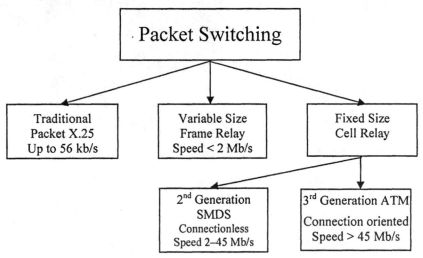

Figure 2.9 The progression of the packet switching capability from X.25 to ATM based cell relay technologies. SMDS - switched multi-megabit digital service using the DQDB protocol [2].

In the ATM environment, cells are routed and relayed by virtual circuits. Such circuits may be fabricated depending on traffic demands and switched and scaled by the ATM switches. These virtual networks may also be switched in the hardware at the ATM switches and/or nodes.

ATM also offers high-speed data transport capabilities. Since the ATM cells are embedded within the SONET frame, they carry all the advantages offered by transport systems carried by SONET. The high speed of transport is derived from optical rates (and thus low buffering delays), optical speeds, and low switching times (because of the simplicity/elegance in the SONET header information).

The features of the packet networks are listed as follows:

X.25	Frame Relay	ATM
Connection Oriented Service	Connection Oriented Service	Multiple Services/Capabilities
- Dial-up	- PVC and	- Constant bit rate (circuit emulation)
- Dedicated	- SVC (future)	- Connectionless services
- Variable bit rate service	- Connection oriented data services	
Range of Bit Rates	Range of Access Bit Rates	Wide Range Access
- Dial up 300 b/s to 19.2 kb/s	- 56 kb/s	- DS3 (45 Mb/s)
- Dedicated 2400 bps to 56 kb/s	- FT1 (64–1.544 Mb/s)	- OC3 (155 Mb/s)
	- T1	- OC12 (622 Mb/s)
Performance	Higher Performance	High Performance
- High reliability	- Low latency	- Low latency
- Wide availability	- High throughput	- High throughput
Network Error	Network Configuration	ATM Network
- Detection and correction	- Streamline	- Scaleable

ATM standards are applicable within LAN/MAN/WANs. ATM standards are applicable to private LANs, campus networks, or any other data network, and thus these networks can be connected to public, regional, or national ATM networks. They can also serve the needs of broadband ISDN by functioning via connection oriented ATM switches. The details of the Cell format for ATM are shown in Figure 2.10. The structure of the ATM layers is also depicted. The transmission path carries the virtual circuits (VCs) that can be set up to satisfy the traffic conditions.

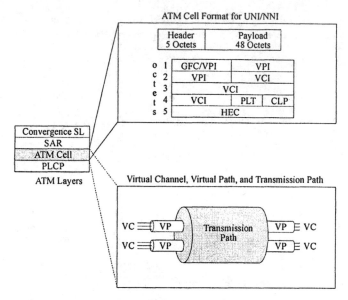

Figure 2.10 ATM cell format: Structure and its transport on the virtual channel, virtual path and transmission path. ATM - asynchronous transfer mode; NNI - network to network interface; PLCP - physical layer convergence protocol; SAR - segmentation and reassembly; SL - sublayer; UNI - user network interface.

2.7 EXPECTATIONS FROM MODERN NETWORK

Increased bandwidth and network intelligence to offer more personalized service are expected from any new network. Reduced network costs are generally expected from network owners, but only competition can drive the economic rewards for customers. Overexpectation beyond the particular network technology is futile. Almost all the social and public service institutions that deploy modern networks expect to be beneficiaries from the increased service capability, capacity, speed, and efficiency of the intelligent and adaptive networks that serve the evolving societies and the public sector at large. Expectations from any new breed of networks without regard to the types of switches, routers, and interconnects can only be misleading. Even the most advanced networks will not provide services randomly in individualistic formats to every customer. Economy of scale and adherence to standards provide the revenue stream to network owners. The economic justification of introducing newer networks is thus feasible.

Realism on the part of network owners and operators is necessary about the extent of services and the quality of service so that these networks can be technologically viable and yet be profitable. For example, basic building blocks of these networks such as the routers, the gateways, and the servers can accommodate certain types of switching and channel allocation depending on the network traffic and quality of service (QoS) constraints. The QoS concept is new and is available in certain types of switches that have the programmability to allocate network resources (such as bandwidth, class of service, and buffer sizes) There is a certain amount of delay and dropped packets/cells that can accrue in the network [10].

Although these types of service parameters may be within the realm of tolerance for service provided, they are impairments. The mean and variance of these impairments (though tolerable) need to be addressed in future networks. These impairments vary depending on the traffic conditions and network/server/link capability and its availability. Furthermore, the current extent of programmability varies considerably between the various types and manufacturers of routers. The allocation of resources (buffers, server space, priority, etc.) and bandwidth also influences the actual QoS based on the actual network conditions. In essence, it is advisable to be aware of the limitations, rather than expecting the best at all times for every customer, as some vendors may claim. In the current era of rapidly changing networks, the precaution for network owners and operators is that the initial awareness of the pitfalls in design of any network is as important as the decision to invest in the network.

2.7.1 Specific Applications

In emerging nations around the world, network-based information service provisioning and the deployment of Internet services are in vogue for two reasons. First, an enormous amount of intelligence and adaptability (that is scarce in less developed nations) can be programmed into the networks. Second, the routine benefits of organizing the information (based on modern IT concepts) in the routers and servers can be tailored to the specific application (such as telemedicine, education/distance learning, and electronic governments). The IT structure within the servers can indeed be successfully intertwined with the organized methodology of doing business, especially for stock markets, taxation, telemedicine, distance learning, and running the government. An information technology (IT) platform for storage, access, usage, and deployment of information is almost inherent for building the network infrastructure. With a certain amount of synergy of IT and network skills at the seminal stages, developing nations can gain significantly in two (IT and network technology) of the most dramatic forces of the twenty-first century.

The Internet plays a dominant force in global communications. Intelligent Internet (i. e, IN and knowledge-based switching capability built within the hardware/firmware of the routers) can bring a developing nation up to par with knowledge-based societies. Specific needs of these three types of such networks for telemedicine, education/distance learning, and electronic government are presented in Chapter 3. Some of their possible architectures are also presented. The IT aspects are not essential for network service. If the servers used as knowledge bases have a classification based on the contents of these knowledge bases, then the access is indeed controlled by the classification of the query or request for service. For example, in telemedicine, the query may be classified as patient/doctor, ailment/disease, doctor/specialty, or drugs/cure, and appropriate knowledge is addressed [11] by the network routers/switches.

In distance learning application, the Dewey Decimal System or the Library of Congress numbering systems may classify contents of knowledge bases. Both numbering systems organize knowledge. The access of relevant information is accomplished in architectural design, incorporating the concepts of IT (for education in the virtual university) and networking (for distance learning). In electronic government applications, the functions at the office of the head of state are coordinated with the offices of the individual ministers/secretaries of divisions in the government. Data and information are organized in the knowledge bases according to the type of office (based on IT concepts and interrelation between the contents knowledge bases) and the access is organized based on the network addressing of the knowledge bases.

2.7.2 Special-Purpose LANs and Generic Backbones

Network components are becoming increasingly more programmable. In fact, new and more versatile components are being introduced more frequently. To rush into architectures that are not mature enough to withstand the demands of the next decade or so would be futile, especially for developing countries. In a sense, it would be like subscribing to the FDDI or SMDS technology of the 1980s when ATM was being evolved and perfected for global deployment. It is our contention that the hardware, such as multiplexers (including the add–drop multiplexers or ADMs), routers, and gateways for all these networks will respond to more complex programs, which are indeed the basis for the flexibility offered by the "soft switches" of the current decade.

With the projected impact of the more sophisticated network operating systems and the intelligence that is embedded in such a blending of networks (hardware and software), the handwriting is already on the wall. Some of the typical networks such as the telephone, the hybrid fiber-coax, and the fiber-based backbones already serving our communities will become more amenable to serve medical, educational, and governmental/social functions. The key to the adaptability of these networks lies in the netware that senses, monitors, and operates the networks in an error-free, secure, and optimal fashion. Such netware programs call for the highest level of application and network programming tailored to the particular application such as medicine, education, or government. Although it is feasible to build networks unique to each of these applications, it is more sensible to have programmable network components that will respond to adaptive netware and perform in a programmable and optimal way. This approach has been adapted and has proved feasible by the evolution of general-purpose computer systems that can solve a great variety of different problems.

2.8 ARCHITECTURAL COMMONALITY

Networks are emerging to be broadband in nature They are scalable and expansive. Networks are becoming service oriented for economic survival. Networks adhere to the OSI standards for interoperability and increased service capability. Packet-based technologies (with TDM, packet, frame and cell relay capabilities) seem to be winning the race against circuit technologies, even though nation to nation and secure communication facilities may be provided by the leased (dedicated long-term circuit-switched) facilities. Specialized applications for financial, banking, and stock market needs are likely to maintain a short-lived status quo for leased circuit-switched networks.

The emerging fiber optic backbone throughout the world makes up for a large percentage of broadband networks. As networks converge, the ATM standard (i.e., the cell relay systems) is likely to dominate. The basic building blocks of the ATM networks (add–drop multiplexers (ADMs), routers, gateways, and servers) and of most high-speed networks are becoming fairly standard, even though the technology and the data rates have gained substantial ground over the last decade.

The recent trend, calling all vendors toward interoperability and international standardization, makes the fabrication of modern networks much like the fabrication of special purpose computers. In the earlier days of mainframes, the trend was to develop the IBM-360s, the CDC-6600s and the Super-Crays for different applications. In the modern days of the Pentiums and multi-GHz systems, the programmability of the chip with its expanded instruction set has driven the last nail in the coffin of the mainframes, except for special applications, such as weather prediction, space exploration and applications that need supercomputing capabilities.

For routine applications, we currently see a similar encroachment by multifunction routers, their programmability, and the WWW IP-addressing operating on the high-speed fiber backbone, thus accelerating the eventual slow demise of electronic switching systems, massive wire centers, and traditional land-line telephone systems in developed countries. The final synergy between the computing and the telecommunication environments is likely to result in the full-scale importation of the microprogrammability of the conventional CPU, to the evolving communication processors embedded within the routers. These communication processors will control the functioning of the intelligent routers of the next decades. From the modern perspective, this type of harmonious interplay between two very fundamental partners (computing and communications) is imminent. Yet another surge of progress of our society is eminent. The platform for the new generation of networks will be founded on the programming of intelligent routers for information and knowledge applications. It will function in both the traditional circuit-switched and ATM environments over the fiber optic backbone.

2.8.1 The All-Internet Solution

Popular as the Internet may be, it is only the tip of an iceberg. On the positive side, we have the IP addressing capability to access a vast number of databases and to gain access into the very broadband flexible networks for the transport of data. On the negative side, even the elementary intelligence embedded in AI concepts (such as adaptive learning, derivation of cause–effect relationships, hypothesis testing, statistical inferencing, evolved pattern recognition, and concept error-correction) is not (yet) incorporated in the operations of the Internet. To some extent, such networks may unnerve the marginal user and cause alienation between users and the network. We have discussed the social impact of intelligent networks [3], (see Chapter 20). Apart from the social effect, the current Internet solutions do provide a basis for cost-effective implementation for ecommerce, telemedicine, and educational networks. Together with very secure coding methods, some government and financial networks may also be initiated. However, for the sake of total privacy and security, special-purpose, sabotage-proof, electronic governments, and financial and banking networks may prevail.

2.8.2 The All-Private Network

This type of customized network has existed in society for a long time. The networks for banks and financial institutions, defense, the internal revenue service (IRS), and the immigration and naturalization service (INS) are examples in the United States. However, developing countries face a dilemma in this regard. Dedicated networks are far more expensive and need a team of specially trained staff to operate and maintain the networks. On the other hand, security and availability can be accurately monitored. In the most rapidly growing network environments (ATM), some of the responsibilities may be shifted to the network owners, and the users may be shielded to some extent. Whereas some networks of a developing country need to be totally private (e.g., electronic government, defense, INS), some other networks can be public (e.g., Internet-based education/library networks, news/information networks). Judicious and well-informed choice is necessary for any country that is proposing to move into the information age and become a reasonable beneficiary of the network revolution. At this stage, the science of network yields to the partly social and partly political foresight of the leadership of the country.

2.8.3 Integrated Network Architectures and Internet

Some of the typical networks, such as the telephone, the hybrid fiber–coax, and the fiber-based backbones, already serving our communities will become more geared toward serving medical, educational and even government functions. The key to the adaptability of these networks lies in the netware that senses, monitors and operates the networks. Such netware programs call for the highest skill in application and network programming tailored to the particular application such as medicine, education, or government.

At present, the Internet uses very elementary netware at its service centers and performs rudimentary and specific tasks within the Internet environment. As the Internet assumes the tasks of delivering intelligent Internet functions, the role of the Internet netware will become more sophisticated during the next few years, bringing a new wave of medical, educational, and government functions to society and the nations of the world. We propose that these new Intranet and Internet services, and their provisioning, will dominate the growth and service sectors for the next decade.

In essence, there is a *threefold* impact of modern networks encompassing SONET and ATM. First, the on-going digital revolution which is alive and well in the computer and communication fields since the days of von Neumann, is coming closer and closer to the telephone customer. Second, the ongoing technological revolution in the fiber optic transmission since 1950s is being implemented closer and closer to work and home environments. Third, the recent, but strong, social revolution demanding more access, precision, and information/knowledge orientation in daily lives is being made possible. The convergence of the *three*— the *digital revolution,* the *information and knowledge processing,* and the *transmission technologies*— is the apparent source.

ATM plays a key role in making the current networks exploit the state-of-the-art technologies (VLSI, optical transmission and optoelectronic) to meet social and socio-economic demands. Even though ATM standards are not direct contributors (as yet) to the state-of-the-art intelligent networks or intelligent communication systems, they play a vital role in making intelligent communication systems economically viable and able to provide newer services anywhere and to anyone at anytime, network permitting.

2.9 INTELLIGENT NETWORKS

Over the last three decades, networks have become increasingly intelligent. They have acquired an aura of being generic, adaptive, and programmable. These features make the evolving networks useful in almost any application, ranging from intensely secure private networks to public global networks that are able to reach anybody at anytime. In addition, they can be tailored to provide almost any type of service, ranging from low-rate monitoring to multimedia broadband duplex communication services. In this section, we provide an insight into the technology and the architectures that make these networks perform as elegantly and as eloquently as the Pentium chip in modern PCs.

The role of technology, the extent of processing, and the bus architecture within the chip are largely comparable to the intricacies that are inherent in modern networks. The microscopic nature of the nanometer chip stands out as the glaring contradiction to transoceanic global networks. Yet, the functionality tracks in both environments in carrying out the right process at the right time, and at the right place. We further expand on these concepts for the networks that are being deployed to serve our society throughout the world.

Intelligent networks (INs) function like massive and widely dispersed computer systems. Both carry out *three* distinct functions. First, they communicate relevant information from one physical or logical point to another. Second, they control the network to facilitate the flow of information. Third, they carry out computations to seek out specific information necessary for the arithmetic/logical functions, switching, and channeling of information.

These three functions are managed and executed by a form of network intelligence that supervises and monitors network functions. The vast majority of computer systems perform arithmetic computations, control the flow of information, and dispatch control signals. In addition, they perform a limited set of switching functions to communicate within the systems and with users. In a broad sense, the four functions of controlling, communicating, computing, and switching also exist within the networks. However, at the design and implementation level, the network functions are far more intricate, more distributed, and more user friendly than the functions in the computer systems. Networks also perform in real time as users begin to utilize the network functions. Today, and in the near future, a more demanding requirement exists for network performance. It is expected that future global networks will serve a vast majority of the entire population and will demonstrate the same kind of innate adaptability that the telephone system offers the public now. Any failure in the network functions and performance is likely to cripple a segment of the population center, bringing about more catastrophic consequences than the failure of computer systems, which is less drastic. Hence, network reliability becomes a dominant consideration in the design of networks, as well as error recovery.

A topological representation of intelligent networks is shown Figure 2.11. This diagram is essentially the same for the topological representation of a computer system. There are four basic groups of functions (control, communication, computation, and switching) and they are interdependent in both systems. This configuration is equally applicable to computer systems, where the generic intelligence corresponds to the adaptive nature of the hardware, the software, and the microcode (and/or firmware). In unison, they monitor the overall computer functionality. Storage and retrieval of information (i.e., the memory function) is another function common to both systems. However, since it is not crucial to the basic functionality of either system, it becomes secondary within the framework of the computer. The proportioning of these four functions (control, communication, computation, and switching) in the two environments (networks and computer systems) can be substantially different. These functions are discussed in greater detail in the following four subsections.

Control and Sequencing of Functions

The control function in computer systems is operative at numerous levels. At the macroscopic level, the operating systems, the job control language, the system security, and so on, each exert their own individualistic global controls. At the intermediate level, the program and the operation code control the computational functions. At the microscopic level, the microcode and the associated control signals exert the control.

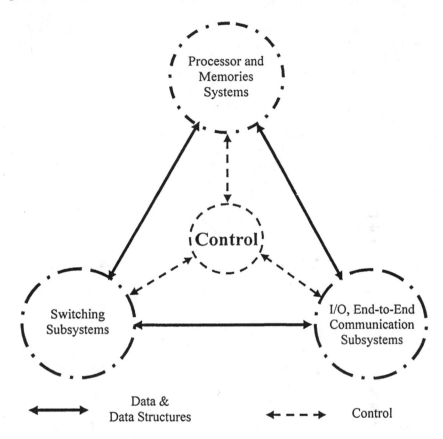

Figure 2.11 Functional Representation of a computer or a communication system.

In the network environment, the levels of control occur at numerous layers of the network. Each layer provides appropriate information for the lower layer to perform the specific function expected from that layer. The structure imposed on the network functions via the network layers is a definite form of control and is standardized in all network architectures.

One widely recognized model for network functions and its hierarchical structure is the open system interconnection (OSI) model, which is discussed in Chapter 4 and which is also used throughout the book. In most computer communications, the OSI layers permit detailed development of protocol. In most communication networks, the role of OSI becomes more diffused and dispersed, even though the concepts are applicable. As a result, the protocol and interfaces in the communication networks are far more variable than those in computer networks.

Communication of Data and Control Signals

Communication within the computer system is handled via bus structures in a dedicated or shared mode. Outside communication is generally handled via dedicated or addressable ports and standard interfaces. In the network environment, the levels for handling communication of information are not easily categorized because of the wide variety of media and channels, and their interconnecting capabilities. Networks also accomplish *two* basic communication functions: (1) Communications within the network, and (2) Communication with the user.

These two aspects of the communication function assume a far greater proportion of hardware and software control than that of conventional computer systems. The interfaces and protocols have become more standard and streamlined in most of the network environments.

Computation, Address Lookup and Dynamic Routing

The arithmetic logic units, the numeric coprocessors, and array processors handle the computational function in computer systems. Most computer applications may have a substantial amount of numerical processing. The flexibility, the hardware, and the utilities for these functions are generally quite exhaustive in most major computer systems. In the network environment, the computational functions play a more limited role. Generally, the calculations are rudimentary and used only occasionally when some network decision becomes critical. Networks are primarily used for exchange of information and not for computation, whereas computer systems are primarily used for computation and not for communication. The database lookup and dynamic routing algorithms assume a great majority of the computational functions in intelligent networks. Simple address transformations are accomplished within the local central offices, whereas address transformations for intricate advanced network services (such as call forwarding and CLASS services [3], (Chapters 10–12]) are carried out at distant databases or knowledge bases. The hardware and architecture differ accordingly.

Logical Channel Switching

Finally, the switching function in the computer system, though essential, is not dominant. Input/Output channel, the direct memory access, and the cache memory channels exist and are switched under the operating system and users' commands. Being akin to the virtual channels in communication systems, they are set up on demand and disbanded after the exchange of information occurs. In network environments, the switching function is essential and dominant. Real-time, concurrent control of many thousands of communication channels is essential at most of the nodes within the network. For this reason, the design and architecture of switching systems is a major area of specialty and can become as intricate as the design and architecture of any major mainframe computer system.

In perspective, computer architecture and network architecture have a similar role for the control function. However, the relative emphasis on the difference between the communication function and the computational function in the two environments is roughly reversed. The networks accomplish a greater proportion of communication functions, whereas the computer systems accomplish a greater proportion of data processing (or computational) functions. In addition, there can be a considerable amount of variation in the admixture of the four functions (control, communication, computation, and switching) depending on the type of computer system or the network under consideration.

Switching functions, and thus the intelligence associated with them, form a major part of the network operations. In general, most of the common public networks have to switch and allocate channels to permit the flow of information from node to node, customer to customer, or from workstation to workstation. The same physical resources are used to carry different channels or even blocks or packets of information. The channels may be dedicated to a certain user for the duration of time of the usage. In the computer environment, the switching of various channels may be considered a subset of the control function. In the network environment, switching is a discipline in its own right.

In particular, special hardware devices tailored to switching channels under software commands have evolved. They form key constituents of any major network switching system. These facilities [2] can be as small as the private branch exchanges switching four lines, or as large as the modern electronic switching systems that switch several hundred thousands of lines and monitor the activity of each one. A typical, modern, large electronic switching system (e.g., the 5ESS® electronic switch built by AT&T, the EWSD® built by Siemens, the AXE® built by Ericsson) may use a hierarchy of up to 3000 microprocessors working under the switch's own specifically tailored operating system with about two million lines of code. Typically, the processing capacity of the 5ESS switch would be about five times that of a typical mainframe computer. Modern networks thus become far more encompassing and inclusive of many of the large computer systems even though a certain amount of functional parallelism may be traced between the two environments.

2.9.1 Intelligent Networks Defined

Intelligent networks (INs) carry and communicate information with distinct algorithmic adaptation. Adaptability occurs at a local or global level. The programs resident at the nodes within the network administer local adaptability. Global adaptability is administered by the coherent functioning of the node to process requests from another node and, thus, to accomplish global and extraneous functions.

Numerous independent networks can and generally do coexist within an IN environment. These subnetworks operate coherently and cooperatively in the intelligent functioning of the overall network. In fact, the predictable and accurate response from the entire network is also a dominant requirement for its acceptance in the user community. The endpoints of the IN refer to the access points to and from which information may flow in any standard form (voice, digitized voice, multimedia, or encoded data bearing any type of information). Typical examples of the endpoints may range from individual user terminals or even plain old telephones, to entire exchanges or even gateway offices tying the network to other national exchanges.

In the context of hardware, intelligence resides in the design, architecture, and algorithmic performance of the integrated circuit (IC) chips. The hierarchical interconnection that permits the ICs to function as network components also contributes to the hardware intelligence. In the context of software, intelligence is coded as programs, utilities, or modules. It resides in the active memories of computers during the execution phase. In the context of firmware, intelligence is placed into the control memories of the monitoring computers through microcode. Thus, the basic computers (the hardware, software, and firmware) that control, monitor, and process the information become an integral part of intelligent networks. The flow of the information takes place over appropriate channels within the network. Information also flows within a diversity of participating networks, such as the circuit-switched, packet-switched, message-switched, or any other digital or analog network. Channels are assigned dynamically, switched, and reallocated to carry the information from node to node, customer to customer, or workstation to workstation. The facilities that actually switch channels may be central offices, switching centers, private branch exchanges (PBXs), or even satellites that relay information. The actual transport of the information is carried out over transmission facilities of the network. Such facilities may span a small laboratory or become extensive to span a nation or the whole world, or be sent into deep space to relay planetary information. The size of the network or its geographical expanse is inconsequential to its nature.

2.9.2 Specific Building Blocks of Intelligent Networks

In the specific and implemented versions of INs in the public domain, the basic building blocks of INs have been defined in a much narrower sense. In the telecommunications industry, some of the basic terminology had been well defined and generally well accepted. However, over the last two decades, a profusion of INs has occurred and slight differences in the nomenclature and functionality can be noticed by comparing the IN architectures around the globe. In the context of this book we follow the original ITU [12] classification of the major building blocks of different types of INs. As an overview, the following *five* basic building blocks have been identified.

2.9.2.1 Service Switching Point (SSP)

The SSP is a central office switch that detects the user (or other central offices) request for IN services. These SSPs are now deployed around the globe and were introduced by AT&T (1980s) and then by Bell Operating Companies (1990s) in the United States and by numerous European vendors during the same time frame.

2.9.2.2 Service Control Point (SCP)

The SCP is one of many massive database (and now information-base) capabilities that honor requests from SSPs to perform address translation and address lookup. Communication between SSPs and SCPs occurs over a secure packet-switched signaling network (X.25 or BX.25 in the U.S. [3], (Chapter 9) known as the CCIS network or the signaling network. This highly secure and dependable network is essential for all IN and advanced network functions in circuit-switched networks. It was first identified and deemed necessary in the early 1980s and has been a cornerstone for the newer networks to evolve and grow since the mid-1980s.

Specialized consideration is due in the design of hardware, software, and database management systems within the SCP. Typically, SCP facilities deploy massive parallel processing to handle very large independent queries that can arrive from any SSP and/or any individual or group(s) of users. In essence, it is a Poisson distribution [13] and follows a pattern similar to the call/traffic intensity distributions. Utmost dependability and latency (in information retrieval) are two basic issues. The hardware components are generally duplicated for quick takeover under hardware failure. The physical location and whole SCP center is also (generally) duplicated in case of fire or natural disasters at any one center.

Hardware Aspects of SCP

There are *four* major hardware components constituting a SCP, as depicted in Figure 2.12. First, an elaborate and highly dependable mass storage system (typically large-capacity disk drives and disk controllers) makes up the database storage. Second, a bank of parallel processors with their own dedicated memory blocks serves to access the bulk storage within the SCP, and also communicates with the input/output devices in the database. Third, a series of front-end processors preprocess the queries received via the SS7 network, or any similar compatible network, with a well-specified protocol. Finally, a series of BX.25 (Bell System specific X.25 protocol) front-end processors complete the major hardware components. These processors receive service management information from the SMS and provide the interface for maintenance, security, and operations of the SCP.

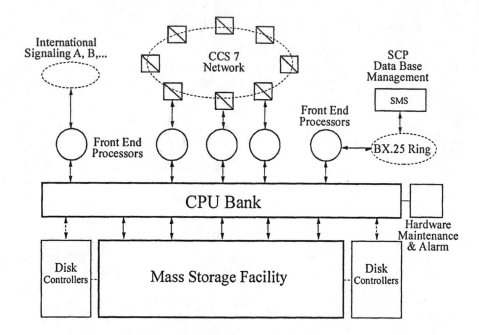

Figure 2.12 One possible hardware configuration for the SCP of intelligent networks. CCS7 - Common Channel Signaling 7; SCP - service control point; SMS - service management system, BX.25 - a front-end processor (hardware), CPU - central processing unit.

It is important to note that any computer hardware architecture with an optimally distributed bus structure can adequately perform the SCP functions. However, certain architectures are more suitable (such as parallel processor, multibus systems). In the interest of high dependability expected from the SCP, duplication of hardware and buses increases the confidence level in the functioning of these special-purpose computer systems. Typically, the downtime on the SCP is under 3 minutes a year, and the wait time in call completion demands both redundancy and speed from the SCP.

Software Aspects within the SCP

There are *two* groups of software structures in the SCP, as depicted in Figure 2.13. The first group deals with the functioning of the SCP as a coherent computational entity, which serves the hierarchical function of the SCP in the IN architecture. The second group deals with the applications that the IN (which hosts the SCP) is equipped to handle.

SCP Functional Software

There are *five major* modules. First, the service networks interface (SNI), receives the signaling information from the CCS7 and other signaling systems querying the SCP and passes the information for response from the SCP. This major and perhaps the most optimally coded group of software routines serves to interface the SSP queries. Second, the support system interface (SSI) provides a software interface for the service management functions to be handled via the SMS. Network management control and customer record entry are updated and handled via this interface. Third, the observation window for the SCP operating personnel, which functions and maintains the SCP, is provided by the operations subsystem (OS).

Software Structure for the Service Control Point (SCP) for IN/1	
FUNCTION Oriented SW	**APPLICATION** Oriented SW
Services Network Interfacing	Alternate Billing Services
Support Systems Interfacing	Area Wide Centrex
Operations Support Systems	800- Toll Free Services
Node Management	Private Virtual Network
Node Administration SW	Software Defined Network

Figure 2.13 Software organization of the SCP for IN/1. The IN/1 configuration is the most rudimentary of intelligent networks. The SW complexity and modules are greatly enhanced for the later versions of intelligent networks; SNI - service network interface, SSI - support system interface, OSS - operations support system(s), NM - node manager, NA - node administrator or node administration, ABS - alternate billing service, AWC - area wide Centrex, PVN - private virtual network, SDN - software defined network.

This interface responds to a system console that monitors the flow of data and information between the SCP components. Fourth, the node manager (NM) subsystem fulfills the startup and shutdown procedures of the SCP. Service continuity and early fault detection, and some possible rerouting, are the critical requirements of the NM subsystem. This software subsystem assures the integrity of the customer database entries and updates without disrupting service. The multitasking and load sharing of numerous central processing units (CPUs) within the SCP are also managed by the NM. In effect, the NM in the SCP environment performs many of the functions similar to the operating system functions in a computer system environment, for example, resource utilization, traffic management, load handling, I/O control, backup procedure, crash aversion, and system boot-up/shutdown. Fifth, the node administration (NA) subsystem permits efficient and optimal database functions and provides for the necessary backup of databases. This function is of considerable importance in the SCP in light of the duplicated databases for fault-tolerance and service dependability (less than 3 minutes downtime a year).

Applications Software and Their Associated Modules

In a broad application framework, the SCP functions can be summarized as validation of the caller to call, the address translation of the called party (from a look-up database, if necessary), and, finally, identification of the carrier authorized to carry the call. The generic capability of the SCP can be tailored to serve a wide variety of special voice services or applications. In the United States, a few of the independent telephone companies have targeted three varieties of special services. Typical of these services being offered and planned are the call rerouting services, alternate billing service, and private virtual networks. Other services in the IN/1 environment can be added by including special-purpose routines (or software modules) directed towards the newer service in the traditional and wireless markets.

2.9.2.3 Signal Transfer Point (STP)

This is a transfer point in the CCIS network that directs the requests from an individual SSP to the appropriate SCP depending on the nature and type of service from the SCP. Hence the SSPs and the SCPs communicate via the STP over the CCIS network in packet-switched mode. Most modern networks have the capability to install STPs, depending on the nature and growth of the service area. Signal transfer points (STPs) are distributed within the common channel signaling (CCS) network. The STP nodes are high-capacity, extremely reliable packet-switches for the transportation of signaling information between SSPs, SCPs, and other STPs. In rare instances, the SSP and STP functions are combined as one node. The four main functions of the STP are performing (1) error-free message routing, (2) protocol processing, (3) address translation, and (4) message routing database look-up.

2.9.2.4 Service Management System (SMS)

This system functions within any SCP environment and is intricately tied with the functions of the SCP. In fact, the SMS is an off-line support facility used to enter customer data into the SCPs databases within the IN/1 environment. It is also used to enter the call-processing software into the SCP. The SMS communicates with the SCP through interface cards that process the BX.25 protocol used for communication between SMS and SCP. The service management systems also need a series of front-end processors to link with the dual buses, which provide data paths between the SCP's other front-end processors and the SCP's bank of CPUs. Generally, these front-end processors may be implemented by deploying microcomputer chips with appropriate interfaces. The details of the SW architecture within the SMS can differ significantly with the type of IN (such as Bellcore's IN/1, IN/1+ architectures or the Universal Services Intelligent Network architecture discussed in [3]).

Service management systems have a wide range of complexity. At the low end, they become no different from database management and data updating systems for the IN/1 type of services. The geographical spread and volume of data and its access play a significant role in the SMS in the communication industry. At the intermediate level, the SMS assumes the flavor of library systems. At the high end, the SMS approaches the sophistication and complexity of knowledge management systems the facilitate knowledge bases to execute library and content-based query handling in real time. Over time, the SMS staff and protocol become specific to the uses and nature of the knowledge bases (such as medical bases, fossil bases, and outer-space knowledge bases) and their applications.

2.9.2.5 Intelligent Peripheral (IP)

Over the last decade, numerous peripherals have evolved to connect different types of networks (e.g., medical, emergency, national security, and Internet) to the circuit-switched and backbone networks. These interfaces are as readily customized as the network interface cards in any large switching system or mainframe computers. The types of service that an IN can provide can be highly specialized. All of these services may or may not be in the legal jurisdiction of the network owners to provide. To supplement the network services and enhance attractiveness to users, outside vendors may offer these services or support functions. The information/service can again be highly variable, ranging from language translation or voice recognition to delivering recorded messages, or digit collection based on the multifrequency tones received at the off-network node (ONN) or IP. In the USIN, the ONN is a remotely located device or module and the IP is a network resident.

2.9.2.6 CCIS Network

This is a robust network for common-channel interoffice signaling. In 1976, the idea of using the telephone set to verify credit card information automatically from remote computers was established by the introduction of the transactions telephone. In the same year, common channel interoffice signaling (CCIS) was introduced in the telephone network to control network functions as intricately as operational code controls the functions in a computer. Throughout the 1980s, use of databases and software to control networks and their functions was firmly in place and, with this, a new generation of intelligent networks had evolved.

This secure signaling network permits the nodes within the network to communicate with each other, such that they cooperate with each other to execute the functions necessary for call processing or service provisioning. Examples of such call processing might be as simple as (1) seize (capture) an available channel, (2) establish voice path, (3) hold during call progress, (4) release channel after call completion, and (5) reallocate channel for future use. In most modern networks, the variety of such commands and the flavor of the services provided by the switching systems are dramatically more elaborate and complex. For this reason, the standards, as they apply to signaling, are necessary not only within an individual country, but throughout the globe.

During the infancy of telephone communication, human operators were deployed for completing message decoding, call completion, call monitoring, and call disconnect. Billing was a human function. The signaling network was the same as the communication network. From our modern perspective, the status of the network was a recipe for disaster.

Automation has taken network signaling through at least two major events: common channel interoffice signaling 6 (CCIS6) and common channel signaling Number 7 (CCS7), even though signaling systems 3, 4 (in Europe), and 5 (in the United States) did exist transitionally. The modern signaling standards (CCIS6 and CCS7) are complex and elaborate. Such topics are generally standardized after exhaustive discussions and detailed analysis by international standards committees. The signaling network is an essential pathway to carry standard signals. It is highly dependable and almost totally duplicated to ensure that its functionality is disaster proof. The signaling functions are vital to all network functions. In emerging nations, the same network is shared to carry signaling and voice or data between customers. Single- and multiple-frequency signaling was used before common channel signaling (CCS), which was approved by the CCITT (now the ITU) in 1968 as System No. 6. However, in most modern telecommunications environments, the signaling network is a distinct and well-developed network in its own right and has a very secure existence in the background. Sometimes referred to as the "backbone signaling network," it conveys and carries the control, operations, administration, and maintenance (OA&M) signals from node to node. Now, in context to the INs, the OA&M becomes OAM&P (for "provisioning").

Also in 1981, a signaling category, distinct from the network control signals, was initiated to facilitate the most rudimentary of the IN functions, that is, the 800 service and the calling card service. This new category was in a query rather than a signal. The query would be for billing authorization (for calling card services) or call completion information (for the 800 services).

The implementation of common channel interoffice signaling (CCIS) started in the United States in May 1976. The CCIS network was simply a robust link connecting two toll offices: the 4A toll crossbar office and the first deployed 4ESS™ switch toll center. After having proved its worth and potential, the link became a network over the eight years that followed until divestiture of the Bell System. The signaling standard used was the CCITT (now ITU) approved System No. 6 and was crucial to proving the advantage of the digital common-channel signals over the single-frequency and multifrequency techniques used earlier.

Typical of the advantages that have been documented are the reduction of call setup time, from about 10 seconds to 2 seconds, thus improving the utilization of network resources. Additional benefits included improved reliability, reduced fraud, call tracing, call-process acknowledgment, and optimal call routing.

The increasing network topology and its geographical expanse in the United States called for nodes in the network. These nodes are called the signal transfer points (STPs). Germane to the CCIS network, the STPs prevailed well before any version of an IN/1 was implemented in 1981. Before the divestiture of the Bell System, the CCIS network operated with 10 regional signaling sectors in the United States. Each region contained two STPs. The locations of these individual STPs within the regions were chosen with due consideration to survival and recovery of the network after natural disasters and disastrous network conditions.

Three types of links span these STPs. Type A links connect the switching offices with the STPs. Type B links connect the STPs of neighboring (adjoining) regions. Type C links are specially balanced, mated pairs that interconnect STPs within regions. In a sense, the links, STPs, and the switching nodes that communicate with the STPs within this network all have unique logical and geographical addressing capabilities.

2.9.2.7 Functionality of IN Components

These functional building blocks of intelligent networks (in conjunction with the CCS network) are essential for the transition of the circuit-switched networks to become intelligent. These components, as they exist in context with the particular intelligent network, differ slightly from network to network. It is important to understand that the phased introduction of intelligent networks during the 1990s has been enhanced dramatically to meet the demands from the newer networks, especially the mobile networks. The older standards committees of CCITT (International Telegraph and Telephone Consultative Committee), and of ANSI (American National Standards Institute), and now the common cooperative role of the ITU Committees have identified a majority of functions, interfaces, and protocols. These standards have been published and are available in most of the major telecommunication libraries. Considerable standardization and uniformity now prevails in the design and functions of signals, protocols, interfaces, and their implementation for all the IN services

A certain amount of intelligence is encompassed in the conventional analog networks, such as the plain old telephone service (POTS) network. The central offices that serve as nodes of the older POTS networks are primarily for the use of analog voice telephones. In modern all-digital networks, the signaling is also digital and it can be enhanced and transformed by digital processes that make the functions of all-digital networks as precise and error-proof as the execution of an operation code in the instruction register (IR) of a CPU. To the extent the CCIS network can carry the digital stream of signals, the network can perform all the switching and channeling functions much as the CPU can execute binary instructions.

2.9.3 Seamless Networks

Modern network technology is experiencing an explosive growth, similar to that of the VLSI technology during the 1970s. The applications are highly diversified and the reach is global, for modern networks are immense. In a sense, it is essential that these networks be self-monitoring and adaptive, and that left unattended they perform well under the vast variety of application functions and intelligent deployment of network resources. Network intelligence becomes an essential feature in regulating the operability, interoperability, and performance of the network. The adaptation ranges from response to the user requirements, nature of service and traffic conditions. In essence, both intelligence and dynamic adaptation become prerequisites to deliver the quality of network service.

The open system interconnect (OSI) model already standardizes the major functions of the network. There are seven layers that are essential to make all networks appear transparent to the user. Programmed network components and customized VLSI chip sets accomplish the layer functions. Any specific needs of the applications and the users are thus accommodated within the networks, provided they are within the OSI guidelines.

The older networks, which were essentially at the physical layer, cannot handle the needs of modern networks or offer the services offered by intelligent networks. The switching systems have to become increasingly programmable to handle the newer types of traffic and user needs such as the CLASS functions [3], (Chapters 9–11]. The concept of "soft-switch" now dominates the traditional grounds of the older electronic switching systems. These soft switches handle the growing needs of all types of circuit, packet, message, and so on switching. More than just satisfying the needs of the particular application at hand, they deploy the network resources in an optimal and adaptive fashion to bring down the costs and enhance the services offered by these networks.

2.10 DATABASE MANAGEMENT

Data in its most rudimentary binary form is generally useless in the information and knowledge domain. The lowest level structure imposed on the. raw data forces its transformation into modules of information such as numbers (e.g., signed integers, floating point, exponential, double precision, complex, coordinates), words (e.g., textual, dictionary, thesaurus) or logical entities (e.g., states, true/false, switch-able machine transitional conditions, etc.). After the second level of structure imposed on data, the lower level or form of information (e.g., amplitude, phase, movement, pixel color/intensity; sentences, paragraphs, pages; and/or state variables, cell boundaries, logical chains) may start to take shape. The number of stages required depends on the levels of encoding necessary to transform the original information into raw data. Conversely, the stages of decoding depend on the steps to convert raw data to useful information. By and large, most designers prefer only one stage encoding and decoding.

The chief advantages associated with the representation of the information and knowledge as raw data occur during its processing, its storage, and its transportation over most digital networks. Processing is done exclusively by computer systems, peripheral processors and the VLSI chips or chip sets functioning under software instructions. Virtual, logical, or connected circuits do transportation over information highways and byways initiated and terminated by switches. However, storage is done in memories: cache, stacks, active semiconductor devices, buffers and long-term storage devices such as drums, disks and other serial, parallel, and/or series–parallel systems. Databases offer a definite structure and methodology for the storage and retrieval of massive amounts of information that is to be stored for active usage, updating, or semiarchival and archival purposes.

Almost all applications demand storage facilities— some small and some large. Small, dynamic or transient data (such as scientific matrices, arrays and potentials) is stored in the active memory during program execution and saved as a file on the secondary storage such as disks, drums, and tapes. Large, relatively stable data (such as corporate human resources files, billing data, and credit card information) is accommodated in the secondary storage facilities of computer systems. Very large and stable databases (such as intelligent network services records, credit call billing, and IRS records) are stored in large data storage facilities and administered and updated by database management systems at regular intervals. Stationary data (such as company records for prior years, medical records of past patients, and inactive accounts) is generally archived onto tapes and stored in vaults. Geographically diversified data access facilities (such as travel agents, Internet bidding and sales, and search engines) query centralized databases via local, national, and global networks.

Design of dependable and efficient databases calls for elaborate database management systems (DBMSs). Intelligent DBMSs permit the search of the stored databases on logical association, search trees, and conditional search algorithms that are generally programmable by the users. The size, the geographical diversity, interfacing, access time, dependability, and interoperability are a few of the concerns in the choice or design of the databases, their structure, and their management. In sections 3.4.1–3.4.4, some of the typical applications and their databases are presented.

2.10.1 Data Management in Intelligent Networks

Data management is necessary in all communication networks and it gets even more elaborate in intelligent networks. Almost all elements of intelligent networks [14], such as service control point (SCP), service management system (SMS), service switching point (SSP), and intelligent peripheral (IP), all store and process data that is customer and service specific. The role of the SCP is especially important since both the user- and network-specific databases are invoked in providing the intelligent network services to the user. In this section only the SCP data management issues are addressed.

Defined as a physical or a virtual node within the intelligent network, the service control point (SCP) for a typical mid-size telephone network contains the active database of customer records. *Three* distinct types of databases (800 number, ABS, and PVN) can reside in the SCP. This database is actively queried from the SSPs within the network to seek and obtain service-completion information; hence, the optimal and effective management and utilization of this database is critical [14] .

Certain sophistication in the hardware and software hierarchy is essential to make the SCP handle the high volume (several million calls per hour) and diversity in the information sought from the SCP, depending on the types of services and sub-services provided. In a sense, the design of the SCP should be considered as a highly efficient parallel processor and data storage-retrieval computer system. The input/output processing needs special attention. The SCP operating environment is relatively well defined, and its functional requirements are clearly delineated both by the architectures of IN/1 and by the CCSS7 requirements. Thus, the hardware design assures consistency with the operational environment (STP, SMS, and SSP), the type of processing accomplished (database functions, their updating, security, error-recovery, and duplication), and the interfaces with the other network components (SS7 network, other signaling networks, service management systems, security systems, etc.).

2.10.2 Data Management for DSL Development

The performance evaluation of the high-speed digital subscriber line (HDSL) depends on the design, linkages, and cooperative role of the extensive databases during simulation studies. Such databases are necessary during component design, performance evaluation, and the overall feasibility studies of the HDSL at the basic data rate (144 kb/s) or at the primary data rate (1.544 Mb/s in the United States and 2.048 Mb/s in Europe). In this section, the design and procedures to build these interoperable databases are presented. The need, consistency, and interdependence of the databases that actually supply the simulation programs are presented. The input data to the simulation programs is derived from large national loop surveys, the cable characteristics, and surveys of noise in the loop plant. The output of the simulation programs generates interdependent and consistent databases that are essential to evaluate the overall performance of the entire subscriber loop survey population at various rates (such as 144, 384, and 768 kb/s and 1.544 and 2.048 Mb/s) in different telecommunication networks of various countries, regions, or even in premises distribution systems. In this section, the success and frustrations in organizing and working with such interdependent and interoperable databases are also presented.

In addition, the organization of the numerous databases for effective ISDN simulations and for the design of components is presented. In contrast to the passive computer-aided design methodology, an interactive and intelligent CAD environment is discussed. This section focuses on the use of three categories of databases. Major loop survey data, cross-talk and impulse noise data, cable characteristics, and relatively static data constitute the permanent databases. The intermediate computational results, excitation data, Fourier components, and loop responses to impulse noise conditions, which contain information of transitory nature, constitute the interim databases. Finally, the important simulation results in the graphic files that constitute the pictorial database. Intelligent techniques for managing and accessing these databases are addressed here.

Simulation procedures introduced in the late 1970s [2] assume the role of elaborate computer-aided design (CAD) when the component values used in HDSL design procedures need optimization [15]. Consistency and interoperability of the simulation programs play a critical role in the CAD procedure. This aspect has been studied in light of the recommendations of the standards committees, since the study of the digital subscriber line started during the late 1970s. The design aspects, data rates, subscriber loop environments, encoding algorithms, and actual devices used on the HDSL applications have changed dramatically.

Multiple databases are essential [16] in the optimal design of high-speed digital subscriber lines (HDSLs). Typically, on the input side, three or four databases need to be accessed, and on the output side, three to six matrices of results are generated. The HDSL itself serves as a crucial link in the deployment of integrated services digital network (ISDN). Most of the regional Bell operating companies and European telecommunication networks are committed to bringing the higher data rates to the customer from the central offices. There can be many thousands of databases in CAD for digital subscriber lines (DSLs) throughout the world.

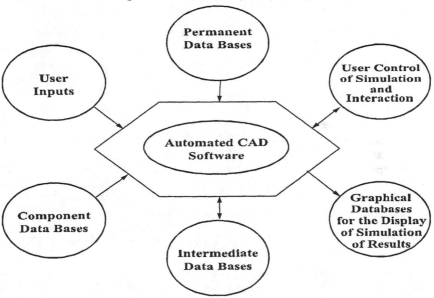

Figure 2.14 Overall Software Organization. CAD-computer aided design.

An overview of the general-purpose CAD software is depicted in Figure 2.14. *Four* major databases (permanent, component, intermediate, and graphical) are activated during the CAD function. The role and usage of these databases are discussed further in this section. User inputs and interaction facilitate the fine-tuning of software to the specific application being processed. In particular, we have been able to use this model in most of the software in both copper lines and fiber optic transmission links (the physical layer of the open system interconnect or OSI model) used in communication networks. Since the CAD procedure involves the verification of the proposed transmission system for an entire country or countries ranging over numerous subscriber loop environments, the inputs to the central analysis module of the software are derived from national loop survey databases for the copper HDSL environment. In the fiber optic CAD facility, other factors such as, multiple vendor fiber characteristics, range of optical characteristics of the devices used, and range of fiber splice characteristics, supply the inputs to the central analysis modules of the fiber design capability.

Databases holding the details of the current environment are essential to ascertain the compatibility of the new high-speed lines and the new components. The *five* major types of databases necessary for the design of the high-speed facilities are (1) the permanent databases, (2) the program databases, (3) the postprocessing program databases (4) the pictorial databases, and (5) the intermediate databases. These are discussed next.

2.10.2.1 Permanent Databases

The variety of these permanent databases depends on the extent and nature of the simulations. Truly global ISDN simulation needs the digital subscriber loop characteristics of different countries. The physical and electrical properties of the overall transmission media, the networking and carrier serving features, and so on are assembled in these databases. A generally localized or a national loop database suffices to initiate a limited study of the ISDN environment. But by and large, the topologies of the loop plant, primary and/or secondary electrical characteristics of the twisted wire-pairs, and cross-talk and impulse noise databases generally constitute the primary databases for ISDN simulations.

In many circumstances, it is necessary to design ISDN components to be functional with those of other vendors. In this case, it becomes essential to retain the interface characteristics of the vendor products. At a more detailed design level, the vendor databases have to become more exhaustive, requiring the physical, electrical, spatial power, thermal, and so on characteristics of these components. Specialized databases need to be developed under such conditions when a viable system is designed by using a large number of existing subsystems.

Four ISDN interfaces (R, S, T, and U) have been standardized. The R interface is necessary for non-ISDN terminals to be connected to the S interface via a terminal adaptor (TA). The U interfaces are necessary to connect the transmission line to connect NT1 (for network channel termination equipment) type hardware. The T interfaces connect the PBX and terminal controllers with the NT1; and S interface connects to the standard ISDN equipment terminals or the non-ISDN terminal equipment via the TA. For designing the compatibility between reference points and the terminal equipment a permanent database of the reference points and vendor characteristic becomes necessary.

2.10.2.2 Program Databases

In streamlined CAD facilities, the main analysis programs are standardized to the extent that they perform as glorified calculators. However, in R&D environments, these programs allow such dramatic variations in the inputs, components, and loop environments, that a database approach to managing their functionality, format, interoperability, and use becomes desirable. For this reason, managing programs and supporting programs are outlined in the following approaches.

2.10.2.3 Postprocessing Program Databases

HDSL simulations provide large amounts of significant results. Most of linear and circular scatter-plots [1, (Chapters 7–10)] are generated by the post processing and display programs. The advantage of separating this set of programs, to be distinct in their own right, is that incremental changes and fine-tuning of the software can be most easily accomplished.

In addition, a very long sequence of simulation runs can be executed by "shell" commands by using batch programs. The computer system does indeed keep a running account of the execution sequence and a detailed documentation of the simulation/optimizations when the machine is left unattended.

2.10.2.4 Pictorial Databases

Unless a systematic strategy for their display and tracking is adopted, the user tends to become overwhelmed in effectively using the results. For this reason, the management of pictorial files for display and interaction falls under the realm of database design. Considerable flexibility is necessary since the user is generally unaware of the intermediate or the eventual expectations of the CAD facility. As the project progresses, the user needs change. Typically, during the early stages, a feasibility study may be the primary goal. Next, system configuration and component optimization become important. During the third phase, compatibility of the proposed data transmission system with other systems already existing in the loop plant dominates the study. Finally, design rules and installation criteria need to be evaluated. Each of these phases, as the project reaches its goal, needs its own formats for display and evaluation of the results. If existing graphic routines are used, then categorizing the displays as recurring groups can minimize the amount of new codes. For example, two eye diagrams (central office to subscriber and subscriber to central office) are generated for each loop simulation. Likewise, two scatter-plots depicting the eye statistics are obtained by one performance evaluation over all the loops in the database. Hence, a hierarchical design of the files and displays facilitates the database management strategy.

Tabulated data is sometimes required to scan the marginal loops. Histograms depict the statistical nature of the loop characteristics. Image impedance is most effectively displayed as scatter-plots. Flexibility in the presentation of the results generally hastens the next phase of investigation. User requirements and component specification also play an important role in the software design.

2.10.2.5 Intermediate Databases

Numerous intermediate files are necessary to conserve core space. Some examples of these write, read-back files are: (1) files containing spectral components of excitation; (2) files containing eye opening statistics [17, 18] for each loop in both direction; and (3) single pulse reflections for echo cancellation. The management of these files can become the system user's responsibility. With an extremely large number of files and updates, the system designer is faced with this additional task. Ideally, when the generated files are to be reprocessed for graphical display in the form of eye diagrams, scatter-plots, signal-to-noise ratios, and so on, then the CAD system should provide a built-in safeguard to ascertain the accuracy of the displayed results. Effective file management is essential if the system has limited disk space. In addition, long and recurring data files should generally be refreshed from the disk rather than by recomputation to reduce the execution time.

A sophisticated human designer can compensate for an archaic CAD environment. The steps that are taken by an intelligent CAD environment can be tediously, but surely, taken by an experienced system designer. However, this approach is highly undesirable for ISDN. An intelligent CAD environment can be duplicated. It is portable, flexible, and systematic, though not creative. An inexperienced designer does not have either of the two desirable characteristics. The current ISDN growth environment needs sophisticated components as the network evolves and grows over a long period of time. For this reason, an enormous amount of intelligent designing of ISDN subcomponents is necessary. Given these conditions for the ISDN evolution and growth, numerous INCAD environments with a large number of designers are more desirable than a few very good designers and passive CAD environments. Database management and access based on the recent AI techniques both become necessary features in designing these intelligent CAD environments.

The purely humanistic approach is undesirable since the results and the performance of transmission systems have to be very dependable. Any probable cause of error in dealing with large databases needs scrutiny and reexamination, calling for sophisticated database capability. The approach proposed in this chapter uses database techniques particularly suited to the HDSL CAD environment. This database environment can be duplicated for other designs, such as the fiber optic system. It is portable, flexible, and systematic for other environments such as fiber optics and microwave systems. The physical layer needs sophisticated components for high-speed digital networks as they evolve and grow over a period of time. For this reason, it becomes essential to compare results under various conditions, components and design strategies. Both refined database management strategy and

AI techniques become necessary for the design process for information and WWW based knowledge management systems.

2.10.3 Data Management for Lightwave Systems

The organization and classification of the databases for fiber optic simulations [2] are not unlike those presented for the DSL studies in Section 2.10.2. From the systems organization perspective, the CAD platforms for DSL, HDSL, ADSL, and so on and that for the lightwave systems are essentially the same. Both are well suited for transferring signals and waveshapes to any other signal processor design package.

The simulation phase is based on *three* categories of files. In the first category, input files containing data to the simulation run are stored. The system does not automatically save all input files unless directed by the user. Thus the current input is likely to overwrite previous input files. The second category of files contains transitory information between one segment of the program and the next. The system does not automatically save these files to conserve disk space, but it can save these files for future reference. The third category of the file contains actual simulation results that may become essential to the signal-processing environment. Systematic saving of these files is a user option. The user may elect to optimize the design of the lightwave system before entering the signal-processing environment or optimize the integrated fiber-IC design. Extreme flexibility exists, since the system is designed to track the history of the procedural steps in the fiber or in VLSI environments.

2.10.3.1 Vendor Databases for Lightwave Systems

Vendor databases follow a hierarchical structure. The first level of classification is the component type. The second level is based the quality of its performance (e.g., rate×distance product or the attenuation and delay characteristics for fiber, noise level for PIN diodes, etc.). Since files and data structures are user definable, there is ample flexibility to store and retrieve data according to any preselected attribute of the device. The storage of noise data for photodiodes and preamplifiers can become quite challenging. If the database holds only the distribution characteristics, computations can become time intensive. In order to enhance execution speeds, the signal-independent to noise values are precomputed and stored in appropriate files. The signal-dependent noise is then computed as the actual simulation proceeds, and the final summation occurs at the device output.

Vendor databases and their organizations are user and applications dependent. At an initial level, it is appropriate to organize these databases as VLSI component databases. From a designers' perspective, the selection of the various components for a microcomputer system is akin to the selection of the optical components for a lightwave system. In many cases, the designer's preferences may also be incorporated in the vendor databases by including the various systems in which the components have been used and their relative performance levels. When a wide range of designs and their components are available, then the CAD facility can be prompted to suggest components in relation to the particular design in progress. When the correlation between the simulation results and the components is complete, the system will be able to identify the components that enhance or degrade the performance objectives.

2.10.3.2 Program Databases for Lightwave Systems

The simulation programs may be classified as *four* categories. First, the generic algorithms for FFTs, transfer function generators, filters, convolution techniques, and so on, and their code that is common to most simulators reside in the program library. Second, the routines for numerical evaluations such as integration, partial differentials, trigonometric approximations, and statistical routines reside in the routines library. Sometimes the computer vendor supplied routines are not adequate or accurate enough for specialized applications and they need to be modified or enhanced for the DSL or fiber optic design studies. Third, the graphics programs for display and postprocessing of the data also become crucial if detailed optimization is necessary. Finally, the programs for cross-comparisons of numerous designs are necessary if various vendors and their components should be analyzed in any given lightwave system. Routine database management techniques may or may not be adequate, depending on the designer's objectives.

The system design flexibility is tailored in the software organization. This software is designed to document and monitor events in the design procedure. The switch between optical signal processing and silicon signal-processing environments can take place at any step with a complete option to retract any false or undesirable steps. Entry and/or exit from one environment to the other are completely discretionary.

REFERENCES

[1] S. V. Ahamed and V. B. Lawrence, *Design and Engineering of Intelligent Communication Systems*, Kluwer Academic Publishers, Boston, 1988.

[2] S. V. Ahamed, Simulation and design studies of the digital subscriber lines, *Bell Sys. Tech. J.* 61, (July-Aug): pp. 1003-1077, 1982. See also, S. V. Ahamed, P. P. Bohn, and N. L. Gottfried, A Tutorial on Two-Wire Digital Transmission in the Loop Plant, *IEEE Special Issue on Comm.*, **COM 29**, pp. 1554–64, 1981.

[3] S. V. Ahamed and V. B. Lawrence, *Intelligent Broadband Multimedia Networks*, Kluwer Academic Publishers, Boston, 1997.

[4] Alcatel, www.alcatel.com/submarine/refs/cables/iaa/semewe.htm, SEA-ME-WE-3, Page scanned January 2006. See also, other WWW pages for SEA-ME-WE 3 cable systems.

[5] (a) Bellcore, *Synchronous Optical Network (SONET) Transport Systems: Common Generic Criteria*, TR-TSY-000253, 1989. (b) *Bellcore, SONET Add/Drop*

Multiplex Equipment Administration Using the TIRKS Provisioning System, *Globecom, Conference Record,* Vol. 3, pp. 1511-1515, 1989. (c) See also Bellcore *SONET Add-Drop Multiplex Equipment (SONET ADM) Generic Criteria,* TR-TSY-000496, Issue 2, 1989. (d) Bellcore *SONET Add-Drop Multiplex Equipment (SONET ADM) Generic Criteria for a Self-Healing Ring Implementation,* TA-TSY-000496, Issue 2, 1989. (e) For SONET Digital Hierarchy, see Ming-Chwan Chow, *Understanding SONET/SDH: Standards and Applications,* Andan Publishers, Holmdel, NJ, 1996.

[6] CCITT (now ITU), *Synchronous Digital Hierarchy Bit Rates,* Rec. G. 707, Blue Book, 1988.

[7] T. J. Aprille, Introducing SONET into the local exchange carrier network, *IEEE Commun. Mag.,* Aug., pp. 34–38, 1990.

[8] N. B. Sandesara, G. R. Ritchie, and B. Engel-Smith, Plans and considerations for SONET deployment, *IEEE Commun. Mag,.* Aug. pp. 26-33, 1990.

[9] Bellcore, *Integrated Digital Loop Carrier System Generic Requirements, Objectives, and Interface,* TR-SY-000303, Issue 1; Rev. 3, Mar. 1986.

[10] (a) T. S. Kazmi, *Simulation and Design Studies of Knowledge Processing Networks,* Ph.D. Dissertation at the Graduate Center of the City University of New York, 2002. (b) Lin Leung, *Local, National and Global Medical Networks,* Ph.D., Dissertation, City University of New York, 2004. (c) Nazli Mollah, *Design and Simulation of International Intelligent Medical Networks,* Ph.D., Dissertation, City University of New York, 2005.

[11] N. Waraporn and S. V. Ahamed, Intelligent medical search engine by knowledge machine, *Proc. 3rd, Int. Conf. on Inf. Tech.: New Generations,* IEEE Computer Society, Los Alamitos, CA. 2006. See also N. Waraporon, *Intelligent Medical Databases for Global Access,* Ph.D. Dissertation at the Graduate Center of the City University of New York, 2006.

[12] ITU, Series I Recommendations, pertaining to terminology, I-100 series, and I-200 series, and I-300 series. 1984.

[13] R. D. Gitlin, J. F. Hayes, and S. B. Weinstein, *Data Communications Principles,* Plenum Press, New York, 1992.

[14] J. O. Boese and R.B. Robrock, Service control point, the brains behind the intelligent networks, *Bellcore Exchange,* Nov.-Dec. 1987.

[15] S. V. Ahamed, B. S. Bosik, N. G. Long, and R. W. Wyndrum, Jr., The Provision of high speed digital data services over existing loop plant, *Proc. Nat. Electron. Conf.,* **33,** pp. 265–270, 1979.

[16] S. V. Ahamed and V. B. Lawrence, Database Organization and Access for ISDN, IEEE International Workshop on Microelectronics and Photonics in Communications, New Seabury, MA, June 6–9, 1989.

[17] M. J. Miller and S. V. Ahamed, *Digital Transmission Systems and Networks Volume II, Applications,* Computer Science Press, Rockville, MD, 1988.

[18] S. V. Ahamed and V. B. Lawrence, PC based image processing system for the two binary to one quaternary (2B1Q) code", *Proc. Southeastern Simulation Conf.* **SESC 88,** pp. 92-97, 1988.

Chapter *3*

Embedded Intelligence

Information processing systems deploy numerous types of embedded intelligence. The software for making systems artificially intelligent is profuse. Intelligence ranges from the controlled triggering of gates in the VLSI circuits, the microprograms encoded in the firmware, to the large array of application programs. It is effectively used from scanning bar codes to genetic tagging of stem cells. The trend and the applications are unlikely to subside. The user-friendly languages, the ease of compilation of very powerful code and the availability of specialized software all contribute to transforming the information domain into a longer lasting knowledge domain.

Intelligence by itself does not directly yield knowledge; however, it facilitates the search for any implicit and underlying relationship between objects. Specialized knowledge about related objects and/or their attributes accrues. In slightly older systems, the balance between artificial (machine) intelligence and natural intelligence was tilted toward the machine, with the human being doing the more delicate and sensitive part of information processing. However, the algorithms and tools of AI have become more powerful and the burden to search for new knowledge is more evenly distributed [1] between the human being and the machine.

To be able to embed intelligence, the interdependencies and interrelationships between objects need expert understanding on the part of human beings. Reasoning and inferencing become two initial steps in extending the thought process into

Intelligent Internet Knowledge Networks. By Syed V. Ahamed
Copyright © 2007 John Wiley & Sons, Inc.

events that follow as a sequential evolution. The process is both numerical and logical. The numerical slant appears as a confidence level [2] in the processing of objects (and concepts during information processing [3] to extract knowledge). In reality, there is a shade of uncertainty in dealing with fuzzy and dynamic situations.

3.1 SEARCH FOR KNOWLEDGE

In the search for entirely new knowledge, the machine by itself is at a loss to extrapolate existing knowledge into an entirely new domain; however, the machine can be predictive to some extent and offers a confidence level in its prediction. A human being can also (intuitively) predict. Along the way, the machine can compute very fast and the human being can be quick in being highly intuitive. At this level of interaction, the cooperative role of the machine and human being becomes evident in searching for long lasting and well-founded knowledge. In the game of creativity, the human being is the clear winner because of the nonprogrammable gift of perception that is yet to be clearly understood by human beings.

In other instances, the musician and the instrument, the painter and the paintbrush, the poet and the words, the writer and the language start to reflect the sensitive dialogue between a human being and the artifact. When the computational power of the machine becomes a match for the creative genius of any user, the synergy approaches the limits of imagination. This dynamic interaction between human beings and artifacts enters a domain of invention. Such interactions have been explored since the Stone Age and are not likely to disappear in the Information Age.

The artifacts (musical instruments, paint brushes, words, language, etc.) like the computing systems are products of the skills of many professionals. They get interwoven and integrated over time as users and technologies mature. When a new user deploys the existing computing systems in a search of new knowledge or wisdom, the entire process resembles a unique combination of synergy of skills catalyzed by the user's imagination. It becomes a process to discover if the human-machine team will lead to genuine new knowledge or wisdom. In addition, the direction and extent of the contribution both start to become vague. It is a rare and historic when the human-machine interaction leads to a new galaxy, a new medical breakthrough, a mathematical identity or even a new drug that may be socially significant.

During the contributions of the nineteenth and twentieth centuries, the human mind extended deep into the faintest dimensions of imagination. In the Information Age, the computational power and Internet access (greatly) push the mind further, extending the frontiers of knowledge deep into every conceivable (mental, psychological, social, physiological, scientific, etc.) space. It appears as if the Information Age is ready for yet another explosion based on computational algorithms and logical relationships that machines can investigate with great ease.

3.1.1 Intelligent Internet Defined

Recent enhancement of network capabilities has triggered the realization of many human achievements. The synergy of science and technology gets further into the realm of what was inconceivable a few decades back. The network performance has benefited from advances in intelligent networks and digital cross-connect switches that provide seamless connectivity throughout networks of the world. The Internet has added another dimension by providing the IP addressing capability and TCP/IP protocol. The Internet is an adaptive all-digital network capable of communicating data and information over the backbone communication infrastructure of any nation.

Intelligent Internet is programmable and supplements human imagination and creativity by using information and knowledge domain functions on the Internet data. The Internet is oblivious to the format of data communicated, thus permitting voice, data, video, graphic, or any information to be transferred from one logical location (IP address) on the network to another. Software and program support provided by any Internet services provider (ISP) making the Internet services powerful but inexpensive to reach any World Wide Web (WWW) site accessible by any backbone communication network. Backbone networks generally deploy just about any mode of communication available to offer Internet services to any user. Internet services far exce! any telephone- or computer-based network service. It is noteworthy that the Internet is itself a computer-based network.

In this book, we add intelligence to the Internet by blending the building blocks of INs into the Internet platform. For this reason, this configuration bears a resemblance to the typical IN architectures. In hindsight, looking at the evolution of computer systems and networks, it is apparent that the intelligent Internet can have numerous flavors. Whereas the Internet has a worldwide protocol (TCP/IP) and IP addressing, the intelligent Internet does not have a standard format. The intelligence in any Internet can be tuned to the provided specialized service. Intelligent Internet deploys knowledge bases throughout the world and provides specialized knowledge services in addition to regular Internet services. Such special knowledge services can range from finding analogies between one branch of science and another, commonalities in success stories and failures, degree of confidence in any axiom of wisdom, to even finding similarities and difference between two universes. Content-based switching permits users to access pages of digital libraries or the subject-based frontiers of knowledge. With an appropriate match to the natural intelligence of the users, the intelligent Internet becomes a viable tool in running a household or a nation. Knowledge processing tools (Chapters 8 and 9) are not immediately available with the ISPs. However, a new era of Internet intelligence is apparent at selected sites like Google and Oracle-PeopleSoft and in specially selected medical environments.

3.1.2 Intelligent Internet from Intelligent Network Platform

One such configuration is shown in Figure 3.1. The Internet is shown as the solid line ellipse and a new secure Internet signaling network (equivalent to the CCS7) is shown by the ellipse with the dash-dot line. Within these two outer ellipses lies a national archive of wisdom, knowledge, ethics, and cultural value of any nation. A full-fledged Internet-based intelligent network configuration is shown with a knowledge transfer point (KTP)— knowledge, wisdom, and other bases that serve as the reference points for the nation. An independent knowledge control point (KCP) holds the content-based address for knowledge and wisdom that is held in the national archive of knowledge and wisdom. Both the knowledge management system (KMS) and knowledge provisioning environment (KPE) are shown. The function of the KMS is to update, validate and consolidate then knowledge held in the archives. The function of the KPE is to provision and dispense selected modules and blocks of information from the archives. The function of safeguarding and preventing abuse of knowledge and information can be shared with the KMS.

There is a three level hierarchy[1] of knowledge providers (national, regional and local) as shown in Figure 3.1. The national level knowledge functions are shown within the two outer ellipses. Other international interconnect blocks are shown as hexagons, the regional knowledge service providers (RKSPs) are shown as pentagons, and the local ISP are shown as triangles. Management of the regional knowledge bases is carried out by a KBMS (equivalent to the DBMS used extensively in computational environments) rather than a KCP, KMS or KPS at the national level. This difference is more a matter of detail than a conceptual difference. In the normal mode of Internet service provisioning, the routine services are provided by the ISPs. When the knowledge seekers tap into the Internet, the knowledge intelligent peripheral or KIP (equivalent to the intelligent peripheral in the IN environment) senses the need to invoke the cooperation of the RKSPs, the national knowledge services providers (NKSPs), or the international KSPs. The Cooperation between KSPs facilitates the Internet users.

If there is a consortium of global knowledge providers, then the national knowledge, and wisdom, etc., bases of all nations can be consolidated under the patronage of the United Nations, much like the health and food programs. This "world bank" of knowledge, wisdom, and culture is the pinnacle at the fourth level (see Figure 1.1(a)) and provides the framework for nations to share values, ethics, and morality much like sharing other world resources. The role of information and knowledge in the growth and stability of some nations has been demonstrated by the recent establishment of cabinet-level offices (e.g., energy, national security) in United States government.

---

[1] This hierarchy is derived from the hierarchy of central offices that provide medium- and long-distance carrier systems for the telecommunications networks.

3.2 PERIPHERALS AND INTERFACES

Peripherals connect the user terminals and devices to the network or to the data processing systems. The complexity of a peripheral device can be significant. Ranging from simple bar code readers to highly intelligent computer systems, these peripherals facilitate the flow of information in a cogent and orderly fashion for the machines to process and for the user devices to communicate.

In addition, the peripheral devices allow users to control the inputs and outputs in a consistent and orderly fashion. Since networks and computer systems are abundant, the nature and classification of peripherals are also abundant. Over the last two decades, interfaces and terminals have become increasingly standardized.

Interfaces generally specify the signals and flow of data, whereas terminals specify the nature and type of physical connections. A wide variety of interfaces and terminals has evolved and changes with the nature of the medium carrying the signals and data. For example, interfaces and peripherals for the coaxial cable systems that carry microwave frequency signals for the L1 to L5 cable systems [4] differ drastically from the interfaces and terminals for the twisted wire pair ISDN systems [5]. Likewise, microwave radio systems deploy different peripherals from those for optical waveguide systems. Peripheral for the computers and networks are also widely varied. Ranging from low-speed teletypewriter (TTY) interfaces to direct memory access (DMA) device interfaces [6], they can provide data rates from a few hundred bits per second to multi-megabits per second. For this reason, interfacing with the appropriate protocol converters needs special attention in global and international data services.

Because of the inexpensive digital devices and profusion of Internet/computer access people all over the world have tapped into vast stores of information and knowledge. In the current information-rich society, communication devices and their interfaces are becoming increasingly generic. Evolution of this knowledge society has been the result of broadband communication and massive information processing capabilities. In this chapter, two of the most important catalysts in the communication industry— the SONET frame relay and ATM cell relay methodologies— are presented. Intelligent networking [7] and knowledge manipulation [3], their counterparts in the information processing environments— become more feasible on a local or global basis.

3.3 GENERIC MEDICAL NETWORKS

Medical networks can assume various formats. In a microscopic version, the network of medical records kept in doctors' offices and accessed by a group of local users qualifies as a miniature medical network. In more extended versions, hospital and insurance companies keep the records of their patients and clients.

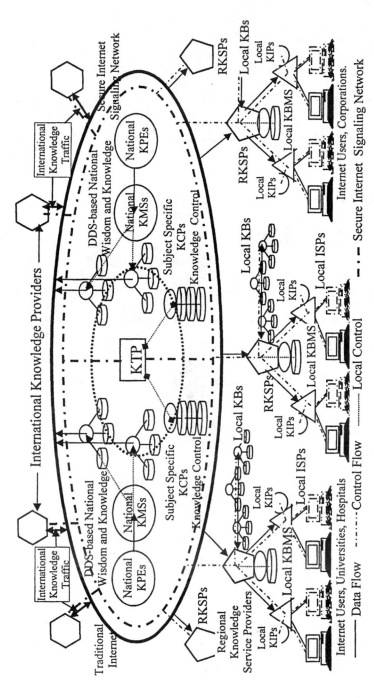

Figure 3.1 Framework of an intelligent Internet-based on IN concepts with traditional IN components. ISP = internet services providers; KIP - knowledge intelligent peripheral attached to ISP local network; RKSP - regional knowledge services providers; KB - knowledge base(s); KBMS - KB management systems; KCP - knowledge control point; KTP - knowledge transfer point; KMS - knowledge management system; KPE - knowledge provisioning environment; DDS - Dewey decimal system/Library of Congress system bases.

Global medical databases can be organized and strictly monitored for accuracy and completeness. The size of databases and the ability to access them for use access and its eventual use become serious concerns. An all-encompassing global medical database would be unfeasible and ineffective. However, a network of medical knowledge bases for a community, nation, or the globe holds scientific and social potential. In this section, the architectural configurations of hospital-based medical networks are presented along with the possibility of expansion to community, regional, or nation-based networks.

3.3.1 Hospital-Based Medical Networks

A hospital-based integrated medical computer system for processing medical and patient information and for evolving medical knowledge, diagnoses, and prognoses is depicted in Figure 3.2. The system consists of a medical processor, including a memory, and a plurality of medical data banks to which it is connected. The medical processor and the medical data banks are designed to work in tandem for executing a plurality of instructions and/or obtaining information. Numerous processor hardware modules are connected to the medical processor.

The modules include a communication module (CM), a switching module (SM), an administrative module (AM) and a knowledge module (KM). This configuration is suitable for handling the traffic of a large community of hospitals or a local medical center. The capacity of the centralized Main Hub of the Hospital (See Figure 3.2) is made consistent with the expected service from the AM, KM and SM. For small local clinics providing routine medical services a standard server environment will suffice.

There are three hardware, firmware and software modules in the processor. These modules function as a communication module— to control data communication between the other modules, the memory, and the medical processor. The effective communication from module to module is thus established. The hardware for the switching module(s) selects and switches between the various medical data banks for solving a particular problem. It also facilitates the administrative module to perform housekeeping functions, including multitasking control with resource allocation, real-time multitasking, and scheduling of tasks. Within a knowledge module (KM), the hardware performs knowledge processing functions and stores pertinent information in the medical data banks.

General patient databases, physician access point units, patient access point units, and service facilities are connected to the medical data banks and medical processor via several buses. In an alternative integrated medical computer system, numerous processors are included with their own memories and modules and are linked together to establish a processor net unit. This system can be used in a campus environment, where several buildings comprise the hospital or where several hospitals are interlinked over local area networks. One such configuration is shown in Figure 3.2. The nature of components and their capacities are matched to the variety of services provided, and sizes of the links and routers are matched to the expected client base that is served by the medical facilities.

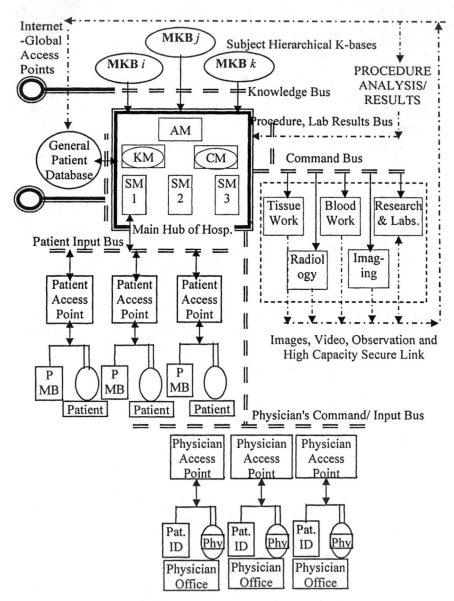

Figure 3.2 Computation and a communication perspective of any medical service provided in a hospital environment. When the medical staff carries handheld and portable devices for communication, total synergy of functions can be achieved within the hospital or medical facility complex. Data and information security issues become paramount under these conditions.

The medical processor in the central hubs shown in Figures 3.2 and 3.3 communicates with the global medical data banks over the Internet. Priming of the local medical knowledge bases (MKBs) with the commonly treated ailments and medical situations reduces the delay in awaiting local expert opinions for routine matters.

The numerous bus connections used in Figure 3.2 can be replaced by router connections in a LAN environment. Typically, if a high-capacity campus LAN is installed, a single router with multiple servers for each service or specialty can be used in each of the buildings within a medical campus.

The design principle of campus networks starts to be a cornerstone of most medical, educational, and electronic government networks. The relative emphasis on the type of service (e.g., research, educational, commerce, legal) influences the components, their size and their capacity rather than the architecture of the network.

Human operators served as switch-board attendants for telecommunications switching during the 1950s and 1960s. As the volume of traffic and the complexity of interconnections increased, automated call handling software was introduced. Entire sequences of steps for all calling scenarios were decommissioned into a series of programmable steps and then reconstituted for any given section of the call progress. Most telecommunication facilities around the world handle telephone calls by a sequence of call processing modules [8]. The sequence is streamlined and highly automated in electronic switching systems.

In designing the automated systems to handle routine medical care [9], a 15-step patient medical process cycle (PMPC) for any patient in the facility is possible. Much as the call processing software would handle telephone calls under all possible scenarios, the PMPC would handle a patient's condition under all the documented stages for any specific branch of diagnosed ailments. It now becomes possible to streamline the flow of diagnostic and procedural steps much like optimizing algorithmic steps (see boxes 3 and 4, Figure 3.4) in a computational process.

In the proposed approach, the possibility of handling a significant number of cases on a computational and artificially intelligent basis is significant thus saving time and energy in handling routine care and shifting the emphasis to expert human scrutiny if the situation demands it (see boxes 6, 7, and 8, Figure 3.4).

Two pitfalls in this approach are (1) undue dependence on the machine functions and (2) the lack of predictability of the patient's health given the patient's medical history and condition(s). Such obstacles have been observed when new software tools are interjected in entirely human organizations and have even been documented when management information systems were brought in to support middle management functions. However, the savings and overall management efficiency are both enhanced considerably over time.

Machines of the modern era are self-analyzing and self-learning to overcome illogical steps and errors. Human involvement in the functionality of the medical machines to execute the PMPC code can be decreased once the medical processor units [8] start to take over minor logical and judgmental functions.

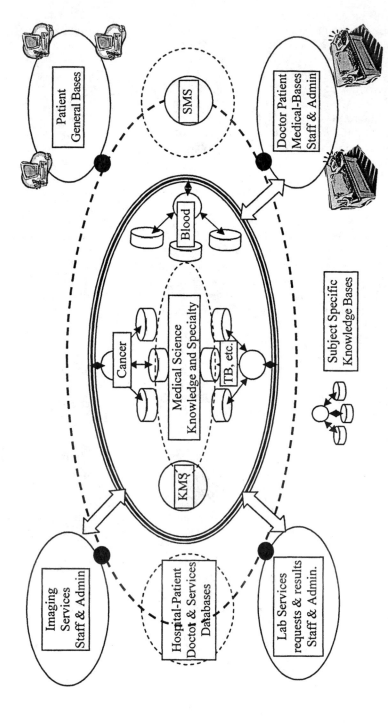

Figure 3.3 A local area network (LAN) implementation of the core hospital-based medical network for doctors, administrators and medical Staff. KMS - knowledge (medical) management systems. SMS service/billing/admin management services.

In the aviation industry, such developments resulted in the autopilot mode for flying large jumbo jets. Most of the intelligent systems involve human supervision but the gradual handover process has streamlined operations by fragmenting and perfecting numerous subprocesses that constitute routine operations.

3.3.2 Architectural Considerations

Figure 3.4 shows a processor-based, local medical data bank integrated medical computer system. Here, the medical processor and the medical data banks are in close proximity such that bus lines can be extended from the medical processor to the medical data banks. The medical data banks include a multitude of subspecialties of knowledge. This generally includes information from medical textbooks, academic information, and information-based on the experience of medical professionals. In general, the information within the medical data banks is complete, thorough, and updated.

Addressing a particular medical database is done via a bus-selector through a knowledge bus tied to the particular medical data bank. The address of the bus may be consistent with the classification of the information stored in that particular bank, thus reducing the seek time in these massive information stores. In such systems, the instruction to the medical data bank is followed by a burst of input data via a direct memory access channel. Note that contact between patients and physicians may be in real-time or via remote access.

Considerable latitude exists in the design of the memory, the processor, and the bus structures. At one extreme, the medical data banks are relaying all relevant information back to the main memory of the medical processor, where the instruction is executed. At the other extreme, a complete instruction is dispatched by the medical processor to the medical data banks and the medical data banks use their own local processors to execute instructions or part thereof. The partial result (in a shorter burst) of the instruction is dispatched back to the medical processor.

This aspect of processing is different from the conventional computing environments. In the proposed system, part of the execution of the instruction takes place in the medical processor and part of the execution takes place in the medical data banks 5, 7, and 9. For example, medical processor 3 performs the functions that are microscopic in nature and bear an immediate outcome from a specific medical instruction. On the other hand, medical data banks 5, 7, and 9 perform a global search and/or contextual search on a medical topic or a procedure within the vast amounts of information stored therein. In a sense, medical processor 3 can be seen as a microcomputer within the environment of a macrocomputer due to the interaction with the knowledge banks.

Alternatively, the network environment drives the medical processor to perform the associated micromedical functions of the macromedical functions. Typical of such macrofunctions in the medical data banks is "Analyze the symptoms of a patient and trace the genealogy of the possible diseases associated with the symptoms." Typical of the associated microfunctions in the medical processor 3 is "For the particular disease for the patient with a given history, weight, age, and other patient data (from the patient database), compute the dosage of Prescription #1 and Prescription #2, and so on, and dispatch the dosage to the pharmacy." Some currently available sophisticated database software packages perform these functions for the integrated medical system. The compromises in cost and performance are evident from the two hardware configurations.

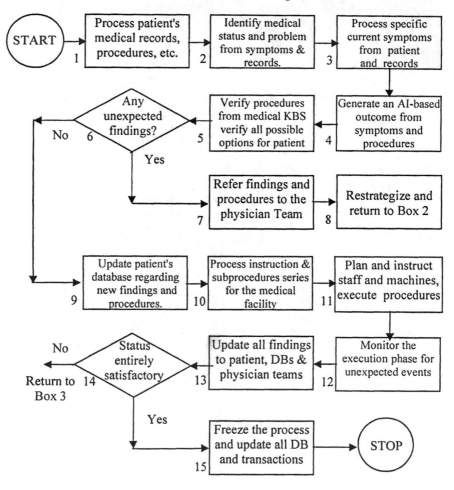

Figure 3.4 Fifteen-step patient medical process cycle (PMPC) for any patient at any medical facility.

The medical processor performs the arithmetic, logical, and the contextual functions that are local in nature, and the knowledge-based, expert system-based, and generic functions are performed by the medical data banks. It is contemplated that the medical data banks perform their functions in conjunction with the search-engines associated with the medical data banks. The most logical place for these search-engines and other such hardware would be in the knowledge map (equivalent of the KCPs in Figure 3.1) of the knowledge bases in Figures 3.1 and 3.5.

Every subprocedure is thus executed and the net result of the procedure is conveyed to the user (or the user program). The output is generated from sub-procedures, procedures, runs, and usage of the integrated medical system in an orderly and systematic fashion. Debugging of the integrated medical system functions becomes as easy as reading the registers and core dump of the medical processor unit or the registers and the core dump of the local processing units of the medical data banks.

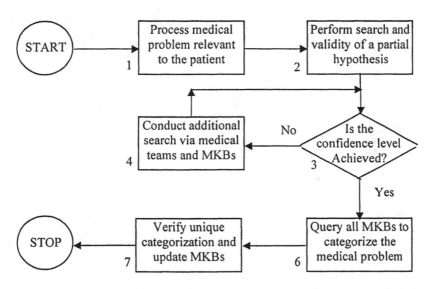

Figure 3.5 Steps in handling new medical situations in the medical facility.

Medical processors necessary to implement the algorithmic flow-charts of Figures 3.4 and 3.5, include a memory and an administrative module, a knowledge module, a communication module, and switching modules (shown in Figure 3.2). The knowledge module executes a plurality of subprocesses. The communication module has software to further control communication between the subareas of the medical data banks and the knowledge module. It controls the subprocesses as they pertain to the inputted medical problem and organizes inputs and outputs of the subprocesses to execute the medical instruction. The processor also generates a medical diagnosis as the solution for a possible input of new medical problems.

Several functions of the administrative module include keeping track of (1) which patient needs to be charged what fees and for which services; (2) which clinical lab needs to be paid, how much, for what services, and for which patient; and (3) accounts receivable and accounts payable for the hospital or medical center.

The administrative module also allocates all resources to the appropriate needs within the hospital and performs the functions akin to the functions of an operating system in a computer environment. The hardware and executable software of the administrative module are the mechanism for the enforcement of overall optimality and a higher level of performance for the system. It also generates reports for hospital management to verify the accountability of every unit of the hospital or medical facility.

The knowledge module stores up-to-date information from textbooks, academic information, and information-based on experience, and the distilled wisdom of medical profession: in short, all of the information that the medical teams can learn in universities, look up in medical journals, research in medical libraries, discover in medical conferences, and so on.

The communication module switches the appropriate query to the right knowledge base. This is done in accordance with preprogrammed instructions, such that the total network access time is minimized. The switching modules provide the pathways via the communication medium (i.e., electrical, microwave, fiber, satellite) on which the hospital-based system is built.

The knowledge-based functions listed above are tailored to the specific patient information that is retrievable from general patient database and procedure/lab information from procedure/result analysis. Output reports from the integrated medical facility may be generated on-demand.   Such essential functions are performed by component-configuration shown in Figure 3.2. In addition to the knowledge bus, there is one or more patient bus(s) connected to general patient database, and one or more procedure/lab bus(s) connected to a procedure/result centers. The output bus is connected to service facilities, which may include tissue work, therapy, blood work, and imaging, such as radiation and biopsy.

The medical processor is connected to numerous patient access point units (Figure 3.2) that may be located at and operated from a remote location from the processor. These units include individual patient medical bases and input to the medical processor as well as output from the processor. These units monitor a patient's condition, input data, and provide instructions to the patient, alert the hospital staff and/or physician about changes in patient's condition.

In its proposed embodiment (Figure 3.2), the medical processor is connected to a number of physician access point units. Through these units, physicians can access services facilities, procedure/result analysis, any or all medical data banks, the general patient database, and patient access point units. Physicians can also access these components through the medical processor as a direct user, or indirectly by query to the medical processor, whereby the medical processor utilizes whatever modules, memory, programs, subprograms, buses, and connected units and facilities as may be necessary or appropriate to respond to particular queries posed by the physician user. Authorized student access and use of integrated medical facility are thus feasible with appropriate security measure. In addition, the physician-based, remotely located physician access point units are connected to the medical processor for operating the processor from remote sources using the processor hardware modules connected to the processor.

3.3.3 Architectures for Telemedicine

In the area of telemedicine, the architecture can be quite small, ranging from a group of PCs on an Ethernet for a private physician's office to a national medical network to monitor and administer medical services for an entire country. An architectural structure for a mid-sized hospital environment is discussed here. This intermediate structure shown in Figure 3.6 may be tailored down to a doctor's office or enhanced to a full-fledged regional or national medical network environment. The design steps for networks of this nature start from the estimation of traffic, the acceptable bit error rate, error free seconds, and the waiting time as a first step to ensure quality of service. In most cases, user preference is reflected as overdesign or redundancy in the network capacity. From the network design considerations, the most inexpensive redundancy is usually the link capacity of dedicated fiber lines. When these links are leased or shared between other network applications, a good estimation of the average response time is obtained by the network simulation studies. Numerous studies [10] of this nature have been performed on commercially available network simulation packages such as COMNET and OPNET. It would not be prudent to design these networks without proper attention to traffic estimation, future needs, scalability, and the quality of service requirements.

3.3.4 MSP-Based Medical Network

In this section, we propose two architectural arrangements shown in Figures 3.6 and 3.7, to build localized and independent intelligent medical networks. These networks constantly monitor the specific needs of the patients and resources of the locality with the involvement of medical service providers (MSP). The MSPs would serve the medical and informational needs of their client patients. A large number of these MSPs would serve a community or a region.

Each MSP(i) will (1) retain a portfolio of each of the client patient(j) and (2) perform a daily check on the status changes in the local or global information or service as it pertains to the medical history of that particular client patient, making the patient aware of any details that may affect the course of action. If the patient goes through the MSP, then the incremental change is updated in the patient database. The system performs routine medical functions much as hospital staff would perform but retains the information over the life of the individual for every ailment and treatment. Details of the databases and their distribution or aggregation, are presented in the two architectural arrangements.

3.3.4.1 INTEGRATION OF MEDICAL NETWORKS

Large groups of independent hospital networks may be integrated (and programmed) to coexist within one larger medical network as independent intelligent networks sharing the network infrastructure. The functionality can also be forced to perform as a group of localized medical networks [9] for the particular hospital rather than one massive medical network for a region or a country. The role of the numerous medical service providers (MSPs) will thus be confined to local area services and information access rather than to a few global medical service providers. The main advantage of having a large number of smaller and localized MSPs is that the cost and complexity of a localized MSP is much lower than a large MSP. The new competition at the localized MSP services will reduce the medical expenses and overall customer costs.

More local MSPs and businesses can offer the medical information and services such as discounted prescription drugs, hospital and nursing services, or physical therapy. Such an increase in the supply side of medical information will facilitate the medical field to become more competitive and thus contain medical costs in the long run.

3.3.4.2 STATUS QUO OF THE MEDICAL NETWORK ENVIRONMENTS

Although smart Internet users can access some of these services, such services have not been tailored to the medical profession. The specialized services that the physicians and hospitals provide and the associated reduced patient costs are still not available to most patients. Over the next decade or so, it is envisioned that specific medical information may be supplied by medical knowledge bases rather than by doctors. In a sense, the initial information gathering and the search for appropriate low-level medical treatment are facilitated by MSPs, medical knowledge bases, and intelligent medical knowledge processing that tailors the medical services and the hospital facilities to the patients. The current approach is to place the patient at the lowest level of service provisioning rather than placing the patient as the paying customer. In the majority of cases, patients are forced to accept medical services and hospital facilities at an unknown quality of service and an unclear billing system. It is also foreseen that the specific information for an individual patient can be retrieved by smart medical databases based on a patient's specific conditions.

3.3.4.3 INTELLIGENT MEDICAL NETWORK OR MSP-BASED INTELLIGENT INTERNET

By enhancement of the basic IN architecture of the 1980s to suit the TINA architectures [11], network designers have brought a sense of interoperability within the framework of all INs. While it is desirable to have this ideology already built in every network, there at least three drawbacks. (1) The standards need a long time to evolve. (2) The standard interfaces and software modules that perform the functional components (service specific feature of the TINA Network) or FC's may not be readily available. (3) More importantly, the backbone network may not be ready to host and execute the network programming language for each of functional components (FCs) for each of the medical subscribers.

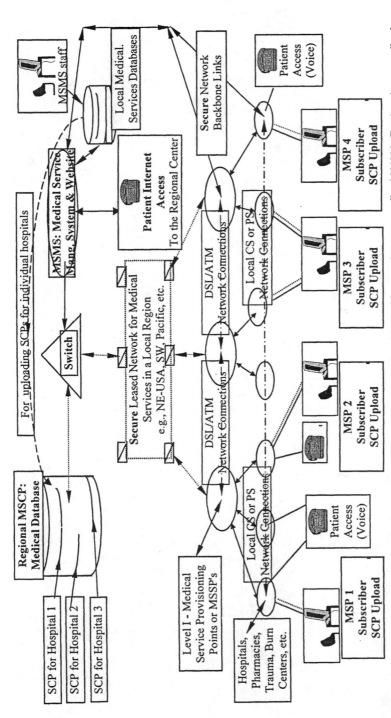

Figure 3.6 A representation of many medical networks being hosted in one larger medical WAN. Each micro medical net is uploaded by the individual MSP Subscriber who can program the network to function as an IN/1, IN/1+, IN/2, or any version of the advanced version of an IN or the AIN. MSP subscribers may also interject their own customized programs to be executed during the operation to provide specialized services to suit the client needs.

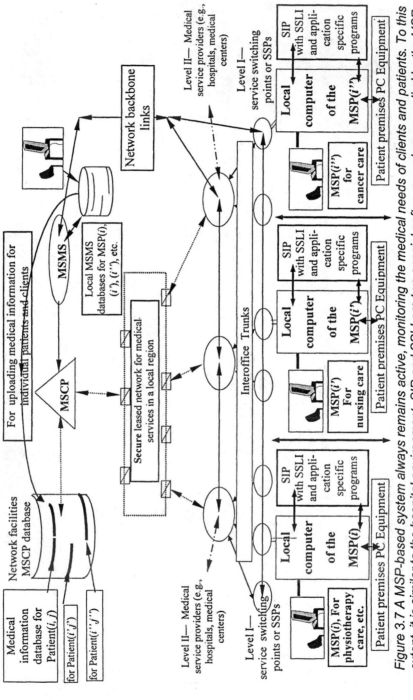

Figure 3.7 A MSP-based system always remains active, monitoring the medical needs of clients and patients. To this extent, it is similar to the hospital environment. SIP and SSLI are two special software package supplied by the MSP for the patient.

A possible configuration of hospital-based integrated medical computer systems for processing medical and patient information using specialized functional Modules is presented in [9]. However, setbacks in the full implementation of such a network environment can cause a delay in bringing the intelligent medical Internet services to patients and users.

At the same time, the marketplace is dynamic and volatile. The business drivers are anxious to get the network services now and take a risk if the price is small enough. In a sense, the proposed network architecture shifts the responsibility back to the MSPs to use their own customized packages that will accomplish their specific goals. These goals are specific for each MSP and the community of patients and users whom the MSP is willing to serve. The MSPs can offer a menu, as the Internet does, but from their own distinct databases. Access via telephone networks for fixed and wireless lines is also feasible. Thus, the blend of services is discretionary, the waiting time is short and patient and user control on the content is made local and immediate. This is in stark contrast to the philosophy of other intelligent network service providers and owners who wish to offer generic and universal services to all customers.

From the architectures of the advanced intelligent networks (AINs) discussed in [8], the adjunct service provider (ASP) and the Internet protocol (IP)-based switching systems provide similar capabilities for their telecommunications clients. However, the programs within the ASP and IP are mentored, monitored, and maintained by the network owners. In the MSP-based Internet, it is proposed that the user/patient-specific functions be programmed and fine-tuned on local computers owned by the MSP subscribers, who will offer a blend of legitimate medical functions (such as dispensing of drugs, physiotherapy, nursing care, paramedical services, or radiation therapy) with authorization from the community of medical professionals and hospitals. Whereas it may take a long time for all the telecommunication-based AIN standards to be written, standardized, debugged and made available to clients, the MSP-based network environment provides patients and users with currently available network technologies. These network and medical functions are blended harmoniously under the supervision of the MSP within the framework of the risk that the MSP is willing to take with the local community of patients and users.

3.3.4.4 PROPOSED MSP NETWORK CONFIGURATION

The proposed MSP-based architectures (Figures 3.6 and 3.7) permit the doctors and hospitals to have an open information policy (such as services, charges, type of care, and so on) brought about by competition on the supply side. It also facilitates a trend for numerous specialized MSPs to participate in the regional, national, or global medical economy. This step is akin to the distribution of localized medical information (from the supply perspective) from local medical data banks rather than sharing very large databanks via global or Internet access. In the ensuing knowledge society, these MSPs will be akin to local banks functioning in cooperation with the regional banks, national banks and the federal reserve system.

Many such MSPs can serve a large number of patients who do not need the very high-speed or intricacies that the high-technology global Internet is capable of providing to all its users. Smaller databases, localized customers, and larger local area traffic will permit smaller MSPs to customize and target their services to a specific clientele and user community.

Under program control, the localized medical knowledge networks (MKNs) that interconnect the MSPs may also be forced to work interdependently, exchanging current information as it becomes available to perform a variety of functions hitherto possible only by human beings. The individual patient and user databases are based on the patient (SS) numbers and assigned secure and logical address within the host network. Each logical medical knowledge network functions as a personal intelligent network (PIN) developed in [8]. It is dedicated to that particular patient only for the illness or for life. These MKNs provide all the medical intelligent network (MIN), [12] and personal communication network (PCN), [8] services and operate under a patient-driven programmable code. The patient has the privilege and freedom to "instruct" the host network to perform all the legitimate and ethically acceptable backbone medical and communication network functions. These functions may be as simple as the banking services (such as account balance, on-line payments, credit card activity, etc.) currently offered by local banks or as complex as the blend of sophisticated hierarchical and cascaded intelligent telecommunication functions that the TINA network is capable of performing.

Figure 3.6 depicts a possible regional medical network architecture that permit the regulation, authentication and monitoring the medical services by a government or a nonprofit entity. The network management system MSMS monitors and tracks the activity to prevent abuse of the medical services in a region, a state or a nation. Many other possible uses of such a network infrastructure (such as child care, nursing home care, or emergency care) are also possible.

3.3.4.5 MSP-BASED NETWORK OR THE INTERNET

In designing Web-based programs, the range and extent of network services become apparent. In a sense, the HTML programs can duplicate the intelligent network functions of the circuit-switched networks for the Internet. Whereas these services are mostly information-based, application-specific client services are usually confined to be stereotyped and minimal. Most application programs are based in distant servers and get communicated via the Internet by packet switches. This can cause substantial delays between screens and during the downloading of programs and data. In addition, when the network programs are uploaded, they reside in the local or distant server, and program execution occurs based on the capabilities of the server. As the volume of data to be exchanged becomes large, the response time also starts to increase due to increased use of the network resources. Most multimedia traffic awaiting broadband networks experiences significant delay. Typically, the bottleneck is in the local fixed line or the wireless loop. This bottleneck can be reduced by the integrated services digital network (ISDN) line or the DSL capability now available in some metropolitan areas.

On the other hand, using local high-capacity servers and a local high-speed LAN may alleviate the problem. For large-scale users, this methodology uses the TCP/IP protocol, high-speed LANs (typically campus networks, educational or medical networks, etc.), and localized high-capacity servers to serve customers. We propose this approach for the countries that will not have their ISDN or the DSL facilities in place for many years. When these services become available, they may be connected to the high-speed LANs and the high-capacity servers. When the problem is taken in the public domain, the local high-speed LANs and servers may be owned by the local fixed loop network owners (rather than Internet operators) and the revenues for such services will revert back to the local telephone companies.

In the case of the MSP-based network, two types of architecture are feasible. Large medical insurance companies can own the larger metropolitan area medical networks or service agencies and the backbone and medical database services will be provided to the local MSPs. This network representation is shown in Figure 3.6. On the other hand, the responsibility and ownership of the services can be retained by the MSPs, and only the network services are obtained from leasing the secure signaling and communication services from the backbone service providers. With the profusion of bandwidth for communication, and the increasing complexity of signaling to provide these backbone services, it appears the latter ownership style is likely to prevail. The MSPs would thus become network-based intermediators between the medical staff (hospitals, etc.) and the patient/user community at large. The network architecture is shown in Figure 3.6 will serve such well for such applications.

3.3.4.6 KNOWLEDGE-BASED PROGRAMMABLE MSP ARCHITECTURES

Another possible architecture of the new MSP-based Internet is shown in Figure 3.7. It deals with small medical centers and typical medical service providers. A large number of businesses (the customers of the service provider) share the SCP of this medical IN. These businesses deal with clients who need specialized services.

In Figure 3.7, the uploading process of the SCP of the subscriber is also depicted. It resides in the SCP of any large telecommunications service provider (under a *new* number and *secured* series of numbers such as 899 or 898). This is an integrated database activated for the client or patient (j) of any medical service provider(i). Special services may thus be activated for that patient (j) provided (1) the patient is within his/her authorized range of special services offered by the hospitals, pharmacies, burn centers, nursing care facilities, and so on and (2) the patient(j) is within his/her own prepaid level or the level of authorization for payment from the insurance companies, and so on. This permits a two-tier service structure (network-based services (such as medical history and treatments, remedies and specialized centers for the particular ailment, counseling, and knowledge dispensing) and patient-based services (such as prescriptions, physiotherapy, nursing care, and ambulatory care)) that the patient may receive.

In Figure 3.7 the operation mode of the network is also depicted. Special and permissible network functions are accomplished by the MSPs via two special units— a hardware unit, the subscriber intelligent peripheral (SIP), and a special software unit, the subscriber service logic interpreter (SSLI). These units are scaled down (into PC size) versions of the IP and SLI that are present in a typical service switching point (SSP) of an IN. These units are necessary for the modern intelligent network (typically IN/2) to provide the special MSP functions akin to subscriber services.

These two functions provided by SIP and SSLI (in Figure 3.7) also can be traced back to the functional architecture of the TINA network documented in [11]. In this TINA network proposed by the International Telecommunications Union (ITU), the functions of IP and of the SDP (see Figure 12-3b in [8]) parallel the functions of SLI shown in Figure 3.6. Likewise, the functions of CCF, the SSF and the SCF at the service node SN of TINA (presented in Figure 12-3b in [8]), parallel the SSLI shown in Figure 3.6.

If a Telecommunications service provider can condense the service node of TINA to a PC-based HW and SW environment for the individual MSP subscriber, then the specialized service creation environment (SCE) of TINA can be handed back to the MSPs. All the advanced intelligent network features now acclaimed by the next-generation intelligent networks, like the TINA network, can be offered in a rudimentary IN environment with the basic SCP, STP, SSP, and SMS as the building blocks for the MSP-based network.

When any patient/client(j) makes a call for the specialized services to the MSP(i), it activates the client-specific service program. The track sector address of the executable code for the client is dispatched from the network SCP database. This facilitates that an executable program code in the databases of patient/client (j), be executed based on the most recent medical information, at the MSP premises to provide the best service for patient/client(j). The enhanced network database furnishes a program address in the subscriber database and redirects the call to the appropriate secondary level service provider (such as a pharmacy, a nursing center, or a counseling service) for additional treatment or help for that patient/client.

In Figure 3.6, the ownership of the regional MSCP medical databases and the MSMS (medical services management system) can be negotiated. One possible variation of the architectures is to permit Internet access to the databases to keep the hospitals and patients updated about the specific changes in these databases. The MSCP and MSMS programs that are customized and uploaded by the MSPs for their patients/clients do the blending of MSP and network services. The segment of the KB that is tagged as (i, j) is invoked and serves according to the contents of the KB uploaded by the MSP(i) for the client/patient (j). The MSP-based network is thus capable of taking the patient request for services through the Internet access or service authorizations from the medical staff or hospitals.

In Figure 3.7, the local subscriber database for the SCP is depicted. In this configuration, the subscriber retains his/her specific database. The SCP now contains all the information to handle customer-specific and authorized network functions. The program database also contains the information for the SSLI functions, and the SIP functions are handled by special hardware to network signaling and network data.

The architectures presented here offer added benefits to the medical community. First, by incorporating the roles of the MSPs (hospitals, medical/ diagnostic centers) and the clients/patients, any client/patient is provided with *all* the information and details of the medical condition germane to that particular client/patient. The human interface is practically eliminated unless it is called for by the patient/client. At the supply side, the MSPs have all the most recent medical information available to them. Their databases include all the codes, coverage, and list of options for treatments. Second, as the client/patient is ready for treatment/hospitalization, the MSPs act as intermediators between the second-level medical service providers (see Figure 3.7) and the client/patients. Third, the medical services provided are based on the procedures of electronic transactions on networks. For this reason the service and turnaround are quick; they are also efficient and inexpensive thus facilitating reduced cost for operating the health industry. Fourth, very large medical network knowledge bases owned by the hospitals and universities can now be fragmented into thousands of small server environments (in any localized area) necessary for smaller specialized MSPs in the local area. Fifth, numerous sophisticated medical intelligent network services can readily be offered by executing special SIP and SSLI programs within the MSP premises computers (see Figure 3.7). Sixth, prepaid and authorized medical services can be dispensed immediately. Each MSP can tailor and fine-tune the medical service provided and can include a personal touch to the client/patient.

The MSP-based network environment effectively taps into the Internet and the wireless telephone networks. Both these networks are growing at an enormous rate with increasing coverage and popularity. The proposed medical networks bring the impact of the new digital technology, knowledge society, and network revolution to the medical community. The MSP-based network quickly and profoundly closes the gap between the medical community and the highly mobile clients and patients within a growing segment of the population [12].

3.4 GENERIC EDUCATIONAL NETWORK

Modern educational networks are intelligent and broadband. In addition, they scan, search, analyze, and deliver content from knowledge bases distributed around the campus or world. Most of the broadband networks are packet-switched and most conventional INs function well in circuit-switched environments. Hence, it becomes necessary to impart the essential IN node characteristics (of circuit-switched networks) to bridges, routers, and gateways (of the packet-switched networks). Router technology (late 1980s) followed the path of ESS technology (late 1960s) two decades later. While the ESS technology is established and definitely program (software) driven, the router industry is struggling to be programmable and intelligent. It appears that this combination of router technology, blended with CPU technology, will give rise to new and more powerful intelligent high-speed networks (typically OC-*n* rates). The switches (typically intelligent and ATM-based), lead to more intelligence than the traditional intelligence of INs of the 1990s.

3.4.1 Network-Based Intelligent Educational Networks

A network-based intelligent information-sourcing system has capabilities akin to an automated universal teacher, researcher, or expert. The system is able to interpret independently and in contextually, and provide comprehensive answers to received queries on substantially any subject. This capability is achieved by enhancing existing telecommunications networks and intelligent networks to incorporate a query and knowledge processing capability. This network uses its communication capability of the network to collect queries from, for example, students in an interactive mode, then passes the question to a "knowledge ring" comprised of numerous knowledge bases arranged hierarchically, and then sends the response back from the system. Such knowledge bases are used in the management of large corporations that deploy intelligent decision support systems embedded in SAP [13] and PeopleSoft [14] applications. Once the query is understood, the system restates the question back to the student in the way the particular knowledge base is integrated and, upon confirmation, the system delivers the response back to the student.

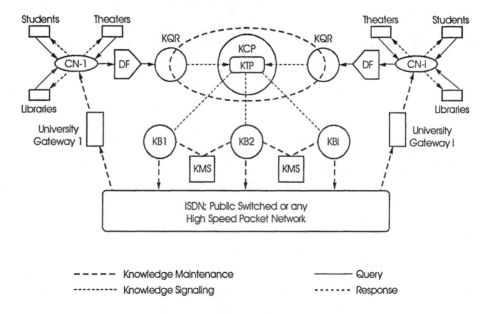

Figure 3.8 A intercampus educational network architecture.

3.4.2 Network Architecture for Distance Learning

Distance learning deals with dispensing knowledge and two-way high-speed communication for an interactive environment [15]. Typically, broadband multimedia features are also necessary to maintain a classroom environment. Two architectures are shown in Figures 3.8 and 3.9. For multicampus universities, the distance learning network can be accommodated through numerous campus networks (CN-*1* through CN-*i*) in Figure 3.8. For larger universities and research institutions, the extensive architecture shown in Figure 3.9 is more suitable. Intercampus traffic is carried by local area networks specific to the campus and intra-campus traffic is carried by public domain digital lines such as the ATM or the broadband ISDN facilities, which also access distant networks and knowledge bases. This two-layer design facilitates the more heavily used local networks to respond to the needs of the local campuses quickly, while the more expensive intercampus lines (via PBXs and DPs or dialog processors) cater only to the lighter traffic reaching out to other campuses or knowledge bases (KB-1, KB-2, etc.). The knowledge bases hold digital libraries and electronic books.

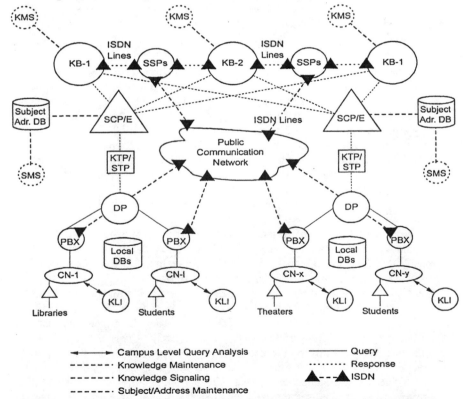

Figure 3.9 A multicampus educational network architecture for a large university or research center.

Students and teachers access these facilities via their PCs, and the subject classification offers access based on any standard library encoding schemes such as the Dewey Decimal or the Library of Congress systems. This type of architecture permits numerous universities to share the facilities of one large high-capacity electronic library. The digital traffic jam during the classroom hours is well handled by intelligent path-finding routers located in the knowledge transfer point/signal transfer point (KTP/STP) switch and the service transfer point (SCP) that actually provides the right address for campus queries. These concepts are already implemented in intelligent network architectures [16] around the world. In the more recent purely digital networks, intelligent routers carry out these functions. These adaptive routers are appearing in the market more and more frequently and their proper usage will facilitate the flow of individualized classroom digital data.

Knowledge bases need to be serviced and updated. Typically, this is accomplished by a group of subject matter specialists in the knowledge management systems (KMSs). In the context of educational networks, Figure 3.9 depicts the use of intelligent network concepts carried into the domain of LANs and WANs.

3.4.3 Design Considerations of Network-based Educational Systems

In this section we enhance the architectures of both the telecommunication networks and intelligent networks to incorporate substantial component of "knowledge processing." It is then reconfigured to meet the needs of educational and research communities Processing of knowledge occurs as information flows through the network in two distinct ways. First when the initial interrogation takes place, the Subject matter is identified *and* linked to other knowledge by forward and backward chaining. Second, the function to be performed on this *subject* matter is also identified and an *operator-operand relationship* is established to facilitate the network response.

Network-based educational systems or NBES have started to emerge as isolated of such networks to facilitate distance learning, interactive distance classrooms and video-based participation of distant classrooms. Such applications [1, 10] need high bandwidth communication links to permit bidirectional video facilities to be implemented. These techniques are currently operational and are successful in creating a classroom environment for college education.

While progress in this direction is noteworthy, progress in the crucial direction of INs, is not being deployed for educational networks. The new breed of INs processes knowledge and its segments intelligently and fabricates the response from a large cross section of knowledge bases (banks). This network uses the communication capability of the network to collect queries from students in an interactive mode. Once the query is understood, the system would restate the question back to the student in the way the particular knowledge base (KB) is interrogated and then poses the question to a "knowledge ring" with numerous knowledge bases arranged hierarchically and then bursts the response back from an "artificially intelligent instructor". Such a response would be consistent with that of an extremely knowledgeable instructor but needing streamlined language interface to comprehend the precise needs of the student.

Upon confirmation of response from the KBs, the system would deliver the response back to the student. In a manner of speaking, this is how the human instructor would have responded in a classroom. We do not promise that this methodology of teaching is applicable in every situation, but there appears to be niche for such a network-based educational system where students are eager and intelligent enough to interact constructively with the system. Typical of this environment is the research and development facility of any organization or the graduate research center of any university.

In this section we present an architectural configuration of the NBES and its components, which have all the advantages, and features of any IN (see Section 2.9.2). We also present the areas where these networks differ from conventional intelligent networks and the need for syntactic rule-based "knowledge processing" and the need for "knowledge control point" rather than a service control point (SCP, See [8,18]) of the traditional IN. Finally, we present how these NBESs are compatible with evolving networks such as the SONET (Section 2.4), campus networks, or any high-speed digital network in the circuit or packet mode of function. The asynchronous transmission mode of the ATM or the hierarchy of SONET rates does not constitute any problem to the evolution of NBES.

We hasten to add that this type of network may not be appropriate for environments where the emotional involvement between the student and teacher is high (e.g., elementary schools, theater, or fine arts) and education is much more than the textual or graphical exchange of information. It is likely to retain some of the pitfalls of AI techniques. Overly intelligent abusers can cause serious problems in the functionality of a NBES and bring about a "dead-locked" situation. However, a NBES can be as useful to the educational community as an IN is to society.

In the following sections, we present the educator's concept of the NBES; the network and communications aspects of the proposed NBES, and how NBES may evolve over the next few decades. These configurations take full advantage of the committed networks such as IN/1, IN/1+, IN/2, AIN, USIN [7, 8], together with ISDN [8], SONET [8], ATM [8].

3.4.4 Features Common to Educational Environments

The discipline of communication is evident in schools and universities, where there is exchange of information and knowledge: It is an age-old methodology at work. The imposition of a new field of data communication upon the oldest institution of the teacher–student relationship is very likely to cause resistance and friction. Be that as it may, if the two are going to be merged, then knowledge bases (KBs) must be installed, interfaces must be designed, and the learning steps can be compiled as incremental processes. Such modules of information are collated, sorted, merged, rearranged, graphed, and evolved as a body of knowledge that will be retained in the minds of the learners. Knowledge engineering is the concern of every teacher to practice and of every student to conceive.

Fortunately, computer scientists have streamlined these basic modular functions in the exchange of information and data. More importantly, human–machine communication via structured language can be parsed based on the rules of syntax and analyzed based on the rules of the semantics, and thus the entire module of communication (i.e., the program) becomes consistent. The assembly and linking functions that generate the executable code are standard. The machine simply processes a collection of binary machine instructions to make computerized instruction and distance learning a reality.

Flexibility of language facilitates communication enormously. If a fault tolerant supercompiler could be instituted at every human-machine interface then any student could "talk" to the machine and any machine could become an "understanding" teacher. The installation of a fault tolerant supercompiler is an outrageously expensive proposition. However, the student can compromise in working with a realistic interface and an inexpensive computer.

3.4.5 Role of Networks in Educational Environments

Ideally, an instructor will able to answer any query on any subject instantly and provide a platform for interactive hierarchy of knowledge. Since the instructor is human, students do compromise. If the logical and retrieval part of the instructor function can be automated, then the source of information can be located in distant knowledge banks and the role of networks in communicating information over long distances becomes evident. In this mechanized environment, the creativity of the instructor to foresee implications— forward vision, and the integration of concepts still remains a human activity. But the capacity to store, monitor and retrieve information over long distances brings memory technology and communication engineering into the realm of the teacher–student relationship.

When the role of networks is only to gap the physical distance between teacher and student via video and audio channels, distance learning ensues. In addition, when the role of networks becomes intelligent and human in processing and controlling the information communicated, the features of intelligent network ensue. When the role of the network further includes the processing of knowledge by dissecting (parsing) and reforming the syntactic and semantic context of the network queries to assemble a logical response from distributed knowledge bases, then the network based education system emerges.

3.4.6 Role of Knowledge Bases in Educational Environments

Mechanized storage and retrieval of information offers well documented [12–14] and distinct advantages to the educational community. We shall not reiterate these benefits; instead, we will discuss the management and updating of such vast electronic devices that serve the interests of the teaching community. Knowledge is dynamic, quantifiable, and classifiable. If the aforementioned aspects are accepted, then knowledge bases need to be maintained, stored in discrete blocks at finite addresses and separated out by the relationship that any finite quantity (e.g., a paper by its title, keywords, etc.; a book by its title, chapter, references, etc; a concept by its origin, its use, its application, etc.) of knowledge has with respect to prior knowledge about the subject (whose address is known or accessible to the software knowledge-bank managers).

In conjunction with any NBES, knowledge bases need to be addressed by subject matter. Knowledge bases need maintenance and management by experts in the field (or local teachers). This concept has been well recognized in the telecommunications, credit-card, and car-rental industries and trained staffs maintain such databases. In context of INs, the service management system (Section 2.9.2.4) is an essential element to maintain, monitor, update, and optimize the service control point (SCP) [17]). And this SCP is itself a large network database: it has 800, 611, ABS, and so on related information in IN/1, and 900, 700, CLASS, etc., related information in the IN/1+, IN/2 networks. These networks are discussed in detail in References [7, 8].

3.5 ARCHITECTURE FOR ELECTRONIC GOVERNMENT

Generally, a cabinet or the democratic process formulates national policy and provides the general direction for a nation. The executive office (head of state) executes the policy as well as assuming full-time managerial and executive responsibilities. For this reason, the electronic government-IT (EG-IT) architecture for any developing nation should have the capacity to retain extensive information of all managerial functions such as planning, organizing, staffing, implementing and controlling most crucial and significant projects, as well commanding, controlling, and coordinating ongoing projects of national importance.

Typically, an electronic government (EG) needs to retain the most recent information for all sectors of the government and the history of that information. Funding and coordination of the other divisions of the government (such as defense, education, commerce, communication, or social welfare) occur at one physical location and a dedicated, secure, and centralized data warehouse is essential to track, update, justify, and explain the important changes in the government on a regular basis. These requirements also exist in most large corporations and multinational organizations. The difference is that of size, security, and importance of programs that national governments have to address, guarantee, and deliver. Some of these considerations are discussed in [12]

3.5.1 Control, Coordination, and Flow of Information

A centralized electronic government (EG) is unique in terms of funding, and coordination of various divisions of government (such as defense, education, commerce, communication, and social welfare) and of projects arising within the government (such as telemedicine, distance learning, and electronic commerce). The organization and structure of the information technology (IT) within the EG has to reflect this rather unique focus and concentration on management and administration (of itself) as well as the other branches of government. A conceptual overview is shown in Figure 3.10.

To accommodate the flow of information based on the nature of functions particular to the executive office and the other ministries, an EG architecture is proposed in Figure 3.11. Whereas the departments, ministries, and the project office may have a unified blueprint for local ITs, the IT of the centralized executive office (head of state) needs special consideration. It is strongly suggested that the network and IT engineers designing the EG of any country incorporate the different functions of the executive office in the initial design of the IT and the networks that support these (coordination, control and command with embedded intelligence symbolized as C^3I) functions. The network is equipped to interface well with the other departments or ministries. If the trend is to use generic programmable network components, then the network and netware that control the operations of these components (to facilitate the EG functions for the executive office) should be endowed with enough intelligence to perform the IT-EG functions in conjunction with the functions of the other ministries. To some extent, this is not trivial, unless the network designers have facilitated these functions as being programmable or already have assigned paths and addresses unique to the offices and databases within the ministries.

This architecture is neither optimized nor customized to any particular country. Only a blueprint of one of many configurations is documented here. Several rounds of optimization of architecture, components, links and server (databases) characteristics are essential before embarking on the direct application of this architecture. The customization of the network to a particular nation is as essential as the funding of the project itself! All the necessary aspects of the detailed planning must be undertaken in the most conscientious way.

Divisions, agencies, or departments of the government handle projects arising within the government (such as telemedicine, distance learning, or electronic commerce). The organization and structure of the IT for the various departments start to differ from those of the centralized government of the executive office (president, prime minister, etc.). The architecture and configuration for the EG for the executive office reflect this rather unique focus and concentration on management and administration.

Figure 3.11 depicts the hierarchy of a typical government structure before the introduction of an EG platform. The EG platform enhances the connectivity between the central command (Prime Minister, in this case) and the various ministries and reduces the workforce over time. The transition to an EG platform is time consuming and the government remains functional during the transition. Entirely self-sufficient electronic government systems have not been successfully implemented in any country.

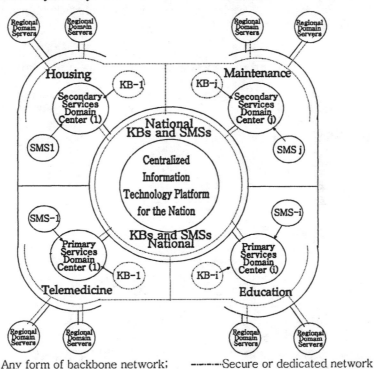

—— Any form of backbone network;   ——·——Secure or dedicated network

SMS – service management system & adminstration of the policy
KB – knowledge bases with SOP's. Any number of primary and/or
secondary domain centers may be added to accommodate the nature
and extent of services provided by the Federal government. Addressing
these domain centers with a logical and physical address permits the agencies
to be contantly updated, monitored and directed by the centralized IT platform.

Figure 3.10 A conceptual overview of an electronic government platform. SMS- service management system and administration of policy; KBs- knowledge bases with standard operating procedures. Any number of secondary domain services may be provided by the centralized government. Addressing these domains centers with logical and physical addresses permits the agencies to be constantly updated, monitored, and directed by the centralized IT platform.

In most cases, the role of EG platforms is essentially that of a communication provider and provider of routine transactions processing, where there are very few policy decisions. In the support facilities for the government, decision support systems help human beings to get better insight into intelligent and informed decision-making. When the role of decision-making becomes sensitive and crucial, Wisdom Machines (Chapter 10) become more desirable with EG platforms providing the intelligent control coordination, and communication within the government. Figure 3.12 depicts the transition of the hierarchy of a typical EG to that of a typical service-based EG.

3.5.2 Configuration of an EG Platform for a Small Nation

In the organization of EG platforms, it becomes desirable to allocate a numbering system to the many branches of the government. Numbering allocation facilitates the allocation of storage, networks, and processes to the documents, interactions and activities in the computer systems that house the IT for the EG.

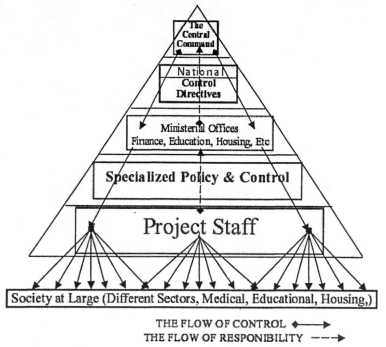

The Traditional Work Environment

Figure 3.11 Hierarchy of a typical government structure before the introduction of an EG platform.

The Migration to an Electronic Government (EG)

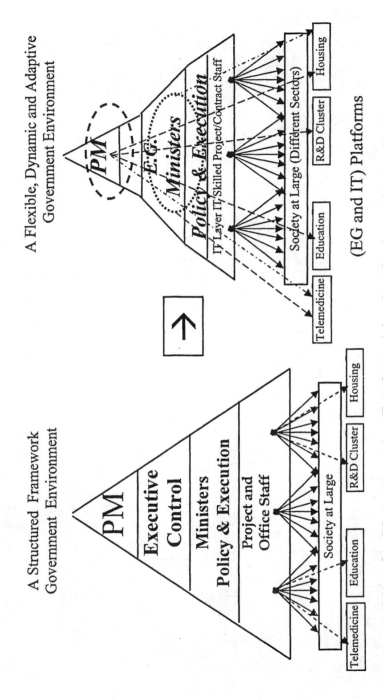

A Structured Framework
Government Environment

A Flexible, Dynamic and Adaptive
Government Environment

(EG and IT) Platforms

Figure 3.12 Use of an EG structure and an IT platform to bring about the changes in a small nation.

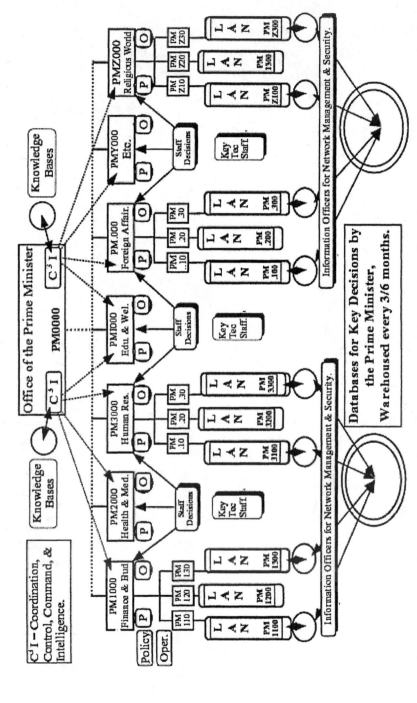

Figure 3.13 An IT platform at the Prime Minister's Office to support the C³I approach.

When document tracking of references to prior or similar tasks becomes necessary, machines can perform most of the routine or AI-based intelligent functions. Design of an electronic government information system (EGIS), can be made akin to a typical large-scale management information System (MIS) or executive information system (EIS) such that a scaled version of current software systems can be used as modular building blocks of the EGIS.

Examples of such numbering systems are the Dewey Decimal System and Library of Congress classification system. These systems draw a boundary (even though a vague boundary) between the branches of knowledge. A similar numbering system that broadly identifies the particular branch of government would facilitate classification of all activities within that branch. Funding, activities, and projects could be tracked and controlled much like the tracking systems in typical human resource applications such a PeopleSoft or SAP.

In the section a simplified number tracking system is suggested. The alpha-numbers are two alphabet, four-digit entity where the first two letters denoting the particular office such as PM, for Prime Minister's Office, EW for Education and Welfare office, HR for Human Resources office, etc. The next four digits signify the organizational segment such as 0000 for the Office of the Prime Minister, 1000 for the Office of Finance and Budget, or 2000 for the Office of Health and Welfare, etc. The tree structure continues. The numbering system is quite flexible and can be adjusted as the structure of the government changes.

In the design of EGs, the location of the center for coordination, control, and command needs precise identification. In the particular example in this book, the logical concentration of power is the Office of the Prime Minister. The physical location can be moved at a later date over wide area broadband networks. If the databases and servers are not physically moved, then the access time for critical information gets enhanced by the transit time between the old and new locations. The logical identification of the center of power serves to strategically place the routers and high-capacity links. Architecture for an IT platform for the Prime Minister's Office to support the C^3I (coordination, control, command and intelligence) approach is shown in Figure 3.12. The communication aspect gets built in the hierarchy of the Prime Minister's own office network in conjunction with the horizontal layout of the local area networks for the various ministries.

Data warehousing becomes necessary to maintain continuity in the operation of the government over an extended period. The long-term economic and growth trends of a small nation can be planned, organized, staffed, implemented, and also monitored and controlled in the EG framework for the country. The three facets of intelligent co-ordination, control, and command starts from the Office of the Prime Minister and the feedback comes from the offices of the Ministries, and from the 13 (key) major indicators measuring the economic activity within the country.

An IT platform for the Education and Welfare (EW) Office for within the country is shown in Figure 3.14. The blueprint can be customized to suit any office reporting to the Office of the Prime Minister. The numbering system provides for organization and document tracking and continuity among the functions in the different branches of any government.

The special PM-EW network EW1000 facilitates linkage with the centralized command facility. This segment can be designed to be physically or logically independent of other networks. Security and network connectivity under fault conditions become important considerations designing this network. The EG computer and network configuration becomes fundamental in monitoring the policy, goals, and projects-completion in any branch of the government.

The execution of the policies set forth by the leader(s) and the roles of the minister(s) and the staff are scanned and documented accurately by the filing system built into the EG infrastructure. Typically, the traditional concepts of planning, organization, staffing, implementation, and control can be achieved efficiently and optimally in any country.

Configuration of the routers and links is shown in Figure 3.15. When the numerous levels of the ministerial offices are dispersed throughout the country, the dependability of the backbone network becomes an issue. Secure and trustworthy connections via independent or leased public domain channels sometimes provide the intraoffice capability.

3.6 BILLING SYSTEMS

Billing systems use databases and their management systems extensively. Geographical separation between the access points and the central database involves network connections. Robust databases, database management systems and network operations become essential. For actively used services such as the telephone company call monitoring and billing, credit card transactions, and hospital-based medical networks, the response time, scalability, and interoperability become the key issues in design, updating and maintenance. The architecture and configuration of the billing network and software generally evolve as the network of any telephone company (Telco) grows. For this reason, there is no specific standard for the billing system configuration.

In this section, key elements of a typical billing system of a small Telco are presented to indicate the nature and complexity of coordinating the numerous databases that make up the billing system. The core nucleus of the billing system is a flexible, fast, and accurate cost engine. The centralized cost engine is constantly fed from numerous databases from many switching centers within the Telco. These centers provide the billing information as a raw data stream for each call. Typically, the call data records (CDRs) are tracked for a few hundred or for many hundred thousand calls per second depending on the number of customers and the busy hour call intensity.

Intermediate databases are consolidated from the unprocessed CDRs and then fed into the cost engine. The cost engine picks the appropriate tariff for each call. Typically, the cost engine for the assigned tariff for every call handled picks up numerous tariff structures. However, new features such as calling cards, convergence billing, prepaid, and special services, all place additional burdens on the entire billing system to compute the total bill for each call for each customer.

For the prepaid and calling card services, the central cost engine accesses the databases and the network and computes the total bill very quickly to prevent any account overruns.

When the same Telco provides numerous services (such as multiple land lines and mobile numbers, long distance, and 900 services), then all the charges need to be reported in one composite bill to the customer. This calls for convergence of multiple bills onto one account. Data and packet communication options and rate differentials also add to the complexity of the convergence process within the billing system.

3.6.1 Interoperability of Databases and Data Formats

Most switches generate the CDRs specific to any call in nonstandard data formats and accumulate them in the switch-specific database. However, many switches may handle the CDRs for the same call as the customer travels from one cell to the next or from country to the next. This situation becomes complicated when cell phone billing and CDR format resolution need intermediate processing, thus demanding additional time to post the most recent bill to any given account. In addition, as newer switches are deployed, the CDR format of the legacy switch can be (and is generally) different for the CDR format of the newer switches (even though they are from the same vendor). The CDR processing is customized and company specific. The CDR data is generally too large for any medium-sized storage facility and a specially tailored DBMS becomes necessary. Special demands are thus placed on the billing system backbone network and the computer systems that handle the processing and DBMS of the CDRs.

3.6.2 Service Options

Flexibility of providing Telco services to enhance revenues was dominant during the late 1990s. However, the billing systems databases had to provide a special tariff for such bundled services. These services differed from customer to customer and trained staff entered these service option preferences via the graphical user interface (GUI) terminals into the databases.

3.6.3 Other Market Demands and Their Influence on Telco Databases

The market forces on the telecommunications industry during the 1990s were phenomenal. In an effort to maintain profitability in excessive competition, the Telco marketing teams offered numerous services at different traffic structures.

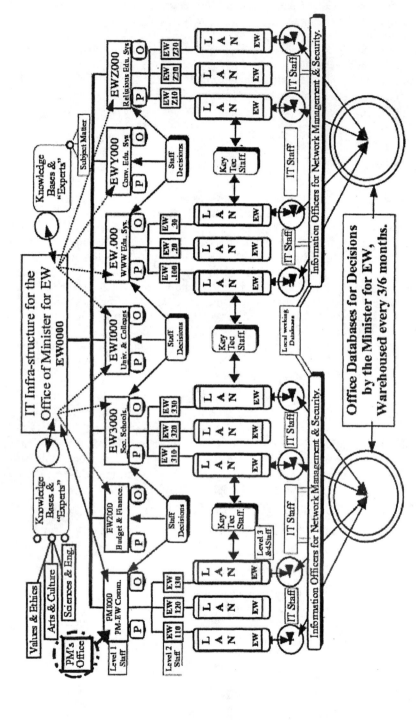

Figure 3.14 An IT platform at the Office of the Minister of Education and Welfare (EW).

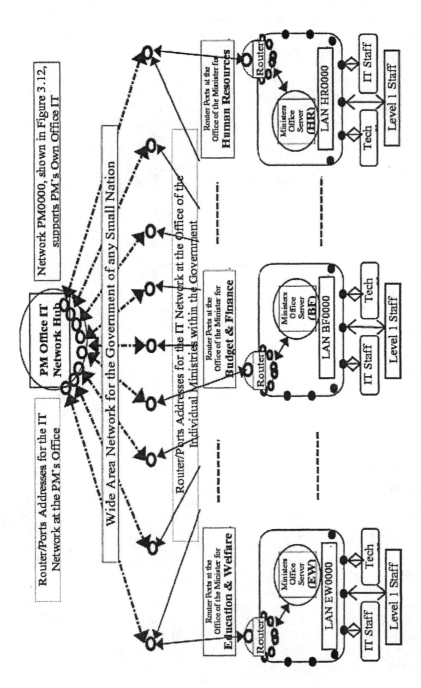

Figure 3.15 Proposed backbone network layout for the EG of a small nation.

Typical of these services being offered in the landline and mobile telephony are voice and data services over existing connection oriented services. Voice over IP depends on the connectionless and high grade ATM/packet networks.

The demands arising from these newer telecommunication services on database design, scalability, and maintenance are intense. For this reason, the problems are addressed individually and solved on a local basis. Numerous separate databases are sometimes designed for specialized services and customer relations. Typical of the newer services are (1) special feature services/downloads: (ring tones, medical alerts, market alerts, emergency alerts, wake-up-calls, (advanced intelligent network functions see [18]), (2) fraud management systems and automatic call blocking, (c) data explosion and the new IP services, (2) customer care and counseling and (5) text messaging and short messaging service (SMS).

3.7 KNOWLEDGE BASES

Knowledge bases (KBs) are relatively new but becoming [13, 14, 16] increasingly popular. Being relatively few, still evolving, and proprietary, the algorithms and techniques for knowledge base management systems (KBMSs) have not become as popular as the DBMSs. The KBs provide logical and textual linkages between the objects stored in databases or objectbases, in addition to storing basic information about the database or object entities. Objects and their attributes are structured in fixed or flexible formats. Both information and the structural relationships between the pieces of information or the attributes of objects are retained for consistency and interoperability. Tight and compact structure provides efficient KB functions such as searches, comparisons, and evaluation of objects/attributes stored. If the run-length of entities such as objects, attributes, or linkages get fixed, then KB functions become highly programmable.

In many instances, any subject matter is assigned a unique identifier number. This methodology is common in the Library of Congress (LoC) classification and the Dewy Decimal System (DDS) used in most standard libraries. The electronic libraries deploy the KB methodology with almost unlimited depth of search algorithms. Close identifier numbers indicate subject/logical linkage and can imply physical proximity of storage space in the massive storage facilities.

Most Internet KBs are highly organized for quick and efficient searches. For instance, IP network addressing is a hierarchy of the physical location of servers and the computer nodes accessible on the Internet. This standard makes WWW addressing, switching, and access very straightforward and quick.

The store and retrieve functions are streamlined. In some cases, vendors of computer hardware and software assign LoC or DDS type numbers to their components and modules. It is more efficient however, to simplify the numbering system to the limited product range of the vendors. This type of simplification can lead to five- or six-digit identifier numbers for information pertaining to the products of a midsized computer vendor.

From a methodological perspective, the encoding of the location of information can be binary. For example, any leaf of binary tree that is eight levels deep has a one-byte address. Such a binary search can lead to a track-sector address or an IP address where the information is stored, leading to the concept of indirect addressing of location of the information. Once the information is recovered, any extent of secondary processing/searching (conditional searching, comparison searching, inclusive/exclusive searching, etc.) can be accomplished. The principle of indirect addressing via the base sector of a computer memory was prevalent even in the IBM 360/370 computers during the 1960s and 1970s. Current DBMSs and KBMSs use a synergy of hardware designs and software algorithms to achieve remarkable speed in the functionality of data and information from DBs and KBs.

Software encoded KB operations are relatively straightforward and programmable. Such operations can be performed on most standard computers. In special cases where the size of data or information is massive and access time is critical (such as providing intelligent network functions to Telco customers), specialized system designs exist. For example, the design of the service control point (SCP, see Section 2.9.2.2) calls for massive parallel processing at the front-end processors to decode the X.25 packets that arrive from the signaling network [8, 17].

Hardware (such as a knowledge processor unit- KPU) to accomplish generic knowledge machine instructions to process knowledge (such as machine instruction with a knowledge operation code (*kopcode*) and objects as knowledge operands) does not currently exist. However, one such architecture of the KPU is presented in Chapter 8.

Peripherals, networks, databases (specifically those used in SAP environments [13]) and knowledge bases (specifically those used in the PeopleSoft environments [14]) are expanding at an alarming rate in the current information-based society. The dramatic fall in the price of IC chips and customized chip sets coupled with the cost of communicating very high-speed data locally and globally has permitted society to enjoy an enhancement in quality of life and literacy. However, the truest contribution of the knowledge worker appears to be in solving the issues of wisdom and values at a global level rather than rehashing the invention issues at a local level.

REFERENCES

[1] S. V. Ahamed, The Architecture of a Wisdom Machine, *Int. J. Smart Eng. Syst. Des.* 5, (4): 537–549, 2003.

[2] S. V. Ahamed, Knowledge processing system employing confidence levels US Patent 5,809,493, 1998, See also, Personal computer-based intelligent networks, US Patent 5,715,371, 1998, Assignee Lucent Technologies, Holmdel, NJ..

[3] S. V. Ahamed, Architectural Considerations for Brave New Machines, Paper presented at ANNIE, Paper MP1.1B, *Proc. Art. Nur. Net. Eng. Conf.*, 71–80, 2005, See also, *Journal of Business and Information Technology (JBIT)*, 2006.

[4] AT&T, Telecommunication Transmission Engineering, Volume II, Facilities, Chap. 12, pp. 317–350, 1985.

[5] S. V. Ahamed, and V. B. Lawrence, *Design and Engineering of Intelligent Communication Systems,* Kluwer Academic Publishers, Boston, 1997.

[6] J. P. Hayes, *Computer Architecture and Organization,* 2 ed., McGraw Hill, New York, 1988. See also, H. S. Stone et al., *Introduction to Computer Architecture,* Computer Science Series, Science Research Associates, New York, 1980.

[7] W. D. Ambrose, A. Maher, and B. Sasscer, *The Intelligent Network,* Springer Verlag, New York, 1989.

[8] S. V. Ahamed and V. B. Lawrence, *Intelligent Broadband Multimedia Networks,* Kluwer Academic Publishers, Boston, 1997.

[9] S. V. Ahamed, et al., Hospital-based integrated medical computer systems for processing medical and patient information using specialized functional modules U.S. Patent 6,272,481 B1 issued on August 7, 2001, Patent Application Number 09/152,809 filed by Lucent Technologies, Holmdel, NJ. 2001, foreign countries, Great Britain, Germany, France, and Japan.

[10] M. Krol, *Intelligent Medical Network,* Ph.D. Dissertation, City University of New York, 1996. See also T. S. Kazmi, *Simulation and Design Studies of Knowledge Processing Networks,* Ph.D. Dissertation at the Graduate Center of the City University of New York, 2002 and L. Leung, *Design and Simulation of International Intelligent Medical Networks,* Dissertation defended Feb. 2005.

[11] CCITT Recommendation M.3010, Principles for Telecommunication Management Network (TMN) TINA Architecture; Rec. M.3200. TMN Management Service; M.3400. TMN Management Functions; Rec. M.3020. TMN Interface Specification Methodology; Rec. M.3180 Catalogue Network Information Model; Rec. M.3300. TMN Management Capabilities.

[12] S. V. Ahamed and V. B. Lawrence, Evolving network architectures for medicine, education and government usage, Pacific Telecommunications Council, Hilton Hawaiian Village, Jan. 14–18, 2002.

[13] *SAP Solutions, and eLearning,* SAP (UK) Limited, Feltham, Middlesex, England, 2002.

[14] R. Rowley, PeopleSoft v.8: A Look under the Hood of a Major Software Upgrade, White Paper, PeopleSoft Knowledge Base, 2005.

[15] B. F Barry, A primer on telecommunication in distance learning, Pacific Telecommunications Conference, 1992.

[16] V. Ramakumar, *eLearner, Solver, Platform and Technology,* Cloverworxs Inc., Austin, TX., <http:// www.cloverworxs.com> URL accessed July 2003. See also M. Krol, and D. L. Reich, Development of a Decision Support System to assist anesthesiologists in operating room, *J. of Med. Sys.,* **24,** 141–146, 2000.

[17] J. O. Boese, and R. B. Robrock, Service control point, the brains behind the intelligent networks, *Bellcore Exchange,* Dec. 1987.

[18] E. G. Sable, and H. W. Kettler, Intelligent network directions, *AT&T Tech. J.,* **Summer,** 2–9, 1991.

PART *II*

Stability of Environments

Machines and gadgets are built to complement human effort. To automate machine-generated response, human ingenuity is directed toward making machines sensitive to changes in the environment. Human beings would be aware of the situation before they would take any action. Rudimentary machine response is an emulation of human reaction such as fight/flee or sense danger/destroy enemy in a conflict situation. Machines respond to direct commands and collect and scan inputs more accurately than human beings could attempt to do in hostile situations. Presently, robots explore and map deep-sea floors and explore planetary surfaces. More recently, war machines and drone planes survey battlefields and enemy strongholds without endangering military personnel.

On the positive side, sensing systems can be built to monitor patient conditions in intensive care units or to monitor, regulate and stabilize production lines in robotic assembly lines. In this vein, we present four chapters (4 through 7) in Part II. Chapter 4 addresses the issues of sensing of large systems, such as multinational corporations, national governments, world banks, and global universities. When the parameters that are measured and sensed are within a defined range, the scan-for-sense cycle continues indefinitely and the (production) process function continues, with the system operating in a healthy and secure fashion. Such ranges are based on design considerations and optimality. All system management parameters are logged on a routine basis. When instability is sensed, the scan rate is adjusted to track the location and reason for the deviation from the normal values of the parameters. The rate of change, and the velocity of change are monitored much like the monitoring of the seismic readings when tremors of the earth are detected. The AI and network techniques are fused together to make the system response quick and accurate, based on the dynamic condition(s) around and within the network.

Chapter 5 deals with sharing knowledge over networks with embedded and programmable intelligence. This concept is particularly useful for global universities and distance learning. In both instances programmability is of paramount importance. When the knowledge bases are updated and monitored for the customer usage, the network management tools and techniques taken from intelligent networks become particularly useful. Both the SCP and the SMS aspects of IN/2 (see Chapter 2) become applicable to monitor, analyze, and stabilize the environment

Chapter 6 extends the sensing of large systems to the control of such systems. In a closed loop feedback system, corrective measures are invoked to return the system back to its normal operating ranges, much like the medicines prescribed for patients in a hospital environment. The extent of artificial intelligence and the mechanisms for control are adjusted to suit the applications and the technology. The entire system acts as an intelligent sensing and control environment. Numerous examples ranging from the control of a simple inventory control item to the economic control of a nation are presented.

Chapter 7 deals with the audio-visual sensory inputs to the human beings who become involved with the control of large systems. This chapter does not cover all the senses and perceptions that play a part in human comprehension and feedback: only the filtering aspects of audio-visual signals are briefly considered in this chapter. However, the human sensory (primarily eyes and ears) organs present a challenge for incorporation into computerized sensory systems. The collation, classification, compilation, collaboration, and confirmation of the all the sensory data from all human and machine-based sensors would also be a challenge to automated control system designers to build and implement.

Chapter *4*

Sensing and Monitoring Networks

In this chapter, we present generic methodologies for networks to sense and monitor environments in which they exist. They are generic to the extent that they can be deployed for any application in which the underlying processes need to be controlled for correctness and/or optimality. Scanning devices routinely sense the parameters that influence the correctness and/or optimality of results. Lexical analyzers [1], in turn, identify the objects whose parameters are being scanned. Pattern recognition (PR) programs [2] recognize the entire scenario from which the objects are drawn. Then the objects and processes are analyzed by a multiplicity of techniques encoded as object-oriented programs [3] to evaluate the optimality of the objects— blending and binding the objects, the particular recognized scenario, and the underlying processes that are occurring within that scenario. Embedded models are invoked to check and monitor the overall efficacy of pursuing the objective functions. Adjustments and corrections are introduced through the network to ascertain the global optimality in realizing the objective function. Learning the behavior of objects and their response to object-oriented programs and the successful negotiation with the objects gives rise to the novel concept of *predictive programming*.

The approach is general enough to be used for any application that has a scientific and numerical rationale. We also disclose a methodology that unifies the

Intelligent Internet Knowledge Networks. By Syed V. Ahamed
Copyright © 2007 John Wiley & Sons, Inc.

aforementioned AI techniques within the intelligent network (IN) [4] framework. Every microstep can be programmed in the network for every application by using the programmability of the telephone switching systems. A new dimension of control and usage for the network results when the switching systems have an attached adjunct processor (typically present in INs). The deployment of the new sensing network becomes akin to the deployment of the intelligent networks. New applications can thus be invoked very quickly, efficiently, and optimally.

We also propose that the generic and the highly evolved architecture of a typical switching systems (for example) be deployed with one additional "knowledge module" for intelligent object processing. Such intelligent objects (scanned and sensed by the global sense networks) are the main players driving our society and are composed of numerous socio-economic [5] variables such as the GNP, consumption, taxation, gross economic activity, the velocity of money, the interest rate, the employment level, and the educational level. These variables are documented in the econometric models of national economies.

Large-scale systems can often become unstable and can function erratically. Such systems respond to discrete changes in their environment. The error function generally restores the functionality by compensating for the change in the environment. In many instances, it becomes impossible to regain control and restore stability if the system performance starts to substantially deviate from its normal range. System performance can become oscillatory and this can damage the components that constitute the system. For simple systems, the conditions for stability can be written down as equations, and while for larger and more complex systems numerical controls of many parameters are generally necessary. Such mechanisms control at least an element of that environment where the system is static.

The control mechanisms may obtain the latest data that is destabilizing the system and utilize programs that are either dynamic or fixed in response to the current data and other environmental conditions. In essence, all the responses of such systems are, preprogrammed as a function of the particular data available up to any instant in time. This requires the programmer to have complete insight into the nature of the problem so that any introduced control mechanism will cause the program to respond properly given in any given situation presented by the data. Furthermore, the effects of a previous change had produced the current environment, are not known the programmer.

To circumvent this innate response from the stabilizing system, large-scale systems can be monitored by employing a knowledge machine that develops programs for at least two machines— the first machine being an information collection system that obtains the latest values of variables, which may be objects, and a second machine that employs the variables in the execution of the program developed for it by the knowledge machine to determine the current state of (input variables from) the large-scale system. In response to the monitoring, an action may be taken. The environment as it would have existed without the program that controls the second machine (which may have taken one or more previous actions) may be known, and this information is used to take further action now or in the future (e.g., in response to the current environment or a similar environment that may exist in the future). Thus, the system is self-learning and self-adjusting, allowing it to optimize the stabilization in an adaptive manner.

4.1 BASIC CONCEPTS FOR SENSING

Concepts from *four* major disciplines are gathered and then reconstituted to implement the network-based sensing system: (1) artificial intelligence [6] for scanning, parsing of the "objects," scenario identification, and selecting the rules of production to optimize the objective function; (2) advanced intelligent networking [7] for gathering all the unique and specialized input information and the specific control information for any particular application at hand; (3) data and model management from decision support systems [8] to manage the data, models, and attributes of the input objects and also the control data for managing the objects and/processes that yield the objective function that needs the optimization; and finally (4) architectural arrangements within typical switching systems that facilitate global network communication.

In a sense the functioning of the network is like the management of a corporate entity. All the essential managerial tasks are embedded in the network functions. However, the capacity to micromanage every aspect of the local operations of a very large number of customers, based on their own individual preferences would not be humanly possible. For this reason, we augment the decision support systems (DSSs see [8, 9]) with clusters of knowledge processing systems (KPSs, see Chapter 8) with the typical switch architectures. The KPS deals with "objects" influencing the objective function. The switching system architectures manage the communication to and from very large numbers of customers and the sensors that "read" the status of specific objects and their attributes.

The network is based on the notion that most work environments and homes are internally networked to monitor the environment. Both the transmit and receive functions of communication are necessary in this network. The sensors provide the periodic input information by sensing the objects. The receptors receive the control information to modify or enhance the objects and/or their attributes. These sensors may be of any type. They could sense the heartbeat of a patient, or sense the activities of the stock market. Typically, they retain the most current reading at the gateway of the LAN on which they reside. This reading is then transmitted to the applications program that brings about a new network-based computer system activity. This, in turn, scans, detects all the objects within the current scenario, analyzes their nature and attributes giving rise to the scenario, evaluates the "health and stability" of the situation, and takes an appropriate action based on the goals prescribed for the application at hand.

The concept of network-based input parameter sensing is generic. It can be deployed in the financial/economic sphere at first and then developed in any format. We envision that the methodology can be deployed at *four* levels (1) the global level, (2) the national level, (3) the corporate/institutional level, and even at *(d)* the personal level. .

4.2 USERS, INTELLIGENCE AND DATABASES

In Figure 4.1, we present a conceptual overview to unify *three* basic functions: (1) the user/external communication functions, (2) the knowledge and (artificial) intelligence functions, and (3) the database and data management functions. Accordingly, these functions are accomplished in *three* Clusters named the *(a)* NCOM (for network Communications) Cluster, *(b)* the KP (for knowledge Processing) Cluster and *(c)* the DM (for Data Management) cluster.

4.2.1 Network Segment Dealing With User Dialogue

The user communication functions permit the proposed network system access to communicate with the customers, with the network management staff, with billing systems personnel, and with the society (at large) in which the network services are being provided. As an interface, it would need to receive inputs from various users in their specific language and it would need to provide information in a format specific to the user. Hence a variety of compilers would be necessary to process the input queries and/or commands, and also a set of output routines to format the information specific to the particular user. Essentially, this segment of the network has *two* basic building components: (1) the language dependent part of the compiler that does the parsing, the lexical analysis, and the syntactic and semantic analysis of the objects to be addressed in the transaction and (2) the machine-dependent assemblers, the code generator, and the loaders and linkers that also reside in this segment of the front-end processors (FEPs), and the software driving these FEPs as shown in Figure 4.1.

The loaders, linkers, and so on that perform the address resolution of the embedded objects and their attributes become machine dependent and are considered as routine SW issues that are resolved at execution time by the compilers and operating systems.

4.2.2 Network Segment Dealing with Knowledge and Intelligence

knowledge and intelligence are necessary to deal with the sensor inputs that continuously scan the environment and also to deal with the user queries and dialog. It is necessary to treat this module (see Figure 4.1) independently for two basic reasons: (1) to verify if the sensor input is routine or needs special low-level decision (via the execution of a "knowledge program" module residing in this network segment) from the network to invoke appropriate action in the

Computer and Network Functionality

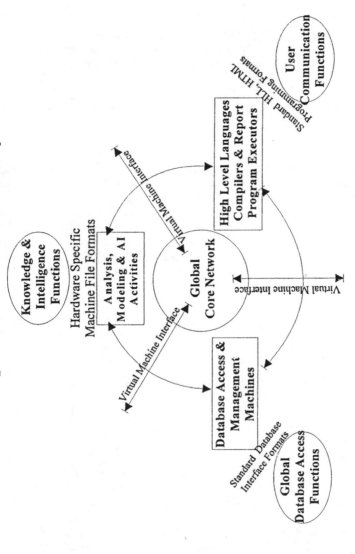

Figure 4.1 The interdependence between the three functional clusters of the sensing network.

environment, and (2) to learn and adapt to the environment such that the next decision is consistent with the new inputs or the behavioral modus operandi of the user whom the network is currently serving.

Because there could be a large number of subscribers active at any given instant of time, a massively parallel-processed knowledge handling environment (see Chapter 11) is suggested. An AI programming environment that can be effectively implemented is a specially designed SW layer that handles C++ type programs to make the object orient programs feasible, inexpensive and realistic.

4.2.3 Network Segment Dealing with Databases and Data Management

Vast amounts of data are accessed, acquired, processed, and communicated during normal operations of the sensing network. A certain chain of programs may be compiled, assembled and executed based on the raw data "sensed" in the network. Hence it becomes necessary to separate the types of data as transient or semi-permanent. Such data is routinely classified in computer environments as "user programs and jobs" and as operating systems programs, compilers, generic I/O SW, utilities, libraries, and math routines. In the same context, the network database information has *two* basic flavors: (1) temporary information dealing with short time data/instructions and response of the network, including the billing information for each users, and (2) more generic information dealing with the mode of operation of the network elements, its HW and SW modules that govern the network performance.

Typically, the former type of data is subscriber specific and the latter type of data dealing with the network policies is network specific. The blending of the two functions is done during the execution of the object-oriented programs in the knowledge module discussed in Section 4.2.2 and is driven by the input data sensed by the "sensors" or the active dialog initiated by the user via the Dialog processors discussed in Section 4.2.1.

4.3 DETAILS OF FLOW OF INFORMATION

In Figure 4.2, we present one level of detail— the role of communication among the *three* basic processes: (1) user communication process, (2) knowledge and object process and (3) process for dealing with data/activities via their own gateways. Basic intelligent modules that govern each transaction through the network facilitate the flow of information. These modules are different from the programs residing in the knowledge machine cluster. Whereas the basic intelligence modules invoke and generate the service module programs to be executed in the three clusters (see Sections 4.2.1, 4.2.2, and 4.2.3) of the network, the knowledge machine cluster only executes the knowledge functions germane to that particular transaction.

Conceptual Architecture of Global Sensing and Control Systems

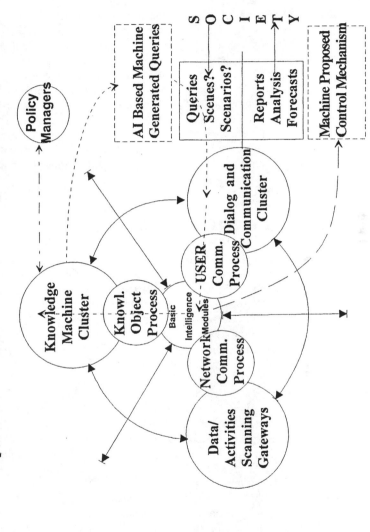

Figure 4.2 The complimentary relationship between human beings and the overall machine.

In a sense, the strategy for the solution and the programs for implementation for the solution to each scenario scanned by the sensors is evolved by the basic intelligence module, while the execution takes place in the three network clusters discussed in Sections 4.2.1, 4.2.2, and 4.2.3.

If there is need for human intervention, the interaction of the mangers is possible with these clusters by setting up a service management system (SMS) type of facility generally provided in basic INs. By and large, the network performs on its own in response to the sensor inputs. Programs are activated and executed to perform network and all related services. Such sensors may scan the social environment and use its AI tools (such as scenario analysis, object and attribute analysis, processing of intelligent objects, pattern recognition, self-leaning, computer-based predictive programming). It also reaches a stable operating condition by learning the individual subscriber responses and preferences. In its own learning mode, the machine also profiles the subscriber, much as a teacher would profile a student or a parent would profile a child, and tries to bring about an (artificially) intelligent, coherent, and expeditious resolution of the situation at hand, if the situation should demand such a recourse.

4.4 DEPLOYMENT OF SWITCH ARCHITECTURE

Switching architectures are completely evolved and the modules function well for both small subscriber groups (a few thousand) and large subscriber groups (a few million). In Figure 4.3, three midsized switches are connected through one centralized switch to facilitate *intra*-cluster communications. In the same way the three remaining switches facilitate *inter*-cluster communication.

It is not essential to use the circuit-switched network type of switch for the sensing network architecture. In general, any switch[1] (circuit switched, packet switched, frame relay or cell relay) will serve the functionality of any typical sensing network.

Selected switching modules (SMs) of the adjoining switches are connected to provide intercluster communications. The remaining SMs of peripheral switches connect to the outside world to perform user communications, knowledge base updating, and access to the user and network data. The architecture (with its administrative module, its communication module and its many switching modules [10]) manages the internal workings of the complex transactions of the peripheral sensors, and also manages the communication of the three functional clusters (1, 2, 3), with the external world and the society. A dynamic equilibrium is thus established by the internal adaptation of the machine and by exercising a renegotiated amount of control within the society. In a sense, the dynamic adaptation of the machine renders its deployment in most robotic, corporate, and socioeconomic situations.

---

[1] Switching is an essential function in all communication systems. It was systematically introduced in Circuit Switched (Public Telephone) networks by AT&T for over six decades since 1940s.

For smaller applications, one switch may also be deployed. The numerous SMs of one generic switch may be partitioned into three groups of SMs— one for each of the three clusters. The communication module (CM) and the administrative module (AM) would need to be shared (this is quite easily accomplished in the UNIX OS environment of the switch). In such cases, the standard software of the switch needs customization.

4.5 ADJUNCT PROCESSING IN THE SWITCHES

Typically, the normal (CS, PS, frame relay or the cell relay) switches are not well suited to sensing objects in the environment, even though line scanners work continuously in the CS environments and the base stations continuously track every active cell phone in wireless environments. In sensing network environments, the sensing is necessarily for objects and their attributes. Such objects are chosen under program control (e.g., the amount of the nth inventory item) and used as a trigger condition. In the CS environment, the equivalent condition would be the "off-hook" status, at which time the scanning rate is substantially increased to collect the digits that are dialed.

To accommodate this variability in the types of objects and their attributes to be scanned in the environment, the complementary functions of the adjunct processor (AP) are invoked. These APs can be programmed for special services and special conditions much like the APs for IN/2 services in typical IN/2 and AIN [2]. The customization of the AP programs and the intelligent peripheral (IP) data takes place much like the initialization of the IN/2 services.

4.6 CONCLUSIONS

The features of this sensing network are listed as follows:

1. The decision support system can be ported in the network environment by arranging the functions of the three switching systems or switching modules of any switching system.
2. one can simulate all the functions of national economy, a corporation, a society, or any midsized social entity by distributing the "sensors" in the environment and then regulating the "climate" of the entity with distributed intelligence modules distributed throughout the network.
3. one can program the response to each sensed scenario as a quantitative measure of the attributes of a set of programmable objects.
4. one can separate the three basic components of any intelligent MIS (the dialog processor, the analytical/simulation module, and the data manager) into three interdependent machine clusters.

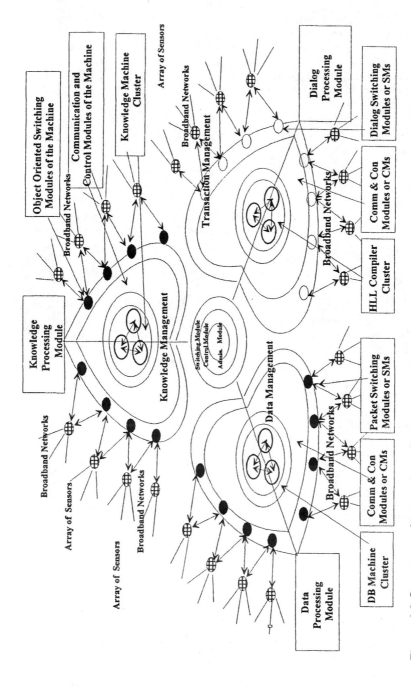

Figure 4.3 One stage of integration of the processing modules into the physical sensing network.

5. one can adapt a switching system to perform the functions of both a natural language processor and any switching system in cluster 1, to perform the functions of both a knowledge machine and a typical switching system in cluster 2, and perform the functions of both a database management system and a typical switching system in cluster 3.

REFERENCES

[1] A. V. Aho et al., *Compilers,* Addison Wesley, Boston, 1986.

[2] C. M. Bishop, and C. Bishop, *Neural Networks for Pattern Recognition,* Oxford University Press, Oxford, UK, 1996. See also *Images, Cyberspace: The World of Digital Architecture,* 2001.

[3] H. M. Deitel and P. J. Deitel, *C++ How to Program,* Prentice Hall, Englewood Cliffs, NJ, 2002. See also O. N. Garcia and Y. T. Chien, *Knowledge-Based Systems: Fundamentals and Tools,* IEEE Computer Society Press, Rockville, MD, 1991.

[4] CCITT Recommendation M.3010, *Principles for a Telecommunication Management network (TMN) TINA Architecture;* Rec. M.3200, *TMN Management Service;* Rec. M.3400, *TMN Management Functions;* Rec. M.3020, *TMN Interface Specification Methodology;* Rec. M.3180, *Catalogue Network Information Model;* Rec. M.3300, *TMN Management Capabilities.*

[5] M. Friedman, *Price Theory,* Walter de Gruyter, Hawthorne, 1976. See also *Columbia Encyclopedia,* Columbia University Press, New York 2002,. See also M. Michael, *Dilemmas in Economic Theory: The Persisting Foundational Problems of Microeconomics,* Oxford University Press, Oxford, UK, 1999.

[6] S. J. Russell and Peter Norvig, *Artificial Intelligence: Modern Approach,* Prentice Hall, Englewood Ciffs, NJ, 1995. See also D. A. Forsyth, J. Ponce, *Computer Vision: A Modern Approach,* Prentice Hall; 2002. Also see D. H. Ballard and C. M. Brown, *Computer Vision,* Prentice Hall, Englewood Ciffs, NJ, 1982; L. F. George, *Artificial Intelligence, Structures and Strategies for Complex Problem Solving,* Addison Wesley, Boston, 2005; R. O. Duda, P. E. Hart, and D. G. Stork, *Pattern Classification,* Wiley-Interscience; ISBN: 0471056693; 2nd edition, 2000.

[7] W. D. Ambrose, A. Maher, and B. Sasscer, *The Intelligent Network,* Springer Verlag, New York, 1989. See also, S. V. Ahamed and V. B. Lawrence, *Intelligent Broadband Multimedia Networks,* Kluwer Academic Publishers, Boston, 1997. For first reading see, S. V. Ahamed, Intelligent Networks, Chapter 9, in *Encyclopedia of Telecommunications,* Academic Press, New York, 1989, pp. 159–174

[8] N. S. Stuart, *Computer-Aided Decision Analysis,* Quorum Books, Westport, CT, 1993.

[9] E. Turban, J. E. Aronson, *Decision Support Systems and Intelligent Systems,* 6th ed., Prentice Hall, Englewood Ciffs, NJ, 2000.

[10] *Telecommunications Transmission Engineering,* Vols. 1–3, AT&T, Indianapolis, IN, 1985.

Chapter *5*

Intelligent Knowledge Sharing

General purpose computing facilitated the popularity of computer systems in the 1950s and 1960s. The introduction of inexpensive personal computers in the 1980s and nineties brought the revolution home. Since the early 1990s, the Internet has provided the access to information highways for the younger generation and brought about a profound revolution in modern society.

Sharing of files in the computer environment is as old as writing code. Computer code that is accurate and optimized serves on any generic computer system and can be shared as macros, routines, libraries and so on. The broadband networks and fiber pathways that encircle the globe have accelerated sharing of data, video, voice, and music. Internet has provided another degree of freedom by providing very inexpensive access to almost any web address.

The Internet is a consolidation of many earlier inventions. During the 1960s and 1970s, the federal government sponsored loosely related research topics as independent projects. These projects generated islands of knowledge that were founded on sound scientific concepts from universities and corporations. Later, these islands were bridged and made into a large body of knowledge by additional investigations lasting for two or three decades from the 1970s through 1990s.

The Internet has brought about the evolution of a highly literate young scientific community. Most of the significant contributions of the last century in the telecommunications arena have systematically culminated in the Internet architecture. The Internet is fueled by the economic motives of participants; the

Intelligent Internet Knowledge Networks. By Syed V. Ahamed
Copyright © 2007 John Wiley & Sons, Inc.

inventions came about because the Internet has sustained its own growth. Over the last decade, the pace has accelerated and the economic forces in a capitalistic society can only add to the Internet to go national, international, and then perhaps spatial.

5.1 INTERNET KNOWLEDGE SHARING

Internet is an adaptive, information-based, all-digital network capable of communicating raw data, digitized information, and video over the backbone communication infrastructure of any nation. *Intelligent* Internet is programmable and supplements human imagination and creativity by performing information and knowledge domain functions on the data over the Internet and its KBs. The Internet is oblivious to the format of the data communicated thus permitting the flow of voice, data, video, graphic or any other information from one logical location (IP address) on the network to another. Connectivity is universal due to worldwide acceptance of the Internet Protocol (IP) and addressing format. Software and program support provided by any Internet services provider (ISP) makes the Internet services powerful but inexpensive, available to World Wide Web (WWW) site accessible by the backbone communication networks. Backbone networks generally deploy just about any mode of communication available to offer the Internet services to any user. Internet services far excel any telephone- or computer-based network services. Internet is itself a computer-based information network reaching deep in every knowledge-based society.

Intelligent Internet deploys knowledge bases throughout the world, thus providing special and knowledge services in addition to regular Internet services. Content-based switching permits users to access pages of digital libraries or the subject-based frontiers of knowledge. Being artificially intelligent, new Internet services are almost limitless. With an appropriately matched with a user's natural intelligence, the intelligent Internet becomes a viable tool in running a household or a nation. Currently all the knowledge processing tools are not available from ISPs. However, the beginning of a new era of intelligent Internet is apparent at selected sites like Google and Oracle-PeopleSoft and in specially selected medical and hospital environments.

5.2 KBS FOR TECHNOLOGY TRANSFER

In this Chapter, we present two architectural arrangements based on the two configurations presented in Figures 3.6 and 3.7. The databases and the supporting computer systems are altered to suit the global technology transfer applications for education, commerce, and industry in developing countries. It is interesting to note that the architectures do not undergo any alteration. Instead, the data and knowledge bases are changed to build localized and wide area intelligent knowledge networks for the transfer of technology.

The technology and knowledge bases can be distributed throughout the world. These networks constantly monitor the specific needs of the information seekers and resources of the locality with the involvement of knowledge service providers (KSP). The KSPs would serve the knowledge and informational needs of their clients and subscribers. A large number of these KSPs would serve a community or a region. Each KSP(i) will retain a portfolio of each of the client/subscriber(j) and will perform a daily check on status change in the local or global information or service as it pertains to the knowledge profile of the particular client. It makes the client aware of any detail as it may affect the course of action. This approach will be particularly useful in manufacturing and production environment, where inventions are constantly made. If the client goes through the KSP, then the incremental change is updated in the client profile database. In addition, the system performs routine functions to accumulate an overall knowledge-based reservoir of the latest information for the transfer of technology. The local staff would perform the retrieval function but the system retains the vital information over the life of the client (company) for every routine activity and its optimal execution. The details of the databases and their distribution or their aggregation, are presented as two architectural networks.

Large groups of independent knowledge and local area networks are integrated (and programmed) to coexist independently within one larger, wide area knowledge network. These independent intelligent networks share the network infrastructure for transport and access the knowledge bases for technology transfer. In addition, the functionality is programmed to perform as a group of localized knowledge networks that seek out specific branches and specialties of knowledge for the particular field. This domain of these networks is local rather than the entire domain of one massive knowledge network for a region or a country. The role of the numerous KSPs will be confined to the local area services and information access rather than that of a few global KSPs. The main advantage of having a large number of smaller and localized KSPs is that the cost and complexity of a localized KSP is much lower than one large KSP. The competition of the localized KSP services thus available will reduce access and storage expenses and thus overall customer costs. Local KSPs and businesses can offer knowledge and information services such as dispensing of patents, special manufacturing procedures, consulting services, or on-line assistance. Such an increase in the supply side of critical knowledge information will facilitate technology transfer (TT) to become more competitive. Furthermore, it brings down the cost of dispensing critical knowledge and information in the long run.

5.3 CURENT KNOWLEDGE NETWORKS

Although smart Internet users can access some of these services, such services have not been tailored to professionals seeking relevant TT-based information. The specialized services that experts, consultants, and local professionals provide are still not available to most clients because of the prohibitive costs. Over the next decade or so, it is envisioned that specific knowledge/information may be supplied by knowledge bases rather than by consultants and their staff that have an embedded profit motive. In a sense, the initial information gathering and the search for appropriate low-level knowledge treatment are facilitated by KSPs, knowledge bases and intelligent knowledge processing that is tailored to the specific needs of the clients. The current approach is to place the client at the lowest level of service provisioning rather than placing the information seeker as a paying customer. In the current scenario, information seekers are obligated to accept knowledge services by the local staff and facilities of unknown quality of service (QoS) and an unclear billing system. In contrast, the architectures and systems proposed supply the specific information for an individual information seeker. It is, in fact, retrieved by smart knowledge processing, based on the client's specific profile and inclusive environmental conditions.

5.3.1 IN and KSP-Based Intelligent Internet

In the enhancement of the basic intelligent network (IN) architecture of the 1980s to suit the telecommunications intelligent network architecture (TINA) [1], network designers have brought interoperability within the framework of all the intelligent networks around the globe. Whereas it is commendable and desirable to have this ideology built in every network, there at least *two* penalties. First, the standards need a long time to evolve, the standard interfaces and software modules to perform the functional components (FCs) a service specific feature of the TINA, may not be readily available. Second, the backbone network should be ready to host and execute the network programming language for each FC for each knowledge subscribers.

A possible configuration of a fully integrated knowledge-based computer system for processing knowledge for information seekers using specialized FCs, is presented in [2]. However, set backs in the full implementation of such a network environment will cause a delay in bringing the intelligent knowledge-based Internet services to the clients.

Developing nations have specific needs and variable socioeconomic settings. It becomes essential for the KSPs to build a national profile of the developing nations around the globe and then build a client profile in context to the national setting of the client. The TT goals are customized to the donor nation and the specific policies restraining the transfer of sensitive information. For example, defense, weapons and nuclear technology is generally restricted by most donor nations. Detailed analysis of the knowledge content can become a part of the economic negotiation in TT. Over a period, only legitimate, ethical, and significant knowledge embedded in science and industry constitutes TT. The socioeconomic significance of knowledge transferred constitutes its value to the recipient nation. The wealth of knowledge (discussed in Chapter 12) needs some consideration by the KSPs, and donor and recipient nations. Appropriate look-up table (based on previous negotiations and TTs), makes TT quick, effective, and economically viable. Security of knowledge in the KBs is a matter of concern to the KSPs.

The control of the information delivered to the client is matched to profile of the client. Legitimate knowledge and information content is made local and immediate. This is a stark contrast to the service of other intelligent network service providers, such as the telephone network owners or the Internet search engines. These generic service providers offer universal services to *all* their customers regardless of their specific needs. From the architectures of the advanced intelligent networks (AIN) discussed in [3], the adjunct service provider (ASP) and the Intelligent Peripheral (IP) based switching systems provide similar capabilities for their clients.

However, the programs within the ASP and IP are mentored, monitored and maintained by the network owners. In the KSP-based Internet, it is proposed that the client's specific needs be programmed, and fine tuned on the local computers owned by the KSPs. These KSPs will in turn offer a blend critical knowledge functions (such as dispensing of patents, special manufacturing procedures, consulting services, on-line assistance, etc.) with approval from the community of knowledge professionals and locals authorities. To this extent, KSP-based network environment provides the clients and developing nations what any current technologies have to offer. These network and knowledge functions are blended harmoniously under the supervision of the KSP within the framework of the risk that the KSP is willing to take with the local community of clients and developing nations.

5.3.2 Proposed Technology Transfer Network

The proposed KSP-based architecture would permit nations of new technology to have an open information policy brought about by competition on the supply side. It would also facilitate numerous specialized KSPs to participate in the regional, national, or global knowledge economy. This step is akin to the distribution of localized knowledge information (from the supply perspective) from local knowledge data banks rather than sharing very large databanks via global or Internet access. In the ensuing knowledge society, these KSPs will be akin to local banks functioning in cooperation with the regional banks, national banks, and the national (Monetary) Reserve System. Many such KSPs can serve a large number of clients that do not need the very high speed or the high intricacy that the high-technology global Internet is capable of providing to *all* its users. Smaller databases, localized customers, and larger local area traffic will permit the smaller KSPs to customize and target their services to a specific clientele and the user community.

Under program control, the localized technology transfer knowledge networks (TTKNs) that interconnect the KSPs may also be forced to work interdependently, exchanging current information as it becomes available to perform a variety of functions hitherto possible only by human beings. The individual client and user databases are-based on the subscriber codes and identification numbers. These databases are assigned logical address within the host network. Each logical knowledge network function becomes a personal intelligent network (PIN) function developed in Reference [4]. It is dedicated to that particular client only for the duration of its use. These TTKNs provide all the technology transfer (for government, banking, medical, educational, distance learning, and commercial clients). These personal communication network (PCN) types of service [5] operate under a client-driven programmable code. The client has the privilege and freedom to "instruct" the host network to perform all the legitimate and ethically acceptable backbone knowledge *and* communication network functions. These functions may be as simple as the banking services (such as account balance, on-line payments, credit card activity, etc.) currently offered by local banks or as complex as the services that TINA is capable of performing— a set highly sophisticated hierarchical and cascaded intelligent telecommunications functions.

Figure 5.1 depicts one of the possible regional knowledge network architecture that permits the regulation, authentication and monitoring of the knowledge services by any authorized entity. The network management system KSMS monitors and tracks the activity to prevent abuse of the facilities and services in a region, a state, or a nation. Many other possible uses of such a network infrastructure (such as child care, nursing homecare, emergency care) are also possible.

5.3.3 Merits of KSP-Based Network

In designing Web-based programs, the range and extent of network services become apparent. To some extent, the HTML programs can duplicate the intelligent network functions of the circuit switched networks for the Internet. Whereas these services are mostly information-based, application-specific client services are usually stereotyped and minimal. Most of the application programs are-based in distant servers and are communicated via the Internet by packet switches. This can cause substantial delays between screens and during the downloading of programs and data. In addition, when the network programs are uploaded, they reside in a local or distant server and program execution occurs-based on the capabilities of the server. As the volume of data to be exchanged becomes large, the response time also starts to increase to the extent that any multimedia traffic becomes too distant in awaiting the broadband networks to be implemented. Typically, the bottleneck is in the local fixed line or the wireless loop. This can be eased by the integrated services digital network (ISDN) line or the ADSL capability now available in some metropolitan areas.

Using local high capacity servers and a local high-speed LAN alleviates the problem. For large-scale users, this methodology uses the TCP/IP, high speed LANs (typically campus networks, educational or knowledge networks, etc.), and very localized high capacity servers, to serve their customers. We propose this approach for the scores of countries that may not have their ISDN or the ADSL facilities in place for many years. When these services become available, they are connected to the high-speed LANs and the high capacity servers. When we consider the public domain, the local high speed LAN's, and the servers are owned by the local-fixed loop network owners (rather than Internet operators) and the revenues for such services revert back to the local telephone companies.

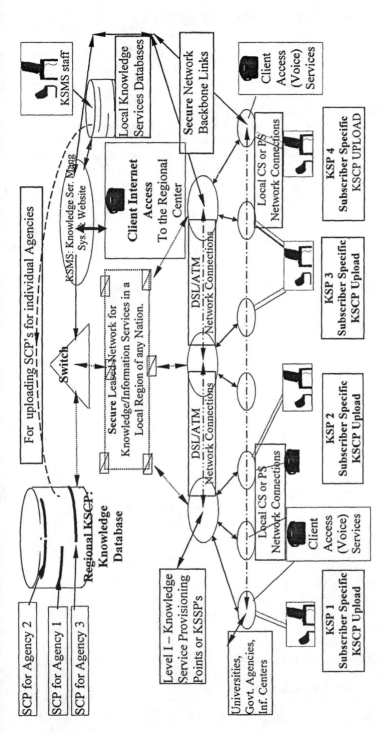

Figure 5.1 Representation of numerous knowledge networks being hosted in one larger knowledge WAN. Each micro knowledge net is uploaded by the individual KSP subscriber who can program the network to function as an IN/1, IN/1+, IN/2, or any version of the advanced version of an IN or the AIN. KSP subscribers may also interject their own customized programs to be executed during the operation to provide specialized services to suit the client's needs.

In the case of the KSP-based network, two types of architecture are feasible. Large knowledge insurance companies, service agencies, and backbone owners of the larger metropolitan area knowledge networks deploy a configuration like that shown in Figure 5.1. knowledge network owners will provide global knowledge database services to the local KSPs.

On the other hand, the responsibility and ownership of the services can be retained by the KSPs, and only the network services are obtained from leasing the secure signaling and communication services from the backbone service providers. With the profusion of bandwidth for communication, and the increasing complexity of signaling to provide these backbone services, it appears the latter ownership style is likely to prevail. The KSPs would thus become network-based intermediators between the knowledge staff (such as specialized consultants, technicians) and the client/user community at large. This network architecture is shown in Figure 5.2.

5.3.4 Programmable KSP-Based Network Architectures

This architecture of the new KSP-based Internet is shown in Figure 5.2. It deals with small knowledge centers and the typical knowledge service providers. Here the service control point (SCP) of this knowledge intelligent network (IN) is dedicated to a large number of businesses (the customers of the service provider). These businesses deal with their clients that need specialized services.

In Figure 5.2, the uploading process of the subscriber's SCP is also depicted. It resides in the SCP of any large telecommunications service provider (under a *new* number and *secured* series of numbers such as 899 or 898, etc.). This is an integrated database activated for the client(j) of any knowledge service provider(i). Special services may thus be activated for that client(j) provided (1) the client is within the authorized range of special services offered by the universities, travel centers, electronic governments, banks, brokerage houses, and so on, and (2) client(j) is within his/her own prepaid level or the level of authorization for payment assigned to this particular client(j). This permits a two-tier service structure: network-based services (such as carrier preference, authentication, service history, and payment record), and client-based services (such as type of information sought, and technical and knowledge profile updates) that the client may receive.

In Figure 5.2 the operation mode of the network is also depicted. Special and permissible network functions are accomplished by the KSPs via the two special units— a hardware unit the subscriber intelligent peripheral (SIP), and a special software unit— the subscriber service logic interpreter (SSLI). These units are scaled down (to the PC size) versions of the SIP and SLI that are present in the typical service switching point (SSP) of an intelligent network. These units are necessary for the modern intelligent network (typically the IN/2) to provide the special KSP functions akin the modern subscriber services.

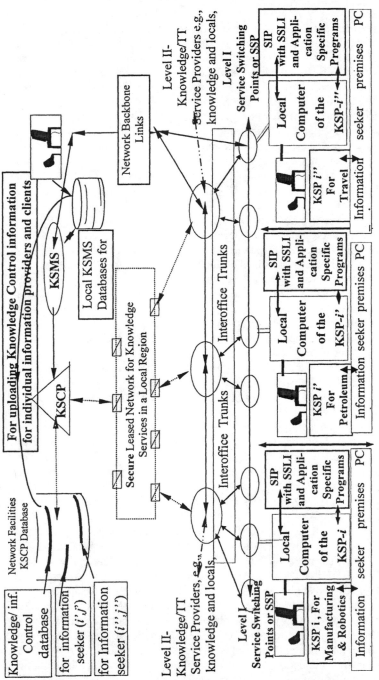

Figure 5.2 The KSP-based system always remains active monitoring the knowledge needs of the clients and subscribers. To this extent, it is similar to knowledge and local environment. SIP and SSLI are two special software package supplied by the KSP for their Level I service providers, their clients and other information seekers.

These two functions provided by SIP and SSLI (in Figure 5.2) are traced back to the functional architecture of the TINA documented in [1]. In this TINA configuration, proposed by International Telecommunications Union (ITU), the functions of IP and SDP [6] parallel the functions of SLI shown in Figure 5.2. Likewise, the CCF, the SSF and the SCF functions at the service node (SN) of TINA parallel the functions of SSLI shown in Figure 5.2.

When a telecommunications service provider can condense the service node of TINA to a PC-based HW and SW environment for the individual KSP subscriber, then the specialized service creation environment (SCE of TINA) is handed back to the KSPs. All the advanced intelligent network features now acclaimed by the next generation intelligent networks, like the TINA, can be offered in rudimentary IN environment with the basic SCP, STP, SSP, and an SMS as the building blocks for the KSP-based network.

When any client/agent(j) calls for specialized services from the KSP(i), it activates the client-specific service program. The track sector address of the executable code for the client is dispatched from the network SCP database. This allows an executable program code in the databases of client/agent(j) be executed (in view of most recent knowledge information) at the KSP premises to provide the best service for client/agent(j). The enhanced network database furnishes a program address in the subscriber database and redirects the call to the appropriate secondary level service provider (such as universities, medical centers, electronic governments, banks, travel agencies, or brokerage houses) to facilitate the request of that particular client/agent.

In Figure 5.1, the ownership of the regional knowledge service control point (KSCP) databases and the knowledge services management system (KSMS) can be negotiated. One possible variation of architecture is to permit Internet access to the databases to keep the local clients updated about the specific changes in the most recent technology or global market conditions. The blending of knowledge services and network services is customized by the KSP and KSMS. The customized service for any particular query is uploaded by the KSCPs for that particular client or agent. The segment of the database tagged as (i, j) is invoked and serves exactly according to the contents of the KSCP uploaded by KSP(i) for client(j). The KSP-based network is thus capable of taking the client request for services through the Internet access throughout knowledge bases around the world.

In Figure 5.2, the local KSP subscriber database containing the specific customer profile for each customer is depicted. Each of the KSPs (KSP-i, i', i'') can program the network via the software SSLIs (service specific logic interpreters). The programs generated by the KSPs are encoded as service instruction programs (SIPs). The service provisioning by the KSPs suits the specific needs of their customers. In this configuration, each customer retains his/her own specific "profile" database and the network may remain active without a specific query from the customer. The KSCP now contains all the information to handle customer-specific knowledge functions and the authorized network functions. The program database also contains the interpreter to assemble the instructions that can be embedded in the SIP programs. The interpretation and assembling of network instructions are handled by special hardware and interfaced to the signaling network. Very specific and precise network *and* knowledge commands (both) may thus be communicated to the KSCP, the KSMS, the knowledge switching points (KSPs) and the various knowledge banks embedded within the knowledge-based network systems.

5.4 KBS IN HOSPITAL NETWORKS

5.4.1 Global Medical Network Environment

Network traffic dealing with any field of medicine can trigger on exploration of opportunities that lead to an inference relationship or a deep-seated statement of medical fact[1]. A chain of events are examined and scrutinized to discover the validity of relationships as medical facts, laws of nature, or even hospital policies.

High-speed information networks for medical applications exist in most hospitals. The global switching centers provide instant Internet access. However, the medical teams dealing with patient welfare follow a much slower, traditional path. Over the last few decades, it has become evident that the gap between the information capacity of the newer networks and the human capacity to derive significant benefits is getting wider. Whereas modern networks are data driven, human understanding is knowledge and wisdom driven. In an attempt to model human oversight, we propose an architecture of machines that works in synergy with the data flow in hospitals and produces initial axioms of medical knowledge that become a basis of derived medical wisdom driven further. These axioms, if approved by the entire medical community, forms a tentative database of axioms or inferences by which physicians may enhance and consolidate the medical field at a faster and consistent pace.

Although smart Internet users can access some of these services, such services have not been tailored to the medical profession. The specialized services that the physicians and hospitals provide and the associated patient costs are still not available to patients. Over the next decade or so, it is envisioned that specific medical information may be supplied by medical knowledge bases rather than by physicians and their staff who may have an embedded profit motive. In a sense, the initial information gathering and the search for appropriate low-level medical treatment are facilitated by medical service providers (MSPs), medical knowledge bases and intelligent medical-knowledge processing that tailors the medical services and hospital facilities to the patients. The current approach is to place the patient at the lowest level of service provisioning rather than placing the patient as the paying customer. In a majority of cases, the patients are forced to accept the

---

[1] The section 5.4.1, is based on a paper by Arif Rana and Syed Ahamed "Knowledge Bases from Medical and Hospital Networks," *Porc. IASTED Int. Conf. Telehealth,* ACTA Press, Anaheim, CA, pp. 64–68. Paper presented at Telehealth Conference, Banf, Alberta, July 19-21, 2005. Mr. Rana is a Doctoral candidate at UMDNJ, Newark, NJ.

medical services and the hospital facilities at an unknown quality of service (QoS) service and an unclear billing system. It will also be possible to retrieve specific information for an individual patient by using smart medical databases-based on the patient specific conditions. Security of information and authentication of recipient are both important design considerations.

Within the perspective of data flow through the networks, data acquisition, categorization, assembly, correlation, switching, and channeling are feasible. The traditional tools and techniques currently used in communication systems and networks technology extract a key summary of events and objects (such as patients, medical conditions, ailments, complications) in hospitals, medical centers, or in any community. This summary exposes the structure, interrelationship, and linkage of the objects embedded within the information carried by the networks. Expert systems, pattern recognition, trend analysis, and statistical analysis augmented by tools of logic and learning, lead to an accumulation of knowledge bases. These prior functions are feasible in the realm of machine intelligence. However, the task of finally deriving an accurate medical diagnosis and inference from knowledge remains divided between a team of physicians and a hierarchy of computers. In the proposed configuration, the consideration of machine-derived axiom or cause–effect relationship (to derive wisdom) still rests with the human medical experts. The network becomes an intelligent agent to derive lower level relationships between causes and their effects to examine their validity and justification.

5.4.2 MSP-Based Intelligent Internet

A possible configuration of the hospital-based integrated medical computer systems for processing medical and patient information using specialized functional components (FCs) is presented in [2]. Full implementation of such a network to bring intelligent medical Internet (IMI) services to patients and users is likely to take some time.

The hospital environment is competitive, dynamic and volatile driven by market forces and laws of supply and demand. The medical service providers are anxious to get the IMI services now and take a risk *if* the price is small enough. In a sense, the proposed network architecture shifts the responsibility back to the MSPs to use their own customized package that will accomplish their specific goals. These goals are specific for the MSP and community of the patients and users whom the MSP is willing to serve. Such MSPs can offer a menu, as the Internet does, but from their own database and via the telephone line on the land-line and wireless networks. Thus, the blend of services is discretionary, the waiting time is short and patient/user control of the content is local and immediate. This is in stark contrast to the philosophy of other intelligent network service providers and owners, who wish to offer generic and universal services to all customers.

The architectures of the advanced intelligent networks for medical application are discussed in Reference [7, 8]. The adjunct service processor (ASP) and the Intelligent Peripheral (IP)-based switching systems provide similar capabilities for their telecommunications clients. The programs within the ASP and IP are owned, monitored, and maintained by the network owners. In the MSP-based Internet, it is proposed that the user/patient specific functions be programmed and fine tuned on the local computers owned by the MSP subscribers who will offer a variety of legitimate medical functions (such as dispensing of drugs, physiotherapy, nursing care, paramedical services, and radiation therapy) with authorization from the community of medical professionals and hospitals. Whereas it may take a long time for all the telecommunications-based AIN standards to be written, and standardized, debugged, and made available to the clients, the MSP-based network environment provides the patients/users what any current network technologies have to offer now. These network and medical functions are blended harmoniously under the supervision of the MSP within the framework of the risk that the MSP is willing to take with the local community of patients/users.

5.4.3 Configurations of the Machine

A three-level configuration for two medical systems are shown in Figures 5.3a and 5.3b. In Figure 5.3a, a generic framework for the hospital medical system is depicted. In Figure 5.3b, a practical implementation of an intelligent medical system is shown. In a large hospital that is patient service oriented, the arrangement in Figure 5.3b becomes immediately attractive. In a large university setting that is research oriented, the arrangement in Figure 5.3a becomes immediately attractive. With reference to Figure 5.3a, the lowest level of functionality [9] to extract information and knowledge from the flow of data within the network, a variety of sensors are embedded within the hospital network. These devices activate the system to indicate a possible scenario to derive significant correlations between events and circumstances. A snapshot of the situation is captured and processed further. At the intermediate level of functionality, the existing search techniques will process the data through the information level and complement the original snapshot with additional details. The AI techniques extract the patterns of change in the flow or the nature of information through the existing knowledge levels to identify unique or repetitive sets of input conditions. Such techniques and procedures are routinely implemented in medical diagnostics [10, 11] and cancer detection.

In the corporate environment, the modern executive information systems [8, 9] deploy similar techniques to discover economic opportunities, and profit potentials and to make intelligent decisions.

At the next level for building the axioms of wisdom, human activity is supported by six computer systems (or subsystems), where the human mind feeds back partial information and knowledge into individualized processes of the machines. Each computer (sub)system performs a step to either forward a new concept in the wisdom-base or to link and classify the realm of current activity to an existing tree of knowledge or as its branch, its twig, or its leaf. The computer component of the network-based medical wisdom machine acts as a preprocessor to the intermediate

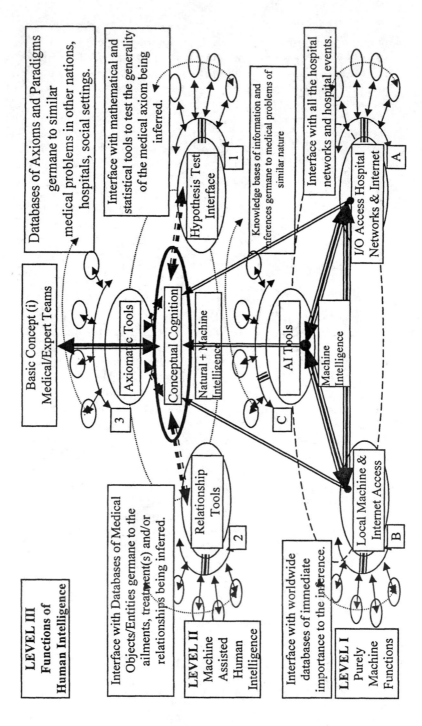

LEVEL III
Functions of
Human Intelligence

Databases of Axioms and Paradigms germane to similar medical problems in other nations, hospitals, social settings.

Interface with mathematical and statistical tools to test the generality of the medical axiom being inferred.

Basic Concept (i)
Medical/Expert Teams

Knowledge bases of information and inferences germane to medical problems of similar nature

Interface with all the hospital networks and hospital events.

Hypothesis Test Interface

1

Axiomatic Tools

3

Conceptual Cognition

Natural + Machine Intelligence

AI Tools

C

Machine Intelligence

I/O Access Hospital Networks & Internet

A

Interface with Databases of Medical Objects/Entities germane to the ailments, treatment(s) and/or relationships being inferred.

Relationship Tools

2

LEVEL II
Machine Assisted Human Intelligence

Interface with worldwide databases of immediate importance to the inference.

Local Machine & Internet Access

B

LEVEL I
Purely Machine Functions

Figure 5.3a Three level system for inferencing and deriving medical knowledge from dataflow in hospital networks.

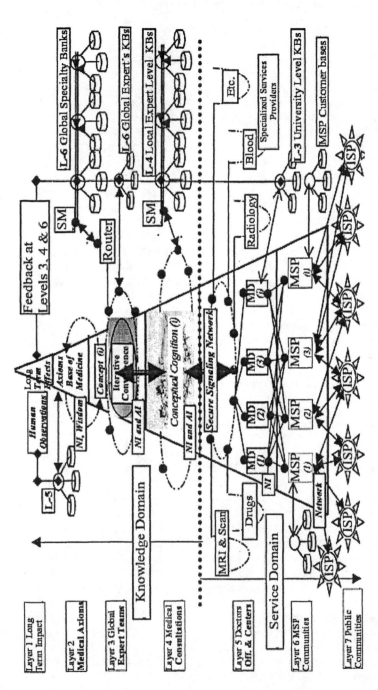

Figure 5.3b A Seven level intelligent hospital environment. *The arrangement provides the public medical needs via the WWW entry (Level 7) into the hospitals. The routine physician–patient transactions are handled at the lower levels (5 to 7). The facilities at the higher levels (1 to 4) provide venues for the physicians and hospital staff to consult with local medical communities and interact with subject matter specialists around the globe. Network security issues are also addressed at all seven levels.*

level functions that examine the validity of a partially developed axiom of wisdom in the field of medicine. Furthermore, these computer systems refine the axiom-based on generality, universality, or a particular set of circumstances in an iterative mode. The underlying concept is thus sharpened and the embedded wisdom is deepened if the situation is novel and uncharted or reported as cause–effect relationship due to known facts documented in the wisdom base.

The basic advantage of the proposed system is that the initial processing of medical information detects the cause of any given chain of events (such as the acuteness of a patient's condition or an increase of costs in any department) accurately on an individual basis. It checks the cause–effect relationship from a set of acceptable circumstances and informs the medical teams or the administration about the dependence. To some extent, the proposed system is similar to tracking the vital signs of any particular patient in an intensive care unit and informing the attending physician.

With reference to Figure 5.3b, the configuration shown caters to the public medical needs via the WWW entry into the hospitals. The routine physician–patient interactions and transactions are provided at levels 7, 6, and 5. When an unusual case arises in dealing with a patient condition (such as bird flue, rare disease like anthrax), the consultation at Level 4 permits physicians and hospital staff to access knowledge bases around the community or around the world (at Levels 4, 3 and 2) to isolate the novelty in the case, to generalize the observations and add to global medical knowledge (at Level 1). The system is quick to implement and offer all the advantages to the medical community that a typical executive information platform would offer to the managerial community of a large corporation.

5.4.3.1 Level I – Routine Medical Functions

All machine tasks are essentially programmable. Even if the machine is capable of altering its own codes and sequence of codes, it is still instructed to do so. Total randomness at this level is a close call to chaos. For this reason, the routine functions that the machine can execute with great dependability and total accountability and tireless accuracy can be made Level I tasks (Figure 5.3a) for a good reason. The human mind with its almost nonprogrammable and creative tasks has a short span of intense attention. During these moments of heightened human activity (or excitement), all necessary information for a conceptual breakthrough is accurately and readily available.

Current technology provides efficient computational, access, database, AI, and network services. Whereas we may install independent machines to perform the core computational, access, database, and AI services, the (inter- and intra-) networking services may be independent or shared. This aspect of the architecture of the human–machine system is not significant at a conceptual level when the functions need to be classified as machine functions or as human functions. To this extent, the functions of all currently available versions of AI-based machines are classified as Level-I functions.

5.4.3.2 Level II – Machine Assisted Human Functions

If the ingenuity and creativity of the medical team can be programmed, the machine can handle such programs. When the solution is specific to a particular task, the team of physicians can handle it; however, the machine will learn the reasons for the human response in order to be able to use the response and the reasoning. For this reason, the greater adaptation for solving any particular problem still resides with the human being. The highest level of programmed rationality of the machine may approach the lowest level of human creativity. But the synergy of tasks between physicians and the machines surpasses the purely inductive reasoning or deductive logic of the machine. For this reason, we propose that the medical inferencing machine have at least one medical expert staff (at Level II in Figure 5.3a) to oversee a group of machines performing all-machine (Level-I) functions in Figure 5.3a.

In interaction between medical staff and machine, the burden for the correct functioning is heavier on the human staff. The multiple processes of the machine need to be vectored and mentored in the mind of a human. A quick and spontaneous inferencing, based on the synergy between the human thought and machine processes, needs to be achieved. This latter task is nontrivial; however, nature has a built-in rescue mode within the thought process. The human mind retains visual and derived information (of significant value) in its medium term memory and the information (by itself) simmers over a period of time until it is recovered and reprocessed or rejected as irrelevant in the context of the solution.

5.4.3.3 Level III – Expert Medical Functions

The role of the medical staff (see Figure 5.3a) is to keep the machines functional and focused in order to derive a medical diagnosis or an axiom. In addition, the machine needs to substantiate the minimum confidence level of any inference or axiom derived.

The human beings (medical and IT staff) keep the overall solution and contributions of several independent and interdependent machines in perspective. More than that, the human being, whose intuition is faster than the computation, forces each machine to function in the direction in which medical wisdom (or inference) is being perceived. This type of human interaction is pursued in solving scientific and corporate problems. Managerial decision-making is supplemented by most program driven MIS (management information system) corrections. Furthermore, false and trivial pursuits are soon eliminated. For example, the wisdom machine (Chapter 10) is perfectly in its bounds to pick up the dictionary meaning of words and rephrase it as classic wisdom. It can also rephrase and replace the statements from an encyclopedia and so on with any given level of confidence. It can restate basic equations as words of wisdom such, as the ratio of circumference of a circle to its diameter, or within the context of its knowledge bases. As the functionality matures, it can guide human beings to function better than machines and to guide machines to think more like human beings.

5.5 KNOWLEDGE-BASED PROCESSES

5.5.1 Intelligent Networks for Telemetry and Data Processing

In this section, we present a generic methodology for networks to sense general or specific environmental conditions. Such networks, in any given environment must process the data and the sensor readings and thus monitor the environments in which they exist. They are generic to the extent that they are applicable for any application in which the underlying processes need to be controlled for validation, security, and/or optimality of operation. Typically, such scanning devices routinely sense and evaluate the parameters that influence the security and optimality of any production or human facility. At a very rudimentary level, the sensors simply provide data or pictures to human beings who monitor the overall activity. For more sophisticated applications and environments, lexical analysis and pattern recognition techniques are invoked to verify and validate the overall environmental conditions. Groups of sensor reading and/or graphical inputs may be processed and checked against the conditions that pose a potential threat to the security of the system or the environment. For more demanding environments, conditions that are a potential threat are deducted from the inference engines or from the expert system rules. Although some of the suggested approaches are deployed in human surveillance activities, we present the methodology and techniques for greatly automating these functionalities, thus reducing the cost and enhancing the dependability of these networks for telemetry and data processing environments.

5.5.2 A Confluence of Four Disciplines

Four major disciplines— artificial intelligence (AI, [10]), intelligent network (IN) design [3], decision support system (DSS) concepts [12] and switching system (SS) design [13]— are embedded in the design of the proposed intelligent networks for telemetry and data processing. In a disjointed form, these overall concepts are prevalent in the management of large multinational corporations and vastly distributed information processing networks. In the human arena the role of the management team is to respond to the local and global conditions as they affect the optimality and stability of the corporate environment. In the information processing environments (such as the Internet), the role of the antivirus programs is to maintain the security of the networks and information they carry.

The essential difference lies in the extent and nature of the role of AI in these networks as compared to the role of natural intelligence in human environments. Programmed machine learning and switching facilitates the detection, arrest, and neutralization of the hazardous events and forces in the environment. Coupled with AI functions, the role of the human being is essentially to mentor and monitor the network to mentor and monitor the environment. To this extent, the highly programmable sensing network functions as a massive intelligent agent that accomplishes the four (AI, IN, DSS, and SS) functions in synergy to produce a highly stable and dependable system.

All essential routine and programmable management tasks are embedded in the network functions. However, the capacity to micromanage every aspect of the local operations of a very large number of sensors or customers,-based on their own individual constraints, would not be humanly possible. For this reason, we augment the facility of the decision support systems (DSSs) with clusters of knowledge processing systems (KPSs) with the switching systems (SSs). The KPS (discussed in Chapters 8 and 9) deals with "objects" influencing the objective function [14] and the management of the entire system. A communications hub communicates with a very large number of sensors that "read" the environment. The hub also distributes the "instructions" to control the environmental conditions on a dynamic basis that monitor the specific "objects" and their attributes. These networks return the system to the normal operating conditions from any unstable or hazardous conditions and thus effectively restore the zone of safe operation.

The centralized sensing interface works in conjunction with the KPS to supply the data structures of the "objects" or "object clusters" periodically, and the control interface supplies the control signals if necessary to restore equilibrium. Both transmit and receive functions of communication are necessary in this interface. The sensors provide the periodic input information by sensing the objects under normal conditions or more frequently during heightened alert. The receptors receive the control information to modify or enhance the objects and/or their attributes periodically or more frequently. These sensors may be of any type. In a hospital environment, these objects may be the heartbeat of a patient, or in a stock market environment, these objects may be market trends, swings, and cycles. Typically, they retain the most current reading at the gateway of the LAN on which they reside.

5.5.3 Implementation

For the implementation of these telemetry and sensing networks, the generic and evolved architecture of modern switching systems (SS) is deployed with one additional "knowledge module" for intelligent object/scenario processing (see Chapter 3). Such intelligent objects or scenarios (scanned and sensed within a given environment) are the main players driving a very restricted community or a very large global society. The network designers share the responsibility of selecting the appropriate parameters to sense and monitor. For example, in governing the economic welfare of a nation, numerous socioeconomic variables, such as the GNP, consumption, taxation, gross economic activity, the velocity of money, the interest rate, the employment level, and educational level, become the key parameters. The key (lagging, current and leading) indicators would also be the inputs for the macroeconomic models of nations. In the proposed network implementation, they are sensed and monitored on a day-to-day basis. These networks, which would enable quick reflexive action if it is deemed necessary, quickly and accurately track catastrophic and major global events.

Sensor readings are regularly and periodically transmitted to the knowledge-based and object-oriented programs that perform real-time optimization to move the whole system towards a new stable and secure area of operation. Security is established on an incremental response basis that is consistent with an overall "objective function." The major advantage is that, since the stabilizing process closely trails the error-function, large swings of the error-functions are not accumulated but are quickly eliminated, leading to a refined control mechanism that was not possible in earlier systems.

5.5.4 The Architecture Dealing with Sensors, Intelligence and Databases

In Figure 5.4, we present a conceptual overview to unify *three* basic modules: (1) the full duplex communication module to read and sense the environment, (2) the knowledge and (artificial) intelligence module to perform the basic AI functions and evaluate a definite course of action-based on the readings, and (3) the database and data management to drive the robotic control mechanism that will stabilize the system.

The network communication functions allow the proposed sensing system to communicate with the environment customers and global KBs. The sensor readings are carried forward to the internal software that monitors the conditions for stability of the environment. Typically, these conditions may be evaluated by system designers or from observation-based on heuristic reasoning. Initial processing of these readings enables the monitoring system to gauge the severity of the instability and to react quickly under hostile or dangerous conditions. The range of response goes from quick and reflexive to slow and data collecting; thus the system response becomes programmable and software dependent. When the sensor readings are numerous, the region of passive observation of the environment without system intervention becomes a hyperdimensional space. In most human response security systems, this aspect of the communication function is performed by observing numerous closed circuit TV screens that display activities within the premises.

As an interface it would need to receive inputs from various devices and users in their specific language and it would need to provide information in a format specific to the device or user. A duality of communication from the system to the devices or users becomes essential. In the first mode, the system may instruct the device or user to alter sensing mode such as the sampling frequency, accuracy, or reporting, and in the second mode, the system may send the numerical control data to restore the stable operating conditions.

Hence, a variety of compilers would be necessary to process the input syntax and/or commands, and a set of output routines would be necessary to format the information specific to the particular device or user. All three aspects of the compile function (parsing, syntactic analysis, and semantic analysis) can be necessary to receive complex object or object strings from the environment. Within the knowledge processing module all the machine-dependent assemblers, the code generator, the loaders and the linkers also reside in this segment of the front-end processors (FEPs), [15]. The software driving these FEPs is shown in Figure 5.5. Thus the software platform for the telemetry, data processing and the associated control mechanism starts to have a triadic profile: (a) input communicating and interfacing with the object processing environment, (b) conversion of the inference-based on the sensed objects to the distribution of the specific data to the numerically controlled machines, and (c) distribution of the NC data to the control machines or robots in the environment.

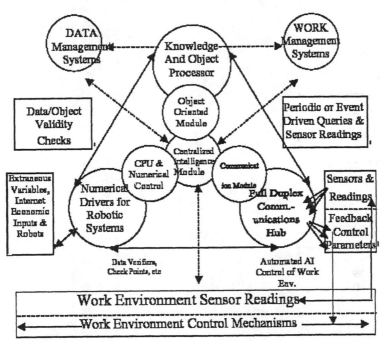

Architecture of a Sensing and Monitoring Network to Stabilize the Work Environment

Figure 5.4 Three level system for sensing, inferencing and controlling the work environments from the flow of data in networks.

The directions for the three types of data is shown in Figure 5.5. Furthermore, the loaders, linkers, and so on, that perform the address resolution of the embedded objects and their attributes, become machine dependent and are considered as routine SW issues that are resolved at execution time by the compilers and operating systems. Expert system rules and deduction and pattern recognition are necessary to deal with the sensor inputs that continuously scan the environment.

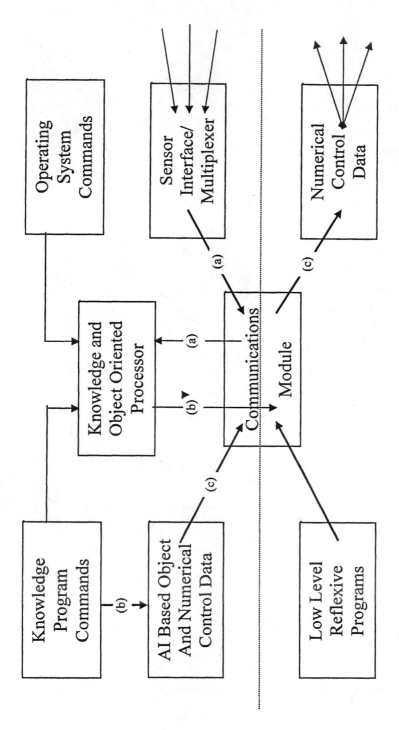

Figure 5.5 Dataflow from sensors (a) provides the input to the KPS for monitoring and analyzing the inputs. The processed control information (b) flows back to the environment as inputs (c) to the numerically controlled machines or to the robotic facilities.

The AI routines enforce the processes by the knowledge and object processor or the KPS in Figure 5.4.

In most cases, the AI programs deploy readings from numerous sensors, and a string of readings or trends that are being detected in the environment. At the interface, the functions of the object-oriented module is to check the validity of the sensor readings individually and collectively and to perform a low-level rationality check about the potentially unstable scenarios in the environment. Machine-generated response sometimes needs human agents to quickly check the validity. Along the same lines, medical information systems and physicians work in conjunction much like management information systems and executives work together in corporations. Human agents may work in parallel with the intelligent agents in severe conditions. User queries and dialog will become necessary during development and debugging of the entire system. If machine learning is a feature of the telemetry and data processing environment, then the KPS learns and adapts to the new environmental conditions and the next decision becomes consistent with the new inputs and consistent with past learning.

If the network is designed to serve a very large environment like a hospital or the economy of a nation, then the network scans a large number of sensors at any given instant of time. A massive parallel processed knowledge-handling environment (see Chapter 11) is suggested. An AI programming environment is effectively implemented in a hierarchically designed SW layer that handles C++ type of programs to make the object orient programs (OOP) feasible, scalable, and adaptable to new hardware and new demands on the system.

Vast amounts of data are accessed, acquired, processed, and communicated during the normal operations of large networks. Long sequences of subprograms may be compiled, assembled and executed-based on the raw data "sensed" in the network. A typical example of such complex sequences of processes occurs when the switching system of a communications facility initiates call processing for any incoming (telephone or data) call. Generally, it becomes necessary to separate the types of data as transient (e.g., routine meter readings, sensor inputs, time and external inputs) or as permanent (e.g., programs, and rules, device characteristics). In computer environments, such data is routinely classified as "user programs and jobs" or as systems programs, compilers, generic I/O SW, utilities, libraries, and math routines. In the same vein, the telemetry and data processing network databases are organized with these two basic flavors.

5.5.5 Program and Data Management in the KPS

Within the architecture of the KPS, the programs for monitoring the environment and routine sensor data needs are handled in different bases in order to maintain a high throughput, especially in complex environments. The management of these bases is done by work management systems (WMS) and data management systems (DMS) in Figure 5.4. Typically, the former type of program enforces the network policies and become network specific, whereas the latter type of data becomes sensor or user specific. The blending of the two functions is done during the execution of the OOPs in the knowledge module and is driven by the input data sensed by the "sensors" or the active dialog initiated by the human agent.

5.6 CONCLUSIONS

The architectures presented in this Chapter offer added benefits to the knowledge community, including the technology transfer agents and users. First, by incorporating the role of the KSPs between the knowledge and technology sources and users, clients (universities, production facilities, hospitals, electronic governments, etc.) are provided with specific information and details of the knowledge condition germane to a particular client. The human interface is practically eliminated unless the client calls for it. At the supply side, the KSPs have all the most recent knowledge information available to them. Their databases include all the codes and coverage and the list of options that are available. Second, when the client is ready for implementation, the KSPs act as inter-mediator between the second level knowledge service providers (see Figure 5.2) and their clients. Third, the KSP services provided are-based on the procedures of electronic transactions on networks. For this reason, the service and turnaround are quick; they are also efficient and inexpensive, thus facilitating reduced cost for the transfer of technology. Fourth, very large network knowledge bases owned by governments and universities can now be fragmented into thousands of small server environments (in any localized area) necessary for smaller specialized KSPs in the local area. Fifth, numerous sophisticated knowledge intelligent network services can be readily offered by executing special SIP and SSLI programs within the KSP's premises computers (see Figure 5.2). Sixth, prepaid and authorized knowledge services can be dispensed immediately. Each KSP can tailor and tune the knowledge service provided and can include a personal touch in its attention to client/patients.

The KSP-based network environment effectively taps into the PSTN, the Internet, and the wireless telephone networks. These networks are growing at an enormous rate and with increasing coverage and popularity. The proposed knowledge networks bring the impact of the new digital technology, knowledge society, and network revolution to the knowledge community. The KSP-based network quickly closes the gap between the knowledge community and the high mobile clients within a growing segment of the population.

The architecture for building generic man-machine medical, educational, or commerce related knowledge processing environment leads to any specified generality; it also yields an estimated level of confidence to the solution. The pursuit of total generality like the pursuit of perfection, is likely to fail: it is a constant drain on resources. Such an indefinite pursuit ends in the collapse of human beings or at the limits of machine precision. We have supplemented the pure search algorithms used in the Internet environments with intelligent searches-based on the medical condition of a patient and on knowledge from local and global medical databases. In general, the wisdom machine supplements the environment from its own knowledge banks of accumulated procedures and inferences about a particular topic under investigation. Human intelligence firmly drives the programmed artificial intelligence of the machine in directions that validate or repudiate an axiom of medical wisdom from a scientific and mathematical perspective.

The novel features dealing with telemetry and data processing networks presented in this chapter are-based on (1) its adaptability to numerous applications (2) use of the established principles of decision support systems, and (3) programmability of the response to any scenario detected within the environment.

The network concepts are adaptable to suit a large number of different applications, such as a national economy, a corporation, a society, or any midsized social entity by distributing the "sensors" in the environment and then regulating the "climate" of the entity with distributed control modules distributed throughout the network. The entire concept of the decision support system can be ported to the network environment by arranging the functions of the switching systems (SSs), the data driven control units (CUs) and the knowledge processing module (KPU, discussed in Chapter 8). Finally, one can program of the response to each scenario sensed as a quantitative measure of the attributes of a set of programmable objects derived from the environment.

REFERENCES

[1] CCITT Recommendations M.3010, *Principles for a Telecommunication Management network (TMN) TINA Architecture;* Rec. M.3200. *TMN Management Service;* Rec. M.3400. *TMN Management Functions;* Rec. M.3020. *TMN Interface Specification Methodology;* Rec. M.3180 *Catalogue network Information Model; M.3300. TMN Management Capabilities.*

[2] S. V. Ahamed, Knowledge and local-based integrated knowledge computer systems for processing knowledge and information seeker information using specialized functional modules, U.S. Patent US6,272,481 B1 issued on August 7, 2001. Assignee Lucent Technologies, Holmdel, NJ. 1998.

[3] W. D. Ambrose, A. Maher, and B. Sasscer, *The Intelligent Network,* Springer Verlag, New York, 1989.

[4] S. V. Ahamed and V. B. Lawrence, *Intelligent Broadband Multimedia Networks,* Kluwer Academic Publishers, Boston, 1998.

[5] S. V. Ahamed, et al., Intelligent networks for sensing and monitoring the environment", filed March 21, 2000, Application, issued in May 2004.

[6] Bellcore TA-TSY-000462, *SSP Capabilities for PVN services,* 1987; Bellcore TA-TSY-000460, *BSDB, SCP Application for PVN services,* 1987; See also, Bell Communications Research, *Integrated Service Management System Functional Architecture,* Bellcore Special Report, SR-TSY-001101, 1988.

[7] M. Krol and D. L. Reich, Development of a decision support system to assist anesthesiologists in the operating room, *J. Med. Sys.* 24, 141-146, 2000.

[8] S. V. Ahamed, et al., Architecture for a Computer System used for Processing Knowledge, U.S. Patent, 5,465,316, November 7, 1995. European Patent 9437848.5- "Knowledge Machine Methods and Apparatus", EP Number 146248, US/05.11.93, Denmark, France, Great Britain, Italy. See also, M. Krol, *Intelligent Medical Network*, Doctoral Dissertation, City University of New York, 1996. Assignee Lucent Technologies, Holmdel, NJ.

[9] S. V. Ahamed, The Architecture of a Wisdom Machine, Int. J. Smart Eng. Sys. Design, **5**, (4): 737–545, 2003.

[10] E. Turban and J. E. Aronson, *Decision Support Systems and Intelligent Systems*, 6th ed., Prentice Hall, Englewood Cliffs, NJ. See also, Salam Z. Al-Sam, Sunil R. Lakhani and Jack Davis, (Eds.), *Practical Atlas of Pseudomalignancy: Benign Lesions Mimicking Malignancy*, Edward Arnold, London, 1998.

[11] C. P. Poole and H. A. Farach (Eds.), *Handbook of Electron Spin Resonance: Data Sources, Computer Technology, Relaxation, and Endor,* Springer Verlag, New York, 1999.

[12] N. S. Stuart, *Computer-Aided Decision Analysis*, Quorum Books, Westport, CT, 1993. For decisions in medical diagnostics, see E. H. Shortliffe, *Computer-Based Medical Consultation, MYCIN*, Elsevier, New York, 1976.

[13] J. W. Johnson, et al., Integrated digital services on the 5ESS™ System, in *XI International Switching Symposium Proceedings*. Florence, Italy. See also, R. Wood, DMS-100, Technology Evolution, *Telesis* **10**, (3), 1984.

[14] F. S. Hillier and G. J. Liebermann, *Introduction to Operations Research,* McGraw Hill, New York, 2002.

[15] C. S. McMahon, *Service Control Point Generic Requirements,* Bell Communications Research, Technical Memorandum TM-TSY 003059, 1987. See also R. Davis, Application of meta level language to the construction, maintenance, and use of large knowledge bases" in *Knowledge-based Systems in Artificial Intelligence,* McGraw-Hill, New York, 1982.

Chapter *6*

Intelligent Control Systems

In this chapter, we present the extension of networks that sense, measure and function intelligently to discern healthy and unhealthy environments. Monitoring of the environment becomes a routine activity: sensors measure parameters that are consistent with the safety and security of the environment. Corrective response is invoked under conditions that deviate or start to deviate from the normal and expected range of parameters. In a sense, a whole set of parameters are sensed routinely and are logged. The rate of change of parameters can also be deduced. In fact, an entire ecosystem for the environment can be charted for that particular system to maintain a healthy and robust relationship between the external destabilizing forces and internal corrective feedback forces.

Such an adaptation occurs in almost all stable and semistable situations for all entities. In fact, a system exists because of some feedback loop that monitors the health and stability of the organism. In a coarse fashion, the basic principles of feedback control theory become applicable to environments and human structures. However, with the extensive programmability of the computer systems monitoring the feedback loop, the older equations for the stability of traditional electrical and electronic systems appear archaic and inadequate. The intelligent control systems have knowledge-based programs and one or more intelligent agent for adaptive feedback control signals tailored to the source and nature of the destabilizing agent. The nature and extent of the analysis, inference, and deduction become highly directional and focused. The artificially intelligent machines fallback into a

Intelligent Internet Knowledge Networks. By Syed V. Ahamed
Copyright © 2007 John Wiley & Sons, Inc.

learning mode and become responsive when the situation reoccurs. The roles of AI and feedback/feedforward get intertwined as the machines get "experienced." If the machines are permitted to alter their execution code, then a certain amount of human intelligence can be channeled to supplement the preprogrammed robotic intelligence. However, the ruthlessness of machines needs to be tamed before the machines show tendencies of total destruction to satisfy their operation research (OR)-based "objective functions" or (OF, see [1]). It appears almost appropriate to program an "objection function"-based on the ethics and values of the society to constrain the objective functions of the machines, humanoids and robots.

6.1 APPLICATIONS

The application of intelligent control systems is encompassing. The applications are (almost) boundless. All rational human functions, ranging from medicine to battlefields, and satellite sensors with missile destroyers become viable for such control.

Over the last few decades human beings have become highly specialized partners with computers offering the venue of expert systems [2] (via AI techniques) to deal with human, organizational, and corporate problems. By the same token, human beings have also acquired a few traits from robots by acting in a preprogrammed fashion without the time, inclination, and wisdom to contemplate. Under the pretext of fear and threat, the robotic instinct takes over in rushing toward an undesirable move (such as corporate crime, wars, emergency rules). It almost appears that some doctors perform senseless surgery to do the right thing but kill the patient. In the more evolved computational environment, the senselessness of execution of preprogrammed instruction has given way to processing of knowledge that surrounds any situation and problem. The processing of knowledge involves discovery of the "objects" embedded in the problem or their attributes. It also involves the discovery of relationships between objects and their interrelationships.

To some extent, when a machine is forced to search and evaluate the interrelationships between objects (embedded in knowledge) and their ensuing attributes, there is more analysis and evaluation involved. The same processes occur in sophisticated decision support systems and the executive information systems (EIS), leading to more valid, wiser, and universal decisions. Current knowledge processing environments are less numerous even though object-oriented programming is becoming more deployed in the UNIX environment.

As object-oriented languages become as easily programmable as scientific and business languages, many routine human functions will become programmable offering human beings to be creative with higher goals and values (see Chapter 12). This transformation in society has been brought about by most of the major inventions that facilitate the resolution of lower level needs (Chapter 12).

Through the development of modeling and simulation techniques, scientists and econometricians have already gained some control over chaotic and unforeseen conditions in industry, corporations, and society. It is our contention that it is possible to construct individual computer controlled feedback systems for any given set of circumstances and in one discipline. It is also our contention that it is possible a generic and programmable machine for (almost) all situations and all disciplines. Through the various applications presented at the end of this chapter, the adaptability of computer-controlled feedback process is illustrated. The feasibility is explored further in the book in the later chapters.

6.2 SENSED PARAMETERS AS "OBJECTS"

When sensed objects within the environment are treated as "objects" in knowledge processing systems (KPSs in Chapters 8 and 9), the computer systems have greater access to the reality of any situation. In traditional computer systems, a "scientific or a business model" of a physical function is simulated to extract and predict its characteristics or performance.

However, knowledge processing via embedded objects leads to the reality of any problem in most situations (as they are documented on the Internet), and the machine has access to knowledge bases in predicting the behavior of the objects under the problem conditions. The problem is viewed from a global perspective. When the problem is entirely new, the machine finds analogies (for the objects and situations) in other disciplines and attempts to solve the problem in an almost human way. The expanse (global) and refinement (local) of the thought processes of programmers limits the human aspect of the machines.

6.3 DEPLOYMENT OF INTELLIGENT CONTROL

To accommodate the variability in the objects and their attributes to be scanned in the environment, the entire system can be subdivided into four distinct functional entities. This concept is documented in Figure 6.1, where a centralized local operation management unit communicates (via the extraneous networks or local bus architectures) with three peripheral units to manage (1) the knowledge processing functions, (2) the database functions, and (3) the transactions and user interaction. The sensors play a more comprehensive role in this configuration. In addition to the local sensing of parameters that would influence the decision and the stability of the environment, the array of sensors would also receive the parameters from the global and social environments.

Electronic governments [3], hospital, and educational environments can be sensed and monitored by these sensing networks that systematically process the localized data and analyze this data in the context of previously known parameters to keep the entire system stable and operational. When additional flexibility is necessary, the role of the adjunct processor (AP) is introduced to support the three modules—

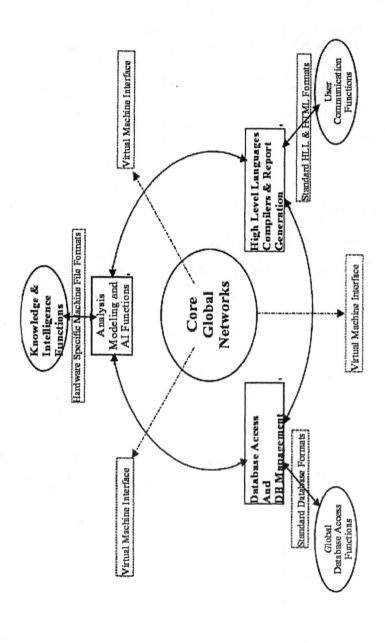

Figure 6.1 A computer and network organization for sensing (as a prelude to controlling) the environment.

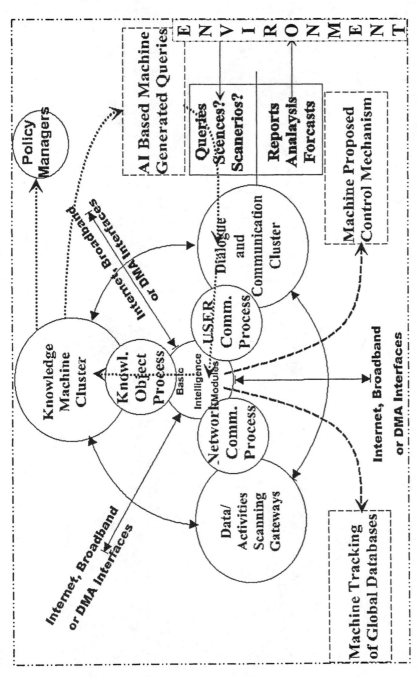

Figure 6.2 A conceptual architecture for global sensing to learn and locally control the environment.

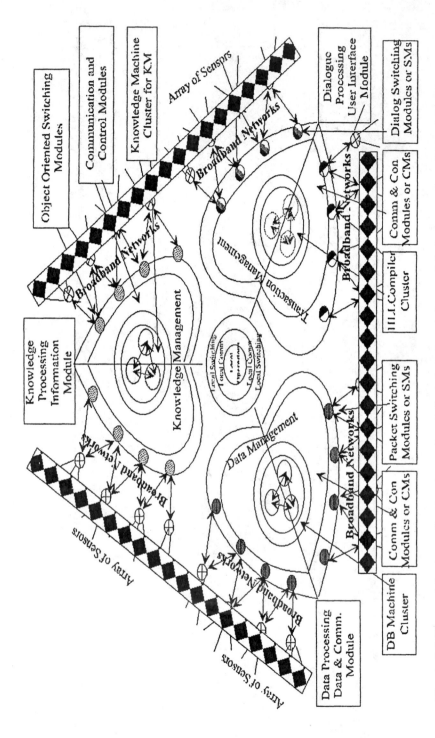

Figure 6.3 The architecture of a sensing network for telemetry and associated processing of the global data.

i.e., the KMM for knowledge management, DBM for database management and TMM for transaction management (see Chapters 4, and 5). The AP facilitates adaptation to the many objects that influence the decision.

These APs retain the programs for special services and special conditions much like the APs for IN/2 services in typical IN/2 and AIN [4]. For smaller applications (i.e., for small businesses), a single switch supported by a single AP would suffice. For larger applications, three or more APs or would serve the higher level functions encountered by a single large switch, a router, or a gateway (Figure 6.3).If the entire sensing network is designed as a stand-alone unit, then the processor banks of the unit can be substantially boosted by numerous arrays of parallel processors. As a unit, these processor banks accomplish both the switching functions and the functions of the clusters for dialog processing, knowledge processing, and database management. The application layer and the operating system would assume the flavor of full-fledged management information systems and that of a network Operating System.

This concept is documented in Figure 6.4, where there is an AP support for the AM, CM, and the SMs of each of the three switches serving the three clusters TMM, KMM and DBM in this configuration. For smaller applications, a single switch would be supported by a single AP or three APs or a multiplicity of APs that would get shared by the shared resource (the AM and the CM).

If central control of the sensing network is designed as an independent stand-alone unit, then a group of parallel processors can also boost the performance. The design of such a central control unit (CCU) within the sensing network as compared to the design of a CPU within a computer, can be optimized in its own right. In Figure 6.5, the APs shown in Figure 6.4 are pulled back into the AM and the CM of the switch architectures and represented as a combined and optimized entity.

A corporate headquarters and premises equipped with a corporate network controlled by a microprocessor (of the type presented in Patent 5,715,371) performs local and external communication as well as inventory control functions. The appliances in the premises are equipped with sensors to monitor the quantity of each inventory item in its storage (e.g., production items, raw materials, spare parts). The sensor information is communicated to the centralized microcomputer-based control, coordination, and communication facility.

6.3.1 Sensing Network Response Complex Via the Sensors

The proposed sensing network response complex depicted in Figure 6.5 senses this condition of the local microprocessor at the subscriber premises as it routinely queries all the control, coordination, and communication centers of all the subscribers. This concept of line scanning is a routine practice in all fixed network systems. The HLL I/O cluster of the transaction management machine (TMM) will receive this information after its scan cycle.

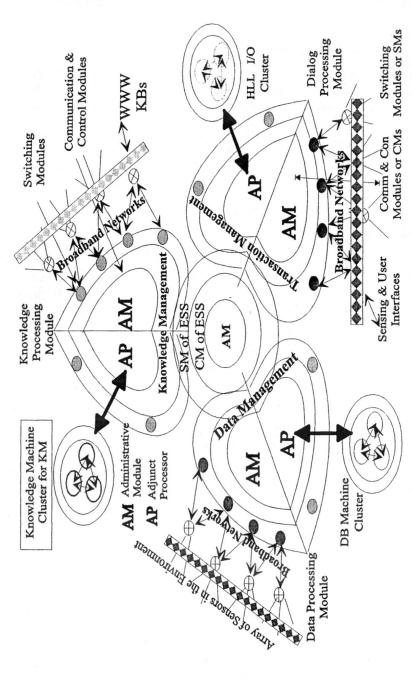

Figure 6.4 Additional level of detail of a network constantly scanning the environment and optimizing the controllable parameters for very large global systems such as seismic and/or weather warning systems.

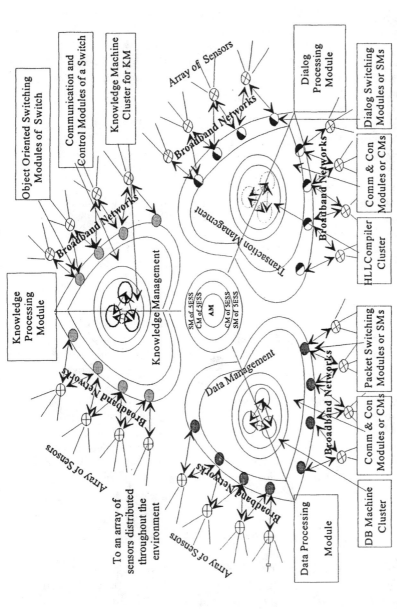

Figure 6.5 Implementation of the control module of the sensing network using the same processors for the switching functions and for each of the three cluster functions (dialog, knowledge, and data management).

6.3.2 Configuration of the Transaction Management Machine (TMM)

The core of this machine is borrowed from any circuit-switched architecture. It has numerous switching modules (SMs) to keep track of the particular line that activated a response and still be able to communicate with a large number of subscribers and to initiate a process request (ID) number.

The communication module (CM) of the TMM will take care of the internal communication within the TMM and communication with the administrative module (AM) of the TMM. For the particular case of the nth inventory item, the role of CM and AM are not critical, but if it were a fire alarm or a life support system, the local intelligence in the TMM would already take the appropriate action without going to data management machine or knowledge management machine. This programmed response of the TMM mimics the human reflex action (fight/flee) that is activated when eminent danger exists in the environment.

The KMM handles generic sets of "object-oriented" scenarios to deal with special conditions scanned by the sensors. These object-oriented programs solve the problems associated by a given set of sensor inputs by finding the best solution for the same process request ID initiated by TMM for that subscriber.

When the problem is complex, such as when both fire alarm sensor and a health alarm for a sick patient in the same premises are activated, the KMM may request the service of a fire response unit and an ambulance unit simultaneously. However, different routes would also be dispatched to the response units, leading to the same premises thus avoiding traffic congestion due to two counts of emergencies. It may also synchronize the travel of the fire unit and the ambulance to be dispatched simultaneously. Any amount of intelligence can thus be instilled in the response of the KMM by the SW hierarchy. The knowledge processing unit for the KMM has been devised and configured by the U.S. Patent 5,465,319. The SMs and CM of the KMM perform the tasks of communicating with the knowledge centers, universities, research and development centers that devise new knowledge algorithms, code knowledge programs and facilitate the knowledge domain functions.

6.3.3 Functions of the Database Management Machine (DBM)

Databases and their updates for all subscribers and their profiles need to be stored in reasonable detail such that the entire sensing network complex responds in an intelligent, coherent, and cogent fashion. This type of individual customer data is stored by most intelligent networks [4] of IN/2 (intelligent network Type 2) or the AIN (Advanced intelligent network) using the intelligent network Conceptual Model (INCM of the International Telecommunications Union).

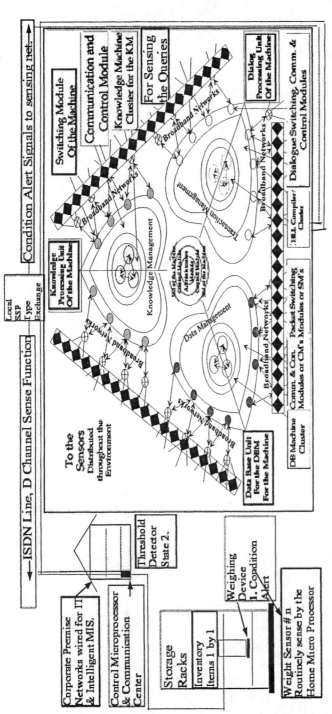

States 1, 2 and 3 are within the Figure. **State 4.** TMM receives Condition Alert & passes it to KMM and DBM for any Special Conditions, Confirmation for the right/strategic decision about the nth inventory item. **State 5.** KMM generates appropriate command to reorder the nth inventory item and sends it TMM. TMM forwards possible the nth inventory item Vendor to deliver it to the corporate customer to satisfy all the constraints subject to the data from the DBM regarding the delivery schedule, sale of the item, comparative shopping, etc.

Figure 6.6 An example of inventory control using the sensing network.

In the typical IN architecture, the service control point (SCP) keeps specific data pertaining to the routing of information for IN services, such as those associated with (800, 900, 700, 411, 911, etc.) caller ID calls. The use and updating of such databases is also covered under the U.S. Patent 5,628,011.

6.3.4 Functions of DBM and KMM, Specific to Inventory Control

For this example, the subscriber may specify that the corporation will be closed for two weeks (data stored in the DBM) and this data will suppress (a function of the KMM) the automatic ordering of the nth inventory item for 1½ (or so) weeks to ensure that the nth inventory item will be delivered only as the corporation resumes production and also will be consistent with the delivery dates and routes of the distribution center. Further, the buyers may also specify that the best price of the nth inventory item should also be scanned and quoted from all the vendors and the order be placed from the cheapest vendor in the vicinity such that the cost of the nth inventory item plus the overhead and delivery charges will be the lowest. Graphical user interfaces (GUIs) can make the functions of the KMM easily available in corporate, medical and educational environments.

Data of these categories will be stored in the DBM and the rules will be stored in the specific Subscriber profile. Combining these rules to optimize the "net objective function" will be governed by the KMM by blending the knowledge rules (KRs), expert system rules (ESRs), based on object recognition (OR), scenario recognition (SR), and pattern recognition (PR). For this reason, the generic nature of the proposed HW and SW architectures (see Figure 6.3) will be useful for a large number of applications.

6.4 CONTROL OF A NATIONAL ECONOMY

A typical nation may be networked enough to generate the numerous parameters that give rise to the economic variables that indicate the economic health of a nation. Some of these parameters are the GNP, employment levels, the rate of inflation, daily bank transactions, consumer spending, the saving rate, international trade balance, consumer price index, the inventory levels, the price of commodities, and types and rates of consumer expenditures. Most of these variables are collected in a centralized data facility and they are compared to their expected values with the normal range of their daily and seasonal variations. When some parameters start to exhibit sudden, inexplicable, or unforeseen variation, trends, or undesirable changes, alarm conditions are triggered. These conditions are registered and a corrective mechanisms may be implemented. In a great majority of the cases dealing with large national economies, these responses are human and committee decisions. But a sensing network may trigger minor corrections, document the environmental conditions and the monitor the condition. Machine learning mode is automatically invoked for future decision makers. The time constants of the variation may permit such scans to be accomplished manually by the staff at the national federal reserve system. But we contend that this process, once automated, can become more accurate, timely, and less subjective.

6.4.1 Sensing Network Response Complex Via the Sensors

The proposed sensing network response complex as it is applied to monitoring the national economy is depicted in Figure 6.7. The raw data from the economic activity of a nation are collected in the initial data banks. The granularity and noise components are smoothed out from the data, thus giving rise to trends, cyclic variations, and business fluctuations. Significant and pertinent parameters are compiled and fed into a second level of data banks. The DBM senses this condition and reanalyzes this data at local divisions and offices. The HLL I/O cluster of the transaction management machine (TMM) will receive this information after its scan cycle.

If an alarm condition is generated and it is consistent with other parameters as well, then the machine can identify historical conditions when such variations were encountered and track them to the root cause of such variations. The machine probes deeper than the human if its pattern recognition programs are activated and it is programmed to explore cause–effect relationships. New relationships between the variable and the parameters may be "discovered" by the machine.

6.4.2 Configuration of the Transaction Management Machine (TMM)

The core of this machine is borrowed from a typical switch Architecture. It has numerous switching modules (SMs) to keep track of the particular line that activated a response and is still able to communicate with a large number of subscribers and also to initiate a process request (ID) number. The communication module (CM) of the TMM will take care of internal communication within the TMM and communication with the administrative module (AM) of the TMM.

For this particular case of mentoring a national economy, the roles of the CM and AM are not critical, but if it was the nuclear fallout or a national emergency, the local intelligence in the TMM would already recommend an appropriate course of action without going to the data management machine or the knowledge management machine. These types of response scenarios are already built in the Emergency Response Systems (ERS, such as 911) of the Intelligent Network (IN/2).

6.4.3 Interaction with Knowledge Management Machine (KMM)

The KMM handles generic sets of "object-oriented" scenarios to deal with special conditions scanned by the sensors.

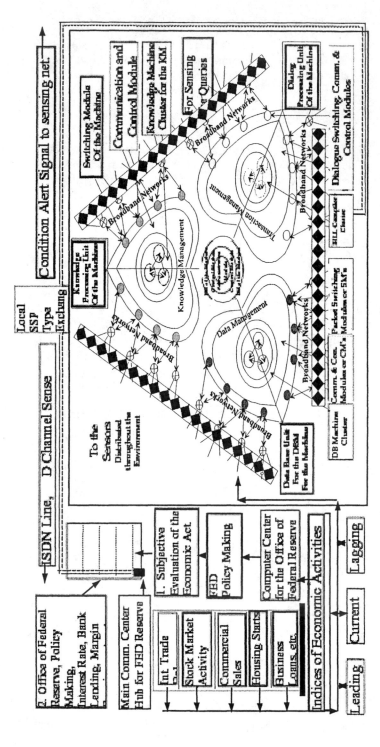

States 1, 2 and 3 are within the Figure. **State 4.** TMM receives control signals and passes it to KMM for typical response to be invoked and to DBM for confirmation, constraints, and/or strategies. **State 5.** KMM generates appropriate recommendations re-stabilize the economy if necessary. TMM forwards possible alerts & special conditions. The correction mechanisms can be e asily governed by the FED policies. These (leading, concurrent and/or predictive) policies are the expert system rules in the

Figure 6.7 An example of KMM to control the national economy of a nation. Historic data available in background.

These OOP solve the problems associated by a given set of sensor inputs by finding the best solution for the same process request ID initiated by TMM for that particular nation. When the problem is complex, such as an imminent natural disaster or a war scenario, the KMM may optimize the solution of a particular economy-based on a complex set of "objective functions." It may also synchronize the mobilization of different combinations of offensive/defensive strategies that will minimize the expected damage or conversely enhance the maximum expected gain. All the scenarios of the zero-sum, non-zero-sum, or no sum at all game theory become programmable. Rules of game theory from many different disciplines (such as military, negotiations, management, medicine, and even ethics and religion) may be optimally combined to seek the best solution. Personal gaming strategies invented by the users of the KMM become just as programmable as the zero-sum game strategy. The knowledge processing unit for the KMM has been devised and configured by the U. S. Patent 5,465,319. The SMs and CM of the KMM perform the tasks of communicating with the knowledge centers, universities, and R&D centers that devise new knowledge algorithms, code knowledge programs, and facilitate the knowledge domain functions.

6.4.4 Functions of DBM to Monitor National Economy

Temporal databases are essential for each economic activity. Their profiles need to be stored in reasonable detail such that the entire sensing network complex responds in an intelligent, coherent, and cogent fashion. These types of databases are stored by most intelligent networks [4] of Bellcore's IN/2 (intelligent network Type 2) or AT&T's AIN (Advanced intelligent network) using the intelligent network Conceptual Model (INCM) of the ITU.

In the typical IN architecture the service control point (SCP) keeps specific data pertaining to the routing of information for IN services, such as those associated with (800, 900, 700, 411, 911, etc.) caller ID calls. The use and updating of such databases is also covered under the U. S. Patent 5,628,011.

6.4.5 Functions of KMM to Monitor National Economy

For this example, the economic development team may specify very targeted goals, such as building a communications infrastructure, main commercial centers, or centers of excellence. Such preferences are programmed into the KMM and are treated favorably in the recommendations of the machine. Likewise, the DBM would operate under enhanced sensitivity to deal with "senses" that may help or hurt the national interests. In a sense, the synergy of the control machine functions can be adjusted to suit any particular economic and political climate. Human response to such situations can only be subjective at best, and the accountability can become questionable.

Data of these categories will be stored in the DBM and the rules will be stored in the specific national interest and the industry profile. Combining these rules to optimize the "net objective function" will be governed by the KMM by blending the knowledge rules (KRs), expert system rules (ESRs), based on object recognition (OR), scenario recognition (SR), pattern recognition (PR). For this reason, the generic nature of the proposed architecture (see Figure 6.3) will be useful for a large number of applications.

6.5 SENSING NETWORK TO REPLACE MIDDLE MANAGEMENT OF A CORPORATION

The functions of a typical multinational corporation are generally networked into its own IT (information technology) platform. Its numerous operations scattered throughout the world are dynamically linked to centralized databases of resources, inventory, sales, and general executive instructions. The senses proposed in this invention scan the vital statistics of the corporation and its diversely distributed divisions. Such vital statistics for corporations have a hierarchical relation and may be linked to the organizational chart of any individual corporation. A large number of management information systems (MISs) [5], and executive information systems (EIS) [6], act as conduits of information to executives and keep them updated about signs and signals of current events, and their trends. This particular invention is a hardware platform on which the EIS may ride. Instead of being a channel switch for the flow of information, it acts as an intelligent EIS network that can process crucial information and monitor the welfare of the corporation, much like the hospital-based monitoring systems that monitor the condition of ICU patients on a second by second basis and also alert the medical staff about any impending danger.

Most of these variables are collected in a centralized data facility and they are compared to their expected values within the normal range of their statistical bounds of the current activities of the corporation. When some of the indicators exhibit sudden, inexplicable, or unforeseen variation, trends, or undesirable changes, alarm conditions are triggered. In a great majority of the cases dealing with large corporations, these responses are executive or committee decisions. But the early identification and early warning system may be triggered, and the sensing network may also monitor the progress of the condition.

6.5.1 Flowchart of Events for Routine Activity

In Figure 6.8, the Master clock initiates the scanning and monitoring activities. The process of collecting the data and feeding it back to the predictive model are shown. The model with the most updated internal parameters is used to predict the production process of the corporation for the next interval. The actual production itself is compared to the predicted production and the error is used to correct the estimation process of the corporate process.

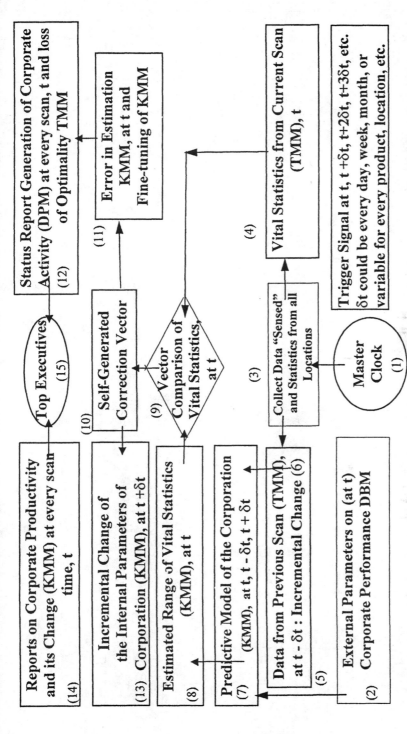

Figure 6.8 Flowchart and the sequence of events (1 through 15) for optimizing corporate functions, productivity, and learning on a continuous and cyclical basis.

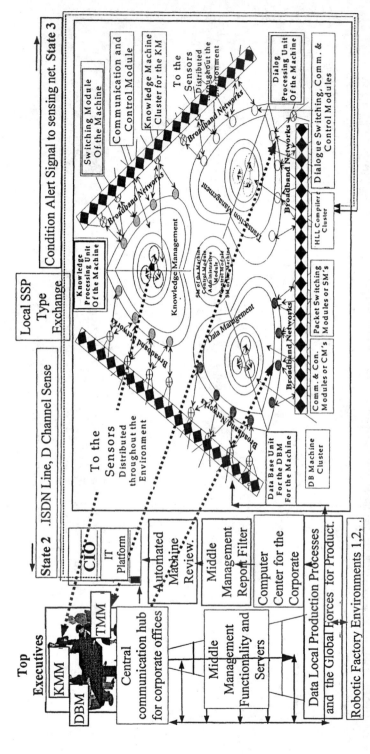

States 1, 2 and 3 are within the Figure. **State 4.** TMM receives Control Signals & passes it to KMM for typical response to be invoked and to DBM for Confirmation, Constraints, and/or Strategies. **State 5.** KMM generates appropriate recommendations re-stabilize the Corporate Parameters. TMM forwards possible alerts & special conditions. The correction mechanisms can be easily governed by the FED policies. These production policies are a combination of the Executive Adaptability and the established Expert System Rules and GEI.

Figure 6.9 Illustrations of sensing and monitoring the stability and profitability of a corporation.

In a sense, the monitoring process takes place on a continual basis and the internal adjustment of the company policies and practices are tuned to the external forces that influence the corporate goals (maximize profit, enhance international trade, capture more market share,

In Figure 6.9, we blend the sensing network in the corporate environment. The process is a dynamic adjustment of the network (and human) control to the production process to optimize any predefined goals. The feedback loop(s) and their time constant(s) are monitored to govern the stability and functionality of the human–machine production and communication environment typical of most industrial environments.

6.6 CONCLUSIONS

Sensing networks combine the roles of networks that measure, monitor, and stabilize environments. They are-based on the decision support systems that can be ported in the network environment by arranging the functions of the three switching systems or switching modules of any switching system. These networks can be scaled down to function in small businesses or they can be scaled up to function as econometric tools to monitor and stabilize the functions of corporations, hospitals, social organizations and even national economies.

Programming of the response to each scenario is sensed as a quantitative measure of the attributes of a set of programmable objects within the environment where the network is placed. The separation of the three basic components of any intelligent MIS (the dialog processor, the analytical/simulation module, and the data manager) into three interdependent programmable units or as machine clusters makes the structural arrangement of the sensing networks quite flexible and adaptive.

The novel features of this sensing and control network are summarized as follows:

1. The entire concept of the decision support system is ported in the network environment by arranging the functions of the three switching systems or switching modules of any switching system.

2. Simulating and paralleling all the functions of a national economy, a corporation, a society, or any midsized social entity by distributing the "sensors" in the environment in feasible. Regulating the "climate" of the entity is done with distributed control modules. These control modules are also distributed throughout the environment.

3. Response to each scenario is computed or derived after the sensors yield a quantitative measure of the attributes of a set of programmable objects, destabilizing the environment.

4. Separation of the three basic components— dialog processor, analytical/simulation module, and data manager— offers sophisticated programming of any intelligent MIS. Three interdependent machine clusters are thus created.

5. Adaptation of a switching system (1) to perform the functions of both a natural language processor and an ESS in cluster 1, (2) to perform functions of both a knowledge machine and an typical switching system in cluster 2, and (3) to perform the functions of both a database management system and a typical switching system in cluster 3 simplifies the implementation of the intelligent sensing and monitoring systems.

REFERENCES

[1] F. S. Hiller, G. J. Lieberman, *Introduction to Operations Research*, 7th ed., McGraw Hill, New York, 2002.

[2] J. C. Gairratano and G. D. Riley, *Expert Systems: Principles and Programming*, Course Technology, Boston, 2004. See also C. M. Bishop and C. Bishop, *Neural networks for Pattern Recognition*, Oxford University Press, Oxford, UK, 1996.

[3] S. V. Ahamed and V. B. Lawrence, Evolving network architectures for medicine, education and government usage, Pacific Telecommunications Council, Hilton Hawaiian Village, Honolulu, Jan. 14–18, 2002.

[4] IEEE, Special Edition on Intelligent Networks, *IEEE Communications Magazine* Feb. 1992. See also J. Meurling, "An intelligent network perspective." *Bellcore Symposium on intelligent networks*, Brussels, Belgium, 1988.

[5] H. C. Lucas, *Information Technology for Management*, Prentice Hall, Englewood Cliffs, NJ, 2004. See also K. C. Laudon, *Management Information Systems*, Prentice Hall, Englewood Cliffs, NJ, 2003.

[6] R. Rowley, *PeopleSoft Volume 8, A look Under the Hood of a Major Software Upgrade*, White Paper, PeopleSoft Knowledge Base, 2005. See also R. Davis, Application of meta level language to the construction, maintenance, and use of large knowledge bases" in *Knowledge-Based Systems in Artificial Intelligence*. New York: McGraw-Hill, New York, 1982.

Chapter *7*

Audio-Visual Sensing in Humans

In this chapter, we examine the special role of audio-visual command language with emphasis on the audio component. In conjunction with specialized audio-visual processor units (AVPUs) that take advantage of the high speed processing of audio-visual information, the programmable user interface provides sensory cues most suited to any group of users or a particular user. In a sense, the interface of the AVPU can be tailored to help less successful language learners improve their language learning strategies and specialized skills. Likewise, users who are aware of the interactive learning methods could be trained to become more effective users. In addition, such users can customize the displays and audio content to better suit their particular needs.

Communication is a human gift. It has strengthened the bondage and cohesion between individuals and groups. In the early days, communication was essential for survival. Signs, gestures, postures, facial expressions all play a specific role of the social accepted and recognized mores. Since then, communication skills are geared toward satisfying the needs (see Chapter 13) germane to existence in the modern society.

Human language has prevailed since the inception of society and plays a key role in survival. In the modern era of information highways and cheap bandwidth, the use of classic written language to convey ideas has become boring and intellectually unappealing to the computer users. This modern generation of users compete with the high-speed Pentium chips in their PCs "talking" to the high-speed

Internet gateways. The firing power of the neuron in the brain has taken eons to change to extract concepts from sounds. However, the mental processes of computer-generated audio-visual information has made some (very sharp) kids excel in quick retrieval of information and in their response time to any intellectual challenge.

When the communication is between human beings of similar caliber, the rate of delivery of the information and the complexity of language [1] are adjusted to prevent mutual boredom. When the communication is between a machine and a human, the conventional machine does not have any means of assessing and adjusting the rate of communication or its audio-visual linguistics to suit the human. In a sense, the rate of delivery is neither controlled nor monitored, and it is generally done at network speeds or the processing speeds of the PCs. The audio-visual output is limited to the speed capability AVPU within the PC. In this chapter we present the syntax of communication of the audio component of information from machine to human. This syntax uses the response time of the individual via the input devices to readjust the delivery time. When it is properly tuned and the reaction times are appropriately damped, the AI program can adjust its response time such that the machine picks up the audio linguistics [2] it used to communicate with any user is tunes to the capacity of the user. The AI program can also gauge the dexterity and the attention span of a user to discover any learning disabilities.

Over the last few decades, a substantially unnatural phenomenon has occurred. The digital revolution has altered the pathways of our thoughts and has intensified imagination. In a very realistic sense, the mind competes with the multi-gigahertz chip in the central processor units and with the terabits per second information highways. For humans to lead and machines to follow, we hope that the human mind continues to hold an edge over the silicon chips and the vastly connected networks. Knowledge is the forte of mind, and speed is the forte of networks.

Traditional language has resurfaced as a new language of thought and perception in the context of interacting with high-speed networks. In this rather demanding environment for mind over matter, the language needs to remain a precise and fast venue for communication between humans and machines. Audio communication stemming from vocal tract to auditory tract mode is much too slow for the super-learners. For the more sophisticated, fast, and creative activity and for the super-fast computers that verify the validity of every newly perceived ideas, a super-efficient language is necessary. At the lower levels of human interaction, the traditional audio-visual contact between the participants will keep the content and the pace of communication at a comfortable level. In the modern era, the problem is to forge a language in which the mind of the super-thinkers will be at par with the wealth of information generated by the supercomputers connected to high-speed backbone networks.

7.1 THE HUMAN EAR AS THE PREPROCESSOR

When the ears become the recipient of high-level information, the paradigm of audio linguistics starts to unfold. Audio language has its own grammar. It also has fairly precise rules of syntax and semantics so that the accuracy and content are not shrouded by fuzziness and confusion. From the human perspective, the slow pace of delivery offers enough recourse to restate the contents in other words and in other context to reinforce the concept. From a computational perspective, accuracy is preserved by the strict adherence to the syntactic rules. Both the syntactic and the semantic laws that govern the audio language govern the content and the interrelation between the "cues."

When the laws of any language become too pervasive, freedom of expression is lost. From a historical perspective, this fact is iterated many times. For example, when machine languages were introduced, only a small number of users could program the machines, even though they could force the machine to do exactly what they wanted it to do with the limits of its hardware (and binary code) capability.

When scientific and business languages were developed, the number of users started to increase, but the burden of compiling the language and of checking out its syntactic and semantic rules was passed along to the machine. The machine faithfully checked out the language, its usage in context to its ability to carry out the higher level language instructions and the associated machine language instructions both at the compilation level and at the execution level.

7.2 THE RULES OF AUDIO LANGUAGE

In order to accommodate the gifted language learners in their imaginative mode of thinking, the language of communication needs very precise syntactic and semantic rules. More than that, the language and the content must be expressed in the manner that is accurate and jitter free. To a large extent, language accommodates to the "cues," processes the audio information and communicates the contents.

In routine human–machine interaction, the imprecision of audio language is tolerated by the adaptability of the human ear. Normal and routine as this process is, it can become time intensive and a source of irritation for the sophisticated user. In the following sections, we present guidelines for the audio linguistics. The needs of all human beings are addressed first as the ground rules (Section 7.2.1) to establish any audio communication at all. The needs of the language learners are addressed in Section 7.2.2 to assure that communication is at par with their (audio) information processing capabilities. For this, two conditions are necessary: (1) the basic ground rules should be satisfied and (2) the content and its rate of delivery should challenge the limits of their perception.

7.2.1 Ground Rules

These rules validate that the format of communication is consistent with the vocal and auditory limitations of all human beings. The human physiology demands certain conditions (such as signal levels, spectral content and emphasis, signal to noise ratio (SNR)) to trigger audio contact. The basic requirement (from a teaching perspective) to even initiate any audio communication is that the wavelength of the sound should be within the specific wavelength corresponding to audible range of frequency i.e., 20 to 20,000 Hertz [3]. Requirements for the signal level and SNR also exist for the ear to comfortable detect the signal in order to continue.

7.2.2 Audio Language for the Language Learners

Emphasis here is on the content, its coherence, and its rate of delivery. The ground rules of Section 7.2.1 remain, but a superstructure of new requirements arise. The main concern is the interaction between the ear of the listener and audio cues containing the significant audio information. In contrast to the eye which carries a bi-directional mode of communication, the ear only receives audio information. As computers and AVPUs become more powerful, a new audio-visual language should evolve to intensify the audio/visual communication to match the capacities and endurance of the listener and of the beholder. If a norm is established, then we would have two individual perceptuality quotients (for audio and visual components of the language) just like we have an individual intelligence quotient. These are measures unique to the individual.

Another unique feature of the AVPU interface is that it will self-adapt to the user's learning abilities based on the input provided by the language leaner. The output produced by the AVPU for the learner will be as comprehensible as the input provided. The AVPU will, in a sense, keep learners within a zone where they are neither too bored with easy material nor perturbed with tasks that are beyond their level of understanding while simultaneously giving them activities that are slightly beyond their immediate range of abilities. The learning process will thus become more efficient as the user will be learning as much as possible in the least amount of time.

7.2.3 A Programmable Audio and Visual Menu for Every User

It is also possible to offer each user the most preferable and comfortable way to hear and to visualize all the audio-visual cues and responses. To provide such a variety of display, a software program driving the AVPU (see Figure 7.1) will become essential. For any application, the user tunes the AVPU to offer the display in a style most preferred by the user.

7.3 COMPUTER AND AUDIO-VISUAL LANGUAGES

In the computer environment, we have numerous languages, such as Machine, Fortran, Cobol, C, C+, C++, and Graphics GKS. These languages and their compilers satisfy specific application needs and reduce the burden on the user. To carry this into the audio-visual domain, we propose that the AVPU designers develop one programmable audio and visual instruction set which can be personalized to the special needs of the user. Such languages for the hearing impaired and the deaf can be specially made for client much as reading glasses or hearing aids are made for routine users. Two major consequences of such an interface are (1) more accurate delivery of the information at a pace suited to the user, and (2) reduced demand on the user's ears, eyes, and mind to process the audio information.

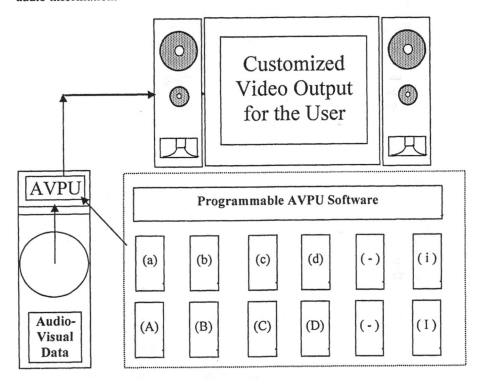

Figure 7.1 Macros (a) through (i) facilitate customization of audio-visual data e.g., data-rates & response times, amount of data displayed, type of coding and coding formats, quality and visibility of the picture. Macros (A) through (I) facilitate user-specific preferences. The suggested customization permits every user to develop a personal audio linguistic code depending on the type of application and to this extent it becomes a preferred signature for listening and interacting with the audio data.

7.4 CONCLUSIONS

Audio systems design engineers should think beyond the typical audio processor units, hearing aids, customized audio amplifiers much like visual system designers should think beyond high definition TVs. The proposed approach provides the software tools for making audio and video presentations from computer systems more user friendly, in addition to tailoring the output to the specific needs of the gifted or the marginal users. In a sense, some customization capability is desirable so that an educator can instruct the new audio-visual system to match the tastes and preferences of the users and students.

REFERENCES

[1] S. V. Ahamed and V. B. Lawrence, *The Art of Scientific Innovation: Cases of Classical Creativity*. Pearson Prentice Hall, 2004.
[2] P. Lightbown, and N. Spada, *How Languages are Learned*. Oxford: Oxford University Press, 1999.
[3] Bell Laboratories, *Transmission Systems for Communications*, Western Electric Co. 1982.

PART *III*

Human Thought and Machine Process

In order to derive information and knowledge from observations, human beings analyze, reflect, and contemplate on an individual basis. As a group, they converse, discuss, and confer. When machines process simple objects like numbers, words, and logical entities, they abide by the established laws of arithmetic, grammar, and syntactic standards. When the object becomes complex, such as arrays, matrices, complex numbers, or series, human beings deal with them on a conceptual basis, and the machines follow the more elaborate mathematical laws for processing such entities. The CPU and banks of processors handle the actual incremental processes that constitute the overall function.

When objects are generalized further and carry attributes, preferences, priorities, and relationships, the architectures of simple CPUs will not suffice. For this reason we propose knowledge processors that handle objects in close proximity and rapidly to be able to interact quickly and efficiently, reducing the execution time for each incremental knowledge process. Much like human beings would keep all pertinent information close at hand as they "weigh and consider" all the details, the KPU would keep all objects under process to carryout the actual incremental knowledge process that constitute the overall knowledge function.

In Chapter 8, the processing power of programmable machines is carried into the information domain. Incremental processes on objects yield fragments of new information. Decomposition or un-compilation of existing information leads to embedded objects. Reprocessing the embedded objects, their attributes, and their interrelationships leads to new information and newer knowledge that can be more significant than the original information and knowledge. Object processing becomes a precursor to information processing and information processing becomes a precursor to knowledge processing. A sequential and orderly chain of processes is established to turn observation and measurement of data into significant and useful knowledge.

In Chapter 9, we present detailed architectures that correspond to single process single object (SPSO), SIMO, MPSO, MPMO, and pipeline object processors. The process and object and attribute caches (akin to instruction and data caches) are embedded in architectures to make the knowledge processors efficient. It may also be possible to build knowledge processors from macrochip computers. These configurations can be derived from the architectures presented in the chapter.

In Chapter 10, wisdom machines are explored so humans to keep the machines on any given track and so machines can quickly and tirelessly explore the venues of artificial intelligence, statistical inferencing, and mathematical techniques. In a synergistic mode, humans and machine explore knowledge and deduce axioms of wisdom in a particular direction of knowledge (based on the DDS or LoC classification) with a finite level of confidence (based on prior or similar knowledge bases within the machine or around the world).

In Chapter 11, the numerous variations of knowledge communication systems (KCSs) and knowledge processing systems (KPSs) that make knowledge environments are explored. It is our contentions that knowledge environments can be customized to a specific discipline and purpose much like computer systems can be customized to any application. The degree of flexibility is much higher in knowledge environments. Intelligent Internets are proposed and examined in this chapter. Such Internets can be tailored to suit the country, the culture and taste of the communities. When used with appropriate care, the path of social progress (or decay) of any society can be measured and predicted by the intelligent agents within the Intelligent Internet configurations that are being installed now.

In Chapter 12, the framework for evaluating the wealth of knowledge is presented. The economic worth is based on the expected gain by using such knowledge in conjunction with existing knowledge. Knowledge machines (Chapter 9) that derive new knowledge based on existing knowledge bases around the country or the globe and on proprietary knowledge (such a patent, a trade secret, or management skill) will provide an initial assessment of the wealth of knowledge for the human counterpart (Chapter 10). The combined effort will provide a mathematical basis for dealing with knowledge as an economic commodity.

Chapter 8

Framework for Processing Knowledge

Knowledge processing systems process objects, their attributes, and their interrelationships. These objects are embedded in a structured body of knowledge or a module of information. Computer systems can process data (numbers, text, images, encoded voice, etc.) that has a pre-specified format and structure. Knowledge machines and knowledge processing systems (KPSs) can process objects (e.g., human beings, universities, governments, corporations, etc.) for which information is gathered. Dynamic linkages with the objects permits processing of objects that undergo modification of their characteristics and attributes over a period of time. This is a fundamental feature of knowledge processing lies in dealing with objects that may undergo a profound change as processing takes place. The nature of objects cannot be held stationary during or after the knowledge process.

A certain amount of complexity and sensitivity is inherent in processing knowledge that has objects embedded in it responding to the process of the knowledge with embedded objects. This circularity instills fuzziness at every step requiring an estimation of a confidence level in the accuracy of the steps within the knowledge process. However, the situation is manageable by assigning a numerical processor to complement the knowledge processor. This combined processing in presented later in the chapter and presented in Figure 8.14. The two processors together keep track of the objects and the extent that the process is within an acceptable confidence level.

In conventional computational processes, the objects such as numbers, logical relationships, shapes, graphical entities, and so on) are insensitive to the process on the system.

In addition to being object processors, KPSs can also change the character and nature of objects and their attributes in a systematic and consistent way to make the enhancement of information a continuous process and in response to external forces or events that bring about such changes. For example, a human being may age, fall in love, get sick, get married, get cured and so on, and the logical events that occur are tracked by the knowledge machines and the entire process is monitored, mentored, or altered by adjusting the future events to be optimal in sequence, strategy, and synergy. These KPS can be programmed to "learn" from previous events and strategies (Section 8.6.9) and can arrange strategic responses to make the foreseeable encounters[1] profitable, healthier, wealthier, wiser, and socially beneficial. Both the learning criteria and the priorities can be programmed within the KPS.

The processing of knowledge is based on *three* hierarchical steps:

1. Any complex knowledge domain function can be decomposed into a series of smaller programmable macro functions and/or executable machine instructions.
2. The solution of any complex problem has some identifiable pattern or programmable structure that follows a sequence of steps. Stated alternatively, a group of programmable macro functions can be identified and executed in an adaptive sequence to accomplish any complex knowledge domain function.
3. Every operation code (opc) in the knowledge domain is a machine-executable knowledge domain function.

Knowledge processing leads to modification and/or enhancement of concepts. Although concepts are abstract, objects, their attributes, and the measure of a given set (of objects) specify and quantify the validity of concepts about the set of objects that make up a "framework" or a body of knowledge. A given set of objects with their initial attributes form and their interrelationships constitute the input to a KPS. The output is also a set of objects and their new attributes and their interrelationships. A different or a derived set of objects with a modified or processed set of attributes results due to the "knowledge process" on the input to the KPS. Zero change in the entropy2 of a knowledge graph by is a "null" knowledge process. Knowledge processing thus monitors the interaction between objects and yields the attributes of each object from the object set during each microstep in knowledge processing. In addition, the processing is based on accepted and documented rules that keep the processes consistent, coordinated,

---

[1] The response is akin to the way a child would learn to deal with reality and society at a young age. It is also the basis for organizational learning in the corporate environment. Many internal body defense mechanisms also retain the success strategies and use them as a basis for building new strategies.

[2] It is suggested that the entropy of knowledge at any stage of he execution of a knowledge program be measured as a graph of the embedded objects, their interrelationships with themselves, and their attributes. The conceptual representation of such a graph is shown in Figure 12.1.

coherent and cogent. Furthermore, the confidence level in the microfunction and in the entire set of functions is also evaluated. At the present time, the repertoire of knowledge functions and instructions is not as highly evolved or standardized as the repertoire of the arithmetic, logical, trigonometric, complex, or even the matrix functions in the scientific domain.

Such an approach is practiced in numerical, text, image, voice, and media processing in conventional computing environments. The basic processing of numbers (integer, floating point, double precision, complex, etc.) follows rules such that the resulting numbers abide by standards for dealing with numbers in the numerical domain. Thus the process remains coordinated, coherent, cogent, and consistent. The processing of other entities such as text, image, voice, and media also follows the same procedure.

8.1 KNOWLEDGE PROCESSING ENVIRONMENTS

The tools, techniques, and methodologies for knowledge processing environments are embedded in computer science, artificial intelligence, intelligent networks, and object-oriented programming systems. The initial platform can come from any one or two of these four environments. However, it becomes necessary to import the concepts, methodologies, and techniques from other disciplines to complete an entire knowledge processing system (KPS). Like computer systems, knowledge systems have numerous flavors. Depending on the platform from where they come, and the design emphasis, the balance of the KPS functionality can be cast in flavor of knowledge processing or knowledge communication— active pursuit of wisdom or solution of mundane daily problems.

In this section, we build the KPS platform on three sets of processes: (1) data processing, (2) call processing, and (3) service provisioning.

The methodologies borrowed from these three environments become germane to the development of knowledge processing. The three sets of processes— data processing, call processing, and service provisioning offer the conceptual modules for constructing a knowledge-processing environment. The physical layers where these sets of processes are executed are the (1) central processor units or (CPUs), from the computer systems, (2) electronic switching systems or (ESSs) from the communication systems, and (3) intelligent network (IN) elements from the intelligent network systems.

The functionality of these systems is decomposed into fragments. These fragments make up the building blocks for KPSs. The physical layer of a general-purpose KPS is thus deduced. These two concurrent and convergent approaches (i.e., decomposition and deduction) yield (1) the concept for constructing a KPS and (2) the hardware (physical) platforms where such concepts may be realized. Accordingly, the three processes are presented in Sections 8.1.1 (CPU), 8.1.2 (ESS), and 8.1.3 (IN), respectively.

8.1.1 Conventional Processing From Computing Systems

In conventional processing of data, the advent of the Institute of Advanced Study (IAS) machine was a turning point [1]. The IAS architecture established the concept of stored program control that permits the main programs as well as the data to be stored in the main memory as binary bits. The format and the representation of these two entities are different. The program and data could thus occupy segments of main memory and the execution of machine instructions could take place systematically according to binary/assembly level programs. The program counter contains the address of the next executable instruction. The design of the central processor unit (CPU) has been the basis of the breakthrough. Many modifications have followed since the 1950s, but the five-step sequence (fetch-instruction, decode-instruction, operand-fetch, execute operation code or *opc*, and store interim results) in the execution of each binary instruction has not changed drastically. The main theme of the von Neumann machine is presented since some architectures of the knowledge processing unit are derived from the original von Neumann's proposals and the subsequent (SIMD, MIMD and MISD, pipeline, array processing, etc.) enhancements.

Von Neumann proposed two embodiments for early computers: EDVAC [2] (Electronic Discrete Variable Computer) and the IAS (Institute of Advanced Study at Princeton) machine. The concepts in EDVAC deployed the stored program control (SPC) concept for controlling the functions within the machine and used the binary arithmetic logic circuits within the CPU. It also used a two-level memory system for the computer: (1) a 1024 word faster memory block, and (2) a second block about twenty times this capacity (but slower), as the secondary memory. Some of these concepts are still in use today.

The IAS machine evolved amid a flurry of innovations in vacuum tube engineering and the inception of semiconductors. A rigorous systems approach to overall design of the (IAS) computer system was launched rather than assembling different gadgets. Some of the basic gating functions of logic were already implemented. The quantum jump that von Neumann proposed was in the design of the entire system. The IAS machine earned an even far greater reputation for von Neumann. The IAS computer [1] has all the features of any recent computer. The most distinguishing and innovative features of this machine are its memory size, word length, operation code (OPC) length, and addressable memory space in binary bits. The machine has 4096 addressable locations in its memory, and the word length at each location is 40 bits, holding two instructions each with one 8-bit byte for the OPC and a 12-bit address field. The machine also uses fixed bit binary format (with 40 bit representation), with the first bit denoting the sign of the number in the next 39 bits. Thus two instructions or one data word would occupy one memory location and the computer could execute one instruction after another and keep computing like any other modern machine.

To detail the IAS machine further, the memory size proposed had 4096; 40 bit words and an address space of 12 bits with 212 = 4096. The way to store a program was in 20-bit half-words with 8 bits for the operation code and 12 bits for addressing. A data format was proposed to have 40 bits and it could be lodged, moved, and shuffled around in the same memory. The size of the address bus and thus the number of bits (in the address register, AR) were both proposed to have 12 bits. Likewise, the size of the instruction bus and thus the number of bits (in the instruction register, IR) were both proposed to have 8 bits. The memory word size and thus the size of the data register (DR) and the data bus each had 40 bits. As a matter of detailed design, the IAS machine has an Instruction Buffer Register (IBR). This is seen as a necessity since the fetch cycle of the IAS machine would bring a two-word instruction (20 bits each) or one data bit (40 bits long). A great many variations of this design can be derived based on the hardware parameters, but they are peripheral to the basic concepts systematically embedded in the design of the IAS machine. The extent of the detailed design provided some boundary conditions for the users trying to solve realistic problems during the 1950s and 1960s.

The CPU architecture was equally well designed with two sections: (1) the program control unit (PCU), and (2) the arithmetic logic unit (ALU). The PCU monitors and facilitates the flow of a program and the execution of the operation code (opc). The ALU facilitates the flow of data through its data register and the execution of the arithmetic and logical instructions.

The choice of instruction sets (i.e., the collection and combination of the operation codes) for the IAS machine is optimally well selected. Five groups of instructions are used for the transfer of data, unconditional branching, conditional branching, arithmetic, and address modifications. Respectively, there are seven, two, two, eight, and two actual instructions in the five groups of instructions.

The most noteworthy contribution to the evolution of computing is the use of common memory for the storage of programs and data and the use of memory addresses and locations, while the earlier machines used separate memories to hold programs and data. In addition, the spark of genius is tightly coupled to the rigor of the invention. Both are manifest in the extremely detailed design of the IAS computer [1].

The IAS computer was not the only possible implementation. Earlier electronic analog computing was attempted in 1938. In 1946, the era of digital computing started with the ENIAC [3] machine as the Electronic Numerical Integrator and Computer. In 1950 [2] the Electronic Discrete Variable Automatic Computer, commonly known as EDVAC was developed followed by IBM's 701 calculator based on electronic tubes, magnetic disk/drum, and tape [4]. This was followed by Bell Laboratories TRADIC (for transistorized digital computer) in 1954 using 800 transistors with printed circuits and magnetic core memories. Software developments during this era were equally impressive with the assemblers, FORTRAN compilers in 1956 [5] and ALGOL compilers [6] in 1960. Digital computing was firmly established during the 1960s.

The CPU plays the dominant role [7] in executing the binary instructions in a predefined, programmed sequence. Architectures of two typical (hardwired and microprogrammable) processors are shown in Figures 8.1 and 8.2. Data address and availability are made feasible by the linking and loading functions.

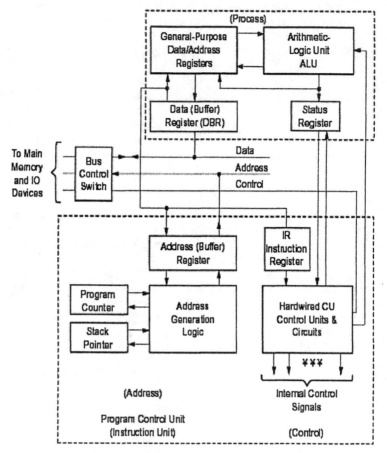

Figure 8.1 Architecture of a typical hardwired CPU with control unit(s) and circuits.

The processes involved to get the executable binary code in the machine include compiling, assembling, linking, and loading the actual program and data in the core of the computer. One process generally forgotten by computer scientists is the higher-level language programming of the problem that is to be solved. Assuming there are no errors in these processes, the machine sequentially executes these instructions, brings the program to a normal termination, and provides the user with the results being sought.

8.1.2 Call Processing from Telecommunication Systems

In telecommunication networks [8] with electronic switching, the switching system(s) [9] plays the dominant role in executing the various steps necessary for call processing. The sequence of the steps necessary for the completion of call processing is much more varied than the sequence of instructions for data processing.

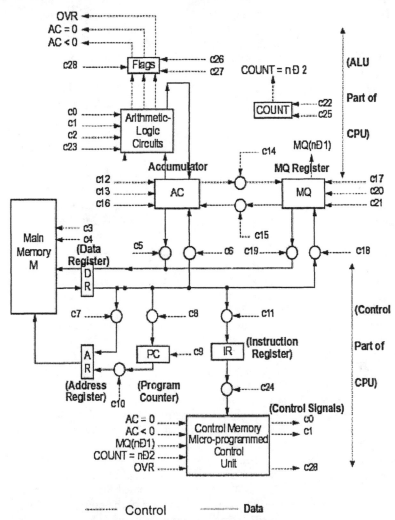

Figure 8.2 Architecture of a micro-programmable CPU with control memory (CM).

The programmability of call processing was made possible with the new concept of electronic switching systems (1ESS™, Version 1) [10] in 1965 by the Bell System in AT&T telephone networks. The 4ESS™ was introduced in 1976 with an initial capacity to receive 107,520 trunk lines and with a capability of handling 500,000 calls per hour. The key component of this toll switch is the 1A processor with busy-hour call-attempt rates of about 800,000 per hour. The switch fits in the network central office hierarchy elegantly by connecting one central office to another. Since 1994, the 1B processor [8], with about 2.4 times the throughput of the 1A processor, has been deployed, being able to implement time slice interchange capability (i.e., having the capacity to multiplex and demultiplex hundreds of voice and data channels to trunk carrier systems). The busy-hour call attempts (BHCAs) with this processor are demonstrated to be well over one million. The architecture of this switch (see Figure 8.3) accommodates a flexible switching fabrics platform. It is the switching platform that contains a space-division (different trunk termination), time multiplex switch that interconnects numerous time-slot interchange channels.

The T1 trunk (with 24 voice or data, 64-kb/s DS0 rate) [11], interfaces with the core switch fabric through a D1 channel bank. A network clock keeps the network and the switching fabric synchronized and retains the synchronization between various signal processors for in-band signaling, maintenance, and control.

This switch serves as a computerized software controlled structure that also uses solid-state switches (rather than the ferreed or the remeed switches [9] used in earlier telephone switches [10]) for making and releasing connections. The time division multiplexing feature implemented in the switches makes multiplexing and demultiplexing of numerous channels (individually or collectively) extremely easy and programmable.

Gates and logical devices, readily available in computer hardware, can be used to perform the channel switching functions in the ESS environment. In fact, the modern ESS performs very much like the modern computer system. All the hardware, software, and firmware concepts are applicable in this environment. However, it has its own operating system, its own specialized version of the office data administration system, and its own special databases. Basic call processing capability is an integral part of the high-level modular software needed to operate the switch. Service-related functions can also be provided by the switch by invoking the service circuit system shown in Figure 8.3.

Typically, at a high level of software control, the switching platform can be instructed to create a 64-kb/s (DS0) voice/data path through the switching fabric to complete a call. Call processing macros can also be implemented. The channel banks provide an interface between the switching fabric and the lines that carry network information in analogue or digital form [11]. The switch, at its highest capacity, can provide 131,072 DS0 paths to 32 expanded time-slot interchanges as shown in Figure 8.3. There is no line concentration at the edges of the switching fabrics platform. The channel banks are physically separated out to serve the individual trunks. In the older systems, one channel unit as deployed for each of the 24 (DS0) channels to constitute a data rate of 1.536 Mb/s of the D1 bank serving a T1 line rate of 1.544 Mb/s.

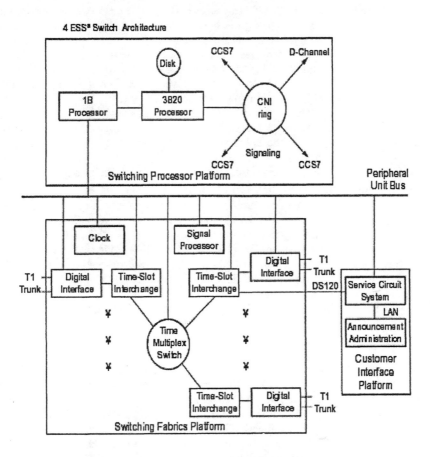

Figure 8.3 Generic architecture of an ESS tandem/toll office switch, typically the 4ESS™ switch. LAN = local area network; CNI = common network interface. IB processor is a 1994 version of call processor for the 4ESS™ switch; 3B20 processor is the complementary process for overall call control.

8.1.2.1 Earlier Configurations of Channel Banks

For the voice circuit, the channel bank provides the D to A (digital-to-analog) and A to D (analog-to-digital) conversion. The signaling bit (which informs the channel units about the signaling/non-signaling state of that particular channel) and the framing bit (to verify that the T1 frame is maintaining synchronization at the transmitter and at the receiver) are added in the channel bank. The carrier systems transfer digital data to and from the central offices. The composite train of these three signals [12] constitutes the T1 carrier digital signal. The lines terminate in the D-type channel banks. The analog-to-digital converter is included for the voice channels during the multiplexing phase for data entering the carrier systems at 1.544 Mb/s. Converse processes occur for the received signal. The digital signals after decoding, demultiplexing, and digital-to-analog conversion go to the line units for traversing to their appropriate destination via subscriber loop or other toll circuits. The filtering, the channel selection, and the multiplexing and demultiplexing of the signals from and to the various customers are carried out by channel banks. The encoding and decoding of the alternate mark inversion (AMI) code or the bipolar code to the unipolar code for the T1 carrier system also take place in the channel banks.

The D channel banks [9] work in conjunction with the digital multiplexer units. These multiplexers (in reality mux–demux units) are essential to traverse the digital hierarchy up and down the six levels in the North American digital hierarchical layers: DS0, DS1(frequently known as T1), DS1C (sometimes known as T1C), DS2 (known as T2), DS3 (also known as T3), and DS4 (occasionally known as T4). The role of the multiplexers (M1C, M12 M13, and M34) is essential to permit six layers in these digital carriers to occupy synchronized time slots in very wide band, long-distance networks. In addition, the correspondence with the CEPT or the European hierarchy is also feasible for international communication networks. The digital communication capability of the network can be enhanced by combining the D channel banks with the cross-connect switches.

8.1.2.2 D Channel Banks in the United States

Four distinct D channel facilities exist in the older central offices within the United States. First, the D1 channel bank facilitates the termination of the T1 lines and the functions associated with the 24 voice channels that they carry in the earlier usage of this digital carrier system. Different versions (D1A, D1B, D1C, and D1D) of the D1 bank perform the specific functions slightly differently. From a network point of view, these variations have insignificant effect except in the final stages of digital data or the voice distribution.

Second, the D2 facility serves 96 channels at 64 kb/s interfacing with four DS1, T1 rate signals. The output of this bank is at the DS2 rate of 6.312 Mb/s and in the DS2 format. Four DS1 rate signals at 1.544 Mb/s can be demultiplexed from this signal. A certain amount of digital interfacing is necessary to sort out the signaling bits and the framing bits before the 96 individual 64 kb/s are recovered from the composite signal. Interfacing between the four types of D1 channels and the D2 channel needs special care, since the differences in companding, channel identification, and subgroups of the individual channels can be significant.

Third, the D3 bank introduced during the early 1970s incorporated the newer technologies that evolved after the introduction of the D1A and D1B banks. The increased numbers of options, smaller size, lower costs, and improved performance all have made this channel bank a more viable option over the D1 bank in newer installation. Since all the factors relevant to the successful introduction of the newer generation of minicomputers are applicable in D channel bank design and architecture, the newer D3 channel banks are the optimal choice in central offices and switching centers. The D3 bank can process the information (digital and digitized voice) with considerably improved dependability at reduced cost and with greater flexibility. Typical of the features as far back as the 1970s are the interfacing with the common channel interoffice signaling (CCIS), capacity for diagnostics and telemetry, and master/slave relationship to internal or external clocking signals. Flexibility in repair and maintenance, fast service restoration and parallel operation of these banks are the result of the IC technology in the design of the D3 bank.

Finally, the D4 bank offers the most flexibility. The functional mode of these banks can be changed by the use of appropriate plug-in hardware modules. Designed to generate DS1, DS1-C (rate of 3.152 Mb/s), or DS2 signaling needs, the D4 channel bank can serve up to a maximum of 48 (= 2×24) DS0 or 64-kb/s channels. One T1C carrier or two T1 carriers may be interfaced to a switching system. Two of the D4 banks (in coupled pairs) can also serve one T2 carrier system. Increased power efficiency, and reduced size make these systems attractive compared to the earlier D banks. The line interface units and multiplexers need special consideration when the D4 system is to be used for terminating the carrier systems. The D4 channel bank can also be used as an interface between the carrier systems and the digroup terminal (an input/output port) for the 4ESS™. Since this switching system uses the TDM principle extensively, it is feasible to interface the D4 system directly or through multiplexers, depending on the rate of the carrier systems.

The D4 system has distinct modularity. The processing is controlled by the seven common control plug-in units. There are two additional units for power conversion and power distribution [9]. Processing in the D4 bank consists of coding and decoding sampled data to PCM pulses. Adaptability of the D4 bank permits it to function in any given type of central office. The channel bank interfaces with processors required for line and far end transmitter banks. It protects the switching office and calls in progress against transmission errors; it processes emergency conditions and invokes the appropriate response; and finally, it processes and buffers data streams when minor differences in carrier rates are detected. This last function is important and is carried out by the Syndes (synchronizer and desynchronizer) plug-in unit.

There are *four* operating modes for the D4 channel banks. First, D4 banks may be directly tied together with a T1C line at 3.154 Mb/s. Second, a D4 bank may be tied to a M1C (which multiplexes two D1 channel banks) with one T1C line. The function of the SU or the Syndes becomes necessary to maintain synchronism between the data in the D1 channel banks. Third, two D4 banks may be coupled to one D4 and two D1 banks via four T1 lines and finally, two D4 banks may be coupled to four D1 banks via two M12 multiplexers and four T1 banks. The need for the Syndes and the line interface units (LIUs) is also shown.

It is important to note the use of digital computer-oriented hardware and software features in the D4 channel bank development. The four designs of channel banks (D1 through D4) are also affected by the IC technology and architectural enhancements. This effect also persists in the last two generations of computers.

The concept of specialized hardware is more dominant in the telecommunications environment than in computer technology, where program control and microprocessors accomplish more generic and more modular functions.

The switching systems may be distributed, and the cooperative role of the various switching systems may become essential. This aspect is not unlike the controlled distribution of the processing in multiprocessor/multicomputer systems. Fortunately, with the evolution of the common channel interoffice signaling system (CCISS) and the standardization of its protocol [10], distributed call processing is not a problem in most modern communication networks. It is interesting to note that the level of programming in the switching systems is at a higher level than the programming level of the third generation programming languages. This jump relieves the programmers of the switching systems from the more mundane functions of generating the executable code for the three modules (communication, switching, and administrative).

8.1.2.3 Later Configurations with High-Speed LANs

Whereas the D channel banks were deployed in telephone exchanges in the past, the modern trend is to provide the ATM backbone switches on the high-speed SONET rings. The explosive growth of high-speed LANs, MANs, and WANs has dwarfed the traditional channel bank configurations; even though they serve the vintage circuit-switched telephone offices. High-speed LANs have altered the modern exchange operations, capabilities, and interfaces. Cell switched ATM LANs and 802.x packet switched, premises networks are now integrated with wide area public and private networks. In response to the ever-increasing deployment of these high-speed LANs, numerous strategies integrate on-premises networks (circuit-switched, ATM and packet-switched) into a converging network environment. The key component that has brought about the convergence is the enterprise communications server (ECS) within the circuit-switched network environment to interface with the other three (ATM, packet, and wide area private and public) networks. Physical network connectivity and internetworking are now a reality with ECS and multimedia communication exchange (MMCX) facilities.

Two types of connectivity are feasible: (1) endpoint connectivity and (2) server connectivity}. In the endpoint connectivity, ECS interfaces with the circuit-switched applications such as ISDN (H.320) and the analog (H.324) multimedia endpoints. Typical applications that constitute this circuit-switched domain are the analog, digital, ISDN, and wireless telephones. The ECS also interfaces with ATM (H.321) and/or LAN (H.323) and propriety multimedia endpoints. Most of the wide area public and private networks provide the PSTN telephone and wireless services, ISDN (H.320), analog (H.324), and point to point (H.323) multimedia endpoints.

Server connectivity opens a new dimension in communication over convergent networks. When these four networks— circuit-switched (CS), packet-switched (PS), ATM and WANs— are supported by server facilities, then additional services become readily available. For example, the CS network with the ECS can facilitate message, fax, conference, system management, wireless call center, directory, call management and feature services. The ATM LANs can facilitate file, print, mail, network management, groupware, message, and conference services. The PS network can also provide file, print, mail, application, network management, group, and Web services. The WANs will also facilitate mail, fax, message, conference, groupware, and Web services.

The role of the ECS is to elegantly integrate most of the older D channel functions in the classic telephony environment with the current high-speed packet network functions. Both private channel and public WANs get included in bridging to and from premises and corporate and proprietary networks. The standardized interfaces and the associated protocol play a decisive role in facilitating the convergent network environment.

The major interconnect between the packet (PS) and ATM networks and the ECS has one or more digital carrier interfaces such as the T1 lines. These lines span between the multimedia communication exchange (in the WAN environment) and the ECS in the basic rate ISDN (BRISDN) interfaces, DCP (digital communication protocol) analog, and so on, (or the CS) networks. A physical interconnect arrangement of this nature permits the integration of PR-ISDN, analog (via simple network management protocol or SNMP) with the extraneous public or private network. The Internet connections are provided via the packet or the ATM networks. Thus, all CS users who deploy similar ECS capability can get interconnected over the backbone networks.

The connectivity between ATM and CS (telephone and multimedia) networks is accomplished over *two* possible (PPN and EPN) configurations. In the first case, the processor port network (PPN) accomplishes system control functions, line and network protocol interface, and service functions for the legacy line and network interfaces on the CS side and provides the ATM user-to-network interface on the ATM side. In the second case, the expansion port network (EPN) also provides the line, network protocol interface, and service functions for the legacy line, network interfaces on the CS side, and provides the ATM user-to-network interface on the ATM side. Thus, a single PPN can accomplish the system control functions for numerous EPNs.

Typical SONET rings at OC-3/OC-12 rates are connected to the ATM backbone switch as shown in Figure 8.4. This ATM backbone carries the PPN and (numerous) EPN interfaces providing legacy T1/E1 interfaces. Group video and other CS services are thus provided for the typical users of the telephone/video type of services over the SONET rings at OC-3/OC-12 rates.

With appropriate interfacing networks (PPNs and EPNs), most of communication functions arc accomplished in closet sized facilities for corporate communication services and campus environments. Inter-exchange carrier networks take the T1 and E1 signaling and the line data everywhere. However, inverse multiplexing for ATM becomes necessary to multiplex numerous T1/E1 lines up to the OC-3c rate that can be tied into the ATM backbone switch thus facilitating a free flow of data to and from the high-speed SONET optical rings.

Intercity networks can also deploy the T1/E1 lines over the inter exchange carriers. The ATM enterprise switches permit direct interconnections between data LANs, ATM backbone switches, and other ATM switches via a call management system and PPN interface makes computer telephony integration entirely feasible within the high-speed networks. An overview of the interconnection of SONET and CS systems is shown in Figure 8.4.

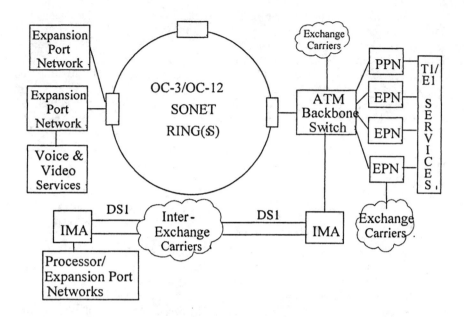

Figure 8.4 Typical internetworking for the evolving convergent networks. PPN, processor port network; EPN, expansion port network; IMA, inverse multiplex for ATM; T1 = DS1 facilities for North American digital hierarchy at 1.544 Mb/s; E1 = Equivalent CEPT hierarchy at 2.048 Mb/s.

The high-speed digital facilities also deploy the add-drop multiplexers (or ADMs) to provide interconnectivity between networks and an overview is shown in Figure 8.5. At a high level, the ATM functionality has been embedded within a fixed size link-layer (i.e., the OSI layer six, data link-layer) entity. This link-layer entity is the "cell" and the size of this fixed length entity is 53 octets (bytes). There are 5 octets for the header block and 48 octets for the payload (or the data to be transported.) Similar to the header of most packet networks, the ATM cell header carries information unique to the nature of data, its functionality, disassemble and reassemble of cells, and their payloads. The typical ATM cell format for the user–network interface and network–network interface is accepted throughout the world. The information contained in the header is encoded to conform to the functions within the ATM sublayers. This advantage in the integrated digital loop carrier [10] environment (deployed in older legacy systems) removes the need for DS1 (1.544 Mb/s) realignment, thus offering these carrier systems better utilization of the switching facilities. Distributed virtual terminal (VT) cross connections, bulk transport/switching of channelized and unchannelized, synchronous or asynchronous DS1s (mapped asynchronously), unchannelized bit-synchronous DS1 transport, DS0 circuit-switched traffic and IDLC byte synchronous mapping are feasible in the floating VT modes of the remote digital terminal or RDTs (see Figure 8.5). The technology and the implementation of the SONET and legacy network interconnections is discussed in detail in [Ref. 8.10]

Three general architectures for SONET transport systems providing point to point DS1, DS1 & DS3 to STS-1 & STS-3, and combinations of *OC-n*, using add-drop multiplexers (ADMs), and digital cross connect switches (DCS) are presented in Chapter 3. Modern digital networks do not deploy the classic architecture of circuit-switched telephone networks. The future networks are likely to all digital in nature providing conventional telephone services via fast packet technology presented in Chapter 3. However, to provide the older telephone networks and the evolving networks to coexist and provide a smooth transition to growing presence of SONET/ATM networks, network architects have evolved architectures depicted in Figures 8.3 and 8.4 with the capability to interface with legacy DS1 and DS3 carriers and also the future all digital networks. The key component in the interconnection is the add-drop-multiplexer (ADM) that provides signal conversion and maintains the synchronization between the various networks.

Whereas the D-channel banks were deployed in telephone exchanges over an extended period (through late 1980s), the modern trend is to provide ATM backbone switches and/or add-drop multiplexers on the high-speed SONET rings. In Figure 8.4, the architectures with ATM Backbone switches, and in Figure 8.5 the ADMs configurations are shown are shown.

8.1.3 Knowledge Service Processing from Intelligent Networks

In intelligent networks,[3] [10, 13] the service provisioning of special services becomes a cooperative role of at least five (SSP, SCP, STP, SCE and IP) interdependent computerized systems. Architecture of a typical intelligent network (Bellcore IN/2) is shown in Figure 8.6. These five systems and their relevance to the KPS are discussed next.

---

[3] Bellcore's IN/2, AT&T's UISN, and the generalized AIN type.

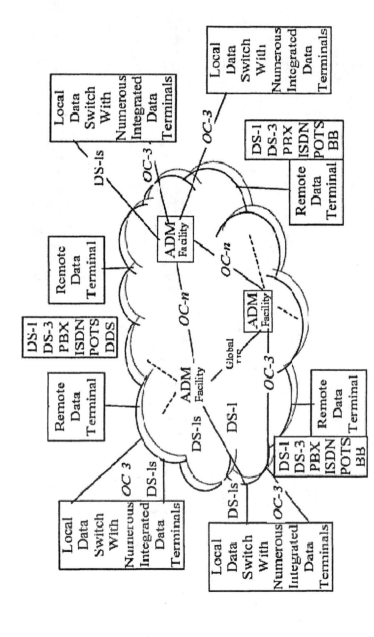

Figure 8.5 Configuration for SONET optical carriers (OCs) and other digital carriers (such as DS1, DS3) and other services (such as POTS, ISDN, and BB) ADM, add drop multiplexers; BB, base band services; CAL, customer access line; ISDN, integrated services digital network; PBX, private branch exchange; POTS, plain old telephone services; DS1, DS3 and DS4, digital signals 1, 3, and 4.

8.1.3.1 Knowledge Switching Points (KSPs) for Knowledge Environments

Consider the service switching points or the SSPs. These are modern switching systems with added capability to recognize the service trigger condition, such as 800, 911, and 700 numbers. The functionality of the SSPs assumes the role of knowledge switching points KSPs in the knowledge environments. Telecommunication services are provided by the network owners and it became necessary for switch designers to make central office switching point aware of the 800, 900, 911 etc., calls. Knowledge services are generally provided over the Internet and special knowledge base owners become aware of special conditions when knowledge services (such as downloading a book, a file, or a patent) are required. To this extent, the traditional role of the SSPs in the intelligent network environment is transformed in the knowledge environment. The equivalent function of the SSP will be the knowledge service point at the ISP locations in the Internet. However, an intelligent peripheral added on the ISP computer network may suffice. The extent and nature of the knowledge service will dictate whether both KSP and ISP are needed or an ISP and an IP will provide the additional knowledge services at the ISP node of the Internet backbone. Some of the intricacies are discussed in Section 8.3.1

8.1.3.2 Knowledge Transfer Points (KTP) for Knowledge Environments

Consider the service transfer points, (STPs). These act as relay points accepting the X.25 packetized information to and from SSPs and service control points (SCPs). The functionality of the STP becomes analogous to the role of KTPs in the knowledge environment. To this day, we still do not have the full-fledged knowledge networks that are comparable to the telecommunication services provisioning networks. It can be foreseen that such networks are likely to become prevalent in the Internet domain. The role of KTPs starts to become obvious when an address translation to a knowledge base location becomes necessary based on the subject matter content of the user queries. To this extent, the traditional role of the STPs as they exist in the intelligent network environment (where service addresses are retrieved from the SCPs) is not crucial to the operation of the knowledge environment. The exchange of information between the various modules (KSPs, KCPs, KMSs, KIPs, etc.) of the knowledge network environment needs a well-designed format and protocol.

8.1.3.3 Knowledge Control Points (KCP) for Knowledge Environments

Consider the service control points, the SCPs. These are extensive databases with information that is well managed, replaceable, and capable of being updated. This makes the queried information available to the SSP as it completes a service or a service process that it is performing at that instant of time and as the provisioning of the service progresses.

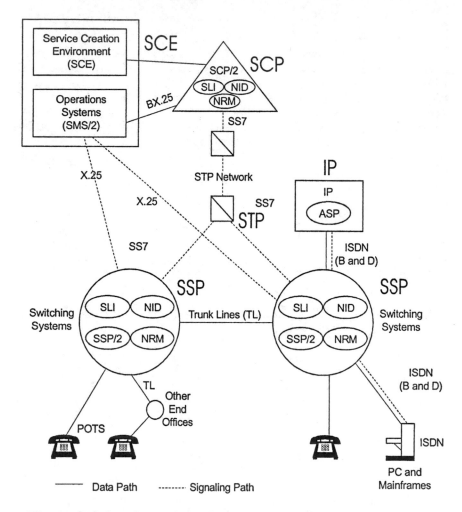

Figure 8.6 Configuration of a typical intelligent network (IN/2 proposed by Bellcore) for offering new services in the telephone network.

In the KPS environment, the storage of information that can be updated becomes necessary so that it acts as a quick reference to the various categories of subjects and the type of derived information about these subjects. The databases in the SCP become equivalent to a "knowledge profile" for the information contained in the knowledge module(s). This provides the machine with the capability to steer any "knowledge process" through the vast maze of information contained in the knowledge module(s).

8.1.3.4 Knowledge Services Control Points (KSCPs) for Knowledge Environments

The switching of knowledge bases to match the subject matter of the user queries with the knowledge profile of the different knowledge bases is done by the KCP. A second level of match is necessary for the knowledge service providers to provide customized services for clients. When knowledge service provisioning need sophistication, the client profile and knowledge base profile are also matched. This level of match is proposed for medical service providers (MSPs) as discussed in Chapter 3 and presented in Figure 3.7. In this case, the ailments of the patients are matched to the services provided by the physicians.

In the KSCP module owned by the knowledge service providers, the knowledge bases are presorted by their attributes. The IP address will also carry an array of attribute numbers. The first level match is done based on the DDS or LoC subject match between the client's queries and the DDS or LoC classification of the knowledge base. At the next level, the user profile or attributes (such as profession, specialty, geographical area, hobbies), is matched with the contents of the knowledge bases on a local, regional, and global basis on a concurrent or timeline basis.

To some extent, organ donor agencies, matrimonial bureaus, and targeted marketing firms, practice the second- and third-level matching functions. However, if the first-level KCP function is followed by automated second-level, third-level, and so on, of KSCP functions in *any* knowledge domain, then the search for optimal solutions to any problem can be totally automated and expedited.

The notion of treating clients and global knowledge bases as "objects" permits a new and extensive variety of services that can be provided by knowledge service providers without human intervention. Installed temporary linkages are automatically uninstalled at the end of the service provided. The feature is implemented in compilers of the higher-level languages to be executed on conventional computer systems. Loading and linking of library functions, routines and macros is a necessary function. In the intelligent network environment, the CLASS II services (such as caller ID, call forwarding, call blocking) are programmed once and automatically continued until they are stopped. In the knowledge environment, the knowledge services are provided by compiling (parsing, lexical scan, syntactic analysis, etc.) the query and then generating a real-time service function based on the functional modules proposed in the INCM model. The INCM model for knowledge domain services does not exist.

The combined function of the KCP and the KSCP is depicted in Figure 8.7. The queries from the clients have *two* components.

The first component deals with the subject (noun equivalent) matter such as DDS and/or LoC classification of the subject matter, type of knowledge, and the context (situation/setting equivalent) part (what, where, when, how, and their combination; origin, syntactic, semantic, contextual; etc.) of service requested. The second component deals with the attributes of the client requesting the query. The KCP provides the IP address of the knowledge base by translating the DDS or the LoC classification into an IP address. The attributes of the knowledge bases and the "context" part of the query are matched to find the best fit of one or more suitable KB addresses.   At the third level of match, the client profile (e.g., profession, specialty, geographical area, hobbies) is matched to the knowledge profile (professional society match, subspecialty publications, geographical preference, hobby information, etc.) of the entire set of the KB attributes.

The architecture shown in Figure 8.7 is scalable to add newer services and also for billing for the knowledge services provided by the ISP. This becomes an attractive feature for distance learning system, global universities, medical services providers, and any other service providers.

8.1.3.5 Knowledge Enablement Environments (KEE)

Consider the service creation environment (SCE). This facility provides service vendors with the programming and debugging environment to try out new service concepts or ideas. In this environment, new services may be "programmed" into the network by "assembling" a new service as a program of various well-defined functional modules. These modules correspond to the macros or routines in conventional computer environments. In a sense, the programming of services into these service-oriented networks is like assembly level programming of an engineering problem. The functional modules provide the bridge for service providers to perform valid network sub-functions consistent with the service they are providing. Such service logic programs (SLPs) are usually interpreted by a service logic interpreter (SLI), which may be housed in a SSP, SCP, or an intelligent peripheral (IP) and may act in conjunction with a local network information database (NID). Hence, the new software interface can be tailored for these types of networks.

In the KPS environment, the knowledge (creation) enablement environment} KEE plays a definite role. Consider the situation when a new inference machine becomes available from the knowledge engineers.

The data for deriving the new inferences can be resident in the knowledge module(s), but the newer implications (obtained from the new inference engine) may not be available to the users unless a group of applications engineers decide to program the new inference engine in the KPS. For this reason, the SCE equivalent in the KPS is seen as an environment that provides new induction(s), inferences, derivations, and so on from old knowledge or that generates new conclusions (germane to the problem at hand) from old data.

8.1.3.6 Intelligent Peripherals for Knowledge Environments

Finally, consider the intelligent peripherals or IPs. These computerized devices may exist as a network node with SS7 (signaling system No. 7) connectivity to a SSP via their own trunk lines or may have an ISDN primary-rate capability. In many cases, the IP may be only bridged to the communication channel for the duration of the call. Because it is a programmable device, we expect that the knowledge intelligent peripherals (KIPs) of the future will provide a great variety of services.

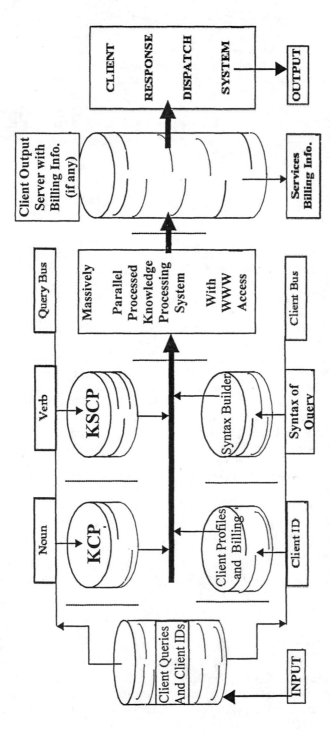

Figure 8.7 Role of combined knowledge control point (KCP) and knowledge services control point (KSCP) for providing intelligent Internet services to clients. The provision for Internet billing is incorporated within the architecture shown. The KCP and KSCP maintenance systems (equivalent to SMS in intelligent network architectures) become essential for updating and enhancing the Internet services.

In the knowledge machine or knowledge processing systems (KPSs) environment, small variations of the response from the KPS are possible to customize derivations specific to the group user needs. For example, a class of pharmaceutical students may be interested in the clinical properties of certain plants, whereas a group of botany students may be interested in the habitat and climatic conditions. Thus, the knowledge IP equivalent (KIP), becomes instrumental in providing the knowledge service back to the user in a fashion, style, and format tailored to the user's needs.

8.2 PLATFORM OF KPS FROM COMPUTER SYSTEMS AND ESS

The existing systems and elements in the previous section are designed to perform specific tasks germane to the system (computer, telecommunication, or intelligent networks). None of these three systems perform functions specific to the processing of knowledge and knowledge engineering. The most flexible hardware platform for the KPS comes from the computer architectures capable of tackling problems of medium- to high-level complexity. A typical configuration of a generic computer of medium complexity is depicted in Figure 8.8. The software layers on a general purpose HW architecture provide the flexibility in the applications domain.

One of the more flexible hardware platforms for intelligent networks is the Bellcore IN/2 platform. The functionality of and programmability of IN/2 are documented and proven. We do not propose the INCM model, even though it is more flexible, because of its lack of total acceptability around the world. One of the more flexible platforms for the switch is the typical 4ESS™ (tandem and regional central offices) and the 5ESS™ generic platform for most types of massive switching applications. The platform for the standard 4ESS™ is shown in Figure 8.9. The enhanced version for the deployment of the switch for knowledge systems is shown in Figure 8.10.

The IN/2, Intelligence platform coupled with 4ESS™ (or especially 5ESS™) capability has the good potential for massive global knowledge processing systems and knowledge machines. The basic fabric of the switching system may be modified to incorporate functions pertinent to the processing of information and the evolution of knowledge by logic and reason. In this section, we propose four major building blocks (CM, AM, SM and the KM) for the KPS with each one being a programmable system.

8.2.1 Communication Module (CM) of KPS

Consider the communication function in the context of the KPS. The capacity to control the communication between all the processes, as they relate to one function upon one piece of information, is not unlike the concentration of the human mind on the solution of one problem at one time. Even though numerous problems are solved simultaneously in the KPS, the communication between the knowledge module(s) and the subprocesses (or tasks within that process) becomes a necessary function of the communication module in the KPS. These subprocesses typically pertain to a specific problem or become generic to a group of function in a given discipline.

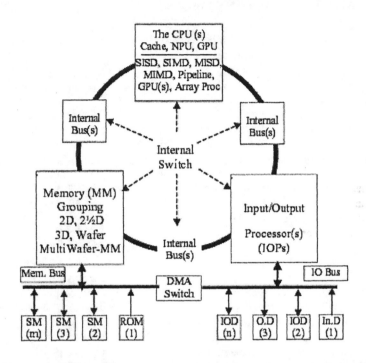

Figure 8.8 Configuration of a general purpose computer of medium complexity. CPU, central processor unit; NPU, numerical processor unit; SISD, single instruction single data CPU architectural design, SIMD, single instruction multiple data CPU architectural design; MISD, multiple instruction single data CPU architectural design; MIMD, multiple instruction multiple data CPU architectural design; GPU, graphics processor unit; D, dimension used for main memory architectures; MM, main memory; ROM, read only memory, SM, secondary memories; IOP, input/output processors; IOD, input/output devices.

At the current state of technology, the collation or assembling of the processes in the solution of knowledge-based problems is a human (rather than machine) function. Standard languages and their compilers do not exist to verify the validity or the relevance of the problem in the context of the knowledge bases accessible to the KPS. The syntax is loosely defined, and the communication module of the KPS may only assemble processes according to the amount of information stored in the knowledge bases. The relationships in the hierarchy of this knowledge must also be considered. Functions of this nature that control and guide the communications germane to the various processes become the task of the communication module.

8.2.2 Switching Module (SM) of the KPS

Consider the switching module in the context of the KPS. Figure 8.8 characterizes the structure of a basic computing machine of the last five decades. Here, the communication facility is minimal and is provided by one or more bus structures. Timesharing of the digital highway (the main bus) connecting the memory, the CPU, and the I/O devices was most common. It was well known that bus access was the bottleneck. Architectures have evolved through the multiple-instruction multiple-data (MIMD) systems, and an additional component (the switching matrix) has been added. The multibus architecture has also significantly eased the congestion and data flow in conventional computers. The configuration in Figure 8.8 depicts a multiplicity of architectures, ranging from the simple MIMD to the specialized array processors, matrices, and transform machines.

Computer systems can have massive parallelism — about 3000 microprocessors are deployed in a mid-sized 5ESS™. A high-level architecture of such a system employed over the last two decades is shown in Figure 8.9. The administrative module provides administration, maintenance, and resource allocation on a system-wide basis. The communication module provides a centralized hardware platform for distributing and switching the voice or digital data, control information, and synchronization signals. One or numerous switching modules provide localized switching and control functions. They also serve to interface subscribers and interexchange circuits and trunks. Traditionally, these switches do not monitor or interact with the subscriber data as it is flowing through the switches.

When such a switching system has the additional burden of processing the contents of the data streams, plus the voice signals, and then relating the information in an educational, beneficial, and creative manner, then the need for a knowledge module[4] (KM) arises. This module channels information based on forward and backward pointers to other pieces of knowledge. The processing is geared toward scanning information, associating it with previous information by pattern matching, and lexically scanning objects that make up the current information. Inferences and evaluations may be accrued in the system to give the machine a knowledge profile of the student (educational networks), or a medical profile of a patient (medical networks), or a financial profile of the client (financial networks). Such machines handle both the call processing inherent to

---

[4] For more detailed information on educational networks, refer to Chapter 15 of [10], "Architectural Consideration in the Design of Network-Based Educational Systems." For more detailed information on medical networks, refer to Chapter 16 of [10], "Integrated Medical Systems." For more detailed information on intelligent home networks, refer to Chapter 18 of [10], "Home Intelligence: Personal Computer-Based Intelligent Home Networks."

communication networks and the knowledge processing inherent to intelligent networks.

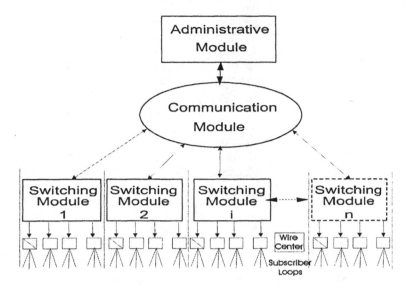

Figure 8.9 Simplest version of a typical switching system in telephone networks.

These machines blend the two types of intelligence and respond with an adaptability to reach the right source and destination with appropriate addressing (physical/logical). They also process what they convey over the channels by compiling and composing the appropriate answer for the user in a logical and consistent fashion.

The capacity to select from, and switch between, large quantities of information from the knowledge bases shown in Figure 8.10, as it becomes relevant to the process of solving a problem, is one of the basic traits of a perceptive mind. The communication module handles the perception, but the switching module handles the contextual switching. The switching module permits the access and direct memory access (DMA) capability between the knowledge bases and the memory necessary for executing the process of problem solving. Furthermore, consider the situation where the local knowledge bases become inadequate, but the KPS has access to other bases on the network. In this case, the function of switching to and from the source of relevant information (wherever it may be) also becomes the function of the switching module of the KPS.

In the electronic switching systems, the switching module functions in a completely duplex mode and any subscriber can be the caller or the called party. In the KPS environment, the switching function is much more confined.

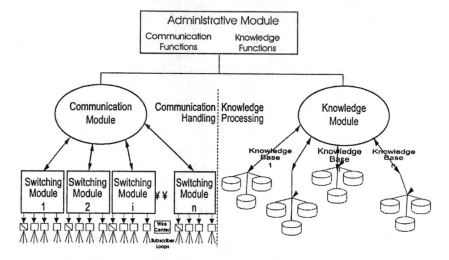

Figure 8.10 Simplest version of an enhanced electronic switching system for content/object based processing.

The processes within a task or a problem have standard and more limited functions. Also, the number of active channels is limited to the number of multiple tasks that the KPS is programmed to handle (in its operating system). The number of addressable and distinct files in the knowledge module can be enormous. Hence, we see that the switching module may be far less complicated than the corresponding module in the telecommunication environment. In fact, from the communication module side, the switch can look like a private branch exchange (PBX) with a limited number of incoming lines. And, from the knowledge module side, the switch can look like a hierarchical star. Each branch is encoded with the successive number of the Dewey Decimal System/Library of Congress subject catalog.

8.2.3 Administrative Module (AM) of the KPS

Consider the administrative module (AM) in the context of the KPS. The KPS may be equipped to handle numerous problems at the same time and operate as a multiprocessor, multitasked system. The housekeeping functions for operating the KPS are handled by the administrative module. Resource allocation, real-time multitasking, and scheduling of tasks in the processing of knowledge become the key functions of the KPS. In many computing systems, the same hardware and memory is partitioned to perform the operating (administrative) system functions and the computing. However, in the KPS, it may be desirable to have the administrative module isolated from the other three modules. This approach is used in telecommunication switching systems to handle the operations, engineering, and maintenance functions distinctly from the network and communication functions.

8.2.4 Knowledge Module (KM) of the KPS

Finally, consider the knowledge module in the context of the KPS. Specially designed, object-oriented programming tools and languages have started to emerge. These tools process entities and establish relationships between them. Forward and backward linkages may be established. Learning machines discover latent causes and effects. Inference engines that seek new relationships between various objects can be codified. Inductive, associative, inferential, and deductive reasoning is programmable, especially with fourth-generation object-oriented programming languages. Since the exact interdependence of this module with the other three modules needs to be optimally configured, we group a class of knowledge processing functions and charge the system (hardware, software, and firmware) housed in the knowledge module with handling some of these functions, depending on the processing power within the module. The remaining knowledge functions are managed in the administrative module. The partitioning of these functions depends on the relative sizes of active memories and processing capabilities of both the administrative and the knowledge modules in the KPS.

It is futile to expect any one of the basic computer architectures to perform optimally the communication, switching, administrative, and knowledge functions germane to the entire cross section of problems that the KPS is expected to handle and manage. Partitioning the system based on its subfunctions leads to the first architectural arrangement. If response time from the machine is to be low, then the balance between the administrative, communication, switching, and knowledge functions needs to be consistent with the average blend of these functions for typical problems that these machines are expected to solve. This aspect of balancing the functional requirements with the relative speed and power of the processors, memories, I/O, switches, and buses also exists in the conventional computer architecture.

8.3 ROLE OF THE KNOWLEDGE PROCESSOR UNIT (KPU)

The architecture of the KPS depends heavily on modules used in either single knowledge processor environments or multiple knowledge processor environments. The design and architecture of the KPU also become critical for the execution of knowledge processes and the execution of binary knowledge instructions. Next, we present the implications of such environments on the KPS architecture.

8.3.1 Processor Environments

We illustrate the configuration of a typical KPU in Figure 8.11. A single processor KPS is shown. The organization of object and instruction registers and caches is presented for a knowledge processor capable of handling each knowledge binary level instruction. From an implementation perspective, the configuration depicted in Figure 8.12 with multiple processors, is more desirable. Additional architectures handling, for example, single-process single-object (SPSO) systems are discussed in Chapter 9.

In the single-processor environments, the communication module and the switching module can be combined into one hardware unit. In the extreme case, it can look like a disk controller that channels the access to certain track-sector addresses when certain subject matters are being pursued. This simplification is feasible because of the reduced requirements placed on the switching module. This module provides a communication path during the allocated time interval between the only processor (or memory) in the administrative module (accomplishing only one individual knowledge-oriented "task") and the knowledge module. To some extent, the simplification is comparable to shrinking an entire switching system to a single-party PBX. All the switching takes place on the knowledge module side.

The role of the administrative module remains the same. This unit does the compilation of the steps invoked in the solution of the knowledge-oriented problems. We can also foresee that the steps invoked in the solution of intricate problems will depend on the results of the prior steps, with a "compile-as-you-go" approach being necessary. Sometimes communication engineers also use this approach during the implementation of network algorithms (such as path routing, use-dependent path assignment, fault tolerance, etc.)

In addition, this administrative unit has the support of a disk-resident "knowledge profile" of the knowledge module. In essence, the profile provides an initial checkpoint when the users invoke operations pertaining to the knowledge stored in the knowledge module(s). It is somewhat similar to the card-file index that older libraries once maintained to facilitate users in finding the exact location of the textbook containing the subject matter they were pursuing. The profile also verifies that users ask questions of the system that are consistent with the knowledge contained therein.

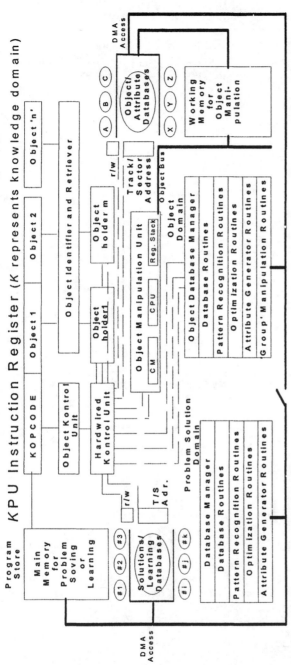

KPU Instruction Register (K represents knowledge domain)

Program Store

Main Memory for Problem Soving or Learning

Solutions/ Learning Databases

KOPCODE   Object 1   Object 2   Object 'n'

Object Kontrol Unit

Object Identifier and Retriever

Hardwired Kontrol Unit

Object holder1   Object holder m

r/w

Track/ Sector Address

Object Manipulation Unit
CM   CPU   Reg. Stack

Object Bus

Object/ Attribute Databases
A   B   C
X   Y   Z

Working Memory for Object Mani- pulation

DMA Access

Problem Solution Domain

Database Manager
Database Routines
Pattern Recognition Routines
Optimization Routines
Attribute Generator Routines

Object Domain

Object Database Manager
Database Routines
Pattern Recognition Routines
Optimization Routines
Attribute Generator Routines
'Group' Manipulation Routines

#1   #2   #3

#i   #j   #k

r/w

T/S Adr.

DMA Access

Switch 1, Open for Execution Mode for Knowledge Domain Problem Soving; Closed for Learning Mode. The Learning programs 'process' the existing solutions and are able to extract Objects, Groups, Relationships, Opcodes, Group Operators, Modules, Strategies, Optimization Methodologies from existing solutions and store them in Object and corresponding databases. The architecture permits the KPU to catalog a new object in relation to existing objects and generate/modify existing pointers to and from new objects.

Figure 8.11 The KPU architecture based on the knowledge instructions being able to process objects embedded in a given body of knowledge or module of information. The unit can serve to execute knowledge instruction to alter the flavor of information or it can learn the attributes of objects and interrelations.

For example, it identifies what action[5] may be applicable to what subject matter (such as, polymers, petrochemicals, Maxwell's equations, and satellite systems). In a simplistic case where the machine is geared toward high school teaching, the profile can be preshrunk from the more elaborate profile of the machine that is oriented to a graduate research center where the subject matters are processed.

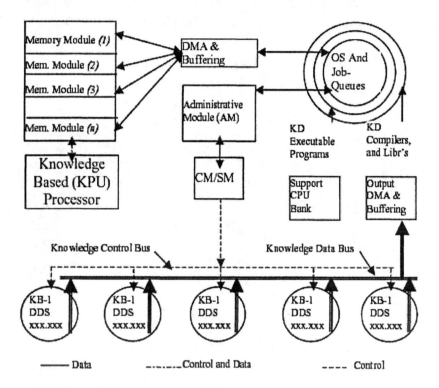

Figure 8.12 Architecture of a Simple Knowledge Processing System with a Single Processor based on the ESS Platform. CM, communication module; SM, switching module; KB, knowledge base.

This customizing of the disk-resident profile is similar to the editing of the table of contents for textbooks covering the same subject for high school or college use. From the perspective of the computer software designers, this customizing is similar to the selection of different compilers for different hardware modules (e.g.,

---

[5] Such as, "what," "how," "when," "where," and "why"; and "what-if," "how-where," "what-when," "then-what" combinations; and also analogize, predict, and simulative combinations. The generalization of this relational concept is presented in Section 10.8.1.

co-processors, array processors, and A to D converters) or software library routines (e.g., trigonometric, hyperbolic, or exponential).

The administrative module may also be invoked to modify and manage the knowledge bases (a function similar to the function of the service management systems in intelligent networks) and the corresponding updating of the knowledge profile. Additional security checks of the access and updating of users, plus their use of the knowledge modules, may also be incorporated here. The compiled and executable task-oriented program may also be made disk-resident or handled in the main memory of the KPS. These routine housekeeping functions are also managed by the AM.

8.3.2 Multiprocessor-Based Environments

Figure 8.13 depicts the four basic modules of the KPS and one of the ways of interconnecting the components. In this arrangement, the switching module (SM) is located between the communication module (CM) and the knowledge bases (KBs). If the various KBs are arranged in some well-defined hierarchical format (such as the Dewey Decimal System, [14] or the Library of Congress classification [15]), then a network configuration (star, bus, ring, dropped bus, etc.) can be used to retain the access methodology in and out of vast databases. Under these conditions, one BISDN (broadband ISDN) link or one access point may be provided between the SM and the KBs.

With its resident operating system, the administrative module (AM) dynamically allocates resources, monitors performance, and prevents deadlocks. The operating and accounting functions of the KPS are confined to the AM. The engineering and maintenance functions are also performed by the AM, such as updating of the KBs, altering the structure and hierarchy of the stored information in the KBs, and modifying the compiling and interpreting processes of the CM for its many tasks. The knowledge rings (KRs) depicted in Figure 8.13 are organized according to the disciplines based on the Dewey Decimal System (DDS) or the Library of Congress (LoC) classification[6].

The AM is also responsible for the execution of each subprocess in the problem solution or query handling by the KPS. In a sense, it becomes the hardware host for the KPS "operating system." We foresee that the AM is a parallel processor system, assuming the KPS is going to be shared between a large numbers of user tasks. Since any processor (in the AM) can access any information in the knowledge base, the switching module will switch between the processors of the AM and the read/write capability of the KBs. The quantity of information and its directionality

---

[6] To be consistent with the memory addresses in 2½D, 3D, and multiple wafer memories, the numbering of the "knowledge rings" can also be binary. The need for external address translation is eliminated and the linkers/loaders can generate the executable code for any given machine. To some extent the scalability of the knowledge bases may be sacrificed because of the limited binary addresses available. This is truly a matter of detailed design of the entire knowledge processing system.

may now be identified. In the great majority of cases, the KBs share large chunks of information with the memory modules of the AM.

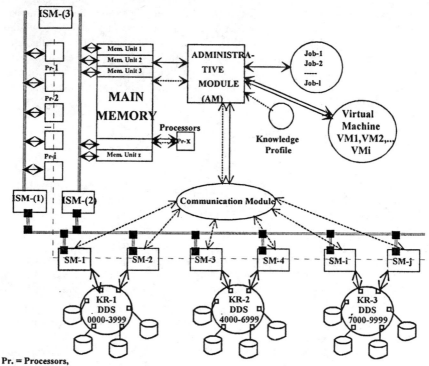

Pr. = Processors,
ISM = Internal Switching Module, SM-i = Typical ESS Switching Module, KR = Knowledge Rings,
– – Control Signals, ══════ Internal Bus Structures,   DDS = Dewey Decimal/Library of Congress System

Figure 8.13 Typical architecture of the knowledge processing system with multiple processors, independent communication module, and switching modules. The "knowledge rings" are partitioned by the subject matter; however, any numbering or addressing system is appropriate. SM, switching module; KR, knowledge ring; KPS, knowledge processing systems or machines. Secondary cache memories (not shown) can also be used to "fetch" object groups from the knowledge bases during processing. Detailed diagrams for parallel and pipeline types of knowledge processor are presented in Chapter 9.

After performing the knowledge functions (e.g., pattern recognition, matching, forward/backward pointing, and inference drawing), the contents of the memory may be discarded. Whereas the interrogation may be only one instruction long, the returned information can be a large block. Thus, the modality of communication between the AM and the KBs can be made asymmetrical, and for this reason a serial query port and DMA for burst-back appears to be a feasible implementation. The SM may also be designed for the low/high rates of data movement.

In traditional electronic switching systems, the SM is located between the trunks (and subscriber links) from one geographic area to the next. In the KPS, the SM accesses the various processors (and memory modules) in the AM and the extensive fragments of knowledge in the KBs. The addressing in the KPS is done by the classification of knowledge and its hierarchy. Typically, the addressing is done via the area codes and exchange numbers. The address translation and seek time is dramatically reduced by the addressing of the subject material, on which the knowledge function is being performed, by its decimal code. The same code thus provides the exact address of that specific piece of knowledge in the KBs.

The bus capacity and memory allocation algorithms affect the performance. Since the amount of information necessary to perform knowledge functions can be vastly different depending on the topic and the type of operation, fixed memory allocation algorithms are soon likely to become constrictive. However, if the operating system has sufficient flexibility (such as dynamic memory allocation), the active memory size is made sufficient to handle complex KPS functions (such as, pattern recognition, cross-compare, find analogies, find supplementary knowledge, and scan other sciences). Then the switching module can provide access between all the AM processors and the file segments in the KBs in real time, and an architecture for intelligent knowledge processing may be generated.

The difficulties that we foresee in this methodology occur when all the users need or access the same information, for example, a class of students handling the solution to a given problem during the laboratory hour. Queue management techniques still lead to long response times. Another instance of such a situation arises if all the users are using memory-intensive subprocesses at the same time. Even though we have listed such functions as "bottlenecks," they are also encountered in all computer systems. Smart operating systems handle contingencies of this nature.

8.4 ALTERNATE ARCHITECTURES

The amount of storage and the extent of processing in the KBs are negotiable. All storage and no processing lead to massive transfers of data from the KBs to the memory modules of the AM whose processor performs all the knowledge-oriented functions. Because this capacity is evidently enough, no storage in KBs eliminates the need for them and also SMs. However, as a compromise, with some processing in the KBs, rudimentary knowledge functions may be attempted and only relevant information may be forwarded to the AM, thus reducing the channel access time and wait time. The intelligent networks have solved this problem partially by having some processing in the SCP. The problems of achieving such a balance are far more delicate in the KPS, and detailed study is desirable.

The resolution and accuracy of the knowledge profile is also a subject of optimal design of the KPS. At one extreme, with perfect granularity in the knowledge profile, the compile time of the problem is longer, but users get the exact response from the KBs. On the other hand, incomplete or imperfect representation of the KBs in the profile will prevent legitimate use of the KBs or cause execution time errors from the KBs. However, we view these issues as secondary but related to the design of the particular KPS.

8.5 A MULTIFUNCTIONAL INTELLIGENT NETWORK

The interplay between the technological frontiers of two dramatic forces (communicating and computing) is important in society. We integrate these trends and investigate telecommunication, computing, and intelligent systems and networks of the last decade. We refocus these technological developments into an integrated Internet, telecommunication and knowledge-processing arena.

8.5.1 Integrated Design Approach

Proper integration of these two forceful disciplines (computation and communication) during the early stages of design and development for a new breed of specialized networks to serve educational, medical, and government needs can save developing countries enormous expense and delays in introducing new features and services. Such features are intended to serve the educational and social needs of the host countries. In a peaceful global environment, human, technological, and financial resources can be focused on the needs of individual countries, creating progress in new directions and forming new links between technologies of the twenty-first century and the most basic of human needs: the need to communicate with anybody, at any time, and at any place.

These goals are in the realm of modern communication systems, which rely heavily on the embedded computer-based switching systems. These objectives have been greatly achieved in the Western Hemisphere. However, we contend that, with very little effort, peoples of the underdeveloped countries stand to benefit substantially and to satisfy their educational and medical needs. Such functions should be viewed as necessary features of the evolving intelligent Internet. Some of the subnetworks become specialized to suit the geographic, demographic, sociocultural (including educational and medical), and communication needs of a particular country.

When the backbone network is not in place, the enhanced signaling functions to perform the specially tailored network features can be built into it. When the backbone network is in place, the enhancements are incorporated into the existing network. Compatibility and integration of the old and new functions become the crucial problem for the network designers. However, with the stored program control of the switching systems presently embedded in most networks, the problem is manageable and has fairly standard approaches to the solution. From the perspective of the network specialist, creating new links between technology and social needs is not a problem but simply a project.

Such network specialty is quite unique and rare. For this reason, the problem for societies and countries is that of coordination between designing the architecture of these specialized networks and implementing them in final form. If the entire project is entrusted to the commercial network designers, the price can become excessively high. Conversely, an ill-designed network brings in a host of follow-up problems. In fact, some networks become a roadblock to the optimized backbone network(s) for any nation. The two extreme approaches to the problem have become important enough for most countries to establish departments or ministries of telecommunications at the highest governmental levels. This is where the problem needs to be addressed.

8.5.2 Proposed Architecture

The platform for the specialized telecommunication services is that of basic intelligent networks [10, 13]. These basic intelligent networks are firmly established in most developed countries and serve specific needs of the network, such as the 800, 900, 700, 911, alternate billing service (ABS), and custom local area special service (CLASS™) type of services. The introduction of the automatic number identification (ANI) and common channel interoffice signaling 6 (CCIS6) triggered these newer services for residential and business customers. A variety of such services and the intelligent networks that perform such services are discussed in [10].

The enhancement of these basic intelligent networks depends on the user needs and character of application, such as knowledge processing for educational, medical, or electronic government. In Figure 8.13, we show the architectural modifications for the basic intelligent network that is designed to serve educational needs and distance learning. The network, can also support and medical services. When the demand of a specific application is not large, the separation of these networks (educational and medical) may be logical rather than physical. Within the same basic building blocks of the network, logical software barriers are introduced so that the same hardware units can serve the traditional applications.

8.6 CERTAINTY IN KNOWLEDGE PROCESSING

In the general realm of rationality, reality and certainty are exclusive. Rationality is based on prior knowledge, reality is based on observation, and certainty is based on flawless and precise inference. Total synergy and congruence of all three are almost impossible. When reality happens, certainty is a conjecture at best. The starkness of reality shapes the notion of certainty. The pursuit of total rationality based on firm reasoning eradicates the basis for absolute certainty. Without being sidetracked into philosophic issues, it appears reasonably accurate (though not totally certain) to say, that in most cases, reality and certainty play an illusive game of interdependence. Reality happens every moment as a successive frame from the previous frames of reality. The capacity to take reasoning to every microsecond and picosecond instants is not matched by our capacity to take measurements of every parameter that gave rise to the events embedded in reality. If it is assumed that nothing incomprehensible has occurred between the instants at which the measurements are taken, then we can assume that reality is a continuous process.

Certainty of a chain of discrete events calls for the fragmentation of time intervals after which the observations of reality are made. Rationality starts to broaden with the assumption that any given parameter at the end of an interval of time $\delta(t)$ is represented by the series of approximations based on the rate of change $(\partial/\partial t$, a velocity term$)$ of parameter (from previous observation), rate of change of the velocity of any parameter $(\partial^2/\partial t^2$, an acceleration term$)$, and so on. The limit of numerical accuracy of the processors terminates the series. In the knowledge domain there is no reason to be sure of the termination of the series. This leads to a continuity of "objects" in the knowledge domain. Knowledge and numbers start to become significantly different. Knowledge is a continuous and life-like process. Numbers have a beginning and an end even though zero remains zero and infinity remains infinity. Knowledge also has no beginning and no end but it carries us along with it, thus leading to many zeros before zero and more infinities past infinity.

Without becoming helpless about the nature of knowledge, we can set a limit to the granularity of knowledge by our (machine's) capacity to comprehend the difference between two bodies of knowledge. In the past, we limited our granularity of numbers by the accuracy of the arithmetic units (AUs). By restricting the accuracy of the numbers to be within reasonable bounds, computing has become a viable technology. Knowledge processing in its infancy is much like numerical processing on a 20-bit integer and floating point number CPU from the von Neumann machine [1].

Two concepts, not necessary in the von Neumann machine were probability and confidence limits. In the 1940s numerical processing (even though numbers have numerous representations) had reached a level of universal acceptability. The uncertainty of numbers (π, Euler's constant e, μ_o, ε_o, etc.) and computed parameters (area of a circle, absolute velocity of light, value of epsilon, etc.) were avoided. In the knowledge domain, it is necessary to address these issues with reasonable (though not absolute) certainty. The concept that every knowledge processor needs a supporting numerical processor [10] was introduced in 1996. The NPU supports an incremental knowledge process with an estimation of the confidence in that increment of the knowledge process. Prior experience (accumulated in knowledge bases around the Web) sheds some light on the objects and extent of processing that is "reasonable" in the knowledge domain.

8.6.1 Knowledge Processing System Based on Uncertainty

We begin with three basic notions:

1. Processing of knowledge gives rise to concepts.
2. Events based on reality augment and enhance or refute such concepts.
3. No concept, or its modifications, is absolute.

Within this framework, we build a dynamic processing system based on the knowledge available, aware of current events that are modifying the knowledge base with some finite probability that its result is accurate. In a sense, the system is limited by its capacity to store and retrieve information (knowledge), its ability to (intelligently) process information, and its ability to compute the confidence level with which it has generated the previous step(s). We fall back on database facilities for storing and retrieving information, on artificial intelligence (AI) techniques for processing, and on basic probability ("fuzzy" set) theory to numerically compute, or at least estimate, the accuracy of its discrete steps. Although any computer system with a complex *software* structure can serve as a knowledge machine, the architecture of the knowledge processing system (KPS) stores and retrieves information; processes, learns, and modifies the information; and finally computes or estimates the confidence level in each step or procedure. These are a subset of macroinstructions to the rather elaborate *hardware*. The KPS processes in two dimensions: the knowledge domain (which generates incremental and integrated conclusions) and the numeric domain (which generates confidence level), confirming the earlier stated notion that the conclusion reached so far is not undeniable.

8.6.2 Basic Building Blocks

The hardware for KPS has *three* distinct components:

1. A sophisticated database management unit (DBU) that provides storage and retrieval service functions.
2. A knowledge-processing unit (KPU) that performs knowledge domain functions.
3. A numerical processing unit (NPU) that provides an estimation of the probability that the last step and the combined probability of all the steps thus far are accurate.

8.6.2.1 Database Unit (DBU)

Database management systems [16, 17] have evolved in most computing environments as a software hierarchy and a generic storage capability. In the communication environment, database facilities have a distinctive flavor. Both hardware and software designs are modified to suit specialized needs especially in the service control point (SCP) applications. Typically, the SCP (see Figure 2.12) architecture has a front-end interface to permit protocol conversion and the decoding of the arriving SS7 packets and other nonstandard, yet acceptable, protocol structure. A bank of central processing units (CPUs) is used and every access is associated with a (call-processing) identifier or task. Once the exact nature of the function is determined, the command is dispatched to a large disk drive store/retrieve system. The data itself is accessed via the data bus and brought to and from the memory. The direct memory access (DMA) quickens the control and access process considerably. Once the databases are logically or physically separated, then the access can be further increased by accessing each field of a data query in parallel. Hence, the databases that store interrelated blocks of information (objects) and their numerous fields (attributes) can be designed to function quickly and inexpensively as memory modules.

In large databases with constant updating and modification, the database itself needs management [18, 19]. Macro database functions require localized CPU support, in which the CPU is dedicated to the database functions, much like the input/output (I/O) processor is dedicated to the I/O functions. In addition, the disk buffering generally needs its own local memory. This memory is dedicated to the database functions, much like the cache memory is dedicated to CPU functions.

In the context of the KPS environment, the database facility is designed to function independently and remotely. Because the KPS has its own architectural identity as a stand alone component, it is termed a database processing unit (DBU). This unit executes its own stand-alone functions based on the assembly-level commands it receives from the centralized KPU, which is dedicated to the knowledge functions.

8.6.2.2 Knowledge Processor Unit (KPU)

The functions of the KPU are at a level higher than those of the arithmetic logic unit or the CPU. Whereas the CPU is dedicated to localized control functions via its control unit and to local arithmetic logic functions via its arithmetic logic unit (ALU), the KPU is dedicated to the execution of assembly-level knowledge instructions that accomplish a stand-alone "binary knowledge instruction." We use the term *KPU* to distinguish it from the CPU, yet to convey the important role that the CPU plays in traditional computer systems. In addition, the traditional binary instruction has two essential parts: its operation code (opcode in plain old computer systems) and its operand(s). In the KPS, we extend this structure into two parts: its *k*nowledge-based *op*eration code (called kopcode), and the object(s) upon which that kop is going to be performed.

The KPU is driven by its assembly-level instructions. These instructions have a knowledge-based operation code and object operands. The kopcode can be a real and distinct knowledge domain (KD) function or a pseudo-kopcode. The real kopcode performs a KD function on objects. Hence, every real assembly-level instruction in the KPU accomplishes incremental KD functions on or from the operands. In a sense, KPU functions are related to the manipulation of objects and/or their interpretation in light of a given set of "events" from the definition or the context of the problem. In light of the previous information stored in its databases, the KPU categorizes, matches, infers, extends, analogizes, and recognizes the events based on the situation or the problem the machine is trying to solve.

8.6.2.3 Numerical Processor Unit (NPU)

During knowledge processing, the problem definition can be vague and the scope of the solution can be considerably wider than the confines of data processing. Concepts, their enhancement, and their modification can be error ridden, reluctant, and uncertain processes. The reluctance and hesitation in inference generation can be characterized by the certainty in the solution to the problem. At the global level, this "certainty" reaches 100 percent in data processing and can only be less than 100 percent in knowledge processing. If a machine has to solve a knowledge-based problem with 100 percent certainty, then it fails, unless the problem is completely defined and is strictly logical and/or numeric. Even under these conditions, truncation and approximations cause inaccuracies.

To reach some solution, though suboptimal and less-than-perfect, we propose that a confidence level on the KPS be imposed that is greater than the lowest acceptable level for solution of similar problems. The machine then strives to present a solution or all feasible solutions that exceed this preset level. This constant checking to meet the confidence level is strictly a numeric process and is confined to conventional computers with its dedicated CPU, memory, and supporting programs. When the machine is processing knowledge, every step of its functionality is assigned a confidence level and the cumulative level of confidence in the collectivity of such steps is updated at every macro knowledge instruction handled by the KPU. The machine thus generates KD result(s) and gives a numeric indication of how confident it is about those result(s). At the two extremes, it can generate an infinitely large number of irrelevant "solutions" with zero confidence level or no solution at all with an absolute 100 percent confidence level. If this number is preset at some reasonable level, the machine can yield or strive to yield acceptable solution(s). The acceptable solution has to generally satisfy additional economic criteria such as minimum expected cost and risk, or maximum expected profit, sales, and so on. Thus the machine offers numerous solutions with composite traits and consequences rather than a single solution.

In most conventional CPU environments, the solution generated has a 100 percent confidence level, since there is no ambiguity in the execution of operation code at binary level and the "solution" is no more than a compiler-generated assembly of binary level instructions. Thus the von Neumann computers are simplistic devices that sequentially execute the instructions associated with the program. But more than that, the "results" are numeric/logical outputs of the arithmetic logic unit obtained from program execution!

8.6.3 Block Diagram of the KPS

Derivation of new knowledge by processing the earlier knowledge differs from generating a new number from previous numbers. The arithmetic and logical functions on operands need to be substituted by learning and deducing relationships between objects. Once a deduction or inference is drawn, it has to be appropriately recycled in other contexts. Furthermore, there is no certainty that the inference is correct and that it has been correctly used in the new context. For this reason, a number is assigned indicating the confidence level to each of the two subprocesses. Hence, the arithmetic unit of the knowledge processor keeps track of the level of certainty of that knowledge step. In fact, every knowledge instruction has two associated numbers: the confidence levels in the particular learning/deduction itself; and the application of the learned/deduced knowledge to the objects being processed. Both these numbers (obtained from input, previous experience, or the best estimate thereof) lead to the numerical "product" of the confidence level of that knowledge instruction.

The basic three basic functionalities are depicted in Figure 8.14. The intertwined character of any microfunction in the KD is decomposed into (1) the database (cache, memory, or network) access of participating objects, (2) the object manipulation, and (3) the computation of the certainty (the "fuzzy" or not-so-sure functions) of the instruction to be executed. However, incremental certainty will not suffice, since the final "conclusion(s)/solution(s)" are achieved after a large number of such incremental knowledge instructions, and the arithmetic unit is forced to track the dependability of all steps that have yielded new knowledge up until this particular step. The weakest link in any chain of rationality or reasoning leading to a subconclusion or the final conclusion can readily be identified and reinforced if necessary.

8.6.4 KPU Execute Cycle

In a conventional computer, the CPU cycle follows four major functions: fetch, decode, execute, and store the result(s) [7] as a binary number for later use. Every CPU cycle executes one complete (or a part of the) machine instruction, and the program execution consists of executing each machine instruction in the loader-generated sequence after compilation and assembly of the program. The hardware's sequential (parallel or pipeline, if possible) execution of machine language instructions yields results, as the programmer had intended.

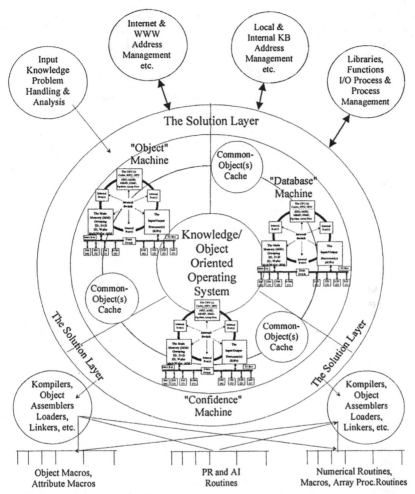

Figure 8.14 Core functions, operating system, and extraneous software of the knowledge processing system. Note that the "numeric" functions, math routines, compilers, and so on with a normal operating system constitute the plain computing environment. Komplition refers to compilation of knowledge domain programs.

Within the very narrow context of the KPS, we define the basis for information as:
1. Objects, their classifications, and interrelationships.
2. Attributes, their classifications, and interrelationships.
3. Events, their classifications, and interrelationships.

In processing information to derive an increment of knowledge, knowledge domain functions are executed. Such functions could range from the execution of one kopcode, macros of assembly-level instructions of kopcodes, to a whole sequence of higher-level knowledge programs. To facilitate the operation of the KPU, a hierarchy of kopcodes can be developed. Special consideration is required to address the following:

a. Numerous types of kopcodes, their functions, and interdependence.
b. Pseudo-kop (defined in the same context as pseudo-op) codes, their KD assembler instructions, and their interdependence.
c. Knowledge macros, their macro KD functions, and interdependence.

Since information does have a predefined boundary, recursion of both objects and procedures is well accepted and welcome. By the same token, new information (knowledge) is an incremental deduction from old information as defined earlier. Information can neither be created (deduced) nor destroyed (deleted) with absolute certainty. The corollary to this statement is that all information as we know it has a discrete level of confidence (unity to zero) in the KD from which it was derived. This last statement is quite important, since two differently primed KPSs can yield different results to the same query, much in the same way that two different individuals (objects) can respond differently to the same situation (event) or two different communication systems can respond differently to the same dialed number and so on.

In the context of the KPS, the KPU cycles have two distinct modes: *solving* a problem at hand and *learning* new knowledge. Implementing the knowledge learned in order to accomplish knowledge in a new context becomes part of the first mode. In both modes, the KPU follows the sequence identical to the CPU sequence: fetch, decode, execute, and store the new knowledge learned for later use. In the solution mode, the kopcodes are distinct from the kopcodes in the learning mode. In the learning mode, kopcodes extract information from the object operand(s) of a knowledge instruction. In the solution mode, kopcodes obtain new knowledge resulting from the instruction upon the object operand(s). In a sense, the two opcodes perform reciprocal functions but do so in the knowledge domain. Typically, the result of the execution of a "solution" kopcode is new knowledge and a number representing a confidence level in the validity of the kop instruction. New information (or knowledge) and a number both result. Procedural learning is also possible. In this case, the next logical step (a microkop or macrokop) in a sequence of knowledge instructions is learned from the previous, similar, or a pattern of previous instructions.

Figure 8.15 depicts a simple overview of the KPS functions. The system executes knowledge programs and learns from outside and from its own programs. In its "solve" mode (see the left side "solve" block in Figure 8.15), the system is solving a knowledge problem; that is, it ascertains the effects of a set of "events" upon a group of objects. At the "start," when a specific problem is posed, the natural language processor identifies the objects and their attributes participating in a set of event(s). If a goal-directed problem is posed, it identifies the subgoals, builds a "solution tree," and forces a series of knowledge macros (from past experience in the databases). A tentative code is thus generated. The code is recycled iteratively through the execute loop until it satisfies a group of acceptance criteria and the machine terminates the program.

In its "learn" mode (see the right side "learn" block in Figure 8.15), the system retrieves programs and objects from its "solutions and results" databases. It learns strategy and rules from its programs. It also learns about objects, their attributes, and the relationships between them. This information is recycled for future use in solving similar problems with different objects or different problems with similar objects. What the system cannot do is solve totally new problems with totally new objects. In an introspection mode (not shown in the Figure 8.15), it studies the problems and their solutions to determine ripple effects and implications, implied relationships, solution similarities, and preferred strategies. This higher level of learning may or may not be desirable in the machine since it is possible for the machine to acquire a collective wisdom of many users and become "smarter" than any single user, unless the human learning process becomes "smarter" than that of the machine.

8.6.4.1 "Fetch" of KPU Instruction

The "fetch" part of the CPU primarily fetches the binary instructions from the main memory. The entire instruction is brought into the CPU. A secondary "fetch" occurs when the operands have a specific (direct or indirect) address. In this case, the operands are brought into the CPU. Operand(s) may exist in a cache, memory, or secondary memory. Generally, the "page replace" operating system routine is used to bring a new segment from the disk. Single-word instruction and multiple-word instructions are brought into the CPU via the different buses during one or multiple clock cycles. The hardware architecture and the operating system utilities play a crucial role in assuring that the right operand is in the right register before the arithmetic logic unit (ALU) or the I/O function takes place.

The "fetch" part of the KPU instruction fetches knowledge instructions into the KPU from the main memory. A secondary "fetch" occurs when the objects have a specific (direct or indirect) address. In this case, the objects and their attributes are brought into the KPU. Object(s) may exist in an object cache, object memory, or one or numerous object databases. The DBU (described in Section 8.6.5) is activated if a long indirect (i.e., indirect address database) operand fetch is necessary. Object(s) may exist in the close environment of the machine, a network environment, or even in remote WWW bases. The fetch of the KPU performs a dual fetch: object(s) are brought into the object handler of the KPU, and corresponding number(s) are brought in the number and logic handler in synchronism[7].

---

[7] True synchronism is not essential. The object processor and the number processor may perform in synchrony at a process level, at a procedure level, at a subroutine level, at a program level, or even at an application level. The entire solution of any knowledge program can also be performed in two distinct phases: (1) the object-phase and (2) the number-phase. The object-phase of the KPU corresponds to the concept level thought process of a human being and the number-phase corresponds to the validity check of each of the steps in the previous object-phase. In reality, a (engineering) solution needs multiple iterations with feed back between the two phases to reach (1) an innovative

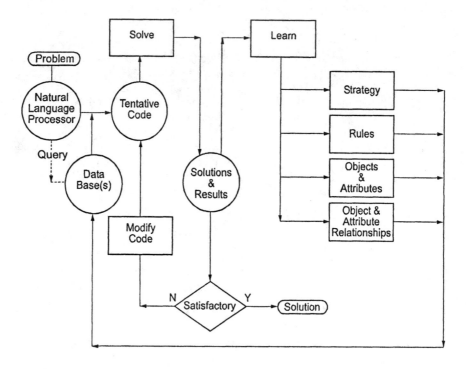

Figure 8.15 A simple arrangement for a KPS with a problem solution mode and learning mode.

They both perform a micro knowledge function during the execution of the kopcode. Object cache memories need to be constructed by either the unique functional specifications, as a specialized VLSI RAM, or even as a cache RAM organized as a data structure or table of numbers. We envision this object cache RAM table organized into numerous columns: the object identifier number, the antecedent, the precedent objects, the numerous contextual objects to which that particular object has been linked in the past (with numerical values of confidence in association with this particular object), and the object attributes (with the numerical value of the confidence level relating to the object with that attribute). For future

---

solution and (2) a viable and practical solution. This iterative approach to the solution is feasible by the innermost software layers that surround the hardware execution of knowledge processes. To some extent, the creative mental processes can be imposed on the machine in the search for (engineering) creativity.

discussion, let us define the environment in which the object exists in the KPU as the object environment[8] (OE) of the object.

Main object memories also need to be constructed. However, the content of this memory is already specified in the discussion of the object cache memories. The main memory thus has the OEs of all the objects participating in the knowledge processing of a knowledge program. The object databases supplement the object memories. Networks furnish specialized OEs from distant object databases or logically joined knowledge processing environments. For example, the records (OE) of a suspected individual may be exchanged between the FBI and the CIA object (suspected individual identification number) databases through a crime network. In another example, the poetic compositions (OEs) of two authors (objects) with similar predisposition (attributes of the objects from the OEs) may be exchanged through a literary network. Such functions now fall under the realm of the execution (see Section 8.6.4.4) of the kopcodes of the knowledge processor.

8.6.4.2 The "Decode" of KPU Instruction

The "decode" part of the CPU decodes the opcode depending on the type of instruction. Essentially, there are numerous types of opcodes (typically, RR, RX, RS, SI, and SS) [20]. These truly modular (operand-independent) micro arithmetic/logic functions constitute the basis of numerical processing. For example, just for addition (the A sub-function of the arithmetic unit), the typical instructions consist of A, AR, AH, AP, AD, ADR, AE, AW, and AU for the fixed point, packed decimal, and floating point operands [20]. Other such instructions exist for logical functions. In microprogrammed CPUs, an additional level of flexibility is provided in decoding the opcode through the microcode in the control memory. Each opcode is a series of microcode instructions that offer the programmer a finer control on the function of the CPU. In the RISC machines, a few selected, but very rapidly executable instructions enhance the CPU speeds but the decoding concept remains the same.

The "decode" part of the KPU decodes the kopcode depending on its mode (learning and/or solving) and its type. This leads to numerous variations of *kopcodes* (L/S times number of types). A set of very specific kopcodes needs to be defined and evolved for each subfunction within the two modes of the KPU functions. At this stage of the KPU development, we envision the kopcodes to be as rudimentary as the opcodes of the von Neumann machine in comparison to the opcodes of the IBM 360/370 [21] computers.

8.6.4.3 "Object Operand Fetch" of KPU Instruction

The "fetch operands" in the CPU of a traditional computer environment are straightforward because the programmer specifies the operands. The memory location of where the operands are stored is determined at the linking and loading

---

[8] The object environment is inclusive of the attributes of the object, its setting (Section 8.1.3.4) and the "context" (Section 10.8.1) in which the object is being processed.

time. Prior to the execution of the instruction, all the operands (or their addresses) are in the appropriate registers within the CPU.

The "object operand fetch" part of the knowledge instruction involves bringing all the other objects or their attributes that may by involved or get affected by the particular kop instruction. The user may specify all other objects or the *K*ompiler may estimate objects that will affect the execution of the current kop. The attribute fetch may be done at the time of "object operand fetch" or may be done at a later time by selecting which attributes need to be fetched. If the object cache is large, then fetching the attributes will reduce the cycle time of the KPU. In cases where the objects are very encompassing (e.g., corporations, governments, universities), the attribute fetch may select which of the attributes may influence or get influenced by the particular kop instruction.

8.6.4.4 The "Execute" of KPU Instruction

During the execution of the opcode in the hardwired CPUs, the control signals are dispatched to appropriate segments of CPU, memory, I/O devices, and so on. In the microprogrammed CPUs, the control signals are provided by the execution of the microcode, which is itself an expansion of the opcode. Each opcode is a series of microcoded instructions that offer the programmer a finer control of the CPUs function at the execution level. In the RISC machines, a few select, but very rapidly executable instructions enhance the CPU speeds, but the execution consists of dispatching the control signals to the appropriate hardware to accomplish a microscopic step in the execution of the opcode.

During the execution of the kopcode in the KPU, the mode of its function (learn/solve) is identified. Next, the type of kopcode is identified and appropriate attributes within the OE are processed. The OE of that object is enhanced and updated in context to that particular knowledge microfunction. Hence every kop modifies the OE of the operand object(s). For example, if an individual (object) is in the process of robbing a bank (a knowledge function program), then the individual's level of performance (the object's OE) is modified in that context. On a positive note, if Shakespeare (object) was writing *West Side Story* (a knowledge function program) then his writing style (OE) would be modified by *West Side Story* setting (the OE of the second object operand).

The learning mode permits the KPU to enhance or enrich the OE of objects. The starting OE of objects would be the basic knowledge level about the objects in general. Typically, this OE for the participating objects in a tabular form or database can be read from dictionaries, databases, technical papers, or specialized documents describing objects. Classification of object attributes can be as painful as writing a special dictionary for each category of knowledge domain functions.

Historically, this has been done by human beings for other human beings as libraries of special disciplines. It has also been done by human beings for computer users as reference tables and databases. The OE for the most frequently referenced objects is far more demanding to write, update, and manage. However, even this has been done in a limited sense in telecommunications environments. For example, the service control point (SCP) maintains a limited amount of customer (object) information (environment) and network information (OE of the network) in its databases. It is maintained and updated [19] by the operator in the service management system (SMS) for the databases in the service creation environment (SCE). Computers also generate dynamic databases in weather-updating systems and meteorological centers for weather forecasting.

In the knowledge machine, the building of exhaustive OEs for all objects is uneconomical, if not impossible. However, an acceptable extent of OE details about a subset of related objects can be built. For example, if a knowledge machine for integrated medical systems is to be built for a localized region, then the OEs of the various objects (patients, doctors, pharmacists, surgeons, patient rooms, nurses, and so on) can be built. The KPU then functions to accomplish its microfunctions in the context of executing a knowledge program in that context. A typical example of such a program would be to find the emergency procedures for third-degree burn patients. People have written such procedures for other people, but the machine may outperform such standard operating procedures (SOPs) in many cases. For example, the machine will give an optimal procedure, depending on the most current object's (i.e., doctors, pharmacists, surgeons, patient rooms, nurses, patient insurance) availability, time of day, day of the week, and any number of additional constraints that the people who wrote the SOPs did not foresee.

8.6.5.5 "Store" the Result of KPU Instruction

In the CPU, the opcode and the particular hardware define where the result will be stored. For example, in the IBM 360/370 [21] environment, the RR and RX instructions leave the result in a register, while the SS instruction leaves the result in the memory (storage). It is the responsibility of the assembly-level programmers to store the result or to use the result when and how it fits the rest of the program. In application programs, the result may get stored as a variable (whose type depends on the declaration statement) location. In an assembly-level program, the result may be stored in one, two, or even a block of memory locations.

In the KPU, the kopcode, the particular HW (yet to be designed), and the declaration of the object type defines the storage procedures for the result. In a sense, it becomes necessary to define objects on the knowledge machine as variables are defined in the binary machine. Participating objects need to be declared as human, animal, inanimate, and so on. The compiler and assembly-level language designer are responsible for optimizing the OE space for classes of objects. Once syntax of the knowledge programs is identified, knowledge programs can be coded as easily as plain old computer system programs can be coded.

After the program is executed, the knowledge machine leaves the OE of participating objects altered and enhances the confidence level of the modified state. In fact, OEs of new objects may be defined or composed, thus forcing the KPS to identify objects not previously envisioned in the problem formulation. Simple deductions or major conclusions may be drawn depending on the program. The programming may be so specific and detailed that a known result is a single and well-defined certainty. Conversely, the programming can be so vague that a large number of results and solutions may be drawn, each with its own level of certainty (or uncertainty). The machine may be forced to dig deep into its own knowledge bases or seek the world over for objects, probable objects, precedent objects, antecedent objects, and all related objects to solve the problem. Validation or disputation of a hypothesis also may be programmed. The machine then identifies the probability of the hypothesis based on the information available for the objects and their attributes.

8.6.6 DBU and Its Functionality

In traditional plain old computing systems, numbers have their identity as integers, fixed point, complex, single precision, double precision, and so on. Word processing formats exist and tables are treated distinctly. In addition, distinct software modules exist for handling integers, complex numbers, and single/double precision numbers; for handling text processing; for handling spreadsheets; for handling graphics; for handling audio visuals; and so on. The more recent trend has been to build integrated environments to handle all user information. Such modules have databases associated with them, but the user assumes the responsibility of storing and retrieving the data and then interfacing it in the appropriate format to other programs also requiring data from these databases.

Objects that participate in events become input to the knowledge machine. The objects and their attributes can be far more complex and more numerous than numbers that are routinely used in numerical programs. Hyperspatial complexity is routine in human (object) transactions (events). The representational format of generalized objects and the representation of their attributes can be highly variable. The database unit of the KPS is designed to manage objects and their attributes like ALUs are designed to handle numbers. Programs for handling procedures, objects, and their attributes can become too many and too varied for simple operating system routines that perform page replacement algorithms from disk to memory and vice versa. For this reason, a sophisticated DBU (software or an equivalent hardware implementation) is necessary for KPS. The DBU handles the disk memory access; disk and memory management; address tracking and translation of objects and attributes; program procedures to associate or disassociate, enhance or curtail, modify or truncate attributes, and so on; and their library/utility routines.

8.6.7 The "Fuzzy" NPU

The "fuzzy" NPU computes: (1) the confidence level of each individual knowledge micro function and (2) the cumulative confidence level in all operations thus far into the knowledge program execution. This type of unit is not necessary in plain old computer systems, since all microinstructions are perfectly executed with 100 percent accuracy and the machine needs to carry out the executable code. However, in the KPS, there is a lurking doubt that something may be inaccurate or inconsistent somewhere. This uncertainty is reflected by the role of the "fuzzy" NPU.

The NPU also can be programmed to track the weakest reasoning by the lowest value of the number signified in the computation of confidence level (see (1)). Ideally, the values of all the numbers for all the knowledge micro functions should approach unity. Initially, the numerical processor in the fuzzy unit can be just a multiplier that evaluates the product of all the individual confidence values. In complex knowledge programs, independent, nonlinear, and/or complex relations may exist between the values of the confidence levels.

8.6.8 Fuzzy Hamming Distance and Its Iterative Control

Hamming distance is traditionally used in error correcting codes to indicate the robustness of any binary coding algorithm. Codes are designed such that the codewords are maximally distant from one another in terms of the number of positions in which they differ. Information received over any noisy channel would have a maximum likelihood that these words would indeed be one of the code words. The notion of deploying Hamming distance in the processing of knowledge needs some enhancement of the a this very powerful concept.

As knowledge processing occurs, intermediate "objects" generated by a knowledge machine should be as close to real "objects" based on reality. Now if the notion of Hamming distance in selected to track the distance between the machine generated "objects" and the real objects, then the processing should be directed towards the machine generated objects to be real. This "reality check" that is used by most scientists in research, can be shifted in the machine domain by allowing the knowledge machine (KM) to generate "objects" that have a sense of reality.

For example, if a medical team (or a knowledge system) is diagnosing a certain ailment that has n symptoms for positive identification and the patient offers only $(n-d)$ symptoms, then error distance in the diagnostic procedure is d. However, the situation gets fuzzy if there are numerous ailments that have similar symptoms and the gap between the ailments is not large (like the Hamming distance between the code words is small). Furthermore, if the patient offers imprecise information about the symptoms, the uncertainty gets even more enhanced. The integer measure of Hamming distance (from coding theory) now becomes probabilistic and multidimensional in the KM environments.

Typically, "objects" have numerous attributes and a perfect match is rare. In a hyper-dimensional space of n dimensions, the KM functions to reduce the error distance by iteratively processing the raw objects until another object is created by the machine that is as close to reality as possible. For example, if a team of genetic engineers are evolving a new gene for cancer control, then the new gene is validated by the "reality check" of other similar genes that are known to exist. The error distance is minimized, and by the same token, the symptom gap between increased by attempting a differential analysis of neighboring ailments (codewords).

Two notions follow: (1) the maximization error distance between objects that are known to exist in reality and (2) iterative control of the uncertainty at any cycle of the knowledge process. The first notion has a parallel in coding theory that offers well-designed codes that are maximally distant from one another in terms of the number of places they differ. The second notion can be derived from Shannon's theory on the extent of information that can be transmitted over noisy channels.

To extend the first notion (of designing codewords) into KM environment, it becomes implicit that the "objects" in the KBs of the machine be as distant from one another as possible. Ill chosen objects primed into the KB's demand more processing time and resources.

The implication of the second notion is that if the distance that is covered to reach the current process in a KM is considered as signal (S) and the distance between the current machine processed "object" and an object in the KB of the machine, is defined as noise (N), then the signal-to-noise ratio (SNR) should be maintained at a high level to ascertain that the KM is as close to reality. If the objects in the KBs are indeed real and distant from one another, then the processes in the KM will have a higher SNR.

Each iteration of the knowledge process reduces the noise level in generating a "real object" from the knowledge machine. This triadic interdependence between objects, knowledge processing software (KW), and iterative control of SNR can be harnessed to make KMs more dependable and precise. In a sense, the KM creates new "objects" from one set of objects (in the KBs) while monitoring the new objects to be real and ascertaining that every knowledge process has a high SNR. The KM moves objects from one location in the hyperdimensional attribute space to another location and creates now real objects.

8.6.9 Design and Implementation of the System

The design and implementation of the KPS is depicted in greater detail in Figure 8.16. In this case its functionality is based upon the duality of its two essential functions: (1) it learns (the learn block in Figure 8.16) all about the objects and their attributes, and it learns procedures and steps from information available; and (2) it applies (the solve block in Figure 8.16) the new information intelligently in the solution of the current knowledge problem.

When the system is in its learning mode, it is actively studying the previous actions of humans or itself to extract rationality and relationships, rules, and strategy. Largely, this can be compared to the process of introspection done by humans. This function does not exist in mechanized systems, but they can be forced into such a function by providing the learning algorithms from pattern recognition and computer vision. The system could learn this series of steps from a study of previous actions taken by humans in solving same or similar problems. This learning mode of the CPU function does not exist in plain old computer systems.

In the later (solve) mode, the KPS is engaged in actively solving a knowledge problem. The KPS follows a series of steps that it has compiled or that have been used in the past to solve similar problems. In this mode, it is actually processing knowledge and deriving new modules of inference to proceed logically to its next step. Each instruction modifies the OE of one or more objects or generates new information about a new or existing object. This mode is similar to the execution phase of a routine computer system where the CPU carries out the *opcode*-dependent hardware functions on a single operand (such as ones complement, twos complement, and NOT), multiple operand opcodes (such as add, multiply, and NAND), register-memory opcodes, device opcodes, opcodes associated with pseudo-operations, and so on.

8.6.10 Program Execution Mode of the KPU

The knowledge-based processor functions like the central processor of any typical computer, except that it processes knowledge domain functions on "objects." The opcode defines a knowledge function, such as "find the locality" of an object, "relate" two objects by their attributes, "generate attributes" of one or more objects, or "find common attributes" of one or more objects, "find the preconditions leading to" one or more objects/conditions. The operands are the objects or conditions. A new knowledge processor (much like the central processor) will now perform assembly-level type instructions on objects/conditions (much like the CPU performing a machine language instruction on binary data operands).

The realization of this knowledge processor can take on at least two architectures (hardwired and microprogrammable). Each knowledge domain opcode (*kopcode* for an abbreviation) flows into a "*k*ontrol" unit (as the opcode flows into the instruction register of the CPU) where it is decoded. Kopcodes are classified much like opcodes. Broad categories may now be identified. Kopcodes and pseudo kopcodes are possible and necessary. When a kopcode accomplishes a definite microfunction on the object(s) to which it is associated, a (real nonpseudo-) kopcode is delineated. When a kopcode accomplishes a function that prepares a machine for the next kopcode, or is an instruction to the machine without any knowledge function associated with it, then a pseudo-kopcode is delineated. An example of a pseudo-kopcode is when the machine exchanges one object for another to find a closer match of the attributes, or when the machine searches its database to find the locality of the most common occurrence of an object. Other classifications of the kopcodes are presented in [10].

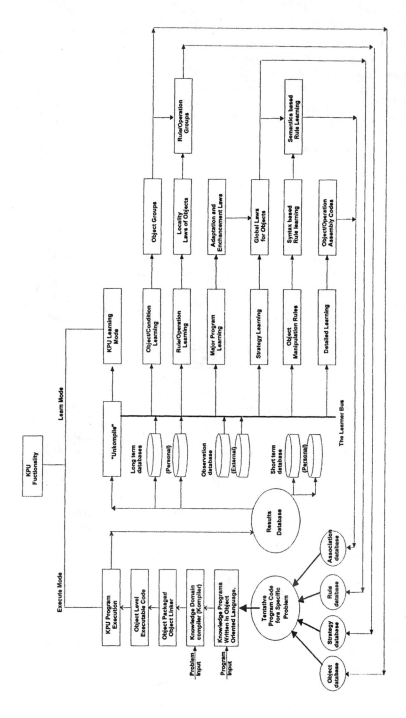

Figure 8.16 A detailed representation of the knowledge processing system functions with two (execute and learn) modes of operation.

After decoding, the actual knowledge domain function associated with that kopcode proceeds by a decomposition of the kopcode into its microscopic hardware functions (much like the hardware functions in the CPU, or the interpretation of the microcode in the micro-programmable CPU). The *kontrol unit* of the KPU dispatches hardwired control signals to perform the microscopic hardwired functions within the hard-wired KPU, or to interpret the "*microkode*" in the microprogrammable KPU. For the complex kopcodes, it may be necessary to launch elaborate macro-assembly routines. Kopcodes may depend on the execution of other kopcodes, and so on. Once a basic set of independent kopcodes are identified and hardwired, then the knowledge machine can be "bootstrapped" like a basic computer from its fundamental, independent, hardwired instructions.

The decomposition of the knowledge domain (KD) macrofunction into a group of kopcodes is as important as the decomposition of a complex KD function into its macros. The three concepts presented earlier will suffice for both orders of resolution. In reality, most organisms and structures follow this methodology. Micromodules are organized into the first level of modular hierarchy; then, the modules are organized into the next level, and so on. Many times, it is necessary to modify or enhance the "rules" to suit the context or the level. It is our contention that KPU-based problem solving and learning both follow a similar organizational hierarchy. Kopcodes can be written for each major KD function, and each kopcode is an assembly of other microscopic machine-realizable subfunctions. For example, consider the kopcode for "find the common attributes of" object X and object Y. First, the KPU invokes the database search for attributes for objects X and Y. Next, the attribute matching is invoked in the context of the attributes, as those defined for X and those defined for Y. The commonality, if apparent and certain, is determined and the result is reported with a given (100) percentile level of confidence. If the commonality is latent or through attributes of attributes, or there is any ambiguity in the matching of the attributes, then the result is reported with a computed percentile level of confidence. An attribute-matching procedure may become as complex as pattern matching, which takes place in artificial intelligence or in computer vision.

8.6.10.1 Execution Sequence for External "Object" Programs

There are two routine modes of execution for solving problems in the KPS. Programs encoded in object-oriented programs, which the KD kompiler accepts (see left side of Figure 8.17), can be compiled, packaged, and linked to generate the executable code and can be run on the processor. The architecture of this "object processor" is shown in Figure 8.11. This processor executes the instructions one by one and generates the final result. The program(s) to solve the problem becomes the "solution(s)" and the new information and its numeric estimate(s) of confidence level becomes the "result(s)." Both are stored in the "solution and results" database (Figure 8.17) for further study as to how the external programmer selected the objects and the rules in the OOL, how the objects are embedded in it, and how the rules are used at the microfunction level and at the macrofunction level. Results are also stored to reinvestigate the optimality of the results. In this limited context, the machine is no more than an object-oriented computer.

In Figure 8.17, the learning programs "process" the existing solutions and are able to extract objects, groups, relationships, opcodes, group operators, modules, strategies, and optimization methodologies from existing solutions and store them in object and corresponding databases. The architecture permits the KPU to catalog a new object in relation to existing objects and generate or modify existing pointers to and from new objects.

8.6.10.2 Execution Sequence for Internally Generated Programs

The processor is also capable of solving problems on its own. When any specific problem is posed (see left side of Figure 8.17), it enters the problem analyzer, parser, and code generator. Here the problem is parsed for what problem is to be solved and in what context the solution is to be attempted. Problem definition specifies some objects to the code generation part, context defines the boundary conditions, and the result sought defines the goal to which the individual (kopcodes) steps are to be directed. The information obtained is used to query the four (or more) databases to obtain all relevant information about the objects, their forward/backward pointers, and the rules of operation (i.e., the kopcodes) used with such objects. But more importantly, the global rules from the "strategy" database are also queried to solve the same or similar problems. If the problem posed to the KPU is totally new and was never before addressed, then an immediate solution is terminated, but the objects (identified in the problem definition) are tagged to perform an external database search (in the form of other network accessible databases) to find more information on the "objects" from the problem parser. The machine gathers each and every byte of information from all accessible databases to attempt to solve the problem once again. Totally nonsensical problems are abandoned.

When enough information is gathered about the problem from its internal and/or external databases, the machine assembles a sequence of codes in OOL or directly in the machine instructions for the processor to generate the steps in solving the problem. This assembly of kopcodes can be much more specific and powerful[9] than the kompiler-generated instructions (based on user code), and can be very specific to the objects about which the machine has specific experience. Syntax-dependent local and global rules may be used by the machine. When the specific executable code is generated, it is taken directly to the object processor shown in Figures 8.12. Both the solution and the results are stored in the "solutions and results" databases in Figure 8.17. The solution is reanalyzed for optimality of execution, and the results are studied for the optimality of the solution to reach the targeted goal. Satisfactory solutions are repeated to solve similar problems and are assigned a number to "mark the excellence" (or lack of it). The machine picks the best solutions to be most frequently repeated when it is in the "solve" mode.

---

[9] Some of the optimizing compliers (e.g., FORTRAN V) perform such code alteration and enhancement to force better performance from the machine. Specific capabilities of the HW and FW are invoked to make the solution faster. In case of the knowledge machine, the code optimization will offer better accuracy of the inferred results by focusing of the confidence level for each knowledge microinstruction.

The functions depicted in Figure 8.17 for the KPS can be realized in hardware via different versions of single/multiple memories, single bus/multiple bus architectures, object/program cache memories, single/multiple I/O processors and spoolers, and so on. It is possible to have two separate sets of primary and secondary memories for programs and objects. It is still to be determined whether single knowledge program and object memory architectures out-perform dual banks of memory (one for objects and one for programs) architecture. The architecture of the traditional von Neumann machine, with the same physical memory for programs and for data, needs to be reexamined for the KPS applications.

8.6.11 Learning Mode of the KPU

Numerous algorithms for implementing the learning process (as shown on the right side of Figure 8.17) in the knowledge-based processor exist. We describe some of the most powerful techniques. Typically, the processor performs assembly-level operations on objects. It learns which objects form groups or entities. It learns which kopcodes and which objects go together. No information (raw or processed) goes wasted. Raw information is tied to objects or their attributes. Processed information is associated with the nature and quantity of the new information to be expected, based on the execution of a kopcode upon that object. The learning of the kopcode groups, in conjunction with a certain class of objects, is an important learning function. Learning the expected outcome of a kopcode upon an object or group of objects is the next learning function. Finally, the cascading of such kopcodes and the relevant object groups to generate complex programs to perform a macro knowledge function is the most advanced learning function. We discuss the learning of the KPU further in the next three sections, which address three major venues of learning.

8.6.11.1 Object Occurrences, Object Groups, and Locality of Objects

The *first* learning procedure deals with identifying the "objects" and classifying such objects in the domain of their occurrence or their locales. For example, the object group "food" may be identified, and the domain of its occurrence may be tied to kitchens, grocery stores, restaurants, and so forth. In the same way, the object "food" is also attributed as being physical, satisfying hunger/thirst, edible, and so on. Another example is that of "income." Its domain of occurrence, from the IRS' perspective, is tied to earned income, interest and dividends, rental income, and so on. Similarly, the object "income" is also attributed as being assessed, spent, accountable, and taxable. Both the identification and the attribute assignment are based on the rules of pattern recognition by which a correlation of the properties of objects with the objects is mapped for future use. This procedure is similar to the subfunction in the compilation phase of a higher language program or routine that a computer system follows. In this case, the machine carries out a lexical scanning to detect the "variables" and separates them by their declarations (i.e., the attributes assigned to such variables) earlier in the program.

The KPS copes with learning and storing the knowledge thus learned. The first part deals with associating "objects" or blocks of information that form customary entities. One example is that the IRS is associated with W-2 and 1099 forms; April 15th is associated with 1040s, and so on. The study of past events bears the clues to such associations. Another example of such "object packaging" occurs in software design and drafting packages, where the designer may form a group of objects in the drawing and be able to collectively move them together or scale them in any proportion. The collection of objects exists and operates as a group rather than as individual items. The context in which the concept becomes important in the KPU functions is that if an "item" is sensed in the process that the KPU is attempting, then the KPU knows that in all probability other items of the same group are also likely to exist and their influence will also be processed. Locality rules are established for items and functions germane to that group and that thus may be applied to the entire group.

Every time an object gets used in the programs, the object itself leaves behind the backward and forward pointers. These pointers indicate which other objects were used in conjunction with the object currently in use. Hence, the locality of objects and the sequence of their use are established by the pointers that point to each other in the group. In addition, the operation used in previous operations with this object is also available to the learning routines. Accordingly, both the syntactic learning associated with the object and the semantic learning associated with the other associated objects provide acceptable kopcode for this object or objects in that group.

8.6.11.2 Laws of Locality for Object Manipulation

The *second* learning procedure deals with the relationship between objects per se; that is, an acceptable range of values may exist for the objects in relationship to each other. An example is that the IRS is highly unlikely to negotiate its tax rates, but it may be liberal to an interpretation of certain deductions. Based on the relationship between the objects, the KPU attempts to follow the strict or relaxed adherence to that relationship. This procedure is similar to the subfunction within the compilation phase of a higher-language program or routine that a computer system follows. In this case, the machine performs a semantic check to see if operations on the "variables" are consistent with the grammar of the language in which the program or the routine is encoded. Consistent operations and values and/or acceptable and unacceptable operations are tagged for user information and for the KPS while it is in the code-generator function (see left side of Figure 8.16).

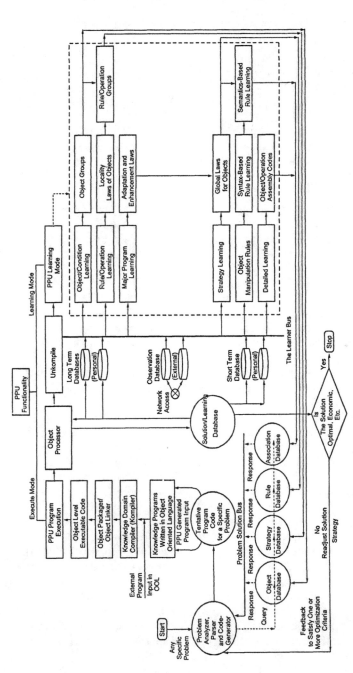

Figure 8.17 Flowchart of the knowledge processing system in the solve mode with database management functions. The learn mode is also shown with the function of 'Un-kompiling' to be able to learn the steps and strategies that have been successful in the solution of previous knowledge-based problems. The term kompile refers to the compilation of knowledge-level programs. Kompilation becomes a more complex and intricate process as compared to the compilation of standard higher level languages currently used for scientific and business applications.

The second part of the KPU, also dealing with learning, encompasses the process of inference generation, that is, deductive reasoning that permits the KPU to conclude that an outcome may be expected within the bounds of a finite probability, based on the previous knowledge and reasoning. One example of such an inference generation is when the IRS is scanning W-2s, it is (in all probability) also finding employer verification of the wages reported on the W-2 form. Results of the inference generation lead to the confirmation or denial of the rules and circumstances that led to the inference. The ensuing step depends on the result, and the functions of the KPU can continue. This is how numerous solutions (with different possibilities) can be generated for the same problem.

8.6.11.3 Global Laws for Object Manipulation

The *third* procedure deals with modifying the "rules" on which major and global actions are based. The KPU learns this when it is analyzing the action of the human being to whom it is assigned and extracting rationality for his/her actions. When it discovers such rationality or reason, the KPU updates its "programs" in the program databases (see Figure 8.17).

If a discrepancy occurs, the KPU brings it to the attention of the human and requests clarification to complete its learning process. When the human does not provide the clarification, the matter remains unresolved, the KPU will not perform rationally, and the function of the KPU may be temporarily blocked. This procedure becomes extremely important for the learning process within the KPU.

In the context of Figure 8.17, four (or more) databases (object database, strategy database, rule database, and association database) are used to store learned information. An additional attribute database may also be used if the nature of the application demands extensive attribute correlation, searching, and other activities. Information stored in these databases is used to solve future problems and flows through the problem-solving bus to generate the new programs for problem solving.

Two types of rules are analyzed: (1) local, immediately applicable rules and (2) global, flexible sets of rules. The local rules deal with reflex actions of humans, such as collision avoidance, falling down when humans/robots slip, or walking into fire. These are universal rules applicable at all times. In the CPU, the arithmetic logic unit (ALU) will not divide by zero; instead it flags an error condition. Global, flexible sets of rules deal with analyzing complex programs. In this case, the human, who may not be an expert in the field, tolerates an ambiguity in order to learn the process. After continued learning, the human develops the expertise (skill) to handle similar complex programs on his/her own. In the context of the KPU, it is this learning of global or long sequences of steps that generated the generic "tax" program (or similar complex sequence of steps) in the first place. The KPU is equipped to scan the database of human functions until it learns a new strategy or challenges an existing one. This process is not generally found in conventional CPU environments. Learning robots sometimes use this approach in a limited sense to solve "collision avoidance" or path finding.

Additional learning methodologies for the KPU may also become necessary to learn the complex and intricate steps that human beings tackle. Systemic approaches for the KPU design are possible when the learning is aimed at a higher and global level. This part of learning deals with the proposed action to follow in the process of inference generation. When numerous alternatives exist, the KPU adapts the certain strategy that the human has adapted in the past. This strategy is learned while analyzing the past data in the "permanent knowledge base" or the long-term memory and also the current "day-to-day" or short-term memory of the KPS (see Figure 8.17). If these strategies can be classified as "risk avoidance," "profit maximization," "minimum cost option," "maximize expected gain," "minimize the maximum expected loss, "maximize the minimum gain," and so on from the classic theories in decision making, then the KPU has a basis for its choice of the next step. Like humans, the KPU is error prone due to a lack of complete knowledge or an inappropriate choice of strategy, but it is accountable for its strategic decision and unlikely to make numeric errors or be inexhaustible in its search. In interpreted programs, this methodology saves a considerable amount of dialog with the user, and the machine intelligently associates the syntax, the semantics, and its own previously selected opcodes.

Considerable latitude exists in the extent to which learning is permitted in the KPS. When global procedures are learned, the KPS scans the knowledge program databases and their libraries to learn strategies, solution charts and diagrams, and major structural relationships between procedural steps. When microrelationships between objects and their attributes are learned, the KPS scans object databases and their libraries to learn the operand (object/event) part of the assembly-level instructions. When micro knowledge instructions are learned, the KPS scans the kopcodes from encoded programs (see "Results" database in Figure 8.16 and "Solutions/Learning" database in Figure 8.17) to associate which instruction formats and which microfunctions are feasible with which group of objects and/or their attributes. To this extent, the coarse and detailed learning process of the KPS is highly deterministic and programmed process and is discussed next.

8.6.12 Program Execution Sequence in the Learning Mode

Solutions in the "solutions" database are retrieved and "unkomplied" (see the right side of Figure 8.17). Here, we depict six branches to learn four major areas of learning.[1] The learning occurs as the KPU studies the solutions in the "solutions" database. It is self-generated and the extraneous "solutions" are both unkompiled to assign them a "mark of excellence" (see Section 8.6.8.2). Information thus learned is stored in the databases of Figure 8.17 and becomes available to attempt new solutions or to find a better solution to a common problem. The learning process forms a feedback to the solution process, and the KPU can cumulate and grow in its ability to become "skilled" in solving problems.

---

[1] The six branches are object/condition learning, rule/operation learning, major program learning, strategy learning, object-manipulation-rule learning, and detailed (local operation rule) learning. The four major areas are objects and their attributes, problem solving strategy, rules for local and global operations on objects, and associations that exist between objects, between rules, and between objects and rules.

8.7 CONCLUSIONS

In this chapter, we have proposed that knowledge processing is concept modification and/or adaptation. We also propose that such incremental knowledge processing has a precise numerical counterpart that defines a confidence level in that incremental process. Thus, the solution of complex problems has *two* numerical quantities at every step: (1) a confidence level in the entire process that has led to the current state and (2) a confidence level in the last step. When the machine reaches its goal (or solves the problem), it then provides two pieces of information: the solution to the problem and its estimate of the probability that the solution is correct. The user has the option of going back and investigating where the machine has the lowest levels of confidence in its logical processes and numbers of such "ill-conclusive" steps.

Furthermore, we propose that the result (each incremental change in the "quantity or entropy of knowledge") also has a number (i.e., the confidence level) associated with the set of events or subconclusions that led to a change. If this confidence level is assigned as the quality of the new knowledge, then each knowledge process has an incremental "quantity" and "quality" associated with it. Well-defined situations and circumstances lead to the total acceptance (which asymptotically reaches 100 percent) of the conclusions and thus new knowledge is generated without (well, almost without) a doubt. When there is some doubt or uncertainty (i.e., low confidence in the results), then results are questioned, challenged, rejected, or even denied.

We have proposed hardware architecture of a knowledge processor that accomplishes a knowledge-related function and also computes the confidence level in that process. When a complex problem is to be solved, the machine is assigned a certain minimum confidence level to which it is targeted. The hardware then takes all steps from its initial "quantity or entropy of knowledge" and proceeds to enhance it with the highest level of confidence consistent with the goals (or the solution of the problem). If the level of confidence drops below its preset level, then it explores other ways to "solve" the problem. One implication of this procedure is that no solution has a certainty level except a purely programmed numeric solution within the level of accuracy of the arithmetic logical processor unit.

We have presented a conceptual framework of knowledge processing systems, and two possible configurations of the processing environments. Functionally, these machines are more sophisticated than data processing environments. Numerous clusters of conventional machines under the control of the central administrative module can process knowledge effectively, much like the electronic switching systems of the telecommunications industry.

In view of the immense amount of knowledge in any branch of science, a multiplicity of knowledge processing systems in a network can be used, with each one dedicated to a particular discipline. The logical and the low-level human functions (including all programmable processing of fragments of knowledge) can be mechanized in this environment.

The administrative module can also program knowledge refurbishing and maintenance. Adequate and authorized sources of new information (such as research laboratories, literature, and meteorological observation centers) also need to be connected to the switching modules to incorporate the "new" information into the knowledge bases.

REFERENCES

[1] A. W. Burks, H. H. Goldstine, and J. von Neumann, U. S. *Army Report Ordnance Department*, 1946. See also G. Estrin, The Electronic Computer at the Institute of Advanced Studies, *Mathematical Tables and Other Aids to Computation, Vol. 7*, IAS, Princeton, NJ, pp. 108–114, 1953.

[2] J. von Neumann, *First Draft of a Report on the EDVAC*, Contract No., W-670-ORD 4926, Between United States Army Ordnance Department and University of Pennsylvania, Moore School of Electrical Engineering, June 30, 1945.

[3] N. B. Stern, From ENIAC to UNIVAC: Appraisal of the Eckert–Mauchly Computers, Digital Press, West Lafayette, IN, 1981.

[4] B. Werner, The system design of the IBM type 701 computer, *Proc. I.R.E.*, 41 (10):1262-1275, 1953.

[5] E. Koffman and F. L. Friedman *FORTRAN*, 5th ed., Addison-Wesley, Boston, See also, IBM FORTRAN IV and V programming manuals during the 1950s and 1960s.

[6] C. H. Lindsey, *Informal Introduction to ALGOL 68*, Elsevier Science, New York, 1977.

[7] J. P. Hayes, *Computer Architecture and Organization*, 2nd ed., McGraw Hill, New York, 1988. See also, H. S. Stone et al., *Introduction to Computer Architecture*, Computer Science Series, Science Research Associates, New York, 1980; W Stallings,. *Computer Organization and Architecture*: Macmillan New York, 1987.

[8] Bell Telephone Laboratories, *Transmission Systems for Communications*. Western Electric Co., Winston-Salem, NC, 1982.

[9] J. L. Cummings, K. R. Hickley, and B. D. Kinney, AT&T network architecture evolution, *AT&T Tech. J.*, 66, 1987. pp 2–12; See also, M. Iwama, "AT&T switching systems: an overview"; *AT&T Tech. J.*, 73, (6), 4–6.; Evolution of the 4ESS switch." *AT&T Tech. J.*, 73, (6), 93–100, 1994.

[10] S. V. Ahamed and V. B. Lawrence, *Intelligent Broadband Multimedia Networks*, Kluwer Academic Publishers, Boston 1997. See also, R. J. Wojcik. Intelligent network platform in the U.S., *AT&T Tech. J.*, Summer, 26–40, 1991

[11] M. J. Miller and S. V. Ahamed, *Digital Transmission Systems and Networks. Volume I, Principles,* and *Volume II, Applications,* Computer Science Press, Rockville, MD, 1987 and 88.

[12] AT&T, *Telecommunication Transmission Engineering, Network and Services* Vol. 3. Western Electric Company, Winston Salem, NC, 1980.

[13] E. G. Sable, Intelligent networks in United States, *1992 International Zurich Seminar on Digital Communications*, Zurich, 1992. See Also P. Miller, Intelligent network/2: A Flexible Framework for the Exchange Services, *Bellcore Exchange*, May/June 1987; J. M. Haas, R. B. Robrock, Intelligent network of the future, in *Proc. of the IEEE Global Telecommunications Conference*, Dec. 1986, pp. 1311–1315; Bell Communication Research, *Plan for Second Generation of the intelligent network*. Bellcore SR-NPL-000444, 1986.

[14] United States Government, *Library of Congress Classification*, <http://catalog.loc.gov> URL accessed June 2003.

[15] OCLC, *Dewey Decimal Classification and Relative Index*, 22nd ed., OCLC, Dublin, OH, 2003. See also, J. P. Comaroni, *Dewey Decimal Classification*, 18th ed., Forest Press, Albany, NY, 1976.

[16] Bell Communications Research, *800 Service Management System General Procedures*, Bellcore Special Report, SR-STS-000741, 1987.

[17] Bell Communications Research, *Integrated Service Management System Functional Architecture*, Bellcore Special Report, SR-TSY-001101, 1987.

[18] Bellcore TA-TSY-000462, SSP Capabilities for PVN Services, 1987; Bellcore TA-TSY-000460, BSDB, SCP Application for PVN Services, 1987; Bellcore TA-TSY-000462, SSP Capabilities for PVN Services, 1987.

[19] J. D. Ullmam, *Database and Knowledge Base Systems*, Computer Science Press, Rockville, MD, 1988. See also, E. Rich, *Artificial Intelligence*, McGraw Hill New York, 1983; S. V. Ahamed and V. B. Lawrence, Knowledge processing system employing confidence levels, U. S. Patent 5,809493, Sept. 15, 1998. Assignee Lucent Technologies, Murray Hill, NJ.

[20] W. G. Rudd, Assembly Level Programming and the IBM 360 and 370 Computers, Prentice Hall, Englewood Cliffs, NJ, 1976. See also, R. C. Detmer, Introduction to 80x86 Assembly Level Language and Computer Architecture, Jones and Bartlett Publishers, Sudbury, MA, 2001.

[21] *IBM System/370 Principles of Operation*, Publication No. A22-6821-3, IBM, White Plains, NY, 1974.

Chapter 9

A New Breed Of Machines

In this Chapter, we propose a new breed of computer systems that actively pursue truth (by scanning the universality of an(y) object, concept, or a notion), contemplate ethics and virtue (by comparing the social benefit derived by similar objects, notions, or concepts), and solicit quality and beauty (by altering the key attributes of an(y) object, concept, or notion to enhance elegance). More than just being artificially intelligent, these brave new machines seek and offer global and wise solutions to any scientific, social, moral, or even ethical problems. The solutions tend to become generic and true (within the framework of mathematical and scientific knowledge bases accessible to the machine), the approach becomes universal (within the framework of major innovations contributed to society), and the implementation becomes elegant (within the framework of artistic contributions and masterpieces that have survived the test of time).

9.1 INTRODUCTION

Machines are mindless slaves of humans. However mindless computers may be, there is an aura of programmed intelligence, quick recall, and global reach that is embedded in machines. Computer programs become the commands to these tireless

Intelligent Internet Knowledge Networks. By Syed V. Ahamed
Copyright © 2007 John Wiley & Sons, Inc.

machines. The tools and techniques of artificial intelligence[1] taught by humans fall short of recursive and reentrant contemplations of wisdom. Machines have been taught to imitate human natural intelligence in a very artificial way. In modern times intelligence appears to be defined better than deeper attributes of human beings such as longing for truth, virtue, and beauty in deeds and words. Many such attributes unified by one common search algorithm (if it exists) approach the elementary modules that constitute wisdom[2].

In a sense, the definition and distillation of wisdom have been evolutionary processes. For this very reason the age of "wise machines" has not dawned in the semiconductor era and core values (truth, ethics and virtue, and order and beauty) have not been cast in silicon or processed in Pentium. With the evolutionary edge favoring the neural pathways and byways in the brain, the speed of thought outpaces electrons in the submicron highways engraved in the VLSI chips or the photons trapped in the optical nets spanning the globe. In being realistic about new breed of machines, it appears logical to explore the synergy of human thoughts based on natural intelligence with (practically) flawless execution of artificially intelligent program modules by computers and networks [1].

Computer designers have shown the utmost skill in building third and fourth generation computer hardware. Software designers have demonstrated the utmost flexibility in encoding binary-level, assembly-level, higher-level and application-level code. The conceptual framework still remains incomplete. If the machines have to serve humankind, then the ideal machine should learn to solve the most basic intellectual and creative needs of human beings. Since human beings expect consistency, dependability, and universality (attributes of truth) of the solutions offered by machines, the new machines will optimize solutions for these attributes for truth. The maximization of the attributes is realistic even though truth itself is totally illusive. To this extent a computationally accurate definition of truth is better than no definition of truth, and it can be totally acceptable in a great many applications. For example, even though the velocity of light, c, or the value of pi, π, or Euler's constant, e, is never "truly" known, for most routine applications, the computed values are accurate enough.

Similarly, because human beings expect optimality, elegance, and perfection (attributes of beauty) in solutions offered by machines, the new machines will find solutions that approach these attributes of beauty. The search of the attributes is realistic even though beauty itself is illusive. To this extent, a computationally close

---

[1] Being intelligent is to be clever, bright, smart, gifted, intellectual, sharp, quick, and /or able. In the context of dealing with traditional machine intelligence, machines can be sharp (precise), quick (fast to respond), and able (resourceful by being programmed and connected to appropriate knowledge bases, sources of information, devices, and peripherals). See *American Heritage Dictionary* for he meaning of words and for meanings of words in the meaning.

[2] Being wise is to be intelligent, shrewd, astute, clever, prudent, judicious and sensible. To perform as a new breed of machines additional attributes [shrewd (adaptive, flexible), astute (smart, incisive), clever (knowledgeable, aware), prudent (cautious, practical, far-sighted), judicious (globally aware), and sensible (sane, rational, sagacious)] are necessary. Even though it is not feasible to make all attributes available to the new machines, some attributes can be encoded as executable macro-commands for the hardware (see *American Heritage Dictionary*).

proximity of beauty is better than an abstention from beauty. Such a manifestation of beauty can be totally acceptable for a great many causal onlookers. For example, the geometry of the Taj Mahal, the shape of the Pyramids or the contours of the Eiffel tower can never be perfect, yet they convey a sense of awe and grandeur to most beholders.

Finally, as human beings expect social benefit, human betterment, and righteousness (attributes of virtue) in solutions offered by machines, the new machines will search for solutions encompassing (at least some of) these attributes of virtue. The search of the attributes is realistic even though virtue itself is illusive. To this extent, a computationally close solution that maximizes the attributes of virtue (in the proposed solution) is searched in a recursive and a reentrant mode. The key constituent of the solutions are sought out and rearranged from the knowledge bases so as to have (at least some) virtuous consequences for the solutions offered. Even though some experts may have better solutions, the machine-generated solution can be acceptable for a great many casual users. For example, character of socially and culturally cognizant leaders (e.g., Martin Luther King or Bill Clinton) or antiviolence attitudes of others (e.g., Jacques Chirac or Mohandas K. Gandhi) may be posed as one of the goals in searching for the CEO of an organization. The long-term rewards of the search for the wise and global solutions to problems can become substantially better than those without Intelligent Internet-based search procedures. Some of ill suited and potentially criminal CEOs would be rooted out before any damage was done.

9.2 HUMAN NEEDS AND COMPUTER SOLUTIONS

Lower-level needs in humans lead to a limited search and quick gratification. Computer programs offering solutions to satisfy such needs are almost trivial. Since the problem is simplistic, the solution is insignificant. The binary code for the machine to offer the solution can even be handwritten. For example, the response to danger (fight/flee) is most impulsive and needs three or four lines of code. Similarly, the response to hunger/thirst (eat/drink) is also trivial and needs very little code for the machine to offer the solution, and so on. The most rudimentary of the hardware will execute the code and generate the solution. At such a low level, the extent of programming is the instruction code and the extent of hardware is an elementary binary CPU, limited memory, and one input/output device. While the hardware structures become quickly complicated and somewhat akin to the von Neumann classic IAS (Institute of Advanced Study) architecture [2], the software also becomes sophisticated when dealing with binary and floating point arithmetic, and the machine offers solutions to mathematical problems with intricate *logical* decision making. Scientific programming becomes feasible and the low level engineering problems may be solved. Such machines can be used to solve lower-level (safety and physiological) human needs. Historically, computers have not been used for finding solutions to these lower-level needs since human beings can find their solutions with very little effort.

However, as human needs become complex and their solutions[3] call for deliberate decision making, programming the machines to offer solution starts to become complex. Operations research [3] tools and techniques are now applicable, and computer programs that offer solution to problems start to assume a definite structure. Decision support systems [4] have been discussed in the literature since the 1970s. For example, if the human need is to maximize return on investment, then the computerized portfolio manager offers solutions to this end. Another example occurs if personality matching is necessary for evaluating the compatibility between two human beings. Whereas the human approach may entail the actual drawing of decision trees, the computer system would offer the solution more quickly and (perhaps more) accurately. As human needs [5] start to cross the third level (i.e., social needs) the role of computers, their hardware and their software starts to unfold.

The newer decision support systems have addressed more intricate problems effectively. For example, for medical problems and diagnostics, AI techniques and expert systems have played a role in Mycin [6] and NeoMycin [7]. For MRI and scanning, special hardware [8] and software platforms [9] have been developed. For anesthesia and surgical applications new AI techniques have been suggested [10].

It becomes clear that the solutions of complex human needs (such as ego and self-realization needs) demand complex computer and signal processing hardware and sophisticated software platforms. Since human needs have a well-defined structure and a hierarchical format [5], it is feasible to extrapolate the hardware architecture and software platforms for the computers to satisfy the realization (or the fifth level) [5], the search (or the sixth level), and the unification (or the seventh level) [11] needs. We present the basic functional hierarchy for new machines in the next Section. Human needs can, thus be mapped on machine functions.

9.3 DEVELOPMENT OF MACHINE INSTRUCTIONS

Consider the lowest level human needs and the lowest level machine instructions [12]. A simple set of instructions (RR, RS, and SI) [12] will suffice for the solution of safety (level 1, such as danger–fight/flee or find refuge), and physiological (level 2, such as hunger/thirst–eat/drink, tired–rest/sleep) needs.

Again, as the needs become more demanding (such as medical attention or prescriptions), the computers that offer solutions also become complex and sophisticated [6, 7]. For this situation, a set of higher-level languages (HLL) and their compilers with at least the complexity of von Neumann hardware [13] become

---

[3] Human beings evolved ways and means of satisfying their social and ego needs long before computers. However, earlier solutions have been less than optimal and sometimes brutal. With sophisticated strategies, the ways and means of satisfying these needs have become elegant, just and fair. We extend this trend further by asserting that newer computer systems will offer human beings the ways and means to satisfy their fourth-, fifth- and even sixth- and seventh- level needs [11] in universal (truthful), socially beneficial (virtuous), and supremely elegant (beautiful) ways.

appropriate. A complete set of basic assembly level instructions (RR, RS, RX, SS, and SI) [12] will be necessary.

Furthermore, as the human needs enter the third (social), fourth (ego), and fifth (realization) levels [5], present-day computers appear to be as rudimentary as the formulations of Liebnitz or the mechanical devices of Babbage. In spite of the recent strides in VLSI and software technology, hardware, higher-level languages, their compilers, and the machine language instruction sets, these giant scientific steps do not address higher-level human needs. The current languages for processing objects (i.e., the object-oriented languages [14]) partially fill the gap to process information and knowledge. To overcome this large void and allow the machine to solve the fundamental needs of human beings, we propose a high-level instruction hierarchy akin to the seven-layer OSI [15] hierarchy for computer communications and telecommunications.

9.3.1 Human Needs and Computer Languages

The binary code for the von Neumann machine and the basic assembly-level instruction set are the lowest level of instructions. These instruction sets are complete to operate the CPUs at their maximum potential and also offer programmers enough limited flexibility to perform scientific, logical, storage, input/output, and store/retrieve functions.

Before higher-level functions are to be executed, the lower-level instruction codes are "assembled" to offer transparency to users. Each higher-level instruction may utilize the lower-level instruction freely to execute the higher-level instruction. When the HLLs were introduced, specific compilers were also designed to isolate users from the intricacies of the hardware. The instruction sets are assembled to let the hardware execute the HLL command exactly the way the user intended. Thus the program is to be precisely compiled, assembled, loaded, linked and finally executed. The CPU and HW execute the lowest-level instruction sets and the overall machine executes HLL instructions either sequentially or in parallel.

When this mode of operation is projected to a set of new machines that attempt to solve the problems associated with higher-level human needs, it becomes futile to design a detailed instruction set for a new series of (human) machines. However, the problem becomes manageable from a top–down perspective. When humans attempt to resolve a social (level 3), ego (level 4) or realization (level 5) need [5], a high-level command structure needs to be emphasized at that need level.

The solutions to the low-level human needs are easily programmable in primitive and current machine environments. For the social and realization needs, the inadequacies of current instructions sets and languages start to become apparent. For example, the pursuit of satisfaction, perfection, or invention of a device or composition of a musical sonata is out of the realm of current instruction sets or machine languages. At these higher levels of human needs, the knowledge level functions (e.g., access knowledge bases, extract relevant information, develop strategies, evaluate strategies, determine benefit/cost ratios, maximize goals, optimize parameters) and implementation functions (e.g., find out the incremental cost for each incremental gain, justify expenditure of resources, allocate resources, alter resource allocation strategy incrementally, reevaluate benefit–cost ratio) become the macros of new language(s). At this stage, all the delicacy of executive decision-making gets implied in making the strategy maximize the satisfaction of the ego or realization needs [5] of a human being.

For the solution of intermediate levels of needs, human beings follow the well-documented Marshall's laws of marginal utility. In reality, two basic rules of behavior are: (1) maximize the incremental satisfaction of need and (2) minimize the incremental resources expended. However, over a period of time a general strategy evolves for the solution of intermediate-level and higher-level needs. A sequence of steps in one such strategy is shown in Figure 9.1. This search for refinement in the solution (for some) could involve the search for universality, elegance, and social benefit. When resources are no longer scarce, the need to solve gets sublimed into a need to search [11]. At the other extreme, when the resources are limited, the search for an immediate gratification of a need could involve deception, arrogance, and social injustice. We examine the role of human discretion further in the choice of gratification of need. Both strategies have worked from archives of civilizations with differing long-term implications.

Traditionally, Marshall's marginal utility theory has no methodology to incorporate social benevolence (virtue) or ethics (beauty). However, if computers are programmed to evaluate the long-term impact in the change of utility and morality as a resource, then marginal utility theory retains validity. The computation of these parameters (like the consumer spending) may not be precise, but their estimation is in order to indicate gross miscalculations that have brought disastrous consequences on some communities and civilizations. Such an approach for the estimation in the changes in utility is proposed for the machines as they pursue social benevolence, or as they pursue social ethics. At an initial stage of building a conceptual frame work for the machine to serve humans in social and ethical dimensions, Marshall's theories become applicable to the extent that they have been applied in microeconomics. In the two social dimensions (benevolence and ethics), the measure for the changes in utilities become less precise than the measure for change of utility (marginal utility) due to material goods and the marginal resources expended.

9.3.2 Simple Needs, Simple Solutions

In general, for most routine resolutions of lower-level needs, the whole process could be as straightforward as (start → Boxes 1,2 → stop) as depicted in Figure 9.1. For the solution of most simpler needs, steps 1 and 2 are simple, concurrent, and combined. In most cases, a satisfactory resolution of a need in repeated without expending the extra energy for finding a new solution. This human tendency needs very little programming to be duplicated by a machine.

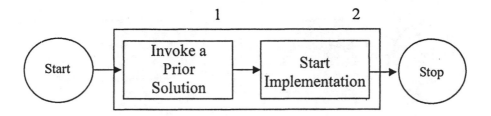

Figure 9.1 Sequential diagrams for the resolution of a simple need.

Human thought is essential in resolving human needs at any level. However some low-level (typically, levels 1 and 2 of Maslow's Need Pyramid [5]) needs are resolved on an impulsive/reflexive basis (safety → fight/fleeing, danger → run, etc.). One does not need any AI programs for the solution. A simple processor and ROM will suffice. For resolution of higher-level needs (such as social, ego or realization needs), the approach and strategy become highly variable.

9.3.3 Complex Needs, Complex Solutions

For the more complex higher-level needs, machines can refine the resolution process by going through six steps, shown in Figure 9.2. At levels 3 through 5 of Maslow's Need Pyramid [5], a sequence of high-level subroutines or instructions is feasible. To this extent the machine can outperform a simple human but may fall short of an experienced and well versed human. This type of scenario is evident in other situations.

For example, if an inventory item is running low at a plant, then the inventory control programs offer quick, efficient, and least expensive solutions far quicker than human counterparts.

The genesis of human thought in the resolution of needs has *two* facets: (1) the embedded objects that can be instrumental in the resolution of any need and (2) the processes involved in resolution. In a sense, the managers of any production line in a corporate environment construct a "process flowchart" and a "critical path" (see CPM techniques in [3]) in the completion of any project based on "nodes" and "processes."

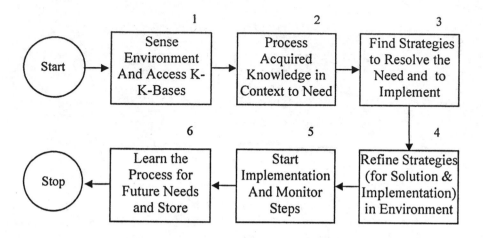

Figure 9.2 Sequential diagrams for the resolution of a complex need.

Each node represents the status of the collectivity of embedded objects for the satisfaction of the need. The organization of objects and processes can become as variable as the way in which people think in resolving their higher-level needs. For addressing these higher-level needs, a higher-level (knowledge) language appears to make the machine conform to solving human problems in a human way. Figure 9.3(a) delineates the status of the current computer languages with definite room at the top for knowledge-based languages. These commands force the machine to perform functions that a human(oid) might accomplish at the fourth- (knowledge) level. In Figure 9.3(b), the processing of the machine is taken into the human domain of being able to scan knowledge to derive concepts from the knowledge. Currently, this activity is in the realm of human functions like multiplication and division were done by human beings about a century back. With an acceleration of machine intelligence, it is foreseeable that knowledge and concept processing will become computerized in a generation or so. The pursuit of a human being who seeks universality (truth), elegance (beauty), and social benefit (virtue) in the solutions may be wisdom-level assembly code for the next generation . Thus the brave new machines offer humanistic solutions to the higher-level needs of human beings. In the Internet era, most human beings seek "wise" solutions rather than mere solutions.

In Figure 9.4, a representation of the first notion is presented. If the smallest programmable function in the KPU is for a single object (e.g., a student) undergoing a single process (i.e., a kopcode, find courses taken), then the execution of this function during a finite increment of time is represented in Figure 9.4.

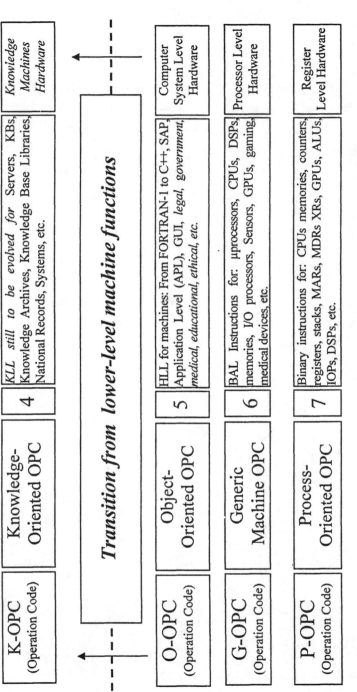

| K-OPC (Operation Code) | Knowledge-Oriented OPC | 4 | *KLL still to be evolved for* Servers, KBs, Knowledge Archives, Knowledge Base Libraries, National Records, Systems, etc. | *Knowledge Machines Hardware* |

Transition from lower-level machine functions

O-OPC (Operation Code)	Object-Oriented OPC	5	HLL for machines: From FORTRAN-1 to C++, SAP, Application Level (APL), GUI, *legal, government, medical, educational, ethical, etc.*	Computer System Level Hardware
G-OPC (Operation Code)	Generic Machine OPC	6	BAL Instructions for: µprocessors, CPUs, DSPs, memories, I/O processors, Sensors, GPUs, gaming, medical devices, etc.	Processor Level Hardware
P-OPC (Operation Code)	Process-Oriented OPC	7	Binary instructions for: CPUs memories, counters, registers, stacks, MARs, MDRs XRs, GPUs, ALUs, IOPs, DSPs, etc.	Register Level Hardware

Figure 9.3(a) A three level transition of computer programmability for machines to approach the knowledge-level machine-humaniod functions starting from the hardware register- level for typical lowest system level function (such binary logic, surveillance, security, door and elevator monitoring) that IC chip systems can accomplish. The knowledge machine platform offers a transition level to accomplish the highest level machine functions.

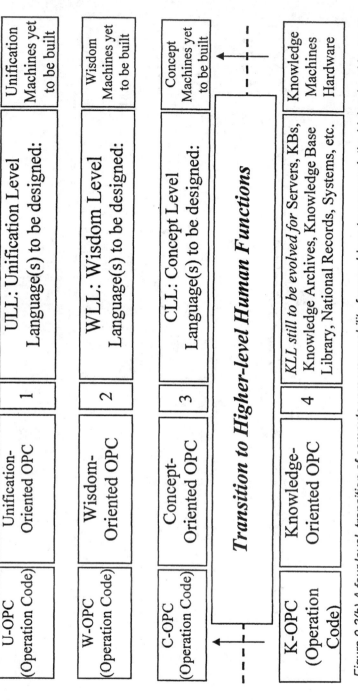

U-OPC (Operation Code)	Unification-Oriented OPC	1	ULL: Unification Level Language(s) to be designed:	Unification Machines yet to be built
W-OPC (Operation Code)	Wisdom-Oriented OPC	2	WLL: Wisdom Level Language(s) to be designed:	Wisdom Machines yet to be built
C-OPC (Operation Code)	Concept-Oriented OPC	3	CLL: Concept Level Language(s) to be designed:	Concept Machines yet to be built

Transition to Higher-level Human Functions

| K-OPC (Operation Code) | Knowledge-Oriented OPC | 4 | KLL still to be evolved for Servers, KBs, Knowledge Archives, Knowledge Base Library, National Records, Systems, etc. | Knowledge Machines Hardware |

Figure 9.3(b) A four level transition of computer programmability for machines to approach the higher-level human functions starting from the knowledge level functions (such as medical diagnostics, intelligent decision support, intelligent robotics, executive information support, intelligent educational support) that machines can accomplish. The knowledge machine platform offers a transition level to perform the lowest level human and humanoid functions.

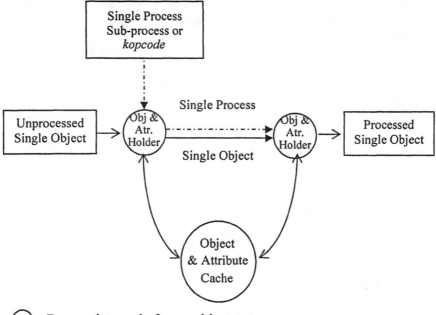

○ Processing node for an object set

⋯⋯► Process flow at any node after the input object set is complete

⋯⋯► Object undergoing a process from node to node

⟶ Object flow

The object set undergoes an incremental change at every node

Figure 9.4 Symbolic representation of one object (with its own attributes) undergoing one kopcode *or one knowledge microprocess.*

After processing, the processed object will carry the required attribute of knowledge associated with it. There is a need for the object and attribute cache. In the example of a student and the number of courses taken, the processor would have to find the student ID, access the university database, supply the authorization code, scan the student records, sum all the course taken, check the grades, and then supply the information about the student in one of the blank attribute fields of the student. For simpler CPU instructions, the need for the operand cache may not be necessary even though it is possible to have it. Typically, the operand stacks or registers are used to hold the intermediate variables. Due to the complexity of KPU functions, the cache (to store partially processed objects and attributes) appears as an integral part of the KPU design.

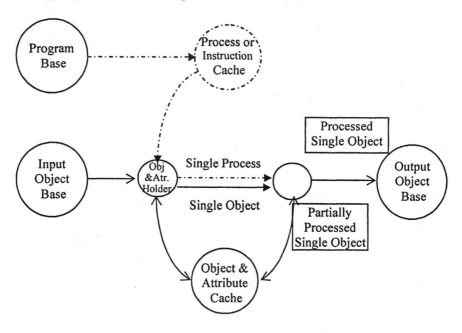

Figure 9.5 Single process single object, SPSO architecture. A single process instruction gets executed on a single object at any one time. Binary level program instructions get executed sequentially.

Architecturally, the KPU designs are amenable to CPU designs and vice versa. The von Neumann machine with a single instruction, single data (SISD) format can be reconstituted as the single process, single object (SPSO) format shown in Figure 9.5. The object and attribute cache(s) are necessary to take account of how the other attribute of the object may affect the execution of the current instruction or how the process may affect a set of attributes, or how the change of one attribute due to the processing of another attribute can affect the stability of the current process.

The execution of the processor instruction by a kopcode upon one or more objects can become more complex than a binary instruction in a conventional computer. For this reason, the handling of different objects and their attributes needs special attention on the input side and then again on the output side. The size of the cache for objects and attributes needs to be considerably larger than the operand cache in conventional computers. A typical example of the SPSO process occurs when the system is seeking (SP) all the attributes of an executive (SO) from a pool of employees one at a time.

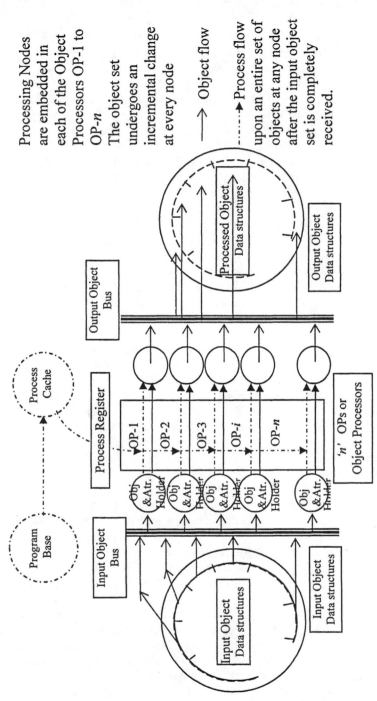

Figure 9.6 Single process multiple objects, SPMO Architecture. The same process flows into the control circuits of numerous object processors (OPs) and multiple objects are processed concurrently. Independent object and attribute caches are attached to each OP, if the SPMO hardware (e.g., multiple employees, single-trait executive search) calls for the use of such caches.

Corresponding to the conventional single instruction, multiple data (SIMD) configuration, single process, multiple object (SPMO) designs are also feasible for a knowledge processing environment. A preliminary architecture is shown in Figure 9.6. In this configuration, objects are processed from left to right and a system executes one instruction on all the n objects during the execution time, thus reducing the overall execution time. A typical example of the SPMO process occurs if the system is searching (SP) for all the executive traits from a large pool of employees and n employees (MO) are processed during the execution time.

In multiple process multiple objects (MPMO) architectures, concurrent knowledge processing becomes akin to concurrent data processing in multiprocessor systems that execute multiple programs MIMD architecture of traditional mainframe computers (e.g., IBM 360 series). The architecture of a MPMO knowledge processing system is shown in Figure 9.7.

The object flow and the process flow are separated into separate buses and the object input bus is distinct from the object output bus. The systems act independently of each other. The operating system tracks the execution in each of the n independent process systems. Typical application of the MPMO knowledge processing environment occurs when n independent processors share memories, I/O subsystems and other peripherals. These logically independent machines coexist in one mainframe environment.

The MPSO and pipeline versions of the knowledge processors can also be built along the same concepts as the MISD [13] since pipeline architectures are well known in conventional computers. In Figure 9.8, representing the MPSO architecture, a single object undergoes a series of knowledge processes or kopcodes. However, the configuration does not offer any specific advantages compared to the MPMO architectures or the pipeline architectures shown in Figure 9.9. A number of objects (e.g., applicants) drawn sequentially from the multiple objects (e.g., employees) base will undergo a sequential set of subprocesses (e.g., search for each of the attributes of an executive) within the pipeline object processor.

The processed objects will appear (on the right-hand side) sequentially in the same order they were drawn from the multiple objects base on the left-hand side with an evaluation sheet for the object (employee listing and the attributes). This observation is validated if the MISD architectures of the conventional computer are compared to MIMD or conventional pipeline architectures [13].

Much like the conventional CPUs and computers, the KPU's and the komputers (the k is for knowledge processing) can be built in many designs. One such design is shown in Figure 9.10 and the processing takes place from left to right. Since the higher-level languages for knowledge processing can be quite cumbersome to execute, the binary-level instructions for knowledge processing are likely to be tedious and elaborate. Such complexity also arises while designing the control circuits for microprogrammable and nanoprogrammable CPUs.

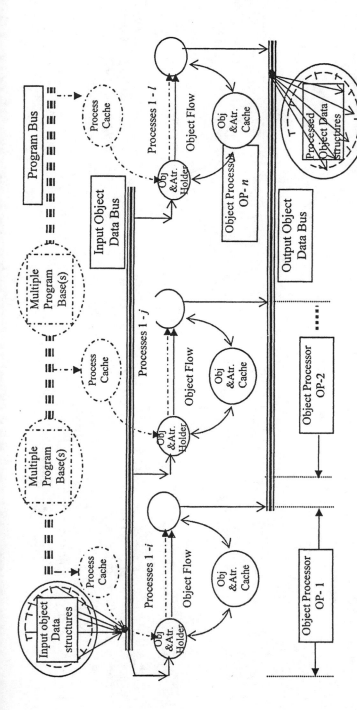

Figure 9.7 Multiple process, multiple objects, (MPMO) architecture. Multiple programs are executed upon multiple objects in multiple processors at the same time. This architecture is akin to the traditional multiprocessor computer systems with the exception that the multiple attribute processing can also take place with each of the multiple object processors (OPs). Such application of the MPMO hardware exists if a search firm seeks multiple executives from multiple databases of applicants based on numerous attributes or requirements.

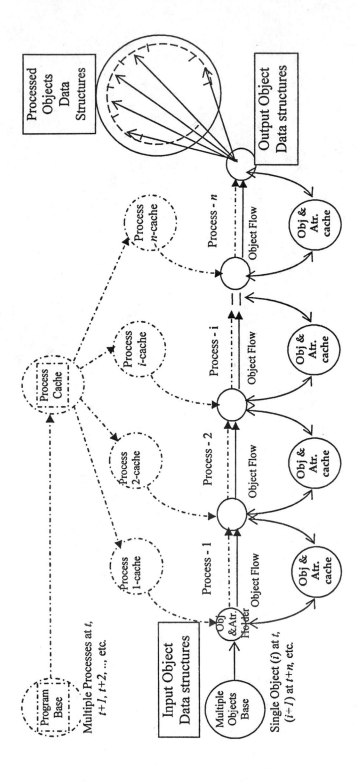

Figure 9.8 Multiple process single objects, MPSO architecture. A multiplicity of processes gets executed on a single object over a period of time. However, numerous objects may flow through the "assembly-line" of a MPSO processor. When each object processor (OP) is totally versatile to perform any function, the MPMO (see Figure 9.8) architectures become more attractive. When each OP is especially suited for a subprocess, the pipeline architectures (Figure 9.9) become more attractive. The allocation of time for each process or subprocess becomes critical to make the MPSO configurations work in an optimal fashion.

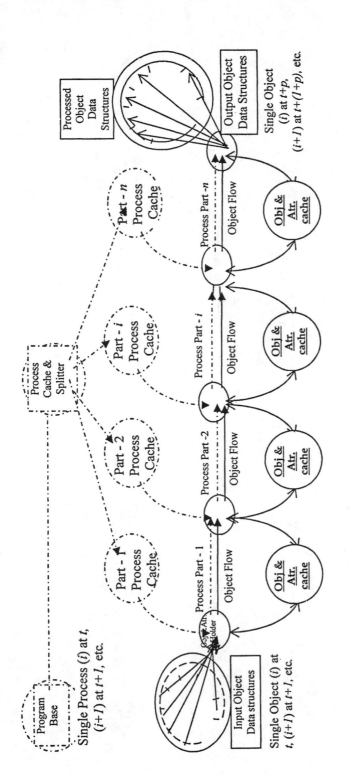

Figure 9.9 Pipeline (or assembly line) object and attribute processor architecture. When each sub-process of an overall process takes the same amount of time (i.e., same number of clock cycles) to execute and each object processors is especially suited for its own function (e.g., evaluate social skills or find work habits) then this architecture works quite satisfactorily. p is the process time for any object to pass through the entire assembly line.

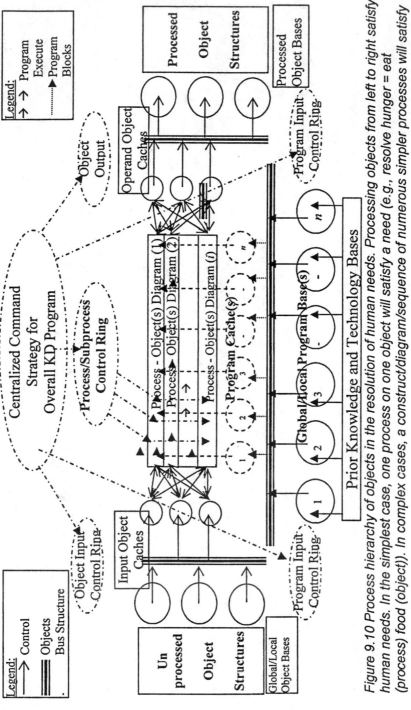

Figure 9.10 Process hierarchy of objects in the resolution of human needs. *Processing objects from left to right satisfy human needs. In the simplest case, one process on one object will satisfy a need (e.g., resolve hunger = eat (process) food (object)). In complex cases, a construct/diagram/sequence of numerous simpler processes will satisfy the complex need (e.g., Shelter = build house = $\sum$(Construction Steps) in proper sequence to follow construction diagram).*

To facilitate the flow of knowledge level instructions and the flow of objects, control rings are shown in the KPU, for I/O and program flow. The flow of data blocks is facilitated through the mainframe komputer much like the flow of packets in networks.

Access to a large number of worldwide knowledge bases becomes a necessity for processing complex objects such as concepts, truth, beauty, or values. The complexity of the komputer design appears to be an order of magnitude higher than the complexity of the design of conventional computers. If the universality of the processed knowledge is a requirement, then IP addressing and protocol for addressing that facilities global access, constitute an integral part of the komputer I/O design. The knowledge level instructions may be assembled from distant knowledge bases before execution of a program. Global knowledge base linkages should be established as the knowledge program start to execute. In these instances, the lower part of Figure 9.10 can be made simpler.

The hardware for processing generalized objects will become more cumbersome than the hardware for integers, floating point numbers, and so on. However, chip designers have built more and more complex processors during the last few decades. For example, the double precision and complex number arithmetic, array processing, are examples of arithmetic processing of the von Neumann era. In addition, recent graphic processors and processors for computer games handle complex (graphical) objects routinely. In processing objects in the knowledge domain, the attributes of the objects can be highly varied needing, specialized hardware registers, stacks, caches, and object arrays.

9.4 ARCHITECTURES

Low-level architectures of the new machines imply knowledge processing systems. In Section 9.3 the arrangements for SPSO, SPMO, MPMO, MPSO, and pipeline are presented. In this section, a concept level diagram is presented in Figure 9.11. The main component in this architecture is the komputer (k for the processing of knowledge). A concept-based switching functionality is added to the normal knowledge domain functions listed in Section 9.3. This facilitates the system function to wisdom, seek out values (if any), and evaluate the presence (or lack of) ethical and/or moral content in the transactions with the processor units of the komputer.

Much like the case of a conventional computer needing input/output and memory function, the komputer also has *two* supplementary structures. The *first* structure supports the conventional computer (which includes its own I/O and memory functions), database (including the relevant data, content, keyword searches), library (based on the Library of Congress [16], Dewey Decimal System [17] or any other knowledge classification systems), and knowledge level (see Section 9.3) functions. The *second* structure performs the local, global, telecommunication and Internet functions.

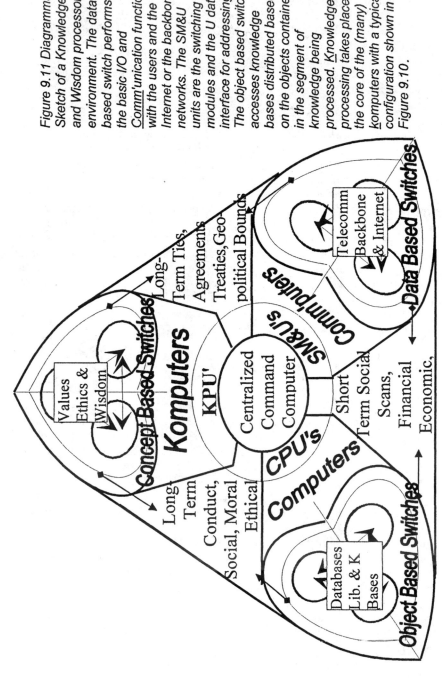

Figure 9.11 Diagrammatic Sketch of a Knowledge and Wisdom processor environment. The data based switch performs the basic I/O and Comm'unication functions with the users and the Internet or the backbone networks. The SM&U units are the switching modules and the U data interface for addressing. The object based switch accesses knowledge bases distributed based on the objects contained in the segment of knowledge being processed. Knowledge processing takes place in the core of the (many) komputers with a typical configuration shown in Figure 9.10.

Values Ethics & Wisdom

Concept Based Switches

Komputers

KPU'

Long-Term Ties, Agreements Treaties,Geopolitical Bounds

Centralized Command Computer

SM&U's Comm'puters

Telecomm Backbone & Internet

Data Based Switches

Long-Term Conduct, Social, Moral Ethical

CPU's Computers

Short Term Social Scans, Financial Economic,

Databases Lib. & K Bases

Object Based Switches

At the initiation of any problem, the user primes the machine and sets the conditions to start the solution of the problem. The user has the option to query the machine with any (rational or irrational) problem. The rationality of the problem is validated by the information in the global data and knowledge bases. This type of a sanity check is also performed in scientific computing by compliers that will prevent illegal mathematical process from the hardware. In the medical field, the AI/ES programs such as Mycin, and Intern. When a patient uses a diagnostic programs, the program leads the patient through a set of queries until the expert system databases can reasonably isolate the symptoms with an acceptable level of confidence. In the knowledge processing environment (KPE), irrational problems are returned to the user for further clarification. The solution of the problem starts with the parsing for the objects embedded in the problem.

In a knowledge environment (KE), an object can be (almost) anything— concept, race, people, society, culture, cr even bacteria and microbes. As far as there is a linkage to the object, the lineage will be explored until all leaves of the knowledge tree are explored. The dictionary, the Internet, and the knowledge bases all become fair venues for the machine to explore for related (precedent and antecedent) objects and their attributes. Thus, the machine leaves no stone unturned or any venue unexplored. The machine starts to build the platform for the origin to the evolution of the objects embedded in the problem after parsing the question and solves the problem in an artificially intelligent fashion with superhuman access and accuracy but without creativity. This aspect of the solution still remains in the ingenuity of human beings who use the machine.

The KPE links the processes within the machine to the current and past processes and inferences stored elsewhere in the world. The universality of any axiom of wisdom derived within the machine is checked for universal validity with Internet access and at Internet speeds. In this configuration, the new machine is capable of many generic high-level functions. If additional attributes of wisdom (such as elegance and social benefit in the knowledge processed) are imposed, then the machine searches for the union-space of the findings for universality (i.e., truth), elegance (i.e., beauty), and social benefit (i.e., virtue).

Depending on the size and computational power of the machine, the solution and searches for the three attributes can be concurrent or sequential. It is interesting to see that all the established concepts generated over the last five decades of conventional computing systems are applicable to the knowledge, concept, and unification machines.

The operating system of the new machine needs extremely robust algorithms to prevent deadlock and abuse of the machine. In a majority of cases, human surveillance may be essential to monitor the execution and functionality, much like a pilot controlling the flight of an airplane or a space vehicle.

9.5 CONCLUSIONS

In this chapter, a number of architectural arrangements for the processing of knowledge and the basic operational code of such knowledge machines are presented. From a technical and design perspective, the question that needs to be addressed is not *how* these machines will be built but *when* these machine will be built. The processing of objects is already evident in the compilers of object-oriented languages that are used extensively in computer graphics, computer games, and superanimation machines. The quantum jump for realizing knowledge processing for solving human problems will occur when a general-purpose *k*omputer (for *k*nowledge processing) is built by the VLSI industry.

A machine of this nature will resolve problems pertaining to the sophisticated human needs, much as a basic computer has helped scientists to deal with simple and sophisticated scientific problems. It is also possible to foresee the use of these machines in tackling generic problems dealing with concepts and methodologies and their long-term implications. It should offer sensible and wise solutions to issues where values and ethics, behavior and society, and culture and progress are concerned.

REFERENCES

[1] S. V. Ahamed, The architecture of a wisdom machine, *Int. J. of Smart Eng. Sys. Design*, **5**, (4): 537–549, 2003.

[2] A. W. Burks, H. H. Goldstine, and J. von Neumann, U. S. *Army Report Ordnance Department,* 1946. See also G. Estrin, The Electronic Computer at the Institute of Advanced Studies, *Mathematical Tables and Other Aids to Computation, Vol. 7,* IAS, Princeton, NJ, 1953, pp. 108–114.

[3] F. S. Hillier and G. J. Liebermann, *Introduction to Operations Research,* McGraw Hill, New York, 2002.

[4] C. W. Holsapple and A. B. Whinston, *Decision Support Systems, A knowledge based Approach,* West Publishing, Belmont, CA, 1996.

[5] A. H. Maslow, A theory of human motivation, *Psychol. Rev,*.**50**, 370–396, 1943.

[6] E. Shortcliffe, MYCIN: Computer-Based Medical Consultations, American Elsevier, New York, 1976. See also, B. G. Buchanan and E. H. Shortcliffe, Rule-Based Expert System: The Mycin Experiment at Stanford Heuristic Programming Project, Addison Wesley, Boston, 1984.

[7] W. Kintsch et al., About NeoMycin, *Methods and Tactics in Cognitive Science,* Lawrence Erlbaum, Mahwah, NJ, 1984.

[8] S. A. Brooks and U. Schumacher (Eds.), *Metastasis Research Protocols, Volume 1: Analysis of Cells & Tissues,* Humana Press, Totowa, NJ, 2001.

[9] C. P. Poole and H. A. Farach (Eds.), Handbook of Electron Spin Resonance: Data Sources, Computer Technology, Relaxation, and Endor, Springer Verlag, New York, 1999.

[10] M. Krol and D. L. Reich, Development of a decision support system to assist anesthesiologists in operating room, *J. Med. Sys.* **24**, (3), 141–146, 2000.

[11] S. V. Ahamed, An enhanced need pyramid for the information age human being, in *Proceedings of the Fifth Hawaii International Conference, Fifth International Conference on Business,* Hawaii, May 26–29, 2005.

[12] R. C. Detmer, Introduction to 80x86 Assembly Level Language and Computer Architecture, Jones and Bartlett Publishers, Sudbury, MA, 2001.

[13] J. P. Hayes, *Computer Architecture and Organization.* McGraw Hill, New York, 1984. See also M. M. Mano, *Computer Engineering Hardware Design,* Prentice Hall, Englewood Cliffs, NJ, 1988.

[14] H. M. Deitel and P. J. Deitel, *C++ How to Program,* Prentice Hall, Englewood Cliffs, NJ, 2002.

[15] S. V. Ahamed, and V. B. Lawrence, *Intelligent Multimedia Broadband Networks,* Kluwer Academic Publishers, Boston, 1997, pp. 95–102.

[16] United States Government, Library of Congress Classification, Refer to http://catalog.loc.gov for a detailed explanation of the LoC classification, coding, and call numbers. URL accessed June 2003.

[17] Dewey Decimal Classification and Relative Index, 22nd Ed., OCLC, OH, 2003.

Chapter *10*

Concepts and Constructs for a Wisdom Machine (WM)

The high-speed information highways may provide instant Internet access but the human mind follows a slower and more contemplative path. A human mind can contour the evolutionary path spanning many millennia and it can reflect on a wide variety of knowledge issues. On the one hand, we have an explosion of data from an information age coercing the mind to comprehend vast amounts of data, and on the other hand, the creative and critical mind needs long stretches of contemplation to weigh and consider the truth and beauty embedded in data streams that traverse the information highways. In order to shelter the mind from irrelevant trivia, we propose that the data be processed initially by high-speed computer banks that filter out the irrelevant data from the wisdom-bearing information necessary for human beings to weigh and consider. These machines will be programmed to become highly sensitive to keywords, information structures, objects and their attributes, and even patterns of data flowing through the networks.

In this chapter we propose that wisdom can be accumulated systematically from knowledge, knowledge can be derived from information, and information can be gathered from data. Within the framework of data manipulation and communication, data can be assembled, acquired, switched, and channeled by traditional tools and techniques currently in use in computers, communication

Intelligent Internet Knowledge Networks. By Syed V. Ahamed
Copyright © 2007 John Wiley & Sons, Inc.

systems and networks technology. In the proposed architectural configuration, the task of finally deriving wisdom is shared between a team of scientists and a hierarchy of computers.

At the first level of functionality of the wisdom machine (WM), a variety of data sensors activate the system to indicate an opportunity to derive wisdom from routine events. At the second level, the traditional AI techniques process the data through the information and the knowledge stages, thus extracting the patterns of change in the flow or the nature of data. At the third level of extracting wisdom, human activity is supported by six computer systems (or subsystems), where the human mind is the super-processor that feeds back from partial information and knowledge. Each computer (sub) system performs a step either in a sequential or a recursive mode of execution to either forward a new concept in the dictionary of wisdom or to link and classify the realm of current activity to an existing tree of knowledge or as detail of known knowledge.

10.1 INTRODUCTION

The notion of *wisdom* originates in the writings of Aristotle. The original context implies the capacity to judge rightly between the many manifestations of good and just life. The word *philosophy* is also rooted in the Greek word for wisdom. A scientific approach to the intersection of the two concepts has not been pursued for a long time. The *Oxford English Dictionary* relating the two words offers a basically interwoven and circular definition for the word *wisdom*. More investigation suggests that the early definitions of wisdom [1, 2] lean heavily toward philosophy. From the writings of early philosophers, the roots of wisdom are spread in nature, soul and psychology, ethics, morality, and art and can be seen to stretch into politics. For a long time (from the third century BC to about AD 1870) the vast umbrella of wisdom had blocked science and mathematics from penetrating the core content and subject matter of wisdom. Even today, the problem continues but computers and networks provide some of the basic tools and systems to examine the mystery and mysticism encompassed in the word wisdom from a numerical perspective.

Over the last few decades, it has become evident that the gap between the information capacity of the high-speed networks within society and the neural networks within the human brain is being driven further apart. Whereas modem networks are fast and data-driven, human understanding is slower and knowledge-driven. In an attempt to bridge this increasing gap, we propose architectures of machines and human beings that work in cooperation and synergy to produce deeply seated axioms of knowledge [3] that are a basis of comprehension and wisdom. Human understanding is thus enhanced. In an effort to offer concrete architectures of computers to buffer high-speed networks from the sensitive human mind, the basic concepts [4, 5] of a wisdom machine were presented earlier.

The premise for the importance and need for a wisdom machine is derived from the structure and organization of modern corporations or national governments.

Both these human structures of the last few decades have had a profound impact on society. In many instances, the shear complexity of the organizational functions and the wide disparity of the array of products, require a middle management to shield the sensitive and delicate executive tasks from the routine and mundane production functions. Both are equally important, but the flavor and impact are different. In a similar vein, the data in the networks which carry the routine and mundane tasks keeping the information society productive and economically stable, need to be isolated to avoid cluttering the sensitive and delicate tasks of guiding policy for social change and progress based on morality, values, and ethics. Thus the long-term search for wisdom to guide society is separated from the short-term objective of performing the routine tasks of keeping the economy going.

Before the advent of the information age and global Internet, the clergy, monks, saints and apostles filled the wisdom space with opinions, teachings, guidance, and sermons. To the extent that the hunter-gatherer survived in the jungle society, the elite thinking human survives in the information age. However, to bring the role of human virtue and values into an information jungle, the beauty and truth that lurk beyond reason and intellect need the long spans of contemplative meditation and consistent reasoning to be realized. To this extent, the wisdom machine serves as an intelligent and resourceful agent that shelters the contemplative mind from the mechanistic mundane. It serves the same function as the IT (information technology) platform serves in corporate environments [6] or as EG (electronic government) networks [7] serve in national and local governments.

One of the chief strategies in science is to set boundaries for the disciplinary area that is investigated and the older and classic definitions of wisdom become too broad and encompassing to be scientifically investigated. To circumvent the inherent problem in building a wisdom machine, we can rely on the strategy still used in some of the libraries, (known as the Dewey Decimal System [8] proposed by Dewey in 1870). This system classifies knowledge into manageable segments and assigns an identifier to each segment. The Library of Congress [9] uses a much finer classification of the disciplines. When the machine is offered this number to *initially* search for an axiom of wisdom through the world knowledge bases, a network-oriented WM can seek out truth, universality and elegance in a *tentative* axiom of wisdom in that direction. As a next step, the WM can look in the databases for interrelated sister disciplines, such as physics and electrical engineering, communications and computer science, or medicine and biology, and so on. Thus the range of search is user controlled and progresses step by step.

Furthermore, the ancient definition of wisdom does not specifically require an absolute (i.e., 100 percent) confidence in the statement of the axiom. Thus the machine strives to achieve the highest feasible confidence. The search thus goes on to find axioms of wisdom constrained by two sets of numbers: (1) by the directionality(ies) imposed by the user and (2) by the prescribed numerical limits (or within limitations bounded by machine accuracy (the NPU)) for confidence in the statement.

From modern perspective, wisdom points to knowledge, virtue and lasting truth. Here, we present an architectural arrangement of a group of computers that examine the flow of data and information through the networks and extract a first level of knowledge from data to evaluate it further to extract any wisdom that is embedded in the data or events that the machines are constantly sensing and processing. The circular definition of wisdom in the *Oxford English Dictionary* is broken by tapping into the flow of information and distilling knowledge and then refining this knowledge to wisdom, if it is wisdom that meets the directional properties (based on the area of knowledge), its confidence level (of the verifiable truth), and virtue associated with social value.

This rationale is derived from the classic works in science (searching for truth), arts (searching for beauty), and philanthropy (searching for social benevolence). *First,* wisdom like truth is illusive; but that has not prevented scientists from writing equations and identities. *Second,* wisdom like beauty is also illusive; but that has not prevented architects, sculptors, and painters from creating masterpieces. *Third,* wisdom like virtue is illusive; but that has not prevented philanthropists from building churches, mosques and shrines for the peace of mind. The list continues. It is evident that even though we cannot define wisdom absolutely, we can pursue it and we can instruct the machine(s) with every (AI) program to track data, information and knowledge upon which wisdom is based.

In the information society, knowledge drives the economy of minds. But the ground rules of the economics of knowledge and information do not completely follow the rules of microeconomics or the rules of macroeconomics [10, 11]. Emotions, passions, and feelings all get activated as sensitive information and knowledge is processed in the mind. Yet, reason and rationality prevail in a majority of cases. Natural/artificial intelligence(s) can verify, with precision and accuracy to verify if a timeless conclusion can be drawn from routine information and knowledge. In a sense, the wisdom has to have the highest quality of reason embedded in it with timelessness of the truth in the statement of the concept being derived from knowledge. Artificially intelligent machines can accomplish a part of this pursuit under the watchful eye of a human mentor with instinct, vision, and creativity.

The premise for perfect wisdom is its total generality in the statement and the perfection within its representation as an axiom of wisdom. In essence, absolute wisdom is not a realistic goal to pursue for either machines or human beings. To be realistic, what the WM can offer is an imperfect statement of wisdom. However, the synthesized statement has a suitable level of generality and a maximum level of perfection of wisdom. Accordingly, its three characteristic constituents— the truth (the accuracy of the statement), the beauty (the elegance encapsulated in the statement), and the virtue (the social benevolence that is conveyed by the statement)— all need to be explored and optimized by the machine and the human element that guides the execution of the machine.

A realm of cooperation and synergy exists between the machines that do not tire and the minds that do not give up. In this vein, we explore the region of intersection and overlap between machines that perform repetitive and numerically accurate functions and humans who dare to break the mundane laws of the known and the discovered. The machines and networks work for us in an extremely disciplined fashion. Likewise, the perseverant minds do not stop until a discovery is made or an invention has been evolved or a new frontier is crossed or a new barrier is broken. Furthermore, the vigor or vitality of the human mind may last a lifetime, even if the goals are abstract. In the WM, the human beings command a set of slave (and emotionless) machines, each having a limited amount of programmed freedom to do its task but also having the ability to quickly abandon fruitless activity at the discretion (or instinct) of the human being.

In this Chapter, we pull together divergent ideas. These ideas stem from AI systems, corporate problem-solving techniques, decision support systems and most of all from being able to assign a vectored notion of dimensionality to wisdom. In the real world, the pursuit of perfect wisdom is much like the pursuit of total generality. In a practical situation, this effort is bound to fail. However, if wisdom is redefined to suit the granularity of present knowledge and its classification, then a sense of generality can be explored, but within the confines of what is known and classified in society. In the world of computation and networks, the pursuit of absolute truth is much like the search for numbers or sets that are undeniably accurate at all limits of computation. Neither one of the two pursuits is likely to lead to anything practical.

In an attempt to reach a compromise between the idealism at one extreme and a real world of numbers that constrains our comprehension and understanding at the other extreme; we propose a negotiated frontier between these extremes and forward two basic concepts. *First,* a directional confine of wisdom is laid down from the granularity of knowledge that is contained and documented in any society by the DDS or the LoC classification; and *second,* the machines that explore any concept of wisdom are not forced beyond the limits of the numerical processor unit (NPU) that computes the confidence level of the wisdom being sought. In most cases, the confidence level need not be computed at the limits of accuracy of the NPU. Suffice it to say that a rough approximation to convince a large audience will facilitate the derivation of wisdom that the WM is going to generate with a certain level of confidence in a predefined direction of knowledge. This approach is implemented in medical diagnostic software [12, 13] systems that help patients and physicians understand and comprehend most health problems at an early stage.

10.2 ROLE OF DECISION SUPPORT SYSTEMS (DSS)

To some extent, the DSS environments [14] shown in Figure 10.1, provide an embryonic precursor to the WM. The composite role of the human–machine interaction is evident. When a query is placed at the input devices via the input bus (A1 in Figure 10.1), the machine recompiles the question. It can also train the human being at A to be precise about the query and type of investigation that the machine is about to conduct. Once the directionality is established, the machine investigates the environmental variables in the operational databases via interface B. This search affirms the context in which the machine would produce a solution relevant to the query and return a confidence level that the solution offered is genuine and appropriate. The nature and type of interfaces and physical location are irrelevant to the functions and the mode of operation of a simple DSS.

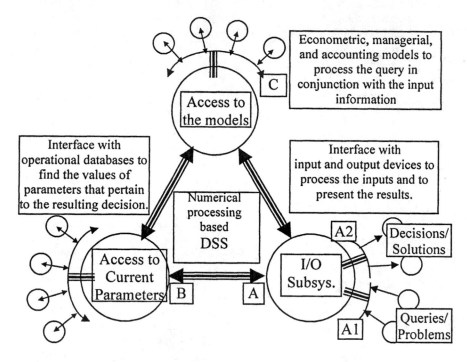

Figure 10.1 A typical decision support system and its implementation on a computer. Managerial queries are received and processed by the (typical) mathematical models in light of the current set of external inputs from the operational databases. Results of possible decisions are presented in view of pros and cons of each decision. Medical, stock market, and educational systems use the DSS approach effectively and extensively.

The DSS also deploys the conventional models from the pure and applied sciences to find valid and acceptable solutions. The nature of databases is consistent with the usage of DSS.

10.2.1 The I/O Subsystem

When a query or a problem is launched by a user at the devices connected to the input bus A1, the system recompiles the question into a problem that the machine is equipped to process. The usual steps in the compilation, assembling, machine code generation are completed and the program execution follows. The results are reported at the output stations via the output bus A2. Any amount of processing is feasible in the I/O subsystem to suit the user needs. Both image and data processing would be appropriate in this subsystem. A rudimentary form of pattern and object recognition can be incorporated to further tune the overall DSS to the individual need of a group of users or any particular user, such as a handicapped person or a genius interacting with the DSS. Numerous applications of this type of a DSS exist in educational, investment and medical fields.

10.2.2 Operational Parameters

Operational parameters are important because the DSS will provide an answer to the problem in the context of previous and/or present environmental conditions and circumstances in which the question is based. The database–network interface at B as shown in Figure 10.1, allows the machine to read and retrieve these parameters. This restriction simplifies the function to the extent that the time domain is restricted to the present and the space domain is restricted to here. In a sense, the question will not be answered if the question was asked in earlier centuries or, likewise, if the question was asked in a different social/cultural environment. Such restrictions will have to be removed if the machine is processing information for knowledge or processing knowledge for wisdom. This question will be addressed again in Section 10.3.2.

10.2.3 Scientific, Social and Mathematical Models

Within the limited constraint of the functions of the DSS, the query is in the context of parameters retrieved at the interface B. The extent to which they would influence any decision is processed by the scientific, social, and econometric/mathematical models stored in database C. In essence, the DSS checks the validity of the solution that it proposes to be consistent with the established scientific principles and concepts embedded in the models. To the extent that these models are static and not dynamically updated by a self-learning and self-healing algorithms, the DSS is not even an artificially intelligent machine environment.

10.3 ROLE OF SENSING NETWORKS

It is possible to elevate the status of a DSS environment to become self-monitoring, self-sufficient, dynamically balanced, and artificially intelligent. In a typical sensing network [15], shown in Figure 10.2, the three major building blocks and the interfaces are retained. Such sensing networks can be used to monitor the security and stability of any given environment. In a sense these elaborate feedback control systems make localized decisions if the sensors detect any threat to the overall functionality as the sensors monitor it.

A real-life example of such sensing networks in conjunction with the rest of the machine(s) is during wars. The movement of the enemy, and the enemy's attack positions, and the enemy's attributes are fed in at the sensors. The position of the friendly attack artillery, the locations of the bombers, and the submarines, and so on are fed into a dynamic and updated database at the current parameter database. Satellite tracking sensors and communicators are used to receive inputs and to dispatch commands. The machine works very hard to maximize any preset goal, such as maximize the losses inflicted, minimize the causalities to the friendly side and maximize the "kill ratio," which can be programmed into the objective function that the machine pursues at an incredibly fast speed and deadly pace. An *abuse* of the machines becomes as feasible as the *use* of the machine. Such war games are seriously pursued by nations at war and the machine becomes an intelligent killer tool in the hands of the humans with shady intentions. We discuss this dark side to the use of the WM again in Section 10.9.

Sensing environment in this rudimentary way has been implemented in security systems and is deployed in almost all automated telephone answering systems. The inputs from the sensors or users prompt the response and the system responds following very predefined and standardized steps. In fact, the traditional telephone system follows this well-known approach before it connects the line to the called party. Any digression from the standard practice in dialing is reported as an error or an operator intervenes. In modern communication systems, a considerable amount of artificial [16] and network intelligence [17] is embedded in completing the communication signals and the evental path between the caller and the called party.

10.3.1 Sensor/Response System

If the I/O subsystem of the DSS can be replaced by a sensor/response system, then the machine can be forced to function as a stable feedback processor that checks an array of inputs (via box A1) and adjusts an array of outputs (via response box A2). The sensors may be local or global, they may provide current or derived information, or they may preprocess the sensor data and act as filters.

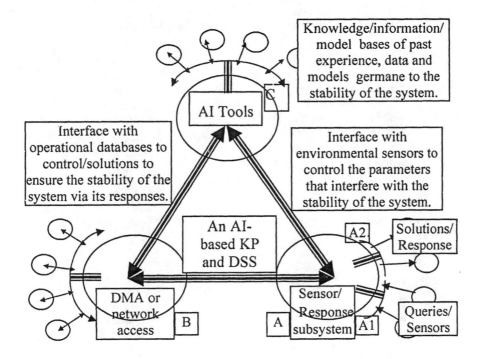

Knowledge/information/ model bases of past experience, data and models germane to the stability of the system.

AI Tools

C

Interface with operational databases to control/solutions to ensure the stability of the system via its responses.

Interface with environmental sensors to control the parameters that interfere with the stability of the system.

An AI-based KP and DSS

A2

Solutions/ Response

DMA or network access

B

Sensor/ Response subsystem

A

A1

Queries/ Sensors

Figure 10.2 Modification of typical decision support system. It can be implemented on a computer with three bus structures: A, dedicated to I/O operations with sensing functions at the input side and control function on the output side; B, automated access to all relevant information that would impact the action being taken to adjust the control parameters; and C, the framework for accessing the knowledge or ground rules that should govern the stabilizing response from the system.

10.3.2 Current Parameter Database

This is akin to the operational database of the DSS. In addition to accessing the parameters that may have an impact on the course of action by the processor, it also predicts the changes of such parameters at the time when the corrective measure will be implemented.

The predictive nature in the estimation of the parameters would impart a greater sense of stability to the system. It also eliminates possibly unexpected oscillations in the transitory behavior of the sensing systems/networks. Critically damped response or incrementally corrective measures may also be invoked from these networks by additional processing at B and C interfaces (see Figure 10.2).

10.3.3 Knowledge, Information, and Models Databases

As the stability of the system gets complicated or it has to be delicately balanced, then the AI tools for handling objects (including personalities of people) embedded as the parameters become active. This methodology would closely parallel the functions of the algebraic/numerical tools that would get activated in handling symbols/numbers in the simpler DSS. As may become necessary, the process of final implementation of the corrective strategy may be a purely humanistic process. This type of approach is frequently seen in the legal [18], managerial [6] and political environments [19]. If the machine is to accurately replace the human (especially during the execution of medically tailored AI programs such as Intern or Mycin), then the confidence level of the machine-based decision needs to be computed along with the inductive reasoning to reach the decision. This approach will be developed in the inductive and (statistically based) estimation functions of the WM.

10.4 ROLE OF ACCUMULATED KNOWLEDGE

There are two major systems for the classification of accumulated knowledge. The first one is based on the Dewey Decimal System (DDS) [8] suggested in 1873; and the second one is based on the Library of Congress (LoC) [9] classification. The latter system further refines the DDS classification and offers more flexibility. Both systems follow a systematic and comprehensive way of constructing knowledge trees in a basic discipline or a subject at the stem of the tree. The branches, twigs and leaves follow. The depth of the tree (subject matter) can be six layers deep in the initial DDS, with six digits to indicate a particular subject. The six-digit number has two, three-digit segments separated by a decimal point, and the body of knowledge is divided into ten grouping (0 through 9). The intermediate numbers between any two six-digit numbers indicate a segment of knowledge.

This classification can become coarse given the explosion of knowledge in the modern society. Fortunately, modern computing systems can handle digits or data stings much longer than the six-digit numbers suggested by Dewey, and the classification of machine-based search can become precise and highly directional. Since the advent of the DDS and then the LoC classification system, the algorithms for the classification of knowledge have not followed any scientific methodology. Related bodies of knowledge do not have any precoded linkages like the databases in computer systems. To this extent, dealing with dynamically expanding knowledge bases can only fall back on established and worldwide platforms (such as the DDS and the LoC classification). The tagging of such knowledge bases by time of the day or by date, may become essential in view of the expansionary nature of current knowledge in certain directions.

Again, the expanding processing power of the central processor units (CPUs) and the broadband of the networks [17] facilitate the search of the knowledge bases. If the rate of expansion of the knowledge bases is faster than the processing power of the WM and the broadband capacity of the networks that feed into the WM(s), then results of the WM can be error prone. The race between knowledge and the machines that process knowledge gets to be time dependent and uncertainty becomes apparent. This principle of this uncertainty is akin to the Heisenberg's principle of uncertainty. The processing of knowledge alters the state of knowledge. However, in a great many cases, the results of the WM can be useful even if the results are a few seconds old and within the framework of the knowledge bases accessed by the machine.

10.5 CONFIDENCE IN THE RESULTS

Wisdom that is absolute at every instant of time and at every point in the globe is impossible to pursue. However, if a region of acceptability is predefined, then the machine can attempt to approach that region in its search for validation. The validity of results is equally important to make a practical search that would otherwise be impossible. An aspect of human behavior can thus be imposed on the machine; the human being first imposes a certain level of confidence in the derivation of wisdom, then gradually tightens the confidence-level number at the expense of greater effort from the machine in searching the knowledge bases more thoroughly and more accurately. This strategy of limited search and relaxing the constraints when no solution exists or conversely tightening the search constraints if too many results exist is well documented in the behavioral theory of corporations.

Modern corporations deploy [20] these two approaches (limited or constrained search and estimation of success) to "weigh and consider" possible solutions to a corporate problem. In the final stages of problem solving, executives tighten or relax the probability of success either by reinforcing every step in the implementation of the solution or by taking a calculated risk at some stages in the implementation. Executives in corporations have indicated the strategy as behavioral modes in dealing with situations that are totally new.

In the WM, these documented human approaches are borrowed to explore a new axiom of wisdom at the lowest (the AI) level. *First,* numerical constraints in the search are implemented by the numerical classification of knowledge and the body of knowledge that immediately surrounds the topic in which wisdom is pursued. *Second,* the estimated confidence level forces the machine to offer practical and realistic results of the search. *Third,* every embryonic axiom of wisdom is reevaluated by examining every fragment of inference that leads to a valid oracle of wisdom.

The ability to assign a numerical level of confidence to any inference becomes a part of the derived wisdom. Thus a tree of knowledge with its own levels of confidence is implicitly structured before any notion of wisdom is drawn. The confidence level becomes the number that pulls the machine to pursue its search in the direction of the classified knowledge. In a philosophic sense, if the strength of the chain is in its weakest link, then confidence in the derived wisdom is the smallest value of confidence in the inference chain leading to an axiom of wisdom. This could either be reinforced by additional search if it succeeds, or become a basis for rejection of the axiom of wisdom if the search fails. In a sense, the WM performs a validity check for every inference much as a physician needs to be convinced (at an appropriate level of confidence) at every stage of diagnosis.

When this number fails to meet a required value, the inferencing algorithms get reinforced to derive a firmer inference. To remain consistent in the search of truth (or elegance, or virtue) in wisdom, human bias (at the second level) is not to compromise the quality of the ultimate scientific truth (or sense of beauty or the goal of social justice) that is pursued. In this area of human-machine decision/search support system, the overlap of artificial intelligence and human virtue can, unwittingly, obscure the truth, spoil the beauty, or deter the social justice. Human integrity plays as important a role as the processing power within the computers or the bandwidth within the networks. Hidden in the union space of the three— human integrity, processing power and bandwidth of networks— lurk the oracles of wisdom waiting to be explored and enunciated.

10.6 THE REALM OF REALITY

The realization of a practical WM relies heavily on the software embedded within a set of at least six computer systems or subsystems. The functionality of these machines is distinct, even though the physical boundaries may not be well partitioned. A six-wafer computer system will serve just as well as an ultrafast computer that is time-shared six times over for each of the six distinct functions. The operating systems and the performance of the two architectural arrangements may be significantly different. In this early design of the WM, three modes of operation are identifiable and discussed in Sections 10.7, 10.8 and 10.9.

In the first level (Section 10.7), the WM performs as a typical HW, SW, and application system with three distinct machine subsystems (discussed in Sections 10.7.1, 10.7.2 and 10.7.3). In the second level (Section 10.6), the WM operates as an intelligent human element driving the machine with three more subsystems, discussed in Sections 10.8.1, 10.8.2 and 10.8.3. In the third level (Section 10.9), the human being(s) performs functions of natural intelligence, such as creativity, instinctive and predictive thinking, perceptual imaging and model building. To assemble the hardware and the interconnection, the first three subsystems constitute level I and second three sub systems constitute level II of the organization. The entire WM is discussed in Section 10.10.

10.7 TYPICAL COMPUTER FUNCTIONS IN THE WM

10.7.1 Dialog Processor (Subsystem 1)

A dialog processor identifies and validates a direction in which the wisdom is being pursued and the expected level of confidence in the axiom of wisdom that is acceptable to the peripheral user of the machine. This access can be direct or it can be remote access via a network. In an idle mode, the machine is tied into a network gate and the Internet/network traffic dealing with any predefined area [such as rainfall, stock market, gross national product (GNP), VLSI, or AI] for searching for axioms of wisdom.

10.7.2 Database (DB) Administrator (Subsystem 2)

A database administrator interfaces with local databases that directly influence the specified area in which an axiom of wisdom is being pursued. This interface permits the machine to explore the relationships between the objects that lead to a basis for wisdom. For example, if an *interim* axiom of wisdom is classified as "the rain in Spain falls mainly on the plain," the machine at this stage (level I) accesses the rainfall data in Spain and, in particular, for the data on the plain of Spain, even though it accumulates the data for the other regions, because the term "mainly" will need a confidence level and a probability number associated with it. Numerical values are assigned to the objects (percentage, inches, drizzle, downpour, etc. for rainfall; percentage, altitude, terrain, etc. for plain of Spain; percentage, seasonal variations, terrain, etc. for mainly). In a true sense, the machine gives a new meaning to the statement because it offers the statistical estimate for the time, season, and geographical spread of the confidence levels and the probabilities that the rainfall is mainly on the plain. To this extent, the WM offers numerical and definite values based on the local databases for the rainfall in Spain.

10.7.3 Knowledge Base (KB) Administrator (Subsystem 3)

A knowledge base administrator interfaces with the knowledge bases dealing with other objects related to the objects in the axiom in which the wisdom is being pursued. The KB functions are significantly different from the DB functions. Use of existing knowledge is generally critical to expounding any axiom of wisdom further by examining the interrelationship between objects or similar objects. For this reason, interface with the knowledge or discipline dealing with the topic becomes necessary. To continue with example in Section 10.7.2, the rainfall data also needs to the correlated to the weather patterns and the barometric pressure/wind velocity data at the time of the rainfall. To support the functionality of the WM at the AI level, the patterns of changes of other related objects are correlated to the actual event of the rainfall by deploying the pattern recognition (PR) programs in this interface.

These PR programs do more than passively search for patterns. They find a pattern of meteorological conditions and the seasons for the plain of Spain, together with the geographical contours of surrounding areas. In a sense, the WM finds whether there is something unique about Spain or whether the prairies of America or the desert lands of Australia would also experience a similar rainfall pattern. If it does find similarities, the initial statement that the "the rain in Spain falls mainly in the plain" would be modified accordingly to reflect all the plains around the world or on other planets, if their databases are available. If no similarity is found, then the wind patterns and the topography of Spain would be investigated to find if any other part of the globe that has similar patterns (via the PR programs) would also experience a rainfall pattern similar to that in Spain. If there are a set of circumstances that are unique to Spain and nowhere else in the world, then the machine would assign a certain confidence level to the extent of its search, that the (truth in) wisdom of the original statement is validated. If we expect the WM to follow Aristotle's teachings, both the beauty and social value (components of wisdom) within the axiom "the rain in Spain falls mainly in the plain" also remain to be verified before the axiom could be classified as genuine words of wisdom.

10.8 HUMAN INTERVENTION

The role of human intervention becomes apparent. Whereas the machine may have exhaustively searched the knowledge bases, the human being will (in all likelihood) quickly link the search to a rhyming dictionary that finds the rhymes and rhythms in the objects (rain, Spain, plain) and detects other patterns (Cain, fain, gain, lain, main, Maine, pain, vain, vein, wain, Wain, etc.). More so, the rhythm is also tracked by counting syllables in the phrase or the axiom and their locations. An extended search follows, based on the rhyming patterns and rhythmic styles. Now the machine can generate other phrases such as "the rain in Spain can be a pain," or "the rain of Spain may not occur in Maine," or "the pain is never in vain," "there is no plain in Maine to have the rain of Spain" and so on. Thus it becomes possible to change an axiom of truth (if any), into words that have the same pattern(s) as that of a previous axiom. The WM now works as a naïve poet much as it acts as naïve musician, or a mathematician, and so on. It is possible to see that, in a higher mode, the WM may be directed (by the human counterpart) to search for more and more truthful statements, or more abstractions of beauty, or solutions that have even more value to the society. Three independent machines can be deployed concurrently (see Section 10.11), or the same machine may be used in a sequential mode but with a different database for the abstractions of beauty and then again with a different database for social benefits. The operating system of the three

WMs or the same WM deployed three times over with reentrant loops becomes complex but viable.

The machine goes further if it is allowed to dig deeper into the rhyming dictionary. For example, if the machine is permitted to search for multi-syllabic objects (terrain, constrain, featherbrain, quatrain, refrain, restrain, etc.) to rhyme with one or more objects (rain), then the WM can search for axioms closer to the truth than the original axiom. For instance, an axiom such as "the terrain of Maine cannot sustain the rain on the plain" is equally truthful. Although it is derived from Professor Henry Higgins's statement, it can be more accurate and it can be successively pushed toward a higher-level of confidence. In the main, the truth is plain; there is plenty to gain from a WM built in this vein.

Even though it is possible to play silly games with the WM, it is a tool of some systemic value. Under the control of serious users, the computer components of the WM function much like the diving gear of an undersea explorer, permitting the humans to dig deeper and probe further into the realm of wisdom. Alternatively, the hardware and AI routines (of the WM) become the glider that lets humans explore unchartered domains of human imagination.

10.8.1 Symbols and Equations (Subsystem 4)

Objects and their semantic and syntactical/interactive processes in search of knowledge are as germane as nouns, adjectives, and verbs/adverbs[1] in any language. In a very direct sense, the objects/symbols, their semantic context, and their interactions are concisely and precisely documented as mathematical equations. To build or search for wisdom in any statement, quickly, efficiently, and optimally, the strategy is to reduce the objects (identified as an object lexical analyzer) and symbols in the axioms to what are already known about these particular objects or similar objects (by relaxing the attributes of identified objects) in knowledge bases. After all, the idea is not to keep spinning the wheels to reinvent the wheel.

To implement this strategy in the WM, an interface to a database of symbols and equations is provided at a higher level. In reality, we do not have the sophisticated AI tools and techniques to detect and remedy a circular search much like a kitten that cannot stop chasing its own tail. A human intervention or an oversight is necessary to allow a machine to make a fruitful search.

As an initial effort, the machine simply lists the symbols that play a dominant role in influencing the symbol for which wisdom is being pursued. To continue with the rain axiom, all the symbols/objects influencing the rainfall, such as humidity, height of rain bearing clouds, ambient temperature, pressure velocity patterns, distance from the oceans, location of the plain, would be identified and

---

[1] In Section 8.3.1 the "noun" equivalent of an object is associated with the "context" equivalent (what, where, when, how, and their combination; origin, syntactic, semantic, contextual setting; etc.) of the object. The concept in this Chapter is more generic than the concept in Chapter 8.

symbolized. The machine searches exhaustively for the symbols that are related in any mathematical/statistical way whatsoever and brings them to the attention of a human counterpart. Any similarity between these variables in any of other discipline would be identified. This machine-based clue forms the basis of any truth/similarity in the statements just as the mathematicians would have seen it from their database of symbols, formulas, and equations.

10.8.2 Axiomatic Tools (Subsystem 5)

Axiomatic tools facilitate the search for truth (elegance or social benefit) that an axiom conveys. After an identification of objects in an axiom (by object lexical analyzer, see Section 10.5), the attributes of the objects and their interrelationships are searched by constructing a hierarchical relation of each objects with its attributes and the linkages and interdependencies. Even though the process appears vague and uncertain, the thesaurus and the dictionary of the language provide the methodology for constructing the attributes and linkages at the first level of direct relationships. When dealing with other disciplines, such as chemistry or computer science, it may become necessary to extend the search in specialized handbooks and link them to the other objects in the axiom. These searches are performed easily if the knowledge banks are addressed by the WM via global gateways.

In searching for truth, the depth of search depends on the confidence level in the refinement of any axiom. In recursive mode of search (i.e., object search first and then an attribute search next, and repeat), the truth within any statement is made arbitrarily deep. Largely, the level of search is limited to truth within an axiom of wisdom. However, if the accuracy of an equation is to be searched, then the WM is forced to expand the search (every object, every attribute; then every attribute, every other object; repeat) until the equation is no longer valid.

The search for elegance is more abstract. Unfortunately, there are no well documented thesauruses or dictionaries of elegance (or refinement, beauty, form, style, grace or polish) to initiate the search in the direction of elegance. However, museums of art document what has been revered in the past. Recognition of the documented patterns (by PR routine) offers some clues about the patterns in the present axioms. When the documentation in the knowledge banks offers no clues, human intuition is the only recourse. For this reason, the human counterpart of the machines (HW, SW, networks, firmware, applications, etc.) in this environment needs to complement the power of the modern machines with multilevel thought and a dictionary of imagination.

The search for social values in any axiom or in any scientific innovation is partially embedded in historical records. Socially significant findings and inventions of the past centuries generally are recorded in record books and by social scientists and as historic events. Over a period of time, the WM can serve as a source for a dictionary or thesaurus of global events that are documented as significant because the machine has a statistical arm to determine how the events have become significant and what percentile of the population have benefited in the community, in a country or around the globe.

10.8.3 Hypothesis Testing (Subsystem 6)

The facility to test a hypothesis for its validity in any partially forwarded axiom is crucial to classifying or declassifying the axiom as a statement of wisdom. This interface is necessary because a statement of absolute truth that is elegant under all conditions and entirely beneficial to every society is scientifically absurd. Hence a compromise is sought by the WM when it can accept an axiom as being close enough to truth (based on statistical calculations), as being partially elegant (based on comparison with other elegant axioms/oracles), and as being acceptably socially beneficial (based on similar axioms of social value).

If a partially processed axiom derived during the operation of the WM has to pass the criteria of truth, elegance and social value (in any combination thereof), then the machine has to perform rigorous tests on the assertion of truth, the presence of elegance and the projection of social value. In this mode, the admixture of the AI methodologies (such as pattern recognition, expert system, and opinion polling) and the traditional tools of statistical inferencing become crucial. If the machine interface cannot tackle both tasks, then multitasking and resource sharing (from the principles in operating systems) become essential.

10.9 ALL HUMAN FUNCTIONS

In the highest mode, the role of the WM is totally human. The goal is to discover the boundary of natural intelligence to probe into artificial intelligence. This interaction extends beyond the realm of programmability. Some humans may have the gifts of creativity, predictive thinking, perceptual imaging, and model building as highly developed personal assets. For this reason, the human counterpart of the computer system in the WM needs to be a perfect (if it is ever possible) match to machine and its capacity. The match extends further to the direction in which the wisdom is being pursued. For instance, depth and breadth of personal knowledge to "weigh and consider" the machine-generated information and deduction will act as the guiding posts to the axiom of wisdom under derivation by the hardware (HW), software (SW), and firmware (FW) of the WM.

Caution in the choice of the human counterpart becomes mandatory. A socially destructive human can force the WM to invent a killer machine. On the other hand, a saint can force the machine to discover the modes of meditation, or a poet can force the machine to express Lord Alfred Tennyson in the words of Gibran Khalil Gibran or express William Shakespeare as Omar Khyyam and so on. The creative applications of the WM depend on the discretionary inputs (see Sections 10.3.3 and 10.8.2) by the user. In a great majority of cases, the WM offers new degrees of freedom to the user just like intelligent networks [17] offer opportunities to the network service providers. In this mode of running the WM, the user has the same degree of control that an astronaut has in flying a spacecraft. In many cases, the machine offers new frontiers at the boundaries of natural and artificial intelligence unified as creativity. Some gifted scientists and artists can execute both types of intelligence without the WM. However, there are no bounds on purely human creativity, or on the bounds of machine-assisted human creativity. It is our contention that machine-assisted creativity can probe deeper into the world of nature still so obscure to us.

In particular, hackers and virus implanters abuse this position of being able to control computers and networks, even though most sane users of computers and networks would attempt to draw benefit from these systems. In the case of the WM, the powers to compute, control, and communicate are each enhanced many times over, because the six subsystems (see Sections 10.7.1–10.7.3 and 10.8.1–10.8.3) work in synergy and in close proximity.

Abuse of the WM is a threat to the social and cultural norms of the society. To some extent, it parallels airplanes (to transport or to bomb), nuclear reactors (to generate power or to enrich uranium for bombs) or even TV networks (to communicate or to agitate). Security and caution are necessary to permit socially beneficial use and, conversely, to prevent its abuse. The synergy of two fundamental partners (six-subsystems and human beings) is essential to the function of the WM. When illegal knowledge base primers corrupt knowledge bases or when users sense the faulty social, moral or ethical deductions from the machine, then either users or operating system of the WM needs to correct the deviation by quarantining the knowledge bases. The security administration and systems operations tools in most computers routinely invoke these steps when corrupted files are encountered.

Moreover, the WM offers users the capacity to retune and refine the axioms, systems, inventions, devices, and so on, iteratively and optimally. Partial concepts can be recycled through the machine to achieve perfection (if it is possible). Making the machine supra-naturally secure like the genomes or the double helix can also prevent abuse of the WM. A sense of moral and ethical dilemma develops at this stage because of the potential of the WM. In the evolution of society such situations are plentiful. For example, nuclear technology, infrared detection, and supersonic transport, or the stealth bombers, land-mines, and dynamite, have earned their place in society as desirable or as undesirable but managed inventions.

10.10 ARCHITECTURE

Figures 10.3, 10.4, and 10.5 depict the three stages of functionality of the WM. In Figure 10.3, the routine data from networks and sensors enters the WM at the lowest level. It may also be used to prime the WM about the general direction wherein wisdom or inference is sought. For example, if electrical engineering (EE) is the direction, the DDS classification for EE is 621 and that should suffice. If the inference or wisdom is sought from Fiji, then the MARC country code for Fiji is fj and that should suffice, and so on.

There is an important difference between the search engines and the WM. The WM extracts any valid concept from the information processed and it manipulates the concept(s) to find if there is truth (accepted level of validity from a scientific perspective), virtue (accepted level of social value and generality), and/or beauty (acceptable level of elegance) in the relationships perceived and then derived and confirmed on an iterative basis. It can be realized that if truth, virtue and beauty are replaced by stocks, bonds and trading practices, the machine will identify the traders and classify their trading practices as legal or illegal, thus catching the wrong doers before another mutual funds (of 2003) or an insurance company scandal (of 2004).

The three computers or subsystems process the data at the preliminary stage in an effort to detect and recognize opportunities to derive wisdom from routine events. The cause-and-effect relationships are deduced at an elementary level during this stage of processing; both the cause and effect are determined by the user or derived by the WM.

In Figure 10.4, the human counterpart in the WM critically evaluates an initially deduced cause–effect relationships or an inference. At this second stage, the human element (creativity, intuition, imagination, etc.) in the derivation of wisdom is injected and the constraints of the search are adaptively adjusted to find if there is truth (validity), virtue (social benefit), and beauty (elegance) in pursuit of the axiom of ultimate wisdom. It is quite feasible to search for truth alone in the machine-derived axiom first, then search for elegance, and then for beauty or grace in any other sequential order, or to search for all three simultaneously. Iterative relaxation of constraints and limits of confidence are interjected by the human being at this stage. To this extent, the inadequacy of the present knowledge bases becomes evident. Whereas the databases to evaluate the truth/validity are scattered throughout the world (as laws of physics, equations in mathematics, or procedures for medical treatment, etc. with their own confidence numbers) and are documented, similar databases to evaluate the beauty/elegance/grace or to evaluate virtue/social benefit/benevolence are harder to find and access. The user of a WM can force the machine to generate its own knowledge bases of virtue/social benefit/benevolence. Some priming of the machine with software and criteria to detect and recognize these three qualities and their attributes becomes necessary. Rule based systems and pattern recognition programs to seek and identify the abstract become harder to encode. Also, the machine, being artificially intelligent can fall back on an expert system database where humans have already identified certain rules and patterns for virtue/social value/benevolence. Later, the WM can reevaluate and modify the rules embedded in the initial priming of the machine. A similar scenario exists for building the knowledge base for beauty/elegance/grace. The WM is quite capable of generating such databases and accumulating more data (beauty/elegance/grace and virtue/social benefit/benevolence) as and when situations arise.

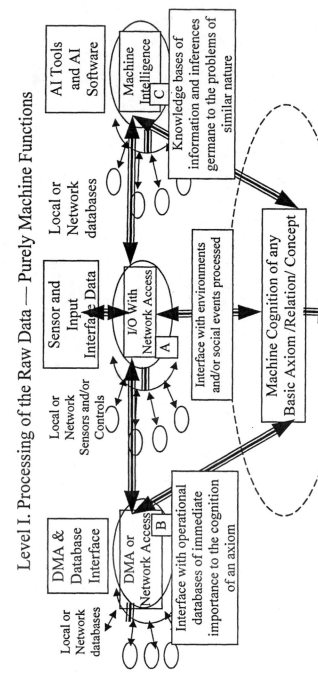

Level I. Processing of the Raw Data — Purely Machine Functions

AI Tools and AI Software

Machine Intelligence

C

Knowledge bases of information and inferences germane to the problems of similar nature

Local or Network databases

Sensor and Input Interface Data

I/O With Network Access

A

Interface with environments and/or social events processed

Local or Network Sensors and/or Controls

Machine Cognition of any Basic Axiom /Relation/ Concept

DMA & Database Interface

DMA or Network Access

B

Interface with operational databases of immediate importance to the cognition of an axiom

Local or Network databases

Initial Verification, Approval, Intuition, Realignment and Fine-tuning by Level II Human–Machine functions

Figure 10.3 Three machines or interfaces deal with the environmental and social setting (A), knowledge accumulated thus far (B), and cross referencing other disciplines (C) at level I.

Level II. Machine-Assisted Human Intelligence

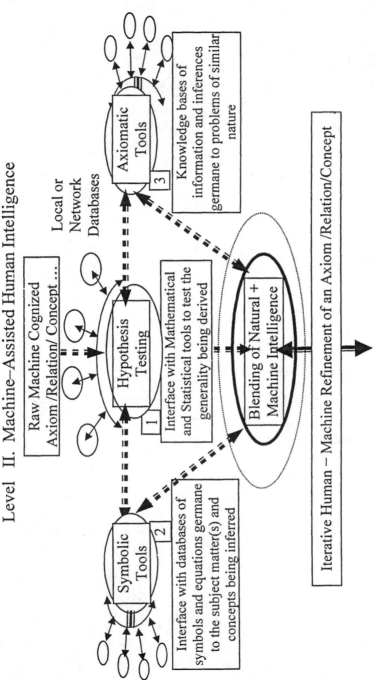

Figure 10.4 Hypothesis testing (1), generality check (2) and axiomatic tools (3), to validate of the axiom from level I. Statistical, symbolic, and axiomatic tools are used. Human creativity and intuition not capable of being programmed into the machine are blended at this level II.

Level III. Functions of Human Comprehension

Iterated and Refined Axiom /Relation/Concept ….

Beauty, Elegance

Grace, Social Value

Universality, Truth

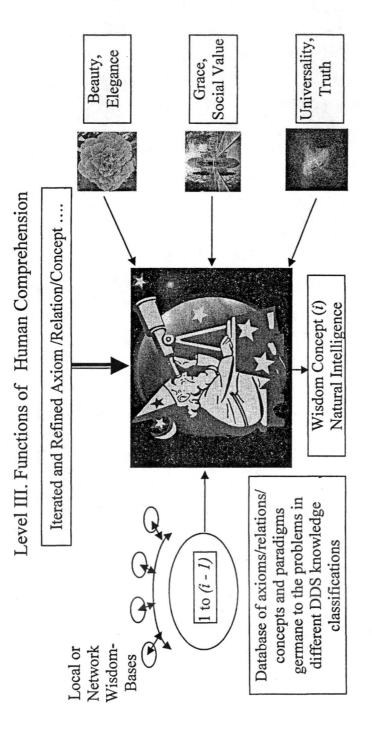

Wisdom Concept (*i*)
Natural Intelligence

Local or Network Wisdom-Bases

1 to (*i – 1*)

Database of axioms/relations/ concepts and paradigms germane to the problems in different DDS knowledge classifications

Figure 10.5 Final Integration of level I and level II functions as an axiom of wisdom by an all-human team. It may become logical and necessary to establish additional perspective from the human counterpart of the WM and polish the processed axiom of wisdom (or an equation in mathematics, or a verse of poetry) for the optimal blend of (at utmost) generality (universality) and perfection (beauty and grace).

The WM now mimics the role of an executive in a corporate environment falling back on standard operating procedures (SOPs). These SOPs suggest the steps to address problem areas when there is no firm mathematical or statistical basis for their solution [20]. Such a heuristic approach is well accepted in building corporate executive information systems.

In Figure 10.5, the all-human activity is depicted to encompass the nonprogrammable (and all) human gift of envisioning the unforeseen. It is quite possible to remove this phase of human polishing of the axioms/relationships/concepts of wisdom. If the human operators decide to force the WM in other modes, such as to assist lawmakers or act as the staff in a hospital to detect new diseases, bacteria, or any other agents, then the final committee will take over the role of this final human appendage to the WM. The results are recirculated through the machine to find the new confidence levels in view of the human enhancements to the early axioms/relationships/concepts.

The six subsystems (level I, see nodes A through C in Figure 10.3; and level Ii, see nodes 1 through 3 in Figure 10.4) are shown as one system. Typically, computer and network architectures do not include human elements as components of the system. However, in most decision support systems (DSSs) the role of the human being is seen as crucial to the output of the system.

For example, in the two medical application programs, Intern and Mycin, the patient plays an important role in the outcome of the system. Multilevel inputs at different levels of execution from the human being can force these medical application [21, 13] programs to offer a dependable diagnosis for the patient.

This type of interaction with the computers of the WM makes the system perform tasks not totally programmable for the hardware to execute by itself. Two features evolve. *First,* the human feedback is based on the partial execution of the search for wisdom. *Second,* the human can fine-tune the progress of the WM to the desired area of investigation and the confidence level sought.

For example, while the machine may be programmed to look for truth, elegance and social benefit in the axiom "the rain in Spain falls mainly on the plain." However, the human counterpart can the force the machine to look for truth in the statement in view of the rhyming pattern and also to generalize the axiom such as "the terrain around the plain in Spain makes the rain fall mostly on the plain," or whatever the case may be. Only the imagination of the user(s) limits the uses of the WM. Human instinct and creativity guide the machine to execute and refine the search or enhance the confidence level. An architectural arrangement of the entire system is depicted in Figure 10.6. The initial user interaction takes place at the dialog processor in subsystem A. The machine may be primed to look for events in an established domain of knowledge (such as electrical engineering at DDS classification of 621) or identify the subject matter. In the execution phase of level I activity, the machine processes all the sensors and monitors the network activity dealing with the subject matter. All the irrelevant information is filtered at this stage. A considerable degree of latitude is possible. Tightening the domain of search retrieves highly specific information while offering the WM a broad area of search results in the collection of very general information.

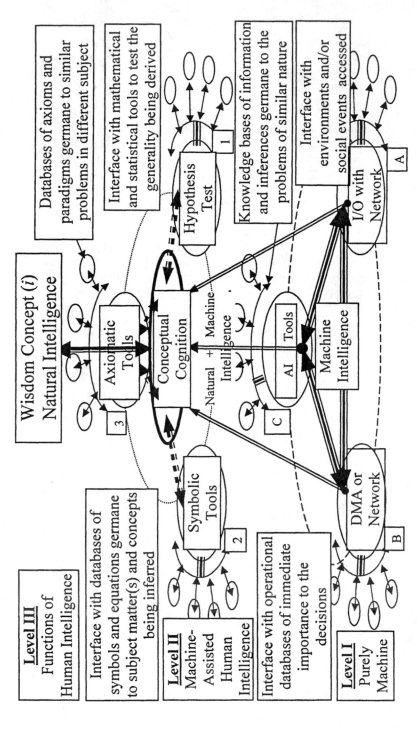

Figure 10.6 Integrated architecture of three-level model for the extraction of wisdom at level III from the knowledge and information at level I.

The processed data passes through interfaces B and C to reject irrelevant data based on collected knowledge databases on problems of a similar nature and to let the machine search for other relevant clues from the experience based on operational databases.

Similar processes at level II polish the raw axiom/relationship/concept further in an iterative mode. The human being will get interactive feedback on the effect of changes made in the processing of information through the sensors and the network.

To some extent, the human being controls the higher processes of the WM much as a pilot monitors a flight until it is complete or as a child learns to play a musical instrument. The rules of engagement are different. After some time, the WM becomes a partner or a tool in the inventions for making very specific contributions to society. We dare to suggest that the role of a WM will be that of human(oid), rather than a robotic, companion of a human being. To this extent, it is our contention that positive use of the WM will outweigh its negative use and the WM will become like any refined computer system that sharpens the human mind by becoming more and more adaptive in its learning algorithms [22, 23]. When its usage becomes extensive, the WM can demand increasingly sophisticated feedback from the human being, thus making the human being more creative and more intelligent at the same time.

10.11 FRONTIER OF INTELLIGENCE INTO WISDOM

The perspective on wisdom is wide and varied. From the teachings of Aristotle [2] to the recent explanations of the String theorists [24], at least three generalizations are drawn. First, a sense of energy and persistence of an axiom of wisdom prevails at all times through eternity (as we know it). Second, a search for the fewest axioms of sciences to comprehend the entire spectrum of behavior within the universe ranging from elementary particles to the cosmic bodies has constantly invoked the human spirit. Third, the intercepted space where three of the highest human values (truth, elegance and social value) overlap is a possible realm of wisdom with a great amount of order, even though we may label the incomprehensible order as chaos. Wisdom becomes as highly dimensioned as the human mind that hosts it and ever ready to overflow its bounds.

From an entirely philosophic perspective, it appears that the architecture of a composite WM is doomed to failure. However, from an engineering perspective, the approach of firmly confining the present problem with finite and realistic bounds offers some venues. We present the most obvious solution in this chapter. If the three human values (truth, virtue or social value, and beauty or elegance) are too many for the human mind to pursue at one time, then three in(ter)dependent architectures of a lower-level WM (see Figure 10.6) are invoked to make up one composite WM. This system now encompasses three WMs; WM-T, along the radial line at $\theta=90°$ or at $\pi/2$; WM-S along the radial line $\theta = 210°$ or at $7\pi/6$ and WM-E along the radial line $\theta = 330°$ or at $11\pi/6$, as shown in Figure 10.7.

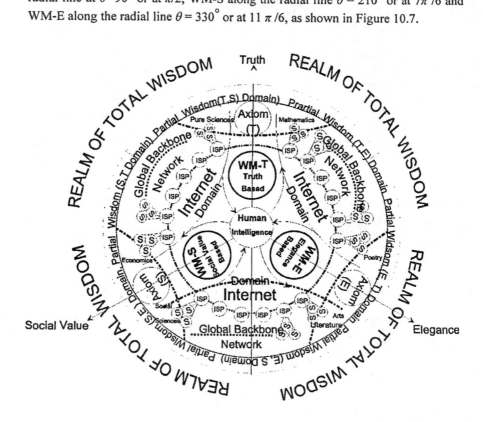

Figure 10.7 Unified role for each of the three wisdom machines WM-T, WM-E, WM-S, depicted in Figure 10.6 as they scan the Internet data and traffic via the numerous ISPs and switches (S). The initially identified axioms of each of the three machines are submitted to the judgment of a panel of human beings to validate or repudiate the findings. The machine search is refined, directed, and targeted by human beings if the machines are likely to offer generalized axioms of wisdom dealing with scientific truth, universal elegance, and/or great social value.

The machine WM-T scans the Internet searching for axioms of truth that are interdisciplinary and universal. Similarly, the WM-S scans the Internet for axioms of social benefit, service to humanity, and/or humanitarian cause. In the same vein, WM-E scans the Internet for beauty, elegance, and/or aesthetics. The radial addresses of the three WMs are quite immaterial to their functions. The placement is only to illustrate the similarity of the functions of each machine. Each WM has access to the Internet traffic and each machine is tailored to the specific nature of wisdom being sought: universal truth in the Internet transactions, genuine human and social virtue or elegance, and beauty in the Internet information or transactions. The switches (see S via the ISP's in Figure 10.7) for these machines permit the three machines to access different segments of the Internet traffic depending on the functionality of the machine and the direction of the pursuit of wisdom.

The interdependence of the three machines starts to emerge after some initial clues are uncovered by any one or all of the WMs. If the clues point toward a genuine axiom of wisdom, then the resources of all the three machines get allocated to that particular axiom and the machine work synergistically until an axiom is identified or it is reclassified as a variation of the existing body of knowledge. This approach is consistent with the human behavioral model of corporations, where most available resources are channeled to the most promising venue in the pursuit of corporate goals. For an individual, the synergy and mix of the modes of thought can be substantially different. If the thread of human thought is mapped into the functional mode of (three) machines, then a triple helix of creativity starts to take shape of an embryonic invention. The invention is also generic to all (DDS or LoC) disciplines embedded as knowledge.

10.12 ORDER, AWARENESS, AND SEARCH

The acceptance and recognition of order involves an act of faith. In the realm of science and mathematics, universities and research institutions have convinced us that an illusive framework of order forms the foundation of nature. Such an order constitutes the Laws of Nature. Electrons do exist, photons do travel at the velocity of light, gravity and laws of electromagnetism can be unified by the general theory of relativity, and so on. Order became evident to Maxwell as he searched for the laws of electromagnetism in an orderly universe that was partially (and practically) explored by Faraday, Ampere, Gauss, and Galvani. However, it was up to Maxwell to write the general equations of electromagnetism. In the same vein, it was up to Einstein to unify gravity, as Newton comprehended it, with the laws of electromagnetic wave propagation that Maxwell wrote. The search for wisdom is the tireless work of all notable scientists.

In Figure 10.8, each of the three wisdom machines [WM-i, i = T, E and S] follows the lead of the scientists, philosophers, and philanthropists. We also propose that the artificial intelligence embedded in these machines be presumptuous (and almost predictive) that one or more axioms of wisdom be derived from the Internet traffic. Partial order is detected first and then the awareness of this order triggers the search for greater and greater order on a cyclic mode until a generalized axiom of wisdom can be derived or inferred. The role of the human beings at this highest level is shown in Figure 10.9. Creativity of numerous participants is triggered by the AI of the machines. To some extent, the thrill of a discovery or an invention triggers more intensified search until the underlying truth, elegance or social value is uncovered. The composition of oracles of wisdom in dictionary accrues making progress a reality.

Role of Order, Search and Wisdom

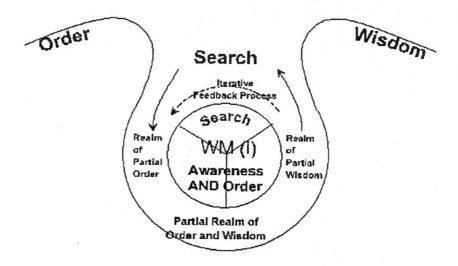

Figure 10.8 High level functionality of each of the three wisdom machines WM-i, i = T for truth, E for elegance, or S for social value, as the Internet data is searched and researched within each of the WM-i, for underlying axioms of wisdom that reflect order in the origin, flow, or final use of Internet data. When the objective functions are defined for different applications, it is quite possible that these machine(s) may uncover abusive users of the Internet and also provide all the forensic evidence to stop criminals, terrorists or those with destructive goals.

10.13 CONCLUSIONS

A conceptual framework for building a generic human–machine knowledge processing environment is presented. This framework leads to understanding the interrelationships between objects and events based on the flow of traffic through the Internet or any specific network. Tentative inferences may be drawn based on the frequency of occurrence and the correlation between objects. The pursuit of total generality, like the pursuit of absolute truth, is likely to fail. However, in a limited sense, artificially intelligent machines and groups of human beings working in unison may explore scientific truths, universal elegance, and/or social values.

The Internet, broadband networks and information highways provide ample amounts of raw data to seek and uncover relationships that are universally true or of lasting value to society. At the first level, very large amounts of data are first filtered by high-speed computers and at the second level, the machines focus on information that carries knowledge and wisdom. With an appropriate set of filter parameters, information and knowledge are gathered in any given direction such as economic activity, national security, or medical emergencies. The complied information may then be fine-tuned to search for cause–effect relationships based on models. For tracking the economic activity of a nation models based on monetary theory [11], Keynesian economics [25], or scarcity theory [26] are invoked. For tracking the factor affecting world peace, models based on global unrest, wars, and UN activities, are invoked. For tracking national security, AIDS, SARS, or bird flue epidemics, tentative models (if any) from global knowledge bases are invoked. Validity and accuracy of such models can also be tracked. The machine provides a buffer between the flow of Internet data and the human beings who make policy decisions.

To a limited extent, the proposed human–machine system supplements the inference that the immediate environment can offer. The lower-level AI functions are programmed to sense and scan specific conditions within the environment. Knowledge generated from the machine's own knowledge banks of accumulated procedures and inferences about the topic under investigation further enhances the search for generality and wisdom in the flow of Internet traffic. Human intelligence firmly drives the programmed artificial intelligence of the machine in directions that validate or repudiate an axiom of knowledge and wisdom from a mathematical and scientific perspective.

The WM stems from ideas drawn from AI systems, corporate-problem solving strategies, decision support systems, and from the ability to assign a direction to wisdom based on the Dewy Decimal System and/or the Library of Congress Classification. In addition, any inference that becomes a part of the derived axiom/relationship/concept retains a level of confidence that the machine evaluates and substantiates. Thus a tree of knowledge is implicitly structured before any notion of wisdom is drawn at any confidence level. Three corporate executive problem-solving techniques that have a direct bearing on the functioning of the WM are (1) the limited search and directional search, (2) the satisficing (i.e., tentatively acceptable) solution rather than an optimal solution and (3) constraint relaxation techniques to find a solution and then to tighten the constraints in order to optimize the solution.

We have also introduced a variation on the computing and network environment so that it can function as an intelligent human agent [16, 27]. The arrangement is inclusive of traditional AI and the scientific/computational environments. It also encompasses the realm of human decision making and offers enough latitude to the human counterpart of the machine to carry out practically all humanoid functions. The realm of true creativity is still in the hands of the human driver who forces the machine to come as close to doing to the data and information what the human being is doing to the embedded concepts and knowledge. The machine, being adaptive and self-learning [23, 28] becomes as effective as the computers that play (and win) most of the chess games against novices. The Internet features embedded in the addressing capability of the machine make it at least three times more

Level III
All human
processes

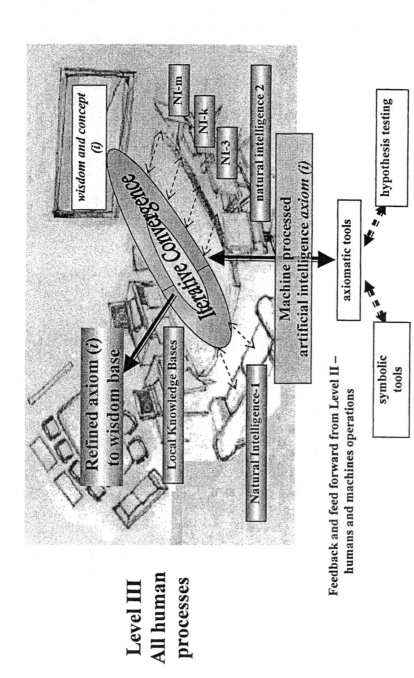

Feedback and feed forward from Level II –
humans and machines operations

Figure 10.9 This figure depicts the synergistic roles between human intelligence/creativity and the AI and Internet access capabilities of a cluster of computers as a final axiom of wisdom is derived from global wisdom bases. Humans and computers play an interactive and integrative role. Compare this function with layer 3 fuctions in Figure 5.3 and with level 5 in Figure 12.5.

powerful. The capacity of the WM to solve problems from a knowledge-based (not subject-based) perspective, with country and IP address-based access, provides sophisticated options to find "a needle in a haystack" as easily as finding a solar system in the Galaxy from the knowledge bases around the world.

REFERENCES

[1] H. B. Hugh, Socratic Wisdom, The Model of Knowledge in Plato's Early Dialogues, Oxford University Press, Oxford, UK, 2000.

[2] J. Barnes (Ed), *The Complete Works of Aristotle*, Vols. 1 and 2, Princeton University Press, Princeton, NJ 1995.

[3] Elsevier Science, *ScienceDirect® A Digital Library of the Future*, 2003 <http://www.sciencedirect.com>.

[4] S. V. Ahamed, The architecture of a wisdom machine, *Int. J. of Smart Eng. Sys. Design*, 5, (4): 537–549, 2003.

[5] S. V. Ahamed, and V. B. Lawrence, "The architecture of a wisdom machine," *Intelligent Eng. Syst. Through Artificial Neural Networks*, 13, pp 81–93, 2003.

[6] *SAP Solutions, and eLearning*, SAP (UK) Limited, Feltham, Middlesex, England, 2002.

[7] S. V. Ahamed and V. B. Lawrence, Evolving network architectures for medicine, education and government usage, Pacific Telecommunications Council, Hilton Hawaiian Village, Honolulu, Jan. 14–18, 2002.

[8] OCLC, Dewey Decimal Classification and Relative Index, 22nd ed., OCLC, Dublin, OH, 2003.

[9] United States Government, *Library of Congress Classification*, <http://catalog.loc.gov> URL accessed June 2003.

[10] M. Friedman, *Price Theory*, Walter de Gruyter, Hawthorne, 1976. See also *Columbia Encyclopedia*, Columbia University Press, New York 2002.

[11] M. Michael, Dilemmas in Economic Theory: The Persisting Foundational Problems of Microeconomics, Oxford University Press, Oxford, UK, 1999.

[12] E. Comunello et al., CycML— a language to describe medical images, *Proceedings of the 16th IEEE Symposium on Computer-Based Medical Systems*, IEEE Computer Society, New York , 2003, pp. 145–149.

[13] M. Krol and D. L. Reich, Development of a decision support system to assist anesthesiologists in the operating room, *J. Med. Sys.* 24, 141-146, 2000.

[14] N. S. Stuart, *Computer-Aided Decision Analysis*, Quorum Books, Westport, CT, 1993.

[15] S. V. Ahamed, et al., Sensing and monitoring the environment using intelligent networks, *U. S. Patent Publication,* US2003/00441013 *AI, Publication,* U. S. Cl. 706/59, Feb. 27, 2003.

[16] M. Wooldridge, *Introduction to MultiAgent Systems,* John Wiley & Sons, Hoboken, 2002.

[17] S. V. Ahamed and V. B. Lawrence, *Intelligent Broadband Multimedia Networks*, Kluwer Academic Publishers, Boston, 1997.

[18] N. S. Stuart, Legal Scholarship, Microcomputers and Super-Optimizing Decision-Making, Quorum Books, Westport, CT, 1993.

[19] H. Robert, The political economy of monetary policy," in *Political Economy of American Monetary Policy*, T. Mayer (Ed.), Cambridge University press, Cambridge, UK 1990.

[20] J. G. March and H. A Simon, *Organizations*, Blackwell Publishers, Cambridge, MA, 1993.

[21] S. V. Ahamed and V. B. Lawrence, localized knowledge based intelligent medical systems, in *Proceedings of the 16th IEEE Symposium on Computer-Based Medical Systems*, IEEE Computer Society, New York, 2003, pp. 89–96.

[22] M. Pinter, Realistic Turning Between Waypoints, and AI Game Programming Wisdom, Charles River Media, Boston, 2002.

[23] V. Ramakumar, *eLearner, Solver, Platform and Technology*, Cloverworxs Inc., Austin, TX., <http:// www.cloverworxs.com> URL accessed July 2003.

[24] N. Arkani-Hamed, S. Dimopoulos, and G. Dvali, The universe's unseen dimensions, *Sci. Am.*, Aug: 62–69, 2000.

[25] R. M. O'Donnell, Philosophy, Economics, and Politics: The Philosophical Foundation of Keynes's Thought and Their Influence on His Economics, Palgrave/ Macmillan, New York, 1989.

[26] R. Tilman (Ed), A Veblen Treasury. From Leisure Class to War, Peace and Capitalism, Armonk, NY, 1993

[27] C. M. Bishop, and C. Bishop, *Neural Networks for Pattern Recognition,* Oxford University Press, Oxford, UK, 1996.

[28] Mathworks and Simulink, *New Real-time Embedded Coder 2*, Release 13. <http:// www.mathworks.com, MathWorks Consulting Services, Novi, MI, 2003.

Chapter *11*

Knowledge Environments

11.1 INTRODUCTION

In this chapter, we present two distinct approaches to the design of knowledge environments. Each design is geared toward the application. Much like the commonality between data communication systems and data processing systems, there is an overlap between knowledge communication systems and knowledge processing systems. After all, information is derived from data and knowledge is deduced from information. In the most rudimentary instance, knowledge communication systems become identical to the data communication systems that carry any specific (binary, alphanumeric, textual, graphical, image, etc.) data from one location to another. As the knowledge communication systems start to get even a little sophisticated, the features of intelligent networks (e.g., address translation capability of the intelligent network/1 or IN/1, call identifier capability of IN/2) become necessary. The architectural designs of the numerous intelligent networks are discussed in great detail in [1]. Knowledge, being more highly evolved than speech or images, needs greater sophistication than the basic versions of intelligent networks. We discuss this aspect in Section 11.2.

Knowledge processing environments have specific features. Such environments

Intelligent Internet Knowledge Networks. By Syed V. Ahamed
Copyright © 2007 John Wiley & Sons, Inc.

are necessary due to the complex nature of knowledge structure encompassing the numerous embedded objects within that segment of knowledge. Knowledge implies objects around which webs of relationships get accumulated. A systematic study and analysis of these relationships give rise to incremental or derived knowledge, which in turn becomes a part of mainstream knowledge. Even though this definition appears to be self-perpetuating, it contributes to the explosion of knowledge on an ever-expanding scale. It also leads to discovery and invention of new objects and concepts that are added to the dictionary as an unending process.

The nature and the relationships between objects (such as the keywords of a paper or an index in a book) constitute a segment or a body of knowledge. These objects and their interrelationships get disoriented due to the processing of knowledge. Only if there is consistency in the processing of all the objects that are implied in a body of knowledge, can the overall processing of knowledge be logical, coherent and legitimate. We discuss this aspect in detail in Section 11.3.

Knowledge environments vary in their adaptation and intelligence. Service intelligence has been successfully deployed since the 1980s [1, 2]. However, three basic categories of intelligence that are feasible in communication systems and computers are in the areas of (1) connectivity to the high-speed backbone networks and Internet, (2) the address and services update capability via the service control point SCP database of the intelligent networks (INs), and (3) the knowledge based intelligence (KI) look-up capability via the Dewey Decimal (DDS) or the Library of Congress (LoC) classification discussed in [3, 4]. (See Table 11.1 for a listing of acronyms.)

Accordingly, knowledge environments or knowledge systems (KS) may have these intelligent features tacked to them. By permuting options available to designers, it becomes clear that three modifications of KSs are possible at the first level— KS + Internet, KS + IN, and KS + KI; three more at the second level— KS+(In + IN), KS + (In + KI), and KS + (IN + KI); and finally only one at the third level— KS + (In + IN + KI). A few of these design options are shown in Figure 11.1.

Figure 11.1A depicts any simple knowledge system (KS) with two *major* variations— the knowledge communication system (KCS) and the knowledge processing system (KPS). It is to be noted that some rudimentary kps (i.e., pure processing geared to communication) becomes absolutely necessary for any kcs (i.e., pure communication geared to processing) facility and vice versa. The value of the operator δ can be very small or very large.

In Figure 11.1B, only the Internet-based KCS and KPS are shown and the two possibilities (KS + IN and KS + KI) can also be derived. The Internet-based KS is discussed in detail in Section 11.5.

In Figure 11.1C, only the KS + (In + IN) possibility is shown but the other two variations can be derived. In Figure 11.1D, the single third-level configuration is shown and discussed in detail in Section 11.6. The realization of any KS is a degenerate case of this configuration. It can be seen that a very large combination of KSs can be achieved by blending the three types of intelligence by varying the value of the operator δ from 0 to large numbers.

A. <u>KS</u> (i.e., Knowledge Systems); plain KS

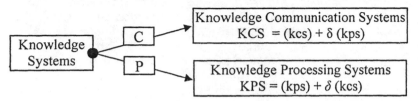

B. <u>I-KS</u> (i.e., Internet-based Knowledge Systems); In + KS. Not depicted are IN + KS, and KI + KS systems.

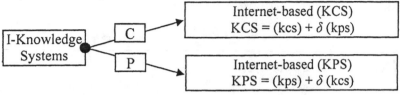

C. <u>I²-KS</u> (i.e., Intelligent Network (IN) + Internet based Knowledge Systems); (IN + In) +KS. Not depicted are (IN + IK) + KS and (In + IK) + KS systems.

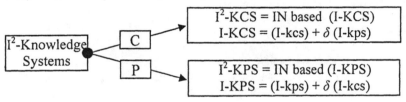

D. <u>I³-KS</u> (i.e., Intelligent Knowledge (IK) + Intelligent Network (IN)-based + Internet (In)-based)

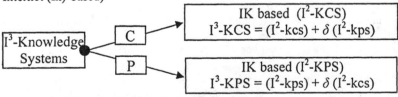

Figure 11.1 General classifications of knowledge systems. See note on page 302 for the explanation of the symbols used in the Figure. Other variations of the KSs, not shown in the diagram are feasible. They can be derived from the architectures shown in Figures 11.2 through 11.13. The admixture of kcs and kps can be varied (by changing the value of δ) to offer large varieties of knowledge systems.

> <u>Note:</u> *C signifies Communication; P signifies Processing: kcs is all knowledge communication system and kps is purely a knowledge processing system. In a practical design, the subprocesses of kcs and kps can be blended to generate new and perhaps more optimal solutions within intellegent knowledge processing environment. Parts (A through D) offer a generic systems integation perspective rather than a specific design. If the distinct breeds of intelligence, 'I', can be written as i, i', i'', etc., then a specific range of values for δ should be associated with each specific breed of intelligence (i, i', i'', etc.).*

Such variations can also be derived in computer and communication systems by changing the relative emphasis between the processing capacity and the switching capacity.

11.2 KNOWLEDGE SYSTEMS

When an entire body of knowledge is complete (e.g., a complete paper, a book, or a report) and self-sufficient (with all the i's dotted and the t's crossed), then the entire module can be communicated from one location to the next as a series of packets, as a series of frames, as a series of bursts, as one or more e-mails, and so on over any backbone of a communication network. Knowledge communication under these conditions is a single transaction that is complete and closed.

When the body of knowledge is segmented or fragmented, then each module still gets communicated but the structure of knowledge needs to be reassembled at the receiver. This function is accomplished by the network-services-provider. Protocols, headers, and packet sequence numbering schemes become crucial in completing the transfer of the entire module of knowledge.

However, it is for the transmitter to send the *complete and consistent* module of knowledge and for the receiver to ascertain that the module of knowledge is *complete and consistent.* Generally, the application layer of the OSI model or human being performs the *completeness and consistency (C&C)* checks in most computer communication systems.

Much like an I/O processor between a computer and a device, or a DMA device between a memory and a disk subsystem, if a rudimentary knowledge enabler is included between the computer and the communication channel, then the enabler will guarantee the *completeness and consistency (C&C)* of the module of knowledge. The knowledge communicator will need the conventional backbone communication facility and a C&C device or a software routine.

11.2.1 C&C Checker

In the conventional communication networks, the C&C checker is not necessary because the human being or the application layer (of the OSI model) will ascertain the validity of a module of exchange. However, if global knowledge processing is foreseen as a possibility, then the C&C of every module of knowledge communication becomes necessary.

11.2.2 Functions of the C&C Checker

When a module or a body of knowledge is communicated between two points in the network, the C&C checker validates all the objects and their attributes before the actual communication. This will permit the receiver to have all the information for processing the received module of knowledge. For example, if a user or a knowledge processing system enquires the GPA of a student at a university, then the C&C checker would make sure that the student ID, the authorization to open the student records, validation of the courses, and the grades are all supplied by the user or a supporting database with the authorization code. The receiver (a knowledge processing system) will be able to honor the query and respond accordingly. The knowledge level transactions will thus be completed without unnecessary transactions.

Such interfaces for data validation have been added to many prior networks such as ISDN, packet and frame networks, and almost all computer networks. For example, when the ISDN interfaces discussed in Refs. [5, 6] were standardized, the U, T and S interfaces were necessary and the two network terminations (NT-1 and NT-2) became very important and were made a part of the ISDN service requirement. When knowledge networks become a part of the Internet service backbone, any specialized interfaces for communication of knowledge will also emerge.

11.2.3 Role of Switching Systems

Traditionally, the architecture of the electronic switching systems (ESSs) evolved to facilitate the telephone environment. Around the globe, telephone systems still play a vital role in communication systems and the introduction of intelligent network services required some basic modifications to the ESS architecture. With appropriate changes, the plain old telephone service (POTS) infrastructure still provides a valuable foundation for KCSs. We hasten to add that the newer all-digital networks also provide an equally firm and valid foundation for KCSs.

Conventional switching systems (SSs) in the POTS environment are too rudimentary for practical knowledge communication systems (KCSs). However, the intelligent network (IN) based SS (i.e., SSPs [1]) become amenable to enhancements for local and global KCS and some KPs. The intelligent networks and their services are based on database switching capability. Thus any new forwarding address (i.e., telephone number of the specific service provider) is derived from 3XX, 4XX, 6XX, 7XX, 8XX, 9XX, and so on telephone numbers.

The architecture of electronic switching system is shown in Figure 11.2. The ESS has three software control modules (AM, CMs, and SMs presented in [5, 7]), for administrative, communications, and switching functions. For the knowledge systems, their operation is unlike either the call processing of overall switching systems or the data processing of conventional computer systems because of their implicit cooperation with and interdependence on a fourth (KM) module. In the original mode of operation, the AM, CM, and SM cannot be trivially modified for knowledge processing. However, if we now add an additional module (i.e., KM or knowledge module) for performing knowledge-oriented communication [7] functions, then some rudimentary knowledge communication may be accomplished.

The functions of the other three modules (AM, CM and SMs) are thus altered to satisfy the true needs to access appropriate knowledge bases in the Internet space. Address translation from the knowledge domain to the network domain (WWW) becomes necessary. Such translation can be carried at a central facility or within the SMs. Specialized functions of service control points, service management systems, intelligent peripherals, and service creation environments within the intelligent networks (IN's), are incorporated for knowledge systems. Storing the Internet knowledge profile and maintaining and updating knowledge addresses can thus be accomplished by the KCP and knowledge management systems (KMSs).

Specialized compilers to respond to a cascaded series of questions and to create new knowledge induction for the knowledge processing systems (KPSs) are also necessary. Practical versions of the KPS have an admixture of kps (purely knowledge processing systems) and kcs (purely knowledge communication systems). Stated alternatively, this assertion can be made as

$$KPS = (kps) + \delta (kcs),$$

(See Figure 11.1A) and a knowledge machine (KM) is defined as a KPS with small or incremental values of δ. In the KM, emphasis is shifted to processing of knowledge. Furthermore, if the number translation capability is based on the Dewey Decimal System (DDS) or the Library of Congress (LoC) classification, then the IN-based switch known as the service switching point (SSP) now accomplishes subject-based switching.

Knowledge based on subject (e.g., sciences, physics, electrical engineering, telemedicine) switching gets accomplished. The established global knowledge bases are accessed from knowledge machines. It becomes more appropriate to call the SSPs by their functionality as knowledge switching points (KSPs). The blueprints of the conventional intelligent networks ranging from IN/1 to the AIN lead to a whole new series of intelligent knowledge network (IKN) architectures (IKN/1 through AIKN— advanced intelligent knowledge network) and correspond to the evolution of IN/1 through AIN. The configurations and architectures are presented in Ref. [1].

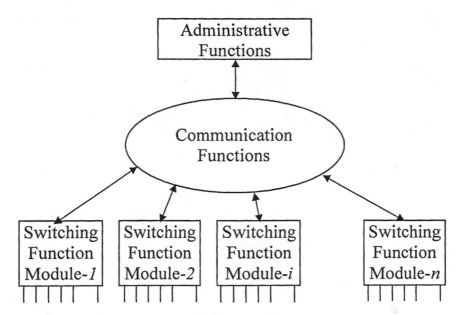

Figure 11.2 Hierarchy of functions in a typical switching system for a circuit-switched network. The switching modules are connected to a "wire-center" (WC) and the subscriber (client) lines are terminated at the WC by typical impedance matching networks to maximize signal energy transfer between the switch and line, and vice versa.

11.3 KNOWLEDGE COMMUNICATION SYSTEMS (KCSs

The processors, memories, I/O interfaces, and switches constitute the components of any typical computer and/or communication system. Both are especially tailored to perform specific tasks germane to that particular system. Neither of these two systems performs functions specific to processing of knowledge even though they are amenable to the mere exchange or communication of knowledge. For the purpose of communicating knowledge, the central component is the typical switching system (SS). The SS is central in the communication of voice and data over the circuit-switched networks deployed in public telephone networks (or PSTN for public switched telephone network). For *communicating* knowledge, the most flexible hardware and software architecture deployed in the SS may be modified. However, to incorporate functions pertinent to generic *processing* of knowledge by content and logical association, both HW and SW need a redesign (Section 11.5). For this section, we propose four major building blocks (Sections 11.3.1–11.3.4). Each block is a programmable computer system in its own right.

11.3.1 Communication Module of KCS

Consider transmission and reception in the context of knowledge communication. The communication modules handle transmission and reception in a full duplex mode. The capacity to control the communication among all the components, as they relate to one function upon one piece of information, is not unlike the concentration of the human mind on the solution of one problem at one time. Even though numerous channels are simultaneously active in the KCS, communication between the knowledge bases and the users become an essential function of the communication module in the KCS. Furthermore, consider the collation or assembling of the processes in the knowledge communication. There is no standard language or compiler especially designed for the communication of knowledge. Functions necessary to verify and validate, or to check the relevance of a user query in the context of the knowledge bases are germane to the operation of the KCS. At the initial stages, the syntax is loosely defined, and the communication module of the KCS assembles the amount of information stored in the knowledge bases. The relationships in the hierarchy of this knowledge must also be considered. Functions of this nature that control and guide communications are germane to the various aspects of the user query and they define the overall task of the KCS. The communication module provides dependable logical channels of communication between the knowledge bases and the users.

11.3.2 Switching Module of KCS

Consider the switching module (SMs) in the context of the KCS. Switching modules translate the logical channels from the communication module into physical (entire or multiplexed) channels. The translation occurs over the localized switching system to/from the users. It also occurs from/to the knowledge bases. By and large, the switching function is complex enough to design SMs as separate modules or addressable entities within the switching system. In the context of the communication system, design of the SM is most demanding and elaborate. In the context of the KCS, the typical SM of any communication system will suffice. However the rest of the KCS needs the elements of knowledge processing just like the conventional telephone communication systems need some elements for speech processing (e.g., encoders, synthesizers, A/D converters). The essential difference between knowledge communication systems (KCSs) and the knowledge processing systems (KPS, see Section 11.4) is that communications aspects in KCSs are greatly emphasized and vice-versa.

In ESSs, the SMs function in a completely duplex mode, and any subscriber can be the caller or the called party. In the KCS environment, the switching function is much more confined. The processes within a task or a problem have standard and more limited functions. Also, the number of active channels is limited to the number of multiple tasks that the KCS is programmed to handle (in its operating system). The number of addresses and in the knowledge module can be enormous;

however, they are classified by their contents and confined to specific locations within the KB. Hence we see that the SM may be less complicated than the corresponding module in the telecommunication environment. In fact, from the CM side, the switch can look like a private branch exchange (PBX) with a limited number of incoming lines. And from the KM side, the switch can look like a hierarchical star terminating at any given file location. Each branch is encoded with the successive number of the Dewey Decimal System/Library of Congress subject catalog.

11.3.3. Administrative Module of the KCS

In the traditional POTS environment, the switching systems also offer the facilities of an administrative module (AM). Most accounting, authorization, verifications and allocation functions take place in the AM. In the context of the KCS, the functions of the AM are marginally enhanced. Authorizations of users and access to knowledge bases will be appended to the AM functions. The authorization, verification, and enablement of the intelligent knowledge network (IKN) services such as library look-up, student services, medical emergency dispatch, and automatic drug dispensation will be monitored by the AM in the KCS. In Figure 11.3, the roles and the hierarchy of the AM, the CM (now shown partitioned to handle local knowledge-based services and global knowledge services), and the SMs is shown.

The capacity to select from, and switch between, large quantities of information from the knowledge bases is also shown in Figure 11.3. The CM handles the channeling, but the contextual switching is handled by the address conversion or look up facility. The SMs permit the access and direct memory access (DMA) capability between the knowledge bases and the memory necessary for any minimal amount of knowledge processing or problem solving. Furthermore, when the local knowledge bases are inadequate, the KCS will access other bases on the wide-area networks. In this case, the function of switching to and from the source of relevant information (wherever it may be) also becomes the function of the SM of the KCS.

11.3.4 Intelligent Network Aspects in KCS

The intelligent network era of the 1980s and 1990s has left a rich legacy of innovations in the communications and services industries. The tools, techniques and methodologies are skewed toward the circuit-switched (POTS type) networks and not totally in synergy with the Internet environment. For this reason, we adapt some of IN features (Sections 11.3.4.1 to 11.3.4.6) to the Internet environment in Section 11.3.4.7.

11.3.4.1 Generic intelligent network Features

Since 1980s, POTS environments have been updated to handle intelligent network (IN) functions. Intelligent networks are discussed in detail in [1]. A rudimentary configuration of an intermediate IN or IN/2 is shown in Figure 11.4. Presently, most of the switching systems are upgraded to SSPs. The CCISS signaling system is now firmly in place and the SCPs enable address translation. The role of these components is discussed in detail in [1]. However, for the communication of knowledge, additional functionality from the units of IN are necessary.

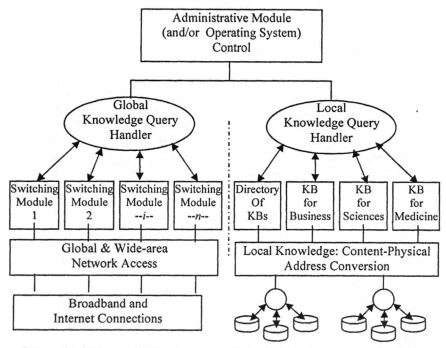

Figure 11.3 Hierarchical arrangement of a knowledge communication system (KCS). AM, administrative module; CM, communication module; SMs, switching modules; and KB, knowledge bases. The three modules and the numerous KBs play tightly interdependent roles in the KCS.

11.3.4.2 Service Switching

These are modern switching systems with the added ability to recognize the service trigger condition that intelligent networks are capable of delivering. In the context of KCS, the functionality gets modified to serve as knowledge switching systems KSSs. These KSSs recognize which specialty of knowledge is being communicated.

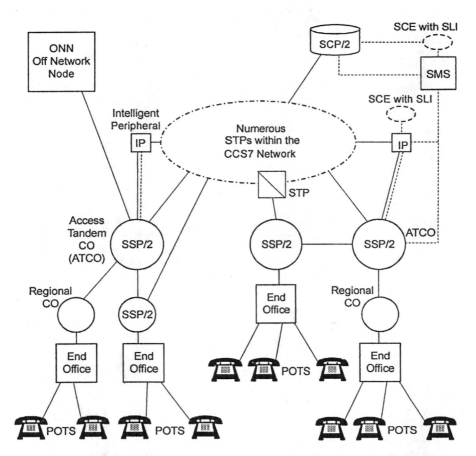

Figure 11.4 Simplified configuration of an Intelligent Network introduced by Bell System1970s and by Bellcore during and 1980s [8]. Five basic components— SSP, STP, SCP, SMS, SS-7 signaling network— are shown. Additional modules for IP and SCE are also depicted. SSP; service switching point: STP, signal transfer point: SCP, service control point: SMS, service management system: IP, intelligent peripheral: SCE, service control environment: ATCO, access tandem central office: POTS, plain old telephone service: and CCS7, common channel signaling 7. The details of this IN/2 network (from Bellcore) are presented in [1, 8].

The Dewey Decimal System (DSS) or the Library of Congress (LoC) classification can be effectively deployed. The user may define the specialty. Alternatively, the KSS may process the query and identify the "objects" around which the knowledge service is requested from the system. The system forwards the request to the appropriate knowledge bank to honor the user request. Rudimentary syntactic verification of the specialty would remove any ambiguity of the word and the multiple meanings and contextual use of the same words. It is possible for the KSS to have an intelligent knowledge peripheral (IKP) that is equivalent to the IP in IN/2, [1].

11.3.4.3 Service Transfer

A service transfer acts as a relay point accepting the X.25 packetized information to and from SSPs and service control points (SCPs) in conventional intelligent networks. The functionality of the service transfer points (STPs) becomes modified to knowledge transfer points (KTPs). In the early stages of building a KCS, the KTPs may be hardwired and permanently connected. The exchange of information between the various components of the KCS needs a well-designed format and knowledge-based protocol.

Over a period of time as ISPs become mature and become knowledge services oriented, the configuration of the Internet is likely to become two tiered. The first, lower-level services will be the typical current Internet services, and the second, higher-level tier will provide intelligent Internet services. The role of the KTP will become crucial in providing access to the KCPs and the KSCP presented in Sections 8.1.3.3 and 8.1.3.4 and shown in Figure 8.7. Knowledge services may also need service processing entailing the unique combination of the KCS and KPS.

11.3.4.4 Service Control

Service control is achieved through extensive databases with information that is highly reliable, secure, duplicated, well managed, and capable of being updated. This makes the queried information available to the SSP as it completes a service or a service process that it is performing at that instant of time and as the provisioning of the service progresses. To be consistent this component should be termed a KCP because the control is in the context of knowledge rather than in the context of services. In the KCS environment, storage of information that can be updated becomes necessary so that it acts as a quick reference to the various categories of subjects and the type of derived information about these subjects. The databases in the KCP become equivalent to a "knowledge profile" for the information contained in the knowledge module(s). This provides the machine with the capability to steer any "knowledge process" through the vast maze of information contained in the knowledge module(s).

11.3.4.5 Knowledge Service Creation Environment

This facility provides knowledge vendors (e.g., educational institutions, universities, libraries, patent offices) with a programming and debugging environment to try out new knowledge vending and marketing concepts or ideas. In this environment, new knowledge related services may be "programmed" into the network by "assembling" new modules of knowledge service as a program of various well-defined functional modules. These modules correspond to the macros or routines in conventional computer environments. In a sense, the programming of services in these knowledge-oriented networks is like assembly-level programming of an educational, learning, teaching or classroom problem. The functional modules provide the bridge for knowledge providers to perform valid KCS subfunctions consistent with the domain of knowledge that they provide.

Such service logic programs are usually interpreted by a knowledge logic interpreter (KLI), which may be housed in a KSP, KCP, or a knowledge intelligent peripheral (KIP) and may act in conjunction with a local knowledge network information database (KNID). Hence the new software interface can be tailored for these types of networks, such as a medical or a hospital network.

In the KCS environment, the KCE plays a definite role. Consider the situation when a new inference machine becomes available from the knowledge engineers. The data for deriving the new inferences can be resident in the knowledge module(s), but the newer implications (obtained from the new inference engine) may not be available to the users unless a group of applications engineers decide to program the new inference engine added on to a KCS. For this reason, the KCE-equivalent in the KCS is seen as an environment that provides new induction(s) from old knowledge or that generates new inferences from old data.

11.3.4.6 Knowledge Intelligent Peripherals

These computerized devices may exist as a network node with SS7 connectivity to an SSP via their own trunk lines or have an ISDN primary-rate capability. In many cases, the KIP may be only bridged to the communication channel for the duration of the call. Because it is a programmable device, we expect that the KIPs of the future will provide a great variety of services such as the IPs of the 1990's in the intelligent networks.

11.3.4.7 Two-Layer Services Architecture for Internet

Internet services are currently confined to the local and global commercial markets that drive national and global economies. Valuable as they are, they do not serve the entire spectrum of human needs. Economic and technological activities drive the nations but knowledge and wisdom drive humans. Circular as it may sound, humans drive the economy, and technology of nations. To include the economics, technology, knowledge and wisdom all in a larger loop driving nations and humans, we propose that services and technology (basis for economic activity) be atop the Internet (as the culmination of all communication methodologies). This two-layer structure is shown in Figure 11.5.

From a practical consideration, the newer Internetworks will blend the KCS and KPS environments to suit the commercial markets of any environment. Such a blending is already evident in the medical, campus and distance learning environments. For this reason, a generic architecture blending the two extremes (purely KCS and purely KPS) is shown in Figure 11.6. Figure 11.6 is a derivative of the IN architecture but adapted to the Internet environment.

It depicts a network combination that offers the capacity to blend existing Internet service with knowledge processing services that society will evolve to need. Such services are available in the medical communities where the medical service providers may subscribe to gain access to clinical, diagnostic, therapy, and drug, procedures and treatments. When the knowledge bases are supported by established medical schools (like the Harvard Medical Group) and centers (such as Sloan-Kettering, University of Pennsylvania, and other Cancer Centers), society stands to benefit. In Figure 8.7, a computer configuration the supports KCP, KSCP and KMS (see Figures 8.7 and 11.6 together) and also provides a venue for billing for special services.

Layer I Multimedia Communication & Processing Services for Information, Knowledge, Wisdom, Concepts, Ethics, etc.
Layer II Older Broadband, Current and Intelligent Internets, Next Generation Internetwork Services.

Figure 11.5 Two-layer service structure providing knowledge and information level services for network users of fast packet technologies.

In Figure 11.6, when the adjunct knowledge service processor (AKSP) detects a request from the ISP user, a trigger condition invoke the participation of the appropriate knowledge service provider (KSP-*i*), The KCP unit of the KSP will start the attribute search for the KBs around the world and does an initial match. Second-level matching takes place based on the client's attributes. After the raw information for the digital libraries and the KBs is processed, the knowledge is again processed to gain the exact information required by the ISP client and is dispatched from the KSP (after knowledge processing) over the global, national, or local backbone networks.

The limited access, high level of security and logical separation from other Internet traffic will ascertain the highest quality of information, knowledge, concept, or wisdom that is returned from the KSPs to the ISP client. Looking back at the early telecommunications industry, in-band signaling systems were a cause of serious concern in the mid-1980s and early 1990s. The common channel interoffice signaling systems, and the ITU-based standards for International signaling networks (CCISS network for local signaling) evolved with a distinct physical identity and standard protocol.

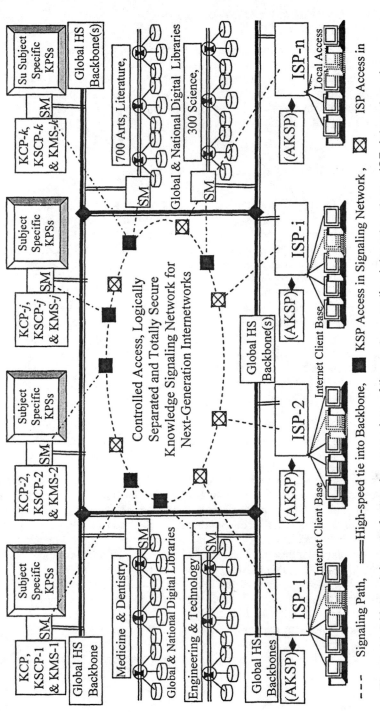

Figure 11.6 Network layouts for two-layer services of the next generation Internet systems. ISP, internet service provider; AKSP, adjunct knowledge services processor; SM switching module; KPS, knowledge service providers; KCP, knowledge control point; KSCP, knowledge services control point; KMS, knowledge management services.

As the Internets start to permeate all the branches (medical, educational, commercial, business, financial, etc.) of activity and all phases of such activities, the need for a distinct signaling network and the participation of knowledge processing providers and systems can be foreseen. We give an example of such next-generation systems, that appears to be financial viable and technologically feasible in, Figure 11.6

11.3.5 KNOWLEDGE CONTROL POINTS IN KCS

In the deployment of practical knowledge communication systems (KCSs) there is little or no knowledge processing involved. In a confined sense, the address resolution can be considered as processing of a WWW address or the resolution of a specific channel address to a particular knowledge base. However, this particular process is in the realm of intelligent routers and address resolution of peripheral processors attached to web routers or to the switching modules (SMs) in circuit/channel-switched networks.

In Figure 11.7, the architecture deploying a knowledge control point (KCP) is shown. The digital libraries communicate with the KCP using the secure packet network[1] for signaling and address resolution. The user queries are forwarded to the appropriate KB and the response is communicated to the user over the circuit/channel-switched network. This approach is different from the current search engines on the Web where the Web address is communicated back to the user and user performs the knowledge search.

11.4 KNOWLEDGE PROCESSING SYSTEMS (KPSs)

Knowledge processing differs considerably from knowledge communication in the same way that data and information processing differ considerably from data and information communication. In addition, since knowledge processing carries far greater intricacies than data and information processing, the knowledge processing unit (KPU) starts out where the CPU and information processing system units terminate. In reviewing the present information processing environment (such as the management information systems (MIS) [9], the corporate information systems (like the PeopleSoft or SAP [10]), and Telco billing systems, we see that numerous database management and network techniques have evolved dramatically over the last two or three decades to suit the applications.

Data and object management become crucial in the processing of knowledge, especially with the KPU. Like typical graphical processor units and caches that have evolved to support the CPU functions, we envision that highly sophisticated

---

[1] This knowledge signaling network would be the equivalent of the traditional CCS7 signaling network using X.25 or BX.25 for communicating the signals between SSPs, STPs, and SCPs in an intelligent network architecture (see Figure 11.4).

data and object manger hardware units (and their specialized software) will emerge to support the KPU functions.

11.4.1 Programmable Steps for KPU

In principle, the knowledge processor unit KPU (akin to the CPU) executes knowledge level (KL) instructions. The KPU works because of *three* basic notions:

1. Any complex knowledge domain function can be decomposed into a series of smaller programmable macrofunctions upon the objects that are implied in any body of knowledge under process.
2. The solution of a complex problem has some identifiable pattern or programmable structure, which follows a sequence of steps. Stated alternatively, a group of programmable macrofunctions can be identified and executed in a predetermined sequence to accomplish any complex knowledge domain function.
3. Every (nonpseudo) kopcode is a machine-executable knowledge domain function.

The rationality behind these three notions is that an identical string of reasoning has prevailed for almost four decades of early scientific programming. In the latter case, overall problems are decomposed into binary executable instructions. Such instructions have two parts: an operation code (or opc) and a (set of) operand(s) represented as an instruction.

In the knowledge domain, a knowledge domain process becomes the knowledge operation code (or kopc) and the concepts, objects (in the most generic sense of the word), and attributes and their interrelationships become a (set of) operand(s). Hence any real or pseudo kopc (or kopcode) and its relevant (set of) object(s) become a complete KPU instruction.

The administrative module (AM) provides administration, maintenance, and resource allocation on a system-wide basis. The communication module provides a centralized hardware platform for distributing and switching the voice or digital data, control information, channel allocation, and synchronization signals. One or numerous switching modules provide localized switching and localized control functions. They also serve to interface subscribers and inter-exchange circuits and trunks. Traditionally, these switches do not monitor or interact with the subscriber data as it is flowing through the switches.

If the electronic switching systems (ESSs) are included in the realm of mainframe computers, then these massive systems function well both as knowledge processing systems (KPSs) and localized knowledge communication systems (KCSs). Computer systems with massive parallelism make up a typical switching system. There are about 5000 microprocessors (with the complexity of a 1B processor, see Chapter 8) in a mid sized telecommunication system (in the POTS environment) of the late 1980s.

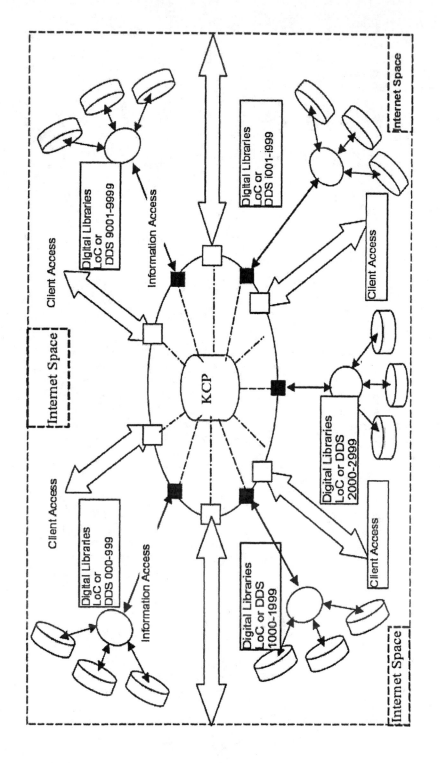

Figure 11.7 Internet and intelligent network version of knowledge communication system (KCS).

There are numerous vendors for such systems, and they routinely service, upgrade and enhance the functions in the voice and data telephony industry[1]. The administrative module (AM) provides administration, maintenance, and resource allocation on a system-wide basis. The communication module provides a centralized hardware platform for distributing and switching the voice or digital data, control information, channel allocation, and synchronization signals. One or numerous switching modules provide localized switching and localized control functions. They also serve to interface subscribers and inter-exchange circuits and trunks. Traditionally, these switches do not monitor or interact with the subscriber data as it is flowing through the switches.

When such a switching system has the additional burden of processing the contents of the data streams, plus the voice signals, and then relating the information in an educational, beneficial, and creative manner, then the need for a knowledge processing module[2] arises. This module channels the information on the basis of forward and backward pointers to other pieces of knowledge. The processing is geared toward scanning the information, associating it with previous information by pattern matching, and lexically scanning the objects that make up the current information. Inferences and evaluations may be accrued in the system to give the machine a knowledge profile of the student (educational networks), or a medical profile of a patient (medical networks), or a financial profile of the client (financial networks). Such machines handle both the call processing inherent in communication networks and the knowledge processing inherent in intelligent networks.

These machines blend the two types of intelligence and respond with an adaptability to reach the right source and destination with an appropriate address (physical/logical). They also process what they convey over the channels by compiling and composing the appropriate answer for the user in a logical and consistent fashion. One or more SMs can be used in conjunction with the SSs to provided access to a modular KPU shown in Figure 11.3. Alternatively, the Internet and intelligent network (IN) may be merged in architectures (as shown in Figure 11.13), and discussed later.

---

[1] With the advent of frame relay and ATM architectures, the older circuit-switched digital capability (CSDC) inherent in the ESS has been overshadowed. In some developing countries, the ESS architectures, integrated services digital network (ISDN), and CSDC are still in good use.

[2] For more detailed information on educational networks, [1], Chapter 15, Architectural Consideration in the Design of Network-Based Educational Systems. For more detailed information on medical networks, see [1], Chapter 16, Integrated Medical Systems. For more detailed information on intelligent home networks, see [1], Chapter 18, Home Intelligence: Personal Computer-Based Intelligent Home Networks.

11.4.2 Computer Processor Environments

Figure 11.8 characterizes the structure of a basic computing machine for the last five decades. Here, the communication facility is minimal and is provided by one or more bus structures. Time-sharing of the digital highway(s) (the main buses) connecting the memory, the CPU, and the I/O devices was most common with early designs. It was well known that bus access was the bottleneck. CPU architectures and configurations have successfully evolved for the last five decades. The types of units (CPUs, NPUs, GPUs, IOPs, etc.) are precisely tuned to the task.

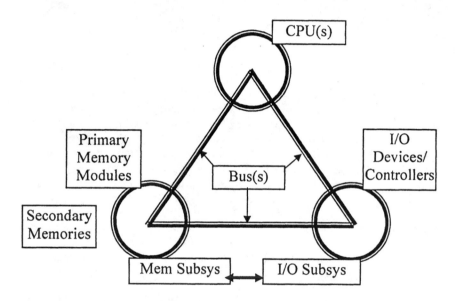

Figure 11.8 Most rudimentary configuration of a basic computer. I/O, input/output; Mem, memory; Subsys, subsystems.

Components, their complexity, their interconnections, and their precision have become optimal for the function. Architectures have evolved from single-instruction, single-data (SISD) type to the multiple-instruction, multiple-data (MIMD) systems, and an additional component (the switching matrix) has been added (see Figure 11.9). This multibus architecture with an embedded switch has eased the congestion and data flow problems of earlier computers. The configuration shown in Figure 11.9 depicts a multiplicity of architectures, ranging from the simple MIMD to the specialized array processors, matrices, and transform machines. Memory control units and I/O processors can also be added.

In conventional processing of data, the central processing unit (CPU) plays the dominant role in executing the binary instructions in a predefined, programmed sequence. Data availability and access are made feasible by the linking and loading functions. The processes involved to get the executable binary code in the machine include compiling, assembling, linking, and loading the actual program and then data in the core of the computer. One process generally forgotten by computer scientists is the higher-level language programming of the problem that is to be solved. Assuming no errors in these processes, the machine sequentially executes these instructions, brings the program to a normal termination, and provides the user with the results being sought.

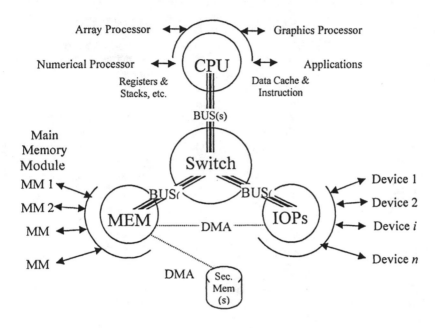

Figure 11.9 Configuration of generic computers with switching capability and specialized processors for specific applications. Array and application processors and direct memory access (DMA) capability are shown. I/O, input/output; Mem, memory; MM, memory modules; Subsys, subsystems.

11.4.3 Knowledge Processing

The fundamental basis of knowledge processing is to process the key objects embedded in any body of knowledge and then process the interrelationships between the objects.

Two levels of processes become apparent. First, the processing of the objects also entails the processing of the attributes of each one of the objects and then the interdependence of the attributes. The interdependence of the attributes offers a clue to the interrelationships between the objects. In a sense, the attributes of any object are documented in the (language or technical) dictionary meaning of the objects. The effective processing of knowledge thus depends on the identification of the key objects embedded in the body of knowledge.

Second, the processing of the interdependence of the objects lies in the identification of the overlapping attributes of the key objects. Obviously, the first and second processes appear to be circular. These are iterative processes and not circular processes. When the body of knowledge is sparsely populated with objects, for example, two objects, the processing is also a simple two-step iterative process with two sets of attributes. When the body of knowledge has n objects with m attributes each, then any two attributes may overlap thus leading to blindly iterative $n \times m/2$ processes. However, with some prior knowledge of regression analysis, the dependent attributes (like dependent variables) may be eliminated or substantially reduced. This process reduces the time and effort to process fewer dependent attributes. Fewer attributes can also lead to fewer objects. Two objects with a vast overlap of attributes can lead to the elimination of one. A smaller set of (independent) attributes and (independent) objects results. Much like regression analysis, the analysis and processing of knowledge is skill-bound and is never totally precise or entirely accurate. However, knowledge processing can provide a reasonably accurate estimate (like the coefficients in a regression) for the influence of objects and their interrelationships in dealing with any bounded body of knowledge.

11.4.4 Low-Level Single KCPU Knowledge Machine

A rudimentary architecture for low-level KP environments is shown in Figure 11.10. A KPU with minor KP functions, labeled as kpu, is appended to the CPU. In this configuration, the machine performs limited KP functions (such as content identification, user-content usage patterns, etc.) in its KCPU. This single-processor (KCPU= KPU + CPU) architectural configuration is primarily a KCS with minimal KPS functions. With numerous SMs, this KM environment is oriented towards the communication of knowledge rather than processing of knowledge. The KM environment in Figure 11.10, demonstrates the organization of the KPS with a single KCPU.

11.4.5 Multiple KCPU Knowledge Machine

The size and capacity of a single KCPU-based machine become extremely limited. Much like the transition from single CPU computers to multiprocessor mainframes, knowledge machines follow similar transitions. From an implementation and economy of scale perspective, the knowledge machine with multiple processors is more desirable. A typical configuration is shown in Figure 11.11.

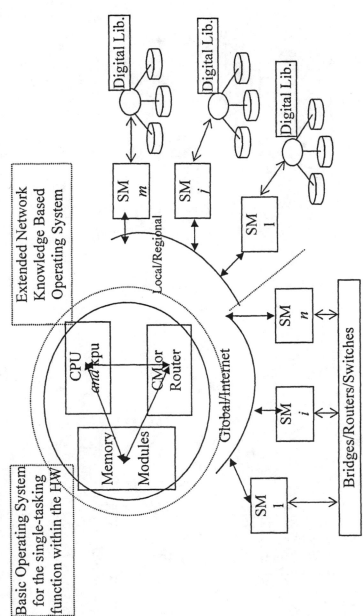

Figure 11.10 Architecture of a rudimentary knowledge communication system (KCS) with a single knowledge processor unit (kpu) that is appended to the CPU. The CPU is dedicated mostly to the administrative and communication functions with the kpu performing rudimentary knowledge level functions. CM, communication module; SM, switching module.

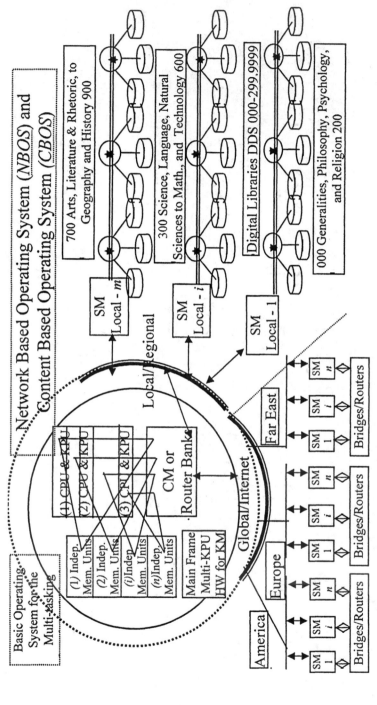

Figure 11.11 Architecture of a multiprocessor (KCPU = KPU + CPU) based system with n multitasking capability. Knowledge processor units (KPUs) are appended to the CPUs. The CPUs furnish administrative and communication functions and KPUs perform simple knowledge level functions. CM, communication module; SM, switching module; DDS/LoC, Dewey Decimal System/Library of Congress classification; KM = knowledge machine.

A multiprocessor architecture that performs multitasking (KCPU) functions can be built by segmenting the memory and a more elaborate operating system that allocates the resources and performs multiple knowledge machine functions concurrently. Even though the knowledge power is enhanced like the computing power of multiprocessor systems, the knowledge processing power remains low. The KCPU architectures (Figures 11.10 and 11.11) do not have the HW-based object processing capability to perform true knowledge-based functions. These architectures fail to accomplish complex wisdom level functions [11] quickly and optimally. In single processor environments, the communication and switching modules (essential for the communication of knowledge) can be combined into one hardware unit. In the extreme case for local knowledge processing, the entire system can look like a disk controller that channels the access to certain track-sector addresses when certain subject matters are being pursued. This simplifying step is feasible because of the reduced requirements placed upon the switching module (for local knowledge processing), which provides a communication path during the allocated time interval between the only processor (or memory) in the administrative module (accomplishing only one individual knowledge-oriented "task") and the knowledge module. To some extent, the simplifying is comparable to shrinking a SS to a one-line PBX. All the switching takes place on the knowledge module side.

11.4.6 Object-Based Knowledge Machine

For intricate and sophisticated knowledge processing (KP) environments, a specialized unit for processing "objects" constitutes the building block for the structure of knowledge (e.g., keywords of a paper, the concepts in an invention, the chapter titles in a book). The most rudimentary format of KPU (presented in Ref. [1]) is shown in Figure 11.12. The KPU functions are logically partitioned into three currently existing functions: *object processing, numeric processing,* and *databases functions.* Object processing is addressed in the design of application-oriented KPUs [1]. In this vein, a hierarchy of knowledge is feasible with data at the lowest rung and concepts/wisdom at the pinnacle. A snapshot of this hierarchy (for processing) is shown in Figure 11.13.

In the case of object-based knowledge machines, the relative emphasis between data processing and knowledge processing can be adjusted to suit the user's needs. The entire basis for constructing powerful knowledge machines is that, even though the frontier of mathematically precise knowledge is vague, firm basic ground rules are commonly perceived and practiced in dealing with knowledge and utilizing it to solve complex problems. For example, a class of pharmaceutical students may be interested in the clinical properties of certain plants, whereas a group of botany students could be interested in the habitat and climatic conditions for the same plants.

In many instances, the deployment of a knowledge-based intelligent peripheral (KIP) attached to the knowledge processor (Figure 11.12) will make customizing the machine more economical than building a KM for each application. Thus KIP or the intelligent peripheral (IP) equivalent becomes instrumental in providing the knowledge service back to the user in a fashion, style, and format exactly tailored to the user's needs.

From a historical perspective, knowledge came before numbers simply because of the inclusive and encompassing definition of knowledge. However, processing came long after numbers. To extend the concept into processing of knowledge, procedural steps from programming of numbers and logical entities are pushed into the knowledge domain. Numbers and logical entities are prone to processing in the CPU environment. A framework of steps for processing of knowledge akin to the programming steps for data processing is proposed in Section 11.1.

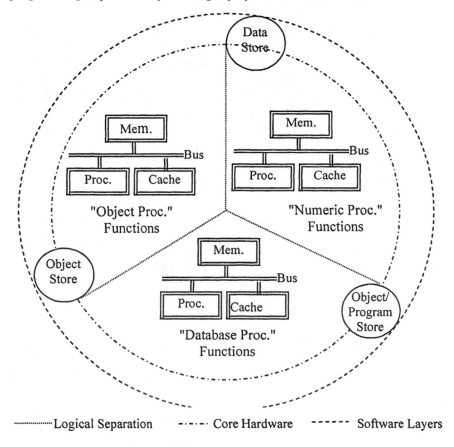

Figure 11.12 A simple knowledge processor with object and number processing with database capabilities. Object hardware details will be handled in the design of the knowledge processor unit.

Much like new numbers can be processed from old numbers, new knowledge can thus be deducted from old knowledge if the computer can execute a specific knowledge program[4]. In this vein, objects in the knowledge domain replace numbers in the scientific domain. The role of the operating system still remains dominant in both domains. The compilation of KM programs also becomes a requirement. Within the compilation, a series of steps (such as lexical scan of objects, syntactic scans of the rules for the use of the objects and object sets, and semantic analysis of the relationship between the objects) are necessary in the solution of knowledge-level programs. These steps invoked in the solution of the knowledge-oriented problems are taken prior to the actual execution of individual kop (knowledge operation) codes on objects. We foresee that the steps invoked in the solution of intricate problems will depend on the results of prior steps, with a compile-as-you-go approach being necessary. However, this approach is already practiced by communication engineers in the implementation of network algorithms (e.g., path routing, use-dependent path assignment for QoS requirements, fault tolerance) and becomes necessary for the design of the software for the knowledge processing environment.

For the purposes of routing information, the administrative and communication units (in Figure 11.8) or the operating system of a generalized KCS and KPS have the support of a disk-resident "knowledge profile" of the local and global knowledge bases. In essence, the profile provides an initial checkpoint when users invoke operations pertaining to the knowledge stored in the knowledge base(s). It is somewhat similar to the card-file index that older libraries once maintained to facilitate users in finding the exact location of books containing the desired subject matter. The profile also verifies that users ask questions from the system that are consistent with the knowledge contained therein. For example, it identifies what action[5] (or process) may be applicable to what objects (such as polymers, petrochemicals, Maxwell's equations, and satellite systems). In a simplistic case where the machine is geared toward high school teaching, the profile can be pre-shrunk from the more elaborate profile of the machine that is oriented to a graduate research center where the subject matters are processed. This customizing of the disk-resident profile is similar to the editing of the table of contents for textbooks covering the same subject for high school or college use.

From the perspective of computer software designers, this customizing is similar to the selection of different macros for different hardware modules (e.g., co-processors, array processors, and A to D converters) or the selection of software library routines (e.g., trigonometric, hyperbolic, or exponential).

---

[4] It becomes imperative that the rules of numeric and logical manipulation (such as $+$, $-$, $\times$, $/$, AND, OR, NOR, EXOR, etc.) be followed appropriately to yield correct results from older numbers used as operands in the CPU. In the same vein, if the laws of AI, deduction, manipulation, and interpretation of the rules and relationships between objects are correctly adhered to then one can obtain accurate knowledge from older objects used as operands in the KPU.

[5] Such as, "what," "how," "when," "where," and "why"; and "what-if," "how-where," "what-when," "then-what" combinations; and also analogize, predict, and similarize combinations.

The administrative module is also invoked to modify and manage the knowledge banks (a function similar to the function of the service management systems [1] in intelligent networks) and the corresponding update of the knowledge profile. Additional security checks of the access and updating users, plus their use of the knowledge modules, are incorporated here. The compiled and executable task-oriented programs are made disk-resident or handled in the main memory of the knowledge processing system. These routine housekeeping functions are managed by knowledge-based operating systems. One or more SMs can be used in conjunction with the SSs to provided access to a modular KPU shown in Figure 11.3. Alternatively, the Internet and intelligent network (IN) may be merged in architectures as shown in Figure 11.13.

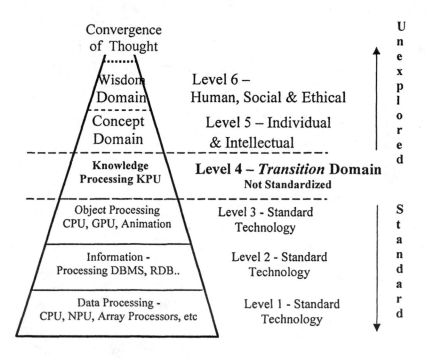

Figure 11.13 Hierarchical representation of the role of computers in processing of knowledge for the intelligent search for concepts and wisdom. The physical world is symbolized as numbers, text, and graphics. Wisdom and concepts are universalities and abstractions, with knowledge at the intermediate level.

11.5 IN AND IK-BASED KPS (I^2-KPS)

Knowledge has definite rules for its classification (DDS and LoC). However, the knowledge bases may be distributed throughout the world. Hence a dynamic address(es) of knowledge locations based on the classification of knowledge becomes necessary to provide a local, regional, national or global search for vital information. The capacity to provide this translation of address based on classification is called intelligent knowledge communication in the same vein as the intelligent network services provisioning based on services rather than the service provider.

Rudimentary knowledge processing (KP) on the Internet takes place in most search engines. However, when sophisticated KP is required, the search engines cannot perform deep knowledge functions (e.g., find objects embedded in knowledge domains and construct hierarchical relationships between such objects to find new objects). For example, if it is necessary to search for the reasons for the spread of Ebola virus, the current search engines cannot find all the locations where Ebola has spread, the attributes common to the locations or the environments, a correlation factor between the spread of Ebola and every attribute of the environment (e.g., climatic condition, cleanliness, diet, physical contact) to the rate of expansion of the Ebola cases and cannot come up with a plausible reason and a confidence level for the reasons for the spread.

However, if the Internet search-engines are coupled to powerful object/numeric processors, Mycin, NeoMycin and Intern type generalized expert systems databases, and graphics/games type of sensors/interpreters and co-relaters, then a global knowledge processing with possible search for generalities and cause-effect relationships can be pursued. In Figure 11.14, the configuration of an Internet-based KP module is shown. For the overall effectiveness, many such independent modules should function in parallel with an architecture as shown in Figure 11.6, that take care of the communication aspects of the KCS.

It becomes apparent that the KPS and KCS will need extensive object-oriented processing capability merged with massive information communication capability. It is envisioned that the centralized KPUs and OOPs in Figure 11.14 will be complementary to the CPUs in Figure 11.8. The architecture of the entire configuration starts to get somewhat complex because of the different natures of processing entailed in the processors. For the gaming industry, the VLSI designers have built sophisticated object processors for translational and rotational movements. The nature of the process in KPS starts to get significantly different from that in the gaming processors. For this reason, it appears logical that the design of KPs be conceived for the nature of knowledge functions rather than the nature of scientific functions. From a conceptual perspective, the scientific processes constitute only a subset of the more global knowledge processes simply because science is a segment of overall human knowledge.

In the recent past, computer system designers have built and deployed specialized hardware-based array processes and complex-algebra (and double-precision) numerical units quite successfully. For scientific and commercial environments, when demand prevails and there is a potential for profit, the computing industry has supplied computers and network components for the banking, transportation, and aircraft industries. For example, the array processors for pressure–velocity distributions in weather tracking or for plotting the electromagnetic field distribution in electrical machines have an elaborate hardware configuration and operating system. The movie industry has also benefited considerably. Special devices and processors are routinely built for military applications such as the moving target missile chasing systems.

11.6 IN AND IN-BASED, INTELLIGENT KPS (I^3-KPS)

Knowledge processing systems (KPSs) gain access to Internet via the backbone networks via the switching modules, bridges, routers, base locations or any standard network interface. Network intelligence is instilled via the use of knowledge control points (KCPs) and knowledge-based intelligent peripherals (KIPs). The indirect addressing and address translation take place because of the universality of the knowledge classification systems such as the DDS or the LoC system. The artificial intelligence is interjected via the use of pattern recognition (PR), expert systems (ESs), and well-placed intelligent agents and sensors throughout the intelligent knowledge processing system or the IKPS.

In Section 11.5, the concepts of Internet-based KPS were introduced by providing access to the backbone via the switching modules for the circuit-switched digital capability (CSDC) or via the routers and bridges for the packet-switched systems. For tuning the capacity of the knowledge and conventional central processor units (KCPUs) to the content of knowledge and the objects embedded in that particular segment of knowledge, a special type of intelligence is needed in addition to the network intelligence.

This new intelligence allocates the processor type and capacity to the specific classification of knowledge that is being pursued. For example, the distinct branch of aviation industry or weather prediction systems that deals with pressure–velocity measurements of air streams needs mathematical routines or hardware processors to deal with the processing and inversion of very large matrices. Conversely, the distinct branch of human psychology that deals with human behavior and cultural influence needs linear and nonlinear regression analysis. Statistical inference engines may also become necessary. Special branches of knowledge need special processors and the assignment of these processors is based on the intelligence embedded in the knowledge operation system for the IKPS or for the I^2-KPS. Traditionally, this type of control intelligence is a part of the operating system for mainframe computers that allocate matrix functions to array processors and graphics functions to graphics processors.

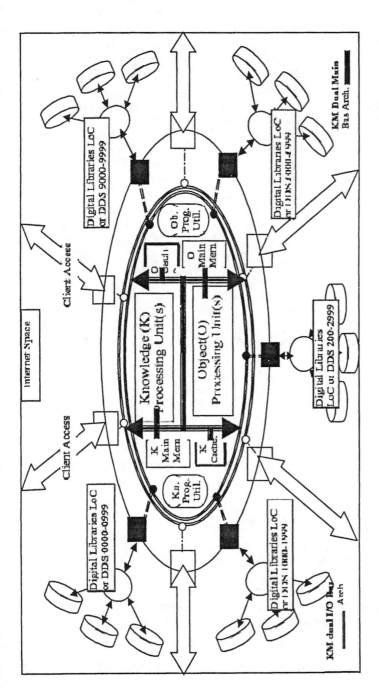

Figure 11.14 Internet-based KCS and KPS knowledge server with knowledge and object processing capabilities (dual bus). The basis of this IKPS corresponds to the I²-KPS because of the Internet and knowledge-intelligent or content-based switching to different digital libraries.

In the context of knowledge processing, we have allocated a special control point called the *processor control point* (PCP shown in Figure 11.15) to match the processor capability to the domain of knowledge being processed. The vast expanse of knowledge in the Internet-user domain and the processes that are specific to certain disciplines (e.g., partial differential equations and array processing to the investigations of nonlinear fields or to weather prediction; or synthesis of new drugs to the pharmaceutical industry) make it necessary to allocate specific processor(s) to specific subject areas. When these knowledge bases span the globe and the many branches of knowledge (as they exist in the LoC classification), the PCP facilitates the flow of knowledge processes within the I^3-KPS environment, and from one KB to the next. It may also facilitate the flow of knowledge/analogies from one discipline to a sister discipline.

The knowledge machine and management system (KMMS, see Figure 11.15) permits the operators of the new knowledge machines to monitor the access of authenticated knowledge bases and maintain security within the flow of knowledge. This type of monitoring of the authoritative, ethical, and socially beneficial flow of knowledge through knowledge machines will prevent the abuse of any powerful machine that is also capable of generating abusive and destructive knowledge from existing knowledge bases. Age-old wisdom that relies heavily on (authoritative and documented) truth, (ethical) virtue, and (socially beneficial) beauty may be enforced via the KCP and KMS components of intelligent knowledge processing systems (IKPSs). The human counterpart of the I^3-KPS plays a significant role in its eventual usefulness to society.

The IN control points (derived from SCP, [8, 12]) and management system (SMS, Ref. [1]) aspects of intelligent network are embedded in the knowledge control point (KCP) and the processor control point (PCP). Any of the seven knowledge processors (see Figure 11.15) can work with any of the memory units; however, depending on the query and the knowledge that is being processed, the processor is appropriately assigned depending on the PCP address and the appropriate knowledge base addressed depending on the KCP addresses. Thus the processor becomes discipline specific.

11.7 WAFER LEVEL KNOWLEDGE MACHINES

The knowledge machine has many manifestations. Like a computer, the knowledge machine can be built as a micro-intermediate or maxi-system. In this section, we confine our attention to what is realizable in the VLSI industry. It appears that the technology is close at hand, if it is not already scattered around in the industry to be able to build large segments wisdom machines (WMs) as ULSI chip sets.

11.7.1 Object Processes and Knowledge Processes

Historically, computer scientists have compartmentalized the processes in the program execution cycle (see Section 8.7) into two phases; the data processes and the program (instruction) processes. Functions associated with the data processes, i.e., data and operand fetch, operands caches, manipulations, storage, fall in the first group of CPU activities. The fields occupy special registers and flow through the designated paths and specialized bus structures. Functions associated with the program or instruction part, i.e., instruction/program block fetch, storage, caches, transfer of control, separation of the "IR" field, program and flow control, etc., fall in the second group of activities. The fields occupy special registers and flow through the designated paths and specialized busses and terminate in control circuits or activate control memories to initiate the execution of microcode.

In the knowledge processors, the operands are "objects" and the instruction code (*opc*) corresponds to the knowledge instruction code (*kopc*). Accordingly the paths and bus structures can be separated and CPU design philosophy can be projected in the KPU architectures. The KPU design shown in Figure 8.11 exemplifies this concept of separation of *kopc* flow and control circuits from the object(s) access and flow circuits. In the processing of knowledge, the number of kopc functions, sub-functions, and associated micro-code can become complex. Similarly, objects, their attributes, their interrelationships, and their interdependencies also become complex. To resolve the complexity of relationships between kopcs and objects (and their attributes), we can fall back on the cross connect switches developed by the communications engineers. Any kopc can thus be forced upon any object, or its attributes. This offers the same flexibility that von Neumann got when he could access any part of his 4096 word memory and hop around the program code during execution. In the design of the knowledge machine we need three microswitch-matrices discussed next.

The first micro-switch matrix resides between knowledge kopc libraries, functions, sub-functions, their microcodes, and knowledge "instruction register(s)", (KIR). The second microswitch matrix resides between objects, their attributes, their interrelationships in the object storage and "object operand register", (OOR). The third microswitch matrix resides between numerous KIRs and numerous OORs of a multiprocessor KPU knowledge machine. These first two architectural layouts are discussed in Sections 11.7.2 and 11.7.3. Two cases of third architecture are presented in Section 11.7.4 and 11.7.5.

11.7.2 KOP Specific Processor Arrays

When knowledge processing becomes specific to a particular discipline, the knowledge-processing unit (KPU) assumes its architecture to suit the discipline. In any general purpose knowledge machine, problems of any of the disciplines may be attempted. For this reason, it becomes necessary to have numerous knowledge operation code (KOP) specific processor arrays. For example, if a series of operation codes are specific to physics, chemistry, or philosophy, then specific groups of such processor arrays will become the domain for solving knowledge problems pertaining the physics, chemistry, or philosophy and so on.

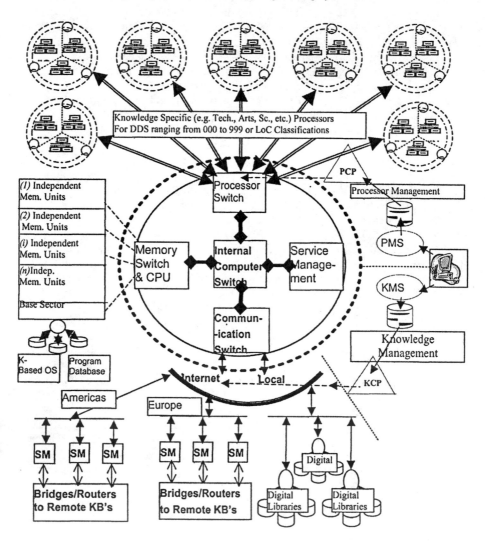

Figure 11.15 An architectural framework of an Internet (In), intelligent network (IN)-based intelligent knowledge, (IK) processing environment (I^3KPS). KB, knowledge base; SM, switching module; OS, operating system; KCP = knowledge control point; KMS, knowledge management system; PCP, processor control point; PMS, processor management system. The basis of this IKPS corresponds to the I^3-KPS.

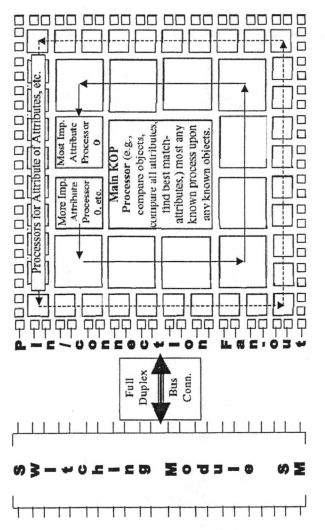

Figure 11.16 KOP specific Processor Arrays. This processor operates on the direct context of the object in relation to the domain of knowledge being processed. The processor of attributes of this object is in context of the attribute that influences the knowledge that is being processed. Multiprocessor chip architectures are amenable for enhancements for object processing. The processors and the attribute handlers are knowledge specific. The DDC or LoC classification of the knowledge domain leads to their designs. For example a physics specific KOP array processor will be different from the Economics specific array processor, even though the numerical and graphics part of the processors may be alike.

Figure 11.16 The configuration of a KOP (knowledge operation code) specific processor array.

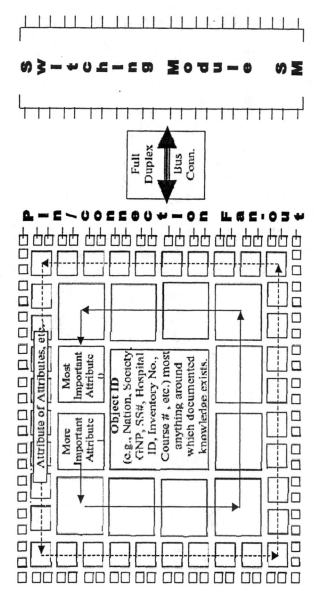

Figure 11.17 A VLSI Wafer/chip/configuration to handle objects embedded in the body of knowledge under process in a KPU environment. The Central object (e.g., the SS# of a patient in a medical network, or the infection in a part of the world, (e.g., chicken flu, Ebola epidemic, etc.)) in the knowledge environment. The attributes of this object are held in the VLSI chip areas, immediately surrounding the Object ID, and attributes of attributes in the next Chip area, etc. each area is accessed via a pin number and the object and its attributes are channeled into the exact processor (see Figure 11.1b).

Figure 11.17 A VLSI wafer/chip/configuration to handle objects embedded in the body of knowledge under process in a KPU (knowledge processing unit) environment.

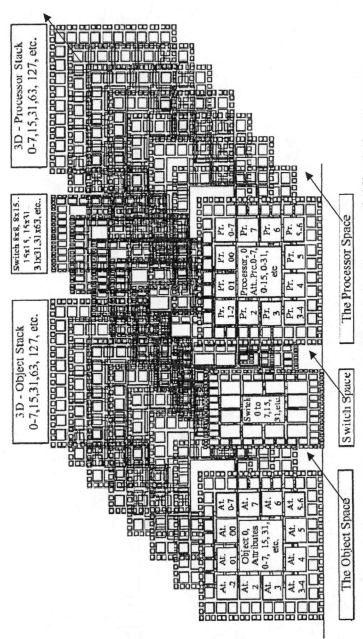

Figure 11.18 A 3-D version of an advanced Knowledge Processing unit (KPU) capable of handling numerous (7,15,32, etc.) objects with numerous attributes (7, 15, 31, 63, etc.) with numerous processors (7, 15, 31, 63, etc.) each capable of handling specific knowledge operation codes (*kop's*) each. The switching matrix (equivalent of a Switching Module or SM) connects any object or attribute to the *kop* specific processor and performs one or more *kop's* concurrently.

Figure 11.18 A 3-D Version of advanced knowledge processing unit.

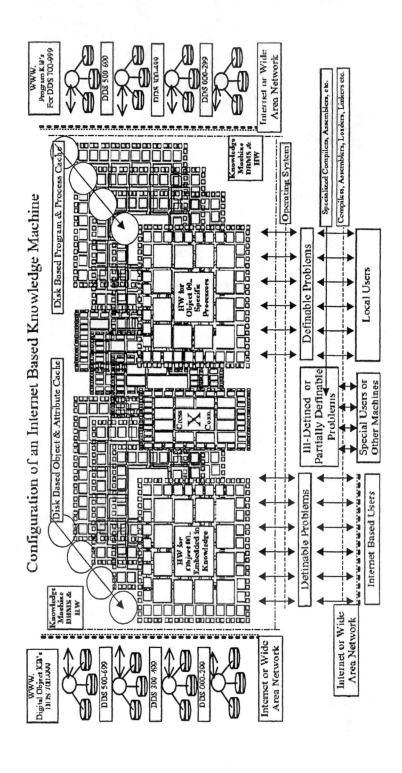

Figure 11.19 Architecture of a wafer-level a generic knowledge machine.

In Figure 11.16 one such processor array is shown where typical objects of any discipline are processed. Hence the KOP executable code gets processed in this particular processor. This partitioning of operation is much like the floating point (FP) operations that take place in FP processors and integer operations take place in fixed-point processors of conventional computers. An external switching matrix is shown on the left hand side to be able to communication with World Wide objects of a similar nature that are being processed in the knowledge machine.

In the knowledge processors, the operands are "objects" and the operation code (opc) corresponds to the knowledge operation code (kopc). Accordingly the paths and bus structures can be separated and CPU design philosophy can be projected in the KPU architectures. The KPU design shown in Figure 8.11 exemplifies this concept of separation of kopc flow and control circuits from the object(s) access

This processor operates on the direct context of objects in relation to their domains of knowledge being processed. The processor of attributes of this object is in context of the attributes that influences the knowledge that is being processed. Multiprocessor chip architectures are amenable for enhancements for object processing. The processors and the attribute handlers are knowledge-specific. The DDC or LoC classification of the knowledge domain leads to their designs. For example a physics-specific KOP array processor will be different from the economics-specific KOP array processor, even though the numerical and graphics part of the processors may be alike.

11.7.3 Object Processors

Knowledge processing gets closely intertwined with object processing. Objects form the nodules around which knowledge gets accumulated in an orderly, systematic and scientific way. Largely, the penetration of science, methodology and order depends on the discipline. On one hand, for hard sciences, the penetration and pathways from concept to the binary bits that encompass knowledge and information are well documented and recognized throughout the world. On the other hand, for soft sciences the pathways are slurry and ill defined. When "objects" are identified as placeholders for "fuzzy" knowledge to accumulate, then processing of objects becomes necessary to bring order and methodology in these soft and viscous sciences such as psychology, sociology, yoga, interpersonal relations, etc. To facilitate the knowledge machines to attempt problems in soft sciences, object processors become necessary just like logic units become necessary in CPUs to navigate the flow of programs and other logical functions and carryout other logical functions

One such object processor is depicted in Figure 11.17. Any central object (e.g., the SS# of a patient in a medical network, or an infection in a part of the world, (e.g., chicken flu, Ebola epidemic, or malaria)) in the knowledge environment occupies the central location. The attributes of this object are held in the VLSI chip areas, immediately surrounding the central object ID, and attributes of attributes in the next chip area, etc. each area is accessed via a pin number and the object and its attributes are channeled into the exact processor (see Figure 11.16) via a switching matrix or module SM.

This is one of numerous ways to design hardware-object-processors. When the direct object-object relations are processed the centralized area of one VLSI chip communicates with the centralized area of adjoining VLSI chip. When attribute-attribute relations are processed, the secondary areas communicate. An orderly influence of one object (and its attributes) with numerous other objects (and their attributes) can be channeled through the allocated silicon areas in numerous VLSI chips

11.7.4 Advanced Knowledge Processing Unit

Knowledge processing units handle numerous objects and their attributes. Objects can have strong or weak (numerically graded) relationships with their own attributes and the attributes of other objects. Attributes can also in turn have strong or weak (numerically graded) relationships with the attributes of other objects. This representation leads to a complex graph structure. Objects and their attributes may have allocated VLSI chips (or a designated real-estate area of a chip). Communication occurs through the switching matrix between such VLSI chips via backplane buses of the KM. In a sense, an advanced KPU needs an embedded switch within its structure. One such configuration is shown in Figure 11.18. This configuration of the KPU is capable of handling numerous (7, 15, 32, etc.) objects with numerous attributes (7, 15, 31, 63, etc.) with numerous processors (7, 15, 31, 63, etc.) each capable of handling specific knowledge operation codes (kops) each. The switching matrix (equivalent of a switching module, SM) connects any object or attribute to the kop-specific processor and performs one or more kops concurrently.

The KPU shown in Figure 11.18 can be implanted in a 2D-VLSI configuration like the 3D semiconductor memories from traditional computer systems can be laid out in a 2D-VLSI chip. One of the challenges to modern VLSI industry will be to build an advanced KPU with numerous object processors and an intermediated switching matrix all on one chip.

11.7.5 Wafer Level Knowledge Machine

Knowledge machines need the support of database management systems, input/output interfaces, and internal KPU to KPU cross communication. In an effort to make a hardware version of the knowledge machine, an architectural arrangement shown in Figure 11.19 is proposed. When VLSI "disk memories" can be mounted on circuit boards and the KPUs and their associated object processors occupy the ULSI (ultra large scale integration) chips on such circuit boards, then the earlier designs of rack-mounted minicomputers configurations will accommodate a full-fledged knowledge machine. The local knowledge banks and WWW interfaces are provided over two interfaces shown on either side of the machine.

The extent of compiler support also gets extensive. Knowledge specific compilers can reduce the complexity of the software design. The local and Internet user interfaces are shown in the lower segment of the knowledge machine configuration.

11.8 CONCLUSIONS

We have presented a conceptual framework of the knowledge machine (KM) and two possible configurations of knowledge processing environments. Functionally, these machines are more sophisticated than data processing environments. Numerous clusters of conventional machines under the control of the central administrative module can process knowledge effectively, much like the electronic switching systems of the telecommunications industry.

In view of the immense amount of knowledge in any branch of science, a multiplicity of knowledge machines in a network can be used with each one dedicated to a particular discipline. The logical and low-level human functions (including all programmable processing of fragments of knowledge) can be mechanized in this environment.

Knowledge refurbishing and maintenance are programmed within the administrative module for a small KP environment. For large national and global knowledge processing systems, the roles of the KCP and KMS (see Figure 11.15) become crucial. A tight control on the security clearance of human beings who manage and monitor these two centers (KCP and KMS) will prevent the abuse of large knowledge machines. Adequate and authorized sources of new information (such as research laboratories, literature, and meteorological observation centers) are connected to the switching modules to incorporate the "new and authenticated" knowledge into the existing knowledge bases.

The use of knowledge machines to process economic data of a nation will facilitate government agencies in monitoring and directing government spending on programs that have mathematical and statistical validity. The knowledge and wisdom gained from prior choices will be weighed and considered in view of current socioeconomic conditions. All the knowledge bases around the world will be consulted to maximize the expected utility that is derived. Gross and expensive human errors will be blocked. A sense of social justice and reinforcement of values can be made a priority in the processing of choices so that the flow of funding and knowledge has no bias and is not based on corruption. Human bias and political interest can be replaced by mathematically precise honesty and integrity.

REFERENCES

[1] S. V. Ahamed, and V. B. Lawrence, *Intelligent Broadband Multimedia Networks*, Kluwer Academic Publishers, Boston, 1997.

[2] S.B. Weinstein, Communication in the Coming Decades, *IEEE Spectrum*, 24, no. (11), pp. :61-67, Nov., 1987.

[3] OCLC, *Dewey Decimal Classification and Relative Index*, 22nd ed., OCLC, Dublin, OH, 2003. See also, J. P. Comaroni, *Dewey Decimal Classification*, 18th ed., Forest Press, Albany, NY, 1976.

[4]United States Government, *Library of Congress Classification*, <http://catalog.loc.gov> URL accessed June 2003..

[5] S. V. Ahamed, and V. B. Lawrence, *Design and Engineering of Intelligent Communication Systems*, Kluwer Academic Publishers, Boston, 1997.

[6] J.W. Johnson et al., Integrated digital services on the 5ESS™ system, *XI International Switching Symposium Proceedings*. Florence, Italy, 1984. Also see, R. Wood, DMS-100, Technology Evolution, *Telesis*, 10, (3), 1983.

[7] S. V. Ahamed, et al., Architecture for a computer system used for processing knowledge, U.S. Patent, 5,465,316, November 7, 1995.   European Patent 9437848.5- "Knowledge Machine Methods and Apparatus", EP Number 146248, US/05.11.93, Denmark, France, Great Britain, Italy.

[8] Bell Communication Research, *Plan for Second Generation of the intelligent network.* Bellcore SR-NPL-000444, 1986.

[9] H. C. Lucas, *Information Technology for Management*, Prentice Hall, Englewood Cliffs, NJ, 2004.

[10] SAP (UK) Limited, *SAP and eLearning*, Bedford, Middlesex, UK, 2002.

[11] S. V. Ahamed, The architecture of a wisdom machine, *Int. J. of Smart Eng. Sys. Design*, 5, (4): 537-549, 2003.

[12] R. A. White, Intelligent networks: perspectives for the future, paper presented at *Zurich Switching Seminar*, March 1992.

Table 11.1 Symbols and Acronyms

δ	Blending factor ranging from 0 to very large numbers. It offers knowledge systems designers the capacity to blend kcs and kps, or vice versa.
AIKN	Advanced intelligent knowledge network
AIN	Advanced intelligent network
AM	Administrative module used in conjunction with ESS
C	Symbol to designate communication of Knowledge
CCS7	Common channel signaling No. 7, used in conjunction with the ITU standards
CM	Communication module if used with ESS, or control memory if used with CPUs
DDS	Dewey Decimal System, used for classifying subject matter in libraries. See also, LoC
DMA	Direct memory access
ESS	Electronic switching systems that came about after the impact of UNIX operating systems and C language initially designed for channel switching functions rather than for computational functions
GPA	Grade point average
I	Prefix added to any current system to make it "intelligent"
IKN	Intelligent knowledge network
In	Prefix for specifying the Internet environment
IN	Intelligent networks, numerous versions such as IN/1, IN/1+, IN/2 and AIN, etc. also exist. Also a Prefix added to any current system to make it IN oriented
IP	Intelligent peripherals; this terminology is borrowed from intelligent networks architectures and signifies additional HW or processor units appended the switching systems (SSs) to force advanced IN services from older SSPs or the older SS [1]
ISDN	Integrated services digital network
ITU	International Telecommunication Union
KB	Knowledge base
KCP	Knowledge control point, used for knowledge-based intelligent (KI) systems; this database carries the address translation from LoC classification to WWW addresses or the dedicated address lines
KCPU	A new breed of CPU that can execute the conventional CPU and also the KPU instructions
kcs	A purely knowledge communication system

KCS	A practical version of a knowledge communication systems
KI	knowledge or content-based intelligence
KIP	Knowledge-based intelligent peripherals
KM	Knowledge machine (see also KPS) or knowledge module within a KCS framework
KN	Knowledge network
KNID	Knowledge network information database
kps	A purely a knowledge processing system
KPS	A practical version of a knowledge processing system
KPU	Knowledge processing unit [1]
KS	Knowledge system
KSP	Knowledge switching point used for switching in knowledge-based intelligent (KI) systems based on LoC classification of content knowledge. The KBs are distributed throughout the world. The content of knowledge carried in the channel determines the Web address of the KB to be accessed. This address is similar to the WWW address but the content determines the appropriate LoC classified KB address that gets translated to the exact WWW address
KSS	Knowledge switching systems akin to the SSP or service switching point (SSP) [1]
KTP	Knowledge Transfer Points akin to the STP or service transfer point (STP) [1]
LoC	Library of Congress classification; a greatly expanded system for classifying subject matter. In the context of the present chapter this alphanumeric classification is used as a pointer to knowledge bases around the world.
NT-x	Types of network terminations used in conjunction with ISDN used for reference only, but the standards committees for knowledge networks can derive such interfaces
OSI	Open system interconnect specification of the ITU
P	Symbol to designate processing of knowledge
PBX	Private branch exchange
PCP	Process control point to match the processor capability to the domain of knowledge processed
POTS	Plain old telephone services (systems) before the intelligent network era since 1980s
SCP	Service control point. This terminology is borrowed from intelligent networks architectures; SCP is a database containing relevant forwarding addresses of service providers or subroutines to

SCP (contd.)	any specific service that a user requests. Such architectures are discussed in greater details in Ref. [1]
SM	Switching module, used in conjunction with ESS
SS	Switching systems (ESS for circuit/channel switching; routers and bridges for packet/frame/cell switching)
SSP	Service switching points to identify IN services calls and type of service requested
U,T,S	ISDN interfaces used for reference only, but such interfaces for knowledge networks can be and should be derived specifically for the flow of knowledge
WC	Wire centers of older switching systems.

Chapter *12*

Wealth Of Knowledge

The wealth of nations has been explored from the perspective of labor, trade, commerce, and affluence since the legacy of Adam Smith (1727 — 1790). The inquiry into the nature and causes of the wealth of nations was launched from monetary and materialistic considerations. In this chapter, we explore *wealth of knowledge*. Knowledge and information in the Internet society bear a different impact than money and affluence do in a materialistic society.

Information and knowledge have numerous implications encompassing personal, social, technical, and scientific domains. Information like scientific parameter(s) can be traced backward and extrapolated forward. The domain of knowledge becomes more encompassing than that of wealth and materials. For dealing with wealth of knowledge, all factors (its scarcity, its total utility, its marginal utility, specifically its diminishing marginal utility, its utilitarian value, its exchange value, etc.) that influence the evaluation need to be considered.

From a computational perspective, we propose the processing of information and knowledge based on the most basic and fewest truisms. These truisms are, in turn, based on reality and they permit the characterization of information and knowledge. To this extent, computational processing does not depend on the philosophic writings of earlier economists. However, the truisms are validated from a longer-term philosophic interpretation of how these truisms have survived so that they can be expanded and reused in scientific and computational environments. This approach permits machines to process information based on the content of a

Intelligent Internet Knowledge Networks. By Syed V. Ahamed
Copyright © 2007 John Wiley & Sons, Inc.

particular piece of information and to enhance content, the presentation and the wealth of knowledge that the information communicates.

The evolution of society is based on the systematic collection, validation, and deployment of gainful information. Information can range from gossip to well-guarded national secrets. Gossip and rumor which have little value, are filtered out of the computational processes. On the other hand, information that is rare or unique enters the computational domain to be examined, refined, and enhanced. Information is collected systematically (from the Internet traffic), validated extensively (from the WWW knowledge banks), and deployed widely (from the dictionary of axioms available from the WWW wisdom bases). The true wealth of knowledge (if there is any) is thus evaluated rather than the raw format of information in which it was presented. Information processing becomes a precursor to the enrichment of knowledge or the distilling of wisdom.

12.1 INTRODUCTION

Many philosophers (Wagner and even Goethe, 1817) and political economists[1] (Petty, Galiani, Locke, and others, through 1871) have dealt with issues of happiness, satisfaction and wealth and welfare in their pre-classical essays. Consideration of materialistic and monetary wealth entered the classic writings of Adam Smith [1]. Ricardo, Malthus, Say and even Karl Marx have contributed to the evolution of the classic theories of economics. Marshall, Menger, and Arrow, have brought the earlier contribution into their respective lives and times. Veblen, Schumpeter, Neo-Marxist have suggested alternative schools of thought and social economics. Of some importance to the wealth of knowledge are the discussions of Thorstein Veblen (1857-1929) who deals with Theory of the Leisure Class (1899) and also with Engineers and their Price System (1921).

Knowledge is derived from information. Processing information leads to initial conjecture. Repeated and recursive information processing[2] refines the conjecture until it can show validity, become stable, and prove reasonably universal. Both the information and the knowledge that are derived enter the domain of truism and philosophic validation over an extended time frame. We extend this chain further into scientific principles derived from truth (as far as known from the current meaning of the word) and its philosophic validation. Furthermore, if the scientific notions can be partially established, then an economic basis is the feasible extension of truth, validation, and scientific notions.

---

[1] The writings of some these renowned scholars are not referenced in this chapter since their contributions are not directly related to the wealth of knowledge presented here, even though some economists may not agree with this assertion.

[2] Information processing is still not as generic as data processing. Just as data processing leads to information, information processing leads to knowledge. To introduce the basic concepts, we use the terms information and knowledge ($I«»K$) to make the presentation smooth. This combined term ($I«»K$) indicates information that is being processed to lead to knowledge and conversely knowledge that is being derived from information.

Material and monetary wealth has been discussed Adam Smith and has evolved as a basis for national and international trade and commerce. John Maynard Keynes (1883–1946) and his fiscal policy issues are still held in esteem in monitoring the growth of nations [2]. Unlike monetary wealth, combined information and knowledge ($I«»K$) has many facets and implications. Whereas the measurement of wealth is scalar and has a numeric measure as the currency value, the wealth of knowledge has more numerous measures. After all, the evolution of society is based on systematic collection, validation, and deployment of gainful information. Information can range from hearsay to well-guarded national secrets. Unfounded information and gossip have only marginal value and such information has no significance. On the other hand, if the information discloses a rare discovery, an invention, or trade secret, then its value is at a premium. If the information has social significance, is rare and is still not disclosed, then the value of that information is high. However, information kept in total secrecy has no value unless it is derogatory or damaging. Even long and extended periods of torture are justified for prisoners of war who supposedly have "information" about the enemy! Rare and damaging information has only blackmail value. For these reasons, the economics and strategy for dealing with knowledge and information need different considerations from those established in typical economics or game theory [3].

A certain commonality exists in the economics of knowledge and traditional macroeconomics. Money that gets stagnant and does not get invested leads to the liquidity trap [2]. The business community refuses to invest and grow because the economic opportunities are too low even though the interest rates may be low. Valuable technological information that does not find its way into production lines remains as paper in patent offices. In a sense, the possibility of an information-rich but stagnant society starts to become real, somewhat like the Japanese society in the 1980s. Valuable knowledge and information (like money) need deployment. Like savings that are invested (Savings = Investment in classical macroeconomic theory), knowledge (Knowledge = Production in knowledge economy) distilled from information needs to be channeled into corporations. Channeling such knowledge into institutions of learning creates a multiplier effect (like that in the national economy) in the ($I«»K$) domain.

A certain *velocity of flow of knowledge and information* ($I«»K$) is necessary for either information or knowledge to be productive. Information that gets too stagnant (like money during liquidity trap conditions) or too fluid (like money during rampant inflationary conditions) loses its potential to be socially valuable. A certain *viscosity in the flow* of ($I«»K$), like money flow) makes the activity rewarding and economically justified. Information that finds no channel(s) for communication has exhausted its life cycle.

A limited commonality also exists in the economics of information and traditional microeconomics. The value of information and knowledge ($I«»K$) that is transacted becomes comparable to the value of goods or assets that are transacted. However, ($I«»K$) does not get depleted like goods or assets that are physically exchanged. The depletion of the value of ($I«»K$) follows an exponential decay rather than a sudden change. The rate of decay can be quite sudden (high exponent) for some types of ($I«»K$), (e.g., weapons and warfare technologies) compared to others (e.g., educational or medical technologies). The sharing of ($I«»K$) may bring down the value as an exponential decay but it still retains some utility for both parties. Both parties benefit from the economic rewards yet retain the wealth of information. Monetary and material wealth that is shared loses value and utility simultaneously. The value of ($I«»K$) varies with server — client relationships. Conflictive and cooperative roles are both feasible, thus altering the laws of economics of knowledge and information.

Mainly, ($I«»K$) that has social, financial, social, ethical, or moral implication is a resource that is not as immediately exhaustible as monetary or materialistic wealth. Like any other resource, ($I«»K$) can be accumulated, enhanced, stored, or even squandered; however, this resource has special properties. The enhancement of ($I«»K$) is a mental/machine activity differing from the enhancement of material wealth, which is a production/robotic activity. For the differences cited above, ($I«»K$), "objects" are treated as hyperdimensional objects that follow the laws of processing but are not quite aligned with the processing of numbers, scalars (such as currency values), or text. Modern computers are capable of processing vectors and graphical objects. Current software packages that handle complex number ($x + iy$), two dimensional space for electrical engineers and mathematicians perform as smoothly as the software packages that handle three-dimensional (X, Y, Z) space for graphics designers and movie makers. In dealing with the ($I«»K$), "objects", special compilers are necessary. Such compilers should perform lexical, syntactic, and semantic analyses of information objects that can identify other information objects and relate themselves to the newly found objects by variable and adaptive role-based linkages. A recursive compiler can handle such a scenario.

The processing of graphics entities [4] starts to assume the initial flavor of the processing of the information objects. Some of the steps suggested in this chapter are initial and rudimentary, but they can be modified and enhanced[3] to suit different types of information object(s) and their interactions. Processing of information objects depends on the application. On the one hand, mechanical and routine transactions of information objects are akin to data processing in banking and commerce. On the other hand, when information has human and social implications, then a new software layer that emulates human processes (such as love, hate, needs, feelings, education, counseling) becomes necessary. Generally, human interactions follow an underlying economic framework of the exchange of resources. On a very short-term basis, the marginal utility theory [5] starts to unfold in most transactions. Perceived fairness and valuation are of essence in most cases. In dealing with information, most humans follow a fairness and value judgment analysis unless it is willfully transgressed.

The rational component of human processes follows simple programming approaches. The emotional component is tackled by suggesting (and adapting) a series of statistical paths ranging from common to rare reactions. Such reactions are documented in the knowledge bases around the world, and steps are adapted in neural networks. In such instances, the machine-generated resolution of

---

[3] For algebraic operations (multiply, divide, matrix, etc.) for complex numbers, the development of software routines followed much later after the assembly level programs for processing real numbers.

information can be superior to all-human solution since machines can evaluate every type of emotional response in every culture and can suggest a customized response closer to the tastes of the humans involved.

While machines are *communicating or exchanging* information, they strictly abide by the I/O commands of humans or of the basic core operating system. While human beings process information, the value and worth of the information are initially assessed, and modified by learning, clarification and negotiation. While machines are *processing* information, the information processing units[4] (IPUs) alter the structural relationships between objects and objects, objects and their attributes, and relationships between object X attributes with object Y attributes. The scenario is depicted in Figure 12.1. The alteration and redistribution of relationships is not altogether random (unless it is the last resort). Instead, they are based on laws of probabilities as to which of the relationships are most common and likely to form secure bonds (e.g., information about automobiles and information about octane values; or information about hang gliders and information about wing span of birds). In the process, the machines also investigate unusual and uncommon relationships (e.g., information about the design of hang gliders for Australian coasts and information about the design of hang gliders for Scandinavian coasts), giving rise to novel and unique information, knowledge, or scientific principles (if any).

Machines have an advantage in processing vast amounts of information quickly and accurately. The incremental changes in information are tallied to the incremental changes in external conditions to optimize and predict the information for a given set of new conditions. Incremental changes over any of the parameters (such as time, attributes, or environmental conditions) are accurately tracked and labeled. Processing the key information object(s) that forms the nucleus (nuclei) of the raw information and then reconstituting the information object(s) identifies opportunities for possibly new and valuable information, knowledge, or scientific principles. This is the fundamental clue to crossing from the information mode to the knowledge mode.

Unlike monetary wealth and the wealth of nations [1] that are depleted, the wealth of information is shared. Unlike monetary wealth, information ($I«»K$) has significantly different attributes. Whereas universal and numerical values can be assigned to monetary wealth, information has overlapping qualities and fuzzy parameters to transact information.

Complexity theory [6] starts to resemble knowledge theory (Section 12.7) because of the highly variable nature of ($I«»K$), "objects" and their interrelationships. Most of the precepts of complexity theory become applicable when dealing with information and knowledge. However, in dealing with ($I«»K$), we limit the processing to a confined number of objects that do not make the

---

[4] Information processing and knowledge processing are used interchangeably in this chapter since the forward processing (distilling) of information leads to knowledge and the backward processing (parsing) of knowledge leads to information. The same machine may be able to process in either direction, perhaps by changing its control memory chip sets. At this stage, it is premature to speak specifically to the many possibilities that still lie ahead.

information processing chaotic. The self-contained structure is statistically prioritized with statistically weighted relationships between the objects that are considered valid for the processing of ($I\langle\!\langle\,\rangle\!\rangle K$) "objects." In addition, the limitations of the computer system (accuracy, memory size, speed, and possible switching capability) define the size and the "body of knowledge" (or the "complex initial object") that the computers will handle.

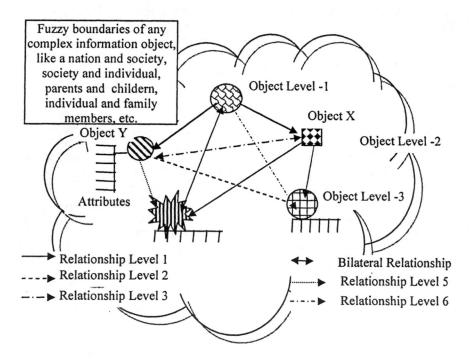

Figure 12.1 Representation of a complex information/knowledge object with five lower-level information objects. Strong, weak, casual, unilateral, and bilateral relationships are shown.

The knowledge processing system filters out any "objects" that are likely to cause chaotic and unstable oscillations in the processing. It refuses to process inconsistent information, much like computers that refuse garbled data. During the execution phase, irrational requests to process information are terminated and the error condition is intimated, just like computers that refuse to execute impossible numeric operations. Unlike complexity theory, the knowledge theory will perform legitimate functions on objects for which some earlier statistical information is available on world-wide knowledge banks. If the extent of information is too restrictive, the learn mode [7] is invoked to build a knowledge base for the unknown object. The machine guards itself from being drawn into an execution mode that ends in catastrophe by establishing non circular forward and backward pointers. Even though recursion is permitted, the depth of recursion is made consistent with the machine capacity. Rationality is given higher priority than the task of execution of a knowledge program. These bounds of rationality contain the fuzzy bounds of knowledge that is under process. To this extent, it regains its own stable operating condition, just as a human being would attempt to do. Thus, overall knowledge processing systems have fair a chance of solving complex knowledge problems that human beings by themselves cannot attempt.

The knowledge processing system limits the size of the body of knowledge processed by a quantitative measure of the capacity of the machine in relation to the requirement of "complex initial object." No such limitation is imposed in complexity theory. For this reason, knowledge theory is based on the computer systems that will attempt to solve a knowledge problem. Knowledge theory is a valid tool in initially formulating the problem and becoming strategic in its solution. The system resource expended to change the status of information and knowledge (see *P3* in Section 12.3) during the course of the solution of the problem will be (in most instances) the bottleneck. In essence, complexity theory is an open-ended theory, but knowledge theory works in the context of machines having discrete (binary or hyperspace) representations, limited in their memory, I/O, switching capacities, and speed of operation.

To this extent, knowledge theory is like information theory that works in most non-chaotic but extremely noisy environments. Knowledge theory does not violate any of the principles (such as auto-organization, edge of chaos, power of connections, circular causality, try&learn, and ologrammatic principle) set forth by complexity theory. To some extent, auto-organization and try&learn are based on the survey of the world-wide knowledge bases on the Internet to find out how other complex knowledge objects have accomplished auto-organization and adaptation. To this extent, quantification within knowledge theory (like that within information theory) becomes totally feasible.

Shared information loses value at a relatively low rate. Whereas there is a suggestion of strict zero-sum game [2] in transacting the wealth of nations and individuals, there is an impression of *elastic zero-sum game* as two parties share knowledge and information. Wealth (i.e., all the utilities combined together) and value rather than price of information are only perceived at the time of sharing information. The sale price of a commodity or an asset can only arise in a free-market environment. The price for sharing information is perceived between buyer and seller and not determined by market forces. Sometimes the value of information in a document, a book, or a scripture far exceeds the price of the book and sometimes the converse can be the case.

In the knowledge domain, an approximation for the scarcity, value and life of the information is feasible. Along the scarcity, value, and lifetime (three dimensional curve) five coordinates points can be readily identified: (1) totally unshared and secret information has no value and indeterminate life, (2) guarded information has high value and relatively long life, (3) information shared with a select clientele has highest value until it starts to leak and slowly erodes in value, (4) media information has a media price and short life, and finally (5) gossip and trivia has junk value and dissipates without a trail.   The value of information in a socioeconomic setting has at least three additional dimensions, the truth contained, the elegance or appeal conveyed, and the social benefit that can be derived from the information.

To deal with the complex nature of information from a computational and processing perspective, we propose four (truism, philosophic, scientific, and economic) dimensions or senses, shown in Figure 12.2, in which information can be characterized. In dealing with information as an object, truism of all information objects (not their content) states the truth (as well as it is known) about the entire object class. Similarly, philosophic characterization of all information objects (not their content) states the philosophic nature (as well as it is known) about the entire object class, and so on.

Processing an information object can alter its four characteristics (T, P, S, E). In fact, constructive processing will make marginal information (objects) into significant information (objects), if there is any significance. Worthless information is filtered out from any scientific knowledge processing[5]. The process can be deduce, interpret, derive, systematize, analogize, categorize, conceptualize, rationalize, and generalize or any other process that has a scientific basis.

In order to initiate the information processing to search out new information or new knowledge from vast amounts of information, three steps are proposed: observation of reality, philosophic validation, and scientific principles that can be generalized and deployed elsewhere. The observation of reality is fundamental to all sciences. Since information has illusive boundaries and flexible formats, the concept resides in the content of information and goes deeper than a statement or representation of information. In a sense, information is the water that can be poured into any vessel. The water is a real information object with its own properties and the vessel is the secondary information object. Together, they form a (partially) stable object group.

The philosophic validation is necessary to provide a long-term continuity and stability of information, such that any inference/scientific conclusion can be drawn. To continue with the earlier example, if the water is poured into a vessel carved out of ice, there will be neither water nor ice over a long enough period[6] of contemplation to form a stable object group (i.e., water in a vessel). It becomes necessary to probe the wealth of knowledge and information (water) in society (vessel) to validate the reality as a stable and dependable basis.

The derivation of scientific principle(s) becomes an act of courage to stand firm in the observation of reality and a philosophic validation to make a universal statement or hypothesize the object — object (H to the OH in H_2O, or electrons beams to electromagnetic fields in cathode ray tubes) relationship as a scientific truth. The bold steps of scientists (e.g., Hamming, Shannon, Bose, Hocquenghem,

---

[5] Most compilers block programs (program-objects) from proceeding to the execution phase unless they are free of all syntactic, all semantic and all linkage errors. In a similar vein, information that is inherently false, malicious, or laden with pornography will not gain access to information-object processing systems

[6] Unless the situation is adiabatic at 32° F, which becomes too specific to draw any general conclusions.

Ampere, Gauss, Maxwell) as they formulated their significant conclusions (based on their own human information processing capabilities) are still valid. To continue with the earlier example, the scientific principle that water (that can be poured) has low viscosity can be used in other instances and situations. In the information domain, very fluid and fast flowing gossip would not have value, since it is not stable enough to become useful as a scientific principle.

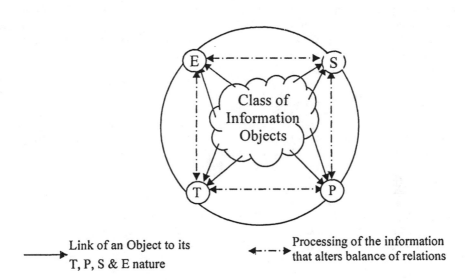

Figure 12.2 Representation of the class of information objects with four characteristics: truism, philosophic, scientific, and economic nature of information.

We attempt to follow the three-step procedure (reality, philosophy, and science) to get a computational handle on processing information. It becomes possible to extend the three-step procedure into a fourth step and derive an economic basis of dealing with knowledge and information. Both knowledge and information are known to have value. The rules of dealing with them as object-based abstract commodities start to become significantly different from the economics of materialistic wealth.

12.2 TRUISMS IN INFORMATION DOMAIN

Observation of reality over long periods leads to generality or truism. In dealing with information, three notions are suggested:

T1. *Information has a life cycle.*
T2. *Information can be altered, but any alteration of information needs expenditure of energy.*
T3. *Information has impact.*

The list is short and other dependent truisms can be derived from the three listed above. The truism layer is shown at the top of Figure 12.3. The T1 to T3 list is kept deliberately short with the hope that the list of derived scientific principles will also be elementary and short. This would reduce the basic operations that a computer system will have to perform while processing information.

12.3 PHILOSOPHIC VALIDATION

Only four philosophic validations (P1—P4) are suggested and the list is deliberately kept short to reduce the instruction set for the machine to process information. It is depicted as the middle layer in Figure 12.3. Based on T1, the justified philosophic validation (at this time) is as follows:

P1. *Information is timely or obsolete and it can change its characteristics over time.* Typically, human or machine processing changes the derived information. It ranges from mere gossip to a scientific principle or an equation in physics. When the linkages to the raw information are not retained, the processed information may assume the identity of a new information object. Hence the concept of Aristotle's beginning, middle, and end becomes fuzzy in the information domain. We refer to this particular validation as P1.

Based on T2, two philosophic validations (P2 and P3) are feasible and presented separately because the implications are different.
P2. *Boundaries of knowledge and information are vague and fuzzy.* Returning to the example of water in a vessel, information is blended in the human perception. Much like the features of beauty that lie in the eye of the beholder, the boundaries of information lie in the mind of the receptor. Human perception becomes a fading memory (or a leaky bucket) to hold information (water). When a machine receives information, the information objects, their structure, and their relationships are analyzed and stored with the timeline for that specific "body" of information. In a sense, the "information compiler" performs a lexical, syntactic, semantic, and timeline analysis on "information inputs" and identifies the information objects, their structures, and their relationships.

Implication P3 based on T2 is
P3. *Information has three qualitative features; truth contained, social value conveyed, and the inherent elegance in content in variable proportions.*

Information can also have the opposite features (falsehood, social malice, and ugliness) in variable proportions. An equally important principle is that the change of status of information implies an effort (equivalent to force) to bring about the change sustained over the displacement of the status (thus invoking a concept of psychological or social energy or the deployment of resources).

To fall back on the example of water and the vessel, if the water carries three partially dissolved solutes (sugar, sweetener, and honey), then the viscosity changes thus altering the fluid mechanics and the concentration levels in different sections of the vessel. Furthermore, any alteration of the concentration level, after an equilibrium condition is reached, needs energy for the change (such as stirring, shaking, vibrating, or adding more water). The scientific basis for predicting the concentration contours becomes quite complex and even unpredictable (like the weather). However, when a machine has a basis of estimating the truth (sugar), the social value (sweetener), and the elegance (honey) independently (based on statistical sampling of other information objects and their relationships), then the raw/processed information can be scientifically evaluated with appropriate confidence levels.

Based on T3, the validation for P4 is stated as follows,

(P4) Sharing of information can bring rewards or retributions in any variable proportion. This particular implication carries little impact in the scientific domain but becomes significant in the social and economic domains. In the socioeconomic realm, it is generally accepted practice to exchange items of similar value (including information, patents, techniques, and ideas). It is also frequent to find the extent of damage inflicted as retribution. In the information domain, litigation and penalties are imposed when negative information and bad publicity are purposely circulated.

12.4 SCIENTIFIC PRINCIPLES

Five scientific principles (S1–S5) are derived from the four philosophic validations (P1–P4). The first principle, S1, results from P1 and is stated as follows.

S1. *It is implied that information is dynamic.* At any instant, information can be segmented (differentiated with respect to time), encoded, communicated, corrected, interpolated, extrapolated, restored and even reconstituted. Information can be grouped (i.e., integrated over time), independently or with current or past information object(s). If information objects are treated as dynamic and continuous in the time domain, then differentiation and integration become possible. The analog and closed-form operations are irrelevant, but finite and event-driven changes are sensed from information and knowledge bases. For instance, every scientific meeting or conference adds or subtracts from the collective information base of a community. Human beings and/or machines can process new information-objects continuously.

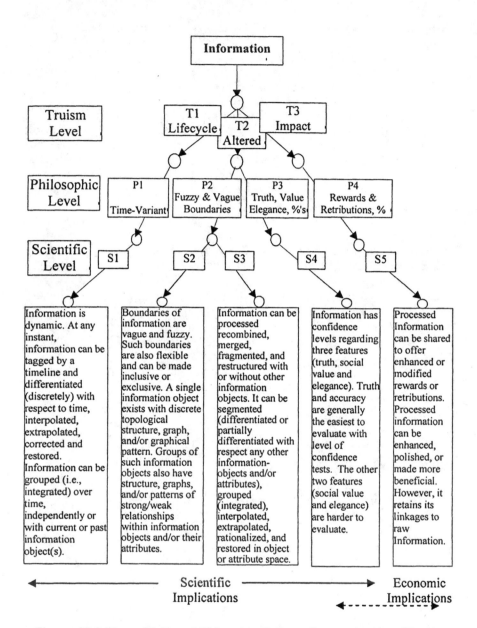

Figure 12.3 Three (T, P and S) levels of information processing. The S Level is consistent with truism and philosophic handling of information-objects, but the scientific principles derived as the third level (S) offer mathematical tools and techniques to deal with information-objects.

When finite changes are necessary then the commitment of resources becomes essential. Hence the concept of (expected) incremental or marginal costs are evaluated and equated to the (expected) incremental or marginal benefit that is gained.

The second principle, S2, is derived as an extension of P2 and is stated as follows:

S2. *Boundaries of knowledge and information are vague and fuzzy.* Such boundaries are also flexible and can be made inclusive or exclusive of other information objects. Single information objects exist as topological structures, "graphs," and/or graphical patterns. Groups of information objects also have structure, graphs, and/or patterns of relationships within the information objects and/or their attributes. Structures, graphs, and patterns (see Figure 12.1) can have scientific implications for stability. In the domain of information, the information objects need reasonable bonds to remain existent for a period. Insecure bonds between objects only results in short-lived rumors and gossip.

The third principle S3 also results as an extension of P2 and stated as follows:

S3. *An information object can be processed, corrected, recombined, merged, fragmented, and restructured by itself or in conjunction with other information objects.* It (they) can also be segmented (differentiated or partially differentiated with respect to other information objects or attributes), grouped (integrated), interpolated, extrapolated, rationalized, and restored in object or attribute space. The basic tools of (discrete) mathematics become applicable in dealing with the continuity of information over time and the continuity of (structural relationships or discrete) contours with respect to other objects or their attributes.

The fourth principle S4 results from P3 and stated as follows.

S4. *Information has confidence levels regarding three features (truth, social value and elegance).* Truth and accuracy are generally the easiest to evaluate in context to other similar single information-objects or other multiple information-objects with level of confidence tests. Generally, (local and global) information bases that contain information about similar objects can provide a basis for confidence tests. The other two features (social value and elegance) become harder to evaluate.

The fifth principle S5 results from P4 and is stated as follows:

S5. *Processed information can be shared to offer enhanced or modified rewards or retributions.* Processed information retains its linkages to raw information. Human processing of information has taken a firm hold in society. Transitory information processed by the human mind is dispersed as conversation. Information that is more important is documented and retained for further reference. In the realm of processing by intelligent machines or systems, information can provide more value (truth, social significance, or elegance) in the processed mode, especially if the processing is done on a scientific basis by following principles (S1–S4). For example, segmentation and recombination offer a slightly different form of truth (that is equally valid) as the original truth. Similarly, mere rearranging of the words can sometimes make a hidden context or idea more apparent and so on. From a computational perspective, simple differentiation tests (i.e., event analysis and correlation studies) can reveal the more sensitive information objects with a complex information structure.

12.5 ECONOMICS OF INFORMATION

Seven extensions of the three truisms, four philosophic validations, and five scientific principles are feasible in the domain of economics. We do not offer elaborate explanations of the economic inferences because the inference chain does not appear immediately obvious. In this particularly human domain, numerous preceding antecedents from truth, philosophy and science influence anyone economic inference. Thus, we simply present them as follows:

E1. *Information and knowledge that are never conveyed or deployed are worthless.* The velocity of flow of information is essential for value. Such a velocity can be altered by events, forces and/or resource expended to accelerate or retard the status of information. The velocity of flow can enhance the information's economic worth, which peaks at an optimum level. Information that is too fluid is as worthless as information that is too stagnant. A bell shaped curve for the worth of information starts to emerge in relation to its velocity of flow.

E2. *Information that is deployed enhances its seepage rate, thus eroding its value.* If the velocity of flow is monitored, the information can retain value over a long period of time, thus maximizing the wealth of information over its life cycle. For example, nuclear technology that is well guarded has offered a "rich" power base for the nuclear nations. Unpublished results by drug manufacturers offer a long revenue stream. However, the sale of the drugs also enhances the probability that other countries will manufacture a similar drug with the same or slightly modified formula, thus eroding the value of the original information.

E3. *Scarcity plays a role in the value of information.* From a historic perspective, the scarcity of the any commodity creates an artificial peak in its valuation. In many instances, corporations and individuals, in order to enhance their own gain and wealth, exploit this artificial peak. In the information domain, information that is scarce can be stolen, copied, hijacked, wiretapped, and so on. In the information age and knowledge society, leaks and tip offs are common and offer a venue for economic gain and profiteering.

E4. *There is no free market price for information.* However there is always a negotiated price between a buyer and a seller. The value of information also depends on the buying party's capacity and willingness to deploy the information.

E5. *Sharing and deployment of information is a non zero-sum game but the depletion/seepage laws are different.* Stated alternatively, sharing and deployment of information is an elastic zero-sum game with elastic laws of depletion/seepage.

E6. *Value of information depends on the buying party's linkage to the other information objects that adjoin the negotiated information object.*

E7. *Expected value of information is roughly equated to expected benefit that can be derived by the deploying that information object in conjunction with other information objects.*

In Sections 12.8 and 12.9, we use the above economic implications to explain some of the behavior that is particularly significant in the knowledge society.

12.6 INTEGRATION AND SOCIAL CHANGE

One of the assertions S1 in Section 12.4 is that information and knowledge can be differentiated and integrated. In this section, an example of the integration of knowledge over a span of time is presented to indicate how nations, corporations, and individuals can experience an enhancement or deterioration of value by integrating current knowledge over time.

Consider a graph with the knowledge level that is deployed by a nation, a corporation, or an individual on the Y axis and time on the X axis. Since ($I«»K$) has a dynamic profile, any point on the ($I«»K$) curve follows an up or a down trajectory, however small the gradient (dI/dt) may be. In order to determine the change in social value (net worth) of the knowledge[7] deployed in a particular discipline (say, electrical engineering classified as 621.34 according to the Dewey Decimal System) over a span T_1 (year 1985) to T_2 (year 2000), the area under the curve is evaluated for that particular discipline, where

---

[7] The change of social value of knowledge can only be evaluated in a given direction, since any nation, corporation or individual has numerous directions of change over time from T_1 to T_2. For example, if a nation is evaluating changes in industrial production, the levels of both technical knowledge and propensity have to be in the direction of industrial production. This particular equation can be aggregated (as it is frequently done in economics) to evaluate national averages. Similar arguments apply in the corporate and individual domains.

$$SV_2 - SV_1 = \int_{T_1}^{T_2} Deployed\,(\,I \ll \gg K\,)\,dt$$

$$Deployed\ information\ (\ \overrightarrow{I \ll \gg K}\ ) = Level\ of\ (\ \overrightarrow{I \ll \gg K}\ ) \bullet Propensity\ of\ organization$$

Typically, the propensity to deploy also exhibits vectorial properties because the national government, corporate management, or an individual has numerous propensities (health, education, welfare, etc). However, only the propensity to deploy the knowledge in a particular discipline (say, EE bearing a DDS direction of 621.34) is meaningful in computing the change in social value ($SV_2 - SV_1$) or net worth (of EE ($I \ll \gg K$) from T_1 to T_2). For this reason, the scalar product (dot product) leads to the deployed ($I \ll \gg K$)

12.6.1 Level of ($I \ll \gg K$)

The level of information and knowledge ($I \ll \gg K$) in any society is dynamic and changing. In reality, it is a function of time and changes slightly during the increment of time δt. However, when its value is to be included in the estimation of net worth, its magnitude can be frozen for a short enough duration over a short enough increment of time Δt, (say, for a month and updated as a moving average). Even though equations that are written on a theoretical basis, they can be implemented in a discrete domain. This procedure is quite common in macroeconomics, where national averages are computed and predicted by econometricians. Information and knowledge again bear similarities to the parameters in economics and can be treated as such. Information-objects permit the manipulation of complex structures of ($I \ll \gg K$) in the computational environment where the linkages and relationships with other information objects or their attributes are essential.

12.6.2 Propensity of Organizations

Organizations like humans have predispositions. The ambitions of the leaders and founding members are reflected in the attitude toward information and knowledge. A bent of mind toward money, research, capital spending, social reform, education, and even war and destruction gets ingrained as the propensities of employees. Such propensities are encouraged or curtailed. The leadership usually lasts for a limited time and the propensity exists for a short enough period of time that it can be treated as a constant or varying so slightly that the evaluation of net worth is not drastically affected. From a theoretical perspective, the propensity is a function of time (t), especially if the interval ($T_2 - T_1$) is long.

Further analysis of propensity has two aspects: (1) the capacity and skill sets to deploy information and knowledge ($I«»K$), and (2) the willingness of human beings to deploy ($I«»K$). Hence it becomes appropriate to write

$$\textit{Propensity (t)} = \overrightarrow{\textit{Capacity (t)}} \bullet \overrightarrow{\textit{Willingness (t)}} \textit{ in that discipline}$$

The capacity of the deployment team is treated as a scalar and the willingness is treated as a vector, or vice versa. However, if both are treated as vectors, the scalar product of the two vectors needs to be evaluated. Additional classification of directions may be necessary. The final equation for the change in social value thus becomes

$$SV_2 - SV_1 = \int_{T_1}^{T_2} \textit{Level of}(I«» K) . \{ \overrightarrow{\textit{Capacity (t)}} . \overrightarrow{\textit{Willingness (t)}} \} \, dt$$

The discrete form of this equation leads to summations of finite changes over increments of time that make up the interval ($T_2 - T_1$). The vector formats are necessary because the classification of ($I«»K$) is in a large numbers of disciplines and the direction of change can be evaluated in particular disciplines. Deployment of ($I«»K$) in one discipline can also yield an incremental change of ($I«»K$) in other discipline(s).

If $C(i,t)$ is the capacity at an instant t in discipline i during a duration Δt, and $W(i,t)$ is the willingness at an instant t during the same interval Δt, with $L(I«»K)$ as the level of (information $I«»K$ knowledge), then the incremental change of value is

$$\Delta \textit{Social Value of knowledge} = L(I «» K) \bullet \{C(i,t) \bullet W(i,t)\} \, \Delta t$$

In its differential form, this equation states that the rate of change of value of knowledge depends on its deployment (see E1 and E2 in Section 12.5) or the scalar product of level of information and willingness to deploy the information. In most instances, only the finite difference form (i.e., $\Delta V/\Delta t$) of this equation relates the change of value with the deployment of the body (or the object) of knowledge for that interval Δt of time.

12.7 THEORY OF KNOWLEDGE

The theory of knowledge is still seminal. The three levels (truism, philosophic, and scientific) can be forced into an algebraic notation, though not a precise one. The qualitative and directional relations that reality, philosophy, and science impose can be restated in quasi mathematical equations. In the science of medicine (state of health = function of cardiovascular parameters, blood test readings, EEG patterns, etc.) and in economics (GNP = C + S + T, + (export − import), etc.), such relationships have been stated before the final refinements that make the relationships more precise and universal.

12.7.1 Algebraic Constructs of Knowledge Theory

Exhaustive and relentless processing of information leads to a tentative foundation of knowledge. Based on the process by which the inference is drawn, certain truisms of knowledge can be perceived. From a quantitative and a mathematical perspective, four theorems are suggested as follows:

I. *The composition of any information object (I«»K) has an algebraic format.* At the most fundamental level, it deals with the composition of the secondary objects that constitute the knowledge about the complex (I«»K)-object. This relationship is represented as

$$Composition(\ I\text{«»}K\ ) = f_c\ (O_1, O_2 .., O_i, .., O_n)$$

The equation affirms that the composition of a complex ($I\text{«»}K$) object is based on a series of n sub-objects, where f_c is an algebraic function (which could be only a summation). The uncertainty of dealing with objects and their correlation to the main object ($I\text{«»}K$) is quantified by the computers connected to Internet knowledge bases (KBs) distributed around the globe. The uncertainty is handled by the numeric confidence limit we have in the relationships that are inherent in dealing with knowledge. Thus the *composition*($I\text{«»}K$) now starts to have a numeric value that is derived by scanning all possible KBs dealing with the same or similar knowledge objects ($I\text{«»}K$). For example, when dealing with the GNP of a nation, numerous secondary objects (like employment, saving, education, and consumption) become important. However, macroeconomics and econometric models around the world have enough parameters for econometricians to construct a GNP model for any new nation. This equation is applicable is other disciplines such as computer architecture or automobiles. If the complex object is a model-T computer (or an automobile) then the equation states that the composition of a computer is a function f_c (e.g., sum) of its CPU(s) O_1, its memories O_2, its buses O_3, its I/O units O_4 and its switching modules O_5.

II. The structure of ($I«»K$) is represented as a function of the structures of its secondary objects. This statement is represented as

$$Structure(\,I«»K\,)\ =f_s\,(O_1,\ O_2,\ ..O_i,\,..O_n)$$

If the complex object is a model-T computer then the equation states that the composition of a computer is a function f_s of its object O_1 (i.e., CPUs with their own structures such as SISD, SIMD, MIMD, parallel and pipeline), The function f_s also relates object O_2 (i.e., memories to their own structures such as 2D, 2½D, 3D, multiwafer, TTL, CMOS, microsecond, nanosecond, picosecond) and so on.

III. *The attributes of each object as they influence the complex object are related.*
This is represented as

$$Attribute\ Relations\ (\,I«»K\,)\ =f_r\,\{R(O_1,\ A_{1\text{-}1i}),\ R(O_2,\ A_{2\text{-}2j})\,,\ ..\ R(O_i,\ A_{i\text{-}ik}),\,..\}$$

If the complex object is a model-T computer then this equation states that the composition of a computer is a function f_r (of the attributes of its object individually) of the attributes of its CPUs O_1 such as speed, opcode length, instruction repertoire, cache and control memories, etc.; of the attributes of its memories O_2 such as the access rate, types of memory(ies), DMA rate, secondary memory features, etc; to its buses O_3 (such 32 bit width, 64 bit width, shared, dedicated, etc.); to its I/O units O_4 (USB, Infra red, optical, parallel port, serial port, etc.), and to its switching modules O_5, (such as step down, matrix, serial, bus, parallel, etc.) and all other possible interconnections via the buses.

IV. *The final form represents the relationships between the attributes of any object*
O_i and the attributes of other object O_j as they influence the complex object.
This representation of the relationships is inclusive of the previous representation III. However, the set of matrices of the Attribute relationships in IV includes the

$$Attribute\text{-}Attribute\ Relations\ (\,I«»K\,)\ =f_{rr}\,\{Matrices\ of\ Attribute\ Relations\}$$

If the complex object is a model-T computer, then the equation states that the composition of a computer is a function f_{rr} (object attributes to the attribute of other objects) of its CPUs O_1 to organization (such as SISD and 2½D memory, MIMD to 3D memory, etc.), its memories O_2 to the memory organization, speed, and so on, (such as 2D to DMA channel, 2½D to parallel ports), ..., I/O devices, ..., and all other possible interconnections via the buses. As can be seen, each of the attribute-attribute relationship becomes a matrix its own right with other matrices {M(OA$_1$, OA$_1$), M(OA$_1$, OA$_2$), ..}, as the individual terms of the main matrix.

$$\begin{vmatrix} M(OA_1, OA_1), M(OA_1, OA_2), ...M(OA_1, OA_n) \\ M(OA_2, OA_1), M(OA_2, OA_2), ...M(OA_2, OA_n) \\ .... \\ .... \\ M(OA_n, OA_1), M(OA_n, OA_2), ...M(OA_n, OA_n) \end{vmatrix}$$

and

$$M(OA_1, OA_1) =$$

$$\begin{vmatrix} R(OA_1, OA_1), R(OA_1, OA_2), R(OA_1, OA_3), ... \\ R(OA_2, OA_1), R(OA_2, OA_2), R(OA_2, OA_3), ... \\ R(OA_3, OA_1), R(OA_3, OA_2), R(OA_3, OA_3), ... \\ R(OA_4, OA_1), R(OA_4, OA_2), R(OA_4, OA_3), ... \\ .... \\ R(OA_i, OA_1), R(OA_i, OA_2), R(OAi, OA_3), ... \end{vmatrix}$$

Where M stands for matrix and R symbolizes individual numeric dependencies. It is interesting to note that $R(OA_i, OA_i)$ terms have a unity relation, i.e., the value in 1.00 whereas all other R terms may have other finite numbers. Attenuation and amplification are both possible leading to values

$$0.00 < R(OA_i, OA_j) < 1.00 \text{ or } R(OA_i, OA_j) > 1.00$$

respectively.

The confidence that one can expect in dealing with knowledge is resource dependent. The machines for processing knowledge become dependent on the knowledge instruction set(s) and their knowledge operand objects and their allocated number of bits for their representation at the KPU level. The extent of memory and the access sets forth another limit of knowledge in machines. The I/O capacity, speed, and I/O processors all contribute to the knowledge that can be handled, held, or processed by the machines.

12.7.2 Systemic Limitations of Knowledge Systems

In the transmission and communication of data, signal-to-noise ratio constrains capacity. In the knowledge domain, three constraints limit the body and the boundary of Internet based knowledge.

1. The limit of knowledge machines is dictated by the granularity of the knowledge handling capacity (the extent of knowledge operation code or kopcode in Chapter 4, and the addressing capacity of the knowledge operands or koprands in Chapter 4) of the KPU in the knowledge machines.

2. The IP addressing capacity and granularity of the IP address space curtail the locations of the WWW Internet knowledge bases. Subbases of knowledge according to discipline based on the Dewey Decimal System or the Library of Congress classification (Chapter 10) and address look-up capability (see SCP in Chapter 2) can greatly enhance the knowledge access based on conventional switching capabilities. The limit of networks is dictated by the bandwidth of the communication system coupled with the addressing granularity.

3. The capacity of human beings is limited by the perception to validate or reject the incremental changes of knowledge that any knowledge system derives from the information domain. Even though the boundaries of knowledge are vague, the granular spacing between one point and the next is limited by the trilogy of computer system, networks and human beings that process, communicate, and perceive incremental changes in the content of knowledge.

Humans and organizations also suffer from similar constraints. The granularity of estimating the incremental changes of knowledge *and* the limit of confidence in such changes are the two fundamental limits to the extent of knowledge that can be perceived by a human-machine system.

There is an advantage in writing algebraic relationships, even though the equations may be qualitative and approximate at first. One concept that such equations bring to the processing of information and knowledge is differentiation and integration of equations. For example, the partial differential of any of the equations with respect to an object, its structure, or its attribute or its attribute to other object attributes leads to sensitivity or sensitivity matrix. There is a qualitative relationships and a quantitative estimate of the effects of how the complex information objects respond to the other independent objects that define the characteristics of the complex-object (i.e., the body of ($I«»K$) or information and knowledge) being processed. Econometricians deploy relationships that cannot be accurately verified in totality. All the same, it is well known that the stagnation of money can be traced to overall economic activity in a nation. In a similar vein, stagnant data in the memory banks of computers is moved to a secondary storage system to make room for more fluid (frequently used) data, thus making the computational activity more productive.   The operating systems perform such activity routinely.

12.8 PROCESSING OF INFORMATION

The processing of sensitive information has been the strength of humans. When machines are involved, the scientific principles derived in Section 12.4 and their economic implications may be programmed into the machines. From a scientific perspective, the processing of information proceeds systematically from one step to the next based on *three* basic concepts listed as follows:

1. Information objects have a certain number of (strong or weak, unilateral or bilateral) relationships with their own attributes or with other objects or their attributes. For example, if water is an information object, then the two hydrogen atoms and one oxygen atom constitute one water molecule (H_2O) in a stable state to be classified as a stable information object. When n number of water molecules interacts with n sulfurtrioxide (SO_3) molecules, then equal numbers of molecules of sulfuric acid (H_2SO_4) are formed. Numerous other examples also exist.

2. Information objects have structures or laws (available from local or global knowledge bases) that hold the internal information objects and/or their attributes in a relational and coherent fashion (e.g., valency of hydrogen = 1 and valency of oxygen = 2). A statistical map of such relationships can be obtained by scanning local or global knowledge banks. An entire collection of information objects acts as a group that can be enhanced, modified, processed or rearranged to suit different events, circumstances, or applications. Numerous other examples also exist.

3. Any change to structure of information needs an event (however slow or fast it may be, like an explosion as hydrogen combines with oxygen or slow corrosion due to condensation) to alter the flavor, content or the composition of information. Without external deployment, information in machines will remain as such, stagnate and turn useless. In human beings, information degenerates due to memory effect over long enough periods.

   Information processing is akin to data processing. Objects rather than variables are processed. Numerical and logical processes become more complex as object processes. The objects, their attributes, and their interdependencies are processed in a coherent fashion to follow the reality and the context of a particular application. It becomes evident that the software layers for object processing are elaborate and extensive to handle real-life information objects.

   The computing and database capabilities of modern machines can handle complex applications (like the PeopleSoft [8], SAP [9], and other decision support systems) quite effectively. Some architectural configurations are presented in chapters dealing with knowledge processing systems. Information processing systems and knowledge processing systems are likely to have similar object processors but differ in the firmware and the control module [10]. The microcode [11] to drive the IPUs and the KPUs is likely to have some common routines and likely to be more elaborate than the microcode of conventional computers.

12.9 ECONOMICS OF KNOWLEDGE

Internet age and high-speed networks make most information readily available to the public. Privacy of information is rapidly becoming a myth of the past. Proliferation in almost all forms of information and knowledge ($I«»K$) raises concerns of security in the minds of most people. In the history of corporations, the technological base and knowledge of a few has nurtured a power base and financial wealth for the founding members of the corporation. More recently, the knowledge base of most corporations is shrinking. The success that a few enjoy is sometimes based on information to which only they are privy. In a sense, the information age exposes this private knowledge base on which the success of a few depends, causing anxiety and fear. The economic implication of this rather serious change brought about by the information age is explored next.

12.9.1 Diminishing Value of Knowledge

In Figure 12.4a, information is classified into different levels depending on its authenticity. The more valuable information is from unbiased world-class authorities in their particular discipline. By the same token, the most worthless information would be the hearsay and gossip in the public domain. A hierarchy for the representation of information is thus possible. At the top of the hierarchical pyramid is the most authentic information that is novel (like the inventions transistor or optical amplification), is scarce (has not been exploited, or mass produced, kept private) and has the highest potential (to positively affect society). In the past, rare and valuable information would retain its value over a long duration because experts were few and only global experts would alter the structure of ($I«»K$) .

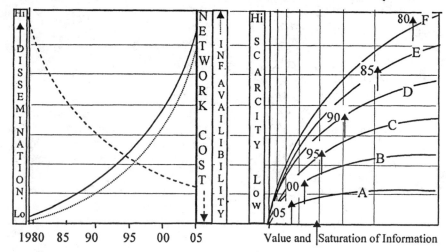

(a) The numerous levels of information ranging from hearsay to global expert level opinions and validations.

(b) The value of information based on its scarcity. Generally, the value of information goes up because of scientific and authenticated process.

(c) The fall in network cost and the increased availability of (all) information over the last two decades.

(d) The fall in scarcity and the consequential fall in the value of information over the last two decades.

Figure 12.4 Multilevel generic knowledge model depicting the dynamics and erosion of the wealth of information due to the impact of Internet and high-speed networks. The information saturates faster and at a lower value.

The notion of Thorstein Veblen (discussed earlier in Section 12.1) relating scarcity to value (of information in this particular context) is drawn out a carve in Figure 12b. The enhanced velocity of flow of information results from high-speed digital networks during the last two decades and depicted in Figures 12.4c and d. This increase in the fluidity of information prematurely depletes the value of technical information for corporations and for individuals who are the sources and creators of novelty. The value of information plunges from the curve E (in 1985) in Figure 12.4d, to curve A (in 2005). More recently, there is no scarcity of information due to high-speed backbone networks.

As discussed in Section 12.1 and presented as E1 in Section 12.5, a certain *viscosity in the flow* of information (like the viscosity in the flow of money) maximizes the potential gain for the owners of that knowledge or information. Other reasons for the unauthenticated depletion of wealth of information are leaks, gossip or irresponsible media exposure. Sometimes this exposure can make significant information worthless or conversely make worthless information significant in the public domain. Both effects take away from the any truth, beauty, and social value that were inherent in the original information object. Due process is thus denied to the worthy information objects.

There are two sides to the higher velocity of flow of information. On the one hand, it brings reward to the consumer and momentarily enhances its utility; yet on the other hand, it depletes the potential gain to owners of the information. In a sense, valuable information can be sold at media (newspaper) prices and conversely worthless gossip can be sold at primetime TV rates. Two serious implications follow.

First, the authenticity is lost (due to leaks, fall-outs, and rumor) and second, the unauthenticated information also gets recirculated at a higher rate due to high-speed networks, causing a multiplier effect in the enhancement of unsubstantiated information. Over a period of time, the higher speeds of the backbone communication networks (cable, TV, Internet, mass-media, etc.) accelerate the flow of unworthy information, causing a downward spiral effect on society.

People tend to consume misinformation more readily than information, simply because validation of authentic information needs additional effort than acceptance of misinformation. At the same time, the flood of insignificant information drowns the significance of worthy information. Truth (T), social value (S), and elegance (E) of ($I«»K$) is replaced by changing social tastes, taboos and mores thus causing instability for ($I«»K$) in the long range. Much like electrical filters that reduce the noise that drowns information in telecommunication networks, an ($I«»K$) filter can amplify the TSE content and block falsehood (F), distaste (D), and corruption (C). Unfortunately, there is only one pinnacle of a unified TSE (see Chapter 13) but millions of peaks of FDC.

12.9.2 Economic Life of Inventions

Corporate inventions have fueled industrial growth and profits. When corporations fund research facilities, they expect that the resulting inventions and innovations will sustain continued corporate growth. However, high-speed networks reduce the timeframe for the possible payoff. Access and speed both deplete the value of the information that is the invention. To this extent, inventions get shortchanged twice. First, the competing corporations can benefit from the principle on which the invention is based and second, researching the WWW can quickly provide the required technology and product lines for the products of the invention.

In a real sense, the risk for corporations to invest in research gets higher as the network service providers make networks faster and access more universal. The circulation of information through networks is shown in Figure 12.5a. The shortness of the cycle time is due to the high-speed and almost unlimited access of the news and Internet media. Worthy and unworthy information both get communicated fast. Earlier, when inventions were disclosed as valuable and scarce information, inventors were given exclusive rights under patent laws. In the last two decades, knowledge processing of inventions opens numerous ways to circumvent the methodology and claims. Principles and concepts now can be fragmented and disassembled [12], (Chapter 4). New inventions can be reassembled, reconstituted, and (almost) tailored, like drugs and vaccines. One of the purposes of the wisdom machine (Chapter 10) is to derive new inventions from old inventions and alter the core concepts of any invention to enhance a partial invention.

The implication of the higher *velocity of flow* of information and misinformation has a profound effect on the profitability for corporations. The product cycle time also gets shortened. From the invention of a concept leading to a product to the demise of the product is quickened as the rate of flow of all relevant information concerning that product is accelerated. Newer products appear quicker and replace the original product. The validity of this recent influence of high-speed networks on corporations is shown in Figures 12.5b and c. During the 1970's and 1980's, corporations could estimate an average (and profitable) product life of a decade or two. After the knowledge and network society has evolved the corporate attitude is to exploit the novelty quickly and maximize the revenues over the narrow slit of opportunity that the high-speed networks provide. This anxiety has adverse influence on human behavior.

12.9.3 Impact of High-Speed Networks on Human Behavior

Human behavior becomes an involuntary participant in a knowledge society where information and misinformation are both communicated at high speeds. When human fears, anxieties and insecurities are factored into the accelerated cycles of information, the foundations of ethics and morality bear the brunt.

Consider a corporate environment where the financial feedback loop has reached a stable condition based on established technical knowledge, corporate management, management information systems, information technology, process information, databases, and archives. Top corporate executives charged with long-term survival of the corporation become aware of the eroding value of information and technical knowledge on which the success of the corporation is based.

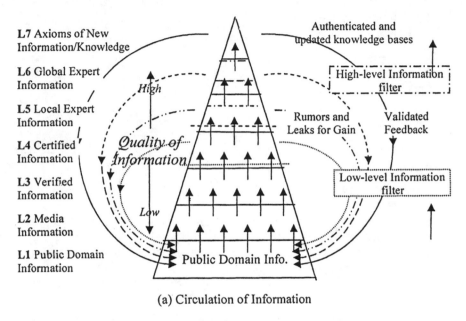

L7 Axioms of New Information/Knowledge

L6 Global Expert Information

L5 Local Expert Information

L4 Certified Information

L3 Verified Information

L2 Media Information

L1 Public Domain Information

Authenticated and updated knowledge bases

High-level Information filter

Rumors and Leaks for Gain

Validated Feedback

Low-level Information filter

Quality of Information

High

Low

Public Domain Info.

(a) Circulation of Information

Figure 12.5 Levels of information with upward flow reinforcing the scientific process to enhance the truth, universality, social value, and elegance in information. The validated feedback path authenticates the true content and concept of information and the fallout paths distort and corrupt the information.

The high-speed networks and knowledge bases will serve as tools for competing firms to offer stiff challenges to its products or services. In fact, the executives who are aware of the pitfalls in the original designs and production line facilities know that the newer corporations will displace the cozy status quo of the traditional corporation.

From a social setting, the information age serves the capitalistic society in bringing newer and cheaper products to market. However, it also awakens the ancient "fight or flight" response in the executives.

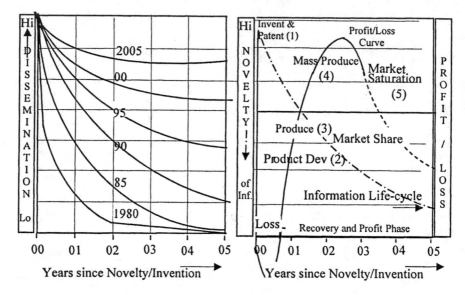

(b) Dissemination curves for an invention since conception over the last two decades. The Internet has enhanced the rate, thus quickly bringing the invention into the public domain.

(c) Information (invention) life cycle and profitability curve of products resulting from invention. When the profitability curve is long and sustained, corporations recover the R & D and initial setup costs.

Figure 12.5 (contd.) Impact of Networks on Dissemination of New Knowledge. Product life cycle gets further reduced due to the dispersion of concepts of the original invention and also due to increased variety of competing products quickly brought to the market place over the Internet.

In this lower response mode, falsehood, distaste, and corruption[8] (FDC) of information becomes a possible recourse, with the executives grabbing corporate resources (money and bank accounts) as they flee. Recent executive scandals at various corporations (Enron, Global Crossing, Arthur Andersen, etc.) bear a painful testimony to the acceleration of unethical behavior. As worthy information grows scarce, deceptive information races through backbone networks, bringing about less

---

[8] The willful human activities encompassing falsehood, distaste, and corruption (FDC) of information get closely intertwined with the deception, arrogance, and hypocrisy (DAH) attitudes of human beings. The DAH aspects of human beings are presented in Chapter 13 and represented in Figures 13.7 and 13.13.

worthy information and more deception (as occurred in the Watergate scandal). The FDC spiral winds faster.

The acceleration grows especially faster with executives whose positions are precarious. The power and position held by such executives comes under scrutiny and gets jeopardized. Any deceptive practices in the past cause heightened anxiety since exposure to the public becomes inevitable. Once more, high-capacity backbone networks play an insidious role, and contribute to the dissemination of any unethical practices of corporate executives.

This modality of behavior also becomes prevalent at the national level. Politicians and elected officials have become involved in unethical practices because of the very rapid exposition of the falsehood, deception, and corruption (FDC) that has given a few members a temporary hideout. To this extent, when the truth about the FDC of a situation or a corporation needs to be exposed, the high-speed networks have benefited society. In a very positive sense, it is networks that can bring truth, social value, and elegance to society as much as they can bring falsehood, deception, and corruption. Implanted intelligent agents within the networks can enhance truth (T), social value (S), and elegance (E), while suppressing falsehood (F), distaste (D), and corruption (C). We propose such a system (of filters) in the architecture of wisdom machines (Chapter 10).

12.10 CONCLUSIONS

This chapter presents two major aspects of knowledge. *First*, in dealing with information, the truism tempered by long-term philosophic validation leads to scientific principles. These principles are formulated as qualitative and statistical relationships to start a basis of knowledge theory by which the differentiation, integration and sensitivity of knowledge can be estimated. Primary and secondary information objects are introduced to offer knowledge structure and dependence. The quantitative basis and content of a body of knowledge are established by the number of secondary objects, their structural relationships, the number of attributes of each secondary object, and their own relation matrices. Granularity of the knowledge space is defined as the smallest prism formed by the numerical precision of the computer systems, the lowest Hamming distance between the code words that the networks can carry at their maximum speed, and the perception of human beings who will sense the microprism of knowledge. At least one dimension of this prism is personality dependent, even though the numerical precision of the computers and lowest Hamming distance through the network can be accurately quantified for that particular human-machine system.

Second, in dealing with the theory of knowledge, the comparison with complexity theory shows that knowledge theory is closely intertwined to the quantity of knowledge (see the paragraph above) in any primary information object. However, knowledge theory is always retractable and (almost) never gets chaotic for three reasons.

(1) The linkage (forward and backward pointers, depth of recursion, size of memory) built in the operating systems of computers will prevent tail-chasing loops through the many information objects.

(2) The seven OSI layers will automatically prevent networks from getting trapped in endless send-resend cycles of any packets, sessions, blocks, information objects and so on.

(3) The human beings who monitor the machines are capable of preventing machines from senseless and silly pursuits.

Knowledge theory is based firmly on the triad of machines, networks and humans working in conjunction and cooperation. Three mechanisms {the machines, (their architectures and operating systems), the networks (their layering and protocol) and the human beings (their natural intelligentsia)} work synergistically in making knowledge environment complex but manageable.

REFERENCES

[1] A. Smith, The Wealth of Nations, Prometheus Books, Buffalo, NY, 1991.

[2] J. M. Keynes, *The General Theory of Employment, Interest, and Money*, Prometheus Books; Buffalo, NY, 1997.

[3] J. Neumann and O. Morgenstern, *Theory of Games and Economic Behavior*, Princeton University Press, Princeton, NJ, 2004.

[4] J. R. Parker, *Algorithms for Image Processing and Computer Vision*, John Wiley and Sons, Hoboken, NJ, 1996.

[5] R. Arena and M. Quere (Eds) *The Economics of Alfred Marshall: Revisiting Marshall's Legacy*, Palgrave Macmillan, New York, 2003.

[6] D. S. Byrne *Complexity Theory and Social Sciences*, Routledge, New York, 1998.

[7] S. V. Ahamed and V. B. Lawrence, *Intelligent Broadband Multimedia Networks*, Kluwer Academic Publishers, Boston, 1997.

[8] R. Gillespie and J. Gillespie, *PeopleSoft Developer's Handbook*, McGraw Hill, New York, 1999.

[9] *SAP Solutions, and eLearning*, SAP (UK) Limited, Feltham, Middlesex, England, 2002.

[10] J. Ganssle, *The Firmware Handbook (Embedded Technology)*, Newnes, Book&CD-Rom, London, 2004.

[11] R. A. Mueller, *Automated Microcode Synthesis*, UMI Research Press (1984). See also H. S. Stone et al. *Introduction to Computer Architecture*, Computer Science Series, Science Research Associates, Boston, 1980.

[12] S. V. Ahamed and V.B. Lawrence, *The Art of Scientific Innovation: A Case for Classical Creativity*, Prentice Hall, Englewood Cliffs, NJ, 2005.

PART *IV*

Persistent Minds and Tireless Machines

In the pursuit of optimal, graceful, and beneficial solutions, the synergy between human beings and machines has found a dynamic blend. Human beings are constantly aware of finiteness of the local problems and the semi-infiniteness of creativity and imagination. Over a period of time, solutions emerge in the union space of science, elegance, and social value. Temporary as any solution is, better solutions will evolve much like the neural nets in the brain.

Two underlying trends can be tracked: the *human motivation* that drives society to solve the problems and the *strategy* in the evolution of the solutions. Human nature is well documented in psychology and social sciences and the strategy of solutions is well documented by the laws of microeconomics and marginal utility theory. Sigmund Freud (1856–1939) has as firmly founded the discipline of psychology as Alfred Marshall (1842–1924) has firmly implanted the direction of microeconomic theories.

In Chapter 13, we initially rely on the theories of Sigmund Freud and Abraham Maslow for the innate forces that drive human beings, but quickly modify them to accommodate the needs of the Internet society. The directions of movement of the human personality at any instant of time in the information age are revealed in subjective fashion. Also in Chapter 13, we initially rely on the theories of Alfred Marshall and upon his mathematical theories in microeconomics, but quickly modify the mathematical framework of his contributions to suit the intellectual

Intelligent Internet Knowledge Networks. By Syed V. Ahamed
Copyright © 2007 John Wiley & Sons, Inc.

properties of information, knowledge, and wisdom. The classical contributions in both directions are fused and merged. From the contribution of Freud, Maslow and Marshall comes a basis for representing the human drive to move from one goal to the next higher goal in an orderly and systematic way rather than in a noisy and chaotic fashion. A computational image of human personality is thus derived as step-by-step progress in view of information age that surrounds a scientist, a philosopher, a poet, saint or anyone the individual wishes to be.

In Chapter 14, we track the progress of human beings and machines along the knowledge trail. Modern machines as supplements to human beings move rapidly along the trail because of the little or no inertia of the machines to execute any compiled code. However, it is for the human being to navigate and move from data to information, from information to knowledge, from knowledge to concepts, from concepts to wisdom and finally from wisdom to the ethics of truth, virtue and beauty. Each of these three ethics resists the erosion of time and the variations of society and culture.

In Chapter 15, we emphasize the role of human beings in the relationship between human intellect and machine capacity, with the constant awareness that the human element has two conflicting sides: the lofty goals for human benefit and the greed for personal gain. The lifelong search for truth, virtue, and/or beauty of some humans stands in direct opposition to the transitory gains attainable via deception, arrogance and hypocrisy. Machines being mindless slaves of humans simply follow the masters.

Chapter 13

Human Needs and Machines

Human needs are as ancient as humans. Needs have driven behavior to claim what is needed for survival. This theme prevailed long before the advent of social scientists and behavioral theorists. Human needs have evolved with the human species. Motivation and behavior have followed subsequently.

Machines serve the human needs in a dramatic way. In fact, most inventions and innovations exist because they serve one or more individual or social needs. Such inventions have evolved and survived in society because they *optimally* serve some human need. Some machines (including systems) serve needs directly like telephones serving the communication need or indirectly like electrical generating plants serving the power requirements for appliances and applications. The driving force is firmly founded in the needs of humans or the needs of society. For this reason, we investigate the needs for the new machines that will prevail rather than machines that exploit a transient economic opportunity. Historically, the inventions that have withstood the test of time satisfy the most dominant (communication, transportation, agricultural, etc.) needs of human beings.

When the basis of breakthrough inventions is projected into the future, it is obvious that human needs are the primary driving force. For this reason, we look at the individual needs and how they have changed in light of the information age and the Internet. The information age offers higher productivity for individuals monitoring efficient robotic [1] production lines, while the Internet offers global communication facilities. The synergy offers humans a greater amount of leisure

Intelligent Internet Knowledge Networks. By Syed V. Ahamed
Copyright © 2007 John Wiley & Sons, Inc.

time for introspection that bring out the best from individuals and that is to search and invent from a practical consideration or to search and unify from a scientific and philosophic consideration.

The synergy between the computer-based information age and the high-speed dominated Internet has somewhat altered the script of human behavior over the last few decades. In modern times, most high school students are computer literate and surf the Internet as easily as adults can enter a conversation. The needs of the next generation may change marginally at the lower levels but the most innate and insidious needs that have evolved over millennia are not likely to be compromised quickly. In the rest of this chapter, we explore two such deeply seated needs (to search and to invent, and to search and to unify) that are not likely to go away because of the information age, the Internet or both.

13.1 FROM AI TO BI

The movement from *artificial intelligent (AI)* to *behavioral intelligence (BI)* is a recent adaptation. Artificial intelligence has permitted machines to emulate human intelligence. The decisions and inferences that a human being might possibly adapt are artificially duplicated in the modular programming steps of machines. The many splinter disciplines of AI are well founded in the rationality of human beings.

As a specific instance, consider pattern recognition (PR) [2]. When the human being sees an image, a scene, or a scenario, the process of identifying the numerous objects, players, or constituents of the scene is accomplished and a mental link is established to the prior experience of the individual dealing with such "objects." The properties or attributes of the objects are embedded into the mental space and interconnected with the properties of other objects to examine the validity of what is seen with what is known. Routine relationships are temporarily stacked to be incorporated into a bigger and global picture. All pieces of relevant information are systematically collated in the mind to evaluate the situation as it is seen in the real world. The machine pretty much adopts the same strategy; it scans the profiles of the objects and identifies them, it calls upon the attribute database of each identified object and ties the various objects "seen" with their perspective relationships with the other objects. In the process of building a table of objects, their attributes, and their relationships, the whole scenario is recognized and the process of pattern recognition is invoked many times to identify different "scenes." It becomes immaterial whether the machine is "looking" at cancer cells to evaluate abnormality or whether the machine is "looking" at a battlefield to evaluate an enemy threat: the same basic principles of PR are invoked many ways in many instances.

As a specific instance, consider robotics [3]. The robot senses the environment and proceeds to perform its preassigned task in a programmed fashion as a human being might have done in performing a routine task. The sensing mechanism of the robot permits it to receive input information about its environment and then map out a methodology to accomplish its objective. To the extent that it can only do part

the user to solve problems in an intelligent way. In a global context, if BI is invoked, then BI makes the machine see the cycle of need, motivation, a course of behavior to satisfy the need, and return to a stable condition to take on another need of the user. To this extent, the machine imitates the behavior of a human being more closely. It becomes clear that a machine based on BI will deploy the AI tools (PR, robotics, ES, IA, etc.) consistently to complete the circle of needs. After all, a circle is a composition of its many segments. The BI aspect of the machine would address the curvature and angular relationship (i.e., r and θ) attributes of the entire small or large circles (and needs) that human beings experience. To complete the circle the machine also deploys the AI tools and techniques at a segment level.

It is unclear if the human beings themselves know or plan the entire circle to satisfy any particular need or the circle is a mere composition of very short lines. Human behavior thus retains an element of randomness, much as the current theorists in quantum mechanics suggest that the entire universe is a mere chance collection of superstrings.

13.1.2 Sigmund Freud's Contributions

Freud was one of the pioneering explorers of human behavior. Even though his perspective has been from the field of clinical medicine (psychiatry), the behavioral model proposed by him is based on the notion that the mind has three basic domains (id, ego, and superego). The Freudian model is based on functions the mind performs rather than the neural pathways in the brain. From a clinical consideration, Freud proposed the very convincing hypothesis that a harmonious blending of these three domains leads to normal behavior and a conflictive overlap of these domains leads to abnormal behavior. Even though modern psychiatry has come a long way from this rudimentary notion of Freud, the basic premise of unresolved conflict leading to abnormal behavior still remains valid. Over the centuries, the conflict leading to severe modalities of behavior existed in humans, tribes, cultures, societies, and even nations. Modern organizations and nations display need-driven collective behavior and succumb to the effects of conflicts in resource allocation, egos, and even in opinions.

In reference to individual behavior and its manifestation, both are subject to genetic tendencies and environmental conditions, conditions that provide or block the means to satisfy the needs. In reference to collective behavior and attitude, both are also subject to the history and resources to satisfy the collective needs. Extremes of behavior, according to Freud, can still be linked to severity of internal needs and the (internal and external) constraints blocking the satisfaction of such needs.

Simplistic as it may be, Freud's model offers a means to understand the rationale behind individual behavior. It is also applicable when dealing with issues at a collective level. The three-level model (Figure 13.1) of Freud is a mere framework for dealing with more complex sets of issues of the workings of the mind, even though no one has really seen the three domains of the mind. In reality, individual behavior is finally embedded in the neural pathways in the brain. To this extent, Freud remains the founder of a simple model for understanding human behavior. In a similar vein, Tesla remains the founder of rotating electromagnetic field based on a model of three (red, yellow, and blue) phase currents even though no one has really "seen" the rotating electromagnetic field.

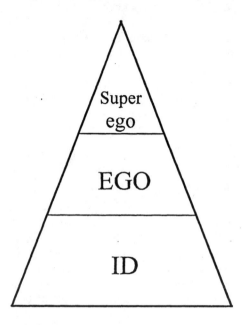

Figure 13.1 Basic three-level segmentation of the human mind proposed by Sigmund Freud to explain behavioral disorders.

Models of this sort also exist in other disciplines. For example, the molecular representations of equations in chemistry offer insight into the interaction of one chemical with another chemical. The organizational models of corporations facilitate mergers, acquisitions, and corporate negotiations. In a sense, when the complexity of the situation needs a coarse investigation, a model of the structure becomes crucial. The representation of internal and external forces on a structure become important since behavior is a result of the dynamics from one stable state to the next. Simple models (like the Freudian model) of this nature are an antithesis to teaching of the current quantum mechanists.

13.1.3 Carl Jung's Contributions

Carl Jung brought a new twist to Freud's theories. A dimension of uncertainty is injected when the influence of the human soul and predictive dreams was included.

Whereas Freudian concepts were based on the mind being predictable and rational, Jung retained that a part of the human mind is beyond rationality. Rather than considering the uncertainty that arises from randomness in the neural paths in the brain and nervous system of the individual, or the environmental conditions, Jung had extended his thoughts into faith as an abrupt jump.

13.1.4 Eric Berne's Contributions

Eric Berne (1910–1970) suggested a transactional analysis model as an explanation of human interactions. Based on the notion "I'm OK, You're OK," smooth transactions can take place, reinforcing the "strokes" that most people exchange. Such transactions could be classified as smooth and balanced or conflictive and crossed (unbalanced). Berne suggested three postures or levels of the mind; child (C), adult (A), and parent (P). This partitioning is somewhat akin to Freud's proposed id, ego, and superego. The transactional analysis approach is in tilted towards psychoanalysis and behavior modification from a medical perspective.

Berne proposed that daily life is based on "I am OK- You're OK," transactions between human beings. Examples of balanced transactions occur when the interaction is between two equals, 1 and 2, at levels C_1 and C_2, A_1 and A_2, or P_1 and P_2. Complementary transactions between parent and child are from level P to level C and vice versa, and so on. A simple working understanding of daily human interactions was thus forwarded by Berne. However, it does not become directly relevant to the behavioral intelligence that is proposed in this chapter.

13.1.5 Abraham Maslow's Contributions

Maslow has discarded the clinical perspective of Freud, the notions behind the reasoning of Jung, and the transactional analysis of Berne. Maslow has taken are a bold new step in tying the needs of healthy human beings to their behavior via the factors that motivate them and society that provides the means to satisfy the needs. In a sense, the relationship between an individual and society (and environment) is implied in Maslow's model but it remains dominant from the individual's point of view. Among the various higher-level models for explaining behavior, Maslow's five-level model is widely accepted in corporate and social settings. It deals with the actions and interactions between highly rational individuals. Maslow studied a cross-section of successful and motivated people and suggested the five-level model (Figure 13.2) to deal with human behavior. When the situation deals with microcosmic real-life issues the five-level model is adequate

However, Maslow's original writings are more profound. Whereas Jung had touched upon an existence and influence of human soul, Maslow did not explicitly incorporate the spiritual dimension in his hierarchy of needs pyramid. Instead, he proposed that human beings have fifteen "B-Values," listed as truth, goodness, beauty, unity and transcendence, aliveness, uniqueness, perfection, justice, simplicity, richness, effortlessness, playfulness, self-sufficiency, and meaningfulness. In essence, Maslow was proposing that a human being is a more complex entity. In an obscure way, Maslow was hinting at the "spirit" of a human being. A contextual correlation emerges between the "spirit" that Maslow writes [11] about and what Carl Jung has explicitly referred to as the "soul" of a human being [8]. This is a sharp contrast to the work of Watson in 1919 and the work of Skinner.

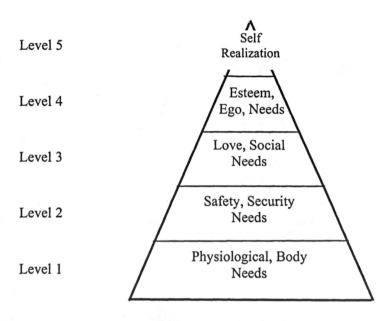

Figure 13.2 Motivations come from human needs. Maslow has proposed a basic five-level motivational model based on human needs. This model is used most often to explain the motivations, aspirations, and organizational behavior of corporate employees and successful human beings.

Human values can also be strong motivators, but Maslow did not include them in a motivational cycle or as driving forces to be considered in a scientific vein. In addition to the five level needs, values could also make a difference. The model proposed by Maslow and his "B-values" form a strong foundation to further the model of human behavior. Unfortunately, Maslow's work does not address the possibility of adapting it to the computer environment and evolving a platform for the behavioral intelligence (BI) proposed in Section 13.1.1.

13.2 INADEQUACY OF EARLIER MODELS

The four models (of Freud, Jung, Berne, and Maslow) and the subsequent scenarios presented earlier do not adequately depict the behavior of modern human beings living in an information age, where lower-level needs are addressed adequately. The by-product of the industrial revolution and the computing era is leisure time. The high productivity within society and the resulting spare time for individuals forces a thoughtful human to probe further into his/herself and the society in which one lives. The models proposed earlier appear transparent and undermine the refinement of thought of the modern human being. In fact, these earlier models tend to be rudimentary for a detailed analysis of how a contemplative human being behaves given the tools and techniques, computers and Internet of modern society.

The social needs of Maslow's third level are based on motivations and behavior explaining how an individual derives the satisfaction from (or suffers at the hands of) society. However, an equally dominant issue is how society may benefit (or suffer) from the individual. Earlier models provide the basis for human behavior from an individual's perspective rather than from the perspective of a human being as a member of society, the environment, and the world community. This resulting equilibrium is dynamic, adaptive, and intelligent. Essentially, the world is not a collectivity of individuals, each driven by a need triangle, but a community of interdependent and interrelated individuals that make up the tribe, the community, society, the nation, and the world. This is in turn a dynamic process.

13.2.1 Two Additional Levels

For addressing needs beyond the individual and for the need to be introspective (resulting from the leisure), we present two additional levels atop Maslow's need triangle. The need within the *sixth-level* drives an individual *to search* for the best solution of needs from a family, group, tribal, social, communal, and/or environmental perspective. Such perspectives may be derived from corporate responsibility and for this the individual is duly compensated. However, it invokes a more fundamental need and that is a need to search. Need to search has infinite dimensions as the self-realization (i.e., level 5) need of Maslow. Modern human living through the information age, have time (the leisure) and means (the information age and Internet) to search and surf almost indefinitely.

Ironically, it becomes a self-defeating proposition to search and never find that which is sought. Searching without an end result becomes frustrating and futile. At this stage, we fall back on Maslow, who suggests that the need is temporarily extinguished even though it is not perfectly satisfied. In this context, the infinite searches at the sixth-level get partially satisfied by the expenditure of leisure and the Internet resources and the individual needs to unify all the (too many) search results. This leads to the *seventh* and final level of need in human beings. This is the need *to unify* the outcome of many searches (hundreds or millions (on the Internet)) into one generic answer, entity, principle, concept that can be searched and searched again and again, time after time, place after place but the conclusion remaining permanently (at least for the time being) valid. The outcome of the search for unification becomes a search in its own right to reach the illusive universal perfection. The need in humans to *unify* (almost) everything into *one* concept, however illusive (like superstring theory, elementary particles, relativity), becomes the final and the seventh-level of needs (Figure 13.3).

Once this level is penetrated, it starts to have the attribute of absoluteness, i.e., the following searches only confirm the process of unification in prior searches. In the scientific domain, such absolutes have been established. For example, the temperature of $-273°$ C or $0°$ K is as illusive as c, the velocity of light, or the true value of *pi*, but the concept is established. Examples of absolute numbers [e.g., e (Euler's coefficient), π (pi), $\hbar$ (Plank's constant), and even ∞ (infinity)), are also documented in the scientific literature.

At the seventh-level, the pyramid is not closed because individuals who get closer and closer to the ultimate goal of unification start to expend all the resources at their disposal in order to find the illusive (like nirvana, true love, perfection) attainment of having reached somewhere or sometime without being able to backtrack. Energy to backtrack has been depleted in the last infinitesimal move forward. An illusive island of no return starts to be perceived. The writing of the greatest philosophers and preachers (Albert Einstein, Martin Luther King, Jr., Mohandas Gandhi, Albert Schweitzer, etc.) from the recent past appear to allude to this state of pure mental/spiritual activity. A sense of faith beyond reason prevails at this outer edge of mental activity and perhaps at this state of attainment, a feeling of detachment starts to set in. We suspect that at this very peak of the need pyramid the human being has little interest in finding a strategy to meet lower-level needs.

13.3 THE NEED TO SEARCH (SIXTH LEVEL)

Beyond Maslow's fifth-level self-realization remains another basic human need— to search; to *optimally search* for the best solution, concept, notion, principle, cause, a perception, and so on, in that particular social or environment. Above the traditional five-level triangle, this need stands out as an entity in its own right. If Marshall's laws of microeconomics were operative during prehistoric times, the hunter-collector-caveman would search for the *best* food that would offer the *most* return for the resources expended to obtain his bounty. Most animal species still prove Marshall's laws during their hunting strategy for prey.

The need to search is almost instinctual from times unknown. Still practiced, the Internet explorers search the knowledge bases around the world much as the ancient mariner explored the unknown islands around the world in the wooden sailboats. Tools and time offered by the knowledge society triples the challenge in search for the modern human beings. The search for novelty, the search for optimality in making the novelty beneficial to society, and the search for the elegance in novelty bridge the gaps between mind, self and society of the information age.

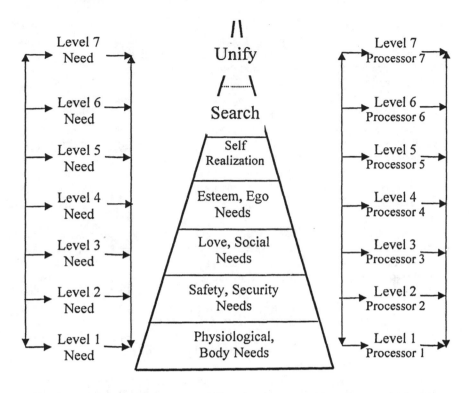

Figure 13.3 Enhanced need hierarchy that addresses all the needs of a modern, thoughtful human being living in the information/Internet age. These include the need to search (for perfection, optimality, invention, etc.) at the sixth-level and the need to unify all the conclusions of all the searches, including one's own search under one basic umbrella of universal wisdom or knowledge at the seventh level. At first glance, a hierarchy of special-purpose processors connected in a dual bus configuration [12] starts to form the basis of a behaviorally intelligent platform to imitate the human need pyramid.

This urge to search is generic enough to influence behavior while a human being seeks to satisfy all other needs, both lower and higher. This need to search becomes dominant at the higher levels of needs (ego, social and realization). After the second-level needs are met, the urge to search and satisfy social needs (third level) becomes dominant with traits to also satisfy ego needs (fourth level) by choosing the best solution just to satisfy one's own ego. Likewise, after third-level needs are met (satisfactorily), the urge to search and satisfy ego needs (fourth level) by choosing the best solution just to satisfy the realization needs (fifth level) becomes dominant, and so on. It is evident that the search to satisfy one-level-up needs also paves the way to satisfy two-level-up needs. The law of optimally utilizing resources to satisfy the ith-level needs from the $(i - 1)$-level also assures that one satisfies the $(i + 1)$ level needs as far as possible. This search for the allocation of resources for dual (i and $i + 1$ level) needs is indeed equivalent to Marshall's second law for maximizing the utility function.

In some cases, the search to satisfy the i th need can invoke a new approach to the $(i - 1)$ need. This multilevel need satisfaction can be directed up or down the need hierarchy. There are two major implications. *First*, the search for optimality is an innate human tendency fundamental to behavior. *Second*, Marshall's first (marginal cost equals marginal gain) and second (maximization of the utility function) laws of economics dominate human behavior. Through the evolution of the human species, these laws have prevailed. But now, as human thought gets more refined, these laws can become more formalized and then can be incorporated into computer software and then into hardware implementation of a behaviorally intelligent machine.

From a scientific perspective, the urge to search has led to some very important findings: Einstein's correlation between space and time; Einstein's correction to Newton's laws in view of the finite velocity of light; Maxwell's search to generalize the findings of Ampere, Galvani, Oersted and Gauss; and Edison's search for the right material for the filament of an electric light. These are examples of the search at work on an individual level. The search for elementary particles in accelerators; the string-theorist's search to generalize the laws of quantum mechanics at a cosmic level; the search of new galaxies in the universe; and the search for generic drugs in the pharmaceutical industry are examples of the search process at-work in organizational circles.

Poets have practiced this intellectual ordeal numerous times. Great writers like Emily Bronte (*Withering Heights*), Omar Khayyam (*Rubiyat*), Charlotte Bronte (*Jane Eyre*), Rabindranath Tagore (*Gitangali*), and Matthew Arnold (*Dover Beach*) and great artists, (like Picasso, Michelangelo, and Rembrandt) portray the legacy of their searches and create beyond the obvious. Their writings and works of art carry their search and longing for an ultimate, an infallible theme, an immortal concept, or an ideal. Along the way, in their struggle, to deal with the abstract, their contributions become classic. Philosophers have pushed the limits of human thought in their search for possibilities beyond the constraints of society. In fact, the exploration of space is to seek (search) the unknown skies and explore the outer galaxies. When the search gets too directed and confined, inventions and masterpieces result. When a sense of freedom rules the search, concepts (velocity of light, gravity, absoluteness of $-273°C$, etc.), wisdom (Buddha's Enlightenment, Gandhi's nonviolence, Lincoln's antislavery, Schweitzer's reverence for life, etc.) and classic theories (relativity, Heisenberg's uncertainty principle, superstring theory, etc.) can emerge. The boundary between sixth-level and seventh-level needs starts to become vague, even though the search to unify is distinct from the search to solve a real or an abstract problem.

13.4 THE NEED TO UNIFY (SEVENTH LEVEL)

Searching in the immediate discipline or neighborhood of the problem and in the context of solving that particular problem falls in the domain of sixth-level needs. In fact, managers use this approach of "bounded reality", [13–15] and "local search" in organizational learning [15], in solving an overwhelming number of routine problems. These approaches— called "limited and local search" —offers a significant way of taking care immediate problems confronting an individual, an entity, a corporation, or even a nation.

The expanded or "global search" seeks to unify the solutions of individuals (colleagues, scientists, or the same individual at different times, etc.) into one universal framework. This search can be quite colossal, leading to whole new way of look at the universe (e.g., superstring theory, the basic building blocks of human genes, or the tiniest component that exists in the universe, etc.). The nature and extent of this search leads to conceptual revolutions and belongs to the seventh-level of needs that push individuals to seek an all-dimensional infinity.

In the context of this book, this concept is important. If machines were built to serve human needs, the newer architectures should be built to address *all* needs of the human beings. In the modern days, we find tools, gadgets, computers, and network systems to address our lower level (Maslow's levels, 1–4) needs adequately. At the fifth, sixth and seventh levels, machines seeking wisdom from information [16] are documented. We do not suggest that there are machines that address the spiritual and virtue needs of human beings. We propose that such needs (to seek the unknown, to explore the stars, "to go where no one has gone before", etc.) do exist (at the sixth and seventh levels). Furthermore, we propose a crude mathematical way in which a human being approaches their solution (see Chapters 14 and 15). The proposed model is incomplete but a first attempt is to define a direction that unifies all dimensions (including the 11 dimensions proposed by string theorists) of human thought and that reaches a stage of absolute knowledge (if it is possible).

Searching for the abstract (solution, concept, notion, principle, cause, or even a divine perception) at different times and in different settings will invariably lead to different results. In essence, the last step toward consolidating the results of the search(es) is to unify the findings under one ideal, concept, notion, or principle. Whereas the sixth level motivates the process of searching, the seventh level need is finding and defining the common umbrella under which all results can be neatly stacked. The need to search for the unified order in the universe becomes all too consuming for a human being.

The sixth- and seventh- needs can take a lifetime to fulfill. Whereas the search (sixth level) is an interactive process with the environment, the abstraction of the generic underlying principle (seventh level) is a very personal process. This personal contribution unifies all the findings of a large number of researchers over a prolonged time. It is a painstakingly cumulative and integrative process. Einstein's extraordinary need to search and generalize his special theory of reletivity; Poynting's [17] need to search and formulate a unified field theory integrating the electric and the magnetic field energies during EM field propagation; the superstring theorists who are still searching for ways to integrate the work of Einstein and Heisenberg all bear a testimony that the need to research all previous concepts into a few laws or principles that drive the whole universe. The search for a solution that leads to an invention, a work of art, a verse of poetry, or a symphony of songs, fall under the sixth-level needs. The unification of all similar human searches into one common universal or super-universal theme falls under seventh-level needs. It is easy to see that at this stage of nirvana there are no neurons to spare leaving no way to backtrack.

From a computational perspective, when a programmer forces a machine to search for a value of pi beyond the limits of the numerical processor unit (NPU), the machine enters an indefinite loop, deciding between two values separated by the limit of precision in the NPU. For the human being, the thought process at the seventh-level claims all the resources of the mind until the last neuron in the brain is left in a stage of indecision. It is unknown to us if such a stage is achievable or can be achieved.

Marshall's laws of economics have no room at the seventh level, even though they monitor human behavior at the lower levels. All the neurons in the brain limit thought and satisfaction of this seventh-level need leaving no resources to be allocated for maximizing the utility function (Marshall's second law). If a human being reaches this stage of being so totally consumed in seeking the infinite, then there is no mental energy to spare. To avoid this internal deadlock, it would be wise to become aware of the law of diminishing returns[1] during the allocation of mental resources. It appears to us that the only path toward approaching this stage is by purity, perfection, and optimality in reaching the goal to unify. Anything less (e.g., greed, selfishness, wickedness) is an insurmountable roadblock to the allocation of all (or an extremely high proportion of) the resources to integrate and to unify.

In synergy with current times to build a reasonably accurate model of behavior, one cannot choose to ignore that there is a negative side to human behavior such as deception, arrogance, and hypocrisy. Whereas philosophers of the past have casually mentioned and dismissed the existence of these negative traits, we propose to include these negative traits in the daily behavior of human beings as they go about finding means to satisfy their needs. The needs remain the same but the mode of operation migrates over from the positive types A and B to the negative types C and D behaviors making the behavioral model complete. The four types of behaviors in human beings explored further in Chapter 14 and incorporated in Figures 14.1 and 14.3.

---

[1] The law of diminishing returns is borrowed from the theory of production documented in W. J. Spillman and E. Lang's book, *The Law of Diminishing Returns,* published in 1924. See also *The Columbia Encyclopedia*, Sixth Ed. 2001-2005.

.

13.5 A MODEL OF HUMAN BEHAVIOR

Microscopic human behavior is as predictive as the movement of an electron. However, at a macroscopic or gross level, the behavior is obvious and predictable. Response to physical threats and danger is programmed in reflexive actions. The reflex to withdraw from a fire, the automatic shrinking of the pupil upon exposure to very bright light, or the quick response during a fall becomes automatic. In the same vein, response to hunger, thirst, and pain (first level) are also predictable. As the level of need starts to increase, the responses diverge but the theme is to satisfy the need consistent with social norms. In this section, we build a model for the behavior as human beings attempt to gratify their individual (or even collective) needs.

13.5.1 Satisfaction of Needs

If the need triangle has seven (or even five) levels, then the innate tendency is to address the lowest level (say, level i) needs first and then proceed to solve the next higher-level need. Even though it can be stated simply, the mind follows distinct patterns in (1) accomplishing and securing the means to satisfy the ith-level need, (2) in being satisfied from the active need, (3) in compromising if satisfaction of the ith-level need is not perfect, (4) in understanding the social structure that provides the means to satisfy the ith-level need, (5) in conforming to the social structure to gain (or earn) the means to satisfy a need, and finally (6) in repeatedly traversing of the loop (1) through (6) as far as the need is basic and recurring. The pattern is shown in Figure 13.4 as a self-propagating flowchart as long as the need persists.

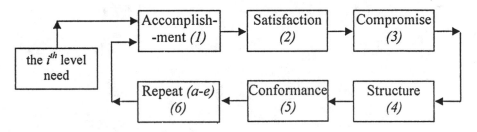

Figure 13.4 Six-stage flowchart of processes involved in the satisfaction of the i th-level need; i ranges from 1 to 7 in the seven-level need structure of a human being. Optimality is reached in (6).

The six discrete steps of Figure 13.4 are rearranged slightly to make the flowchart follow the contours of the need hierarchy. A transformed figure is shown in Figure 13.5. It is not crucial that there should be only six discrete steps in the need resolution strategy. As far as a repetitive pattern and closed cycle is at work, this model will suffice. The repetition reinforces the six steps thus making the pattern stable and error-free (also as friction-free as possible) in that particular social setting. In a very obvious way, the expenditure of resources is minimized and the need satisfaction is maximized (Marshall's law to maximize marginal utility).

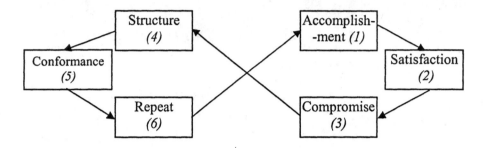

Figure 13.5 A transformed depiction of the six-stage flowchart of processes involved in the satisfaction of the i th-level need, i ranges from 1 to 7 in the seven-level need structure of a human being. The cycle repeats every time the i th-level need recurs. An optimal solution in any social structure is reached in (5) by repeating the solution in (6).

When any basic need surfaces, this symbolic loop (cycle or flowchart) comes into play. It is immaterial where the loop starts as far as there is an awareness of the need. If there is local blockage in the steps to satisfy, the process of local search takes over, the flowchart is updated, and the cycle continues. If the problem is recurrent, the whole loop may get reexamined to find a lasting and error-free means to satisfy the need.

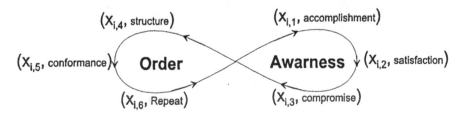

(x_i) denotes the Need at the *i-th* level

Figure 13.6 Symbolic representation of the need extinction process in the human mind.

In most cases, an orderly way to satisfy the need is learned and retained for repeated use. The diagram in Figure 13.6 can be further reduced to its most rudimentary form as a sequence of six digits 1 to 6 and the sequence in the steps 1 through 6, or 2 through 1, or 3 through 2, and so on. This model is shown in Figure 13.7. If a human being remains trapped in this loop, then there is no more energy or motivation to satisfy the $(i + 1)$st need. According to Maslow, this state of entrapment of mind exists at the fifth-level (or realization) need and according to the seven-level model proposed in this chapter, the state of entrapment (of body, (last neuron), of mind (the thought process) and of soul (the state of nirvana)) occurs at the seventh-level (or unification) need.

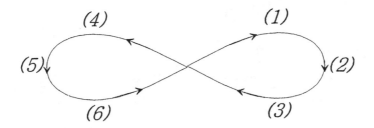

Rudimentary diagram of response to a need

Figure 13.7 In this rudimentary form, the normal response to the satisfaction of any need consists of (1) accomplishment (2) satisfaction (3) compromise (4) social structure (5) conformance and (6) the repeated traversing of the loop.

Whereas Maslow has indicated that the realization (fifth-level) need is for one's own self to realize one's own potential, the need to search (sixth-level) and the need to unify (seventh-level) are dynamic, interactive with the entire society and the universe. Such an approach can bear a positive return (in most cases) to society (e.g., Maxwell's equations, relativity theory, quantum mechanics theory, etc.).

13.5.2 Repetition and Boredom at (6)

Repetition breeds boredom. Being trapped in any loop such as the cycle shown in Figure 13.7 forces an individual to optimize the traverse of the cycle. Optimality and efficacy of the need satisfaction are actively sought and when the law of diminishing returns gets firmly established, human beings move on from the *i*th-level need to the $(i + 1)$st-level need or reoptimize the processes embedded (*1–6*) in the lower-level needs.

When all the processes in the lower-level needs (i.e., 1 through $(i - 1)$) are close to being optimal, the loop at *i*th-level breaks apart into a trajectory that explores the possibilities of satisfying $(i + 1)$st through seventh-level needs preferably all at once or at least the $(i + 1)$st-level need. The symbolic diagram now assumes an additional (vertical) lobe starting at the intersection point of the awareness (right) lobe and the order (left) lobe (see Figure 13.7). This process of breaking open the cycle to accommodate the third lobe is shown in Figure 13.8.

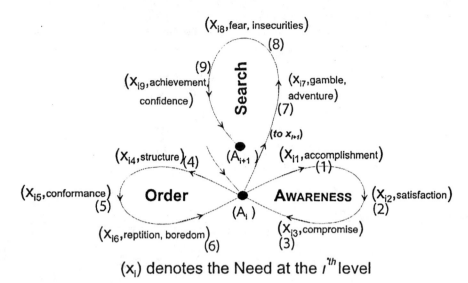

(x_i) denotes the Need at the ith level

Figure 13.8 The migration of the mind from node A_i to A_{i+1} in an attempt to satisfy the needs at the (i + 1)st level. The six steps (1-6) are left intact for the i th-level need but the process of migration adds three more steps— 7,8 and 9— to reach node A_{i+1}.

When the break of the cycle occurs at node A_i, two forces are at work: first, the need to escape from the boredom of being trapped in the loop (1–6) shown in Figure 13.7 and second, a sense of adventure, gamble, and thrill to search new possibilities to satisfy the (i + 1)st level need. Note that the human being is already in the search (level 6 need) mode while migrating from lower-level needs to higher-level needs. As the next step, a sense of insecurity or fear dominates and the urge to return toward node A_i forces the mind to try accomplish the means to satisfy the (i + 1)st level need in a way similar to the way, the *i*th-level need was satisfied. A certain sense of achievement or joy is found at step 9 and the human being attempts to enter the loop (1–6) for the (i + 1)st level need. In a symbolic way the Figure 13.8 may be represented as Figure 13.9 with nine steps (1-9).

The actual number of steps that may be encountered in the process of migration is unimportant. The duration to migrate can also vary drastically. For example to satisfy the hunger, one may find a restaurant with a sense of adventure (7), without feeling insecure (8) about the price tag for the meal and leave with a feeling of having found (9) a new place to eat. In other cases, like finding a spouse, the migration can take years or decades and the number of steps will also be more numerous. Numerous iterations are also likely. Indecision and procrastination (available from the personality profile database) can force entrapment in any loop.

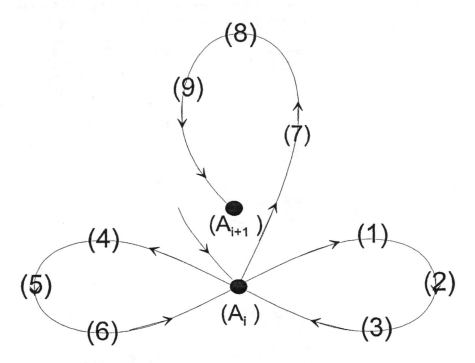

(A$_i$) denotes the Focal Node for
Need at the *ith* level

Figure 13.9 A symbolic diagram for the migration of the mind from node A$_i$ to node A$_{i+1}$ in an attempt to satisfy the needs at the (i + 1)st level. There are three steps—7, 8 and 9 in Figure 13.8— that permit the mind to choose a suitable strategy in tackling the next need at node A$_{i+1}$.

13.5.3 The New Cycle (1–6) for (*i* + 1)st Need

When the needs are similar (like finding shelter and finding food, both falling under level 2, safety needs) and alike, the tendency is to quickly reach an optimal solution for the (*i* + 1)st need. According to Marshall's third law, the individual maximizes the expected gains and minimizes the resources expended. A limited search approach and a targeted search (March and Simon) will usually dominate and the needs are quickly resolved. When the needs are radically different, such as level 5, (realization needs) and level 6, (search needs (see Figure 13.3)), the resolution can be a lifelong process. The same scenario can repeat between level 6 and level 7 needs.

The handover at each of the nodes A_i in Figures 13.8 and 13.9 can sometimes be quite variable and complex. It is not amenable to the standardization or blue print process; however, the steps to satisfy next higher level of needs tend to become streamlined and follow the same steps for last need that was resolved. This is especially true if the needs are similar and the means of satisfying are readily available. In dealing with lower-level needs (i.e., levels 1–4), the handover process can be approximated and depicted in Figure 13.10. The top lobe from need $(i - 1)$ returns to solve the need at (9) and proceeds to step (1) of need i and the cycle (1–9) repeats at ith-level need.

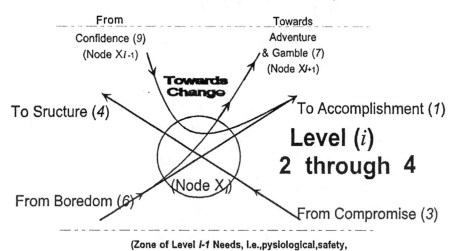

(Zone of Level *i+1* Needs, i.e., safety, social, ego, actualization, search and unification needs)

(Zone of Level *i-1* Needs, i.e., pysiological, safety, social, ego, actualization and search needs)

Figure 13.10 The handover of the need satisfaction strategy from node A_{i-1} to node A_i .

The branching from the left lobe into the vertical node for need i occurs because of the repetition of the cycle (1–6). As the processes in the loop get streamlined, there is more time and energy to address the $(i + 1)$ need and the focus shifts toward change. Change of modality brings back the thrill of living and the process continues.

13.5.4 Integrated Patterns for (1–7) Needs

When the pattern (1-9) is repeated for the lower six needs, Figure 13.9 gets superposed six times over. Each figure is displaced vertically by one need level. In an ideal case, the nodes A_i all line up on a vertical axis. In reality, many variations and distortions of the combined figure are just as likely (see Figure 13.11).

The need and migration pattern after the sixth need deserve special consideration. At this last and final stage that is perhaps reached at the highest stages of maturity and emotional development, the vertical leap to the seventh-level can be high and drawn out in time. The stage, when approached without normal human shortcomings (like fear, jealousy, hate, deception, arrogance, and hypocrisy; see Section 13.5.5) can be an island of no return. All human resources (including the last neuron in the brain) can be drawn into unification of all the infinite dimensions of a unified infinity. This rather rare phenomenon is seen in a few individuals (e.g., Gautama Buddha, Jesus Christ, St. John the Baptist) who have achieved a status of being almost supernatural.

The basic pattern embedded in Figure 13.11 remains the same as that shown in Figure 13.9, but the size and shape of the pattern can change drastically from one individual to the next and with the level of maturity. These loops can also be recursive and modified every time they are revisited. But like human nature, these loops are cast in the neural nets of the brain and are hard to change radically. The progression of human behavior from early days to modern times can be traced by locating the height of the need hierarchy at any stage of evolution. If the modern human is most evolved, then it appears the mode of behavior can vary between the most rudimentary as the hunter-killer (in modern wars) to the most profound, patient, and perseverant as Mother Theresa, or Albert Schweitzer (see his famous prayer for animals).

In the pattern shown in Figure 13.11, an additional level is depicted as $(7)^*$. Such needs at the $(7)^*$ level in human beings are extraordinary. We can only guess at this need structure since there are people who would resort to extreme behavior (e.g., starve themselves to death, or enter a stage of willful coma before their natural death, or even wantonly kill themselves) for a cause on the positive scale.

13.5.5 The Semi-infinite Search Space at Each Level

If there is a pyramid of needs, then there is a need frustum at every level. History has shown that the escape from boredom shown in Figure 13.9 does not always have to be vertical. A variation in the way in which any particular need is gratified also yields an aversion from boredom. This is a powerful venue for escaping from the routine of gratifying any given need in the same repetitive way. Without taking bold step in resolving the next higher level need, many people vary the configuration of the loops within the same level of need.

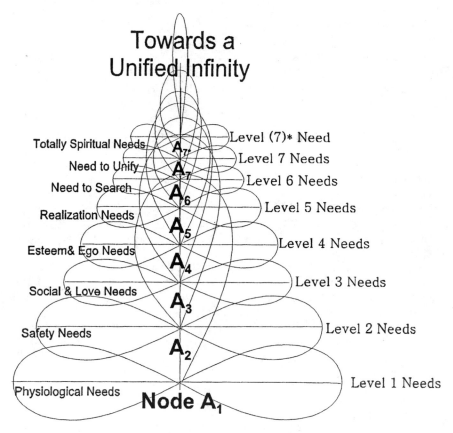

Figure 13.11 Superimposed migration pattern for all seven nodes A_1 to A_7. As the individual follows the timeline of life, the size and proportions may change but the movement and progression lingers on.

The need space for any given need now constitutes a frustum as shown in Figure 13.12, derived from the pyramid of needs. If the need pyramid (Figure 13.3) is allowed to spin freely about the centerline of the triangle, a cone gets generated and a section of the cone forms the frustum. The loops shown in Figures 13.6 –13.11 start to have a three dimensional perspective. Hopping between cycles in the same frustum (e.g., changing category jobs, swapping partners, changing restaurants) offers relief from boredom but not progress. Hopping between frustums without a contemplated path of migration for the transfer of mental resources can become chaotic and cause intellectual fractals causing disorderly behavior.

Search gets ingrained in the resolution of needs and continues beyond the fifth-level, thus entering the search level (level 6) for solving a scientific, social, cultural, moral, or ethical issue rather than searching for personal gain. The human being thus gets drawn into society and culture beyond the "self" notions embodied in Freud's and Maslow's models. G. H. Mead [18] acknowledges the search in the sixth-level as the quest for the "whole" in his book *Mind, Self and Society*.

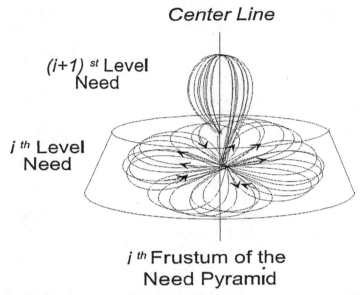

Center Line

(i+1) st Level
Need

i th Level
Need

i th Frustum of the
Need Pyramid

Figure 13.12 Model of an iterative process (in the mind) searching for the best solution to resolve the need at any level i. The process gets repeated thereafter in developing a new (or similar) strategy for resolving the next higher need at (i + 1). These loops are reentrant and recursive in the search for the best solution.

13.5.6 The Sevenfold Semi-infinite Search Space

The semi-infinite space comes to light because of the innumerable ways to satisfy any particular need. The sevenfold increase takes place because there are seven levels of needs. However, there are fundamental differences. The society and culture provides streamlined ways of solving the issue of needs, especially at the lower levels. Restaurants, motels, residential complexes, and so on are numerous and widespread. The means of gratifying the higher-level needs can vary dramatically. Hence, the sevenfold increase in the search space follows an exponential law being limited to a few standard choices (accepted by the social and cultural norms) and then becoming innumerable for the higher-level needs (social, ego, realization, search and unification).

It is appropriate to note that human beings tend to subconsciously lean toward the means that maximize the expected gratification consistent with the resources expended. For this reason, the process of search is limited by the expected marginal gain. Individuals like organizations [14] thus curtail the search and maximize the rewards. By the same token, almost every activity and behavior appears to become confined to the seven frustums of a human need structure.

The sevenfold semi-infinite search space may not be evident or attainable by a great majority of people who become overly content by the gratification of the needs at the third, fourth or fifth-levels. In any social setting, the need to be resourceful, optimal, and benevolent is felt by leaders (e.g., Abraham Lincoln, George Washington, Thomas Jefferson) of that era. The drive for the higher needs is a personal attribute even though the social rewards may be monumental. Historically, there are few who attain and master the search (sixth) and the unification (seventh) level search space unless they are genetically or circumstantially driven in this realm of thought.

13.6 MOVEMENT WITHIN PATTERN (1–9) FOR ANY ONE NEED

Individuals resolve their needs in different ways. It would be futile to attempt to standardize the microsteps in need satisfaction for each individual. However, the guidelines go back to Aristotle and their reinforcement by Maslow.

Aristotle suggested that there are two sides to the human nature: (1) the positive side[2] (type-I) where truth, virtue, and beauty dominate the tendency and (2) the negative side[3] (type-II) where deception, arrogance, and hypocrisy dominate. Maslow has written about "B-values" and built an array of fifteen attributes (see Section 13.1.5) for such individuals. In order to merge the concepts of Aristotle and Maslow, and make them applicable to the behavioral model (proposed in this chapter), we introduce the concepts of a phasor representation.

In this representation there two phasors: type I and type II. Both phasors are active as an individual traverses the cycle (1–9) for each of the lower six levels of needs (i.e., physiological through the search). Each individual leaves a trail of phasor angles at every step in the resolution of needs. In essence, a character trail is

---

[2] There is a contextual overlap between age-old Aristotle's type I classification of information-age nature and attributes of human beings who control and monitor (see Chapter 14) the wisdom machine (Chapter 10) in a *positive* sense. In the modern age, Aristotle's type I has *at least* two manifestations: type A (the philosopher, scholar, etc.; see Section 14.6) and type B (the pragmatic problem solver, scientist, etc.; Figures 14.1 and 14.2, Section 14.6).

[3] There is a contextual overlap between age-old Aristotle's type II classification of Information-age nature and attributes of human beings who control and monitor (see Chapter 14) the wisdom machine (Chapter 10) in a *negative* sense. In the modern age, Aristotle's type II has *at least* two manifestations type C (the warmonger, the tyrant king, etc; see Section 14.7) and type D (the mobster, the thug, etc.; see Figures 14.3 and 14.4, Section 14.7).

left behind and a study of the trail (on the computer) generates a personality signature of the individual. Much like a handwritten signature, the personality signature has a smooth and predictable pattern unless one person has numerous personalities and the modality of personality change is abrupt.

The approach to build a database of the personality is to classify the needs (1 through 7) and nine steps germane to each pattern of need satisfaction at each of the seven levels, and then represent the phasor angle from (+15 attributes to –15 attributes according to Maslow, or +3 to –3, according to Aristotle) of the nature portrayed at each of the 63 (i.e., 7 times 9) discrete points. This 3-D space (7 × 9 × 30, for Maslow or 7 × 9 × 6, for Aristotle), should provide a low-resolution portrayal of an individual's personality. In reality, the gradation of needs, the stages in satisfying the need, and the migration path can be many times more than the numbers 7 and 9 suggested here. The actual number in unimportant since the range of attributes and sub-attributes of need-objects in a computer can be quite large. Changes of personality and styles of behavior do not actually follow the Aristotle's or Maslow's guidelines. However, modern computer systems offer ample storage and memory to capture the many personality variations of very sophisticated or very primitive human beings.

We incorporate this concept into the behavioral model by taking a cross section of the lines in the diagram 13.9. In fact the lines and curves in Figure 13.9 are not lines at all but multistring threads. The twist of the threads depicts the type-A and type-B phasor angles in the nature of the personality. The concept is depicted in Figure 13.12 according to Aristotle's model of conduct. There are only three (120 degrees i.e., 3 × 120 = 360°) segments in each of the two phasor (types A and B) diagrams. The coarse attributes are highlighted as Truth, Virtue, and Beauty with the type-A side and Deception, Arrogance, and Hypocrisy on the type-B side.

Over the last few decades, social scientists have become aware of the negative side of human personality. The classic thinker Erich Fromm has presented modes of behaviorism [19, 20] quite the opposite of his own findings in his earlier classic *The Art of Loving* [21]. Fromm (a psychoanalyst by profession) classifies these unhealthy personalities as receptive (takers), exploitive, hoarding, and marketing characters and they become segments of the DAH (see Figure 13.13b) circle. More recently, Noam Chomsky offers a similar insight in his book, *Distorted Morality* [22].

We have selected the type-I and type II attributes (Figure 13.13) to be tied to personality traits of human beings. The finer classification of Truth as honest, sincere, open, frank, and candid is preferred rather than reality, actuality or conformity to knowledge. In a sense, the dictionary of ideas becomes more comprehensive than the dictionary of words.

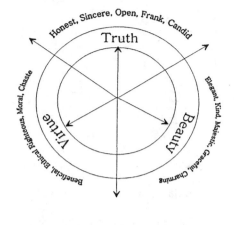

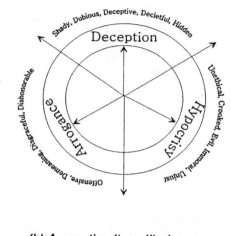

(a) A positive (type I) phasor diagram where the pursuit of any need (1 through 7) also entails an innate personal tendency toward Truth, Virtue, and/or Beauty (TVB) with attributes shown in the outermost ring.

(b) A negative (type II) phasor diagram where the pursuit of any need (1 through 5) also entails an innate personal tendency toward Deception, Arrogance, and /or Hypocrisy (DAH) with attributes shown in the outermost ring.

Figure 13.13 Tendencies of humans and their representations in a (r, θ) coordinate system indicating intensity and direction of the predisposition.

In Figure 13.13, the circles have three 120° segments pertaining to the TVB or DAH attributes of an individual's personality. Similarly, for the type-A phasor according to Maslow there are 15 (18°, i.e., 15 × 18° = 360°) segments in each of the two (types A and B) phasor diagrams. These two figures are not shown but they can be deduced from Figure 13.13.

The granularities of the three segments in the two circles of Figure 13.13 are not important since the individual can have any blending of TVB and/or DAH. Like the three primary colors (red, yellow and blue) can be blended to yield any shade or hue, the basic traits blend together to yield any character of a human being. Maslow's 15 type-A and type-B phasor classifications simply become one or more angular coordinates in the TVB or DAH (r, θ) coordinate system. It is interesting to note these numerical identifiers are dynamic but generally stable in healthy personalities but oscillate drastically in unstable personalities.

If a wisdom machine (WM), discussed in Part III of this book, has access to a worldwide knowledge bases of different personality and behavioral types, then an initial mapping of any particular individual may be accomplished based on the "action profile" of how that individual has resolved lower-level needs. It is possible to identify the saint–benevolent scientist/artist genius in the TVB space and the terrorist in the DHA space, with the full understanding that a genius terrorist and an idiot saint lie at the extremes of a normal distribution curve. There are six extremes (TVB and DAH) and six normal distribution curves (T to D, V to A, and B to H; D to T, A to V, and H to B)[4], if not 18 (= 2 × 3 × 3)[5] normal distribution curves for the basic personality variations according to the writings of Aristotle.

The number increases to 450 (= 2 × 15 × 15) normal distribution curves according to the writings of Maslow. The fine granularity that Maslow has indicated by his 15 shades of the type-A phasor[6] ("B-Values," listed as truth, goodness, beauty, unity and transcendence, aliveness, uniqueness, perfection, justice, simplicity, richness, effortlessness, playfulness, self-sufficiency, and meaningfulness, see Section 13.1.5) and the 15 shades of the type-B phasor can be derived from the space encompassed within the 18 normal distribution curves from Aristotle's classification.

13.7 OSCILLATIONS OF BEHAVIOR

Over time, variations in human and cultural behavior are to be expected. The level of individual maturity, the cultural evolution, the changes in social norms all influence the long-term migration in patterns of behavior. However, it is also possible to witness violent swings in attitudes and behavior (and even cultural outlook) due to strong forces of conflict such as wars, plagues, or famines. The movement does not have to be smooth. This mode of violent change is most obvious in conflict-ridden and unstable personalities and in nations going through revolutions such as the French, Chinese, and Russian Revolutions.

When order and rationality prevail, the process transition and migration are manageable and fall within the level of acceptance of society. From the days of Freud, conflict has been identified as the cause of instability and its resolution has been envisioned as a cure. In this chapter it is suggested that the rational and step-by-step (see steps 1–6, Figure 13.9) approach in satisfaction of any need and then the migration (steps 7–9, in Figure 13.9) to the satisfaction of the next need can be approached on a mathematical basis and by computer-assisted techniques rather than by the tools and techniques of modern psychiatry. When a machine is

---

[4] We have differentiated between the distribution curve X to Y as being distinct from the curve Y to X because the human personality change from positive to negative is a different mode when changing from negative to positive. In most other mathematical representations, these two curves would overlap. This type of hysteresis effect is known to exist in magnetic materials during the reversal of a magnetizing field.

5 The other 12 extremes are T to H, T to A; V to H, V to D; and B to D, B to A in the set that extends from the TVB phasor to the DAH phasor; and D to V, D to B; H to T, H to B; and A to B, A to T in the set that extends from the DAH phasor to the TVB phasor.

6. The 15 positive values can be seen as B+ values of Maslow and the 15 negative values (opposite of the B attributes) can be seen as B- values.

programmed to trace the pattern of behavior of any given child or individual, it is feasible for the machine to suggest a strategy that is consistent with social attitudes and venues and resolves the next stage in need satisfaction or progression to the next stage. Typical knowledge banks and Internet access may facilitate the most suitable if not an optimal guide to behavior at any stage in human life and in any cultural or social setting. Much like modern medicine, the solution can be tailored to individual needs. The gift of being graceful, charming, and highly intelligent in the satisfaction of any human need can be programmed. The guide to etiquette now becomes a computational process.

The basic premise of this approach is that all motivations tend to follow a personality profile and the machine, from the prior actions of the individual, learns this personality profile. The extrapolation of this profile onto other social and cultural settings relieves the anxiety and tension associated with facing an uncertain situation. Currently, electronic government and IT platforms assist nations and organizations by suggesting the best course of action in any given setting and a similar personalized decision support system can suggest how an individual can achieve his/her goals in everyday life quickly and optimally, thus avoiding oscillation or impertinence of unexpected social behavior.

13.8 EFFECTS OF PHASORS ON PATTERN (1–9) OF BEHAVIOR

The type-A and type-B phasors in Figures 13.13 influence the structure of the pattern (1–9) shown in Figure 13.9. Human beings with either the TVB or DAH phasors pursue the satisfaction of their needs. Individuals with the type-A TVB phasor show a mature and sophisticated approach, whereas individuals with the type-B DAH phasor show a degenerate and opportunistic approach. There are short-term and long-term consequences.

The immediate short-term effect of the TVB phasor on pattern (1–9) is that the diagram tends to be repetitive and uniform because of the absence of deception, arrogance, and hypocrisy in the approach to finding a socially acceptable satisfaction to their needs. The diagram (1–9) gets less cluttered and the steps appear to be clearly delineated. The path is smooth and requires less effort to traverse and sustain as shown in Figure 13.14(a).

Conversely, the short-term effect of the DAH phasor on pattern (1–9) is that the diagram tends to be uniquely tailored to each situation and jagged because of the presence of deception, arrogance and hypocrisy in the approach to finding a satisfaction of their needs as shown in Figure 13.14 (b).

In the long run, the effects of the type-A (TVB) and type-B (DAH) phasors become more pronounced. The process of constructing the pattern of behavior for each need and its variations requires emotional and psychological energy. Whereas the type-A individual has a mental blueprint for the response that is consistent with the TVB approach, the type-B individual has to construct a unique plan for *each* need and its variations, to be consistent with the DAH approach. The net long-term effects of the two types A and B are shown in Figures 13.14(c) and (d).

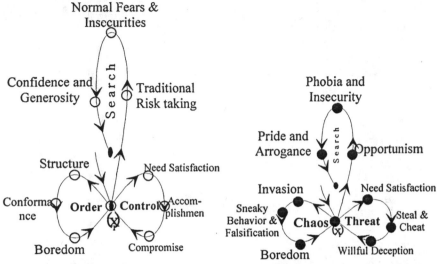

Pattern of Behavior with Positive Phasor Leading to Migration of Human Needs From Level Xi-1, to Xi and to Xi+1

POSITIVE-base Contents

Pattern of Behavior with Negative Phasor Leading to Migration of Human Needs From Level Xi-1, to Xi and to Xi+1

NEGATIVE-base Contents

(a) Effects of positive or TBV phasor. The diagram is taller, repetitive for each need and its variation, making the adaptation and behavior easier and streamlined.

(b) Effect of negative or DAH phasor. The diagram is short, jagged for each need and its variation, making the adaptation and behavior harder and strenuous.

Figure 13.14 Short-term effect of positive and negative phasors on the overall evolution of behavior patterns (1-9) and the migration path from (i)th level need (i + 1)st level need.

The greater expenditure of time and energy for type-B individuals deplete resources more rapidly at the higher need levels, leaving less time and energy for the highest level needs and their response patterns. The DAH individual spends part of the time in hiding or camouflaging the opportunistic mode of achieving the earlier goal or satisfying the needs. It appears unlikely that a DAH personality will succeed at the sixth and seventh-levels of needs, if there are any such needs, for this type of personality. The finiteness of the time, energy, and mental capacity becomes the final seal of true achievement.

In a great majority of cases, when truth, social benevolence, and/or the pursuit of perfection or an ideal are not the innate nature of the human being, the growth of the personality gets sealed at the fifth (self-realization) level, unless the personality evolves to truly discard (not camouflage) the DAH personality in favor of the TVB personality. We depict the short- and long- term effects of the TVB and the DAH personalities in the four diagrams in Figure13.14. The seven composite patterns (1-9) in Figures 13.14(c) and 13.14(d) are noticeably different.

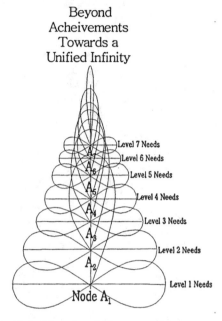

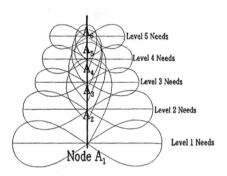

Deficit Needs of Human Beings   Deficit Needs of Human Beings

(c) Effects of positive or TBV phasor. The pyramid becomes taller and focused on needs beyond ones own self.

(d) Effects of negative or DAH phasor. The pyramid becomes restricted to fewer lower-layers focusing on ones own needs.

Figure 13.14(contd.) Long-term effect of positive and negative phasor on the overall evolution of behavior patterns (1-9) for the entire seven-level need diagram.

The natural fear and insecurity within the personality of the TVB individual move freely into the top excursions of the (7–8–9) segment of the behavior pattern. Over a period of time, factors restricting the height of this segment are overcome by consistent and prolonged migration pattern. Historically, evidence [e.g., the Bay of Pigs deliberations (Kennedy), abolition of slavery (Abraham Lincoln)] reinforces the nature and attitudes of such leaders.

On the other hand, the DAH personality faces the constant threat of being exposed to society for negative attributes inherent with this mode of behavior. A certain amount of mental and emotional energy is lost in reinforcement of the attributes associated with the DAH personality. The finiteness of resources (time, energy, and capability) will take its toll on the DAH personality. In the public domain, this status quo is most prevalent in corrupt officials and hypocritical politicians. The achievements survive until evidence (e.g., the White House tapes (Nixon), Monica Lewinsky's confessions (Clinton)) dawns on the entire picture exposing the nature and attitudes of such leaders.

Effect of Positive Phasor
Truth,red;
Virtue,blue; Beauty,green

(a) Hopping between traits such as truth, virtue, and elegance or honest, sincere, and kind. The clustering effects of related traits become dominant.

Effect of Negative Phasor
Deception,black;
Arrogance,Gray;Hypocrisy,brown

(b) Hopping between traits such as deception, arrogance and hypocrisy, or lying, selfishness and cruelty. The clustering effects of related traits become dominant.

Figure 13.15 Effect of the two phasors on the human tendency to hop between closely associated traits.

Human behavior tends to be dynamic and contextual. Behavior is also a conscious and controlled process. However, the personality traits are innate and ingrained. For this reason, the very short term results from the model and thus the behaviorally intelligent (BI) platforms can become error prone. Integrative and average performances together become as accurate as the macroeconomic models for the behavior and performance of national economies or the test results of a patient with a dubious illness.

In a sense, the BI platform develops a personality profile based on a lifetime of study of past behavior and then extracts features that are known to form clustered relationships, such as honesty and truthfulness, benevolence and generosity, lovingness and kindness. Conversely, the platform also evolves clustered relationships such as deceitfulness and lying, thoughtlessness and selfishness, hatefulness and cruelty. The model assigns psychological distances (much like Hamming distances [23] between encoded information) between these traits. Shorter distances are assigned within clusters and longer distances between clusters. Thus the energy required for the behavior to flip between the patterns in Figure 13.15a and Figure 13.15b becomes more than to flip within the patterns. Artificially intelligent systems would routinely search the innate and ingrained personality much more effectively (and inexpensively) than psychiatrists as they search during psychoanalysis.

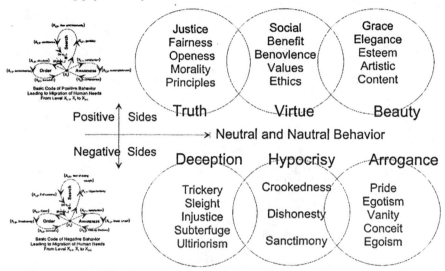

Figure 13.16 Clustered behavioral patterns of humans tend to keep actions reasonably confined and predictable. In most social settings (e.g., corporate, executive), the legal and ethical frameworks focus the range of expected behavior leaning toward the positive side.

The clustering effects are depicted in Figures 13.16, with the relatively short and long behavioral distances. Flippant behavior is a rare phenomenon in healthy personalities. Thus the BI platform explores for interclustered behavioral traits before exploring for intraclustered traits, even though they are possible. An alternate representation of the clusters is shown in Figure 13.17. In this diagram, the BI platform recognizes the pattern by using the same approach that is used in most statistical PR programs [24].

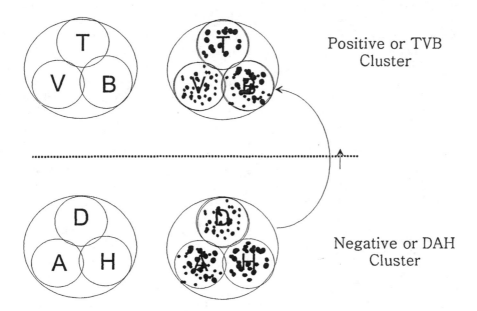

Positive or TVB
Cluster

Negative or DAH
Cluster

Statistical Distribution of the Human Behavior
within the TVB and the DAH Cluster.

*Figure 13.17 Alternate depictions of the statistical variations of human
behavior. T, V, and B signify (Aristotle's type I) Truth, Virtue, and Beauty.
D, A, and H signify (Aristotle's type II) Deception, Arrogance, and Hate.
This representation facilitates the pattern recognition processes within the
behaviorally intelligent machines. Machines are programmed to move
from one domain to the other by the inherently positive gravity in the three
clusters T, V, and B; or conversely by the inherently subversive gravity in
the three clusters D, A, and H. Every incremental movement of human
behavior gets translated as a change in finite-state variables within the
machine. The BI machine thus emulates the human behavior much as a
AI robot would emulate the human actions.*

Human behavior starts at the inception of life and continues as a lifelong process.
The blueprint of the embryonic baby is written in the cells of the womb as a tale of
the genes that become the maps of the mind. Millions of other possible
embodiments disappear and only one fertilized egg remains, carrying the potential
personality of one human being. Clusters of cells and neurons evolve. The drama
begins, and the pattern of behavior starts to take shape.

Machine behavior starts at the program level and continues through the execution
of robotic code in the hardware. The flowchart of the robotic code is conceived in
the mind of a human being. Being prone to positive and negative social pressures,

the (Freudian) slip of an operation code in the CPU can mean the difference between a nuclear power plant and a nuclear bomb. The human surveillance of machine becomes an integral part of imparting a sense of direction in the information age as machines take over some of the thought processes from human beings.

From a contemporary perspective, modern humans are beyond the models Freud, Maslow and even Fromm [21]. Modern humans need at least two more levels for the longing mind that cries to contribute to a society of which one is only a part. The search to be a pioneer continues. For the body, modern humans have the id (Freudian), an ego (Freudian), and a set of lower-level needs (physiological and safety—Maslow's need pyramid). For the mind, the modern humans have a set of higher needs (the ego (Freudian), the social (or the Freudian superego) and realization (Maslow's need pyramid)).

Finally, the contemplative modern humans have two levels (search and unification) atop the models of Freud and Maslow that will form the basis of a seven-level personality. This model is complete basis for human behavior and is a model for the machine to impersonate a human. The complete human being with a body, mind (Freud and Maslow) and longing (soul by Jung; see also Crick [25]) is represented in this model. These two outermost levels of personality represented as sixth- and seventh-level needs, let the thoughtful, meditative, and contemplative individual leap into the realm of the unknown and unexplored. The individual explores a little more into the outer reaches of human perceptions, "having gone where no one has gone before" in the perceptual space of the mind. The evolution from Freudian model to the seven-level model is depicted in Figure 13.18.

13.10 CONCLUSION

In this chapter we present a theme for developing a (computer) model for human behavior starting from Freud (based on observation of a large number of patients). Maslow's contributions are equally impressive while he developed his five-level need pyramid as he observed a large number of healthy and successful people. This chapter extends Maslow's five-level model to a seven-level model to encompass the struggle of the modern thoughtful and contemplative human being in the information society and Internet age. This model also explains the contemplative meditations of the type–I human being working as a saint or a scientist at levels 6 and 7 of the model. It also explains the killer instincts of the type-II human being acting as a most primitive human in the information age and Internet society.

Both constructive and destructive tendencies of a human being are included in the model by (Aristotle's) type-I and type-II phasors. These phasors govern the behavioral variations of the human at a microscopic level as the individual achieves the ways and means of satisfying innate needs.

In a positive sense, the framework of a human self and society dominates as an individual resolves the third-, fourth, and fifth-level needs. At the resolution of the sixth- and seventh-levels needs, the modern humans with the type-A phasor or bent of mind portray the originality by contributing to society and understanding. Human beings who live in a purely materialistic world do not invoke the top two levels.

This chapter presents an alternate way to assess the personality of modern humans by considering that the overlapping portrayals. First, from the Freudian perspective; the id, ego and superego in proper proportions. Second, we can follow a motivational perspective based on Maslow's writings, where self-realization tops the need pyramid. Finally, from the seven-level perspective, there is motivation beyond the self-realization of a human being.

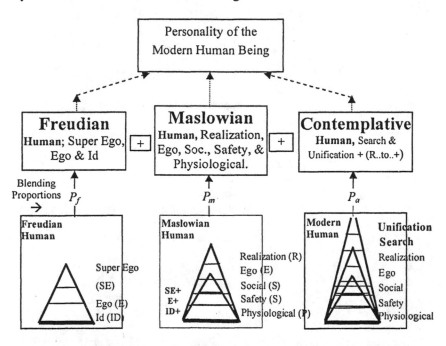

Figure 13.18 Evolution of the behavioral model from the Freudian model to the model of behavior of the modern human searching beyond the materialistic and mundane of living for one's own self. The symbols SE, E and ID denote the superego, the ego and the id from the Freudian school of thought. The symbols R, E, S, S, and P denote the fives classes of human needs (realization, ego or esteem, social or love, safety and physiological needs) derived from Maslow's Need hierarchy. For the modern human the two top levels of need (search and unification) are also added. This hierarchy is the basis of motivational theory that leads to the foundation of human behavior of the human being who looks to all aspects of living as an integral part personal and social responsibility.

This perspective projects a human being beyond the individual's own self into society. It explains the contribution of scientists, poets, philosophers, and artists as they contribute by searching for the best, the optimal, and the most beneficial. It also extends longing (if it can be considered a need) and the need to unify into the realm of the unknown and uncover a universal law, or a new order.

REFERENCES

[1] C-T. Chen, *Linear System Theory and Design,* 3rd ed., Oxford Series in Electrical and Computer Engineering, Oxford University Press, New York, 1998.

[2] R. Hartley and A. Zisserman, *Multiple View Geometry in Computer Vision,* Cambridge University Press, Cambridge, UK, 2004.

[3] A. J. Stubberud, et el.,, *Schaum's Outline of Feedback and Control Systems,* 2nd ed., McGraw-Hill, New York, 1994.

[4] J. C. Giarratano and G. D. Riley *Expert Systems: Principles and Programming,* Course Technology; 3rd ed., Boston, 1998.

[5] M. Mohammadian, *Intelligent Agents for Data Mining and Information Retrieval,* Idea Group Publishing, 2004.

[6] J. Mena *Investigative Data Mining for Security and Criminal Detection,* Butterworth-Heinemann, Woburn, MA, 2003.

[7] S. Freud, *Basic Writings of Freud,* Modern Library, New York, 1938.

[8] C. Jung, *Modern Man in Search of a Soul,* Routletdge & Kenan Paul Ltd., London 1933 and 1961

[9] A. H. Maslow, A theory of human motivation, *Psychol. Rev.* **50**, pp 370–396, 1943.

[10] A. H. Maslow, *Motivation and Personality,* Harper & Row, New York, 1970.

[11] A. Maslow, *Farther Reaches of Human Nature,* Viking Press, New York, 1971.

[12] J. P. Hayes, *Computer Architecture and Organization,* 2nd Ed., McGraw Hill, New York, 1988.

[13] H. A Simon, A behavioral model of rational choice, *Q. J. Economics,* **69**: 99–118. 1955.

[14] H. A March and J. G. Simon, *Organizations,* John Wiley & Sons, Hoboken, NJ, 1958.

[15] R. Cyert and J. G. March, *A Behavioral Theory of the Firm,* Prentice Hall, Englewood Cliffs, NJ, 1963.

[16] S. V. Ahamed, The architecture of a wisdom machine, *Int. J. of Smart Eng. Sys. Design,* **5**, (4): 537–549, 2003.

[17] J. D. Kraus, and K. R. Carver, *Electromagnetics,* McGraw Hill, New York, 1973.

[18] G. H. Mead, *Mind, Self and Society,* University of Chicago Press, Chicago, 1934.

[19] E. Fromm, *Anatomy of Human Destruction,* Holt, Rinehart and Winston, Austin, TX, 1973.

[20] E. Fromm, *Man for Himself, An inquiry into Psychology of Ethics,* Owl Books, NewYork, 1990.

[21] E. Fromm, *The Art of Loving*, Harper and Rowe, New York, 1954.

[22] N. Chomsky *Distorted Morality*, Production Koch, Studio Wea Corp., DVD released, Mar. 2003.

[23] E. R. Berelkamp, *Key Papers in the Development of Coding Theory*, IEEE Press, New York.

[24] J. R. Parker, *Algorithms for Image Processing and Computer Vision*, John Wiley & Sons, Hoboken, 1996.

[25] F. Crick, *The Astonishing Hypothesis – The Scientific Search for the Soul*, Simon & Schuster, Touchstone Book, New York, 1995.

Chapter 14

The Practice of Wisdom

An accepted structure of values forms the basis for the practice of wisdom. The classical works of the Greek writers (Plato, Socrates, as well as Aristotle) and of Roman scholars document the structure of logic, inference, and knowledge. A framework and a code of ethics exist from the days of Aristotle. Even though he does not draw out the shape and levels in a hierarchy of values like that of Maslow's pyramid of needs [1], the notion of values is evident. To the extent that values have changed over time, the structure of values (shape and levels) is dynamic.

Over the many thousands of years between Aristotle and Maslow, the pursuits of kings and emperors modified the values of Aristotle to suit the times. A questionable sense of justice has challenged the domain of equality and respect for human life and faith. In the history of human thought, the approach to immortality was in the propagation of timeless goals. Being intangible, capable of being falsified, and being negotiable, the timelessness of goals is replaced by timely goals. A sense of immortality of values is replaced by materiality of possessions. The structure of values appears as heaps of money where values are stepped down to make way for a new generation of wealth mongers and pyramid climbers.

One of the goals of the capitalistic society is the enhancement of personal wealth by bringing novelty and sophistication in the production and distribution process. In most civilized societies, the greed in capitalism is restrained by legal and ethical frameworks. However noble the restraint may be, the erosion of values is a steady and gradual process, especially when the attainment of values requires steps contradicting the maximization of wealth. While economists have offered numerous econometric tools for the pursuit and achievement of wealth, philanthropists have not offered any scientific methodology in the preservation of values. The act of willful negligence on the part of corporations has left no personal recourse in the minds of the most thoughtful executives. The corruption of values at highest corporate levels (like Enron and Arthur Anderson [2]) is along the downward trend that Aristotle was trying to prevent in his spectrum of "moral virtues." The perceived need to survive sometimes conflicts with the elusive need to preserve moral virtues.

14.1 THE HUMAN ASPECTS

The adaptability of the human mind has been a primary tool for survival. The primitive reaction of the mind is instinctual. The adaptation of behavior is based on the capacity to think and prolonged adaptation shortchanges the thought process. Over a period of time, human thought starts to get minuscule and minimal. This process poses a grave danger to values that are based on wisdom derived from knowledge and based on rationality and thought. In a sense, the quality of intelligence is being deprived of the capacity to adapt. This appears to be pointing to a downward spiral of values until the ultimate collapse of society. The cyclic nature of social growth and its decay stems from age-long swings of values. The philosophic and saintly notions in society are eroded by exploiters and profit seekers[1]. An uneasy cycle of social growth with high values and then its decay into moral bankruptcy goes on. One fact remains firmly supported by history; the decay time can be short and chaotic if mass hysteria catalyzes the initiation of change.

In the modern information age, the preservation of knowledge is securely founded. The written word and the nonvolatile, self-refreshing memories can preserve the knowledge bases and the axioms of wisdom over long durations and almost indefinitely. The preservation of such axioms of wisdom can be made much longer than the whims and fancies of abusers of society and manipulators of values. However well preserved, the nature of conflict between the founders of values and the interpreters of the laws becomes evident. In a great many cases, the role of a new Supreme Court of values to preserve the dignity of all humanity becomes as critical as the Supreme Court of Justice to preserve the freedom of a small group of humanity in a given nation. Here the machines can analyze more rationally than human beings who react more emotionally.

In the information age, knowledge banks and axioms of wisdom are linked via the Internet. A global IT platform for wisdom and values is a viable contribution to humanity. More recently, some individuals have committed crimes against

---

[1] We do not impose our own values but we are constrained by the words of language that have evolved as the values themselves have evolved over the history of humankind.

humanity. It appears just as logical that some just philanthropists can build tamper-proof IT platforms to enhance human values and block the microscopic individual exploitation and prevent macroscopic societal deception. Such a platform will catch a criminal on a real-time basis. Even though the scope of the platform appears vast, the implementation is quite feasible with the current IT, Internet, and networking technologies. Information processing, knowledge processing, wisdom processing, and value processing all achieve convergence within the platform.

14.2 THE SOURCES OF WISDOM

Sources of wisdom can be an ordeal if one does not know what wisdom is or how it is defined[2]. Over a period of time, for any human organization or for a human–machine team of opposite perception, wisdom and evil can be switched around. Without a long-term reference or perspective, a human organization or a human–machine team with negative goals will perform equally well, gradually depleting the very constructs of well organized society.

Short of a revelation, wisdom can only be accumulated over a period of time (or processed at incredible speeds) since the accumulated wisdom has to survive over far longer periods. In view of the nanosecond cycle times of computers and gigabit/sec rates of the networks, the wisdom can be pursued relatively quickly to build wisdom bases. The architecture of wisdom machine (WM) was presented in Chapter 10. As was suggested, the WM will function equally well as an evil machine if it is primed from corrupted knowledge bases.

The normal operating systems block the hardware from executing false arithmetic (e.g., divide by zero, go into infinite loops, request a precision exceeding the precision of the numerical processor unit) and illogical functions (e.g., exceed the allocated resources, cross program boundaries) and even avoid deadlocks during multiprocessing. However, the operating systems do not stop the machine from executing deadly social functions or making illegal recommendations. It appears ironic that we build fast computers and even faster networks without querying what the computers process or what information the networks carry. The bug and virus planters have taken full advantage of this loophole. Disaster in the values and wisdom domain is feasible when every computer and network gradually and systematically depletes society of its ethical values. The operating systems perhaps need a socially intelligent (SI) component to enhance values or suggest socially acceptable solutions. Value protection algorithms can be conceived just as easily as the capital preservation algorithms in financial analysis environments.

One environment where an entire sequence of programs has come into existence in a very short time frame is the telephone billing system (See Section 3.6). These fraud management programs are an integral part of the billing system. The purpose has been to prevent the abuse of telephone networks by fraudulent customers,

---

[2] In the words of an Indian poet: "How unjust am I, that I seek love from the one who does not know what love is?"

subscribers, and intruders. The practice of fraud is common in developing countries (especially where mobile telephony is being introduced). Overcharging of the depleted and prepaid credit cards had become a serious drain of company revenues. These programs use AI techniques to detect the abusive practices of the fraudulent users and then block them from running up excessive bills that the company cannot collect.

In the AI platform for monitoring values, the activities of suspected individuals and corporations (e.g., Enron, insurance companies, Arthur Anderson) would be under nonintrusive information surveillance for their corporate practices (much like activities of spies, terrorists, suspected criminals, and child molesters). The platform warns society of the possible dangers from the organizations before the damage is done. In the corporate accounting programs, the concept of accounting ratios has been established. Much like the vital signs of patients, these programs monitor the financial ratios continuously and check if they fall within the range of acceptability for healthy companies.

In addition, an eminent possibility of value-fraud exists. Viruses that belittle the existing social and ethical values can infect a network of human beings. Human beings and machines can get affected by a set of corrupt values or a willful negligence of existing values. In localized environments, (such as Enron, insurance companies, Arthur Anderson) toward the end of the twentieth century, the corruption of ethics, values and responsibility has unfolded. In a reverse society if every exploitive activity can be revamped to be legal and every ethical practice is made illegal, society can be as primitive as a brave new stone age.

14.3 VIRUSES IN HUMAN NETWORKS

The minds of socially ethical human beings drive society but corrupt individuals incubate, implant, and propagate deadly social viruses in human networks. Much like terrorism, the goal is to inflict damage and propagate suffering. Such viruses have a life story much like the viruses in computer networks.

Numerous organizations build sophisticated antivirus and antispy programs. Much like the viruses and spy programs that steal computer, network, and information resources, human viruses trigger human beings to steal social and organizational resources. The extent of damage can be as extensive as the damage by the computer and network viruses and spy programs.

14.4 PERIPHERAL ACCOMPLICES IN HUMAN NETWORKS

Accomplices actively connect human elements engaged in illegal or unethical activities. The disservice to society is facilitated and can reach chronic proportions[3]. Unlike the flow of money in a capitalistic society which enhances economic activity, the flow of information between accomplices spreads disease and suffering in society.

Accomplices act like the peripherals in computer systems. These peripherals connect the user terminals and devices to the network or to the data processing systems. The level of sophistication of an accomplice can be significant. Ranging from a simple informer to a highly intelligent ring of spies or the Mafia, these accomplices facilitate the flow of social viruses in an otherwise sane and civil society. In addition, the accomplices can impede the legal and ethical functions within a society. Like the functions and dealings of any productive society are abundant, the nature and classification of the social disrupters are also abundant.

Over the last two decades, the role of police and law enforcers is becoming increasingly standardized. These agencies generally monitor the nature and legality of social events and transactions. A wide variety of tools and techniques have evolved ranging from wiretaps to mathematically precise snoopers. These tools and techniques vary with nature of the human networks who carry the socially poisonous contaminants and infectious viruses.

The information age and a knowledge society have altered the life of most people because of the inexpensive digital devices and the profusion of Internet/computer access. However, these very tools and techniques can be used by socially and morally corrupt individuals and their accomplices. In the current information-rich society communication devices and their interfaces are becoming increasingly generic. The downward spiral of a knowledge society stems from the abuse of information processing and communication tools.

14.5 CONVICTION AND WISDOM

In a realistic sense, every society incorporates the far-reaching advantages and stability of rational, just, legal and ethical conduct. Since the dawn of civilization (Greek and ancient Indian), society has documented the preservation of ethics and morality. The reigns of cruelty and barbaric behavior that taint history are preserved in the trails of deeds rather than in words of wisdom. There is enough historical evidence to deduce that the savage behavior of the Incas and the Aztecs would not find worth in being preserved in books of learning. In a sense, we contend that only the pursuit of positive values (virtues) yields axioms of wisdom.

At the opposite end of the spectrum, the negative values of rulers and emperors have the flavor of tyranny and infliction of suffering. However, from a very short time perspective the dynamics of tyranny are not unlike the dynamics of virtue. Both are catalysts of change, and sometimes some change is better than no change, but no change is better than negative change. If a corrective mechanism is not in place, society can more easily fall into a degenerate tailspin.

---

[3] The corrupt governments in many nations, the cruel union of powers, the street gangs, and the Mafia are examples of such sick human psychological institutions.

From the perspective of WM, the error-proof and tamperproof security of the wisdom bases (WB's) becomes essential. Bugs and viruses implanted in the functions and operations of WMs and networks extracting values from wisdom can result in a form of knowledge AIDS in the information society.

14.6 MODULES OF POSITIVE WISDOM

In the context of the WMs presented in Chapter 10, the machines at levels I and II perform related database, networking, and AI statistical functions. However, when human beings get entirely involved at level III, a new perspective is interjected. The scientists who "weigh and consider" the tentative axioms of wisdom proposed by the six computers (see Figure 10.6) at the two levels (I and II) can pose two extremes of modalities.

First, if the group of humans at level III has an open view of the universe, a sense of unrestrained wisdom will result from the human–WM team. A similar scenario emerged in the 1980's in the telecommunications industry[4]. The capacity of the human beings to assume a global perspective of wisdom results in a breed of *global, universal,* and *timeless* axioms of wisdom. If it is possible to tentative label such a group of human beings as type A, then the axioms will have long lasting and far-reaching implications. The resulting axioms can be stored in a type A *wisdom axiom base* (A-WAB). This classification of human beings is discussed further in the next section.

Second, if the group of humans at level III has a local and narrow perspective, a sense of restrained wisdom[5] will result from the human–machine WM team. The area of specialty can be narrow and focused or broad and encompassing. It can also be in any particular domain, (e.g., physics, chemistry, mathematics, sciences, arts). If it is possible to tentatively label such a group of human beings (with a restricted perspective) as type B, then the axioms will have innovative and immediate implications. The resulting axioms can be stored in a type B wisdom axiom base (B-WAB). This classification of the human beings is also discussed further in the next section.

The dynamics of the entire WM were discussed in Chapter 8. The processing of machine instructions in the lower two levels I and II, (see in Chapter 8) and the participation of human teams make up the entire WM function in isolating the axioms of wisdom. The influence of the two types of users (type A and type B) is

---

[4] Communication scientists during the 1980s evolved the open system interconnect (OSI) design; the networking field had two options: (1) The networking standards could have been individually tailored to each mode, (i.e., telephone, TV, data, computer, etc. communications) or (2) one networking standard (currently being used) could have been established for *all* communication channels. After due diligence, the latter option was selected and now we have seamless communication facility throughout the world. Each network abides by the same OSI standard, even though some protocol converters may be necessary.

[5] From the previous comparison, when the human team is strictly from the telephone circuit-switched networks, then the derived axioms of wisdom will be slanted toward that particular discipline.

shown in Figure 14.1. Whereas the machine functions are deterministic, the human participation is driven largely by the predisposition and creativity of the users. Commitment to positive social values (such as pursuit of truth, search for social elegance, and the enhancement of social benefit), becomes imperative in forcing the levels I and II of the WM to be an instrument of virtue. Conversely, if the commitment is to negative values (such as psychotic fear, selfish greed, and irrational hate), then levels I and II of the WM will perform as precise instruments of vice. This scenario is addressed in Section 14.7.

The users of WMs may not have an exact blueprint of any of one type (a philosopher, a scientist, a tyrant or a thug) of individual. However, the collective personality profile of anyone user or a team of users can lean towards the (positive) philosopher (type A) or (positive) scientists (type B). At the other extreme, the collective personality profile may lean toward a (negative) tyrant king/leader (type C) or a (negative) mobster/thug (type D). From the discussions presented in Chapter 13, Aristotle's perceptions of his type-I human nature corresponds to type A and B personality profiles in this Chapter. Conversely, Aristotle's type-II human nature corresponds to type C and D personality profiles in this chapter.

14.6.1 Positive Predisposition of the Human Team

Human beings have an infinite variety of predispositions. Any attempt to classify them would be futile. However in the context of being wise, it appears that there are two extremes of the modality: being infinitely wise in an immortal and universal sense or being wise enough to deal with problems and solve the problems for a (very long) time for a (very large) cross section of humankind.

14.6.1.1 Type A: Individuals Favoring Unrestrained Wisdom

Even though mathematical and precise definitions of philosophers and saints do not exist, their contributions have acted as prolonged and insidious catalysts of positive change in society. The individual traits can vary significantly. Even so, it is possible to distill a collective composition of their traits, their inclinations, and their predispositions. We present this concept based on documented approaches (via typical PR programs and humanistic search) in recognizing patterns common to great minds, explorers, and scientists or common to terrorists, criminals, and thugs.

In this section, we present the characteristics of the type A users. Ideally, these users would have liked to solve all the needs of all the peoples of the world and for all times. Impossible as the mission is, such individuals sometimes find partial solutions and still become low-level benefactors to humanity, at least for the time being and at least for the immediate society. In searching for the traits that drive the type A individuals, we present a small basis of their personality profile. Five dominant attributes (A1 to A5) are presented to map a very large intellectual space of positive thinkers who have left a mark on society.

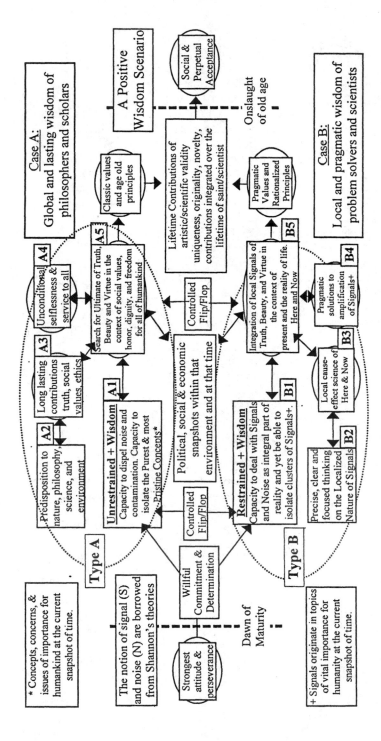

Figure 14.1 Scenario for the philosophers (type A) and scientists (type B) to track their lifelong interaction(s). Please see note on the next page for a detailed explanation of this diagram.

Note for Figure 14.1. *Creative blending of talents and deeds becomes as much of a reality as the creative blending of the contributions and philosophy of life. The elements in the two ellipses are fully and adaptively connected (e.g., neural net to suit the problem) rather than what is shown in this rudimentary diagram. If the entire diagram is allowed to vacillate (be indecisive) about the central X-axis (i.e., the horizontal centerline of the diagram), then these boxes assume more humanistic thought/behavioral processes.*

Some reference to such attributes can be found in the discourse on Aristotle and the teachings of Socrates. In reality, these attributes of the type A human teams can be very general or individualistic.

A1. Capacity to dispel secondary effects and insignificant roles from the underlying principles and notions that are fundamental to lasting statements of generality. A capacity to be unrestrained in thinking and to pursue axioms of wisdom that are longlasting. A capacity to isolate the purest and most pristine concepts that are (almost) eternal and independent of current events. A profound capacity to deal with concepts, concerns, and issues of importance for humanity at the current snapshot of time. A clue to such concerns may be found in the writings of Aristotle [3], Socrates [4], and Maslow [1] and enhanced need pyramid discussed in Chapter 13.

A2. Predisposition toward remaining focused on philosophy, human nature, philanthropy, society, sciences and environment. The goal is to derive and implement the axioms of wisdom that are fundamental to making quality of life more amenable to a large cross section of humanity and to search for and invent new ways to meet global and universal needs of society. A passion (at least an attempt) to address and solve the basic problems of hunger, health, energy, and pollution. The contributions of Fleming [5], Edison [6], Bell [7], and Tesla [8] are some noteworthy examples.

A3. Capacity to make universal and cross-cultural contributions that bring peace, joy and contentment to large segments of human populations. Long lasting achievements, contributions, to society based on true long lasting social values and an ethics framework of society. (e.g., Gandhi [9], King [10], Abraham Lincoln, [11])

A4. Unconditional and selfless surrender of one's own personal interest; dedication to the betterment and welfare of humanity in any field of activity (Buddha [12], Christ [13], John the Baptist [14], King [10])

A5. Almost endless search for ultimate of truth, beauty and virtue in the context of social values such as honor dignity and freedom for all of humankind (Khalil Gibran, Tennyson, Arnold).

These traits A1–A5 demand unusual sensitivities in human beings. Suffice it to say that one lifetime and one personality may not be sufficient to become all the great saints and all the great philosophers. However, any one of the traits practiced at the highest level practiced for a long enough time can lead to a type-A person. Furthermore, when the type A team working in conjunction with numerous wisdom machines (see Chapter 10) primed with knowledge bases of the collective consciousness of type A human beings, can discover axioms of (type A) distilled wisdom such as that espoused by all the philosophers and saints who have lived on the earth. Some very skilled negotiators (Henry Kissinger [15], Kofi Anan [16], etc.) appear to display a fragmented but yet a sophisticated combination of some of these traits.

14.6.1.1 Type B: Individuals Favoring Restrained Wisdom

A considerable amount of commonality occurs between the type A and type B teams of individuals. The fundamental differences lie in moderating the goals of a lifelong search toward immediate and realizable results. The boundaries for the search and practice of this type of wisdom lie in being able to realize and deliver the results of the wisdom in a more realistic and materialistic sense. When the boundaries are drawn very tight, the activities of the type B individuals become that of (wisdom) machine-assisted problem solving (Chapter 10). When the boundaries are stretched further, type B individuals follow the classic style of "constrained search" practiced by executives [17] in corporate environments. When more freedom is permitted, the activity follows the classic research strategy of scientists. Strict adherence to the ethics and the values is a requirement of the typical activities of the type B individuals. The outcome of the search can become as generic as the gasoline for energy, water and air filters for public buildings, or electricity to homes. Five dominant attributes (B1–B5) are presented to map a very large intellectual space of positive contributors who have left a mark on society. Some reference to such attributes can be found in the discourse on Edison [18], Bell [18], and Tesla [18]. In reality, these attributes of the type B human teams can be as variable as the scientists themselves.

In the context of these directed and motivated individuals, two terms (signal and noise[6] are introduced. Signal refers to the events and circumstances that can possibly lead to an axiom of wisdom. Noise refers to the contaminating events and circumstances that clutter and confuse the role-playing signals that lead to a precise axiom of wisdom. In many cases, the admixture and overlap of signals and noise are almost indistinguishable. The human mind in pursuit of truth, virtue and beauty can filter out the relevant signals from the irrelevant noise because (we think) the signals themselves affirm the truth, virtue, and beauty embedded in signals but not in noise. The constructs of a pure mind favor (we think) the thrill of wisdom. Accordingly, the attributes of B type individuals are listed as follows:

B1. Capacity to deal with signals and noise as an integral part of reality and yet be able to isolate (decode/correct) clusters of signals from the contamination of noise. Initially, there is no value judgment a ssociated with noise but it is

---

6 The terms signal and noise have a special connotation in communication theory. In the context of knowledge processing and wisdom creation, these two terms retain similar validity. When the signal-to-noise ratio (SNR) is very high, the possibility for reaching a correct axiom of wisdom is also high.

considered as a factor within the environment. The signals denote topics of grave importance for humanity at the current snapshot of time. If and when the effects of noise are known or determined to be harmful (e.g., side effects of medicinal drugs, porno on the media, bias in news) to society, then the noise is blocked or cancelled as much as possible.

B2. Capacity to practice precise, clear, and focused thinking on the localized nature of signals. In a sense, trait B2 is in part the practice of trait B1 upon one's own self. In addition, when directed upon the origin, nature, and validation of localized signals, the amplification, enhancement and reconstruction of the local signals are greatly facilitated. The practice of B2 in any discipline will lead to an understanding of other disciplines thus leading to a general axiom of wisdom.

B3. Capacity to practice the highest level of reasoning, logic, and association to analyze signals to enhance, refine and reconstruct them. The converse capacity of reasoning, logic, and association to analyze noise itself to suppress, attenuate, and deter noise also becomes equally important. Unabated noise seriously alters the magnitude and composition of signals. Corrupted signals cause serious flaws in the derivation of any wisdom, whereas the purest signals and their hierarchy of relationships can lead to valid and general axioms of wisdom.

B4. Capacity to seek out simple local cause–effect and cause(i)–effect(j) relationships or combinations thereof. Capacity to concentrate with great precision on the immediate or prolonged chain of relationships in any given or generic setting of a bounded problem, situation or event. Capacity to "see" through feedback and feed-forward stabilizing and destabilizing signals and noise sources in nature and in society. The capacity to concentrate on the present time and place to produce an immediate and lasting solution(s) to a(ny) problem or series of problems.

B5. Capacity to integrate and differentiate local variables (or components) in underlying authenticated and universal scientific equations and relationships that give rise to signals and noise in the local setting. Capacity to identify and enforce reasons that enhance simplicity, grace, and elegance in the axioms of wisdom and knowledge bases. Capacity to enhance the potential use of the solutions to local problems to become useful to a large segment of humanity.

These traits B1–B5 demand unusual sensitivities in human beings. Suffice it say that one lifetime and one personality may not be sufficient to become so many great inventors and scientists. However, any one of the traits practiced at the highest level for a long enough time can lead to a type B individual. Furthermore, a type B team, working in conjunction with a wisdom machine primed with knowledge bases of collective consciousness of type B individuals (problem solvers and scientists) can discover some axioms of (type B) distilled wisdom such as that espoused by all the inventors and scientists who have lived on the earth. Some very skilled scientists (Einstein [19], Maxwell [20], Braittain [21], Schalow [22], and

Townes [23] have displayed [18] a sophisticated combination of some of these traits.

14.6.2 Realizations of the Axioms of Positive Wisdom

The realization of wisdom by a human–machine team is achievable with some degree of confidence because the humans have some known (type A, type A/B, type B/A, and/or type B) bent of mind and the machines have programmed software modules. It starts to become clear that the human beings using the wisdom machine (Chapter 8) can be assisted with their own wisdom bases (WBs). This scenario is becoming popular when we see members of Congress carrying their own laptop computers to the floor.

Figure 14.1 depicts the sequence of functionalities that are expected from the human counterpart of the machine (Chapter 10). The two ellipses portray the type A and the type B attitudes in human beings. Both attitudes are distinctly feasible and universally acceptable. In the endeavor of knowledge and wisdom, human attitudes play a unique role. To accommodate the wide range of such attitudes, the two ellipses in Figure 14.1 are portrayed to indicate that human beings can be philosophers and scholars (at one extreme (top ellipse, A types) of the thought process) and they can be pragmatic scientists and problem solvers (at the other extreme (lower ellipse, B types) of the thought process).

The situation can be addressed by having an admixture of type A and type B traits. When the human team displays a philosophic perspective, the wisdom machine will supplement a set of accumulated wisdom (i.e., an expert system's knowledge base) from philosophers of the past. This accumulated wisdom is tentatively stored in a wisdom base, WB-A. Conversely, when the human team displays a scientific perspective, the wisdom machine will supplement a set of accumulated wisdom (i.e., an expert system's knowledge base) from scientists of the past. This accumulated wisdom is tentatively stored in a Wisdom Base, WB-B. There are two more converse modes possible. The first mode occurs if the operation of the wisdom machine is to be complementary to the human team with a philosophic predisposition. The second mode occurs if the operation of the machine is to be complementary to the human team with a scientific predisposition.

14.6.3 Flavors of Positive Wisdom

The two wisdom bases (WB-A and WB-B) are derived from the axioms of the philosophers (type A) and of the problem solvers (type B) can either supplement or complement a current group of users of the wisdom machine whether they have a philosophic (Ph.) or a scientific (Sc.) predisposition. Four vectors of forces influence (philosophic and scientific WM WBs derived from wisdom of prior generations, and philosophic or scientific predispositions of the current users) guide the outcome of wisdom. This leads to the four scenarios shown in Figure 14.2.

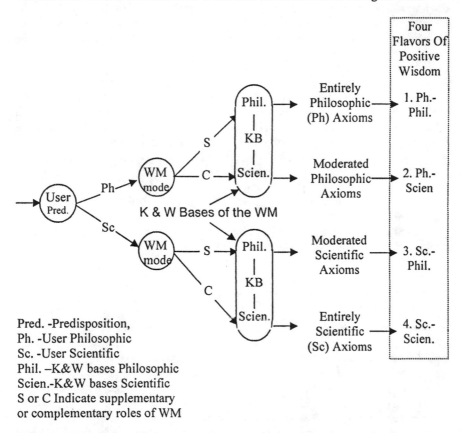

Pred. -Predisposition,
Ph. -User Philosophic
Sc. -User Scientific
Phil. –K&W bases Philosophic
Scien.-K&W bases Scientific
S or C Indicate supplementary
or complementary roles of WM

Figure 14.2 Representation of the four main databases of positive wisdom that can be primed into any WM. In reality, human creativity dominates this chart. Infinitely large number of flavors of wisdom are possible by altering the predispositions of the current users and/or slightly altering the gradations of the KB contents. In a sense, the creative, resourceful and intelligent human being still comes out in command of the situation.

The human–machine team of any wisdom machine can invoke responses from the machine that either complement (C) the thought processes of the users or supplement (S) the thought processes. The two knowledge bases can also be labeled as Phil. or Scien. depending on the nature of the axioms in these two knowledge bases.

We thus see four logical flavors of wisdom that can be expected from the continuous use of the wisdom machines by human beings. The machines being armed with AI learning tools will profile themselves to the users and the applications. However, creativity remains with the humans since the composition of the human team is neither very philosophic nor precisely scientific. Similarly, the wisdom bases (WB-A and WB-B) of the WM are neither very philosophic nor precisely scientific. For this reason, the axioms of wisdom resulting from the machine will only be leaning toward the four logical flavors. The role of creativity becomes as boundless as the bounds of wisdom; both remain as flexible as before. However, the new breed of wisdom will suit the current times far more closely.

Human creativity plays a critical role in refining the axioms of the earlier philosophers and scientists to suit the current use. Human creativity of the current users alters the balance between the embedded axioms of wisdom of prior philosophers and scientists and the most recent trend of thought, thus making up infinitely many flavors of wisdom. It is logical to infer that the first (Ph.-Phil.) of the four flavors of wisdom in Figure 14.2 tends to change slowly as compared to the fourth (Sc.-Scien.) because of greater emphasis on truth, beauty and virtue (that tend to be long lasting) in Box A5 shown in Figure 14.1. Furthermore, the nature of axioms in the fourth (Sc.-Scien.) of the four flavors of wisdom tends to become diversified and discipline oriented because of the emphasis on practicality and pragmatics of the axioms of wisdom in Box B5 shown in Figure 14.1.

14.6.4 Symphony of Positive Wisdom

If wisdom can be composed like music with string instruments on the one hand and percussion instruments on the other hand. It is that both types of instruments make equally beautiful music. On the one hand, wisdom derived from a *weighted balance* leaning toward being too philosophic can bring beauty, truth, and virtue to any society to suit the times and nations. An emerging knowledge and information society are both dynamic, calling for wisdom based on shifting values. The wisdom machines and the human teams can help foster a society with longer lasting truth, elegant beauty and immortal virtue, rather than society randomly forging values and wisdom to suit the times. On the other hand, wisdom derived from a *weighted balance* leaning towards being too scientific can bring novelty, innovations and technology to any society to suit the times and nations. Both modalities of the human–machine teams are equally beautiful.

While it is possible to see the two extreme forms of wisdom (Ph. and Sc. in Figure 14.2), it is also possible to see a detailed script of wisdom. The two positive predisposition of the human team (type A and type B in Figure 14.1) have been discussed earlier. Each of the two types has five sub-classifications A1 through A5 and B1 through B5. If these ten sub-classifications were blended and merged, as a composer would blend and merge the music from a variety of instruments, then many compositions of wisdom would result.

If such a composition were attempted by a purely human team (without conflicts and selfish interests), then it is possible to "see" a form of wisdom (perhaps a form of intelligent wisdom) that is dynamic and adaptive. It will guide values and ethics based on the values and ethics of the human teams. However, if the human teams were to degenerate and become corrupt, then the degeneration of society will have started. From a practical consideration, we do not see this as a problem because the constitution of any country is also interpreted and slightly adapted by the Supreme Court Justices to suit the times.

From a purely human consideration, the blending of the two types (A and B) would become laborious and time consuming. There is every reason to believe that such a peak of human creativity cannot last as long. However, if the computers holding the ten knowledge bases (for A1 through B5) are permitted to interact and offer blended cross sections of expert opinions and derivations, then the symphony of wisdom can be composed as a symphony of computer-generated music. A super-base of values and ethics will become essential to prevent the negative admixtures of wisdoms such as type C and type D, discussed in Section 14.7.

For the sophisticated scientists and philosophers, there is no need for the level I and level II counterparts of the wisdom machine presented in Chapter 10. At the extreme of intellectual and psychological endeavor, such individuals outperform the machine (levels I and II) functions in their private intellectual and psychological space. Positive wisdom becomes a gift of sustained practice and maturity. Such individuals continue to contribute to the social welfare over their entire life with or without the wisdom machine. For such individuals, there is little or no chance to be swayed into the dark side (see type C and type D classifications) of human nature.

Impossible as it may sound; a total personality switch (from Dr. Jykle to Mr. Hyde) is not inconceivable. In the business world, numerous executives have perpetuated the dark side of human personality and hidden motives and is documented [2]. In machine environment, the finite probabilities are amenable to representation provided such low values are with the limit of accuracy of the numerical processor unit. Furthermore, the gradual movement from type A or type B humans (or their attributes) to type C or type D humans (or their attributes) can be tracked accurately and substantiated from documented information on the WWW. The accuracy of WM offers a new methodology in detecting and documenting subtle drifts in outlook of humans or nations.

14.7 MODULES O F NEGATIVE WISDOM

Wisdom machines were presented in Chapter 10. When the human beings bring a new perspective at level III, new dimensions of the user preferences are interjected in the composite axioms of wisdom derived from the human–machine team. Tyrant kings, the mafia and the thugs can overrule any tentative axioms of wisdom proposed by the six computers at levels I and II. Even amid such gross abuse of the lower levels of the machine, the human teams can pose two extremes of modalities.

First, consider a group of humans at level III, with intent to cause total destruction[1] and damage to a maximum number of people and for as long a time as possible. These abusers of computers and networks would like to inflict an unlimited amount of damage. There is no limit to this type of fear, jealousy and hate can an evil human mind and heart can hold; it is the opposite extreme of openness (truth), sharing (benevolence) and love (beauty) that a philosophic human mind and heart can hold. Much as it is distasteful, some leaders (e.g., Adolf Hitler [24], Augusto Pinochet [25], Slobodan Milosevic [26]) in the modern era have displayed it. The alarming situation is that if a human element plants the knowledge bases of evil wisdom in all the network bases, gradual decay in ethics and values can be triggered. The capacity of human beings to be proponents of negative wisdom results in statements that are global, universal, and very destructive. If it is possible to tentatively label such a group of abusers as type C, then the statements will have implications for long lasting and far-reaching chaos and destruction. When there is prolonged abuse of computers and networks, the knowledge bases will hold the procedures and strategies for negative wisdom. The resulting statements of negative wisdom can be stored in a type C wisdom axiom base (C-WAB).

Second, if the group of abusers at level III has a local and narrow perspective, then restrained damage (such as civil wars, missile attacks, invasions, suicide bombings) will result from the human–WM team. The area of harm can be narrow and focused or broad and encompassing. It can also be in any particular domain (e.g., war tactics, bombing missions, stealth bombings, street crimes, muggings and rape). If it is possible to tentatively label such a group of abusers (with a restricted perspective) as type D, then the statements in the knowledge bases (lists of crime gangs, e-mail porno bases, directory of mafia members, location of sex bars, etc.) will have locally nasty and demeaning implications. The resulting statements of negative wisdom can be stored in a type D wisdom axiom base (D-WAB). This attributes of these abusers are also presented further in the next Section.

The influence of the two types of abusers (type C and type D) is shown in Figure 14.3. Whereas the machine functions are deterministic, the human participation is driven largely by the predisposition and attitude of the abusers. Indulgence in negative social factors (such as fear, jealousy and hate etc.), becomes instrumental in coercing the level I and level II functions of the WM to be instruments of destruction. If the commitment is to negative values (such as psychotic fear, selfish greed, and irrational hate), then levels I and II of a WM (Chapter 10) will perform as precise instruments of vice.

---

[1] Every conceivable damage that could possibly be inflicted is included here ranging from physical, material, psychological, emotional to mental. Even though the total damage is also self-destructive, it is evident at very microscopic levels, in the case of suicide bombers. Some leaders of nations have used such strategies on their own people and on others with a selfish intent for themselves. The words of an ancient poet who asks, "Does ill-fame not have the word fame in it?" makes human beings aware that acts of war and crime give some "fame" to otherwise insignificant human beings. In the recent history, Native American Indians had been treated with this type of attitude to displace a whole race.

14.7.1 Negative Predisposition of the Abuser Team

Human beings have an infinitely large variety of negative predispositions. Any attempt to classify them would be futile. However, in the context of being vile, it appears possible to identify two extremes (types C and D) of predispositions: being infinitely baleful in a global and devastating sense or being wicked enough to deal with local situations and satisfy the selfish needs for a (long) time in spite of injury to a (large) cross section of humankind.

14.7.1.1 Type C: War Mongers Favoring Maximal Injury and Destruction

Even though the psyche of tyrants, warmongers, and evil leaders is not documented accurately, their misdeeds have left a dark imprint on society. Their personalities can vary significantly since the role of evil can shroud the lives f people for (quite) some time. Even so it is possible to distill a collective composition of their traits, their inclinations and their predispositions. We present this concept based on a documented approach (via the typical PR programs and humanistic search) in recognizing patterns common to abusive leaders, killer kings, and even warlords, terrorists, criminals, and thugs.

In this section the composition of the type C abusers is presented. Ideally, these abusers would like to destroy everything and start a new world for themselves as absolute rulers. Greed and self-glory are exposed. In a psychotic way, type C abuser would like to be a type of antichrist doing the maximum damage to all people and for all times. Impossible as the mission is, such abusers sometimes find partial solutions and still become low-level destructors to humanity, at least for the time being and at least for the immediate society. In searching for the traits that drive such type C users, we present a small basis of their personality profile. Five dominant attributes (C1 to C5) are presented to map a very large baleful space of negative thinkers who have abused society. Reference to such attributes can be found in the discourse on John the Baptist [14] and in the writings about Aztec leaders [27]. In reality, the wickedness of the type C human teams can be the depth of darkness without a glimpse of light.

C1. Capacity to be unrestrained killers and destroyers. A capacity to be totally callous and blind toward anything or anybody. Total myopic vision to see no farther than themselves. The capacity to assume the total selfish gravity of a black hole. A profound capacity to internalize and deploy concepts, concerns, and issues of harm to humankind at the current snapshot of time. A clue to such personalities may be found in writing about the antichrist.

C2. Predisposition toward remaining focused on the fear and hate tactics that they can invoke in people, surroundings, and environment. The selfish and greedy goals that are to propagating their own political and power base. To search for and invent new ways to deprive society of the satisfaction of basic and universal needs, to be able to convince frightened followers that they are "saviors". Leaders in the modern times try to control global food production, energy supplies, drugs and even water to drink.

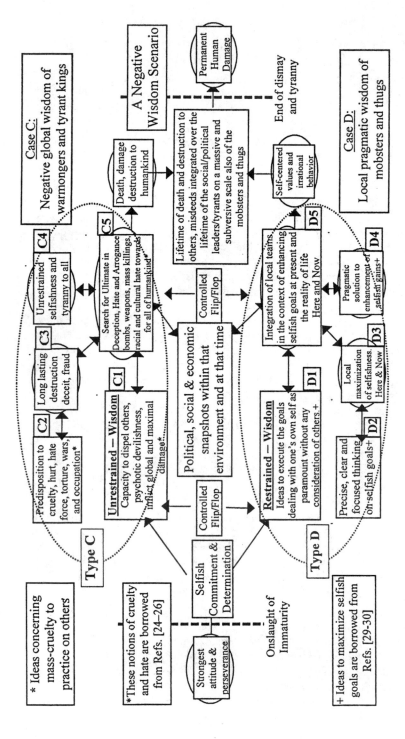

Figure 14.3 Scenario for the global war-mongers (type C) and local thugs (type D) to track the lifetime of misdeeds. Please see Note on next page.

Note for Figure 14.3. *Destructive blending of skill and misdeeds (at a global level) is as much of a reality as the destructive blending of evil and cruelty (at a local level) in life. The elements in the two ellipses are fully and adaptively connected (e.g., neural net to suit the destruction) rather than what is shown in this rudimentary diagram. If the entire diagram is to vacillate (be indecisive) about the central X-axis (i.e., the horizontal center-line of the diagram), then these boxes assume more and more of the mafia patterns and processes.*

C3. A capacity to provoke universal and cross-cultural conflicts that bring war, fear, and oppression to large segments of human populations. Capacity to bring long lasting fear and dismay to society based on deprivation of basic needs of society (e.g., British viceroys during the occupation of India, British occupation of American Indian lands, Spanish Conquistadors in South America, Crusaders in Spain).

C4. A total and targeted preoccupation with one's own personal interest resulting in fear, hate and global disharmony within humanity in every field of what should be orderly activity.

C5. An almost endless search for the ultimate of fear, jealousy and hate to invoke commotion and unrest with a degeneration of social values such as honor dignity and freedom for all of humankind (Communist rule under Mao and Stalin, Portuguese slave-traders from Africa, McCarthy's persecution, Russian/Chinese prosecution of the elite and poets)

These traits C1–C5 demand unusual cruelty in human beings. Suffice it to say that one lifetime and one personality may not be sufficient to become that cruel person. However, any one of the cruelties practiced at the highest level for a long enough time can lead to a type C person. Furthermore, a type C abuser working in conjunction with a wisdom machine primed with knowledge bases of collective consciousness of type C personalities can embed the distilled cruelties of all the tyrants and evil leaders who have lived on the earth. The databases (C-WAB) are primed from the lives of all the greatest tyrant king and war-criminals who have lived on earth.

Some very dangerous majors, leaders and thugs (Lord Clive (in India), British Indian Killers (1750s to 1770s), the Spaniards and their deadly diseases, the Portuguese and British slave-traders, the infamous Captain James Cook against the Native Hawaiian Tribes (1770s)) appear to display fragmented combinations of some of these traits.

14.7.1.2 Type D: Thugs Favoring Local and Controlled Injury

A considerable amount of commonality occurs between the type C and type D teams of users of a WM. The fundamental difference lies in moderating the lifelong goal of cruelty into immediate and realizable goals for themselves. The boundaries for the search and practice of this type of balefulness lie in being able to act in a more realistic and materialistic sense. When the boundaries are drawn very tight, the activity of type D users becomes that of a (wisdom) machine-assisted search for cruelty (e.g., the French guillotine [28]). When the boundaries are stretched more, type D users follow a "constrained search" for the acts of injury practiced by thugs, mobsters, suicide bombers, kidnappers, and rapists. When more freedom is permitted, the activity follows classic conquer-and-enslave strategy of street gangs and criminals. The outcome of such actions can become as typical as the street crimes, open mugging or open bribery. Five dominant attributes (D1 to D5) are presented to map a very large criminal space of negative abusers of society who have left dark and cruel imprints on society [29, 30].

D1. Capacity to enact and play out all the steps to achieve vile and destructive goals against a targeted population. Capacity and predisposition to eliminate anybody perceived as a threat to the realization of their goals. Firm commitment to the goals and their fulfillment by all (just or unjust) means. Initially, there is total indifference to others; they are considered dispensable and incidental to the goals. These goals are of grave importance for the individual at that current snapshot of time. When the effects of others are perceived to be harmful, then they are blocked or cancelled as much as possible.

D2. Capacity to practice precise, clear, and focused thinking on localized goals by using the tactics in D1. In addition, when directed upon the origin, nature, and the validation of localized goals, enhancement and reconstruction of the local goals are greatly facilitated. The practice of D2 in one direction will also lead to the realization of vile goals in other directions, leading to a general strategy of negative wisdom.

D3. Capacity to practice the highest level of reasoning, logic, and association to analyze the steps in realizing the vile goals and to enhance, refine, and reconstruct them. The complementary capacity of reasoning, logic, and association to analyze other people to suppress, deter and eliminate others if they are seen as a potential threat to the achievement of their goals. Sometimes, flawed strategies can cause serious problems in the derivation of an overall goal directed toward self-interest thus containing the extent of damage inflicted.

D4. Capacity to seek out simple local cause–effect and cause(i)–effect(j) relationships or combinations thereof. Capacity to concentrate with great precision on the immediate or prolonged chain of goals to maximize pofit and self-interests in any setting of a bounded situation or event. Capacity to "see" through feedback and feed forward to destabilize others who are perceived as a block in achieving wealth, power, or political gains. The capacity to concentrate on the present time and place to produce an immediate and lasting personal gains in any situation.

D5. Capacity to integrate and differentiate local causes (or components) in the underlying use of power, coercion, and unjust or illegal means to achieve the selfish goals in the local setting. Capacity to identify and enforce injustice, disservice, and social, moral and ethical corruption. Capacity to enhance the potential use of violence and injustice to achieve one's objectives with brutal indifference to others.

These traits D1–D5 demand unusual insensitivity in human beings. Suffice it to say that one lifetime and one personality may not be sufficient to become that great a great criminal. However, any one of the traits practiced at the highest level for a long enough time can lead to a type D person. Furthermore, a type D team working in conjunction with a wisdom machine primed with knowledge bases of collective consciousness of type D persons (criminals and thugs) can lead to a Mafia (type D) type of organization. The databases (D-WAB) are primed from the lives of all the greatest criminals who have lived on earth.

14.7.2 (Derivations of) Statements of Negative Wisdom

Like human beings, a wisdom machine can also be coerced into negativity and balefulness. Much as a tyrant king can force his authority when he takes over the reigns of a kingdom or nation, human teams can remains dominant over the wisdom bases in the machine. The wisdom machine (at levels I and II, see Figure 10.4) is configured to remain subservient to the ultimate authority of the humans (at level III, see Figure 10.5)

The realization of wisdom by a human–machine team is achievable with some degree of confidence because the abusers have some expected (type C, type C/D, type D/C and/or type D) bent[1] of mind and the machines have programmed software modules. It starts to become clear that the abusers of the wisdom machine (Chapter 10) can be assisted by their own wisdom bases (WBs). This scenario is becoming popular when we see members of the Mafia carrying their own laptop computers to the courtroom.

Figure 14.3 is a diagram of the sequence of functionalities that can be expected from the human counterpart of the machine. The two ellipses portray the type C and type D attitudes in human beings. Both attitudes are distinctly feasible though not universally acceptable. In the endeavor of crime and cruelty, human attitudes play a unique role. To accommodate the wide range of such attitudes, the two ellipses in Figure 14.3 are portrayed to indicate that abusers can be tyrant kings and leaders (at one extreme of the thought process) or be pragmatic members of Mafia and thugs (at the other extreme of the abuse of the wisdom machine).

The situation can be addressed by having an admixture of type C and type D traits. When the abuser team displays a tyrant perspective, the wisdom machine will supplement a set of accumulated wisdom (i.e., an expert systems knowledge base) from tyrant kings of the past. This accumulated wisdom is tentatively stored in a

---

[1] In reality the combination of negative traits can be highly variable. Types such as C_iD_j (C1,C2,D3,C4,C5; $C_xD_yC_z$ or D_l,C_m,D_n, etc.) are all feasible. In fact, the trait map can start to look like a genome map.

wisdom base, WB-C. Conversely, when the human team displays a pragmatic criminal perspective, the wisdom machine will supplement a set of accumulated wisdom (i.e., an expert systems knowledge base) from scientists of the past. This accumulated wisdom is tentatively stored in a wisdom base, WB-D. Two more converse modes are possible. The first mode occurs if the operation of the wisdom machine is to be complementary to the abuser team with a tyrant predisposition. The second mode occurs if the operation of the machine is to be complementary to the human team with a pragmatic criminal predisposition.

14.7.3 Flavors of Negative Wisdom

The two negative wisdom bases (WB-C and WB-D) derived are from the strategies of the tyrant kings (type C) and of pragmatic criminals (type D). These bases can either supplement or complement a current group of abusers of the wisdom machine who can have a tyrant (Tr.) or a pragmatic criminal (Prag.) predisposition.

Four vectors of forces (strategies from WB-C and WB-D derived from strategies of prior generations of tyrant kings, or pragmatic criminals together with the two predispositions of the current abusers) guide the outcome of the abuse of the wisdom machine. This leads to four scenarios shown in Figure 14.4. The human–machine team of any wisdom machine can invoke responses from the machine that either complements (C) the thought processes of the users or supplements (S) the thought processes. The two knowledge bases can also be labeled as Tyr. or Prag., depending on the nature of the strategies in these two knowledge bases.

14.7.4 Chaos and Fractals of Negative Wisdom

As much as the symphony of positive wisdom is possible, the clamor of negative wisdom is also plausible. If a WM has been abused by warmongers (type C)/ local thugs (type D) over a long period of time, then negative wisdom bases (WB-C and WB-D) get accumulated and reinforced. The entire process of the tainted human–machine interaction goes on in an bizarre sense of harmony. The entire orientation of positive and negative is conveniently switched to suit the personalities of the type C and type D individuals in a bizarre society.

14.7.5 Positive and Negative Modes of Wisdom

Positive and negative wisdom bring opposite social value structures to the processing of information and knowledge. Whereas wisdom is traditionally associated with positive values, negative wisdom is associated with negative values but retains the capacity to be intelligent, adaptive, and scientific about pursuing vile goals. In the current Internet age, intelligence, adaptation, and scientific approach is the forte of the networks, computers, and switches that constitute the Internet.

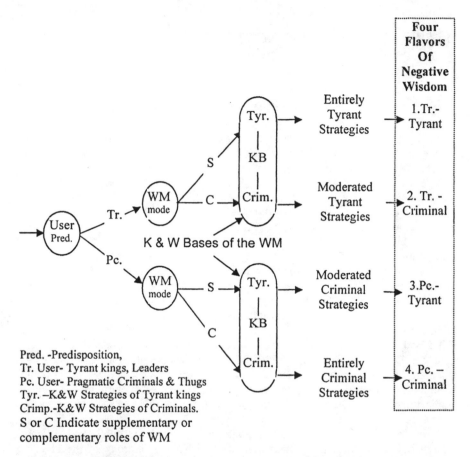

Figure 14.4 Representation of the four main databases of negative wisdom that can be primed into from any WM. In reality, the human creativity dominates this chart. Infinitely large numbers of flavors of balefulness are possible by altering the predispositions of the current users and/or slightly altering the gradations of the K&W base contents. In a sense, the resourceful and intelligent abuser still comes out in command of the situation offering more and more ways to be injurious and destructive.

Hence, the user maintains the option to derive positive or negative wisdom from the Internet or any special hierarchy of computers, networks, and knowledge bases that constitute a wisdom machine (see Chapter 10). The catalyst determining the use or abuse is the human element of intelligent Internets and the knowledge processing in the framework of the WM.

14.8 IKW&V BASE MANAGEMENT

14.8.1 Wisdom Base Management (WBM)

Knowledge bases (KBs) are relatively new but are becoming increasingly popular. Being relatively few, still evolving, and proprietary, the algorithms and techniques for knowledge base management systems (KBMSs) are not as popular as the database management systems (DBMSs). The knowledge bases provide logical and textual linkages between the objects stored in databases or object bases, in addition to storing basic information about the database or object entities. Objects and their attributes are structured in fixed or flexible formats.

Both information and the structural relationships between the pieces of information or the attributes of objects are retained for consistency and interoperability. Tight and compact structure provides efficient KB functions such as searches, comparisons, and evaluation of objects and/or attributes stored. When the run-length of entities such as object, attributes, or linkages, remains fixed, knowledge base functions become highly programmable.

In many instances, any subject matter is assigned a unique identifier number. This methodology is common in the Library of Congress (LoC) classification [31] and the Dewey Decimal System (DDS) classification [32] and used in most standard libraries. The electronic libraries deploy the knowledge base methodology with almost unlimited depth of search algorithms. Close identifier numbers indicate subject/logical linkage and can imply physical proximity of storage space on the massive storage facilities.

Most Internet knowledge bases are highly organized for quick and efficient searches. For instance, the IP network addressing is a hierarchy of the physical locations of servers and computer nodes accessible on the Internet. This standard makes the WWW addressing, switching, and access very straightforward and quick.

The store and retrieve functions are streamlined. In some cases, vendors of computer hardware and software assign LoC or DDS type numbers to their components and modules. It is more efficient however, to simplify the numbering system to the limited product range of the vendors. This type of simplification can lead to five- or six-digit identifier numbers for information pertaining to the products of a midsized computer vendor.

From a methodological perspective, the encoding of the location of information can be binary. For example, any leaf of a binary tree that is eight levels deep has a one-byte address. Such a binary search can lead to a track-sector address or an IP address where the information is stored, leading to the concept of indirect addressing of location of the information. Once the information is recovered, any extent of secondary processing/searching (conditional searching, comparison searching, inclusive/exclusive searching, etc.) can be accomplished. The principle of indirect addressing via the base sector of a computer memory was prevalent even in the IBM 360/370 computers during the 1960s and 1970s. The current DBMSs and KBMSs use a synergy of hardware designs and software algorithms to achieve remarkable speed in the functionality of data and information from DBs and KBs.

Software-encoded knowledge base operations are relatively straightforward and programmable. Such operations can be performed on most standard computers. In special cases where the size of data or information is massive and the access time is critical (such as providing intelligent network functions to Telco customers), specialized system designs exist. For example, the design of the service control point (SCP, see Section 3.4) calls for massive parallel processing at the front-end processors to decode the X.25 packets that arrive from the signaling network [33].

Hardware (such as knowledge processor unit, KPU) to accomplish generic knowledge machine instructions to process knowledge (such as machine instruction with a knowledge operation code (*Kopcode*) and objects as knowledge operands) does not exist yet. An architecture of the KPU is presented in Chapter 8 and in [34].

14.9 THE ECONOMICS OF IK&W

Information (I) , knowledge (K) and wisdom (W) blend seamlessly like the primary colors in light. In this section we apply the principles of the economics to exchange and utilization of information and knowledge. Unlike the wealth of individuals and nations, expending and utilizing information and knowledge do not deplete them. Instead, the immediate environment benefits from utilizing information and knowledge in a positive direction, or conversely, the environment suffers when information and knowledge are used in a negative direction. The original pool of information and knowledge is not depleted but requires enhancement to the information and knowledge banks to stay ahead in the knowledge game. Public information and knowledge are worthless and top-secret information and knowledge are priceless. To paraphrase Thorstein Veblen [35], the value of significant information also lies in its scarcity[2]. In reality, the situation is more complex because the value of information is not generated by the sale of information but by the depth of knowledge (understanding) that is derived from the information. In addition, the value of knowledge is not generated by the sale of knowledge but by the quality of wisdom that is derived from the knowledge.

---

[2] Veblen is credited as the founder of the "scarcity theory" of value by affirming a direct relationship between the scarcity and value. Thorstein Veblen wrote the Article, "Imperial Germany and the Industrial Revolution," in 1935, and correlated the "scarcity of weapons" to the "defenseless distribution of settlements." In the twenty-first century, the correlation between "scarcity of knowledge" and the "defenseless masses of information-deprived societies" still exists. If knowledge and technology are used as weapons, then ignorant societies become the slaves.

Finally, the value of wisdom is not generated by the sale of wisdom (if it can be sold) but by the esteem of values[3] that is derived from the wisdom. It is our contention that individual and social values cannot be sold but they can become the (intellectual) joy and pride of most individuals and almost all nations, although we can foresee that it is possible to sell human values in the direst of needs and pride tumbles before a fall.

Computers and network systems process data, information, and knowledge. Databases, information servers, and knowledge centers are becoming key elements for all IT-based systems. As the processing becomes intricate and highly adaptive, the human intuition starts to outweigh artificial intelligence. Wisdom and values are still in the domain of human endeavor. The information and knowledge that machines and networks process enter the wisdom and value domain that humans cherish, thus enforcing a IKWV chain.

14.9.1 The (Shortened) IKWV Chain

Utilization of information and knowledge brings about changes in society. In capitalistic societies, the creation of wealth is based on the sale of goods and services. The cycle consists of production of marketable goods and services followed by the economic compensation for such sale of goods of provision of services. Thus a whole transaction ends in an exchange of goods or services for money. The cycle time can be quite short (e.g., a few minutes for a meal) or quite long (e.g., securing a fleet of airplanes). Such transactions are well bounded. In a sense, the positive utilization of information and knowledge is self-sustaining. Society survives by enhancing the satisfaction of the needs it has itself invented or by solving the problems that it has itself created.

The economics of information and knowledge starts to differ significantly from the economics of goods and materials because of the much longer time constants involved in dealing with the creation of an information, knowledge, wisdom and values (IKWV) chain and then the dispersion and utilization of this chain in society. The by-products of deployment of an IKWV chain alter the socioeconomic structure of individuals, societies, and nations. This is especially the case when there is no depletion in the deployment: the consequences are greatly beneficial for the positive IKWV chain and gravely grim for the negative IKWV chain.

The economic forces driving the IKWV chain may last for a few generations. The social and political stability is altered by the insidious nature of the chain (I$\rightarrow$K$\rightarrow$W$\rightarrow$V, in a recursive and reentrant mode) reaction. Used in a constructive fashion by the drivers, the chain is sustained and self-propagating. The progress or degeneration of society appears to be by-products of this long chain starting from basic information within society and ending as values for society. The long and

---

[3] All measures of value become significant. Financial implications, intellectual rewards, relationships between embedded objects, emotional joy and so on play a role in determining the value of an axiom of wisdom.

insidious nature of the IKWV chain can last for several major business cycles. The wisdom and values within society affect the nature and duration of business cycles. In a utopian knowledge society, the height of (economic) expansion and the depth of recession both are moderated. The wisdom starts to control overspending during the expansion phase and values would control fear during recessions. Both greed and fear are tempered by the wisdom and values evolved by the underlying knowledge and information that is driving society in the first place.

Used in a selfish and greedy fashion by the drivers, the chain is short-lived and the last two nodes of the chain (i.e., wisdom (W) and values (V)) are generally shortchanged. Information and knowledge are bought and sold for economic gain without regard to the social benefit or the social evil that they may bring. By and large, the positive and negative trends in any society are reflected in the dynamics of slow (forward and backward) oscillations of the IKWV chain.

When the information engines, knowledge distillers, wisdom machines and value builders are working in harmony, synchrony, and ethical accord, global computers and Internets catch a glimpse of human virtue and welfare in their knowledge processing units and routers and in their arithmetic logic units and switching systems. This utopia of the positive recycling of knowledge is a snapshot of perfection and the goal for all knowledge workers and their leaders. However, there is a dark side to the tainted and negative wisdom.

The response time of human beings to greed is quite short. Likewise, breakdowns for information engines, knowledge distillers, wisdom machines, or value builders can be frequent. Since the number of components that need to function consistently for the entire IKWV chain is very large, the probability of machines and human counterparts functioning in harmony, synchrony, and ethical accord starts to become small. With the current technology and space age components, it is as likely that the entire chain of machines and human beings will function without failure over the IKWV chain. It is expected that this chain may need many years before it will come with a comprehensive set of values for humankind to fulfill all the goals for a perfect society. However, an overall conceptual plan can be implemented with computers operating at accelerated internal cycle times and offering solutions within a few years. Two essential requirements are that the human beings do not become corrupt and hostile to a system that can complement their own thinking.

If positive wisdom that was derived from information and knowledge is reused in a positive context in the current usage of the WM, the benefits could be far reaching. Positive feedback leads to long sustained and stable societies. The converse is also true; if negative wisdom is reused in a negative context to inflict tyranny and suffering to humankind, this will lead to short lived and unstable societies. The science and mathematics dealing with the stability of systems [36] with positive and negative feedback and feed forward become applicable to the stability and oscillations of social systems and organizations. It appears that the WM will be able to use a heuristic approach to solving such social stability problems.

14.10 CONCLUSIONS

Peripherals, networks, databases used in corporate executive information systems and knowledge bases are expanding at an alarming rate in the current information-based society. The dramatic fall in the price to design specialized IC chips and customized chip-sets coupled with the cost of communicating high-speed data locally and globally has permitted society to enjoy an enhancement in the quality of life and literacy. A new mindset for the computer and communication designers to evolve systems that solve social and ethical problems will bring about a new era of behaviorally intelligent machines.

Wisdom machines will be able to offer practical guideline to enhance the core values within a society over many years. Wisdom machines and intelligent educational systems working in synergy to maintain stable values will be equivalent of Federal Reserve System and banks working in synergy to maintain a stable economy in a nation. The potential use of wisdom machine by human beings can be extrapolated from the current use of computer systems by students. Whereas the computer systems are tuned to solving technical and numerical problems in academia, the wisdom machine can solve personal and societal problems.

REFERENCES

[1] A. H. Maslow, A theory of human motivation, *Psychol. Rev,*.50: 370–396, 1943; See also George Norwood, Maslow's Hierarchy of Needs, http://www.connect.net/georgen/maslow.htm, June 1996, and A. H. Maslow, *Farther Reaches of Human Nature*, Viking Press, New York, 1993

[2] R. Bryce and M. Ivins, *Pipe Dreams: Greed, Ego, and the Death of Enron*, HarperCollins Canada / Public Affairs; 1st ed. 2002. See also B. Cruver, *Anatomy of Greed: The Unshredded Truth from an Enron Insider*, Carroll Graf Publishers, 2002. See also P. A. Bernstein, What's wrong with Telecom, *IEEE Spectrum*, 26–29, Jan. 2003.

[3] J. Barnes (Ed.), *The Complete Works of Aristotle*, Vols. 1 and 2, Princeton University Press, Princeton, NJ 1995.

[4] C. Taylor, *Socrates,* Oxford University Press, Oxford, UK, 1999. See also H. H. Benson, *Essays in the Philosophy of Socrates*, Oxford University Press, Oxford, UK, 1992.

[5] J. Bankston, *Alexander Fleming and the Story of Penicillin,* Mitchell Lane Publishers, Hockessin, DE, 2001.

[6] M. Josphson, *Edison: A Biography*, John Wiley & Sons, ISBN 0471548065, Reprint 1992. See also C. Cramer, (Ed.) *Thomas Edison (People Who Made History)*, Greenhaven Press, San Diego, CA, 2001.

[7] E. S. Grosvenor and M. Wesson, *Alexander Graham Bell,* Harry N. Abrams, Inc., New York, 1997.

[8] M. J. Seifer, *Wizard: The Life and Times of Nikola Tesla: Biography of a Genius,* Citadel Press Book, New York, 1998.

[9] M. K. Gandhi, *Gandhi An Autobiography: The Story of My Experiments With Truth,* Beacon Press; Boston, MA, 1993.

[10] C. Carson *The Autobiography of Martin Luther King, Jr.,* Warner Books, New York, 2001.

[11] J. W. Shenk, *Lincoln's Melancholy: How Depression Challenged a President and Fueled His Greatness* Houghton Mifflin, New York, 2005.

[12] S. Bercholz and S. C. Kohn (Eds.), *The Buddha and His Teachings,* Shambhala, Boston, MA 2002.

[13] J. D. Pentecost, J. Danilson, *The Words and Works of Jesus Christ: A Study of the Life of Christ,* Zondervan 2000.

[14] J. E. Taylor, *The Immerser: John the Baptist Within Second Temple Judaism (Studying the Historical Jesus),* Wm. B. Eerdmans Publishing, 1997.

[15] H. Kissinger *A World Restored,* Weidenfeld & Nicholson, New York, 2000.

[16] K. Anan, *Annual Report on the Work of the Organization:* United Nations Publications, New York, 2001.

[17] H. A. March, and J. G. Simon, *Organizations,* Wiley, 1958. See also R. Cyert, and J. G. March, *A Behavioral Theory of the Firm,* Prentice Hall, Englewood Cliffs, NJ, 1963. See also H. A. Simon, A behavioral model of rational choice, *Q. J. Econ.,* **69**, 99–118, 1955.

[18] S. V. Ahamed and V. B. Lawrence, *The Art of Scientific Innovation: Cases of Classical Creativity.* Pearson Prentice Hall, 2004.

[19] A. Einstein, Preface in Where is Science Going? by Max Planck. Translation by J. Murphy, George Mien & Unwin Ltd., London, 1933.

[20] J. C. Maxwell, *Treatise on Electricity and Magnetism,* 3rd ed., Dover Publications, New York, 1991. See also Ref. 18 for the noteworthy contributions of scientists.

[21] J. Bardeen and W.H. Brattain, Application June 17, 1948 Three-electrode circuit utilizing semiconductive materials, U.S. Patent 2,524,035, 1950.

[22] A. L. Schawlow and C. H. Townes, Infrared and optical masers, *Phys. Rev.,* 112, 1940-1949, 1958.

[23] C. H. Townes and P. A. Miles, *Quantum Electronics and Coherent Light,* Academic Press, New York, 1964. See also C. H. Townes and A. L. Schawlow, *Microwave Spectroscopy* Dover Publications, New York, 1975.

[24] J. Toland, *Adolf Hitler: The Definitive Biography* Anchor, Wilmington, NC, 1991. See also, W. L. Shirer, *Rise and Fall of the Third Reich,* Simon & Schuster, New York, 1990.

[25] P. Constable and A. Valenzuela; *A Nation of Enemies: Chile Under Pinochet* W. W. Norton, New York, 1993.

[26] B. Magaš and I. Žanic, and F. Cass, Eds. *The War in Croatia and Bosnia-Herzegovina, 1991–1995,* Portland, OR, http://www.frankcass.com, 2001.

[27] M. E. Smith, *The Aztecs (Peoples of America),* 2nd ed., Blackwell Publishers, Cambridge, MA, 2002. See also P. Tierney, *The Highest Altar: The Story of Human Sacrifice,* Viking Adult, New York, 1989.

[28] G. Abbott, Execution: *The Guillotine, the Pendulum, the Thousand Cuts, the Spanish Donkey, and 66 Other Ways of Putting Someone to Death,* St. Martin's

Press New York, 2006. See also W. H. Carroll, *Guillotine & The Cross*, Christendom Press, Chicago, IL, 2004.

[29] F. R. Scarpitti, A. Nielsen and A. L. Nielsen, (Eds.) *Crime and Criminals: Contemporary and Classic Readings,* 4th ed., Roxbury Publishing Company 1999. See also D. C. Gibbons, *Society, Crime, and Criminal Behavior,* Prentice-Hall, Englewood Cliffs, NJ, 1982.

[30] J. Kobler, *Capone: The Life and World of Al Capone,* Da Capo Press, New York, 2003.

[31] J. Ganendran, *Learn Library of Congress Subject Access,* Scarecrow Press, Lanham, MD, 2000.

[32] M. Mortimer, *Learn Dewey Decimal Classification,* 21st ed., Scarecrow Press, Lanham, MD, 1999.

[33] S. V. Ahamed, and V. B. Lawrence, *Intelligent Multimedia Broadband Networks,* Kluwer Academic Publishers, Boston, 1997.

[34] S. V. Ahamed et al., Knowledge processing system employing confidence levels, U.S. Patent 5,809493, issued on Sept. 15, 1998, assigned to Lucent Technologies, Murray Hill, NJ.

[35] R. Tilman, (Ed.), *A Veblen Treasury. From Leisure Class to War, Peace and Capitalism,* M. E. Sharpe, Armonk, NY, 1993.

[36] H. Ozbay, *Introduction to Feedback Control Theory,* CRC Press, Boca Raton, 1999.

Chapter *15*

Looking Ahead:
Social and Ethical Implications

Computers have brought a scientific revolution to society. From kindergarten to the workplace computer facilities penetrate modern social settings. The computer revolution since the 1950s can be compared to the Industrial Revolution from 1750 to 1830. The passport to white-collar jobs has become computer proficiency and fluency of computer languages. The key to four-window offices bears the inscription of the cardinal knowledge of global financial markets working off computers and networks.

Networks have brought an information revolution to society since the advent of the *T1* line (or carrier systems [1]) since the early 1960s. From high schools to boardrooms, the availability of critical and time-sensitive information has become paramount. Networks facilitate the distribution of this critical information at marginal cost. Scarcity also determines the cost. Most of the public domain information is available at the cost of an Internet connection.

Intelligent networks have facilitated almost every type of (information) service to the customers and corporations that can pay for the services. The concept of introducing service control points [1] within the networks that routinely perform switching functions enables IN services to be provided at a minimal/marginal cost. Intelligent networks have evolved into third- and fourth-generation INs since the early 1970s.

Fiber optic and broadband networks have enabled global access of prime, sophisticated and detailed information for every desktop since the late 1970s. The development of compound semiconductors [2], laser sources, dense wave division multiplexers/demultiplexers [2], and passive optical switches has brought down the cost of optical transmission so much that the capacity of the global information highways is grossly underutilized.

The Internet has brought a cultural revolution to most households. The synergy of numerous technologies of the last few decades now makes the skilled Internet children more knowledgeable than teachers and parents. The reminiscent effect of this most recent change is loss of respect for wisdom and ethics. In prior generations, society and culture has inculcated a sense of right and wrong. In essence, the purpose of this book is to make the machines and networks themselves "artificially wise" and "socially ethical." We presented some of those concepts in Part III of the book.

A knowledge society differs significantly from an industrial society. The laws of economics that deal with information, knowledge, and maturity (wisdom) start to deviate from the laws of microeconomics based on utility theory (Marshall's laws) or the laws of macroeconomics based on Keynesian formulations. However, the economics of knowledge deals with the value of scarce and cardinal information (resource) and its use and deployment for building a personal and national power base. The laws of scarcity (derived from the writings of Thorstein Veblen) start to become applicable in evaluating knowledge and its worth. Precise information at the right time and right place becomes more important than all the information at "any time, at any place." Transparency does not have value in knowledge economics. Once knowledge and information are in the public domain, they start to lose value. A hierarchy of knowledge starts to emerge and is evolved in Chapter 12 and depicted in Figure 12.5. Axioms of wisdom are shown at the top and seminal and cardinal information are at the lower levels. Whereas seminal and cardinal information can be squandered (like VLSI technology), axioms of wisdom (like binary arithmetic and Boolean algebra) retain significance over a long period of time. The human counterpart of wisdom machine presented in Chapter 10 and shown in Figure 10.4, selecting new axioms of wisdom to be added in a dictionary of wisdom.

Knowledge, concept and wisdom machines are likely to reinforce the impact of unprecedented technologies to solve the innermost human needs; that is to be able to use computers, networks, intelligence, and global connectivity to provide *valid and wise* information to all users from children to critical decision makers, and thus provide a better society for every distant global community. The accumulated knowledge, concept, and axiom bases through the knowledge trail should be able to provide answers to the highest of human needs— the search for truth (T), virtue (V) elegance and social justice (B for beauty) of Aristotle's ethics. It appears that nature in mysterious ways has solved the riddle and placed it before human beings to discover all three (T, V, and B). However, the path to discovery needs the most ingenious tools, techniques, and methodologies that a new breed of knowledge, concept and wisdom machines is likely to provide.

15.1 THE KNOWLEDGE TRAIL—

MIGRATION FROM BINARY DATA TO SOCIAL ETHICS

Scientific concepts are deduced from a chain of observation, accumulation, processing, grouping, hypothesizing, deducing, concluding, and generalizing. The cycle is iterated until the concepts become firm enough to be useful in the future. Confirming each step is a continuum of intellectual activity to retain or enhance the major conclusions. In tracking the steps in intellectual activity, certain key guidelines exist in the organization of computer systems. These approaches (e.g., graphing, branching, algorithms, and optimization, minimizing resource utilization) have been deployed in the past to streamline many generic processes. For the migration of machines and humans from raw data on the Internet and broadband networks to social ethics, we propose a simple six-node sequential process. In most cases, these concepts arise from the data that was observed in the first place. Since the path is final, long, and tedious, we propose, a simple "graph" approach with nodes and links to start *the knowledge trail.*

The initial configurations are quite simple but get progressively more complex. The concepts that humans deploy in resolving obscure problems also get more intricate. The processes leading human beings to any solution occupy a special place in the strategy for developing the overall migration path. The growth of complexity (from Figure 15.1 to 15.15) is faster than linear and likely to follow a geometric pattern if not an entirely exponential pattern.

The representation of the migration path by a "graph", or a series of graphs, enables highlighting and generalizing the migration trail with key nodes and links within the graph. Any patterns that repeat and get recursive can more easily be represented and later encoded as computer routines or as recursive processes. In establishing a path between the data domain and the ethical value structure of any given society, the crucial nodes are shown in Figure 15.1.

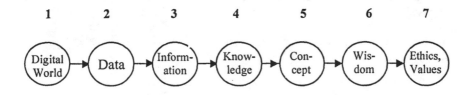

Figure 15.1 Progression of binary data from an entirely digital domain to the key concepts, wisdom, and ethical values in any given society. Seven nodes are shown with reality of digital data that flows through the networks on the left side and ethics on the right side.

The condition that prompts the movement from one node to next is that all the necessary and sufficient processing is complete at the previous node. Accuracy and confidence in the processes reinforce the transition. The process after any node involves iteration and affirmation that the parameters of the next node can be duplicated at a high enough level of confidence or total certainty. At the left side of Figure 15.1, the transformation rules are stringent and data can be accurately drawn from bits by following the rule for structuring data. The rules for encoding the bits into data structures are also well documented for most scientific applications.

Bytes, words, hexadecimal, and ASC structures are accurately derived from bits much like pictures are derived from pixels, provided scanning and framing algorithms are in place. There is no limit to the complexity of encoding the bits to generate the data structures, and conversely there is no limit to the complexity of the decoders to replicate bits from data structures. The necessary and sufficient condition is that the syntactic rules of the code are accurately written and precisely followed at the encoder and the decoder.

Two basic strategies facilitate the solution of many complex scientific problems in the computational domain. First, the symbolic representation of objects is classified as binary, floating point, exponential, complex, graphical, and so on entities or some complex data structures. Second, the algebra of relationships between objects is symbolized as computer processes, such as $+$, $-$, $\times$, $/$, logical operations (.OR., .EXOR., .NOR., etc.), and graphical operations (MOVE, ROTATE, SLANT, COLOR, etc.), lumped as numeric operations and logical processes that are machine executable hardware operations or software macros. Trigonometric object operations, series expansions, complex matrix operations, Fourier transformations, animations, and graphical transformations, all fall within the realm of legitimate processes on specific and predetermined object/variable sets.

Representing objects by symbols, their relationships start to become progressively fuzzy toward the right side of Figure 15.1. The symbols for representation and the transformations of symbols from data to information, information to knowledge, knowledge to concepts, concepts to wisdom, and wisdom to ethical values are neither completely investigated, documented nor processed by well established and universal scientific rules. In essence, the movement from knowledge to wisdom (on the right side of Figure 15.1) is fuzzier than the fuzzy movement of binary bits to data structures (on the left side of Figure 15.1) one century earlier.

15.1.1 Flexible Representation of Objects

However, there are *two* feasible approaches. First, the generic definition of an object and its attributes can be expanded (by the initial declaration statement) to suit the entity being processed. For example, if a book is being processed, then the data structure for this object will be declared to have 20, 30 or 100 (depending on accuracy of its representation) attributes starting from its ISBN and LoC call number, author(s), and so on to the number of words[1] or the words themselves. A truncated representation is traditionally used in storing the statistics (social security numbers with vital statistics in hospitals, social security numbers for taxpayers, etc.) of human beings depending on the application. However, a table look to a database (a typical SCP function [1]) will provide other detailed statistics if they are necessary. In the processing of knowledge, the application is uncertain. The context-dependent look up pointer will solve the immediate problem of object space allocation in knowledge processing environments.

Second, the relationships between objects can also be situation or context dependent. For this reason, a set of syntactic rules that are germane to any particular situation are initially selected and then reiterated to find the best fit. In pattern recognition [3] problems, this approach is well deployed. For example, when an interaction (e.g., between two cells) is being investigated, the most common rules of interaction are investigated first (as being the most probable) and then the more obscure rules are investigated. In the processing of knowledge, it is suggested that the rules of an established AI approach (e.g., PR, ES, CV, intelligent sensing and feedback/feed forward corrective mechanisms) are used first and the improbable/obscure rules of interaction between objects are used later. This is an almost human way to proceed, when the rules of solution of problems are fuzzy or there is no good strategy for solution. A child while learning a new language also deploys this approach.

Initially, the "fuzzy" rules of representation of complex objects and a set of "probable" rules of interactions are used in the migration path from left to right in Figure 15.1. Rudimentary knowledge processing software can evolve even for the traditional computer hardware that currently processes numbers and objects. Unfortunately, we have not entered the software era for processing matrices (collectivities) of "objects." The KPU and its assembly-level knowledge software (KSW) are likely to evolve for the knowledge processing environments much like the early CPU hardware and its basic assembly-level programs.

15.1.2 Object Processing Along the Knowledge Trail

The seven-node path in Figure 15.1 is labeled as the knowledge trail since the knowledge node is the middle node. Processing any particular class of entities (e.g., numbers such as binary, floating point, double precision, complex) in the knowledge trail of Figure 15.1 become quite precise at the left side of the figure and becomes progressively fuzzy towards the right side. It becomes evident that the root node is the start of the path from "raw data" or the observation of the real

---

[1] Generally, the representation of a limited set of attributes (and their truncation) is desirable to facilitate quick processing. In scientific applications, we use this methodology without too much ado. For instance, if the GNP of a nation is computed in any econometric study, the value is approximated to the last million dollars rather than to the last penny. An acceptable extent of fuzziness is tolerated for the variable. For moving from left to right in Figure 15.1, it is proposed that objects be represented in a "reasonably accurate" way rather than a "totally accurate" way.

world. It probably terminates at some basic "truth," or a universal concept, such as the law of economics, law of marginal utility, law of conservation of mass and/or energy, relativity, or the principle of uncertainty that gave rise to the raw data observed as reality in the first place. The cycle time for the entire process can be microseconds or eons. In this situation, time is of no essence because data/knowledge banks integrate all the information available.

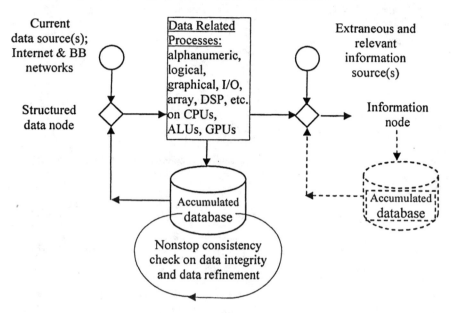

Figure 15.2 Key module in the path from data to information.

Reality as the starting point is consistent with the scientific basis of all information leading to knowledge. Current data pulled out of context can lead to suspicious information and flaky knowledge. However, consistently accumulated, classified, and organized "raw data" can be a good basis of valid information and sound knowledge. A simplified representation of the process between the two nodes (data to information) and one link process to progress from data to information is shown in Figure 15.2.

The migration from data to information involves accumulation, categorizing, classifying, labeling, and synthesizing the raw data. These machine executable processes and/or human activities become the link/edges of the graph. The raw data storage becomes the antecedent (parent) node and deduced information storage becomes the descendant (child) node.

It becomes feasible to generalize the steps and processes in the migration from any node (i) to the next node ($i + 1$). The link between the two nodes needs the programs or the hardware to process the inputs at the i-th node. In general, it is not sufficient to be able to process at the i-th node inputs; it is also necessary to cumulatively check the consistency of the prior processes (i.e., between node *1* through $(i - 1)$ in view of the process at the *i*-th node. Generally, this backward compatibility of processes is a requirement for almost all software revisions. For example, when the updated version of any software is released, the new version is made compatible with rules and files processed by earlier versions of the same or similar software.

In a sense, the progression of knowledge hinges on the adherence to the laws that have been used to generate prior (information or) knowledge. In certain special cases (such as the correction of Maxwell's equation because of Einstein's theory of relativity, or inclusion of Heisenberg's principle of uncertainty in the measurement of physical parameters, or quantum mechanics integration into wave propagation), the prior laws are modified rather than being rejected.

A diagrammatic representation of the movement of inputs from the *i*-th node to the $(i + 1)$st node is shown in Figure 15.3. Validity and consistency checks become essential to maintain accuracy and sanity in the processing and accumulation of bits, data, information, knowledge, concepts, wisdom, and social values at the seven nodes of Figure 15.1. The dashed loops in Figure 15.3 perform the checks and balances for the contents of the local bases at every node. The process becomes iterative and continuous because of the three possible inputs (the output of the prior node, accumulated contents from the same node, and extraneous and relevant contents from WWW; see three arrows into the switch and server platform in Figure 15.3) at each of seven nodes.

Reentrancy at the switch from its own database can make the process tedious at each node, and the return loops for the slight variation of an acceptable process at any one of the nodes can also lead to a ripple (or unstable feedback) effect through the entire system.

This type of instability in the system makes the processing on the right-hand side of Figure 15.1 increasingly demanding; however, with a sufficiently well organized operating system, the machine(s) can provide ample information, knowledge, concepts, and wisdom. Processing algorithms and capabilities for each node are consistent with the format and input into that particular node for the progression along the trail.

On the one hand, we have the universally accepted rules for bit manipulation (for arithmetic and logical operations being implemented as binary gate logic at node 1, Figure 15.1) and alphanumeric processing (including all byte, word, and structured variable representations and the associated algorithms and algebra at node 2 in Figure 15.1). Yet, on the other hand, rudimentary representation and manipulation of concepts (node 5, Figure 15.1) are not documented enough for a computer to assemble, process, verify, regenerate, and amend concepts on the trail to deriving wisdom from knowledge.

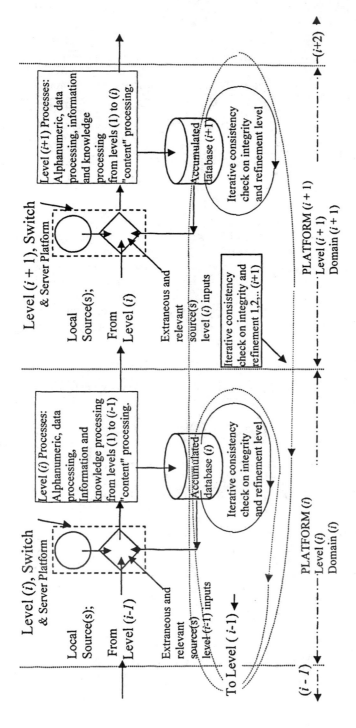

Figure 15.3 Domain migration pattern from level (i) domain (e.g., data, information, knowledge, concept) to level (i + 1) domain (e.g., information, knowledge, concept, wisdom). All the processing (e.g., data processing, information processing, knowledge processing, concept processing, wisdom processing) in the appropriate level becomes applicable to generate a platform (as shown in the Figure) to move from domain (i) to (i + 1). Inadequate processing in any domain (i) is likely to lead to a failure in domain (i + 1).

During the 1970s, lack of the open system interconnect (OSI) model had temporarily curtailed the interfacing of global digital networks. In the 1980s, a consorted effort by world bodies (reconstituted as the ITU) to resolve the protocol and interfacing issues at the (seven) OSI layers paved the way to global interconnections of computer and communication networks. The lack of such standardization (like the OSI Standards for all the global communication systems or the X.25 protocol for local packet-switched networks) makes processing more difficult and disorganized in the knowledge and wisdom domains. At an early stage of establishing the seven-node "graph," to move from raw data (node 1) on the Internet to ethics (node 7) in society, the lack of any standards for the implementation on machines appears to be an early barrier.

The strategy for the solution of the problem of establishing the path for migration for data on Internet to ethics in society becomes progressively cumbersome. For this reason, we suggest a universal and documented protocol for the flow of bits into data (node 2) all the way to the flow of wisdom into ethics (node 7). These nodes and levels are shown as a diagram in Figure 15.1 and in a hierarchical fashion in Figure 15.4. The hierarchy representation of the movement from bits to ethics and social values (Figure 15.1) can also be depicted in a vertical fashion with ethics and social values at the top of the pyramid.

The use of this vertical representation is to stress that the lower levels are subjugated to the higher levels in a progressive format; that is, processing at any level (i) has the potential and capacity to command processes at any of levels 1 through ($i - 1$) including checking for parity, error control, and consistency (as in the OSI model).

In comparing Figures 15.1 and 15.4, the seven nodes (Figure 15.1) correspond to levels <u>B</u> through <u>E</u> (Figure 15.4). In an effort to establish the knowledge model of Figures 15.1 and 15.4 as a practical and computational reality, we depict the migration and process trail in Figure 15.5. In this figure, the migration pattern from node 1 (Figure 15.1 or the <u>B</u>its level in Figure 15.4) to node 7 (Figure 15.1 or <u>E</u>thics level in Figure 15.4) is interleaved with computational processes.

The hardware (HW), software (SW) and application programs (APP) aspects are depicted at each node. The computational tools as they exist at the lower level are emphasized. The processing as it already exists for bit, data, and information environments to the projected processing for knowledge, concepts, and wisdom are shown. Knowledge processing environments are depicted but not built with sufficient skill, technology, and sophistication to make them as dependable as computers. However, it is our contention that such machines will process knowledge, concepts, and wisdom to move societies and civilizations forward just as computers and communication systems are currently moving the education, economy, and society forward.

Machines start to fail in the higher levels of functions, such as deriving knowledge from information or deriving concepts from knowledge. Over a period of maturity of the scientific processing at nodes I, K, C, and W, these processes are more likely to become machine functions gradually as the AI tools and techniques become more universal. The movement is likely to be as much of a breakthrough as data processing appeared to be in the 1940s.

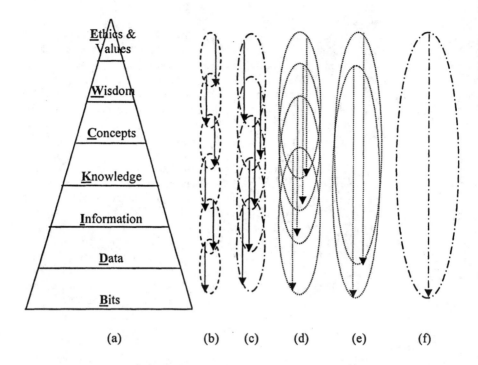

Figure 15.4 Vertical Integration of the BDI-K-CWE pyramid from binary bits to ethics and social values. Loops (b) through (f) indicate the downward compatibility of any higher level rules with the prior rules of the lower level(s). For instance, the rules in the Ethics and Values level (Layer 7) will be compatible and be validated by the rules in all the lower levels.

15.2 ROLE OF HUMANS

Gathering information is a raw instinct, just in case it may become valuable. Birds and animals do it for food and shelter. Curiosity and primitive intelligence tempted Stone Age humans, to search and gather strategies. In the information-rich society, human beings still search for gold mines and hidden treasures on the Internet. The role of human beings becomes evident in the early sensing of patterns in data, gathering of sensitive information or searching for clues.

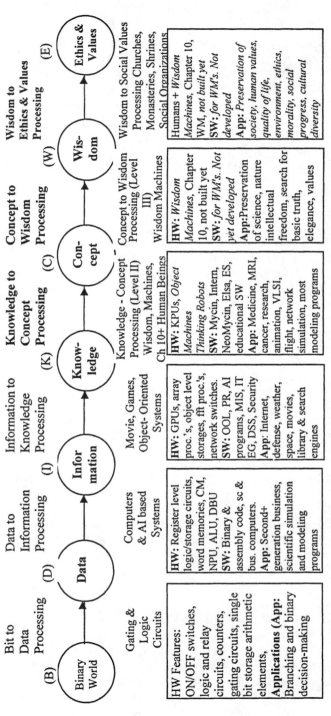

Figure 15.5 Migration pattern from level (B) domain (i.e., bits) to level (E) domain (i.e., ethics and social values). Processing as it already exists for bit, data and information environments to the projected processing for knowledge, concept, and wisdom are shown. The role of human beings starts to become crucial as the machines start to fail in the higher levels of functions, such as deriving knowledge from information or deriving concepts from knowledge. These processes are likely to become machine functions gradually as the AI tools and techniques become more dependable.

Willful data mining is now a deliberate search for information and we extend this willful search to knowledge, concepts, and wisdom. The willful searching of global knowledge banks for hidden concepts can be a deliberate and programmed activity. Similarly, the concepts in theoretical physics, pure mathematics, number and string theories, relativity, evolution can be deliberate and programmed activities, and so on.

15.2.1 Economic Basis of Human Search

A biological basis for the functioning of the body and mind starts to unfold at this level. The energy expended at the higher levels (like thinking) suddenly appears to be more economical to resolve the lower-level needs (such as food and shelter). The energy expended in the search and store activity in the human mind and senses is low in comparison to the expected gain in the physiological energy or safety by the knowledge gained from the expenditure of the mental energy.

The laws of microeconomics play a dominant role even in the rudimentary duties of life since early civilization. Survival being the most basic need would permit the search and store activity by all means, provided the marginal cost of search is low in relation to the expected gain from the search. In more recent times, exploring (rather than searching) and investing (rather than storing) have become a positive side of social activity. Human as people are, the converse syndrome also prevails. Snooping (rather than searching) and hoarding (rather than storing) have become a downward side of social activity.

This pursuit of a potential or expected gain is a highly rewarding economic game. The expected marginal gain from the use of prior information (already stored in knowledge and databases) can be far in excess of the cost of the marginal energy expended in gathering and tagging the information. If the intent of this search and store activity in modern days is not defined early enough, the abuse of information and knowledge lurks as a danger in society. Such incidents have been repeated numerous times in recent history. Nuclear research has produced nuclear bombs, new drugs have brought on addiction, disgruntled software designers have implanted computer viruses, genetic research can cause cancer in cattle. As history has documented, even if the intent is genuine, the final use can well be an abuse. One way to circumvent the problem is to reinforce the positive aspects throughout the entire BDI-K-CWE trail in all human beings.

15.2.2 Conflictive Directions of Human Role

The human role becomes crucial in the BDI-K-CWE trail. Human beings drive machines, define the purpose, write the software, and hold the intent of the use of machine output(s). For example, a satellite can be launched as accurately for tracking weather and storms as it can launched for spying and guiding missile attacks. As an additional example, a robot will serve as a production agent (in VLSI facility) or as a killer agent (on a battlefield). After all machines are mindless slaves and agents of humans. At any node in the trail (Figure 15.4), human intent alone holds the clue for eventual use for the output of that node. Processing of data (D node) to explore (scientific truth) or to snoop (user activity), to gather information (I node) and to use (facilitating dialog) or abuse (create animosity), to infer knowledge (K node) and to facilitate welfare (share tsunami warning) or to deduce weakness (to kill and oppress), they all have become suddenly feasible with the synergy of programmable techniques for computation, broadband networks and WWW- based Internet for communication. In a probabilistic sense, both directions of movement are equally possible. Positive or negative intelligence (embedded in the human mind and embedded by humans in machines) facilitates social progress or hastens social decay. The syndrome becomes crucial as the machines share crucial information with thugs, the Mafia, underworld and mindless leaders.

The human counterpart at any node (i) in Figure 15.4 has the capacity to direct the vector of movement to the node ($i + 1$). Poorly designed machines (model-T cars) and well-intentioned humans (Henry Ford) can bring enormous benefits to society (1920s). Conversely, well-designed machines (and inventions) and ill intentioned operators[1] can drag society to death just like well-engineered cars can kill the driver and the occupants in a deadly crash. The power of a human being to instantly override the collective wisdom of decades can suddenly lead a nation to an ill-conceived war. In essence, unexpected behavior/error on the part of human beings can turn a highly scientific project into a deadly project (Bhopal disaster, India; Three-Mile Island nuclear spill, United States; Chernobyl nuclear accident, Russia).

15.3 HUMAN DISCRETION: PROPHETS OR PLUNDERERS

In the evolution of machines, the biggest unknown is human indiscretion toward creativity. Positive inventions are as feasible as negative inventions. In the recent evolution of humankind, the greatest unknown is the new creed of inventions and breakthrough machines. Though humans and machines are cyclic in interdependence, the human being still drives the cycle. Historically, constructive and destructive machines have been built and rebuilt. Inventions start out being positive, well intentioned, and beneficial to society; society thrives beyond its natural limits; competition for resources creates new negative intentions; inventions start to become negative and destructive against (the "other") society. The conflictive societies and their (constructive and destructive) inventions both survive in a delicate balance for some time longer.

---

[1] History has many instances from the recent past such as flying jumbo 747s into the World Trade Centers on September 11, 2001, bombing of bystanders, children's hospitals, and national infrastructures; Eron, Global Crossing, and Tyco executives siphoning corporate funds into private accounts.

15.3.1 Human, Still the Unknown

The unknown is still the human being because of the tendency to flip-flop. Early humans resorted to fighting or fleeing; modern human resort to love or hate. Many attitudes are changed at the drop of a hat. In the absence of certainty, some human beings resort to a sudden change of attitude and the instability arises due to the duality of human nature. Unable to hold a steady course on a long path, sometimes pious people can turn savage. Holy wars offer as much contradiction as an insane saint. Scientists can turn against other scientists. Savage leaders can show very human feeling. To this extent history is full of documented facts.

In reaction to fear and insecurity bombs are dropped on the innocent rather than penalizing the culprits. A flip-flop of attitude can deploy positive knowledge with negative wisdom, or positive wisdom for a negative concept, and so on. It needs a true saint to do the opposite, that is, to move over to a positive realm from a negative domain and sustain the positive self-drive with the positive social drive. Some notable examples prevail in history. Buddha after every type of worldly indulgence founded Buddhism. Ashoka after the brutal Kalinga war[2] embraced nonviolence and Buddhism.

In the realm of human consciousness, rationality is controversial and nonprogrammable. However, over a period of time, emotions are filtered out of rationality and it is laid down as laws of behavioral logic or rules of adaptation. At the present time, when such laws of human rationality are not totally written down for every discipline, some rules are better articulated than others. Even though the laws may be unwritten as certainties, they are probabilistic in nature. For this reason, we suggest that a probability be assigned to each operation at the I, K, C, W, and E nodes in Figure 15.5. This approach has been successfully used in Mycin, Intern, and NeoMycin [4].

15.3.2. Machine, Still the Mindless

In the realm of machines, laws of logic or mathematics define rationality. Rationality becomes a prerequisite to mechanized choice. However, it is implied that rationality is universal for every situation in which the machine executes a

---

[2] It is easy to picture him (Ashoka) walking the still smoking battlefields saying to himself: "Ah, so this is what I mustn't do. Now that I have done it, I know it. These are the dead. These are the wounded. This is suffering. These are the fruits of my actions. This is the result of the failure of Kingship."

"The conquest is no conquest, for there was killing, death (and) banishment of the people. Injury or death or deportation of beloved relations may happen. This may befall all men. There is no part of the world where (the effects of my orders are not felt.) Nor is there any part of any country where there is any individual who is not attached to one form of religion or another. All beings should be left unhurt, should have equal (impartial) treatment and should lead happy lives. The only true conquest is conquest by Dharma. Let (us) not think that conquests by the sword merit the name of conquest. Let (us) see (our) ruin, confusion, and violence."

(Extract taken from http:/www.katinkahesselink/Tibet/asoka3.html)

program. In processing numbers and physical entities, the laws of logic or mathematics are written, accepted, and well documented. These laws are rigid and applicable in the context of the solutions for most scientific, physical, or engineering problems that the machine is simulating. After the solution, the initial conditions and the final conditions of the physical entities are unaffected by the solution of the particular problem. In most cases, the properties of the physical entities are not modified by the solution.

In processing information and knowledge, the social, economic and optimization laws that are applicable to the objects embedded in the information or knowledge are ill defined. The solution is not attempted for a stand-alone problem, but it is attempted for the web of interrelated objects and their interwoven attributes. The global perspective of the problem can alter the solution significantly. Humans are better equipped to tackle the solution at a more universal and global level. Hence, the mundane and lower level rationality is better handled at the machine level and the global optimality (especially for complex objects) is better handled by the human being. For this reason, we have proposed a three level architecture for the wisdom machine in Chapter 10.

The admixture of human discretion to offer directionality for the processing of information and knowledge also brings bias and predispositions. The solution can lean toward positive or the negative over a period, even though it may appear neutral over a much shorter period. The imbalance of knowledge and wisdom can work for the better informed and wise. For this reason, we offer two venues (up and down) for the migration pattern for any node (i) to the next node ($i + 1$) in Figure 15.1. This pattern of migration is evident in Figures 15.6 to 15.14 along the knowledge trail.

Prior to the open information society, the balance of power thrived on an imbalance of knowledge and wisdom. In an open Internet age, bluffs and blahs are generally unsustainable. If a perfect balance can be found (with the help of knowledge processing systems and wisdom machines) then a new leap forward towards harmony and elegance is likely but without the circumstances that led to earlier conflicts for resources—selfishness, greed and ultimate chaos— if the human–machine system is not stabilized. Systemic movements in both (positive and negative) directions are equally feasible with the human being in control.

15.4 A NEW BDI-K-CWE TRAIL

The role of humans is implicit in the evolution trail shown in Figure 15.4 at two stages. First, the direction of the trajectory after any node can be willfully altered by humans and second, the process code can be willfully enhanced to provide results that the group of humans wishes to see. The first role is akin to a political pressure on to scientific process (e.g., nuclear research) and the next role is akin to tampering with the code to alter the composition of (positive or negative) results (as in the case of news reporting).

15.4.1 A Simplified Graph Representation

From an immediate perspective, bits, data, information, knowledge, and so on serve some well-defined purpose such as banking, trade, commerce, or IT. This corresponds to the routine use of computers and networks in modern society. From a slightly distant perspective, the two sides of human nature start to surface: the constructive and the destructive.

It becomes realistic for humans to evolve machines that facilitate activities leaning towards longer lasting ethical purposes (e.g., medicine, education, commerce) or leaning toward destruction (e.g., terrorism, violence, crime) in the social fabric of society. With accurate sensing (over long periods of time), of the *incremental gradients* of the movement in the BDI-K-CWE trail, wisdom machines (at node 6 in Figure 15.1) can warn human beings of the danger of any downward trend and/or enlighten human beings of the potential benefits from the positive trend bringing prosperity to humankind. In fact, the wisdom machine (node 6) serves as a social barometer, analyzing the flow of information in the high-speed networks and the Internet.

Humans have a duality of nature: they can be constructive or destructive. This duality of humans who eventually control machines is not shown in Figure 15.4 or in Figure 15.5 and to this extent the figures are incomplete. More than that, the tendency of humans to flip-flop is not totally binary. If the positive side has an array of prerequisites and the negative side also has an array of opposite prerequisites, then a gradual (and almost imperceptible) slippage can occur rather than a total flip-flop. The process becomes a slow-moving matrix trace rather than an inversion. Unfortunately, the mathematical tools to track an instantaneous slippage of human tendencies do not exist at this time, but a graphical depiction is possible.

We start the diagram for humans and machines as a simplistic pattern in Figure 15.6. The diagram gets enhanced to include the dual-minded human beings who can change course midstream after any of the nodes or during the transition from one node to the next by altering the rules of processing for the output of the node (i) as it moves to the input of the node ($i + 1$) in Figure 15.3.

The inception of this graph is founded in flow of binary data over the networks and Internet, on the left-hand side. The binary nature of bits makes representation and manipulation simpler for machines to process and makes logic and programming easy for humans. To deal with the reality of machines of the current era, the binary bits (see Figure 15.6) are assumed to be the initial node of the current BDI-K-CWE trail. The content at the output of each node (D through E) is blended by external databases, Internet content, network traffic, prior databases, and so on and processed by the programs appropriate to the content (e.g., data processing programs for data, object processing programs for objects, knowledge processing programs for knowledge and so on).

Much as operands undergo an operation code (OPC) in a typical CPU environment, the array of contents at the output of each node undergoes an operation, a process, a program, or a application. These operations, processes, programs and applications transform data to information, information to knowledge, knowledge to concept, and so on. At the present time, it appears that only the binary to data, data to information processing, object processing, and graphical manipulations are firmly established in computer science.

The completed graph for Figure 15.6 is a much more complicated configuration. Even the concept of a binary flip-flop makes the graph appear with D+ to I−, D− to I+, I+ to K−, and so on. If dual stage hopping (i.e., D+ to K−, D− to K+, etc.) is permitted, then many more links appear between the nodes of the graph. Forward and backward linking makes the diagram even more complex. Asymmetric hops imply different energies for moving forward and backward. We do not show these graph forms but they can be extrapolated from the graph shown in the figure.

15.4.2 Movement from Node (i) to Node ($i + 1$)

In Figure 15.6, there are seven nodes. The pattern of movement from any node (i) to the next node ($i + 1$) can be generalized. There is considerable similarity in the approach in the progression of knowledge and science, in building one computer platform after an earlier one, or even in introducing one computer language after an earlier version (e.g., FORTRAN V after FORTRAN IV, C+ after C, C++ after C+).

When sufficient expertise is gathered in processing at each of the seven nodes (B through E), under the current rules of compilation, a more generic, powerful, and encompassing format is conceived or invented for the nodes I, K, C,W, and E. Backward compatibility is generally adhered and sometimes abandoned in light of a breakthrough process, technology or invention. In applying these guidelines to machines for processing information, knowledge, concepts, wisdom, and ethical/social values, the generic migratory path from any node (i) to next node ($i + 1$) is extrapolated and shown in Figure 15.7.

The role of human beings for content processing becomes evident and assumes a role similar to OPC on operands. From a macroscopic perspective, the contents of the databases at each of the nodes become the operands and the human control by using the appropriate programs or applications becomes the OPC. Globally, the human beings retain all the control by providing the access to the correct data and content bases and again by choosing the most appropriate programs/ applications to process the contents.

The platform for the next-generation computers to process information, knowledge, concepts, or wisdom starts at platform (i) in Figure 15.6. The content (full lines) can come from all the databases of prior domains and from all sources including Internet, WWW, knowledge bases, broadband and digital networks, and library databases. It is important that the content satisfy the processing capability of content at that particular node.

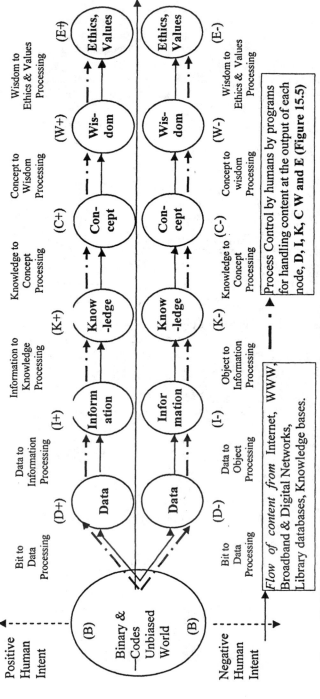

Figure 15.6 Migration pattern from level (B) domain (i.e., bits) to level (E) domain (i.e., ethics & social values) under the control of human beings. Processing as it already exists for bits, data, and information environments to the projected processing for knowledge, concept and wisdom can be used or abused. The role of human beings starts to become dominant as machines need programs and intelligent-knowledgeware (IKW) for deriving knowledge from information or deriving concepts from knowledge. The contents of databases that support each of the nodes in the BDI-K-CWE trail are likely to get tainted by the intent of the human teams that monitor the machines.

For example if graphics/Internet objects are a part of the content, then the program should be able to handle these objects (e.g., Microsoft Word rather than Notepad). In the same vein, knowledge bases should be handled by knowledge processing systems like business data is handled by business processing systems, or like the personnel data files are handled by PeopleSoft or SAP programs.

The content that flows into any node (i) arrives from the platform of node ($i - 1$) and the accumulated database for node (i), and all authenticated sources of bases containing (i) type of contents. For example if the C node (Figure 15.6) is processing concepts pertaining to HIV, then all the concepts pertaining to every type of HIV and all general class of viruses will be drawn into the C node to process the generality of concepts as they pertain to HIV. An underlying concept is deduced with a given confidence and probability that it is universal, partially true, or locally true. Insufficient data leads to lower probability until there is no confidence in the derivation of any tentative hypothesis.

In order to reduce the complexity of the entire seven-node transition (B→D→I→K→C→W→E) trail in Figure 15.6, the B and C nodes are tentatively removed from Figure 15.8. The diagram now has five nodes. The representation for each node removed is akin to the nodes represented in Figure 15.7 and they can be readily inserted in Figure 15.8. Two arrows show the role of human beings from each of the four D, I, K, and W platforms.

The human role is not uniform or standardized. The role can be discretionary and it can fluctuate from being constructive and benign (snooping) to actively harmful and disruptive. Well-intentioned data and knowledge bases can be abused over a period of time. The converse is also possible: the ill-intentioned bases can be reused in a positive light. However, the human role is generally long drawn and it can get protracted from one administration to the next. Change can be so gradual that it goes unnoticed by human observers.

The nodes (D, I, K, W, and E) are depicted as + and − to indicate that data and codes on the Internet and backbone networks depend on the discretion and intent of human beings. Security and encryption can temporarily protect the data and codes from the general public, hackers, and abusers. This measure is well used by the corporate and government agencies. However, the data already accumulated in declassified knowledge banks can be abused. The only barriers are the human wisdom, social values, and etiquette. As the norm of abusers and hackers starts to slide down the negative side, the decline is likely to be cataclysmic. As documented during the last decade, corporate crimes, information and knowledge abuse, and human greed have been on the upswing.

15.4.3 Charting of the Knowledge Trail

Movement along the knowledge or B→D→I→K→C→W→E trail is a time-intensive process. By placing the seven nodes along the X-axis, we can represent the migration path. Being time intensive, it also carries the time axis T.

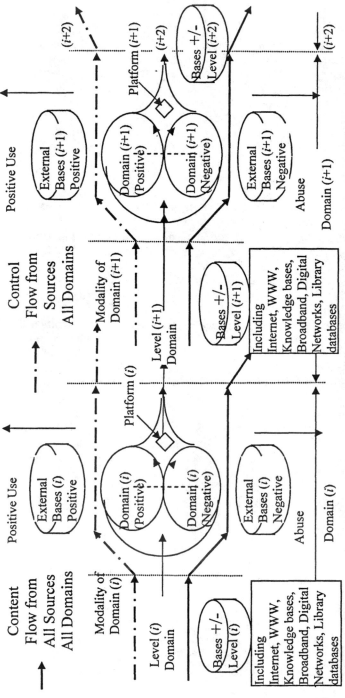

Figure 15.7 Domain migration pattern from level (i) domain (e.g., information) to level (i + 1) domain (e.g., knowledge) under the control of human beings. The content flows from attitudes and temperaments (dashed dark lines) of human beings who command the machines and sources of the content. It is interesting to note that without human control, there would be chaos in the networks and machines.

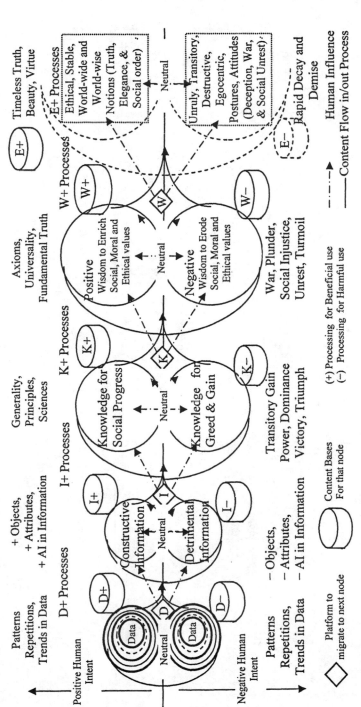

Figure 15.8 Diagram for migration along the B→D→I→K→C→W→E trail with B and C nodes removed. The human being influences the direction of movement (+ to +, + to −, − to −, − to +, or − to −) from node to node and within the nodal processing. Note the similarity in seven-level transition diagrams of human behavior shown in Figures 13.9–15, suggesting that machines have evolved in a pattern to solve the simplest to the most complex of human and social needs.

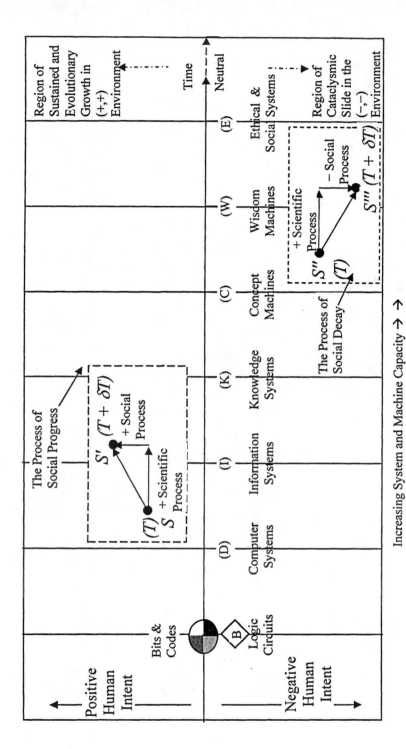

Figure 15.9 Snapshot of movement along the knowledge trail with positive and negative human interference.

The Y-axis has positive and negative propensities of human use/abuse for the content bases at the seven nodes. Such a propensity can be labeled human intent.

The XY (Figure 15.9) plane now carries significant relationships. Around the X-axis the migration path remains neutral and gets driven by the scientific, information, and knowledge processes. Around any vertical line the forward migratory path get temporarily frozen but the contents of the nodes get used for enriching (by scientists, social workers, doctors, musicians, artists, etc.) society or depleting (by corrupt leaders, corporate executives, Mafia members, thugs, etc.) society. Every point in this XY plane represents the status of society at any given time. The X coordinate represents the stage of the current technology along the migration path and the Y coordinate represents the current aggregate human intensity to use/abuse the contents of the bases at the current and prior nodes.

The XY (migration path along knowledge trail (X direction); human intent (Y direction)) diagram, shown in Figure 15.9 is also indicative of the instantaneous movements (jitters) of any point S that the aggregate society occupies at any time T. If the movement of point S to S' takes δT^4, then the rate of change of momentum of the point S in the X direction depends on aggregate (and integrated) *scientific/intellectual/technological pressures* systems designers of the knowledge trail. The rate of change of momentum of the point S in the Y direction depends on aggregate (and integrated) *social/educational/government pressures* on systems designers of the knowledge trail. The propensity is much like a vector force or a pressure with magnitude and direction.

Any point S also has a history of how society arrived at that point. Over a period of time (0–T) two vector forces (scientific (X-axis) and social (Y-axis) pressures)) on society made the migration to point S possible. This integrated effect of the two pressures over millennia explains the status of different nations in the information age and knowledge societies.

---

[4] δT should be measured on a suitable time scale. This duration can vary from seconds to centuries. When the human propensity for change is low (like periods of slow growth, low innovation and static societies), the time scale can range from years to decades. When the human propensity for change is high (like industrial or French revolutions, wars, national emergencies) the time scale can be short, thus generating new machines for that particular purpose. Examples prevail in history. For example, vaccines, antibiotics, industrial robots, the aircraft industry, Cray machines, and encryption on the positive side have evolved quickly. Computer bugs, viruses, dynamite, nuclear bombs, battlefield robots on the negative side have also evolved relatively quickly and efficiently. As an extreme case, δT can last for a few seconds when a new invention is conceived or a new lyric is written on the positive side or a new bombing strategy is formulated on the negative side.

The product of scientific[5] inertia of a society and the short-term velocity of movement at S in the X direction offers the scientific momentum of society. The product of social[6] inertia of a society and the short-term velocity of movement at S in the Y direction offers the social momentum of society. Stated symbolically, the two analogous equations are written

$$Momentum_{\text{scientific}} = Inertia_{\text{(scientific/intellectual/technological)}} \cdot dx/dt \qquad (15.1)$$

$$Momentum_{\text{social}} = Inertia_{\text{(social /educational/government)}} \cdot dy/dt \qquad (15.2)$$

The two directions for movement (scientific and social) are treated as orthogonal on a short-term basis. Over a longer term, the overlap starts to become dominant. The cumulative effect of a scientific, intellectual, and technological society is also likely to be orient toward a higher degree of social, educational, and government activities. In effect, when long-term movements in the XY plane are considered, the different societies of the world need to be located in different regions of the XY plane. Each region would have its own specific inertia(s) to change. Even though the equations would show the effects of scientific and social pressures, the mass(es) and inertia(s) need to be evaluated on a region-to-region, society-to-society, and culture-to-culture basis.

Differentiating equations (15.1) and (15.2), we have

$$Scientific_{\text{pressure}} = (Inertia/mass_{\text{scientific}}) \cdot (x\text{-}acceleration = d^2x/dt^2) \qquad (15.3)$$

$$Social_{\text{pressure}} = (Inertia/mass_{\text{social}}) \cdot (y\text{-}acceleration = d^2y/dt^2) \qquad (15.4)$$

Stated in the vector notation, the equations (3) and (4) can by written as

$$\overrightarrow{PR} = (I/M) \cdot \overrightarrow{Acceleration}$$

where the PR vector is the aggregate pressure on designers and (I/M) is the scientific or social inertia to change.

It is interesting to note that the change can be positive or negative and depends on the human beings who surround and use the (knowledge, concept, and/or wisdom) machines with positive or negative intents for or against society. Even though measure of the pressure cannot be entirely numeric (as it is in the FPS or MKS systems), it is generally manifest as the amount of money and effort that are

---

[5] The inertia signifies the resistance of that particular society to changes in at least three directions, namely, *scientific/intellectual/technological*.

[6] The inertia signifies the resistance of that particular society to changes in at least three directions, namely, *social /educational/government*.

expended to effect a change. Although the measure for inertia/mass cannot be entirely numeric (as it is in the FPS or MKS systems), it is generally captured in the socioeconomic structure and educational constitution of society[7].

The movement on the right side of the knowledge trail (right side of Figure 15.8) is vague and fuzzy. The fuzziness can be tackled by assigning probabilities to the incremental steps of the migration path in the charted space within the XY space of the rectangle. When extreme nonlinearity is encountered in the human realm, the knowledge trail model (shown in Figure 15.8) starts to become inaccurate. As an extension of the migration of any given point S (in the XY plane) to S' for any society over an interval of time, the equations can be generalized and related to the scientific and social pressures on society.

15.5 FROM BITS TO ETIQUETTE

From a global perspective of the knowledge trail, one can find discipline, consistency, and rigor. In many instances, the trail ends as a manifestation of a well-defined pursuit. The observation of reality as bits and pieces of data sometimes ends as a new axiom and truism in the mind if the trail is relentlessly followed. We dissect the knowledge trail from a computational framework in six progressive steps, listed as (a) through (f) as follows.

(a) *B → D Transition:* When "binary bits and codes" of data are observed in the real world, low-level mental activity (a sort of subconscious pattern recognition) isolates the repetitions and patterns of the observed bits and packets. A cause–effect relationship is discovered, leading to the reasoning for the observation that was made earlier and could be implemented as simple logic circuits (during 1930s to 1940s).

(b) *D → I Transition:* When the bits and codes cannot represent the real world with sufficient flexibility for manipulation and processing, "data structures" are introduced. These data structures linger in the information domain and constitute words, numbers, parameters symbolic names, and logical entities to represent the information domain much like bits, bytes, and register and memory contents represent the data domain. When the chain of reasoning becomes too cumbersome for logic circuits, parameters and variables are introduced to include multiple cause–effect relationships, memory effects, and communication with the real world. Observations, interactions, and

---

[7] The Newtonian relations between force, mass, and acceleration (or torque, moment of inertia, and angular acceleration) get reshaped in the movement of societies through technological changes. Societies can and do exhibit different masses and inertias for different types of changes. For this reason, group velocities and aggregated mass and inertia numbers should be used. Also, the dot product rules do not apply since human beings behave differently for different pressures. On a very local basis the piecewise linearization techniques will become applicable and the prediction may be dependable for the immediate future. Similar situations also occur in the prediction of weather and traffic patterns.

numerically measured observations are programmed by Fortran, Cobol, and spreadsheet and accounting languages into computer systems (during 1950s to 1980s). A complex chain of processes are analyzed, modeled and simulated in these environments.

(c) *I → K Transition:* When the words, numbers, parameters, symbolic names, and logical entities assume greater complexity, the user-defined "objects" take over the representations. The representations and manipulations need greater flexibility. Based on compiler and operating system design, processing of more and more complex situations and scenarios are symbolically represented, logically and mathematically related, and chained to deal with intricate and delicate observations in the real world. New machines and languages such as C, C+, and C++ (during the 1980s and 1990s) started to facilitate the application-level programmers dealing with knowledge functions and knowledge bases. The system designers now have adequate flexibility to contend with most real-world problems and situations. Human beings interpret the results and make the amends to the suit the real world situations. At this stage the AI-rich languages and applications (e.g., HR application programs, medical and management Information systems, intelligent decision support systems) attempt to ease the human processes that follow I→ K transition.

(d) *K → C Transition:* In the knowledge intensive society, "object" programmability and functions start to become inadequate. Many extrapolations and predictions are based on concepts rather than purely predictive computations and logic. Such concepts can indeed be weighed and considered by contemplating human minds rather than charted and extrapolated by computer systems. It starts to become evident that if concepts are inferred from the knowledge domain and then generalized, some elementary knowledge processing is necessary. When knowledge trees and intelligent decisions are derived from the information domain, then it is logical to enforce object processing methodologies upon such knowledge trees and intelligent decisions. The process becomes partially human even though it is possible to conceive concepts machines with new methodologies, algorithms and architecture to perform the knowledge specific functions.

We fall back on the adaptations of the hardware designers about forty years back as they were designing complex, double precision numbers or array processors for the computers of the 1960s and 1970s. The approach was to take many single-precision systems and recombine their modular functionality to achieve the desired operations for complex, double-precision numbers or array processors. If hardware object processors are built for processing objects in the information domain, numerous whole or modular subprocesses of such object processors can be enhanced and reconstituted to perform whole or modular subfunctions in the knowledge or concept domains. The concept can be realized in hardware, software, or firmware implementations.

(e) *C → W Transition:* Concepts flowing into wisdom has been proposed in Chapter 10. Human beings do the highest level of processing at level-3 of wisdom machines. It is inconceivable that machines can outperform the highest level of human talent. Machines at their higher level of processing can still outdo the lower level functions of human beings. The frontier of the higher-level machine functions is artificial and any willful systems designer can push such a frontier. Thus a systematic approach to crossing the frontiers at strategic locations will make $C \rightarrow W$ transition as real as the von Neumann machine made in the1940s. As machines and humans interact to derive wisdom from concepts, the machine will learn from the many strategies that will be iterated to derive any one concept of wisdom from the contents of the concept base at node C.

(f) *W → E Transition:* The role of wisdom for ethics, social justice, and values has been the domain of philosophy since the days of Aristotle and Socrates. Values, political and social justice, and Aristotle's ethics have not been represented as numbers or figures. However, it seems that attribute space of the object constellation can be declared in concept and wisdom languages of next generation computers. Machines have the tireless agility to accurately retract content bases from many decades and many nodes and learn from the axioms of wisdom from Aristotle [5] or from Greenspan [6]. AI-based machines and intelligent Internet environment are likely to become influential in balancing social values with the wisdom that is derived from fundamental/derived concepts.

An overview of the knowledge trail with the types of machines and the caliber of human beings is shown in Figure 15.10. It is possible to conceive that machines and intelligent Internets will provide services and facilities to make human life far more enjoyable to societies around the world. It is also possible that the newer technologies will make knowledge processing as practical as object processing in the HW/SW mode of implementation. The confluence of the synergies should lead to an ethical society if the human intent is for the enhancement of values and rewards. It could be equally devastating if the intent of the leaders turns negative.

15.6 MIGRATION OF SOCIETIES UNDER EXTERNAL INFLUENCES

The XY space of Figure 15.9 can now be generalized to represent the dynamics of societies under the influence of different agencies and different directions. It becomes necessary to introduce the concept of social inertia or mass to write down the laws of dynamics. The position of society at any point S on the XY plane at an instant T is indicative of its inertia/mass. Consider an interval δT immediately prior to the instant T. If the position of society was at S_{-1} at $T - \delta T$, then $\delta x_1 / \delta T$ is the velocity at $(T - \delta T/2)$. Next, consider the location S_{-2} of society 2 δT intervals back. The acceleration in the x direction at S_{-1} becomes the rate of change of velocity computed as $((\delta x_1 / \delta T) - (\delta x_2 / \delta T))/\delta T$, where δx_1 is the x distance between S and S_{-1} and $\delta x2$ is the X distance between S-1 and S-2 .

Unlike particle dynamics, societies have distinct humanistic characteristics. Yet, some basic rules apply in most of orderly migration of societies and cultures. Over long time frames, needs (see Chapter 13) drive societies. In an immediate time frame, external pressures such as federal funding, policy decisions, campaign funds, money spent, political pressures account for the movement. Incremental changes occur.

In the context of machines that serve human beings, two directions need to be considered. First, consider the dimension of scientific progress (X dimension in Figure 15.10) that yields the new and novel machines such as the object machine, the knowledge machine (Chapters 8 and 9), the concept machine, and the wisdom machines (Chapters 10 and 11) lurking on the horizon. Second, consider the orthogonal dimension of the social progress that fosters society to use these machines to affect society. The pressures that impact the incremental movement of society can come from within society itself or from extraneous forces such as discovery of oil reserves or gold mines or even incidents such as global warming, earthquakes, etc. Societies can and generally do monitor themselves for gradual social progress and for rapid scientific progress to invent and build new machines. Most civilized nations do follow a blueprint of what society should be even if the constitutions are different.

The independent variable (over the short term[8]) is the pressure vector (PR). The movements (δx, δy) of society in the XY plane follow over a period δt. Thus, the three incremental parameters ($i.\delta x$, $j.\delta y$ and δt) become evident in Figure 15.10. The unit vectors i and j indicate the scientific and social directions, respectively.

Societies exhibit inertia/mass effect and the effects of the pressure vector Pr[9] over a period δt changes the velocity of point S shown in Figure 15.11. The inertia/mass effects can vary significantly from area to area, discipline to discipline, society to society, and culture to culture. However, the location of the point S at T is a historical record of the pressures that have moved society to the point S'. For example, if the Department of Energy Grants money \$(Grant) to the General Motors Corporation over a period of three years for manufacturing electric cars, then the inertia of the GM Corporation during the contract period would be \$(Grant)/rate of change of velocity to move GM from a status (S) of no electric car production to the status (S') of manufacturing electric cars. The change of momentum in general, is not uniform over long periods but an aggregated average can be estimated over short enough durations. The concept of social dynamics and social inertia is introduced here. Aggregated rates of change over similar projects are also indicative of momentum.

---

[8] In the long term, the tendency is to enhance social progress and curtail social decay. However, some changes that are slow and insidious hardly noticed at first gather momentum that appears impossible to curtail. Corruption, lobbying, false advertising, gambling, Mafia influence and so on survive.

[9] The dimensions of Pr would be per unit time basis (such as \$ spent/day or campaign contribution/month), such that total pressure (force equivalent or $PR = \int Pr.dt$, integrated from T to ($T + \delta T$)) is to bring a social change from S to S' would last for δt. There is a difference between particle dynamics and social dynamics to the extent the physical energy expended is (force×displacement), in the first case and the social energy expended is (effort×duration), in the second case.

Numerous external variables (such as resource allocation, management team, nature and excellence of the technical staff) enter the picture in the estimation of the inertia of any social organization. Accumulated statistics over a long time offer an insight into the future movement of projects and undertakings.

Similar examples abound in universities, medical institutions, townships, and municipalities. The estimation of the acceleration to any given stimulation, the momentum gained in accomplishing the goal at some finite status (S at (x_1,y_1)), and the ($dX = x_2 - x_1$) and ($dY = y_2 - y_1$) displacements can be tracked in a predictive way rather than in retrospect. The difference between the prediction and the reality also makes the appropriate correction to the management of future projects involving social organizations.

The proposed technique offers an estimation of the movement ($x_2 - x_1$ and $y_2 - y_1$), momentum (inertia/mass × rotational/linear velocity) and the acceleration (rate of change of rotational/linear velocity). In Figures 15.12 and 15.13, the momentum and displacement equations are shown. The most obscure variable in the strict formulation for momentum and displacement is the mass/inertia of a social organization. We have proposed a simple approach for calculating the velocity by retracting from the position S to S_{-1} for δT and then for $2\delta T$, for calculating the acceleration. In this simplistic approach, the integrated effects of changes to inertia/mass are not reflected. A more rigorous approach is to accumulate the changes of the particular social environment to components of the PR vector. When the estimations are carried out for a long period, the values for inertia/mass become dependable as most of the econometric constants for a nation or an industry.

For example, when federal spending (G) is changed, its effects on unemployment and gross domestic and gross national products are computed in most of the econometric models. In economic models used to predict the behavior of national economies or corporate models, the estimation of inertia is implicit. Numerous categories of such inertia/mass systems exist in economic environments. For an additional example, the response to federal spending for medical and hospital environments is significantly different from the response to federal spending for education, welfare, or social security and so on. Aggregate values for the displacement (δx, δy, etc. movement) of economic numbers (such as unemployment, 0.1%, 0.2%, etc.) for different pressure vectors (PR, $spent (0.1% GDP, 0.2% GDP, etc.), lobbying done (1 TV appearance, 2 TV appearances, etc.,) and so on) are tracked for some time before these coefficients used in economic models become accurate and yield dependable results.

15.6.1 Coefficient of Corruption

Two aspects of social dynamics become evident: (1) the resources expended over a period ($t = T_1 - T_2$) in Figure 15.13, and (2) the energy consumed for the society to move from x_2 to x_1 and from y_2 to y_1. First, consider the expenditure of resource to bring about a change in society in either x or y directions is computed by integrating the vector Pr from an instant of time T_1 to T_2. This integral (PR) has its two components (PR_x and PR_y) in the x and y directions. Second, consider the energy consumed for the society to moved in these two directions. The energy consumed is computed as the product of inertia/mass and the rotational/linear acceleration in the x and y directions. Under ideal conditions the law of conservation of energy (resources) will apply and the vector PR would equal the vector sum of the x and y energies consumed.

However in corrupt societies, the vector PR exceeds the energies consumed. The proportion of wasted resources to the resources spent leads to a *coefficient of corruption* (*CC*) reaching a value of one and indicating an absolutely corrupt society. In such a society, no resources are ever delivered[10] to make an actual change in the society. In some social settings, when deception, greed and arrogance (see DAH component in Figure 13.17) are high, *CC* approaches unity indicating that all the resources are diverted by the corrupt agencies. At the other extreme, where honesty, truth and virtue (see TVB components in Figure 13.17) are high, *CC* approaches zero indicating that all resources are delivers and consumed to make the social change. The coefficient of corruption can be a vector with numeric value of *CC* such as CC_x, and CCy, to quantify the extent of corruption in numerous directions (x and y, in this case). Historically, some societies have been more corrupt in directions such as betting and gambling rather than in education and welfare.

Correlation studies based on computational analysis (by studying the Internet traffic), will indicate if corruption occurs together with DAH attributes of individuals, organizations, societies and nations. Furthermore, trend analysis of *CC* offers clues about any slow drift of a society from one decade to the next.

15.6.2 Discrete Event Analysis and PERT

Management techniques including project evaluation and review technique (or PERT [7]), offer a qualitative insight into the project based on a timeline for each task within the project. In the proposed methodology, it is suggested that any discrete movement ($x_2 - x_1$ and $y_2 - y_1$), momentum (inertia/mass times velocity), and acceleration (rate of change of velocity) approach will offer a predictive tool and corrective mechanism in project management and econometrics. When the project is likely to affect the managerial team (the social effect or the y dimension), then two-dimensional analysis (proposed in Figures 15.10 and 15.11) becomes a useful technique.

As it has been witnessed in some highly specialized projects (such as the space flights), the social effect of success in prior projects leads to the slackening if standards thus bringing a catastrophic end (*Challenger*) to similar projects.

---

[10] A situation of this nature exists in lossy transmission line, where the transmission impedance is so high that very little power gets delivered to the load impedance at the end of line; instead all the power is consumed in the line In such instances, the characteristic impedance Z_0 of the line [2] becomes far greater than the load impedance. However, if the source, line, and load impedances are matched, then a maximum transfer of energy can take place between the source and the termination.

Two-dimensional effects are numerically quantified by simultaneous tracking of the changes in both the x and y directions. The predictive nature of the proposed inertia/mass approach leads to incremental study of the social behavior and movements within the organizations rather than the gross overall project analysis possible by PERT. When projects assume complexity by encompassing two, three, or more dimensions, then the proposed analysis of finding the inertia/mass effect to different types of pressures (vector PR, Figure 15.10) will correlate the effect from the matrix PR to its matrix effects (movement, momentum, and acceleration of projects) in the many dimensions. The extended control of other factors in the management of projects (such as resource allocation, management team, nature and excellence of the technical staff) can thus be adaptively deployed as corrective or compensating tools.

In Figures 15.12 and 15.13, four additional coefficients— $R(F_x)$, $R(F_y)$, $R(D_x)$, and $R(D_y)$— are introduced to deal with social resistance. The first two coefficients— $R(F_x)$ and $R(F_y)$— account for sticky-friction effects. Societies ignore pressures until a critical level is reached and this effectively reduces the initial response to pressures in the x and y directions. If societies are instantly responsive, these coefficients would assume values of unity. The second two coefficients— $R(D_x)$ and $R(D_y)$— account for the plain friction effects to slowly move social positions. Societies put up different amounts of friction to movements in the x and y directions.

Sometimes, societies exhibit different values for these coefficients in the positive (+) and negative (−) directions. If societies assumed robotic properties (e.g., in prisons or tightly controlled productions lines) these coefficients would tend to have values of unity.

The integrated response of society to knowledge and wisdom machines is depicted in Figures 15.14 and 15.15. The desirable human adaptation to a knowledge society is to absorb and propagate the positive effects that the machines can offer. Human discretion to use or abuse the new machine leads to the symbiotic relationship between humans and machines in the two sections above or below the horizontal centerline of Figure 15.14. On the positive side, stable civilizations have emerged and thrived with or without computers and networks. However, the modern technological framework allows individuals (who implant viruses and bugs) and independent entities (who sponsor global unrest and violence) to shift the impact from positive to negative. Concepts and notions need the nucleus of wisdom and justice to gravitate. Machine activity can turn chaotic without humans, and human activity can become paralyzed without machines. For these reasons, the newer machines can help humans to become contemplative and wise just as the computer systems of the 1970s and 1980s helped human beings to become precise and efficient.

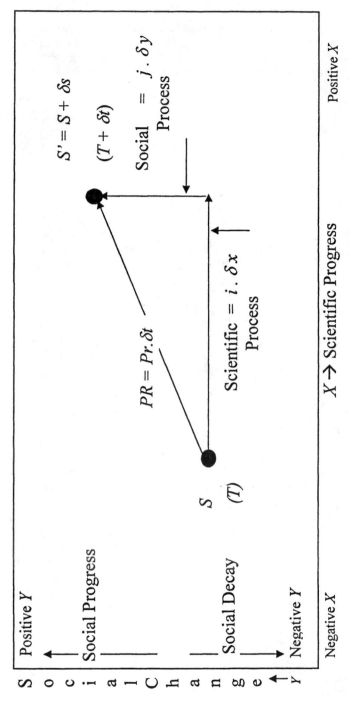

Figure 15.10 Movement of any society through (scientific, social) progress (or decay) over a period δT. The XY space is a snapshot of the status of any (micro- or macrocosmic) society that responds to external influence and shifts its position from S to S'. Over a period, the history of movement in response to various external pressures and incentives is traced out. A two dimensional regression analysis indicates the types of inertia/mass society exhibits to the movement in the X and in the Y directions. The unit vectors in the X (scientific) ad Y (social) directions are i and j.

Influence of Aggregated External Influence (*PR*, e.g., federal funding, policy decisions, campaign funds, money spent, political pressures, etc.) at *S* during an interval δT.

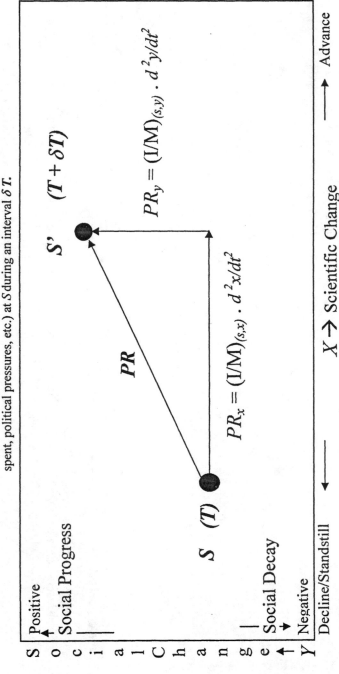

Figure 15.11 Incremental movement of a society through (scientific, social) space. The aggregated external influence brings about two effects: acceleration in the X (scientific progress/decay) direction and acceleration in the Y (social progress/decay) direction. The inertia/mass effects can be different, nonlinear, and unpredictable over very long periods of time. For short-term studies, these effects can be considered static.

Change of Momentum (Scientific and Social) at S over a period t

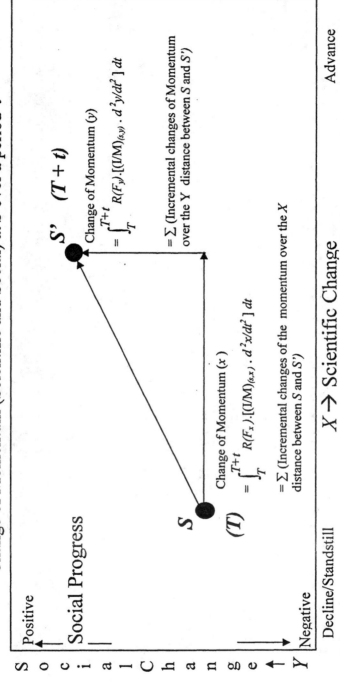

Social Progress

S (T)

S' $(T+t)$

Change of Momentum (x)

$$= \int_{T}^{T+t} R(F_x).[(1/M)_{(s,x)} \, . \, d^2x/dt^2] \, dt$$

$= \Sigma$ (Incremental changes of the momentum over the X distance between S and S')

Change of Momentum (y)

$$= \int_{T}^{T+t} R(F_y).[(1/M)_{(s,y)} \, . \, d^2y/dt^2] \, dt$$

$= \Sigma$ (Incremental changes of Momentum over the Y distance between S and S')

S o c i a l   C h a n g e : Positive ... Negative

$X \rightarrow$ Scientific Change

Decline/Standstill   Advance

Figure 15.12 Change of momentum of the overall society over a period of time t due to an aggregated external pressure lasting for the duration (t = T_2 − T_1). The inertia/mass can show considerable variation over the XY space, from society to society and from generation to generation.

Change of Status of a Society from S_1 to S_2 in an interval $T_2 - T_1$ And Energy Consumed during the Change. The Pressure Vector (Pr) influences the change.

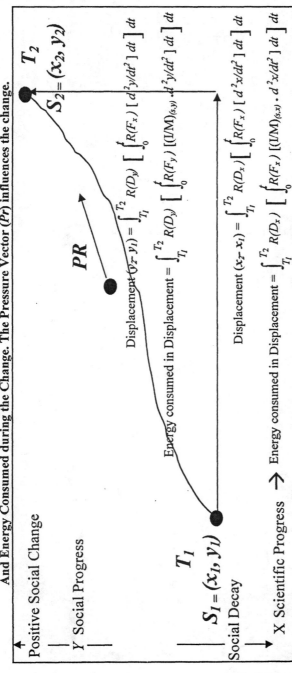

$$\text{Displacement }(y_2 - y_1) = \int_{T_1}^{T_2} R(D_y) \left[\int_0^t R(F_x) \, [\, d^2y/dt^2 \,] \, dt \right] dt$$

$$\text{Energy consumed in Displacement} = \int_{T_1}^{T_2} R(D_y) \left[\int_0^t R(F_y) \, [(1/M)_{(s,y)} \cdot d^2y/dt^2 \,] \, dt \right] dt$$

$$\text{Displacement }(x_2 - x_1) = \int_{T_1}^{T_2} R(D_x) \left[\int_0^t R(F_x) \, [\, d^2x/dt^2 \,] \, dt \right] dt$$

$$\text{Energy consumed in Displacement} = \int_{T_1}^{T_2} R(D_x) \left[\int_0^t R(F_x) \, [(1/M)_{(s,x)} \cdot d^2x/dt^2 \,] \, dt \right] dt$$

Figure 15.13 Movement of a society from point S_1 to S_2 in a time frame of t = $T_2 - T_1$. The equations for the displacement (actual change) and the energy (socio–economic–political effort) required to move society in x and y directions are shown. The time integral of the Pr from T_1 to T_2 should equal the work done (PR, total effort) in moving society in both dimensions. Finite summation forms of the four equations can be written down from the integral form shown above.

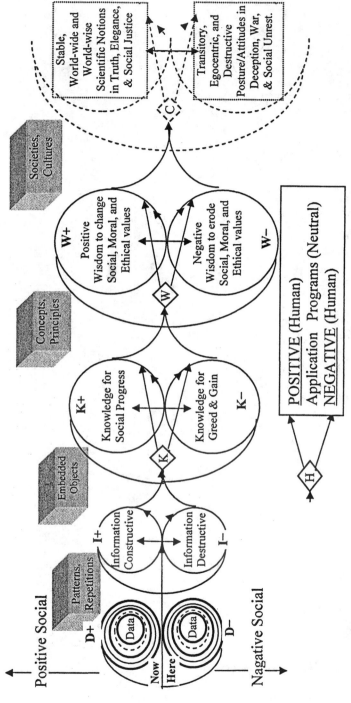

Figure 15.14 Diagram to indicate the positive and negative directions in which society can move from "here and now," depending on the willful migration path of human beings. Three platforms are shown as K for the knowledge that is generated by information processing systems, W for the wisdom that is generated by knowledge processing systems and concepts derived from the knowledge, and finally C for the combination of virtue and elegance derived from the processing of wisdom.

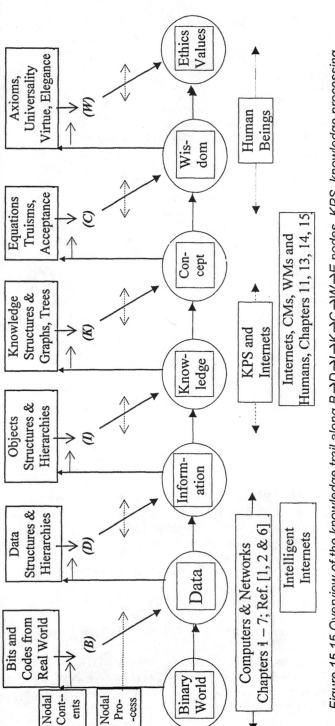

Figure 15.15 Overview of the knowledge trail along B→D→I→K→C→W→E nodes. KPS, knowledge processing systems, CM, concept machines, WM, wisdom machines. The boundary between the machine functions and the human functions has shifted substantially over the last few decades. Most of the applications facilitate human functions rather than performing such functions. A new breed of computer systems that accomplish knowledge domain functions (such as find common graph sections between one discipline and the next, explore cosmic charts and thought patterns, find commonality between Beethoven's music and classic ragas) can push the frontiers of human comprehension beyond the boundaries of sciences and cultures.

15.7 CONCLUSIONS

In this book we examine the challenge to take the computer systems into the next era. One must be able to redefine the object space (of the modern "object machines") and the universe for humans can write knowledge and concept programs with the same confidence as they write application programs. The uncertainty that may linger in the results needs to be quantified as a confidence level. Modern computers also suffer from similar constraint since the numbers are accurate only to the "last bit" of the machine representation.

Some concepts presented in the functioning of the wisdom machine where computers, network elements, and human beings actively interact to distill many tentative axioms of wisdom, are applicable in building concept machines with little or no interference from human beings. Some of the knowledge processing environments that deploy matrices and arrays for attributes of objects are also discussed in Chapter 9. The traditional linear matrix and array equations are not applicable to modeling array-based objects, their attributes, or their interactions. It appears that a newer mathematics for processing of knowledge, concept and wisdom should be evolved for objects and their attributes as numbers and their fractions or as symbols and their features. A representation of objects and their attributes in a string format akin to the IP address with n substrings provides a methodology for storing, accessing and processing objects. Processed object-string and the substrings will need forward and backward pointers to identify the intermediate objects and the substrings.

REFERENCES

[1] W. D. Ambrosch, A. Maher, and B. Sasscer, *The Intelligent Network*, Springer Verlag, New York, 1989. See also S. V. Ahamed, and V. B. Lawrence, *Intelligent Broadband Multimedia Networks*, Kluwer Academic Publishers, Boston, 1997.

[2] S. V. Ahamed, and V. B. Lawrence, *Design and Engineering of Intelligent Communication Systems,* Kluwer Academic Publishers, Boston, 1997.

[3] C. M. Bishop, *Neural Networks for Pattern Recognition*, Oxford University Press, New York, 1995.

[4] G. F. Luger, *Artificial Intelligence, Structures and Strategies for Complex Problem Solving*, Addison Wesley, Boston, 2005.

[5] J. Barnes, *The Complete Works of Aristotle*, Princeton University Press, Princeton, NJ, 1997.

[6] A. Greenspan, Gold and economic freedom, Newsletter article from *The Objectivist*, published 1966 and reprinted in *Capitalism: The Unknown Ideal*, by Ayn Rand, et al., Signet; New York, 1986.

[7] F. S. Hillier and G. J. Liebermann, *Introduction to Operations Research*, McGraw Hill, New York, 2002.

List of Acronyms for the Entire Book

δ Blending factor ranging from 0 to very large numbers. It offers knowledge systems designers the capacity to blend purely knowledge communication systems (kcs) and purely knowledge processing systems (kps), or vice versa to deal with a large variety of knowledge systems

1

1A processor   Special communication processor for call-processing applications in electronic switching systems.

2

2B1Q code	two binary to one quartinary code
2-D trellis coding	two dimensional $(x + iy)$ code algorithm for data communication
2G, 2G+	coding standards by ITU cordless telephone (CT) usage.

3

3G,	Third generation wireless technologies for CT applications
3XX, 4XX, 6XX,	Numbering System for special services in the CSDC
7XX, 8XX, 9XX,	environment

4

4ESS, 4ESS™	electronic switch toll center Part of the ESS developed by Bell system 1970s to 1990s
48 octets	payload in the ATM cell

5

5ESS,	A generic electronic switch for handling a wide variety of telephone switching services
53 octets,	ATM cell size

8

800-network	first generation Intelligent network IN/1 toll free calling
899 or 898	numbers and numbers for specialized services to the customers

800, 900, 700, 411, 911	numbers reserved for special services
802.x, 192	ITU standards for packet switched networks

9

900 services,	Reversed charges special services network services
9-row/13-row	SONET frame configuration debates and deliberations

A

ABS,	alternate billing service
ADMs,	Add-Drop Multiplexers for the new and older generation networks
ADSL, ADSL/ADSL Lite,ADSL2+,	Numerous versions and configurations of the asymmetric\ digital subscriber line (ADSL)
AI,	Artificial Intelligence
AIKN	advanced intelligent knowledge network
AIN,	advanced intelligent networks proposed by Bellcore.
ALUs,	Arithmetic Logic Units in the CPU environment of a computer
AKSP,	Adjunct knowledge processor for knowledge functions in knowledge environment
AM,	Administrative module
AM, CM, and SM,	Administrative communications and switching modules in a ESS facility
ANSI,	American National Standards Institute
AP,	adjunct processor
AT&T,	American Telephone and Telegraph Company, no longer in existence
Atlantis-2,	One of the many Atlantic crossings for voice and data communication listed on page 27 in this book
ATM,	Asynchronous transfer mode for cell relay systems
AUs,	Arithmetic units embedded in the ALU and CPU environments.
AVPU,	Audiovisual processing unit
AXE,	A generic European switching environment for data and voice communications by Ericsson.
A-WAB,	Wisdom axiom base for the type A human being (philosopher)

B

(B1–B5),	B1 to B5 attributes of a scientist in a flow chart of behavior
BAL,	Basic assembly language
BDI-K-CWE,	A chain or a trail the permits linkage of binary, data, information, to the knowledge, and then to the concept, wisdom and ethics of human beings
Bellcore,	Bell Communications Research, no longer in existence
BI,	behavioral intelligence evolved to solve routine human problems at a behavioral bevel.
BRISDN,	basic rate integrated services digital network (ISDN)
BB networks	broadband networks
B-values,	Maslow's concepts of the values of human being (see page 383)
BX.25,	A version of X.25 protocol/network developed by Bell system

B-WAB	Wisdom axiom base for the type B human being (scientist)

C

C	symbol associated with knowledge systems to designate communication of knowledge
C, C+ and C++	computer languages for generic programming applications
C&C check,	completeness and consistency check of data modules communicated.
C1 to C5,	C1 to C5 attributes of a tyrant king/leader in a flow chart of behavior
CAD	computer aided design
CAMEL	Intelligent network services for mobile users to select specific service. (one of the numerous services, see pare 25 for details)
CANTAT-3,	one of the numerous Trans Atlantic Cables for data/voice services
CATV,	cable TV
CCIS,	Common Channel Interoffice Signaling
CCISS,	Common Channel Interoffice Signaling System
CCITT,	consultative committee of the ITT
CCS	Common Channel Signaling
CCS7,	Common Channel Signaling #7
CDRs,	call data records
CEPT	central European post and telegraph
CSDC	circuit-switched digital capability
CLASS	special group of IN/2 services provided by second generation INs
CM,	communication module or concept machine
COMNET,	A network simulation program
CPM,	critical path method
CT2,	cordless telephone 2nd generation
CT3,	enhanced CT-2 telephone services towards the 3rd generation
C-WAB	wisdom axiom base for the type C human being (tyrant king)

D

D channel banks	CO equipment for multiplexing and demultiplexing the DS0 and DS1 signals through the Circuit switched networks.
D, I, K, W, and E,	Data, information, knowledge, wisdom and ethics levels of progression.
(D1 to D5),	D1 to D5 attributes of a criminal/thug in a flow chart of behavior
DACS	digital access cross connect systems
DAH,	deception, arrogance and hate for the (C1-C5) and (D1-D5) type of human beings
DBM,	database management
DBMSs,	database management systems
DCS,	digital cross connect systems in the SONET environment
DDS,	digital data services (in context to digital transmission systems)
DDS,	Dewey decimal system (in context to classification of knowledge)
DM,	Data management/data manager
DMA	direct memory access (in traditional computer systems)
DMT,	discrete multi tone (for DSL transmission)
DQDB,	distributed queue dual bus
DS0,	digital signal 0 is 64kb/s channel at the lowest level of digital hierarchy

DS1,	digital signal 1 is 1.544 Mb/s signal with 24 DS0 channels + signaling bits, also known as T1 signal
DS1C,	digital signal 1C is at 3.152 Mb/s
DS2,	digital signal 2 is at 6.312 Mb/s also known as T2 signal
DS3,	digital signal 3 is at 44.736 Mb/s
DSL,	digital subscriber line
DSLAM,	uplink multiplexer typically converts the DSL data and signal onto the Layer 2 ATM format
DSSs	decision support systems

E

E1,	CEPT digital hierarchy signals at 2.048 Mb/s
E2, E3,	CEPT digital hierarchy signals
EG	electronic government
EG-IT	the IT platform and numbering system for EG operations
ESs,	expert systems
ESS,	electronic switching systems
EW1000,	Education and welfare wing of electronic governement systems
EWSD	a variety of ESS facilities built by Siemens

F

FCs,	functional components of the intelligent network conceptual model
FDC,	falsehood, distaste and corruption of type (C1-C5) and (D1-D5) individuals
FEPs,	front end processors of the SCP facility
FLAG,	one of the numerous transoceanic fiber optic networks 9see page 27)
flip-flop	attitude of human beings in doubt or under stress
FTTC,	fiber to the curb distribution data/voice/video networks
FTTH,	fiber to the home distribution data/voice/video networks
fuzzy NPU	A numerical processor unit working with imprecise rule for manipulating the attributes of objects.

G

G.992.2,	ADSL standards for ADSL Lite discrete multi-tone
Gb/s	gigabits per second optical rates in FO networks
G.DMT,	ADSL standards for ADSL discrete multi-tone
GNP,	gross national product
GPRS,	global packet radio services
GPU,	graphical processor unit
GUI,	graphical user interface

H

H.323,	One of the ISDN applications. See page 192 for other H.3XX applications
HDSL,	high-speed digital subscriber line
HDTV,	high definition TV
HLLs,	higher level languages

I

I«»K,	information under process for refinement to the knowledge level
IKPS, I-KPS	intelligent, Internet-based, or IN-based knowledge processing system
I^2-KPS,	intelligent and Internet-based; Intelligent and IN-based; or Internet-based and IN-based knowledge processing system
I^3KPS, or I^3-KPS	Intelligent, Internet-based and IN-based knowledge processing system
IAS,	Institute of Advanced Study known for von Neumann's SPC machine
IC,	integrated circuit
IKN,	intelligent knowledge network
IKWV chain,	information, knowledge, wisdom and (human) values chain
IN,	intelligent network
IN/1,	first generation intelligent network
IN/1+,	enhanced version of the IN/1
IN/2,	second generation IN
INCAD	intelligent computer aided design
INCM,	intelligent network conceptual model
INKW	intelligent knowledgeware
IP,	intelligent peripheral or Internet protocol
ISDN,	integrated services digital network
ISP,	Internet service provider
IT	information technology

K

kb/s	kilobits per second
KBMS,	knowledge base management system
KBs,	knowledge bases
KCP,	knowledge control point
KCPU,	a hardware unit to accomplish knowledge functions and CPU functions
kcs,	A purely knowledge communication system
KCSs,	knowledge communication systems
KD	knowledge domain
KEE,	knowledge enhancement environments
KI	knowledge or content based intelligence
KIR,	knowledge instruction register
KIP,	knowledge intelligent peripheral
KM,	knowledge machine
KMM,	knowledge management module
KMSs	knowledge management systems
KN	knowledge network
KNID	knowledge network information database
Kompilation,	compilation of knowledge programs
kopc,	knowledge operation code
KPE,	knowledge processing environment
kps,	A purely knowledge processing system
KPSs,	knowledge processing systems
KPU,	knowledge processing unit
KS,	knowledge systems
KSCP,	knowledge services control point
KSMS,	knowledge system management system

KSP,	knowledge switching point used for switching in knowledge-based intelligent (KI) systems based on LoC classification of content knowledge. The KBs are distributed throughout the world. The content of knowledge carried in the channel determines the Web address of the KB to be accessed. This address is similar to the WWW address but the content determines the appropriate LoC classified KB address that gets translated to the exact WWW address
KSW,	knowledge software or knowledge switch
KTP,	knowledge transfer point

L

LoC,	Library of Congress
LUs,	logical unit

M

M1C, M12, M13, M34	Group of digital multiplexers used in the American digital hierarchy
MAN,	metropolitan area networks
Mb/s	megabits per second
MIMD,	multiple instruction multiple data CPU architecture
MIN	medical intelligent network
MISD,	multiple instruction single data CPU architecture
MKNs,	medical knowledge networks
MPMO,	multiple process multiple object KPU architecture
MPSO,	multiple process single object KPU architecture
MRI,	magnetic resonance imaging
MSMS,	medical services management system
MSPs,	medical service providers

N

NA	node administration
NBES,	Networkbased educational system
NCOM,	network communication unit
NKSPs,	network knowledge service providers
NPU,	numerical processor unit in the CPU or KPU environment
NT-1 and NT-2,	network terminations 1 and 2 for ISDN serices

O

OA&M,	operations, administration and maintenance
OAM&P,	operations, administration, maintenance and provisioning
OC-n,	optical carrier systems in the SONET environment
ONN	off node netwok
OOL,	object oriented language
OOP,	object oriented programs
OPNET	a discrete event networks simulation package
OSI	open system interconnect

P

PBXs,	private branch exchanges
PCM,	pulse code modulation
PCP	processor control point to match the processor capability to the domain of knowledge processed
PCU,	program control unit
PIN,	personal intelligent network
PLCP,	physical layer convergence protocol
PMPC,	patient medical process cycle
PMPC code,	machine instruction code to drive the different stages in the PMPC
PMR,	private mobile radio
POTS,	Plain old telephone service
PPNs and EPNs,	processor port network and expansion port network
PR,	pattern recognition
PROLOG,	one of the numerous OOLs

Q

QAM coding,	quadrature amplitude modulation
QoS,	quality of service

R

$R(F_x)$, $R(F_y)$, $R(D_x)$, and $R(D_y)$,	resistance factors in social dynamics
RACE, Europe	research and development projects for advanced communication in
RDTs,	remote data terminals

S

SANs,	storage area networks
SAP,	one of a series of intelligent MIS and EIS programming systems
SAT-3/WASC /SAFE,	one of the newer fiber optic transoceanic network spanning the globe (see pages 27-29)
SDSL,	symmetric DSL
SDTV,	standard TV
SCE,	service creation environment
SCP,	service control point
SEA-ME-WE 2, SEA-ME-WE 3,	segments of the newer fiber optic transoceanic network spanning the globe (see pages 27-29)
SIMD,	single instruction single data CPU architecture
SIMO,	single instruction multiple data CPU architecture
SIP,	service intelligent peripheral
SM,	switching module of an ESS facility
SMDS,	switched multi-megabit digital service
SMS,	service management system (in conventional INs)
SNI,	Service network interface
SNMP,	simple network management protocol
SNR,	signal to noise ratio

SONET,	synchronous optical network
SONET/SDH,	SONET/SONET digital hierarchy
SPC,	service control point (in conventional INs)
SOPs,	standard operating procedures
SPSO,	single process single object KPU architecture
SS7	signaling system 7
SSI,	small scale integration
SSLI,	special services logical interface
SSPs,	service switching points (in conventional INs)
SST,	spread spectrum technique
STM-*i*,	STM-*i* designation, with i (= $n/3$) for the STS-*n* designation
STPs,	signal transfer points (in conventional INs)
STS-*n*	synchronous transport signal at level *n*

T

T, P and S,	true, philosophic and scientific validations
T, P, S, E,	true, philosophic scientific and economic validations
T, V, and B,	truth, virtue and beauty
T1,	Signal at DS1 rate of 1.544 Mb/s
T1/E1 lines,	T1 or E1 lines
TAT-8 and 9	transatlantic telecommunication fiber optic systems
TCP/IP,	transmission control protocol, connection oriented transport protocol of the Internet architecture; reliable byte stream delivery service. IP Internet protocol that provides a connectionless best effort delivery service across the Internet
TINA,	TMN + IN, (telecommunication management network + intelligent network)
TMM,	transaction management machine
TPC-5,	trans Pacific cables
TT,	transfer of technology from one nation to another
TTKNs,	TT knowledge networks
TVB,	truth, virtue and beauty borrowed from Aristotle's writings
type A,	behavioral database of type A individuals (philosophers) from a social and cultural basis
type B,	behavioral database of type B individuals (scientists and engineers) from a social and cultural basis
type C,	behavioral database of type C individuals (tyrant kings and political leaders) from a social and cultural basis
type D,	behavioral database of type D individuals (Mafia figures and thugs) from a social and cultural basis
type-I,	Aristotle's notion of the socially beneficent leaders (positive side, see page 400)
type-II,	Aristotle's notion of the socially disruptive persons (negative side, see page 400). See also, Maslow's fifteen attributes or "B-values", he has identified in individuals
Type B links	STP-STP connections between neighboring regions
Type C links pairs	STPs connections within region specifically balanced and mated wire

U

U, T and S	interfaces for ISDN
UMTS,	universal mobile telephone system
UNIX,	a powerful operating systems developed by Bell System to operate ESS type of telecommunication nodes and network functions. It is generic enough to operate most computing environments.
USIN,	universal services intelligent network proposed by AT&T during late 1980s, but never finally implemented.

V

VCs,	virtual circuits through the network environments
VDSL,	one of the numerous versions of the digital subscriber lines
VHDSL,	very high-speed DSL
VLSI,	very large scale integration for IC chips
VoIP,	voice over Internet deploying established IPs
VT	Virtual terminal

W

WAN	wide area network
WC	wire center of a typical switching node where the subscriber line terminate at the central office
WDM	wave-length division multiplex for FO transmission

X

X.25	ITU recommendation that specifies the interface between users data equipment (DTE) and the packet-switching data circuit terminating equipment (DCE)

CLASSIFICATION OF EIGHT INDICES

Eight indices (established concepts, new concepts, human aspects, knowledge, social settings, technology, wisdom and information/words) are presented in this section. Eight indices (rather than just one index), are necessary to cover the expanse of topics covered in this book. These indices facilitate a casual reader to enter the subject matter of the book in eight directions. Concepts that are prevalent and those that are presented in this book make up the first two indices of concepts. If the reader is looking for the concepts that form the foundation for the new machines and their knowledge bases then the index of established concepts will provide a platform to search the book and so on. The index of new concepts evolved in the book, knowledge, wisdom, and word indices follow. The eight indices are as follows.

- Index of established concepts to build a platform for the new machines and concepts
- Index of new concepts to build the new machines and their core functions
- Index of human aspects to relate human need that will eventually drive the new machines
- Index of knowledge related functions to migrate from information domain to knowledge domain and move from knowledge to wisdom domain along the knowledge or (B→D→I→K→C→W→E) trail
- Index of social settings for the new machines to function appropriately and intelligently in different cultural settings
- Index of technology related factors that enable the new machines to be realized and implemented
- Index of wisdom related topics from Aristotle to Carter who have a framework of viable approaches to deal with age old or very modern information age problems
- Index of words and (uncorrelated) information as it appears in the book.

The index dealing with knowledge presents the topics that are necessary to move information into the knowledge domain and then move knowledge to the wisdom domain. The index of words and uncorrelated information topics the last and the longest index the simply lists the words and the page numbers where these words occur. Such an index will become useful to look for an idea the is defined precisely by certain key words. Fuzzy ideas are tackled by the first five indices.

There is an overlap of all these directions of approach to the core subject matter of the book that deals with intelligent Internet knowledge networks and introduces the methodology for processing of concepts and wisdom.

The computer, communication and network specialists may find the Index of Technology on pages 505-506 most useful. Inventors and research students should benefit from the Indices of Knowledge and Wisdom on pages 501-502 and 507-508. Chapters 8–10 should provide insights into building systems that move concepts into realizable machines architectures. The social scientists are likely to find the Indices Human Aspects and Social Settings on pages 499-500 and on pages 503-504 useful. Chapters 13–15 present a new insight in the motivations and drives of individuals and social organizations embedded in information age and Internet society. Poets and Philosophers are likely for find topics referenced in Index of Wisdom (pages 507-508) interesting. Finally, the Index of Words (pages 509-521) provides the subject matter as it pertains to individual and independent words.

I -.Index of Established Concepts

A

Adam Smith (concepts from), 345, 346, 347
Albert Einstein, Martin Luther King, Jr., Mohandas Gandhi, Albert Schweitzer, (concepts from), 386
Albert Schweitzer and Mother Theresa, (concepts from), 397
Aristotle, 268, 280, 291, 296, 354, 400, 401, 403, 409, 410, 415, 416, 421, 423, 442, 446, 471, 482, 483, 485
an ultimate, an infallible theme, an immortal concept, or an ideal., 388
any valid concept, 284
axiom/relationship/concept, 291, 295

B

Buddha's Enlightenment, Gandhi's nonviolence, Lincoln's antislavery, Schweitzer's reverence for life, (concepts from), 388

C

concept by its origin, 99
concept for controlling the functions, 184
concept in processing of knowledge, 324
concept into the behavioral model, 401

Concept of human needs, 389
concept modification and/or adaptation., 240
concept of (expected) incremental or marginal costs, 357
concept of "soft-switch", 60

concept of Aristotle's beginning, middle, and end, 354
concept of electronic switching systems, 188
concept of indirect addressing, 111, 439
concept of line scanning, 159
concept of network-based input parameter sensing, 117
concept of providing a computer on a chip, 16

concept of psychological or social energy, 355

concept of relocatable programs, 11

concept of social inertia, 471

concept of stored program control, 184
concept of the decision support system, 151, 171
concept of wisdom, 271, 471

concept resides in the content of information, 352
concept, or wisdom, 312
concepts and wisdom, 20, 27, 326

D

DAH, disception, arrogance and hate concept, 372, 401, 402, 403, 404, 405, 406, 407, 474, 485

E

entity, principle, concept that can be searched, changed and altered 385

G

Gautama Buddha, Jesus Christ, St. John
   the Baptist, 397
Goethe writings, 346
Greek writers (Plato, Socrates), 415

H

Hamming distance, concept, 229, 373

I

INCM, (intelligent network conceptual
   model) 7, 162, 167, 199, 202
internal combustion concept, 17
invention of a concept
   product life cycle, 370

K

Karl Marx, 346
knowledge, concept, and unification, 263

M

Maxwell, Ampere, Galvani, Oersted and
   Gauss; and Edison, 388
manipulation the concept, 284
Marshall, Menger, and Arrow, (concepts
   from), 346
Marshall's Laws, 388

N

new concept in the dictionary
   wisdom, 268
new concept in the wisdom-base, 139
nirvana, true love, perfection
   concepts, 386
No concept, or its modifications, is
   absolute, 217

O

optimally search for the best solution,
   concept, notion, principle, 386

P

Petty, Galiani, Locke (concepts from),
   346
positive wisdom for a negative concept,
   458
processing for knowledge concept,, 455
programmable intelligence. This concept,
   114

Q

QoS concept, 43

R

reinforce a concept, 175
Ricardo, Malthus, Say, (concepts from),
   346

S

search for truth (T), virtue (V) elegance
   and social justice, 446
signal transport concept, 39

T

Thorstein Veblen, Scarcity concept 346,
   369, 439, 446
TVB Concepts for truth, virtue and
   beauty, 402, 403, 404, 406, 474, 485

U

underlying concept, 142, 463
Unification, 386

V

Veblen, Schumpeter, 346

W

wealth of knowledge, 130, 180, 345, 346,
   347, 352

(

(A1 to A5)
traits, of philophers in flow-chart 421
(C1 to C5)
traits of tyrant kings, in flow chart 431

B

behavioral intelligence, 378, 379, 380, 383, 384

C

concept programs, 482
concept banks, 21
concept derived from knowledge, 270
concept domains
Six transitions, 470
concept error-correction, 46
concept for constructing a KPS, 183
concept for controlling the functions, 184
concept into processing of knowledge, 324

Sixth and Seventh Level human needs, 389
concept level diagram, 261
concept machine, 472

concept of hierarchy of information, 371

concept of predictive programming., 115
concept of psychological or social energy, 355

concept of separation of *kopc*, 331, 338

concept processing, 250, 452

concept programs, 482

concept resides in the content of information, 352
concept that every knowledge processor needs a supporting numerical processor, 216
concept that such equations differentiation & Integration, 365
concept to the binary
Fuzzy knowledge, 338

concept, as an Object such as race, people, society, culture,, 263
concept-based switching functionality, 261
concepts to wisdom, 20, 27, 326

D

DAH 372, 401, 402, 403, 404, 405, 406, 407, 474, 485
decoding concept, 225

E

Economics of IK&W Concept, 439
entity, principle, concept that can be processed 385

F

Fuzzy Hamming Distance, in the knowledge domain 229
"fuzzy" knowledge, 338

I

iterative control of maximization of SNR in the medical field, 230

K

knowledge to concept, 461
knowledge, concept and wisdom machines, 446
knowledge, concept, and/or wisdom machine search, 468

M

manipulation the concept, 284

N

No concept, or its modifications, is absolute, and it can be modified by a machine, 217

O

optimally search for the best solution, concept, notion, principle, 386

P

positive wisdom for a negative concept, 458
processing for knowledge concept,, 455
programmable intelligence. concept, 114

S

search for truth, machine based, for virtue elegance and social justice, 446
sixth-level and seventh-level needs concept, 388
SNR for concepts, 176, 230, 424

T

Three (T, P and S) concept levels, 356
(T1-T3) Concept for truth, 354
    (P1-P4) Philosophic validations 354-355
    (S1-S5) Social value, 355-357
    (E1-E7) Economic value,358
Machine-based search for TVB, truth, virtue and beauty, 402, 403, 404, 406, 474, 485

U

unified infinity, 397
unify (almost) everything into *one* infinite and immortal concept Unification, 386
One universal concept,, 450
universality of an(y) object, concept,, 243

W

wealth of knowledge, 130, 181, 347, 349, 351, 357
wisdom bases Positive, (WB-A and WB-B) for human interactions, 434, 436
wisdom bases Negative (WB-C and WB-D) for human interactions, 444

III - Index of Human Aspects

A

Abrham Lincoln's, antislavery, 388
Aristotle's type-I and II classification of
human nature 437, 446

B

Berne, I'm OK, You're OK, 383, 385

C

Conflictive human roles, 348, 456
control, human, 461, 464
cooperative, human roles, 59, 62, 72,
192, 195, 348

D

D, I, K, W, and E, knowledge and
wisdom trail, 463

E

Enlightenment, Buddha 388
etiquette, human, 404, 463

F

Freud, Sigmund, 375, 376, 380, 381,
382, 383, 385, 399, 403, 410, 412

H

Human evolution, 8

Human, needs as they are referenced in
this book, 2, 3, 4, 5, 8, 9, 12, 14, 16,
17, 23, 26, 27, 29, 30, 33, 34, 41, 43,
45, 60, 62, 64, 65, 66, 75, 83, 84, 85,
87, 88, 95, 96, 99, 100, 105, 117, 118,
123, 129, 130, 131, 133, 135, 136,
141, 142, 143, 149, 154, 173, 174,
175, 177, 178, 190, 191, 197, 202,
207, 214, 215, 216, 218, 223, 225,
228, 229, 235, 244, 245, 246, 247,
248, 249, 250, 254, 260, 263, 264,
267, 273, 276, 277, 279, 282, 283,
284, 299, 302, 304, 306, 310, 311,
323, 324, 328, 339, 347, 348, 354,
355, 361, 366, 369, 373, 375, 377,
378, 379, 380, 381, 382, 383, 384,
385, 386, 387, 388, 389, 390, 391,
393, 394, 395, 396, 397, 398, 399,
400, 401, 402, 404, 405, 410, 411,
415, 421, 423, 431, 433, 440, 446,
450, 456, 458, 465, 472, 482
human wisdom, 463

M

Marshall, 248, 346, 374, 375, 376, 386,
388, 390, 392, 395, 446
Maslow, 249, 264, 375, 376, 380, 383,
384, 385, 386, 389, 393, 399, 400,
401, 402, 403, 410, 411, 412, 415,
423, 442
motivation, 3, 264, 375, 380, 381, 393,
411, 412, 442

N

Need Pyramid, Maslow, 249
nonviolence, Gandhi and King, 388, 458

O

organization (s), human, 14, 20, 55, 62,
67, 68, 97, 99, 100, 102, 105, 106,
156, 208, 245, 250, 268, 278, 320,
351, 363, 417, 435, 447, 473

P

phasor representation of the TVB and
DAH tendencies in humans, 400, 404,
405, 407, 410
Philosophers, 388
Poets, 388

R

reverence for life, Schweitzer, 388

S

Scientists, 458
seventh level, 246, 387, 389, 390

sixth level, 246, 389
social values
human, 10, 282, 294, 421, 423, 433,
440, 451, 453, 454, 455, 461, 462,
463, 471
structures, 10, 14, 21, 50, 54, 67, 81, 106,
107, 145, 153, 204, 233, 245, 261,
267, 269, 275, 318, 331, 338, 354,
357, 360, 363, 366, 436, 448, 469

T

type A, humans, 379, 390, 400, 420, 421,
422, 423, 424, 426, 428, 429
type B, humans, 379, 390, 400, 420, 421,
422, 424, 425, 426, 428, 429
type C, humans, 400, 421, 429, 430, 431,
432, 433, 435, 436
type D, humans, 400, 421, 429, 430, 432,
433, 434, 435, 436
type-I and II classification of human
nature from Aristotle, 437, 446

IV - Index for Knowledge

I^3-KPS, 328

I

Information – Knowledge Transition Stage

($I«»K$), 346, 347, 348, 349, 350, 359, 360, 361, 362, 363, 365, 367, 369

B

Knowledge Trail

Binary to Data to Information to Knowledge to Concept to Wisdom to Ethics Transformation and Trail B→D→I→K→C→W→E Trail or BDI-K-CWE trail, 456, 460, 462

Classification of Knowledge

DDS, 76, 110, 180, 199, 211, 271, 276, 284, 289, 293, 300, 304, 322, 326, 328, 342, 360, 438
Dewy Decimal System, 110, 295

LoC, 110, 180, 199, 211, 265, 271, 276, 293, 300, 304, 309, 322, 326, 328, 330, 338, 342, 343, 438, 448
Library of Congress, 44, 76, 95, 105, 110, 206, 211, 242, 261, 265, 269, 276, 295, 296, 300, 304, 306, 309, 322, 341, 343, 365, 438, 444

Knowledge Systems

IKPS, 328, 329, 332
I^2-KPS, 326, 329

Knowledge Base

Knowledge Bases
KB, 76, 92, 95, 96, 110, 111, 200, 210, 230, 279, 306, 308, 314, 330, 332, 342, 343, 427, 438
KBs, 97, 101, 110, 111, 128, 130, 137, 146, 211, 212, 213, 214, 230, 308, 312, 343, 362, 438, 439
knowledge base,
base, 20, 76, 84, 94, 96, 110, 122, 197, 199, 210, 211, 217, 239, 261, 279, 284, 285, 314, 325, 330, 332, 350, 367, 426, 435, 436, 438, 439
bases, 96, 99, 110, 438
knowledge database, 134

Knowledge Management

KBMSs, 110, 111, 438, 439
KMS, 74, 76, 80, 312, 313, 330, 332, 340

Knowledge Control Points
KCP, Knowledge Control Points, 74, 76, 197, 199, 201, 304, 310, 311, 312, 313, 314, 330, 332, 340, 342
KSPs, knowledge switching points, 137, 197, 304
KSPs, knowledge service providers, 74, 129, 134, 150, 199, 313
KSPs, 74, 129, 130, 131, 134, 136, 137, 150, 197, 304, 312

Knowledge Machine

Knowledge Machine (KM), 69, 111, 116, 120, 125, 172, 202, 217, 227, 228,

229, 230, 233, 234, 251, 252, 304, 320, 322, 323, 330, 331, 338, 339, 340, 439, 472

Knowledge processing (KP), 28, 73, 111, 181, 182, 216, 242, 299, 314, 328, 337, 338, 339, 343, 444, 453

Knowledge processing systems (KPSs), 8, 30, 117, 145, 155, 180, 181, 202, 212, 240, 261, 299, 304, 306, 315, 330, 340, 351, 367, 459, 463, 480, 481

Knowledge Processors (KPs), 179 180, 256, 330, 331, 338

Knowledge Processing Unit, KPU, 111, 151, 179, 207, 208, 209, 217, 218, 219, 220, 222, 223, 225, 226, 227, 231, 233, 234, 235, 236, 238, 239, 250, 253, 254, 256, 261, 314, 315, 317, 320, 322, 323, 325, 326, 331, 335, 338, 339, 342, 343, 364, 365, 439, 449

Knowledge Networks

networks, 21, 90, 128, 129, 131, 132, 133, 134, 150, 197, 303, 343, 344

systems, 9, 183, 202, 300, 301, 304, 342

Knowledge Systems (KSs), 300, 301 knowledge networks; medical, 90

Knowledge Operations

Knowledge Processing System, KPS, 74, 117, 145, 148, 149, 182, 183, 195, 198, 200, 202, 203, 204, 205, 206, 207, 208, 211, 212, 213, 214, 217, 218, 219, 220, 221, 222, 224, 227, 228, 230, 231, 233, 235, 236, 239, 300, 304, 306, 310, 311, 313, 320, 325, 326, 327, 328, 329, 330, 332, 343, 481

operands, 111, 365, 439

kopc, operation code, 111, 315, 331, 365, 439

ring, 94, 96, 212

trial, 376, 446, 447, 449, 459, 466, 467, 469, 471, 481

Search for Knowledge

Search for knowledge, 72

B

BDI-K-CWE, Chain and its social
impact, 473, 475, 479, 480, 483

C

CC, 498
CC$_x$, and *CCy,* 498
coefficient of corruption (CC), 498

D

DAH, deception, arrogance and hate,
negative forces in social settings 378,
412, 413, 415, 417, 418, 419, 420, 498

N

Negative social factors, 447

O

Organization, 15, 20, 55, 62, 67, 68, 97,
99, 100, 102, 105, 106, 156, 210, 247,
252, 270, 280, 322, 355, 369, 432,
452, 465, 496
Organizations, 8, 67, 79, 99, 371, 389,
410, 417, 434, 459, 498, 500

P

Positive social,
factors 10, 438, 478
positive
social values, 10, 438
PR, Social Pressure Vector

17, 115, 165, 169, 195, 282, 284, 330,
385, 387, 389, 421, 438, 448, 468,
489, 494, 496, 497, 498, 500, 504

S

Social
(level 3) needs, 249
(*Y*-axis) Representation, 488
activity, 475
and cultural norms, 286, 409
and economic domains, 359
and ethical problems, 460
and ethical values, 434
and political stability, 457
and public service institutions, 42
barometer, 480
benefit, 10
benevolence, 250, 272, 419
bias, 10
change, 271, 494, 498
conditions, 8
decay, 476, 494
demand, 2
directions, 494
economics, 349
elegance, 438
energy, 359, 494
entity, 123, 151, 172
environments, 4, 155
ethics, 250, 465
events, 435
evil, 459
fabric, 480
functions, 44, 432
gains, 9
growth, 431
impact, 46
implications, 3, 5, 352

inertia, 489
injustice, 250
interdependence, 3, 5
malice, 359
needs, 8, 9, 17, 30, 216, 217, 248, 383, 393, 396, 486
or love needs, 425
organizations, 172, 496
potential, 77
pressures, 422, 489, 490
problems, 8, 30
progress, 5, 17, 181, 476, 494, 502
reform, 365
responsibility, 425
revolution, 47
scientists, 284, 383, 388, 412
skills, 261
structures, 10
systems, 459
value, 3, 10, 272, 282, 285, 287, 293, 294, 295, 296, 358, 359, 362, 364, 365, 367, 375, 377, 379, 381, 453
values, 284, 297, 440, 450, 457, 470, 472, 473, 474, 482, 483, 484, 492
virtue or elegance, 295
viruses, 434, 435
welfare, 99, 446

workers, 488

social, ego or realization needs, 251
social, moral and ethical corruption, 452
social, moral or ethical deductions, 286
social, technical, and scientific domains, 347
social/cultural environment, 275
socially beneficial flow of knowledge, 332
socially destructive human, 285
socially intelligent, 432
socially poisonous, 435
socially valuable, 351
societies, 9, 27, 42, 43, 217, 389, 430, 435, 456, 457, 459, 472, 477, 488, 489, 490, 492, 494, 498, 500
socio-economic, 47, 116

T

TVB, truth, virtue and beauty,
    Positive traits in social settings 413, 414, 415, 417, 419, 498
two social dimensions, 250

VI - Index of Technology

DSL, 22, 23, 24, 29, 62, 67, 68, 93

A

Add-Drop Multiplex, 69
ADM, 37, 39, 69, 214, 215
architecture
  computer, 51, 227, 392
Architecture, 97, 109, 115, 116, 131,
  159, 165, 167, 180, 203, 204, 214,
  230, 235, 265, 266, 280, 290, 338,
  349, 350, 366, 370, 405, 449
ATM, 21, 22, 24, 25, 26, 27, 30, 31, 33,
  34, 35, 37, 38, 39, 40, 41, 42, 44, 45,
  46, 47, 76, 96, 97, 99, 114, 209, 211,
  212, 214, 345

C

C+, 13, 18, 126, 131, 162, 193, 290, 507,
  517
chain
  Knowledge trail, 7, 126, 147, 154,
    196, 236, 241, 303, 375, 388, 464,
    473, 481, 482, 483, 490, 515, 517
chip sets, 11, 15, 16, 19, 60, 61, 115,
  358, 378
confidence level, 10, 54, 73, 155, 197,
  199, 237, 239, 241, 243, 246, 248,
  250, 252, 256, 258, 264, 295, 296,
  297, 301, 302, 304, 305, 307, 314,
  321, 355, 530
current technology, 1, 483, 513

D

Digital Hierarchy, 69

E

EG
  systems, 101, 102, 103, 104, 105, 107,
    109, 110, 113, 294
ESS
  switches, 13, 15, 36, 95, 188, 199,
    205, 206, 222, 230, 330, 345, 371,
    373

F

Fiber Optics, 26
FORTRAN, 12, 201, 258, 265, 507

H

Hamming, 252, 382, 403, 444

I

IAS machine, 13, 200, 201
IN architectures, 53, 74
ISDN, 22, 23, 25, 27, 33, 35, 41, 63, 65,
  67, 70, 76, 92, 93, 97, 99, 140, 209,
  211, 215, 219, 231, 330, 338, 345,
  371, 372, 373

K

KM, 78, 222, 224, 227, 252, 253, 331,
  333, 348, 350, 352, 353, 368, 369, 372
knowledge machine, 70, 115, 120, 126,
  131, 188, 222, 237, 248, 250, 252,
  253, 256, 258, 275, 277, 331, 348,

350, 351, 358, 359, 367, 368, 369, 479, 520

Knowledge machines, 196, 197, 368

Knowledge processing, 29, 74, 115, 197, 198, 236, 266, 325, 341, 356, 366, 367, 368, 372, 487, 497

knowledge systems, 9, 199, 222, 326, 328, 330, 331, 371

L

levels, 7, 11, 49, 50, 61, 68, 110, 115, 123, 151, 153, 154, 179, 190, 192, 207, 235, 241, 252, 264, 266, 271, 272, 273, 302, 304, 314, 347, 384, 385, 387, 389, 392, 397, 409, 415, 418, 420, 423, 424, 425, 430, 433, 434, 436, 441, 446, 447, 448, 452, 453, 457, 459, 468, 469, 474, 478, 487, 489, 497, 499, 500, 501

M

medical diagnostics, 151, 167, 276

N

network
  medical intelligent, 92, 95
  TINA, 92, 94
network architecture, 51, 91, 92, 93, 97, 98, 128, 137, 140, 144, 149, 265, 341
networks
  electronic Governements, 80
  Intelligent, 20, 21, 46, 47, 48, 50, 52, 54, 55, 58, 59, 60, 61, 70, 74, 87, 91, 94, 96, 98, 99, 115, 116, 118, 120, 135, 137, 138, 146, 149, 156, 177, 183, 188, 199, 214, 222, 225, 231, 233, 235, 308, 322, 325, 326,

330, 331, 335, 337, 338, 345, 354, 371, 372
  knowledge, 21, 92, 134, 135, 138, 140, 142, 144, 163, 216, 330, 372, 373

R

routers
  switching, 35, 42, 43, 44, 45, 46, 78, 95, 98, 109, 110, 341, 356, 373, 483

S

simulation, 20, 25, 62, 63, 65, 66, 67, 68, 87, 129, 169, 187
SNR, 192, 253, 462
SONET, 21, 22, 23, 31, 32, 33, 34, 35, 36, 37, 38, 39, 41, 47, 69, 76, 99, 209, 211, 212, 214, 215

T

TCP/IP, 7, 74, 93, 140

U

UNIX, 13, 16, 18, 129, 169, 371

W

wireless
  networks, 21, 25, 26, 149
wisdom machine, 27, 151, 155, 164, 289, 293, 294, 322, 370, 400, 434, 437, 449, 454, 464, 465, 466, 468, 472, 474, 476, 477, 484, 489, 504, 505, 530
wisdom machines, 31, 196, 318, 319, 320, 358, 403, 462, 466, 467, 483, 489, 504, 505, 518, 520, 523, 529

(

(truth in) wisdom, 280

A

absolute wisdom, 270
Age-old wisdom, 330
Aristotle, 268, 280, 291, 296, 354, 400,
    401, 403, 409, 410, 415, 416, 421,
    423, 442, 446, 471, 482, 483
axiom of wisdom, 73, 142, 263, 269,
    270, 277, 278, 279, 282, 283, 288,
    291, 293, 424, 425, 440
axioms of wisdom, 5, 7, 8, 17, 139, 180,
    269, 278, 292, 293, 294, 416, 419,
    420, 423, 425, 428, 429, 446, 471, 482

C

concepts and wisdom, 20, 27, 326
concepts/wisdom, 323
constructs of wisdom, 10

D

definition of wisdom, 269, 270
derivation of wisdom, 271, 277, 285
dictionary of wisdom, 10, 268, 446
directional confine of wisdom, 271

E

extraction of wisdom, 4, 290

F

first level, 67, 199, 233, 268, 270, 278,
    279, 282, 295, 300, 391
foundations of wisdom, 2

G

generality and wisdom, 295

I

interim axiom of wisdom, 279

K

knowledge and wisdom, 9, 17, 74, 137,
    295, 311, 340, 426, 453, 459, 475
knowledge to wisdom, 270, 448
knowledge, and wisdom *4, 74, 376*

N

notion of wisdom, 268, 277, 295

P

perfect wisdom, 270, 271
perfection of wisdom, 270

S

search for wisdom, 15, 269, 281, 289,
    293
second level, 60, 67, 150, 165, 199, 268,
    277, 278, 295, 300
Socratic Wisdom, 296

W

wisdom

embedded, 142
extraction, 1
    machine, 27, 101, 143, 150, 264, 268,
    269, 296, 341, 370, 400, 402, 412,
    417, 425, 426, 427, 429, 433, 435,
    436, 437, 442, 446, 459, 460, 482
    medical, 137, 139, 143, 151

WM, (Wisdom Machine), 267, 268, 269,
    270, 271, 274, 276, 277, 278, 279,
    280, 281, 282, 283, 284, 285, 288,
    289, 291, 292, 293, 294, 295, 296,
    402, 417, 420, 421, 426, 427, 428,
    429, 430, 433, 436, 437, 438, 441, 481

wisdom and values, 111, 416, 440, 441
wisdom base, 142, 426, 436
wisdom bases, 346, 417, 420, 426, 428,
    435, 436
wisdom from knowledge, 8, 451
wisdom level functions, 323
wisdom originating from, 10
wisdom-base, 139
WM-E for elegance, 292
WM-i, i = E, T, or S, 294
WM-T, T for truth, 291
WM-S, S for social value, 294

VIII - Index of Information (Words)

(

"last-link", 24
"Store" the Result in CPU and KPU, 227
(B1–B5), 424
(T), social value (S), and elegance (E),
  373

1

1940s, 1, 122, 216, 453, 469

1950s, 1, 11, 26, 47

1960s, 12, 15, 17, 19, 26, 79, 93, 111,
  127, 185, 241, 439, 445, 470

1970s, 12, 14, 21, 26, 60, 63, 111, 127,
  190, 191, 246, 439, 445, 446, 453,
  470, 475

1980s, 12, 13, 16, 21, 26, 28, 30, 44, 53,
  57, 86, 93, 127, 130, 195, 300, 307,
  309, 312, 315, 343, 347, 420, 453,
  470, 475

1990s, 15, 16, 21, 22, 26, 27, 53, 59, 93,
  107, 127, 307, 312, 470

1A processor, 13, 188

2

2B1Q code, 22, 23
2-D trellis coding, 22
2G, 21
2G+, 21

3

3G, 21, 25
3XX, 4XX, 6XX, 7XX, 8XX, 9XX, 303

4

4ESS, 13, 58, 188, 189, 191, 202, 241
4ESS™ switch toll center, 58

5

5ESS, 13, 51, 202, 204
53 octets, 40, 194

8

800-network, 20
899 or 898 numbers 91, 134
800, 900, 700, 411, 911 networks, 164,
  167
802.x, 192

9

900 services, 107
9-row/13-row debate, 31

A

abstractions, 280, 326
abuse, 74, 90, 132, 263, 274, 283, 284,
  330, 340, 417, 419, 429, 430, 435,
  436, 438, 456, 457, 463, 467, 475
Adam Smith, 345, 346, 347
adjunct processor, 116, 123, 155

administrative module, 77, 83, 122, 123,
    162, 165, 204, 206, 207, 208, 211,
    240, 241, 307, 308, 315, 317, 323,
    325, 340
ADMs, 35, 36, 37, 39, 44, 45, 194, 195
ADSL, 22, 23, 29, 67, 132
ADSL/ADSL Lite, 23
ADSL2+, 23, 24
AI, 4, 15, 17, 20, 46, 66, 67, 71, 105,
    114, 116, 120, 122, 139, 142, 144,
    145, 146, 149, 154, 174, 217, 246,
    249, 263, 268, 270, 271, 275, 277,
    278, 279, 280, 281, 282, 295, 296,
    297, 325, 378, 380, 381, 409, 418,
    420, 428, 449, 453, 455, 470, 471
AI concepts, 46
AI programming, 15, 120, 149
AI tools, 122, 275, 281, 381, 453, 455
AIDS, SARS, 295
AIN, 87, 89, 97, 123, 131, 133, 139, 159,
    162, 167, 195, 304, 342
ailment, 44, 85, 91, 229
airplane industry, 15
ALUs, 11, 228
AKSP, 312, 313
Alfred Marshall, 374, 375
algorithmic adaptation, 51
alternate billing service (ABS),, 215
AM, Administrative Module
        25, 77, 123, 159, 162, 165,
    202, 206, 211, 212, 213, 303, 304,
    307, 308, 315, 317, 342
AM, CM, and SM, 304
antivirus and antispy programs, 418
ANSI, 59
architecture, 11, 15, 23, 25, 47, 50, 51,
    52, 54, 57, 79, 85, 86, 89, 90, 91, 92,
    94, 95, 99, 100, 106, 111, 116, 122,
    127, 130, 131, 132, 134, 136, 137,
    138, 142, 145, 149, 150, 157, 158,
    162, 164, 167, 168, 184, 185, 188,
    189, 191, 195, 200, 201, 202, 204,
    207, 208, 209, 212, 213, 215, 217,
    218, 223, 233, 234, 235, 240, 241,
    245, 246, 254, 256, 257, 258, 259,
    261, 264, 290, 291, 296, 303, 305,
    311, 314, 318, 320, 323, 327, 331,
    341, 362, 373, 412, 417, 439, 459, 470
architecture of the KM, 207
archives, 74, 248, 371

Aristotle, 268, 280, 291, 296, 354, 400,
    401, 403, 409, 410, 415, 416, 421,
    423, 442, 446, 471, 482

AT&T, 35, 51, 53, 112, 122, 125, 167,
    188, 195, 241
Atlantis-2, 27
ATM, 21, 22, 24, 25, 26, 27, 30, 31, 32,
    34, 35, 36, 38, 39, 40, 41, 42, 44, 45,
    46, 47, 75, 93, 95, 97, 110, 192, 193,
    194, 195, 317
Ashoka, King, 9, 458
AT&T, 35, 51, 53, 112, 122, 125, 167,
    188, 195, 241
attribute, 67, 122, 180, 199, 225, 226,
    230, 233, 235, 238, 253, 254, 255,
    257, 259, 282, 312, 327, 338, 339,
    357, 363, 365, 378, 386, 400, 471
AUs, 11, 216
AVPU, 173, 174, 176, 177
AXE, 51
A-WAB, 420
axioms of wisdom, 5, 7, 8, 17, 139, 180,
    269, 278, 292, 293, 294, 416, 419,
    420, 423, 425, 428, 429, 446, 471, 482
Axioms of wisdom, 446
Aztec leaders, 431

B

BAL, 11
Babbage, 247
balanced transactions, 383
base cells, 25
basic building blocks of intelligent
    networks, 52
billing system, 86, 106, 107, 130, 138,
    417
BDI-K-CWE, 454, 456, 459, 460, 462
beauty/elegance/grace, 285
behavioral intelligence, 378, 379, 380,
    383, 384
behavioral models, 379, 380
behavioral theory, 277
Bellcore, 151, 242
Berne, 383, 385
best solutions, 234
BI, 378, 380, 381, 384, 407, 408, 409
Block Diagram of the KPS, 220
Boole, 8, 18
breeds of intelligence, 302

BRISDN, 22, 27, 193
broadband networks, 20, 22, 36, 45, 90, 93, 105, 127, 132, 294, 446, 447, 457
Buddhism, 458
building blocks, 4, 8, 11, 13, 19, 20, 42, 43, 45, 52, 59, 73, 92, 105, 118, 136, 139, 150, 167, 182, 183, 202, 215, 227, 244, 248, 269, 270, 273, 278, 283, 285, 289, 294, 305, 310, 323, 378, 389, 446, 461, 482
business records, 14
B-values, 384, 400
BX.25, 53, 54, 56, 314
BX.25 protocol, 56
B-WAB, 420

C

C language, 12, 13, 14, 15, 342
C&C checker, 302, 303
CAD environment, 62, 66
calculated risk, 277
call monitoring, 58
Call Processing, 187
CAMEL, 25
CANTAT-3, 27
CATV, 30
CCIS, 53, 56, 57, 58, 59, 191
CCISS, 192, 307, 312
CCITT, 58, 59
CCITT-approved System 6, 58
CCS7, 54, 55, 58, 74, 309, 314, 342
CDC-6600s, 45
CDRs, 106, 107
cell format, 40, 42, 194
cell relay, 22, 39, 40, 45, 75, 122, 123
centralized sensing interface, 145
CEPT-1, 31
characteristic impedance, 474
chicken flu, Ebola epidemic, or malaria, 338
chromatic dispersion, 26
Common Channel Signaling (CCS), 58
Common Channel Signaling (CCS) network, 56
circularity, 181
circuit-switched, 13, 22, 24, 36, 38, 40, 45, 52, 53, 57, 59, 90, 93, 122, 162, 192, 195, 305, 307, 317, 328, 420
CLASS, 30, 50, 60, 99, 199, 215
clergy, monks, saints and apostles, 269

client(*j*), 92, 134, 136
client/agent(*j*), 136
CM, 11, 77, 123, 159, 162, 165, 167, 187, 202, 210, 211, 303, 304, 306, 307, 308, 321, 322, 342, 481
coefficient of corruption, 474
Coefficient of Corruption, 473
communicating knowledge, 305
communicating, computing, and switching, 48
Communication Module of the KM, 202, 305
communication module, 77, 83, 84, 122, 123, 146, 162, 165, 203, 204, 205, 206, 208, 210, 211, 212, 305, 306, 308, 315, 317, 321, 322
COMNET, 85
compilers, 12, 14, 118, 120, 146, 147, 149, 177, 185, 199, 203, 211, 221, 247, 264, 304, 340, 348, 352
complex objects, 261, 449, 459
Complexity theory, 349
compound semiconductor, 26
Computing environments, 4, 5, 10, 14, 17, 19, 26, 45, 72, 81, 127, 183, 184, 185, 204, 207, 214, 216, 218, 221, 228, 263, 276, 295, 317, 323, 327, 360, 366, 380, 385
concept, 3, 4, 11, 16, 17, 21, 27, 39, 43, 46, 60, 97, 98, 99, 111, 114, 115, 117, 139, 142, 151, 155, 159, 171, 175, 183, 184, 188, 192, 210, 216, 217, 223, 225, 229, 236, 240, 243, 250, 261, 263, 268, 270, 271, 281, 284, 291, 295, 312, 324, 331, 338, 352, 354, 355, 357, 365, 370, 371, 385, 386, 388, 389, 401, 418, 421, 431, 439, 445, 446, 450, 452, 455, 458, 461, 462, 463, 468, 470, 471, 472, 481, 482
concept banks, 21
concept-based switching, 261
concepts, 7, 8, 13, 17, 20, 27, 31, 43, 44, 46, 48, 50, 72, 76, 96, 98, 106, 144, 151, 174, 182, 183, 184, 185, 188, 200, 216, 217, 233, 243, 250, 256, 261, 263, 264, 268, 271, 273, 284, 289, 295, 300, 310, 315, 323, 326, 328, 346, 366, 370, 372, 376, 383,

388, 390, 400, 423, 431, 446, 447,
448, 451, 453, 455, 456, 461, 462,
463, 470, 471, 480, 482
conditions for stability, 116, 146
confidence level, 10, 54, 72, 143, 181,
183, 217, 219, 220, 222, 225, 227,
228, 229, 233, 234, 240, 270, 271,
276, 277, 279, 280, 282, 289, 295,
327, 482
Connection oriented data, 41
Connectionless services, 41
control signals, 48, 49, 58, 145, 153, 226,
233
control, communication, computation,
48, 51
control units, 151, 318
coordinated, coherent, cogent, and
consistent, 183
Corning Glass, 26
corporate crime, 154
corrective strategy, 275
CPM, 249
creativity, 7, 20, 72, 73, 98, 128, 143,
263, 270, 278, 283, 284, 287, 289,
293, 295, 375, 421, 427, 428, 429,
437, 457
criminal CEOs, 245
criminals, 294, 418, 421, 431, 433, 434,
435, 436
cross-talk and impulse noise, 62, 64
CT2, 21, 24
CT3, 21, 24
culture, 74, 180, 263, 264, 349, 376, 399,
446, 468, 472
customer care, 110

D

D channel banks, 190, 192
D, I, K, W, and E, 463
D1 to D5, 434
DACS, 35
DAH, 372, 401, 402, 403, 404, 405, 406,
407, 474
data link-layer, 40, 194
data transmission system, 65
database management systems, 20, 53,
61, 106, 339, 438
data manager, 123, 171
DBM, 159, 164, 165, 167
DBMS, 74, 107

DBMSs, 61, 110, 111, 438, 439
DCS, 33, 34, 35, 195
DDS, 76, 110, 180, 199, 211, 271, 276,
284, 289, 293, 300, 304, 322, 326,
328, 342, 360, 438
decision
support, 4, 9, 11, 43, 50, 94, 101, 117, 118,
120, 123, 143, 144, 145, 149, 151, 154,
155, 159, 164, 171, 239, 245, 246, 248,
252, 265, 271, 272, 273, 275, 276, 278,
289, 295, 296, 366, 380, 404, 446, 470
destructive goals, 294, 434
design of networks, 48
Dewey, 44, 76, 95, 105, 206, 211, 242,
261, 265, 269, 276, 296, 300, 304,
306, 309, 322, 341, 342, 359, 365,
438, 444
Dewey Decimal System, 44, 105, 206,
211, 261, 269, 276, 304, 306, 309,
322, 342, 359, 365, 438
direct memory access, 50, 75, 81, 205,
218, 307, 319
distance learning, 20, 43, 44, 95, 96, 98,
99, 100, 112, 114, 132, 200, 215, 311
distillation of wisdom, 244
DM, 118
DMA, 75, 205, 213, 218, 302, 307, 319,
342, 363
DMT, 22, 23
DQDB, 22, 40
domain of search, 289
DS0, 30, 35, 36, 37, 188, 189, 190, 191,
195
DS1, 21, 30, 31, 33, 35, 37, 38, 40, 190,
191, 194, 195, 196
DS1C, 31, 190
DS2, 31, 39, 190, 191
DS3, 21, 31, 33, 35, 37, 38, 39, 40, 41,
190, 195, 196
DSL, 22, 23, 24, 29, 62, 67, 68, 90, 91
DSLAM, 24
DSSs, 117, 145, 289
duality of human nature, 458
duality of nature, 460
dynamic equilibrium, 122

E

E1, 21, 23, 27, 193, 194, 358, 361, 369
E3, 21, 38, 358
echo cancellation, 23, 66

economic activity, 105, 116, 145, 165, 167, 295, 311, 365, 419
economic motives, 127
ecosystem, 153
Edison [18], Bell [18], and Tesla [18], 424
Education and Welfare, 105, 108
education/distance learning,, 43
education/library networks, 46
educational networks, 30, 46, 93, 96, 204, 317
EG of a small nation, 109
EG platform, 100, 102
EG-IT, 99
Einstein [19], Maxwell [20], Braittain [21], Schalow [22], 425
elastic zero-sum game, 351, 359
electronic government, 20, 21, 43, 44, 46, 79, 99, 100, 101, 105, 215, 269, 404
elegance, 3, 8, 10, 20, 31, 41, 243, 244, 248, 250, 263, 269, 270, 277, 281, 282, 284, 285, 289, 291, 292, 293, 294, 352, 354, 355, 357, 369, 371, 373, 375, 421, 425, 446, 459, 480
elementary particles, 291, 386, 388
embedded intelligence, 71, 100
Enron, 372, 416, 418, 442
Enron and Arthur Anderson, 416
Enron, Global Crossing, Arthur Andersen, 372
entropy, 182, 240
epidemics, 295
ethical dimensions, 248
ESs, 17, 328
ESS, 12, 14, 35, 93, 172, 183, 188, 189, 202, 210, 303, 317, 342, 344
expansion port network, 193, 194
EW1000, 106
EWSD, 51

F

Faraday, Ampere, Gauss, and Galvani, 293
FCs, 86, 130, 138
FDC, 369, 372, 373
fear and threat, 154
federal government, 127
federal sponsorship, 17
feedback loop, 8, 153, 171, 371

FEPs, 118, 147
fiber optic, 17, 21, 26, 27, 28, 29, 30, 31, 33, 45, 47, 64, 66, 67, 68
field of medicine, 137, 142
fifteen "B-Values,", 383
financial networks, 14, 46, 205, 317
FLAG, 27
flip-flop of attitude, 458
Ford Motor Company, 17
frame relay, 21, 22, 24, 40, 75, 122, 123, 317
fraud management, 110, 417
from node A_i to A_{i+1}, 394
Fromm, 401, 410, 412, 413
FTTC, 23, 24, 26, 27, 29
FTTH, 23, 26, 27, 29
fuzziness, 175, 181, 449, 469
Fuzzy Hamming Distance, 229
fuzzy NPU, 228

G

G.992.2, 23
G.DMT, 23
global unrest and violence, 475
GNP, 116, 145, 164, 278, 362, 449
Goethe, 346
GPRS, 25
GPU, 15, 203
graphics processors, 13, 328
greed for personal gain, 376
GUI, 107

H

H.323, 192
Hamming distance, 229, 373
Hamming Distance, fuzzy in the medical field, defined as symptomatic distance between known diseases 229
Hamming, Shannon, Bose, Hocquenghem, Ampere, Gauss,, 353
Hardware Configuration for the SCP of Intelligent Networks, 54
hardware for KPS, 217
HDSL, 22, 23, 34, 62, 63, 64, 65, 66, 67
HDTV, 23, 30, 35
Heisenberg's principle, 276, 451
Henry Ford, 457
Henry Kissinger , Kofi Anan, 424

hierarchy, 3, 7, 21, 31, 33, 51, 62, 74, 97, 98, 100, 101, 105, 110, 138, 162, 188, 190, 194, 204, 211, 213, 218, 222, 233, 246, 247, 260, 268, 306, 307, 323, 367, 383, 387, 388, 391, 397, 411, 415, 425, 437, 438, 446, 453
higher-level needs, 248, 249, 250, 394, 399
HLLs, 12, 13, 247
high-speed LANs, 22, 91, 132, 192
high-speed lines, 64
hospital-based medical networks, 77, 106

human activity, 20
human aspect, 155
human behavior, 5, 277, 328, 370, 378, 379, 380, 381, 382, 383, 384, 385, 388, 390, 391, 397, 409, 410, 411, 465
human being, 17, 71, 72
human beings, 2, 3, 4, 8, 9, 20, 30, 71, 72, 90, 101, 113, 114, 121, 131, 143, 144, 150, 154, 174, 175, 176, 179, 181, 226, 238, 244, 245, 246, 247, 248, 250, 263, 267, 268, 270, 271, 284, 292, 294, 295, 340, 349, 351, 361, 365, 366, 372, 373, 374, 375, 376, 377, 378, 379, 380, 381, 383, 384, 385, 389, 390, 391, 393, 397, 400, 401, 410, 416, 418, 420, 423, 425, 426, 427, 429, 430, 433, 435, 441, 442, 446, 447, 449, 454, 455, 456, 457, 458, 460, 461, 462, 463, 464, 468, 469, 471, 472, 475, 480, 482
Human bias, 340
human designer, 66
human errors, 340
human integrity, 278
human intellect, 7, 376, 379
human interactions, 348, 383
human needs, 3, 5, 8, 214, 245, 246, 247, 248, 249, 260, 264, 311, 377, 380, 384, 389, 411, 446
Human Search, 456
humankind, 7, 8, 21, 244, 416, 421, 423, 431, 433, 441, 457, 460
human–machine interaction, 175, 271, 436
human-machine system, 365, 373
Human Resources, 105
humanoid functions, 295

hyperdimensional objects, 348
hybrid fiber coaxial, 23
hypothesis, 46, 228, 282, 381, 463

I

I, K, C, W, and E nodes, 458

I«»K, 346, 347, 348, 349, 350, 359, 360, 361, 362, 363, 365, 367, 369

I-KPS, 328, 329, 332
I_2-KPS, 326, 328, 329
I_3-KPS, 328, 330
I^3-KPS, 332
IAS, 11, 13, 18, 184, 185, 241, 245, 264
IBM 360/370, 11, 111, 225, 227, 439
IC, 16, 52, 67, 111, 191, 192, 251, 442
IKN, 304, 307, 342
IKPS, 328, 329, 332
IKWV chain, 440, 441
imaging, 2, 14, 16, 23, 29, 84, 278, 283
in-band signaling, 188, 312
IN/1, 20, 55, 56, 57, 59, 62, 87, 97, 99, 133, 299, 304, 342
IN/1+, 57, 87, 133, 342
IN/2, 87, 92, 97, 99, 114, 123, 133, 134, 159, 162, 165, 167, 195, 198, 202, 299, 307, 309, 310, 342
INCAD environments, 66
INCM, 7, 162, 167, 199, 202
incremental gain, 248
incremental gradients, 460
inertia/mass effect, 472, 475
information age, 5, 46, 265, 267, 269, 358, 367, 371, 375, 376, 377, 378, 385, 410, 416, 419, 467
information and knowledge, 4, 6, 17, 30, 45, 47, 60, 61, 73, 74, 75, 97, 128, 139, 179, 180, 247, 268, 270, 295, 345, 346, 347, 349, 351, 355, 359, 360, 361, 365, 367, 436, 439, 440, 441, 456, 459, 463
information processing, 4, 71, 72, 75, 144, 175, 180, 314, 346, 349, 350, 352, 353, 356, 419, 452, 461, 480
Information processing systems, 71, 367
information, knowledge, wisdom, 20, 440
innovation, 3, 16, 282, 467

innovations, 3, 5, 29, 184, 243, 307, 370, 377, 428
intelligent agents, 149, 180, 328, 373, 379, 380
intelligent communication systems, 47
intelligent decision support, 94, 252, 470
Intelligent hardware agents, 15
intelligent human agent, 295
Intelligent Internet, 43, 73, 74, 86, 128, 130, 138, 180, 245
intelligent information-sourcing system, 94
intelligent Internet, 7, 47, 73, 76, 128, 201, 214, 310, 471
Intelligent internets, 9
intelligent instructor, 96
intelligent medical Internet, 89, 138
intelligent medical knowledge processing, 86
intelligent networks, 20, 21, 46, 47, 48, 50, 52, 54, 55, 57, 59, 60, 61, 69, 73, 85, 89, 92, 94, 96, 97, 111, 112, 114, 116, 129, 130, 131, 136, 138, 144, 162, 167, 172, 183, 195, 202, 205, 211, 213, 215, 283, 296, 299, 300, 303, 304, 308, 310, 311, 317, 326, 342, 343
intelligent robotics, 252
intelligent-knowledgeware (IKW), 462
intelligent systems, 81, 214, 408
intermediate databases, 64
Intern, 263, 276, 289, 327, 379, 458
Internet environment, 47, 307, 311, 342, 471
Internet netware, 47
Internet platform, 73
Internet services, 27, 43, 47, 73, 89, 128, 201, 310, 311
interoperability, 45, 60, 61, 63, 65, 86, 106, 110, 130, 438
IP, 1, 7, 23, 24, 29, 30, 45, 46, 57, 61, 73, 89, 90, 92, 110, 111, 123, 128, 131, 132, 136, 138, 139, 195, 197, 199, 200, 202, 261, 296, 309, 310, 324, 342, 365, 438, 482
ISDN, 22, 23, 25, 27, 33, 34, 41, 62, 63, 64, 66, 69, 75, 90, 91, 95, 97, 132, 192, 193, 196, 200, 211, 303, 311, 317, 342, 343, 344
ISP, 24, 30, 73, 74, 76, 128, 197, 200, 293, 312, 313

IT aspects, 43
IT concepts, 43, 44
IT engineers, 100
IT platform, 101, 103, 104, 105, 108, 416
ITU, 21, 23, 31, 32, 34, 52, 58, 59, 69, 92, 136, 167, 312, 342, 343, 453
invention, 26, 72, 111, 168, 185, 247, 271, 293, 300, 323, 347, 370, 372, 387, 390, 461, 467

J

job control language, 48
John the Baptist, 397, 423, 431, 443
Jung, 380, 382, 383, 384, 385, 410, 412

K

KBMS, 74, 76
KBs, 97, 101, 110, 111, 128, 130, 137, 146, 211, 212, 213, 214, 230, 308, 312, 343, 362, 438, 439
KBMSs, 110, 111, 438, 439
KCP, 74, 76, 197, 199, 201, 304, 310, 311, 312, 313, 314, 330, 332, 340, 342
KCPU, 320, 322, 323, 342
KCS, 300, 303, 305, 306, 307, 308, 310, 311, 314, 316, 320, 321, 325, 327, 329, 343
KCSs, 180, 303, 306, 314, 315
KD function, 219, 233
KEE, 200
killer machine, 283
King Ashoka, 9
KIR, 331
KIP, 74, 76, 202, 311, 323, 343
KM, 77, 202, 204, 207, 229, 230, 303, 304, 306, 320, 322, 323, 325, 339, 340, 343
KMM, 159, 162, 164, 165, 166, 167, 168
KMS, 74, 76, 80, 312, 313, 330, 332, 340
KMSs, 96, 197, 304
knowledge and wisdom, 9, 17, 74, 137, 295, 311, 340, 426, 453, 459, 475
knowledge bank, 27, 309
knowledge base systems, 20
knowledge bases, 4, 8, 29, 43, 44, 50, 57, 73, 74, 77, 79, 83, 86, 93, 94, 95, 96, 97, 98, 99, 101, 111, 114, 128, 129, 130, 136, 137, 138, 142, 143, 150, 152, 155, 172, 180, 199, 200, 203,

204, 205, 211, 212, 217, 228, 241, 243, 244, 245, 248, 261, 263, 269, 276, 277, 279, 280, 281, 284, 285, 295, 296, 304, 305, 306, 307, 308, 312, 325, 326, 330, 340, 343, 348, 351, 355, 362, 365, 366, 371, 402, 416, 417, 424, 425, 427, 429, 430, 433, 435, 436, 437, 438, 442, 461, 463, 470
knowledge dispensing, 91
knowledge domain, 71, 162, 167, 182, 199, 216, 217, 219, 221, 222, 226, 231, 233, 261, 304, 315, 324, 325, 338, 351, 365, 470, 481
Knowledge engineering, 97
knowledge environments, 180, 197, 299, 300
knowledge instruction, 209, 218, 219, 220, 222, 226, 331, 338, 364
knowledge machine, 69, 111, 116, 120, 125, 172, 202, 217, 227, 228, 229, 230, 233, 234, 251, 252, 304, 320, 322, 323, 330, 331, 338, 339, 340, 439, 472
knowledge machine cluster, 120
knowledge machines, 8, 182, 202, 264, 304, 320, 323, 330, 338, 340, 365
knowledge module, 77, 83, 84, 116, 120, 145, 150, 198, 200,
203, 204, 206, 207, 208, 304, 306, 310, 311, 323, 343
knowledge network, 90, 129, 131, 132, 134, 197, 304, 307, 311, 342
knowledge processing, 1, 4, 8, 9, 27, 30, 47, 77, 86, 94, 96, 97, 117, 128, 130, 137, 145, 147, 150, 151, 154, 155, 159, 162, 167, 180, 181, 182, 183, 184, 202, 205, 207, 211, 212, 213, 215, 217, 219, 221, 225, 229, 230, 232, 237, 240, 256, 261, 263, 264, 294, 299, 300, 302, 303, 304, 306, 307, 312, 314, 315, 317, 319, 320, 323, 325, 326, 327, 328, 330, 331, 336, 340, 343, 349, 350, 351, 352, 367, 370, 417, 424, 438, 441, 449, 452, 459, 460, 463, 470, 471, 480, 481, 482
Knowledge processing, 28, 73, 111, 181, 182, 216, 242, 299, 314, 328, 337, 338, 339, 343, 444, 453

knowledge profile, 129, 134, 198, 199, 200, 204, 208, 211, 214, 304, 310, 317, 325, 326
knowledge program, 118, 182, 223, 225, 227, 228, 235, 239, 261, 325, 351
knowledge ring, 94, 96, 212
knowledge service providers, 74, 129, 134, 150, 199, 313
knowledge society, 75, 89, 93, 131, 150, 358, 359, 370, 419, 441, 446, 475
knowledge services, 73, 74, 76, 128, 130, 132, 136, 150, 197, 199, 200, 201, 307, 310, 313
knowledge software, 449
knowledge systems, 9, 183, 202, 300, 301, 303, 304, 342
knowledge theory, 349, 350, 351, 373
knowledge trail, 376, 446, 447, 449, 459, 466, 467, 469, 471, 481
knowledge tree, 263
knowledge-oriented functions, 213
knowledge-oriented problems, 208, 325
knowledge, wisdom, and culture, 74
Kompilation, 237
kompile, 237
kopc, 315, 331, 338

kopcode, 111, 218, 219, 222, 224, 225, 226, 227, 231, 233, 235, 236, 250, 253, 254, 315, 365
KPE, 74, 76, 263
KPSs, 117, 145, 155, 180, 181, 182, 183, 202, 222, 304, 314, 315, 328
KPU, 111, 151, 179, 207, 208, 209, 217, 218, 219, 220, 222, 223, 225, 226, 227, 231, 233, 234, 235, 236, 238, 239, 250, 253, 254, 261, 314, 315, 317, 320, 322, 323, 325, 326, 331, 335, 338, 339, 342, 343, 364, 365, 439, 449
KS + (In + IN + KI), 300
KS + (IN + KI), 300
KS + (In + KI),, 300
KS + IN, 300
KS + Internet, 300
KS + KI, 300
KS+(In + IN), 300
KSCP, 136, 137, 199, 201, 310, 312, 313
KSMS, 132, 136, 137
KSP, 129, 130, 131, 132, 133, 134, 135, 136, 150, 197, 311, 312, 343

KSP(*i*), 129, 136
KSW, 449
KTP, 74, 76, 96, 197, 310, 343

L

laser, 5, 26, 27, 446
large-scale systems, 116
learning routines, 236
leisure time, 380, 385
Levels of information, 371
lexical analysis, 12, 118, 144
Lexical analyzers, 115
Library of Congress, 44, 76, 95, 105,
  110, 206, 211, 242, 261, 265, 269,
  276, 295, 296, 300, 304, 306, 309,
  322, 341, 343, 365, 438, 444
Liebnitz, 247
Life of Inventions, 370
Lightwave Systems, 67, 68
limited search, 245, 277, 295, 395
LISP, 13
LoC, 110, 180, 199, 211, 265, 271, 276,
  293, 300, 304, 309, 322, 326, 328,
  330, 338, 342, 343, 438, 448
longer-term benefits, 17
loop (1–6), 394
lower level needs, 154
LUs, 11

M

M1C, M12 M13, and M34, 190
machine-humaniod functions, 251
Mafia, 419, 435, 457, 467, 472
MAN, 22, 38, 41
March and Simon, 395
Marshall's marginal utility, 248
maser, 5
Maslow's pyramid of needs, 415
Maximal Injury and Destruction, 431
Maxwell, 210, 293, 325, 353, 388, 393,
  425, 443, 451
Maxwell's equations, 210, 325, 393
Mead, 399, 412
medical computer system, 77, 81
medical data bank, 81
medical databases, 77, 86, 92, 138, 150
medical diagnostics, 139, 152, 252
Medical networks, 75
medical processor, 77, 79, 81, 82, 83, 84

Mendel, 8, 17
message-switched, 24, 52
microcode, 48, 49, 52, 225, 226, 233,
  331, 367
microcodes, 331
microeconomics, 248, 270, 347, 375,
  386, 446, 456
microwave communications, 24
MIMD, 184, 203, 204, 256, 318, 363
ministries, 100, 105, 215
MISD, 184, 203, 256
MKNs, 90
Models Databases, 275
Modes of Wisdom, 436
modular
  functions, 4, 25, 97, 105, 188, 192, 225,
    233, 317, 326, 378, 470
monetary theory, 295
moral content, 261
MPMO, 180, 256, 257, 258, 261
MPSO, 180, 256, 258, 261
MRI, 2, 14, 16, 246
MSMS, 90, 92
MSPs, 85, 86, 89, 90, 91, 92, 137, 138,
  199
Multicast service, 24
multimedia traffic, 90, 132
Mycin, 246, 263, 264, 276, 289, 327,
  379, 458

N

national economy, 123, 151, 165, 166,
  171, 347
natural intelligence, 5, 7, 71, 73, 128,
  144, 244, 278, 283, 380
NBES, 96, 97, 99
NCOM, 118
need extinction process, 392
Need Pyramid, 249
negative side, 46, 390, 400, 401, 460,
  463, 467
negative use, 291
negative wisdom, 430, 434, 436, 437,
  441, 458
NEGATIVE WISDOM, 429
NeoMycin, 246, 264, 327, 458
netware programs, 44, 46
Network service, 27
networks and machines, 464
neural networks, 268, 348

new breed of computer systems, 243, 481
nirvana, true love,, 386
NKSPs, 74
node manager, 55
Noise, 424
noisy environments, 351
novel
  configurations, 4
NPU, 203, 216, 217, 219, 228, 229, 269,
  271, 390
NT-1 and NT-2, 303
numerically controlled, 15, 147, 148

O

OA&M, 58
object management, 314
object process, 120
objective function, 115, 117, 145, 146,
  164, 168, 274
object-oriented languages, 154, 247, 264
object-oriented programs, 115, 120, 146,
  162, 233
OC-1, 31, 32, 33
OC-12, 27, 32, 193
OC-192, 31, 32, 33
OC-3, 32, 33, 34, 35, 36, 38, 193
OC-48, 27, 32
OOL, 233, 234
OOP, 149, 167
operand cache, 253, 254
OPNET, 85

operand stacks, 253
optical carrier systems, 22
optical network terminations, 30
Optical systems, 26
optimality, 84, 113, 115, 144, 233, 234,
  244, 387, 388, 390, 459
optimizing compliers, 12, 234
organizational behavior, 384
oscillatory, 116
OSI
  model, 5, 7, 21, 40, 45, 49, 60, 64, 194,
    247, 302, 343, 374, 420, 453

P

Packet-based, 45
packet-switched, 24, 25, 40, 52, 53, 56,
  93, 192, 328, 453

passive optical networks, 29
patient information, 77, 84, 89, 112, 138
pattern (1–9), 404
pattern recognition, 17, 46, 122, 138,
  144, 147, 164, 165, 168, 212, 213,
  230, 235, 279, 282, 285, 328, 378,
  409, 449, 469
Pattern recognition, 115
payload, 31, 32, 33, 34, 38, 40, 194
PBXs, 24, 25, 52, 95
PCM, 23, 30, 31, 191
PCU, 185
peace of mind, 270
PeopleSoft, 73, 94, 105, 111, 112, 128,
  172, 314, 366, 374, 463
perfection, 150, 244, 247, 270, 284, 288,
  384, 386, 387, 390, 403, 406, 441
pharmacies, 91
Physicians, 84
physiological, 72, 245, 246, 400, 410,
  411, 456
philosopher, a scientist, 421
philosophic (Ph.), 426
physician–patient, 141, 142
pictorial databases, 64
PIN, 67, 90, 131
Pipeline, 259
plain old telephone services, 29, 196
Plato, Socrates, 415
PLCP, 42
plesiochronous, 31
PMPC, 79, 82
PMPC code, 79
PMR, 25
political economists, 346
positive and negative phasors, 405
Positive inventions, 457
positive side, 46, 113, 400, 408, 456,
  460, 467, 475
positive values, 403, 419, 436
Positive Wisdom, 426, 428
POTS, 24, 30, 59, 196, 303, 307, 309,
  315, 343
PPNs and EPNs, 193
PR, 17, 115, 164, 168, 193, 279, 282,
  328, 378, 379, 381, 408, 421, 431,
  449, 468, 472, 473, 474, 475, 479
predictive programming, 115, 122
primary driving force, 377
Prime Minister's Office, 104, 105
primitive

humans, 5, 247, 401, 410, 416, 418, 454
prior knowledge, 99, 215, 320
private virtual network, 24, 55
Process hierarchy, 260
processing of knowledge, 7, 8, 10, 98,
  154, 182, 202, 206, 229, 261, 264,
  276, 300, 304, 305, 314, 319, 320,
  324, 326, 331, 343, 449, 482
processor control point (PCP), 330
processor port network, 193, 194
program instructions, 254
program databases, 64, 238, 239
programmed intelligence, 243
PROLOG, 13
protocol, 7, 22, 25, 38, 39, 40, 42, 49, 53,
  56, 57, 73, 75, 89, 91, 192, 193, 197,
  218, 261, 310, 312, 374, 420, 453
psychological, 72, 355, 404, 408, 419,
  429, 430
psychotic fear, selfish greed, and
  irrational hate, 421, 430

Q

QAM coding, 23
QoS, 23, 24, 43, 130, 138, 325

R

R(F_x), R(F_y), R(D_x), and *R(D_y)*, 475
RACE, 25
Rationality, 215, 216, 351, 458
raw data, 60, 61, 106, 120, 128, 149, 165,
  294, 447, 449, 450, 453
repeaters, 27, 29
RDTs, 35, 36, 195
Ricardo, Malthus, Say and even Karl
  Marx, 346
Rolls Royce, 17
rotary switches, 19
routers, 35, 42, 43, 44, 45, 77, 93, 96,
  105, 106, 314, 328, 344, 441

S

SANs, 22
SAP, 94, 105, 111, 112, 296, 314, 341,
  366, 374, 463
SAT-3/WASC/SAFE, 28
scarcity theory, 295, 439

SDSL, 23
SDTV, 30
SCE, 92, 136, 195, 200, 227, 309
scenario identification, 117
SCP, 20, 53, 54, 55, 56, 61, 62, 91, 92,
  96, 97, 99, 111, 114, 134, 136, 151,
  164, 167, 195, 198, 200, 214, 218,
  227, 242, 300, 309, 330, 343, 344,
  365, 439, 449
SCPs, 53, 56, 197, 307, 310, 314
scientific (Sc.), 426
scientific revolution, 445
SEA-ME-WE 2, 28
SEA-ME-WE 3, 28, 29, 68
search for wisdom, 15, 269, 281, 289,
  293
security, and encryption., 14
self-adjusting, 117
self-destructive, 430
self-learning, 79, 117, 273, 295
semantic analysis, 12, 118, 146, 325
semi-conductor technology, 11
Semi-infinite Search Space, 397, 399
sense and monitor, 115, 145
sensing network, 116, 119, 120, 122, ·
  123, 124, 145, 158, 159, 161, 162,
  163, 164, 165, 167, 168, 171, 273
service provisioning, 23, 24, 30, 43, 58,
  74, 86, 130, 136, 137, 183, 195, 199
sevenfold semi-infinite search space, 400
seven-level model, 393, 410
short-term objective, 269
Sigmund Freud, 375, 381, 382
Signal, 31, 32, 56, 424
SIMD, 184, 203, 256, 363
SIMO, 180
single object, 180, 250, 254, 256, 258
SIP, 88, 91, 92, 93, 134, 135, 136, 150
Six-stage flowchart, 391
sixth-level, 385, 387, 388, 389, 390, 393,
  399
sixth-level drives, 385
SM, 77, 202, 203, 204, 210, 211, 212,
  213, 303, 306, 307, 313, 321, 322,
  332, 339, 344
SMDS, 22, 40, 44
SMS, 53, 54, 55, 56, 57, 61, 62, 80, 92,
  101, 110, 114, 122, 136, 201, 227,
  309, 330
SNI, 55
SNMP, 193

SNR, 176, 230, 424
social activity, 456
social and cultural norms, 283, 399
social benefit, 243, 245, 248, 250, 263,
    281, 285, 289, 292, 352, 421, 441
social effect, 46
social ethics, 248, 447
social justice, 8, 277, 340, 446, 471
social problems, 30
social setting, 286, 371, 392, 400, 404
social structures, 10
social values, 10, 282, 294, 421, 423,
    433, 440, 451, 453, 454, 455, 461,
    462, 463, 471
socially destructive human, 283
socially intelligent, 417
societal problems, 442
soft and viscous sciences, 338
software defined network, 55
software layers, 12, 202, 366
SONET, 21, 22, 23, 30, 31, 32, 33, 34,
    35, 36, 37, 38, 39, 40, 47, 68, 69, 75,
    97, 192, 193, 194, 195, 196
SONET frame, 34, 37
SONET/SDH, 22, 69
sophisticated feedback, 291
SPC, 11, 19, 184
spin–lattice, 14
spin–spin, 14
SOPs, 227, 289
SPSO, 180, 208, 254, 261
SS7 network, 53, 62
SSI, 11, 55
SSLI, 88, 91, 92, 93, 134, 135, 136, 150
SSP, 53, 55, 56, 61, 62, 92, 134, 136,
    151, 195, 197, 200, 242, 304, 309,
    310, 311, 343, 344
SSPs, 53, 56, 62, 197, 303, 304, 307,
    310, 314, 342
SST, 25
standard operating procedures, 101, 227,
    289
Still as Mindless, 458
STM-1, 24
STM-*i*, 32
Stone
    age, 5, 72, 112, 241, 374, 454
STP, 56, 62, 92, 96, 136, 195, 197, 309,
    343
STPs, 56, 59, 197, 310, 314

strategies, 20, 38, 66, 167, 173, 182, 192,
    223, 234, 237, 239, 246, 248, 269,
    295, 430, 434, 436, 448, 454, 471
STS, 31, 32, 33, 34, 35, 37, 195, 242
STS-1, 31, 32, 33, 35, 37, 195
STS-3, 32, 37, 195
Supreme Court, 10, 416, 429
Supreme Court Justices, 429
switching centers, 52
switching modules, 19
switching system, 26, 51, 57, 117, 123,
    125, 144, 149, 171, 172, 187, 191,
    202, 204, 205, 206, 208, 303, 305,
    306, 315, 317
switching systems, 4, 12, 13, 14, 16, 19,
    20, 24, 26, 45, 51, 58, 60, 79, 89, 116,
    117, 123, 131, 138, 145, 151, 171,
    183, 188, 192, 197, 206, 207, 213,
    214, 215, 240, 241, 303, 304, 307,
    308, 315, 340, 342, 343, 344, 441
Symbols and Equations, 281
synergy, 1, 7, 11, 30, 43, 45, 72, 73, 78,
    111, 137, 143, 145, 167, 182, 216,
    244, 268, 270, 283, 293, 307, 375,
    377, 378, 390, 439, 442, 446, 457
System performance, 116
syntactic analysis, 12, 146, 199

T

T, P and S, 356
T, P, S, E, 352
T, V, and B, 409, 446
T1, 22, 23, 27, 29, 30, 34, 40, 41, 188,
    189, 190, 191, 193, 194, 354, 359,
    360, 361, 445, 473, 478, 479
T1/E1 lines, 193, 194
TAT-9, 27
technology transfer, 128, 129, 131, 132,
    150
TCP/IP, 73
telecommunications industry, 14, 52,
    107, 240, 312, 340, 420
telecommunication networks, 20, 38, 62,
    63, 96, 187, 369
telecommunications, 4, 14, 24, 52, 58,
    74, 79, 89, 91, 94, 99, 107, 127, 130,
    132, 134, 136, 139, 192, 215, 226,
    240, 247, 312, 340, 420
Telcordia, 31
Telco, 106, 107, 111, 314, 439

telemedicine, 4, 43, 46, 85, 99, 100, 304
telephone switching systems, 116
terrorists, 294, 418, 421, 431
Tesla, 8, 17, 24, 382, 423, 424, 442
The New Cycle, 395
Thorstein Veblen, 346, 369, 439, 446
timeless axioms, 420
TINA, 86, 90, 92, 112, 125, 130, 132,
    136, 151
TMM, 159, 162, 165, 167
to search and to unify, 378
TPC-5, 27
traits A1–A5, 423
traits B1–B5, 425
traits C1–C5, 433
traits D1–D5, 435
transfer of technology, 128, 129, 150
Transition, 469, 470, 471
transmission, 5, 22, 25, 26, 27, 28, 42,
    47, 64, 97, 191, 305, 365, 446, 474
transmission media, 64
transmission system, 64
trigger condition, 123, 197, 308, 312
triple helix, 293
truism, philosophic, scientific, and
    economic, 352, 353
truth, 3, 10, 20, 243, 244, 250, 261, 263,
    267, 269, 270, 271, 277, 280, 281,
    282, 284, 285, 289, 291, 292, 293,
    294, 330, 346, 352, 353, 354, 355,
    357, 358, 369, 371, 373, 376, 383,
    400, 403, 406, 421, 423, 424, 428,
    430, 446, 450, 457, 474
truth, virtue and beauty, 284, 376, 424
TT, 129, 130
TTKNs, 131, 132
TVB, 402, 403, 404, 406, 474
two ellipses, 423, 426, 433, 435
type A, 379, 390, 400, 420, 421, 422,
    423, 424, 426, 428, 429
type B, 379, 390, 400, 420, 421, 422,
    424, 425, 426, 428, 429
type C, 400, 421, 429, 430, 431, 432,
    433, 435, 436
type D, 400, 421, 429, 430, 432, 433,
    434, 435, 436
type-I, 400, 401, 410, 421
type-II, 400, 410, 421
Tyrant kings, the mafia and the thugs,
    429
tyrant or a thug, 421

U

U, T and S interfaces for ISDN, 303
UMTS, 25
uncertainty, 72, 216, 228, 229, 230, 240,
    276, 362, 382, 383, 388, 450, 451, 482
underworld and mindless leaders, 457
unethical behavior, 372
unify, 118, 146, 293, 378, 385, 386, 387,
    388, 389, 390, 393, 412
United Nations, 74, 443
universal scientific rules, 448
universality, 20, 142, 243, 244, 248, 250,
    261, 263, 269, 288, 328, 371
universality of wisdom, 20
UNIX, 12, 13, 15, 18, 123, 154, 342
unstable feedback, 451
user communication process, 120
USIN, 97

V

value processing, 417
values and ethics, 264, 428, 429
VCs, 41
VDSL, 23, 24
VHDSL, 34
velocity of flow of information, 347,
    358, 369, 370
velocity of money, 116, 145
VLSI, 1, 5, 11, 13, 15, 17, 21, 30, 47, 60,
    61, 67, 71
virtue/social benefit/benevolence, 285
virus implanters, 283
virtual university, 44
VoIP, 24
von Neumann, 18, 47, 184, 216, 219,
    225, 235, 241, 245, 247, 254, 261,
    264, 331, 471
viscosity in the flow of information, 347,
    369

W

Wafer/chip/configuration, 335
Wagner, 346
wars, 154, 274, 295, 397, 403, 430, 458,
    467

Syed V. Ahamed received his Ph.D. and D. Sc. (E.E.) degrees from the University of Manchester and his MBA (Econ.) from the New York University. He taught at the University of Colorado for 2 years before joining AT&T Bell Laboratories in 1966. In 1982 he became a Professor of Computer Science at the City University of New York and a member of the Doctoral Faculty in 1985. He has taught at New York Polytechnic at Brooklyn as a visiting Professor of Computer Science from 1982 to 1986. Professor Ahamed has been a Telecommunications consultant to Bell Communications Research, AT&T Bell Laboratories, Lucent Technologies, Timplex Corporation, Telecom Australia, ETH Zurich, and to Celcom, Malaysia. In Malaysia, he worked as a Management consultant to establish an IT platform and to design the high-speed backbone network. He is the co-recipient of the 1981 IEEE Communications Society, Leonard G. Abraham Prize Paper Award and the co-recipient of the 1964 Honorable Citation for the IEEE Aerospace Society paper. With Professor Michael J. Miller he has written two books "Digital Transmission Systems and Networks," - Volumes I & II in 1987 and 1988. In 1992 he became a Fellow of the IEEE for his seminal contribution to the simulation and design studies of the High-speed Digital Subscriber Lines. The results published in the Bell System Technical Journal in 1982 form the basis for the later versions of the DSLs described in this book. He is listed in Marquis 1995, Who's Who in the World and holds many such honors. He has also written two other books: "Intelligent Broadband Multimedia Networks," and "Design and Engineering of Intelligent Communications Systems," based on his investigations of subscriber networks around the world for high-speed data. His doctoral students continue to contribute to knowledge processing systems and wisdom machines proposed by him in 1999 and 2002. In 2004, he wrote the book "The Art of Scientific Innovation," for new doctoral students. The book is based on his teaching and mentoring scores of Ph.D. students at the City University of New York. He holds over 20 American and European patents ranging from slip-meters for induction motors to medical networks for hospitals. He has also published over 200 papers and numerous chapters in books.